Family Problems

Family Problems

Stress, Risk, and Resilience

Edited by

Joyce A. Arditti

WILEY Blackwell

This edition first published 2015
© 2015 John Wiley & Sons, Inc.

Registered Office
John Wiley & Sons, Ltd, The Atrium, Southern Gate, Chichester, West Sussex, PO19 8SQ, UK

Editorial Offices
350 Main Street, Malden, MA 02148-5020, USA
9600 Garsington Road, Oxford, OX4 2DQ, UK
The Atrium, Southern Gate, Chichester, West Sussex, PO19 8SQ, UK

For details of our global editorial offices, for customer services, and for information about how to apply for permission to reuse the copyright material in this book please see our website at www.wiley.com/wiley-blackwell.

The right of Joyce A. Arditti to be identified as the author of the editorial material in this work has been asserted in accordance with the UK Copyright, Designs and Patents Act 1988.

Wiley also publishes its books in a variety of electronic formats. Some content that appears in print may not be available in electronic books.

Designations used by companies to distinguish their products are often claimed as trademarks. All brand names and product names used in this book are trade names, service marks, trademarks or registered trademarks of their respective owners. The publisher is not associated with any product or vendor mentioned in this book.

Limit of Liability/Disclaimer of Warranty: While the publisher and authors have used their best efforts in preparing this book, they make no representations or warranties with respect to the accuracy or completeness of the contents of this book and specifically disclaim any implied warranties of merchantability or fitness for a particular purpose. It is sold on the understanding that the publisher is not engaged in rendering professional services and neither the publisher nor the author shall be liable for damages arising herefrom. If professional advice or other expert assistance is required, the services of a competent professional should be sought.

Library of Congress Cataloging-in-Publication Data is available for this title

PB: 9781118348284

A catalogue record for this book is available from the British Library.

Cover image: © Yurz Kuzmin / Photos.com

Set in 10/12pt Bembo by SPi Publisher Services, Pondicherry, India

Printed in Singapore by C.O.S. Printers Pte Ltd

1   2015

Contents

Part III   Family Challenges Over the Life Course   183

Part IV   Policy and Practice Responses to Family Problems   271

Part V   Conclusion   355

Notes on Contributors

Elaine A. Anderson is Professor and Chair in the Department of Family Science, School of Public Health, at the University of Maryland. Her work focuses on the impact of policies on the health and well-being of families. She has used her research to inform state and federal legislators about how best to modify programmatic and policy initiatives on behalf of families. She is the former President of the National Council on Family Relations. She earned her Ph.D. from The Pennsylvania State University.

Joyce A. Arditti is Professor of Human Development at Virginia Tech. She received her doctorate in Family Studies from the University of North Carolina, Greensboro. Her research interests include family disruption, parent–child relationships in vulnerable families, and public policy. Her scholarship is recognized nationally and internationally and she has published numerous empirical and review articles in therapy, human services, family studies, and criminal justice journals. She is the author of the book *Parental incarceration and the family: Psychological and social effects of imprisonment on children, parents, and care-givers* published by New York University Press, for which she was the 2014 recipient of the Academy of Criminal Justice Sciences (ACJS) Outstanding Book Award, an honor awarded to a member of ACJS who has authored a book representing an extraordinary contribution in the field of criminal justice. Joyce recently served as the Editor in Chief of *Family Relations: The Interdisciplinary Journal of Applied Family Studies*. She is a Fellow of the National Council on Family Relations (NCFR), and Chair of the Research and Theory

Section (NCFR). She is an Associate Editor for the *Journal of Child and Family Studies*, serves on various editorial boards, and is actively involved in research projects dealing with families involved in the criminal justice system.

William R. Avison is Professor of Sociology, Paediatrics, and Epidemiology and Biostatistics at the University of Western Ontario and Chair of the Division of Children's Health and Therapeutics at the Children's Health Research Institute. His research focuses on the effects of socio-economic disadvantage and social stressors on the health of families and children. He is the founding editor of *Society and Mental Health: The Journal of the Sociology of Mental Health Section of the American Sociological Association*. He received the Leonard I. Pearlin Award for Distinguished Contributions to the Sociological Study of Mental Health from the American Sociological Association in 2009. He earned his Ph.D. from the University of Alberta.

Ozge Sensoy Bahar is a recent doctoral graduate of University of Illinois at Urbana-Champaign, School of Social Work. Her research interests include inner-city communities, ethnic families, migration and women, the intersection of race/ethnicity, gender, and class, and resilience. Her dissertation explored how low-income Kurdish migrant/displaced mothers reconstructed their lives in an inner-city neighborhood of Istanbul, Turkey after migrating from the southeast of Turkey. Dr. Sensoy Bahar has co-authored multiple publications and conference presentations on the challenges encountered by inner-city residents both in Turkey and the United States as well as the resilience of female members of these communities in navigating multiple challenges created by structural factors.

Kristen Benson is Assistant Professor of Human Development and Family Science at North Dakota State University. A licensed Marriage and Family Therapist and Certified Family Life Educator, her research and clinical focus is on supporting lesbian, gay, bisexual, transgender, queer (LGBTQ) people and relationships. She is a clinical fellow of the American Association for Marriage and Family Therapy and a member of the National Council on Family Relations. She received her Ph.D. from Virginia Tech.

Adrian Blow is Associate Professor in the Department of Human Development and Family Studies at Michigan State University and Program Director of the couple and family therapy program. He is involved with several studies related to military deployment, including post-deployment adjustment of National Guard couples, evaluation of the Buddy-to-Buddy program (a peer-to-peer support program), resiliency processes in National Guard families, and other family-based interventions. He received his Ph.D. from Purdue University.

Gary L. Bowen is Kenan Distinguished Professor and serves as Lead Scientist in the Jordan Institute for Military Members, Veterans, and their Families, School of Social Work, the University of North Carolina at Chapel Hill. He also co-directs the School Success Profile (SSP) project and is a Fellow of the National Council on Family Relations (NCFR), the Society for Social Work and Research (SSWR), and Armed Forces & Society (AFS). He is past President of NCFR (2009–2011). He received his Ph.D. from the University of North Carolina at Greensboro.

Patricia A. Brennan is Professor of Psychology at Emory University. Her primary area of research is developmental psychopathology. She employs longitudinal and treatment research designs to assess biosocial risk factors for aggression, as well as the intergenerational transmission of depression and related disorders. Recently she has been examining the utility of biological factors as predictors of

outcome in the context of Multisystemic Therapy. She received her Ph.D. from the University of Southern California.

Linda M. Burton is James B. Duke Professor of Sociology at Duke University. She directed the ethnographic component of Welfare, Children, and Families: A Three-City Study and is Principal Investigator of a multi-site team ethnographic study (Family Life Project) of poverty, family processes, and child development in six rural communities. Her research integrates ethnographic and demographic approaches and examines the roles that poverty and intergenerational family dynamics play in the intimate unions of low-income mothers and the accelerated life course transitions of children, adolescents, and adults in urban and rural families. She received her Ph.D. from the University of Southern California.

Hans Saint-Eloi Cadely is a doctoral candidate in the Department of Human Development and Family Studies at Auburn University. His research focuses on adolescent identity development and changes in romantic relationships throughout the transitional period of adolescence to adulthood. Hans currently has four refereed journal publications that address adolescent romantic relationships, identity development, and intervention programs. He has also been involved in the implementation of relationship education programs across the state of Alabama such as Relationship Smarts.

Jinette Comeau is a doctoral candidate in Sociology at Western University and graduate research fellow at the Children's Health Research Institute. Her dissertation examines the impact of socioeconomic disadvantage, neighborhood context, and family processes on children's mental health over the life course. She is co-author of "The impact of mental illness on the family" in *The handbook of the sociology of mental health*, 2nd edn.

Patrick W. Corrigan is Distinguished Professor of Psychology at the Illinois Institute of Technology and a licensed clinical psychologist for more than 30 years. He is the Director of the National Consortium on Stigma and Empowerment (NCSE), a research center supported by NIMH. Central to NCSE is the Center on Adherence and Self-Determination (CASD), supported as a developing center in services research by NIMH. Corrigan is a prolific researcher, having authored or edited 12 books and more than 300 papers. He received his Psy.D. from the Illinois School of Professional Psychology.

Kimberly A. Crossman is a doctoral candidate in the Department of Human and Community Development at the University of Illinois at Urbana-Champaign. Her research focuses on women's experiences of violent and nonviolent intimate partner abuse in the contexts of marriage, divorce or separation, and co-parenting with a current or former abusive partner. She is particularly interested in the roles of coercive control and the influence of gender in women's experiences of abuse.

Phillippe B. Cunningham is Professor in the Department of Psychiatry and Behavioral Sciences, Family Services Research Center at the Medical University of South Carolina. He has had a longstanding commitment to addressing the psychosocial needs of children and adolescents, especially those who are disadvantaged and underserved. Much of this work has taken place within the context of federally funded studies aimed at further validating and disseminating Multisystemic Therapy. In 2000, Dr. Cunningham received the Theodore H. Blau Early Career Award from the American Psychological Association's Society of Clinical Psychology. He received his Ph.D. from Virginia Tech.

Patt Denning is Director of Clinical Services and Training at the Harm Reduction Therapy Center (HRTC) and has been a primary developer of Harm Reduction Treatments (HTC). She is a Diplomate-Fellow in Psychopharmacology and a certified addiction specialist through the American Psychological Association's College of Professional Psychology. She has worked in public and private treatment settings since 1975. She received her Ph.D. from the San Francisco School of Psychology.

Megan L. Dolbin–MacNab is Associate Professor of Human Development, Associate Professor of Health Sciences, and a faculty affiliate of the Center for Gerontology at Virginia Tech. She is also a licensed Marriage and Family Therapist and the Clinical Training Director at the Family Therapy Center of Virginia Tech. Her research on grandfamilies has explored grandchild experiences and well-being, parenting and family dynamics, and best practices for community-based interventions. She is the author of numerous journal articles and book chapters about grandfamilies, and has also developed variety of resources for practitioners working with custodial grandparents and their grandchildren. She received her Ph.D. from Purdue University.

Ana Rocío Escobar-Chew is an international Fulbright scholar and a postdoctoral fellow in the program of Couple and Family Therapy at Michigan State University. She is the project manager of various mix-methods studies focused on evidenced-based services for Latinos (including an NIMH-funded study on parenting and a program evaluation study for IPV Latina survivors). Her research experience includes community-based research, cultural adaptation of evidenced-based interventions, gender-based violence, and immigrant families. Her doctoral dissertation explored the life experiences and parenting needs of Guatemalan women exposed to violence. She is a member of the MSU Research Consortium on Gender-Based Violence at MSU. She earned her Ph.D. from Michigan State University.

Anne F. Farrell is Assistant Professor in the Department of Human Development and Family Studies at the University of Connecticut. She is a translational scholar whose work encompasses at-risk and underserved populations, including children with special health care needs (CSHCN) and their families. Recent projects and publications address family-centered practices, positive behavior interventions, cross-systems collaboration, family resilience, supportive housing in child welfare, and military families with CSHCN. She serves on the editorial boards of *Infants and Young Children*, *Family Relations*, and *Early Childhood Research Quarterly*. She received her Ph.D. from Hofstra University.

Sharon L. Foster is Distinguished Professor at the California School of Professional Psychology at Alliant International University in San Diego. She is the author of numerous articles and book chapters on children's aggression and peer relations, assessment and treatment of parent–adolescent conflict, and research methodology. She also co-authored *Helping adolescents at risk* (2004) and *Negotiating parent–adolescent conflict* (1989). She received her Ph.D. from the State University of New York at Stony Brook.

Natalie R. Gela is a doctoral candidate in Clinical Psychology at the Illinois Institute of Technology, Chicago, Illinois. Her research and clinical interests include working with individuals, couples and families coping with mental illness.

Samantha A. Goodrich is Senior Research and Evaluation Scientist in the Office of Health Systems Research and Innovation within the Lehigh Valley Health Network. Her research interests include evaluations of prevention and intervention programs for children and families. In particular, her focus is on the implementation of programs that aim to improve the health and well-being of families and communities, including home visiting, parent education, early education, early intervention, and wrap-around programs. She received her Ph.D. from the University of Connecticut Department of Human Development and Family Studies.

Lisa Gorman is Program Director for the Michigan Public Health Institute and a licensed Marriage and Family Therapist. She works collaboratively with families, public health, universities, policy makers, and other community partners on innovative solutions that will improve health outcomes and quality of life for families. Dr. Gorman has been engaged in program development, evaluation, and research activities on behalf of military families since 2005 and is co-principal investigator of Risk, Resiliency, and Coping in National Guard Families, a Department of Defense-funded study. She received her Ph.D. in Family and Child Ecology from Michigan State University.

Jennifer L. Hardesty is Associate Professor of Family Studies in the Department of Human and Community Development at the University of Illinois at Urbana-Champaign. Her research focuses on mothers who separate from violent partners, with specific attention

to the separation/divorce process, post-separation violence and coercive control, parenting with violent former partners, and the health and safety of mothers and children after separation. She received her Ph.D. in Human Development and Family Studies from the University of Missouri-Columbia and completed a postdoctoral training fellowship in violence research in the School of Nursing at Johns Hopkins University.

Bert Hayslip, Jr. is Regents Professor Emeritus at the University of North Texas. He is a Fellow of the American Psychological Association, the Gerontological Society of America, and the Association for Gerontology in Higher Education. An Associate Editor of *Experimental Aging Research* and of *Developmental Psychology*, his co-authored books include *Emerging perspectives on resilience in adulthood and later life* (Springer, 2012), *Resilient grandparent caregivers: A strengths-based perspective* (Routledge, 2012), *Adult development and aging* (Krieger, 2011), and *Parenting the custodial grandchild* (Springer, 2008). He is Co-principal Investigator on a NINR-funded project exploring interventions to improve the functioning of grandparent caregivers. He received his Ph.D. from the University of Akron.

Robin L. Jarrett is Professor of Family Studies in the Department of Human and Community Development, and Professor in the Department of African American Studies at the University of Illinois at Urbana-Champaign. Her research interests include positive child and adolescent development, African American family functioning and resilience, and building supportive inner-city communities. As an urban ethnographer, Dr. Jarrett uses an array of qualitative data collection strategies in her research, including participant observation, neighborhood observation, individual and group interviewing, photo-documentation, and GIS. She has published widely in journals that reflect her interest in child/youth development, families, and neighborhoods, including *Journal of Children and Poverty*, *Journal of Family Issues*, *Journal of Family Psychology*, *Journal of Poverty*, *Journal of Research on Adolescence*, and *International Journal of the Constructed Environment*. She received her Ph.D. from the University of Chicago, Department of Sociology.

Jennifer Kerpelman is Professor of Human Development and Family Studies and Associate Dean for Research and Graduate Studies in the College of Human Sciences at Auburn University. Her research focuses on the examination of adolescent development and adolescents' relationships with parents and peers. She has over 50 refereed journal publications that address individual development, close relationship functioning, and adolescent outcomes such as educational goals, sexual health, relationship knowledge and quality, and identity development. She also has created resources designed to promote positive youth development in areas of self-development, civic engagement, parent–adolescent relationships, and adolescent peer and dating relationships. She received her Ph.D. from Auburn University.

Robin Gaines Lanzi is Associate Professor and Graduate Program Director of Health Behavior in the School of Public Health at the University of Alabama at Birmingham. She is a developmental psychologist with a maternal and child health background whose research centers on reducing maternal and child health disparities and promoting positive youth development. A central theme throughout her research is "putting research into practice" through multiple pathways, including a focus on community-based participatory research in the design, planning, implementation, and dissemination of findings. She received her Ph.D. from the University of Alabama at Birmingham.

Sara Lappan is a doctoral student in the Department of Human Development and Family Studies with a concentration in Couple and Family Therapy at Michigan State University. She is currently involved in program evaluation research. Sara is a student affiliate of the American Association of Marriage and Family Therapy. Her clinical experience includes providing family, couple, and individual therapy working in the Adolescent Partial Hospitalization Program at Borgess Medical Center, at Western Michigan University's Center for Counseling and Psychological Services, Michigan State University's Couple and Family Therapy Clinic, and Perspectives Therapy Services.

Bethany L. Letiecq is Associate Professor of Human Development and Family Science at George Mason University. She teaches courses on family relations and family law and social policy. Her community-based and action research focuses on the health and well-being of families marginalized by social, economic, and political forces. Most recently, she has worked in partnership with Mexican migrant families settling in new destinations to ameliorate poor mental health conditions among migrant families and promote migrant justice. She received her Ph.D. from the University of Maryland at College Park.

Ann Booker Loper is Professor at the University of Virginia's Curry School of Education. Her research focuses on the mental health and adjustment of prisoners and their family members, with a particular emphasis upon the parent–child relationships in justice-involved families. Dr. Loper has collaborated with prison, jail, and community partners in the development of a parenting program for incarcerated mothers. She has consulted with local and state agencies concerning the rehabilitative needs of returning prisoners, particularly as related to family reunification. She received her Ph.D. from the University of Texas at Austin.

Chris Marchiondo is a doctoral student in Human Development and Family Studies, with a specialization in Couple and Family Therapy at Michigan State University. His research focuses on the risk and protective factors facing veterans and their families after combat deployments. Previously, Chris served as an active duty Army officer.

Alyssa McElwain is a doctoral candidate in Human Development and Family Studies at Auburn University. Her research focuses on interpersonal and individual factors associated with adolescent sexual development including romantic relationships, parent–adolescent relationships, and identity exploration. She has worked in outreach in the state of Alabama by assisting with the implementation of sexual health and relationship education programs, writing website content, and providing technical assistance and program evaluation. She has also coordinated undergraduate service learning courses that implement positive youth development and relationship education programs targeting adolescents in the local community.

Marvin McKinney is Research Fellow at the Frank Porter Graham Child Development Institute at the University of North Carolina at Chapel Hill and Co-principal Investigator for Promoting Academic Success for Young Boys of Color. He is also a member of the Research, Policy, and Practice Alliance Supporting Excellence in Black Children and serves as senior consultant to University Outreach and Engagement at Michigan State University. He has over three decades of experience working as a strategist and an advocate for young children in urban communities. He received his Ph.D. from the University of Michigan.

Ezella McPherson has expertise in qualitative research, STEM education, mentoring, academic advising, K-20 retention, persistence, and graduation for underserved populations. Her dissertation centered on the persistence of African American women in STEM fields. It examined why some African American women stayed in or departed from STEM majors. Her current research projects focus on college student persistence and success for underrepresented populations in STEM fields at PWIs and HBCUs. Other research interests include: resilience, mentoring, health, neighborhoods, environmental studies, and urban studies. She recently received her Ph.D. in Educational Policy Studies from the University of Illinois at Urbana-Champaign

Marya C. McPherson is Executive Director at Mental Health America of New River Valley in Blacksburg, Virginia. She has over 20 years' experience working with families, children, and older adults through educational and community-based programs. In recent years, Ms. McPherson has acquired additional credentials and expertise in adult development and aging, research, and grant-writing, with a primary focus on family violence prevention and mental health across the lifespan. Her current role involves advocacy, education, and program development for improved community response to mental health challenges. She received her Master's degree from Virginia Tech.

Lenore M. McWey is Professor in the Marriage and Family Therapy Doctoral Program at Florida State University. Her research and clinical interests involve working with families at high risk for child maltreatment. She is particularly interested in systemic interventions aimed to improve outcomes of families involved with the child welfare system. She received her Ph.D. from Florida State University.

Rob Palkovitz is Professor of Human Development and Family Studies at the University of Delaware. His research interests are in fathering and intergenerational relationships and development, with a particular emphasis on the relationships between patterns of father involvement and developmental outcomes for men and their children. His teaching, research, and community service focus on applied systems perspectives for facilitating life opportunities for persons at risk. He received his Ph.D. from Rutgers University.

José Rubén Parra-Cardona is Associate Professor in the program of Couple and Family Therapy at Michigan State University (MSU), Department of Human Development and Family Studies. He is also Associate Director of the MSU Research Consortium on Gender-Based Violence. His NIMH-funded research is focused on the prevention of child abuse and neglect through the cultural adaptation of evidence-based parenting interventions for Latino immigrant populations. His violence research is focused on: (a) investigating the cultural relevance of services for Latina survivors and Latino men who abuse, and (b) understanding intervention processes associated with men's elimination of abusive behaviors. He received his Ph.D. from Texas Tech University.

Kathleen W. Piercy is Professor in the Department of Family, Consumer, and Human Development at Utah State University. She teaches undergraduate and graduate student courses in family policy, and graduate courses in personal relationships and in qualitative methods. Dr. Piercy's primary research focus is on the dynamics of family care of older adults. Her first book, *Working with aging families: Therapeutic solutions for caregivers, spouses, and adult children*, was published by W. W. Norton in 2010. She has authored or co-authored 40 refereed journal articles, mostly on aging topics, and three book chapters. She received her Ph.D. from Virginia Tech.

Craig T. Ramey is Distinguished Scholar of Human Development at the Virginia Tech Carilion Research Institute and Professor of Psychology at Virginia Tech. He is a lifespan developmental psychologist who has conducted randomized controlled studies of the impact of high-quality early childhood education on the cognitive, social, and educational outcomes for vulnerable children (including the Abecedarian Project, Project CARE, and the Infant Health and Development Program). These studies have affirmed that positive early childhood experiences exert a large effect on adolescent and adult outcomes, including health and educational attainment with benefits to the entire family. He received his Ph.D. from West Virginia University.

Sharon Landesman Ramey is Distinguished Scholar of Human Development at the Virginia Tech Carilion Research Institute and Professor of Psychology at Virginia Tech. She is a developmental scientist who has studied the changing American family. She has developed and tested interventions for children with developmental disabilities and with family risk conditions, often resulting in large and sustained benefits that exceed what had been predicted based on their biology and life circumstances. She also conducts research on stress and resilience effects across multiple generations. She received her Ph.D. from the University of Washington at Seattle.

Karen A. Roberto is Professor and Director of the Center for Gerontology and the Institute for Society, Culture and Environment at Virginia Tech. Her research focuses on health and social support in late life and includes studies of rural older women, family relationships and caregiving, and elder abuse. She is the author of over 180 scholarly publications and the editor/author of 11 books. Dr. Roberto is a Fellow of the Gerontological Society of America and the National Council on Family Relations. She is a recipient of the Gerontological Society of America Behavioral and Social Sciences Distinguished Mentorship Award. She received her Ph.D. from Texas Tech University.

Kevin M. Roy is Associate Professor in the Department of Family Science at the University of Maryland, College Park, School of Public Health. His research focuses on the life course of young men on the margins of families and the work force, as they transition into adulthood and fatherhood. He explores the intersection of policy systems, such as welfare reform, community-based parenting programs, and incarceration, with caregiving and providing roles in kin networks. He received his Ph.D. from Northwestern University.

Stacy R. Ryan is Assistant Professor in the Department of Psychiatry, Neurobehavioral Research Laboratory and Clinic at the University of Texas Health Science Center at San Antonio. Her primary research interests center on identifying factors that influence outcomes for treatment of youth substance use and related aggressive/delinquent behavior. She is particularly interested in using this information to understand the utility of current evidence-based programs for underserved families. She received her Ph.D. from Emory University.

Howard Stevenson is Constance E. Clayton Professor of Urban Education and Africana Studies at the University of Pennsylvania in the Applied Psychology and Human Development Division at the Graduate School of Education. His research interests include the development of racial socialization interventions to promote racial coping strategies that increase youth and family well-being. His latest book, *Promoting racial literacy in schools: Differences that make a difference*, focuses on how educators, community leaders, and parents can resolve face-to-face racially stressful encounters that undermine student achievement and health, racial profiling, and social conflicts within neighborhoods of color. He received his Ph.D. from the Fuller Graduate School of Psychology.

Pamela B. Teaster is Professor at the Center for Gerontology and Department of Human Development at Virginia Tech. She previously served as Director of the Geriatric Education Center and Director and Chairperson of the Graduate Center for Gerontology/Department of Gerontology, Director of Doctoral Studies, and Associate Dean for Research for the College of Public Health at the University of Kentucky. Dr. Teaster is a member of the editorial board of the *Journal of Elder Abuse and Neglect* and is a Fellow of the Gerontological Society of America and the Association for Gerontology in Higher Education. She received her Ph.D. from Virginia Tech.

Brad van Eeden-Moorefield is Associate Professor in the Department of Family and Child Studies at Montclair State University. He also is a Certified Family Life Educator and has previously worked as a clinical therapist. His research focuses on how the social context influences relationship processes and outcomes among diverse families, including step-families and those headed by same-sex couples. Much of his work uses a queer feminist lens to understand these influences. He earned his Ph.D. from the University of North Carolina at Greensboro.

Damian Waters is a doctoral candidate in the Family Science Department at the University of Maryland. His research interests center around understanding the processes and contexts shaping fatherhood, particularly the intersection of paternal and child health. His current project explores father involvement in pediatric caregiving among low-income, emerging adult men. He is also a Licensed Graduate Marriage and Family Therapist and coordinates fatherhood services for a teen parenting program at Children's National Medical Center.

Mathilde Whalen is a doctoral candidate in Clinical and School Psychology at the University of Virginia's Curry School of Education, where she received her Master's degree in 2011. Her research focuses on behavioral outcomes of youth who have experienced the incarceration of a close family member. She has worked to revise and implement a parenting curriculum designed for incarcerated mothers at several correctional facilities across the state of Virginia. Ms. Whalen's clinical interests include forensic assessment and providing mental health interventions within the correctional system.

Michael Whitehead is a doctoral student in the Couple and Family Therapy program at Michigan State University. He is currently involved in research focusing on the statewide implementation of an efficacious parenting program. He has also been involved in a number of research projects ranging from theory evaluation to intervention development. His current research focus is primarily on the experience of children in bi-racial families, and more broadly on evidence-based interventions for children and families.

Joanna Will is a doctoral candidate in Clinical and School Psychology in the Curry School of Education at the University of Virginia. She is a former probation officer who has provided assessment and intervention to justice-involved individuals across a variety of community, forensic, and inpatient settings. Her research interests include domestic violence, inmate adjustment and mental health, and the impact of incarceration on the family.

Donna-Marie Winn is Research Scientist at the Frank Porter Graham Child Development Institute at the University of North Carolina at Chapel Hill. Her areas of expertise include mental health and well-being, race, and culture. Dr. Winn has been involved in the development of numerous national, evidence-based programs to enhance children's social, emotional, and academic skills. She has extensive experience in conducting research on resilience in African American families. She currently leads the Research, Policy, and Practice Alliance Supporting Excellence in Black Children and the Promoting Academic Success of Boys of Color Project. She is a licensed clinical psychologist and received her Ph.D. from the University of North Carolina at Chapel Hill.

Armeda Stevenson Wojciak is Assistant Professor at the University of Iowa in the Couple and Family Therapy Doctoral Program. Her research focuses on identifying and using protective factors to improve outcomes for children and families involved with the foster-care system. She received her Ph.D. from Florida State University.

Acknowledgments

This textbook resulted from the efforts and contributions of many different people. I would like to first gratefully acknowledge Wiley Executive Editor Julia Teweles for her early input in developing this project and her encouragement to assemble an edited volume that addressed contemporary challenges and strengths among families. Thanks also to Julia Kirk, Wiley Senior Project Editor, for her excellent assistance in organizing the details of the book project and overseeing its execution. I also want to acknowledge those who assisted me in the final stages of copyediting this book and preparing it for production: Wiley staff Ian Critchley and Christopher Feeney, and Virginia Tech students Cailin Clinton, Sara Spiers, and Kendra Woodley.

Most of all I would like to thank the 20 contributors of this textbook and their willingness to share their knowledge and viewpoint on vulnerable families and how best to respond to diverse family contexts of care and community. *Family Problems* is truly an interdisciplinary endeavor; authors represent varied academic disciplines and professional backgrounds and I appreciate the obvious effort that went into each and every chapter.

Finally, this textbook is a means for me to acknowledge my own family in all their complexity. We are a resilient bunch, and it is from them that I learned to endure, and ultimately be transformed by, family problems.

1

Introduction and Conceptual Overview

Joyce A. Arditti

Case Example: Nick

Nick, a 16-year-old, moved with his family from a large city in the Northwestern United States to a Southern rural town during the summer before his eleventh-grade year. Nick is a second-generation member of a Chinese family; his grandparents immigrated during the 1950s; his father, whose job transfer caused the move, is an engineer and his mother an elementary schoolteacher. Up to the point of the move, Nick's medical and psychological histories had been "unremarkable to date." In his home city, he was an avid gaming enthusiast, and a natural on the baseball field. Nick was well liked by his circle of friends who accepted his bisexual orientation without judgement. In contrast to his large, racially diverse high school in his home city, his new school was small, and comprised 550 predominantly white students. Cliques among students were well formed and hard to penetrate. In his new environment, Nick had trouble making friends, was terribly homesick, and kept his sexual orientation a secret for fear of being bullied. By the end of the fall semester, Nick's grades had dropped to an all-time low and he was spending most of his time in his room alone, either sleeping or gaming. He had not touched a baseball in months. Additionally, he was having a great deal of stomach pain and was diagnosed with a bleeding ulcer, causing him to miss a great deal of school. Nick's family realized he was in trouble.

As we can see from the case examples on pages 1 and 2, both Nick's and Martina's family are in trouble, and affected by an array of problems stemming from caregiver stress, economic inadequacy, adolescent development, social exclusion, and health challenges. Whether Nick or Martina and their families will be able to effectively deal with the problems they are faced with depends on a number of individual, family, and societal factors including how they define their situation, their ability to respond to family demands, resources and assets at their disposal, individual competencies and strengths, social support, and societal tolerance and understanding regarding the conditions and situations with which each family is confronted. For example, whether Nick will thrive, survive, or deteriorate during his junior year and beyond is contingent on his ability to get the help he needs, find support, and transform his experience into something that has meaning and ultimately enhances his development. How might this happen? First, Nick is lucky: he is

Family Problems: Stress, Risk, and Resilience, First Edition. Edited by Joyce A. Arditti.
© 2015 John Wiley & Sons, Inc. Published 2015 by John Wiley & Sons, Inc.

Case Example: Martina

Mexican-born Martina is an 81-year-old widow with an array of medical needs. She has painful arthritis and is showing the early signs of dementia. Martina lives with her daughter, Lisa, and her four grandchildren aged 4 to 14. Lisa is a single mother who does shift-work at a local poultry factory near an urban center. She, Martina, and the kids live in a third story two-bedroom apartment in a tough neighborhood punctuated with occasional gang-related violence. Once a caring grandmother and a help to Lisa and the children, Martina has increasingly become a "burden" to the family. Martina has trouble walking and caring for herself and personality changes include irritability and forgetfulness. For example, recently after making dinner, Martina left the stove on overnight. Now, 14-year-old Johnny is left in charge of Martina and the children while Lisa works evenings. However, Johnny has taken up with a new set of friends and rather than holding down the fort, he is out most nights on the streets leaving Martina and the younger children to fend for themselves. Lisa is at a breaking point – she is unable to carry the load of caring for her children, work, and dealing with Martina's caregiving and health needs. Lisa is also grieving the loss of the loving mother she once had, before Martina's dementia. While Martina has Medicare coverage, Lisa's earnings are barely enough to get by. Based on Lisa's commitment to keeping her family together and caring for her mother at home, Lisa has taken an extra shift on weekends to make ends meet.

smart and has loving and supportive parents and siblings who believe in him. Nick's family has health insurance and financial resources and are able to get him in to see a counselor who understands the challenges Nick is facing and is nonjudgmental about Nick's bisexuality. Nick also receives the medical attention he needs for his ulcer. He begins to feel better about himself, breaks his isolation, and with his family's support, decides to try out for the baseball team the spring of his junior year. A new family moves in next door and Nick becomes friends with the teenage daughter, Zoe, who is also into gaming. Nick feels safe with her – she too was a city girl and a non-conformist in her politics and dress. She has a small group of gaming and political friends and Nick decides to "come out" and with his counselor's help, Nick shares his sexual orientation with his new-found friends and joins their causes for civil rights. Between medical and psychological treatment, making the baseball team, and the support of his friends and family, Nick's senior year looks bright. Nick's path is one of transcendence over adversity. But he did not necessarily do it alone.

Perhaps Lisa, Martina and their wider family are not so lucky. Lisa is teetering on the poverty line, and without the financial resources that Nick's family has, she will have a tough time meeting the demands of her situation. Lisa's children are at risk of endangerment unless adequate supervision and developmentally enhancing care can be found. Martina will continue to deteriorate without the proper medical and physical care. Johnny may end up joining one of the gangs in his neighborhood without some kind of intervention to promote his well-being. It is clear he cannot handle the adult-like family responsibilities Lisa has given him. Lisa has too many responsibilities as a single-mother and caregiver to Martina. She needs support and help and since she has no kin to rely on, it will have to come from the outside. Tired and alone, Lisa, herself is at risk for burn-out.

All families have problems. Some of these problems stem from change within and outside the family. Other problems are connected to developmental transitions and challenges inherent in certain caregiving arrangements, such as caring for an elder or infirm family member. Further, problems may be intensified or seemingly irresolvable due to discrimination and social inequality. *Family Problems: Stress, Risk, and Resilience* examines an array of critical challenges faced by contemporary families such as Nick's and

Lisa's, and digs deep into their origins, effects, and perhaps most importantly how families may still thrive and grow in the face of adversity. Additionally, an essential question posed throughout the book is: when do family issues become "problems"?

What is a Family Problem?

The field of family studies has long considered the issue of family problems, with particular attention to how families cope with stress related to various life transitions and difficult life events. Key trends within family science that emerged during the 1990s have been influential in how we define and conceive of family problems. These developments include a focus on individual and family resilience, as well as feminist and ethnic minority critique that has given way to recognition of the diversity of family experiences (Doherty, Boss, LaRossa, Schumm, and Steinmetz, 2008). The diverse "postmodern" family is fluid and distinct from previous generations, essentially broadening the scope of family problem definition, as well as expert interpretation of the challenges families face in their everyday lives and how best to solve these challenges. There are three broad perspectives that can be applied in thinking about family problems today and these perspectives or *theories* are utilized throughout the book: (1) a constructivist perspective, (2) the family stress perspective, and (3) ecological systems theory.

Constructivist reflections on the nature of family problems

First, a phenomenon is a family problem when it is seen as such by family members themselves or defined by a great many others in the family's social world. This criterion is rooted in "constructivist theory," which emphasizes how people view the relationships and situations they are involved in. For example, some of Nick's difficulties were rooted in his concern that his bisexuality would be viewed as abnormal or different by members of his new school and community. This fear is warranted given the likelihood of negative and homophobic attitudes that more often characterize both rural and Southern regions of the United States (Eldridge, Mack, and Swank, 2006; Snively,

Krueger, Stretch, Watt, and Chadha, 2004). Thus real or imagined discrimination was a force that was adding to the difficulties Nick was having in adjusting to his new life after his move.

From a constructivist perspective, all knowledge systems are "ever-changing human inventions" to help people make sense of their lives (Raskin, 2006, p. 212). Constructivism also involves an increasing emphasis on understanding families in context, in their social world, with a sensitivity to the oppressive power of larger social forces. Power may be manifested to the extent to which people can get others to accept and live according to their preferred discourses. From a constructivist viewpoint, social inequality is in part a byproduct of one's inability to gain this acceptance – thus problems signify a gap in how families experience the world and social pathologizing of that experience.

At the core of constructivism is a central assumption that human beings – individually and through their relationships (e.g., Gergen, 1994), "create meaningful mental frameworks of understanding," which are the basis for self-understanding and comprehending the surrounding world (Raskin, 2006, p. 212). By extension, families construe their interactions with the world and these constructions may serve to organize families around specific problems (Doherty and Baptiste, 2008). In contrast, a hallmark of positivistic social science was the belief that "facts" about the world and more specifically about families were givens that could produce generalizations that could be tested by gathering more facts (Doherty and Baptiste, 2008). Therefore, family health, well-being, and other specific child and family outcomes rested on a certain pattern of facts and objective conditions. Concurrently, deviations from these facts, typically defined in terms of traditional family forms, role functions, and normative developmental trajectories, were characterized as *problems* located within people and within families. Now, with family science's recognition of the postmodern family, the question of whether a particular role variation, family structure, or interactional pattern is defined as a problem is more complex. Family phenomena can be defined one way within the family by its members, and defined outside the boundaries of the family by society in another manner altogether. Consider for example the controversy that swirls around the notion of the "family bed." Is sleeping with your child a problem? Medical experts argue that co-sleeping can be physically dangerous for children, emotionally unhealthy, and compromise marital intimacy. Parent advocates cite benefits such as increased bonding and access between parents and child(ren), as well as more confident and secure children. A polarizing illustration such as the family bed illustrates how family and social definitions may be at odds. From a constructivist perspective, people are viewed as actively creating meaning – and as we see from the family-bed example, meaning systems can be wildly different among people and contexts.

Thus problems, sometimes defined as psychopathology or family pathology, occur not only as a result of social rejection, but when individual, familial, and cultural ways of construing are incongruent or become ineffective. Problems are inherently rooted in meaning because they involve a "felt discrepancy between the way things are and the way they are … supposed to be" (Mahoney, 2003, p. 45). Lisa's family is a case-in-point, based on her cultural heritage she believes she should be able to take care of her mother Martina and keep her at home, yet the way things are and the necessities associated with Martina's care is creating a great discrepancy for her which has become a source of distress. Therefore, problems can be viewed as expressions of a family's attempt to protect itself, and pursue directions that feel "immediately satisfying" (Mahoney, 2003, p. 45). From this standpoint, *problems are often attempts at solutions* (Mahoney, 2003), and in this manner, important mechanisms of development and systemic reorganization. Lisa's shift work, which takes her out of the home and leaves vulnerable family members unsupervised, is a problem, but also an attempt on her part to resolve the family's economic inadequacies.

In sum, constructivism highlights that problems are rooted in discrepant or ineffective meanings and often products of collective definition – particularly in relation to social and cultural norms pertaining to family dysfunction and deviance (Schneider, 1985). However, it is also worth noting that some family conditions fail to be identified as "social problems" and thus remain invisible to society in that they are not deemed important issues of concern (worthy of resources and intervention) (Schneider, 1985). Society and even family

experts may not recognize a problem per se, and yet a certain set of conditions, behaviors, interactions, can be defined within the family, or by one of its members, as problematic. Moreover, family problems of devalued groups (such as the poor, minorities, prisoners) may be particularly invisible and thus collective definition of an issue may dominate, effectively obscuring the families' experience.

Family stress theory and family problems

A second perspective applied in deciding whether an issue is a "family problem" involves the extent to which the degree of stress reaches a level that is more than the family "can handle." Family members may become dissatisfied, compromised, or show other signs of disturbance. We can clearly see this happening in Lisa's family. The fact that Lisa is feeling that she is "ready to snap" suggests the demands of her situation are exceeding her ability to respond to them as well as compromising the healthy functioning of the family and the well-being of its members. This perspective focuses on how change, loss, and disturbance can create stress (Boss, 2002). Lisa's stress is further intensified by the loss she feels due to the changes in her mother's mental and physical health.

Traditional approaches to studying family problems draw heavily from a family stress framework, which historically pathologized hardship and adversity. The study of family stress began in the 1930s, during the Great Depression. Its classic formulation was embodied by Ruben Hill's ABC-X model (1949), developed as a result of his research on war-torn families. This work established the study of families in crisis, and a conceptual and empirical tradition for the study of distressed families that remained virtually unchanged until the early 1980s. A central deficiency of Hill's model was its static nature and dysfunctional definition of crisis. A second model of family stress was subsequently developed, the double ABC-X model (McCubbin and Patterson, 1982), which highlighted the adjustment process of the family and how an imbalance of resources and demands, as well as the family's inability to stop change, gave rise to distress. This model of family stress became the predominant framework for considering family problems for the next decade. However, deficiencies still persisted in that the model was static and mechanistic and considered change as pathological. Personal and environmental factors were considered to exist separately and prior to their connection to the "stressor event," and as a result, there was an overemphasis on action and reaction or cause and effect (Smith, 1984). Dynamic processes and positive adaptations were thus ignored.

The Family Adjustment and Adaptation Response (FAAR) model (Patterson, 1988) represents family stress theorizing that considered active processes and varied adaptations, including the possibility of positive family adjustment. Families are viewed as actively engaging in ways to balance *family demands* with *family capabilities*. Demands can be normative (e.g., stress associated with parenting and adolescence), and non-normative (e.g., change events such as an act of violence or, as in Nick's case, the family move across the country). Demands can also encompass ongoing family strains, which tend to be unresolved, such as Lisa's caregiving burden, and daily hassles (e.g., minor day-to-day disruptions) (Patterson, 2002). Family capabilities include tangible (e.g., income) and intangible (psychological coping or social support) resources of the family.

A growing emphasis on meaning and the family's "world view" is apparent in the FAAR model. From the FAAR framework, consistent with family stress theory, the process of adapting to major stressors involves changing prior values and beliefs in order to make sense of what is affecting the family (Patterson, 1993). If family demands significantly and persistently exceed family capabilities, families experience crisis, which is a period of disorganization in which the family cannot function or carry out its normal responsibilities. Or families may poorly adapt in their attempts to strike a balance between demands and capabilities, making them *vulnerable*. For example, if Lisa started drinking to the point of dependence to cope with the imbalance of demands and capabilities in her family, we can predict a poor outcome and family vulnerability.

The contextual model of family stress

Marriage and family therapist and scholar Pauline Boss advanced a Contextual Model of Family Stress, which draws from ecological theory (next section) and also builds on elements of Hill's original ABC-X model. Boss (2002) conceptualized family stress processes as

---

Box 1.1 Daily Hassles

Research has found that "normal stressors," that is, the ongoing strains and repeated hassles of everyday life, have been found to figure more prominently in predicting negative health outcomes and pain (De Benedittis and Lorenzetti, 1992; DeLongis, Coyne, Dakof, Folkman, and Lazarus, 1982), depression in adolescents (Dumont and Provost, 1999), and certain aspects of family functioning (Crnic and Greenberg, 1990) than major life events (e.g., divorce or relocation). Hassles are the "irritating, frustrating, distressing demands" that characterize everyday life and can involve practical problems (e.g., losing things, traffic jams), disappointments, feeling as if one has "too much to do," and stress stemming from the ongoing care of children and aged parents (Kanner, Coyne, Schaefer, and Lazarus, 1981, p. 3). Beginning in the late 1970s, Richard Lazarus and his colleagues published a series of theoretical papers proposing

the significance of relatively minor stresses on health outcomes. The central ideas behind this scholarship were that minor stresses are *cumulative* and *proximal* – that is, they build up and people's experience of them is direct and immediate (for example, think of how you felt the last time you were stuck in traffic and late for an appointment or had an argument with a family member).

Some hassles may be situationally determined and infrequent (as in the case of bad weather and a canceled airline flight), while others are more repetitive because the individual remains in a context that is characterized by predictable demands – as in the case of parents with young children (Crnic and Greenberg, 1990). Protective factors such as family support, self-esteem, positive experiences and effective coping strategies help individuals tolerate or minimize the effects of daily hassles and normative stress (Dumont and Provost, 1999; Kanner et al., 1981; Lazarus, 1990).

influenced by *internal* and *external* contexts. External contexts are those components outside of the family, such as war or economic recession, over which the family has no control. According to Boss, these outside "macro" influences can profoundly affect how family members perceive, experience, and manage stress. Elements that the family can control and change to reduce stress were labeled the internal context by Boss. These include family boundaries, or definitions about who is in and out of the family, and family rules and roles. For example, a lack of clarity about whether a family member is in or out of the system (such as in the case of a parent's incarceration, Chapter 4; a family member's mental illness, Chapter 3, or dementia, Chapter 10; or in the case of military deployment, Chapter 13) is a source of boundary ambiguity and can cause stress to the family unit (see Boss, 1999, for more information about the concept). Family perceptions and values about stressful experiences are also elements of the internal context. According to Boss, stressor events that are ambiguous and contain a great deal of uncertainty are the most difficult to resolve and therefore cause a great deal of stress for family members. Family members' ability to tolerate uncertainty, and empower themselves to gather information, solve problems, and move ahead, even in the face of ambiguity, are all internal contextual strengths in response to stress.

In sum, more contemporary variations of family stress theory, such as the FAAR or the Contextual Model of Family Stress, are flexible and have expanded to acknowledge more varied responses to adversity and crisis. Furthermore, family stress frameworks increasingly pay attention to individual, family, and community interpretations of reality (Boss, 2003). Finally, a growing recognition of enhancing and protective family processes has served to draw greater attention to family success and competence (Patterson, 2002). Modern variations of family stress theory often focus on intervening psychological and relational processes that determine in part how a particular stressor event connects with a family outcome. For example, *the family stress model* (K. Conger, Rueter, and Conger, 2000) focuses on how the experience of poverty (stressor event) leads to emotional distress and strained spousal relationships (intervening processes), which in turn are linked to less effective parenting (outcome).

Ecological theory and family risk

Ecological theory suggests the importance of environmental contexts and proximal processes in understanding behavior and patterns of adaptation (Cicchetti, 2006). Proximal processes typically involve those day-to-day relationships that are most important to the developing individual and bear directly on critical psycho-social outcomes. Psychologist Urie Bronfenbrenner (1979) conceptualized developmental contexts as resembling a set of Russian dolls, which are nested inside each other, with the smallest at the core.

These contexts, or ecological layers, can be visualized as concentric circles of context set in time. Risk and protective factors unfold over time, and the contexts are continually changing. According to Bronfenbrenner, there were five contexts of development. The smallest of the contexts is labeled the microsystem, which encompasses the relationships and interaction in the child or developing individual's immediate environment. It is within the microsystem that proximal family processes are particularly important in driving development. Mesosystems are "systems of microsystems" and involve interrelations among contexts containing the developing person. A common example would involve interaction between parents and schoolteachers. Research has found that strong and positive interactions between home and school enhance school achievement (Comer and Haynes, 1991), although this relationship varies according to race and ethnicity and is strongest for White (European American) families (Lee and Bowen, 2006). The child or developing person may not be directly involved with mesosystems, but is affected by them. Exosystems typically involve broader contexts, which affect the developing person, but with whom that person is not directly involved. The policies and practices associated with Lisa's job (i.e. late-night shifts) *indirectly* affect her children and her mother. Changes in Lisa's life stemming from her workplace impact her family. Finally, the macrosystem, or outside circle, refers to overreaching cultural prototypes. These include the attitudes and ideologies and values and customs of a particular culture or subculture. Families are embedded in a broad sociocultural network that either supports them or stigmatizes them. Stigma and discrimination are "risks" at the macrosystem level.

In thinking about family problems, ecological theory gives us a framework to consider multiple influences and the balance of risk and protective factors connected to a particular individual, family, or situation. Risk factors are those features or characteristics associated with the family and its environment that contribute to vulnerability and maladaptive, psychopathological outcomes (Cicchetti, 2006). As evident in both Nick's and Lisa's stories, risk factors tend to co-occur rather than occur in isolation. For example, Lisa's family is impacted by multiple risks such as living in an unsafe neighborhood, the absence of stable and high-quality care for both Martina and the children, Lisa's work schedule and low wages, and Johnny's and Martina's developmental status. Risk factors are considered in light of any protective factors, which function to counterbalance the negative impact of risk factors (Luthar, 2003). Nick's supportive relationships with his parents and counselor were important protective factors that contributed to his ability to overcome his social isolation. Lisa's history of a loving relationship with her mother may serve to enhance the chances that she will take the necessary steps to find ways to help care for Martina.

According to ecological theory, these risk and protective factors are thought to occur on multiple systemic levels or *developmental contexts*. Contexts represent a cluster of characteristics that may constrain or enable development; these characteristics may be subject to change or fixed. For example, age is a factor that is subject to change, while prenatal exposure to toxins is fixed. Contexts may include the family, peers, and the multiple social institutions that surround the developing individual. Societal attitudes and norms can also be thought of as a context because deviation from them gives rise to stigma, discrimination, and stereotypes. Stereotypes are false generalizations applied to all members of a particular group (Pennington, 2009). For example, like other non-heterosexuals, Nick's experience moving was made more difficult because of social stigma and negative stereotyping pertaining to his bisexuality, also known as "biphobia" (see Ochs and Rowley, 2005). Hence, biphobia is a contextual factor that can be thought of as *constraining* Nick's development. His new friendship with Zoe, the girl next door, and the support derived from it may be thought of as *enabling* or enhancing his

development. In sum, ecological theory helps us identify what risk and protective factors are important, why certain problems change individuals and families, and how family problems connect with developmental outcomes and family relationships. Ecological theory suggests that family relationships are best understood by examining the changing and reciprocal interactions between individuals and the multiple contexts within which they live (Lerner, Noh, and Wilson, 1998).

Resilience: going beyond family problems

Social and behavioral scientists who study family problems are increasingly asking questions about why "some stay healthy and do well in the face of risk … and others do not?" (Ganong and Coleman, 2002, p. 346). Family scholars have long been focused on difficulties and problems, with less attention being paid to family strengths and positive adaptations to adversity. All three perspectives or theories of family problems described above support a focus on resilience. Throughout this book, the consideration of family problems goes beyond family pathology, or *what is wrong* with families, and also highlights *what families are doing right* in the face of adversity. An emerging literature is beginning to document the resilience of parents, their children, and families as a whole. The term "resilience" refers to "patterns of positive adaptation in the context of significant risk or adversity" (Masten and Powell, 2003, p. 4) and represents two judgments about an individual. The first judgment is an inference that a person is doing "OK"; the second is that there is or has been significant adversity (Masten and Powell, 2003). A family-resilience framework extends these judgments from the individual to the family and suggests that even under extreme hardship and duress, positive family outcomes are possible (Luthar, 2006; Masten, 2001; Walsh, 2006).

A family-resilience perspective identifies protective factors and processes within the family system that seem to "buffer" or lessen a family's vulnerability to adversity, as well as enhance their ability to adapt and demonstrate competence under stress (R. Conger and Conger, 2002). For example, qualitative research on Chicago's urban poor affirmed resilience processes among even the most "hard luck" families. Within contexts of extreme disadvantage, resilient families were characterized as very resourceful, placed a high value on the parenting role (especially motherhood), protected their children from harm and promoted their well-being, and were committed to collective responsibility and strength of character (Jarrett, 2010). Further, family boundaries in resilient families tend to be broad and flexible. This means that family members may share breadwinning and nurturing roles as needed (for example, one family member may take care of the young children of the extended family so that more members may work and pool resources). Given that many family problems are experienced within contexts of extreme disadvantage, one can infer that family resilience can help, and also, to the extent that the seeds of family strength are present in a given family, resilience may be cultivated. Lisa's commitment to her family and cultural identity are important sources of resilience. Although she is spread thin due to her workload, if she is able to get help from neighbors, friends, schools, or agencies, it may tip things in a positive direction. Similarly, Nick's ability to persevere in the face of change and exclusion, along with his parent's help, is a source of resilience.

Overview of Book

The theories discussed in this chapter are utilized throughout this book in the discussion of family problems. For example, a social construction perspective is at the heart of van Eeden-Moorefield and Benson's chapter on gay, lesbian, bisexual and transgender families: "We're Here, We're Queer, and We Count: Perspectives on Queer Families" (Chapter 2). An ecological perspective guides Roy *et al.*'s discussion of challenges faced by young, low-income fathers (Chapter 6), Dolbin-MacNab and Hayslip's chapter on grandparents raising grandchildren (Chapter 9), and Ryan and colleagues' chapter on multisystemic therapy with multiproblem families (Chapter 19). Family stress theory is an underlying foundation of Chapter 7 ("'Do What You Gotta' Do': How Low-Income African American Mothers Manage Food Insecurity") by Jarrett, Bahar, and McPherson. These authors focus our attention on positive family coping

in response to the stress of food insecurity. Ramey, Lanzi, and Ramey (Chapter 12) provide a new way of thinking about family stress by not only specifying how various physical, social-emotional, and societal stressors contribute to poor child outcomes, but also how family stress can be an opportunity for growth. These authors remind us that stress can serve an important function in families: "without challenges to development, resilience may be virtually impossible to promote" (this volume, p. 196).

In addition to these major perspectives on family problems, other theories or "lenses" are introduced to help us understand specific topics such as a typology of intimate partner violence (Hardesty and Crossman, Chapter 14), childhood adultification (Burton *et al.*, Chapter 11), familism and the care of aging family members (Piercy, Chapter 10), adult role models and adolescent development (Kerpelman *et al.*, Chapter 16), and a human rights lens for analyzing family policy (Anderson and Letiecq, Chapter 18). While theories help us understand family problems, no one perspective explains everything, and the authors in this collection of chapters rely on a variety of concepts to help readers understand the nature of a particular family problem or set of challenges.

Part themes

Chapters in this volume address the challenges and strengths of a diverse spectrum of families in varied structural arrangements, cultural orientations, socioeconomic conditions, and developmental contexts. The chapters are organized in four parts based on common themes or concerns. A brief introduction precedes each chapter in order to highlight relevant themes, substantive issues, or theoretical concepts.

Social inequality and marginalization

Part I critically examines how social inequality may underpin family problems, and includes chapters that illustrate how marginalization processes are an important feature of the family's experience. Social inequality and marginalization have bearing on how challenges are defined and responded to, and outcomes pertaining to child and family well-being. Social inequality is typically reflected by *disproportionality*, that is, the overrepresentation of a particular group of people with certain problems, lifestyle, or sets of issues such as involvement in the child welfare system (Dunbar and Barth, 2007). This disproportionality translates into unequal patterns of goods, wealth, opportunities, rewards and punishments, or burdens. Social inequality may connect with injustice (Dorling, 2011) and different social positions (e.g., one's occupation) or statuses (e.g., race and gender) (Grusky 2001).

Marginalization is the process by which social inequality is constructed and perpetuated (Arnold, 1995). It has been said that marginalization is the most "dangerous form of oppression" (Young, 1990, p. 53). Marginalization occurs when people are systematically excluded from meaningful participation in economic, social, political, cultural, and other forms of human activity that are normally available to members of a given community and society. Marginalized persons are thus denied the opportunity to "fulfill themselves as human beings" (Jenson, 2000, p. 1). This part includes chapters that touch on the issue of social inequality, marginalization and family problems, either by virtue of the characteristics of the group of people or families being discussed, the challenges they face, or a combination of both. Topics include the stigma of mental illness by Natalie Gela and Patrick Corrigan; parental incarceration by Ann Loper and colleagues; gay, lesbian, bisexual, and transgendered families by Brad van Eeden-Moorefield and Kristen Benson; family health disparities by Jinette Comeau and William Avison; and low-income fathers by Kevin Roy, Ron Palkovitz, and Damian Waters.

As you read through the chapters in Part I, ask yourself how social inequality and marginalization may undermine child and family well-being. Sometimes exclusionary practices and processes may not be readily apparent, but operate "behind the scenes" (e.g. health disparities, poverty). Also, consider the ways in which families adapt to their circumstances and find ways to transcend their circumstances and participate fully as parents, family members, and citizens within the communities that they live.

Parenting and caregiving in diverse contexts
Part II of the volume is focused on how family members care for each other in diverse contexts. We often hear family scholars talk about "diversity," but

what does it really mean? Historically, diversity referred to variations of the traditional family, with all other family types considered deviant or dysfunctional (van Eeden-Moorefield and Demo, 2007). Although a more contemporary focus on family diversity acknowledges the multitude of family types and processes, there is still much debate about the family due to the dramatic and widespread changes in family structure, roles, and functions that have occurred over the past few decades. Primary among these changes are the increased separation of childbearing and child-rearing from marriage – that is more children than ever before are in single-parent households, or being reared by other family members and caregivers. Single women in particular make up an increased and growing percentage of those having children. A second major change impacting families involves the aging of our society. Due to declining mortality and morbidity and advances in medicine, older people are living longer than ever before. The increased health and life expectancy of elders raises questions about their role in society, their care, and, increasingly, their ability to provide assistance to their families.

In Part II, family diversity is considered as it pertains to parenting and the provision of family caregiving. Caregiving is broadly defined to encompass caring for another adult. Even a pluralistic and tolerant view of family diversity does not negate that certain family problems involving the care of children and elders exist. The chapters in this part examine the care of children and family members in a wide array of developmental contexts. Part II includes topics such as foster care by Lenore McWey and Armeda Stevenson Wojciak, caregiving for aging and disabled adults by Kathleen Piercy, grandparents raising grandchildren by Megan Dolbin-MacNab and Bert Hayslip; low-income single mothers by Robin Jarrett and colleagues; and childhood adultification by Linda Burton and colleagues.

Many of us pay "lip service" to the idea of family diversity. As you read through the chapters, ask yourself what values and biases you may have about the "best family" for children and adults to live in. Consider the essential ingredients of caring family relationships and how families might compensate for less than optimal circumstances.

Family challenges over the life course

As we have discussed, development implies an unfolding pathway, or change of some sort and is best understood in the contexts in which it occurs. Contexts of development include family, peers, and multiple social institutions that surround the developing individual. Here we extend our view of development beyond the individual to consider how families change over time, deal with challenges associated with specific life events and intimate relationships, and locate family problems in broader socio-historical and economic systems (Bengtson and Allen, 1993). This broader view of development is the basic premise of a "life course perspective" which recognizes the structural diversity of families, the interdependence (connections) of family members, and the timing of processes and events in lives (Elder, 1984). A life course perspective also recognizes the linkages between childhood and adolescent experiences and later experiences in adulthood, although there is considerable diversity in the ways in which individuals and families may respond to experiences over time. Variation originates from the different ways in which families give meaning to their experiences, as well as by virtue of gender, race, ethnic and socioeconomic differences (Bengtson and Allen, 1993). Family scholars have become increasingly interested in how meaning is constructed around the changes that come with age, intergenerational relationships, and an array of family transitions and challenges that stem from normative events (e.g., parenting young children; adolescent development, aging) as well as the discontinuous effects of a changing social environment (e.g., military deployment during war).

In Part III, "Family Challenges Over the Life Course," we are reminded that intimate and family relationships can be developmental contexts for both harm and resilience. The topics in this section include young children and parental resilience and stress, by Sharon Ramey and colleagues; resilience in military families by Adrian Blow and colleagues, intimate partner violence by Jennifer Hardesty and Kim Crossman; elder abuse by Karen Roberto and colleagues; and the challenges of romantic relationships among adolescents by Jennifer Kerpelman and colleagues.

As you read through the chapters in this part, think about how social structures and norms create or uphold certain family problems. Consider how the timing of certain experiences and stressors enhances vulnerability during particular developmental periods. Conversely, what contextual factors and family processes seem to promote resilience throughout the life course?

Policy and practice response to family problems

The call for evidence-based policy and practice has become commonplace across a wide range of fields that connect to families such as education, child welfare, mental health, juvenile justice, youth programs, and health care (Tseng, 2012). The term "evidence-based" generally implies that policy, programs, and interventions are informed by rigorous scientific evidence. Sometimes, evidence-based policy and practice also means including clinical expertise and client perspectives so that that clinical outcomes or the quality of life can be optimized (APA Presidential Taskforce, 2006). Thus research and scholarship on family problems can be very useful to the extent that it can be translated by policymakers and practitioners and disseminated to those who work closely with at-risk youth and families. Moreover, federal, state, and local governments, as well as other funding organizations are under increased political and economic pressure to demonstrate "accountability" and effectiveness of prevention and intervention programs targeting the needs of children, youth, and families (Small, Cooney, and O'Connor, 2009). Vital connections between research, policy, and practice are necessary to ensure innovation and relevance. Suggestions to improve collaboration and inspire innovation could include the development of partnerships between researchers and community members, as well as embracing emancipatory approaches to research aimed at social change and the empowerment of vulnerable populations (see for example, Small, 2005).

The chapters that follow in Part IV, "Policy and Practice Responses to Family Problems," all utilize scientific research in the development of innovative practice and policy responses to some of the most pressing contemporary family problems. Anne Farrell, Gary Bowen, and Samantha Goodrich focus on a community capacity approach to strengthening vulnerable families. Stacy Ryan and colleagues outline a strength-based approach to multisystemic therapy for working with troubled youth in multiproblem families. Other topics include the use of community-based programs for Latino immigrant families by José Rubén Parra-Cordona and colleagues; harm-reduction approaches to addressing substance abuse by Patt Denning; and analyzing family policy from a human rights perspective by Elaine Anderson and Bethany Letiecq.

As you read through the chapters, consider the ways that the social scientific research is applied to help address a specific family problem. What kind of information is most necessary in designing a program or intervention? In addition to research, think about how theories guide policy and practice. Since most family problems are multifaceted, notice how theories may be integrated and synthesized to fit a particular situation.

In sum, this volume is designed to serve as a core textbook for students in an array of disciplines (family studies, sociology, psychology, social work, counseling, human services) who study families and development. The cutting-edge knowledge presented here, authored by distinguished scholars at the forefront of their field, can help inform not only how we think about family problems and family strengths, but also inform intervention, community programs, and social policy aimed at enhancing the well-being families and children.

References

American Psychological Association (APA) Presidential Task Force. (2006). Evidence-based practice in psychology. *American Psychologist, 61*, 271–285.

Arnold, J. (1995). Social inequality, marginalization, and economic process. In T. D. Price and G. M. Feinman (eds), *Foundations of social inequality* (pp. 87–103). New York: Plenum.

Bengtson, V., and Allen, K. R. (1993). The life course perspective applied to families over time. In P. Boss, W. Doherty, R. LaRossa, W. Schumm, and S. Steinmetz (eds), *Sourcebook of family theories and methods: A contextual approach* (pp. 469–504). New York: Springer Science.

Boss, P. (1999). *Ambiguous loss: Learning to live with unresolved grief.* Cambridge, MA: Harvard University Press.

Boss, P. (2002). *Family stress management: A contextual approach* (2nd edn). Thousand Oaks, CA: Sage Publications. doi: 10.4135/9781452233895.

Boss, P. (2003). Preface. In P. Boss (ed.), *Family stress: Classic and contemporary readings* (pp. viii–x). Thousand Oaks, CA: Sage Publications.

Bronfenbrenner, U. (1979). *The ecology of human development: Experiments by nature and design.* Cambridge, MA: Harvard University Press.

Cicchetti, D. (2006). Development and psychopathology. In D. Cicchetti and D. Cohen (eds), *Developmental psychopathology*, vol. 1, *Theory and method* (pp. 1–23). Hoboken, NJ: John Wiley & Sons, Inc.

Comer, J., and Haynes, N. (1991). Parent involvement in schools: An ecological approach. *Elementary School Journal, 91*, 271–277.

Conger, K. J., Rueter, M. A., and Conger, R. D. (2000). The role of economic pressure in the lives of parents and their adolescents: The family stress model. In L. J. Crockett and R. J. Silbereisen (eds), *Negotiating adolescence in times of social change* (pp. 201–223). Cambridge, UK: Cambridge University Press.

Conger, R. D., and Conger, K. J. (2002). Resilience in midwestern families: Selected findings from the first decade of a prospective, longitudinal study. *Journal of Marriage and Family, 64*, 361–373.

Crnic, K., and Greenberg, M. (1990). Minor parenting stresses with young children. *Child Development, 61*, 1628–1637.

De Benedittis, G., and Lorenzetti, A. (1992). The role of stressful life events in the persistence of primary headache: Major events vs. daily hassles. *Pain, 51*, 35–42.

DeLongis, A., Coyne, J., Dakof, G., Folkman, S., and Lazarus, R. (1982). Relationship of daily hassles, uplifts, and major life events to health status. *Health Psychology, 1*, 119–136.

Doherty, W., and Baptiste, D. (2008). Theories emerging from family therapy. In P. Boss, W. Doherty, R. LaRossa, W. Schumm, and S. Steinmetz (eds), *Sourcebook of family theories and methods: A contextual approach* (pp. 505–529). New York: Springer Science.

Doherty, W., Boss, P., LaRossa, R., Schumm, W., and Steinmetz, A. (2008). Family theories and methods: A contextual approach. In P. Boss, W. Doherty, R. LaRossa, W. Schumm, and S. Steinmetz (eds), *Sourcebook of family theories and methods: A contextual approach* (pp. 3–30). New York: Springer Science.

Dorling, D. (2011). *Injustice: Why social inequality persists.* Portland, OR: The Policy Press.

Dumont, M., and Provost, M. (1999). Resilience in adolescents: Protective role of social support, coping strategies, self-esteem, and social activities on experience of stress and depression. *Journal of Youth and Adolescence, 28*, 343–363.

Dunbar, K., and Barth, R. (2007). *Racial disproportionality, race disparity, and other race-related findings in published works derived from the National Survey of Child and Adolescent Well-Being*. Casey Family Programs. Retrieved May 30, 2014 from http://www.aecf.org/~/media/Pubs/Topics/Child%20Welfare%20Permanence/Other/RacialDisproportionalityRaceDisparityandOther/Dunbar%20Barth%20Racial%20Disparity%20report%2012808.pdf.

Elder, G. H., Jr. (1984). Families, kin, and the life course: A sociological perspective. In R. Parke (ed.), *Review of child development research*, vol. 7 (pp. 215–241). Chicago: University of Chicago Press.

Eldridge, V., Mack, L., and Swank, E. (2006). Explaining comfort with homosexuality in rural America. *Journal of Homosexuality*, *51*, 39–56.

Ganong, L., and Coleman, M. (2002). Family resilience in multiple contexts. *Journal of Marriage and Family*, *64*, 346–348.

Gergen, K. J. (1994). *Realities and relationships: Soundings in social construction*. Cambridge, MA: Harvard University Press.

Grusky, D. B. (ed.) (2001). *Social stratification: Class, race, and gender in sociological perspective* (2nd edn). Boulder, CO: Westview.

Hill, R. (1949). *Families under stress*. New York: Harper.

Jarrett, R. L. (2010). Building strong families and communities: Lessons from the field. Research presentation at the Children, Youth, and Families at Risk Annual Conference, May 5, San Diego, California.

Jenson, J. (2000, November). Thinking about marginalization: What, who, and why. CPRN-Backgrounder (Web version). Canadian Policy Research Networks Inc. Retrieved May 30, 2014 from http://www.cprn.org/documents/15746_en.pdf.

Kanner, A., Coyne, J., Schaefer, C., and Lazarus, R. (1981). Comparison of two modes of stress measurement: Daily hassles and uplifts versus major life events. *Journal of Behavioral Medicine*, *4*, 1–39.

Lazarus, R. (1990). Theory-based stress measurement. *Psychological Inquiry*, *1*, 3–13.

Lee, J., and Bowen, N. (2006). Parent involvement, cultural capital, and the achievement gap among elementary school children. *American Educational Research Journal*, *43*, 193–218.

Lerner, R., Noh, E. R., and Wilson, C. (1998). The parenting of adolescents and adolescents as parents: A developmental contextual perspective. Paper presented at Parenthood in America conference, Madison, WI, April 19–21. Retrieved May 30, 2014 from http://parenthood.library.wisc.edu/Lerner/Lerner.html.

Luthar, S. S. (2003). *Resilience and vulnerability: Adaptation in the context of childhood adversities*. New York: Cambridge University Press.

Luthar, S. S. (2006). Resilience in development: A synthesis of research across five decades. In D. Cicchetti, and D. Cohen (eds), *Developmental psychopathology*, vol. 3, *Risk, disorder, and adaptation* (2nd edn) (pp. 739–795). Hoboken, NJ: John Wiley & Sons, Inc.

Mahoney, M. J. (2003). *Constructive psychotherapy: A practical guide*. New York: Guilford Press.

Masten, A. S. (2001). Ordinary magic: Resilience processes in development. *American Psychologist*, *56*, 227–238.

Masten, A. S., and Powell, J. L. (2003). A resilience framework for research, policy, and practice. In S. Luthar (ed.), *Resilience and vulnerability: Adaptation in the context of childhood adversities* (pp. 1–26). New York: Cambridge University Press.

McCubbin, H., and Patterson, J. (1982). Family adaptation to crisis. In H. McCubbin, E. Cauble, and J. Patterson (eds), *Family stress, coping, and social support* (pp. 26–47). Springfield, IL: Charles Thomas.

Ochs, R., and Rowley, S. (eds) (2005). *Getting bi: Voices of bisexuals around the world* (2nd edn). Boston, MA: Bisexual Resource Center.

Patterson, J. M. (1988). The Family Adjustment and Response Model, II: Applying the FAAR Model to health-related issues for intervention and research. *Family Systems Medicine*, *6*, 202–237.

Patterson, J. M. (1993). The role of family meanings in adaptation to chronic illness and disability. In A. Turnbull, J. M. Patterson, S. Behr, D. L. Murphy, J. G. Marquis, and M. J. Blue-Banning (eds), *Cognitive coping research and developmental disabilities* (pp. 221–238). Baltimore, MD: Brookes.

Patterson, J. M. (2002). Integrating family resilience and family stress theory. *Journal of Marriage and Family*, *64*, 349–360.

Pennington, S. (2009). Bisexuality. In J. O'Brian (ed.), *Encyclopedia of gender and society*, vol. 1 (pp. 68–72). Thousand Oaks, CA: Sage Publications.

Raskin, J. D. (2006). Constructivist theories. In J. Thomas and D. Segal (eds), *Comprehensive handbook of personality and psychopathology*, vol. 1 (pp. 212–230). Hoboken, NJ: John Wiley & Sons, Inc.

Schneider, J. W. (1985). Social problems theory: The constructionist view. *Annual Review of Sociology*, *11*, 209–229.

Small, S. (2005). Bridging research and practice in the family and human sciences. *Family Relations*, *54*, 320–334.

Small, S., Cooney, S., and O'Connor, C. (2009). Evidence-based program improvement: Using principles of effectiveness to enhance the quality and impact of family-based prevention programs. *Family Relations*, *58*, 1–13.

Smith, S. (1984). Family stress theory: Review and critique. Paper presented at the National Conference on Family

Relations, San Francisco, October 16–20. Retrieved May 30, 2014 from http://www.eric.ed.gov/ERICWebPortal/search/detailmini.jsp?_nfpb=true&_&ERICExtSearch_SearchValue_0=ED255819&ERICExtSearch_SearchType_0=no&accno=ED255819.

Snively, C., Kreuger, L., Stretch, J., Watt, W., and Chadha, J. (2004). Understanding homophobia: Preparing for practice realities in urban and rural settings. *Journal of Gay and Lesbian Social Services*, 17, 59–81.

Tseng, V. (2012). The uses of research in policy and practice. *Social Policy Report*, 26, 1–16. Retrieved May 30, 2014 from http://www.wtgrantfoundation.org.

van Eeden-Moorefield, B., and Demo, D. H. (2007). Family diversity. In G. Ritzer (ed.), *The Blackwell encyclopedia of sociology online*. Blackwell Reference Online. Retrieved May 30, 2014 from http://www.blackwellreference.com/subscriber/book?id=g9781405124331_9781405124331.

Walsh, F. (2006). *Strengthening family resilience* (2nd edn). New York: Guilford Press.

Young, I. M. (1990). *Justice and the politics of difference*. Princeton, NJ: Princeton University Press.

Part I

Social Inequality and Marginalization

2

We're Here, We're Queer, and We Count

Perspectives on Queer Families

Brad van Eeden-Moorefield and Kristen Benson

"Queer families" are the subject of Chapter 2. Here, van Eeden-Moorefield and Benson explain how public opinion toward sexual orientation and alternative family structures impacts the politics of exclusion. For example, homophobic attitudes characterized by a fear and hatred of same-sex couples serve to perpetuate discrimination. Discrimination can take many forms and same-sex couples may be barred from certain privileges (e.g., marriage) afforded to their heterosexual counterparts. Education efforts that promote tolerance may lessen stigma and promote acceptance of LGBTQ families.

Introduction

"We're here, we're queer, get used to it," was a chant often heard at gay pride rallies during the gay rights movements of the 1960s and 1970s. In the 1980s, and in response to the HIV/AIDS crisis, a new catch-phrase emerged – "Act up, act now, fight AIDS." Since then other slogans have permeated the social fight for equal rights, including those related to marriage. Such slogans included, but are not limited to, "Hey, hey, ho, ho, homophobia's got to go," "What do we want? Equal rights! When do we want them? Now!!" and "Gay, straight, Black, White, marriage is a civil right." Although each phrase is seemingly different at first glance, the message behind them is quite similar. The message is a simple one, actually – it is about a group of individuals demanding to be made visible, counted, and valued. To be clear, although the best-known gay

rights movement (the Stonewall Riots) occurred in 1969, queer (i.e., bisexual, gay, lesbian, transgender, and all other "non-conforming" people) individuals and families have been fighting against exclusion and for the civil right to be included as American and global citizens since before the term homosexuality was first coined in the 1860s (Gibson, Alexander, and Meem, 2013).

In fact, the first American gay rights group, the Society for Human Rights, was established in 1926, whereas the first published use of the word "faggot" occurred in 1913. Additionally, it is well documented that queer people have existed and faced varying degrees of exclusion and inclusion since recorded history (Gibson *et al.*, 2013). In spite of all of this, queer people continue to be largely excluded in significant ways (e.g., it is still legal to fire someone for being perceived as gay or transgender in over half of the

Family Problems: Stress, Risk, and Resilience, First Edition. Edited by Joyce A. Arditti.
© 2015 John Wiley & Sons, Inc. Published 2015 by John Wiley & Sons, Inc.

states in the United States). There have been, however, important strides in progress toward inclusion (e.g., the passage of several marriage laws permitting same-sex marriages). This chapter uses a queer feminist lens (van Eeden-Moorefield, Martell, Williams, and Preston, 2011; Weed and Schor, 1997) to explore the ecology of exclusion of queers and their families. Specifically, we review research related to exclusion of queer individuals and families in various levels of society (i.e., ecological contexts, such as the macro, exo, and interpersonal contexts). Next, we focus on information related to within-group marginalization of those who identify as bisexual, transgender, or are in mixed-orientation marriages. Finally, we conclude by presenting research findings related to the strengths of queer families and offer several implications for policy and practice. It should be noted that although we use term such as queers, gays and lesbians, and the acronym LGBTQ, which stands for lesbian, gay, bisexual, transgender and queer, people should be referred to using language with which they are comfortable and identify. In other words, it is more inclusive not to categorize or label people.

Queer Feminist Ecologies of Same-Sex-Headed Families

From an ecological perspective, the macrosystem embodies the attitudes and beliefs of a particular cultural setting (Bronfenbrenner, 1979, 1989). This is the context in which all others are embedded and in which individuals and families live, work, and play. Individuals, their families, and friends form the microsystem, whereas laws, policies, and other major social institutions comprise the exosystem. These contexts, or systems, interact and influence each other directly or indirectly in the mesosystem, and such influences unfold over time (i.e., the historical context). As influences unfold, change and growth occur.

A queer feminist lens is a way of viewing and asking questions about the way change and growth can, and do, happen (Halberstam, 2012). A primary objective then is to identify potential underlying assumptions, biases, and discourses that work to maintain *exclusion*. In this chapter, exclusion refers to the

ways that people are marginalized and denied access to rights and privileges, and inclusion refers to the ways in which people are included and allowed access to rights and privileges. Examining the discourse of inclusion/exclusion is part of the deconstruction process, which is followed by (re)construction through the correction of assumptions and biases found in discourse, and then altering discourse through action (i.e., change and growth). Simply put, a queer feminist lens can be used to ask questions of *why* things might happen and be the way they are with an end-goal of creating and promoting change that is equitable, inclusive, and socially just.

Additionally, this lens contends that families represent the interactions between ecological systems and between social ideals about how families should look and act and how actual families choose (or not) to look and act like the ideal. This is the social construction and queering of families. Further, families gain a sense of identity from such interactions and subsequently perform, or *do family*, in a way that creates and shares their family identity with themselves and others (Oswald, Blume, and Marks, 2005). A queer feminist lens also suggests that heteronormativity, or the belief that heterosexuality is the only valued way of being, pervades each system such that the belief that to be a family you must act and look like *the one family* – the Standard North American Family (SNAF) – is endemic. For example, the SNAF is an idealized family form comprising a heterosexual married couple with children, such as the Dunphys on the popular show *Modern Family*. As such, everyone in the United States should attempt to create a harmonious and stable White, heterosexual, middle-class family with one husband, one wife, 2.5 children, and a white picket fence – the one natural family. Idealizing SNAF is part of the privileging of the natural to the exclusion of the unnatural (Butler, 1990).

A core tenet of a "queer perspective" is that no one can achieve the natural because it is perfection, and perfection does not exist in reality – it is simply a social construction (Butler, 1990; Oswald *et al.*, 2005). As such, all families are queer, or unnatural, therefore all families should be equal. Additionally, homonormativity exists and refers to those who believe queer families that attempt to recreate the heterosexual "natural" family are engaging in assimilation (van Eeden-Moorefield et al., 2011). As such, it can place queer families in the middle of conflict between homo/heteronormativity. This prompts questions about how queers navigate and negotiate being minorities in a majority culture. For example, why do some queers choose to disclose their sexual orientation when they do and to whom? Why do some gays enter a heterosexual marriage, later disclose their sexual orientation, and then choose to remain in a heterosexual marriage? If queers want to create families, why do some believe they require legal marriage to do so? Answers to these questions are a few examples of topics discussed in this chapter. On a final, albeit important note, a queer feminist lens also seeks to define difference, or the unnatural, as simply different, with no value or exclusion placed on difference. In fact, queer scholars believe that difference should be advocated for and celebrated. As you read through the rest of this chapter we hope you consider how each of the contextual influences and family processes presented may serve as negotiation and navigation strategies, and how such strategies can serve to resist or promote change for equality and social justice of queers.

Queer Lives in Context

Macro context of exclusion

Our everyday lives are impacted by many factors that we cannot see and feel directly (Bronfenbrenner, 1979, 1989). These macro or broader level environmental factors, however, can have profound negative and/or positive impacts on queers and their families through the creation of an (dis)affirming context in which queer people live, work, and play (Biblarz and Savci, 2010). In this section, we focus on how public opinion, representing macro-level social attitudes and beliefs, creates such context and how it impacts queers and their families.

The most influential macro factor impacting the exclusion and inclusion of queers is public opinion. The average general public's attitude toward queers can create one layer of acceptance (i.e., inclusion) or rejection (i.e., exclusion) that can influence laws, policies, etc. – all of which will be discussed in the next section on the exosystem (Bronfenbrenner, 1979,

1989). These same attitudes can also indirectly impact how some same-sex couples interact (Gibson et al., 2013). For example, most heterosexual dating couples enjoy holding hands when on a date. These desires are no different for same-sex couples. What is different is a same-sex couple's likelihood of engaging in this important symbolic relationship activity.

For any couple, engaging in hand-holding can be considered a relationship-maintenance activity in that it is a way for the couple to connect with each other and demonstrate to themselves and others that they share a romantic connection. In turn, this can help build the couple's sense of being a couple, or their identity as a couple (McWhirter and Mattison, 1984). Research consistently demonstrates the positive effects on various relationship outcomes (e.g., relationship quality, liking, stability) when couples engage in relationship-maintenance strategies and forge stronger couple identities (Burke and Stets, 1999).

How the macro context impacts couples is different both between and within same-sex couples. One can argue that most heterosexual dating couples, regardless where they live in the United States, would hold hands at some point while on a date. However, the picture is different for same-sex couples. Same-sex couples, on average, are less likely to hold hands on a date when they are in public due to a fear of non-acceptance, exclusion, and possibly falling victim to homophobic acts, including hate crimes resulting in severe victimization, hospitalization, or even death, as has been reported by the media many times in previous decades (Frable, Wortman, and Joseph, 1997). When queer couples perceive their macro context as non-accepting they can feel excluded from participating in basic relationship-maintenance strategies. Again, this differs when the macro context is perceived differently. For example, whereas same-sex couples who live in largely disaffirming contexts (e.g., rural Alabama) may be less likely to hold hands while on a date, those in more affirming contexts (e.g., urban New York) may choose to hold hands. The point is that the macro context has a daily impact on perceptions of being included or excluded.

Multiple public opinion polls (e.g., Gallup, n.d.) gauge general social attitudes, including those about being queer and being in queer families. Although public opinion varies greatly by state, communities, etc., understanding overall public sentiment can tell us much about the exclusion and inclusion of queers in the United States. Here we focus on Gallup's polls, as they have asked various questions about queerness for more decades than other polling firms of which we are aware (since the late 1970s, for many questions) and always use a random sample. Gallup poll data provide the ability to explore how opinions change over time and, by proxy, how inclusion/exclusion changes over time. We refer the reader to a full list of the polls from which we drew for our discussion here (http://www.gallup.com/poll/1651/Gay-Lesbian-Rights.aspx). We do note that most polls focus solely on gay and lesbian individuals and same-sex couples, and we know little about the social attitudes toward those who identify as bisexual or transgender.

In general, Americans are more accepting of gays and lesbians today than any other previous decade, and more consistently so (Gallup, n.d.). For example, beginning in 1999 the majority of Americans now consistently believe that relations between gays and lesbians should be legal (64% in 2012 compared to a low of 43% in 1977). In each year since 2010, a majority of Americans also believe gay and lesbian relationships are morally acceptable (52%, 56%, and 54%, respectively). Being female, younger, having higher education, and being an Independent or Democrat all are associated with higher acceptance levels. Historically, heterosexual women have been more accepting of same-sex relationships. However, recent polls show the opposite, with heterosexual men as most accepting. Interestingly, in every poll since 1978, Americans believed that gays and lesbians should have equal rights, beginning with 56% in 1978 and consistently in the 80% range since 1993. Currently, the percentage is 89. However, rights in this context only refer to individual rights (e.g., protection in employment) and not couple and family-level rights (e.g., marriage).

When asked whether same-sex couples should be allowed to marry, a somewhat similar picture emerges with the majority of Americans now favoring allowing same-sex couples to legally marry (53%) compared to 68% favoring exclusion in 1996 (Gallup, n.d.). Additionally, both 2012 polls indicate a majority (50% and 53%) of Americans believe same-sex married couples should receive the same rights as couples in "traditional" marriages. Of those that support the inclusion of same-sex couples in the institution of marriage, 32% believe it is an equal rights issue and another 32% believe love and happiness, rather than their sexual orientation, should determine if people should be allowed to marry.

In addition to asking about legality and acceptance of gay and lesbian relationships, including the right to marry, Gallup (n.d.) also polls Americans related to their opinions of several other beliefs, rights, and protections. Scholarly research has found more support for biological determinants of sexual orientation compared to environmental determinants (e.g., parenting, choice). Accordingly, a shift in public opinion about the same issues has been parallel. In 1977, 56% of the American public believed being gay or lesbian was related to their environment (i.e., a choice), whereas 13% believed it was genetic and 14% believed it was both. In the 2012 poll, 36% believe it is a choice, 45% believe it is genetic, and 10% believe it is both. Also during this time, research has demonstrated that knowing someone who is queer positively influences someone's likelihood of acceptance, and when asked in 2012, 78% of the public reported knowing someone who was queer, a sharp increase over previous decades. Clearly, this has played a significant role in altering public opinion.

Polls also explore public opinion regarding which rights gays and lesbian should have, and these also have increased over previous decades (Gallup, n.d.). Today, 61% of the public believes gays and lesbian should be able to adopt children, 77% believe same-sex couples should have access to employee benefits, and 78% believe same-sex couples should have access to inheritance rights. Further, 89% of the public believe gays and lesbian should have equal rights and protections in the workplace. Lastly, over half of Americans (51%) are dissatisfied or very dissatisfied with the acceptance level of gays and lesbian in the United States, and 67% of Americans favor including sexual orientation to the federal hate-crime laws.

Taken together, the majority of Americans favor a more inclusive approach to the treatment and rights of gays and lesbians, and this is an increase over previous decades. Unfortunately, the largely inclusive macro context does not match parts of the exo context (i.e., employment policies), presented below, which tend to be more exclusionary in the actual treatment of queers as well as their provision of access to equal rights and protections under the law. This inconsistency represents a stark tension, but is moving in an inclusive direction.

Exo context of exclusion

Economic

The economy has been a topic of importance for many years, as countless Americans, their families, communities, and businesses have suffered through one of the more difficult economic periods in US history. Even before this most recent economic downturn, queer individuals have been excluded in many ways, and with many consequences. These consequences range from employment and pay (Horvath and Ryan, 2003) to the ability to rent or purchase housing (Page, 1998), and they have severe negative impacts. Imagine for a moment you are in a lesbian partnership and you view an apartment and decide it would be a nice place to live. The prospective landlord then tells you both that she cannot rent to you because you seem to be a lesbian couple and she does not believe being lesbian is morally acceptable. Depending on the state in which you reside, this type of discrimination, based on your perceived sexual orientation, may be completely legal. In fact, there is no federal law protecting queer individuals and families from being denied housing. However, in 2012 the Federal Housing and Urban Development (HUD) department did issue an order that no facility receiving HUD funding could discriminate based on whether someone is LGBT (Department of Housing and Urban Development, 2012). Although this certainly is an inclusive step, it remains legal to deny someone housing based on their perceived sexual or gender identity in 29 states, and based on gender identity in an additional 5 states.

Sears and Mallory (2011) used data from the 2008 General Social Survey (GSS) and found that approximately 27% of queer workers experienced or witnessed discrimination related to either sexual orientation or gender identity at their workplace in the previous five years, and the rate increased to 42% ever experiencing discrimination in the workplace. For those workers who were "out" (i.e., work colleagues knew they were LGBT), the rate was 38% in the previous five years

and 56% ever experiencing discrimination. Reporting on other survey data, Sears and Mallory (2011) found that among transgender workers only the rates of workplace discrimination were 70% and above. Clearly, such acts can create uncomfortable and even hostile work environments, and research suggests such exclusionary acts are related to a host of negative outcomes for workers (e.g., depression, illness) and businesses (e.g., lower productivity, missed work) alike. Considering the public overwhelmingly believes queers should be protected and have equal access to the workplace (Gallup, n.d.), exclusion in the workplace is running at a high level.

Although Congress has attempted to pass the Employment and Non-discrimination Act (ENDA), which would prohibit discrimination based on sexual orientation or gender identity, multiple times, it remains legal in most states to not hire, promote, or to fire someone for their perceived identity as gay or transgender. In fact, this type of employment discrimination is illegal in only 15 states, with an additional 4 states making discrimination based only on sexual orientation illegal, a few states protecting queer state workers only, and 19 states offering no employment protections for any queer workers (Human Rights Campaign, 2011). It should be noted that some cities and businesses have developed their own inclusive non-discrimination policies and these represent an important avenue for more immediate inclusive change. Again, it is important to reiterate that although public opinion about queer workplace issues is significantly inclusive, the actual actions in the workplace are more exclusive on average.

Legal and political

Although the previous section mentioned some laws and policies, or the lack thereof, here the focus is on those legal and political issues specific to same-sex marriage and dissolution. Although public opinion is more inclusive of allowing same-sex marriage in the United States, the laws and policies of the United States do not match such general public attitudes (Gallup, n.d.). This is changing fairly rapidly, though, with three new states just legalizing same-sex marriage as a result of the most recent (2012) election. Currently, same-sex marriage is allowed in 12 states and the District of Columbia, with others expected in the coming months and years. Additionally, Rhode Island recognizes same-sex marriages performed elsewhere.

Although legal fights for marriage equality have been in the system for decades, two crucial cases were recently heard by the Supreme Court. The results of these cases allowed California to provide same-sex couples access to marriage and struck down Section 3 of DOMA, allowing the federal government to provide over 1,000 rights to married couples (see Box 2.1). These Supreme Court rulings lay legal groundwork for couples living in states that fail to recognize their relationship to challenge non-inclusive marriage laws.

For those less familiar with DOMA, it was signed into law in 1996 by former President Bill Clinton and although marriage laws are determined by each state, DOMA prevented federal recognition of same-sex marriages. Importantly, this excluded same-sex couples from the right to marry as well as all the rights, privileges, and protections offered at the federal level. In all, 19 states followed DOMA's lead and also amended their state constitutions or established laws to prohibit recognizing same-sex marriages and or unions of any type (e.g., domestic partnerships; van Eeden-Moorefield et al., 2011).

In addition to same-sex marriage recognition, three states offer civil unions, six offer domestic partnerships, one state designates beneficiaries, and one more state offers reciprocal beneficiaries. Although the names vary by states, to truly understand what couples are afforded in each state it is important to examine

---

Box 2.1   DOMA

DOMA (Defense of Marriage Act) defined marriage as being between one man and one woman between 1996 and 2013. On June 26, 2013, the Supreme Court of the United States ruled in *Windsor vs. United States* that Section 3 of the DOMA created unfair treatment and therefore deemed it unconstitutional. All legally married couples who reside in states where inclusive marriage laws exists are now recognized as married by the federal government and are eligible for federal protections and rights.

---

the specific benefits offered within a particular state (Gates, Badgett, and Ho, 2008). For example, same-sex couples who register as domestic partners in Washington state receive almost identical benefits compared to heterosexual married couples. However, in Wisconsin same-sex couples who register as domestic partners receive few rights (van Eeden-Moorefield et al., 2011). From this we can conclude: (a) even when same-sex couples can legally marry their marriage only appears to be an inclusive act; (b) all same-sex couples remain excluded in some form; and (c) it is simply confusing for these families and practitioners who work with them to understand the options available for some type of recognition of protections (e.g., preparing wills, health care power of attorney documents).

With the confusion and complications of same-sex marriage, the idea of dissolving a partnership or divorcing is almost never discussed, and it is even more complicated for queer families (van Eeden-Moorefield et al., 2011). Politically, to acknowledge that some same-sex couples dissolve partnerships, or divorce, runs counter to fighting for same-sex marriage rights. It also helps to establish an idea that if same-sex couples marry they will automatically create only harmonious and *perfect* family lives, an idea filled with heteronormativity (Brower, 2009). As such, little attention has been paid to the experiences and needs of queer families who do end their partnerships (dissolution) or marriages (divorce).

Typical divorce proceedings occur in family courts, and these courts have case precedents, which help judges rule over divorce proceedings, guide outcomes, and establish some ethic of equity for the divorce couple (e.g., equitable division of property; Brower, 2009). For same-sex couples who are legally married, state divorce proceedings are generally comparable to heterosexual divorce. In essence, the same precedents apply equally to all divorcing couples, regardless of the sexual orientation. Exceptions occur at the federal level. For example, if money is part of a divorce settlement for a same-sex couple, it could be considered income and subject to a higher tax because it would not be viewed as an exchange of family money.

For couples who live in states where they are legally recognized as a couple, but not as a married couple (e.g., civil union partners), most divorce laws and rulings are also the same as those for divorcing heterosexual couples (Brower, 2009). Residency requirements exist for same-sex partners, though. For example, Washington state has no residency requirement. However, Connecticut requires that at least one partner of any couple wishing to dissolve their relationship must reside in the state for at least one year prior to filing for a legal dissolution. Let us assume Ben and Mark obtained a civil union in Connecticut and subsequently took new jobs and moved to Virginia, which does not recognize their civil union, nor confer any benefits. While living in Virginia, Ben and Mark decided to end their partnership. Because neither partner lives in Connecticut, they will never be able to legally dissolve their partnership unless at least one of them moves back to Connecticut for at least one year. Further, assume that they continued living in Virginia for another 10 years and both met and created families with new partners. Eventually, and without the other couple knowing, both new couples moved back to Connecticut. Mark and his new partner decided to have a civil union, and after going to the court house to file the necessary papers found out the state still recognized Mark as being in a civil union with his now ex-partner Ben. Thus, Mark cannot enter into a new civil union for at least one year, but now would be able to file and begin dissolution proceedings 10 years later. Clearly, the different types of inclusion and exclusion create unique and potentially harmful circumstances for these queer couples.

For couples who live as partners in states without any form of legal recognition and later wish to dissolve their partnerships the process can be clearer in some ways, but more devastating in others. For these couples, their only real choices to dissolve their partnerships include developing their own terms for the dissolution, or attempting to work with a professional (e.g., divorce mediator or therapist), assuming they can afford these services. We know that many dissolutions are acrimonious. So, to expect former partners to be able to settle their own dissolution in a fair and equitable way may be to expect a lot, especially if children are present. These couples can turn to the courts. However, their cases would be heard in civil court, which has no case precedent for handling family matters (Hoogs, 2003). As such, these dissolutions often are more expensive, time-consuming, and often end in less than equitable ways.

Interpersonal context of exclusion

Anti-gay groups (e.g., the Family Research Council) promote the misguided understanding that being LGBT causes negative outcomes such as drug abuse, depression, suicide, and contracting a sexually transmitted infection (e.g., frc.org/homosexuality). We label these examples as "misguided" because social scientific research suggests such negative outcomes are associated with negative treatment by society (DiPlacido, 1998; Meyer, 2003); queer people are not inherently broken. Rather, LGBTQ people face a range of prejudices, are more likely to experience cut-off in their families, and are subject to stereotypes (Meyer, 2003). Homophobia, or the negative attitudes and hostile feelings about people who identify or are perceived to be gay, can be expressed through name-calling, jokes that make fun of gay people, and even through acts of violence (DiPlacido, 1998).

Stigma consciousness

Stigma refers to the social disapproval of a person based on perceived flaws of the group to which they belong. Queer people may expect to be stereotyped or discriminated against based on their awareness of negative stigmas against LGBTQ people, which is known as *stigma consciousness* (Pinel, 1999). Being worried about how one might be stereotyped impacts how they engage in social interactions and can increase the likelihood that they avoid scenarios where they expect to be stereotyped. For example, a lesbian woman may avoid spending time in public with lesbian friends who do not dress in feminine ways out of concern that she will be associated with butch women. The more concerned she is, the more likely she is to notice when people look at her with her friends, believe that a mistake on the bill was intentional, and the more likely that person will expect to be stereotyped.

Internalized homophobia

LGB people may struggle to come to terms with their sexual orientation due to the negative messages they received about what it means to be queer. They may even reject their own sexual orientation because of their negative beliefs about queer people. Prejudices about queer people that exist socially can be directed towards oneself, which is referred to as internalized homophobia (Herek *et al.*, 2009). People with high degrees of internalized homophobia tend to hold anti-gay beliefs which lead to negative outcomes for relationships (Frost and Meyer, 2009; Otis, Rostosky, Riggle, and Hamrin, 2006).

Disclosure

Heteronormativity reflects the social framework that values heterosexuality as the standard sexual practice (Oswald *et al.*, 2005). From this frame, we can view the processing of coming out, or the belief that LGBTQ people *should* disclose their sexual orientation and gender identity, as necessary because it is assumed that all people are heterosexual until proven otherwise. The metaphor of being "in the closet" represents the secrecy experienced by LGBTQ people who hide their sexual orientation and gender identity for fear of negative treatment. Therefore, the term "coming out", or disclosing one's sexual orientation, refers to opening the closet doors and no longer hiding. More importantly, as LGBTQ people live more openly, they challenge stereotypes and myths about what it means to live as a queer person. Conversely, not all friends and family are supportive of queer identities (Savin-Williams, 1998), and prejudice can lead to uncertainty, harassment, or rejection. For example, the Gay, Lesbian and Straight Education Network (GLSEN) conducted a National School Climate Survey of 8,584 LGBT students and found a decline in anti-LGBT language and victimization; yet, over 63% of students continued to feel unsafe at school, over 81% experienced verbal harassment, and over 38% were physically harassed because of their sexual orientation (Gay, 2011).

Research on LGBTQ populations tends to include samples of White middle- to upper-middle-class populations, which has resulted in an underrepresentation of queer people of color (Moore, 2011; Peplau, Cochran, and Mays, 1997; Sandfort and Dodge, 2008), and more specifically, their coming-out experiences (Mays, Chatters, Cochran, and Mackness, 1998). Although myths reinforce the belief that Black and Asian American people are not gay, research suggests queer people are found in every demographic category (Moore, 2011; Narui, 2011). We do know a little about the experiences of Black lesbian women and gay men (Moore, 2012). For example, research shows that gay Black individuals are more likely to disclose their sexual orientation to mothers and sisters and less often to extended family, which may be due to roles women play in Black families (Mays *et al.*, 1998).

Expectations of masculinity among men of color may lead to varying experiences in regards to openness about their sexual orientation and the gender of their sexual partners. Disclosure of sexual orientation and same-sex behaviors among Black and Latino men may be less likely due to a perception that gay culture is predominantly White, gay and bisexual men are viewed as more feminine, the increased likelihood of discrimination based on the complexity of homophobia and racism, as well as lack of gay acceptance in communities of color (Sandfort and Dodge, 2008). "Men who have sex with men" (MSM) is a term used to reach out to men who engage in sexual relationships with other men yet may not identify as gay. Similarly, the term "on the down low" or "DL" has developed as an identity label to indicate both masculinity and the desire to remain private about same-sex behaviors (Sandfort and Dodge, 2008).

LGBTQ adults vary in when and how they come out. They tend to choose people in their social networks that they anticipate will be accepting of their sexual identity (Beals and Peplau, 2006). Disclosure literature has focused on children and adolescence; however, more recently research examines disclosure across the lifespan. For example, recent research found that the process of gay grandfathers coming out to their grandchildren is largely facilitated by adult children (Fruhauf, Orel, and Jenkins, 2009).

Gender identity

The terms sex and gender are frequently used interchangeably, yet they have distinct meanings (Kessler and McKenna, 1978). "Sex" refers to the classification of people as either female or male, usually assigned shortly after birth based on a combination of physical characteristics which include: genitals, reproductive organs, hormones, and chromosomes. The term "gender" is a reference to the ways our society determines what is considered feminine or masculine, and how people experience those understandings psychologically and culturally (Kessler and McKenna, 1978). Words like "woman" and "man" denote gender categories, creating a gender binary that differentiates those who do not conform to gender stereotypes from those that do (Oswald *et al.*, 2005). Gender norms change across location and time. For example, a man who wore pink nail polish might be thought of as feminine 10 years ago, yet today he might be seen as punk rock or emo, which is viewed as more acceptable.

Gender identity represents a person's person-experience of their gender (Kessler and McKenna, 1978). People who are transgender may not identify with the sex they were assigned at birth (Lev, 2004). Gender identity is often confused with sexual orientation; however, it is important to know that everyone has both a gender identity and a sexual orientation. Gender identity is a person's deeply held sense of their gender and sexual orientation refers to who a person is emotionally and physically attracted to (Lev, 2004). People express gender in various ways (e.g., mannerisms, hair styles, clothing). Gender is not only a core aspect of our identity, it also helps us to make sense of how we understand other people according to social norms. There is little research about the process of transgender people's disclosure to friends, family, and coworkers. Benson (unpublished data) argues that distinctions be made between coming out in reference to sexual orientation and transgender people's disclosure of gender identity.

Queer, but Not Queer Enough: Marginalization in the Queer Community

The acronym LGBT may refer to a unified population of lesbian, gay, bisexual, and transgender people who are marginalized based on their sexual orientation and gender identity; however, all are not equal. Sexual orientation and gender identity are believed to exist within a two-gender system that limits gender to two categories: gay or straight, woman or man (Kessler and McKenna, 1978). In a culture that values either/or binary classifications, bisexual and transgender people challenge socio-political categories of sexual orientation and disrupt what it means to be a man or a woman (or not) (Israel and Mohr, 2004). Though members of the queer community experience social oppression, they also can assume the role of oppressor (excluder) (McLean, 2008). For example, some members of the queer community have questioned if bisexual and transgender are valid identities (Alexander and Yescavage, 2003). Slurs like "bicurious" and "she-male" are sometimes used by gay men and lesbian women to further 'other' bisexual and transgender identified people. These terms are offensive, yet most recognizable at this time and demonstrate that marginalization happens within marginalized populations.

Bisexuality

As recognition of same-gender relationships and queer identities grows, bisexual identities remain invisible (Diamond, 2008; Erickson-Schroth and Mitchell, 2009). Negative attitudes about bisexual people exist not only among straight people, but among gay men and lesbian women who maintain dichotomous understandings of gender and sexual orientation (Israel and Mohr, 2004). Bisexual people are subjected to the de-legitimization of their sexual identity (Erickson-Schroth and Mitchell, 2009; Israel and Mohr, 2004). For example, straight people often believe that bisexual people are gay, and gay people often hold the belief that bisexual people are straight. The stereotype of the bisexual female coed, which is frequently depicted in pornography, reiterates the belief that bisexual women are only interested in sex with other women to please their male partners. Bisexual men, on the other hand, tend to be viewed more negatively as they are thought to be closeted gay men, which is grounded in heteronormative beliefs about masculinity (Eliason, 2000).

Many bisexual people have expressed concern that their sexuality is viewed as simply who they have sex with, rather than recognizing the complex nature of human relationships (Israel and Mohr, 2004). They may be mistakenly viewed as promiscuous and unable to choose a gender to partner with, thus limiting their perceived ability to be trusted in a monogamous relationship with a man *or* a woman. Bisexual people may have only been in opposite-gender relationships or same-sex relationship, causing them to be seen as straight or gay or not seen at all, yet embrace the capacity to be attracted to and in relationship with people who express a range of genders (Eliason, 2000;

Rust, 2001). Overall, there are few empirical studies that explore bisexual discrimination within queer communities (e.g., McLean, 2008).

Transgender identities

The within-group marginalization of transgender people was most notably recognized in 2007, when Barney Frank, the first out-gay member of the US House of Representatives, initially proposed the Employee Nondiscrimination Act (ENDA), mentioned earlier, which specifically excluded transgender people. Frank later reintroduced a transgender-inclusive version of ENDA after much debate and backlash from transgender advocates, which was the most public conversation about transgender exclusion in history at that time. The National Center for Transgender Equality and National Gay and Lesbian Task Force recently released a study highlighting the pervasive discrimination that transgender people endure with the largest number of transgender participants to date (Grant *et al.*, 2011). While this report shed light on the injustices that transgender people face in virtually all areas of life, transgender people still remain under-studied and least visible as a group. Media depictions have come a long way since transgender people were portrayed as mentally unstable oddities on the *Jerry Springer Show*, as transgender adults and children are now featured as dynamic people with compelling life stories on more notable shows such as *20/20* and *Oprah*.

Many straight and LGB people live with gender privilege, or the advantages a person experience when their gender identity is congruent with the sex they were assigned at birth (Schilt and Westbrook, 2009). For example, a woman has been designated female at birth and identifies as a woman. A transwoman may have been designated male at birth and identifies as a woman. This type of privilege allows people who express their gender in normative ways to have regular access to safe restrooms, not have people question their "real" name, avoid strangers' questions about the appearance, and not have their gender validated by how many medical procedures they have undergone. "Transphobia" refers to negative attitudes and feelings towards transgender people, which can be due to their gender presentation (Lombardi, 2009).

Many LGB people view transgender people as having vastly different political goals (Devor and Matte,

2004; Stone, 2009) that focus on protections related to gender identity. While there is little research on this subject (e.g., Stone, 2009), political conversations regarding the non-inclusive version of ENDA included LGB people's public statements that trans issues are not gay issues, that our larger culture does not "get" transgender people, and that by including them in political initiatives it will take longer to attain equal rights for LGB people. Transgender activists have stated that top priorities of the gay community, such as same-sex marriage, fail to recognize that transgender people are still denied basic needs. For example, consider how challenging it might be for a transman who appears masculine to locate a health provider willing to administer gynecological services – a crucial element of preventative care.

Mixed-orientation families

Mixed-orientation families are those in which one spouse, or partner, discloses a different sexual orientation after engaging in a committed relationship or marriage. There is little research about this type of family and their experiences, and almost all of it focuses on married opposite-sex families in which one spouse comes out as gay or lesbian sometime during their marriage (Buxton, 2012). Sometimes this disclosure comes as a complete surprise to both spouses, sometimes one spouse knew of previous same-sex sexual encounters of the other spouse that occurred prior to their marriage, and other times one spouse knew of their same-sex sexual attractions, and possible gay or lesbian orientation before the marriage. As such, they felt pressure to conform to social heteronormative norms and they married while trying to exclude the part of their identity that is gay or lesbian as a result of internalized homophobia.

To be clear, there are other pathways to becoming a mixed-orientation family, although research is so limited that we have yet to fully explore and understand the full array of pathways and experiences (Buxton, 2012). What we do know is that for the entire family this is beyond a difficult experience and one that often includes a grieving process. For some who come out as gay or lesbian during a marriage they have been denying this part of their identity, and as a result often experience depressive and anxious symptoms – symptoms that spill over and affect the way spouses communicate, resolve conflict, express affection, parent, etc. (Swan and Benack, 2012; Tornello and Patterson, 2012). They also can create risk for the unknowing partner if the disclosing partner has engaged in risky sexual behavior outside of the marital relationship (Klaar, 2012). Often, but not always, these couples ultimately break up or divorce.

Any outcome for the family involves a need to navigate and renegotiate the functioning, and for some the structure, of their family (Swan and Benack, 2012). This is especially true when children are involved. For the disclosing partner this can produce a tremendous amount of fear of lost custody or visitation rights. However, some states no longer allow sexual orientation of a parent to dictate custody and/or visitation, or divorce settlements (Brower, 2009). This is another reason the legal context in states and at the federal level is important to help guide such decisions in an inclusive and socially just manner that is best for the child and family. Alternatively, some states continue to exclude such recognitions and losing access to children becomes a legitimate fear.

More contemporary research has examined coping among heterosexual spouses. This research finds that these spouses often confront exclusion and dismissal from social support systems, including therapists (Grever, 2012). This comes after a considerable internal struggle to admit they have a spouse who came out as queer. With increased clinical attention and changing social views this is changing to create a more inclusive and supportive environment for these spouses, although much additional work is needed. Interestingly, some spouses cope by focusing more on parenting and turning to the spouse who came out. Some of these coping methods appear to be slightly more specific to heterosexual male spouses, compared to heterosexual female spouses (Buxton, 2012). Many online support groups and some face-to-face groups in communities also are increasing and these will play an important role in reducing exclusion.

Queer Strengths and Resilience

In spite of being told they are mentally ill, sexually perverse, immoral, incapable of forming families, etc., and living daily lives in which the fear of enduring a homophobic act against them, ranging from harsh

---

Case Example: Levon and Dirk

Levon and Dirk, an interracial gay couple in their early 40s, have been together for 15 years. They adopted their son Marcus five years ago, when he was 9 years old. Due to the laws in their state, which restrict unmarried partners from jointly adopting, Levon first legally adopted Marcus and Dirk later filed for second parent adoption so that they would both have full parental rights and responsibilities. Levon's mother used to express concerns about the hardships that Marcus may endure as a boy with two dads; however, both fathers have remained present in his schooling and social activities without major incident. Marcus has many friends and does well in school. They have experienced some discriminatory behavior, such as the time that Dirk took Marcus to a new pediatrician and the receptionist questioned his role as a father because the intake paperwork indicated that Marcus already had a father who shared his last name (Dirk's last name is different from Levon and Marcus's). Recently, a constitutional ban on gay marriage was introduced to their state legislature. Although Levon and Dirk have not pursued legal marriage, their family is subjected to harsh political advertisements and news segments on TV. Lawmakers have been debating the merits of a gay marriage ban in the media, which include disparaging claims about gay people and same-sex relationships. Each time Marcus is exposed to discrimination based on the formation of his family, Levon and Dirk discuss the influence of homophobia on people, what to do if Marcus is directly confronted, and they talk about the love present in their family. Both dads agree that people do not always act in fair ways, but love and open conversation help to create safety for their family.

words and general threats to death, as we have seen in too many media reports (e.g., Matthew Shepard), which may pervade their every thought, queer families demonstrate great levels of resilience (Oswald, 2002; Weston, 1991). Although we do not intend to dismiss the great hardships that many queers continue to endure (Gibson *et al.*, 2013), on average, we believe American queers in particular have created many strengths in order to help them navigate and negotiate often exclusionary contexts.

These strengths promote great resilience and help fuel the fight for socially just inclusion. From early studies of female same-sex relationships among prisoners (Selling, 1931), to the seminal work of Weston (1991) and more contemporary work (Goldberg, 2010), we have learned that queers create their own inclusive families, even in harsh social contexts, including contexts which involve exclusion by biological kin and society. Queers often create their own families based on connecting people through the power of choice, as opposed to marriage, adoption, or blood. Oswald (2002) developed two overarching types of resilience strategies found among queers: intentionality and redefinition. Choosing one's own family is an example of being intentional (i.e., engaging in behaviors that work to support queer families), whereas redefinition includes acts that help queers make meaning. For example, using "daddy" and "papa" as a way for children to recognize two men as their parents.

Gay- and lesbian-headed families experience high rates of social exclusion, which has been shown to have negative effects on this population (Meyer, 2003). Yet research clearly demonstrates that same-sex couples are doing well creating and maintaining meaningful family relationships (Biblarz and Savci, 2010; Goldberg, 2010; Patterson, 2000). In fact, decades of research have shown that children raised by same-sex parents are happy, healthy, and well adjusted (Biblarz and Savci, 2010; Goldberg, 2010; Patterson, 2006). These families tend to exhibit strengths that buffer the negative effects of exclusion. Gay and lesbian couples are unique in that they are highly likely to be intentional in choosing to have and raise children, which is related to their satisfaction as a couple (Goldberg, 2010). Such is the case with Levon and Dirk, who were happily partnered for 10 years prior to pursuing adoption.

As a result, they tend to maintain a child-focused approach to parenting which contributes to positive child outcomes (Wainright, Russell, and Patterson, 2004). This is important because research has found the quality of parental relationships, not gender or sexual orientation, to be significant for the healthy development of children (Patterson, 2006).

Findings consistently show that these children are doing well in many areas. More specifically, studies have repeatedly found that children of same-sex parents score well in relationship quality, psychological well-being, social adjustment, and parental investment (Biblarz and Savci, 2010). For example, Wainright *et al.* (2004) found that children of same-sex parents who reported higher levels of parental warmth experienced higher levels of self-esteem and were more likely to have positive relationships at school. Similarly, the effects of Marcus's close relationship with his dads on his academic success are evident in the case example. Children of gay and lesbian parents also tend to be more open and tolerant of diversity (Goldberg, 2010), as families like Levon and Dirk's often discuss the diversity of their own family. Although gay- and lesbian-headed families exist in a social context of homophobic exclusion, these families continue to thrive as they exhibit many strengths that contribute to their resiliency (Goldberg, 2010; Patterson, 2000).

There is also a strong history of navigating harshly homophobic contexts to create and sustain inclusive communities such as those made visible during the LGBT rights movement and the response to the AIDS crisis, as well as the more contemporary movements for transgender and same-sex marriage rights (Gibson *et al.*, 2013). Visibility also has been gained through a highly symbolic queer community. For example, a pink triangle was used in concentration camps during World War II to identify queers. Since then the queer community has (re)used the pink triangle to symbolize a resilient community identity, and to serve as a reminder of the monstrous atrocities that occurred against queers in concentration camps, as well as to demonstrate an active fighting back against other social persecutions. Much of the research on queer strengths and resilience comes from noncomparative studies (i.e., those that look at the diversity of queer families rather than comparing them to various types of heterosexual families). Although comparative studies are important, especially to help the general public stop seeing queer families as deviant or immoral, we believe more non-comparative studies of strengths and resilience are needed if we are to be truly inclusive of recognizing queer families as families in their own right. In this manner, we can really begin to understand their strengths, challenges, and problems without pathologizing these individuals or their families.

Implications for practice and policy

Discrimination and homophobic attitudes towards LGBT people have been shown to negatively affect their individual and relationship well-being (Meyer, 2003). Initiatives to provide critical information regarding LGBTQ-inclusive education should be paramount in family studies and family life education (Allen and Demo, 1995). As family and relationship structures continue to change and the public advocates for more inclusive laws, family life educators are charged with teaching students various means to understand and cope with discrimination. Premier family life education textbooks do not currently include queer families (e.g., Powell and Cassidy, 2007); doing so in future editions could contribute to the likelihood of queer-inclusive curriculums. The larger political climate may create polarizing positions on social issues; however, the classroom is a space for dialog about relevant issues that affect families today. Classrooms can be conversational spaces where students engage in critical thinking regarding the differences between ideology, science, and social injustice (Allen, 2009).

Efforts to promote resilience and education about legal issues should begin by developing accurate and accessible information for public consumption. Awareness about policies and laws helps community members to understand the need for legislative initiatives to change and create laws that impact LGBT

individuals and families. Additionally, organizations like Lambda Legal (www.lambdalegal.org), the National Center for Transgender Equality (www.transequality.org), Human Right Campaign (HRC) (www.hrc.org), the Gay and Lesbian Task Force (www.ngltf.org) provide important policy information that raises consciousness about unnecessary and archaic state and federal laws that keep discrimination legal.

Are you wondering how you can fight exclusion and advocate for social justice? Here are some suggestions. Understand policies in your place of employment and advocate for inclusive change by contacting human resources departments. Connect with LGBT colleagues and peers and ask how the policies in your community impact their families. Find out if LGBT children are protected under local and state anti-bullying policies. Be aware of state and federal legislative initiatives that seek to protect LGBT people, as well as legislation that can limit freedoms and equal rights. Know who your state and federal senators and representatives are and where they stand on relevant issues. Vote.

Critical Thinking Questions

1. In what ways might we remake the institution of marriage in the United States to be more inclusive, but in a way that also respects the current heteronormative institution?
2. How might stigma consciousness and internalized homophobia influence a queer person's beliefs about themselves and likelihood for successful relationships?
3. How does the research about children of same-sex parents compare to socially biased concerns about child outcomes in these families?
4. What policy recommendations would you make to create more equality for LGBTQ people?

References

Alexander, J., and Yescavage, K. (2003). Bisexuality and transgenderism: InterSEXions of the Others. *Journal of Bisexuality*, *3*, 1–23. doi: 10.1300/J159v03n03_01.

Allen, K. R. (2009). Keeping the feminist in our teaching: Daring to make a difference. In S. A. Lloyd, A. L. Few, and K. R. Allen (eds), *Handbook of feminist family studies* (pp. 351–359). Thousand Oaks, CA: Sage Publications.

Allen, K. R., and Demo, D. H. (1995). The families of lesbians and gay men: A new frontier in family research. *Journal of Marriage and the Family*, 57, 111–127. doi: doi:10.2307/353821.

Beals, K. P., and Peplau, L. A. (2006). Disclosure patterns within social networks of gay men and lesbians. *Journal of Homosexuality*, 51, 101–120. doi:10.1300/J082v51n02_06.

Biblarz, T., and Savci, E. (2010). Lesbian, gay, bisexual, and transgender families. *Journal of Marriage and Family*, 72, 480–497.

Bronfenbrenner, U. (1979). *The ecology of human development: Experiments by nature and design.* Cambridge, MA: Harvard University Press.

Bronfenbrenner, U. (1989). Ecological systems theory. In R. Vasta (ed.), *Annals of child development*, vol. 6 (pp. 187–249). Greenwich, CT: JAI.

Brower, T. (2009). It's not just shopping, urban lofts, and the lesbian gay-by boom: How sexual orientation demographics can inform family courts. *American University Journal of Gender, Social Policy and the Law*, 17, 1–39.

Burke, P. J., and Stets, J. E. (1999). Trust and commitment through self-verification. *Social Psychology Quarterly*, 62, 347–366.

Butler, J. P. (1990). *Gender trouble: Feminism and the subversion of identity.* New York: Routledge.

Buxton, A. (2012). Straight husbands whose wives come out as lesbian or bisexual: Men's voices challenge the "masculinity myth." *Journal of GLBT Family Studies*, 8, 23–45.

Department of Housing and Urban Development. (2012). Equal access to housing in HUD programs regardless of sexual orientation or gender identity. A rule by the Housing and Urban Development Department on 02/03/2012. *Federal Register*, 77, 5662–5676.

Devor, A. H., and Matte, N. (2004). One Inc. and Reed Erickson: The uneasy collaboration of gay and trans activism. *GLQ: A Journal of Gay and Lesbian Studies*, 10, 179–209. doi: 10.1215/10642684-10-2-179.

Diamond, L. M. (2008). Female bisexuality from adolescence to adulthood: Results from a 10-year longitudinal study. *Developmental Psychology*, 44, 5–14. doi: 10.1037/0012-1649.44.1.5.

DiPlacido, J. (1998). Minority stress among lesbians, gay men and bisexuals: A consequence of heterosexism, homophobia and stigmatization. In G. Herek (ed.), *Stigma and sexual orientation* (pp. 138–159). Thousand Oaks, CA: Sage Publications.

Eliason, M. (2000). Bi-negativity: The stigma facing bisexual men. *Journal of Bisexuality*, 1, 137–154. doi: 10.1300/J159v01n02_05.

Erickson-Schroth, L., and Mitchell, J. (2009). Queering queer theory, or why bisexuality matters. *Journal of Bisexuality*, 9, 297–315. doi: 10.1080/15299710903316596.

Frable, D. E. S., Wortman, C., and Joseph, J. (1997). Predicting self-esteem, well-being, and distress in a cohort of gay men: The importance of cultural stigma, personal visibility, community networks, and positive identity. *Journal of Personality*, 65, 599–624.

Frost, D. M., and Meyer, I. H. (2009). Internalized homophobia and relationship quality among lesbians, gay men, and bisexuals. *Journal of Counseling Psychology*, 56, 97–109. doi: 10.1037/a0012844.

Fruhauf, C. A., Orel, N. A., and Jenkins, D. A. (2009). The coming-out process of gay grandfathers: Perceptions of their adult children's influence. *Journal of GLBT Family Studies*, 5, 99–118. doi:10.1080/15504280802595402.

Gallup (n.d.). Gay and lesbian rights. Retrieved December 16, 2012 from http://www.gallup.com/poll/1651/Gay-Lesbian-Rights.aspx.

Gates, G., Badgett, M., and Ho, D. (2008). Marriage, registration and dissolution by same-sex couples in the U.S. Williams Institute, UCLA School of Law.

Gay, L. (2012). The 2011 National School Climate Survey: Key findings on the experiences of lesbian, gay, bisexual and transgender youth in our nation's schools. Executive summary. New York: Gay, Lesbian and Straight Education Network (GLSEN).

Gibson, M., Alexander, J., and Meem, D. (2013). *Finding out: An introduction to LGBT studies* (2nd edn). Thousand Oaks, CA: Sage Publications.

Goldberg, A. E. (2010). *Lesbian and gay parents and their children: Research on the family life cycle.* Washington, DC: APA Books.

Grant, J., Mottet, J., Tanis, J., Harrison, J., Herman, J., and Keisling, M. (2011). *Injustice at every turn: A report of the national transgender discrimination survey.* Retrieved May 30, 2014 from http://transequality.org/PDFs/Executive_Summary.pdf.

Grever, C. (2012). Unintended consequences: Unique issues of female straight spouses. *Journal of GLBT Family Studies*, 8, 67–84.

Halberstam, J. (2012). *Gaga feminism.* Boston, MA: Beacon Press.

Herek, G. M., Gillis, J. R., and Cogan, J. C. (2009). Internalized stigma among sexual minority adults: Insights from a social psychological perspective. *Journal of Counseling Psychology*, 56, 32–43. doi: 10.1037/a0014672.

Hoogs, J. (2003). Divorce without marriage: Establishing a uniform dissolution procedure for domestic partners through a comparative analysis of European and American domestic partner laws. *Hastings Law Journal*, 54, 707–708.

Horvath, M., and Ryan, A. (2003). Antecedents and potential moderators between attitudes and hiring discrimination on the basis of sexual orientation. *Sex Roles, 48,* 115–130.

Human Rights Campaign (2011). Federal laws: Employment Non-Discrimination Act. Retrieved January 5, 2011 from http://www.hrc.org/laws_and_elections/enda.asp.

Israel, T., and Mohr, J. J. (2004). Attitudes toward bisexual women and men. *Journal of Bisexuality, 4,* 117–134. doi: 10.1300/J159v04n01_09.

Kessler, S. J., and McKenna, W. (1978). *Gender: An ethnomethodological approach.* New York: John Wiley & Sons, Inc.

Klaar, C. (2012). Straight wives of HIV-positive husbands who contracted the virus through male-to-male sexual contact. *Journal of GLBT Family Studies, 8,* 99–120.

Lev, A. I. (2004). *Transgender emergence: Therapeutic guidelines for working with gender-variant people and their families.* New York: Haworth Press.

Lombardi, E. (2009). Varieties of transgender/transsexual lives and their relationship with transphobia. *Journal of Homosexuality, 56,* 977–992. doi: 10.1080/00918360903275393.

Mays, V. M., Chatters, L. M., Cochran, S. D., and Mackness, J. (1998). African American families in diversity: Gay men and lesbians as participants in family networks. *Journal of Comparative Family Studies, 29,* 73–87.

McLean, K. (2008). Inside, outside, nowhere: Bisexual men and women in the gay and lesbian community. *Journal of Bisexuality, 8,* 63–80. doi: 10.1080/15299710802143174.

McWhirter, D. P., and Mattison, A. M. (1984). *The male couple: How relationships develop.* Englewood Cliffs, NJ: Prentice Hall.

Meyer, I. H. (2003). Prejudice, social stress and mental health in lesbian, gay and bisexual populations: Conceptual issues and research evidence. *Psychological Bulletin, 129,* 674–697. doi: 10.1037/0033-2909.129.5.674.

Moore, M. R. (2011). Two sides of the same coin: Revising analyses of lesbian sexuality and family formation through the study of black women. *Journal of Lesbian Studies, 15,* 58–68. doi: 10.1080/10894160.2010.508412.

Moore, M. R. (2012). Intersectionality and the study of black, sexual minority women. *Gender and Society, 26,* 33–39. doi: 10.1177/0891243211427031.

Narui, M. (2011). Understanding Asian/American gay, lesbian, and bisexual experiences from a poststructural perspective. *Journal of Homosexuality, 58,* 1211–1234.

Oswald, R. F. (2002). Resilience within the family networks of lesbians and gay men: Intentionality and redefinition. *Journal of Marriage and Family, 64,* 374–383.

Oswald, R. F., Blume, L. B., and Marks, S. R. (2005). Decentering heteronormativity: A model for family studies. In V. L. Bengston, A. C. Acock, K. R. Allen, P. Dillworth

Anderson, and D. M. Klein (eds), *Sourcebook of family theory and research* (pp. 143–154). Thousand Oaks, CA: Sage Publications.

Otis, M. D., Rostosky, S. S., Riggle, E. D., and Hamrin, R. (2006). Stress and relationship quality in same-sex couples. *Journal of Social and Personal Relationships, 23,* 81–99.

Page, S. (1998). Accepting the gay person: Rental accommodation in the community. *Journal of Homosexuality, 36,* 31–39.

Patterson, C. J. (2000). Family relationships of lesbians and gay men. *Journal of Marriage and Family, 62,* 1052–1069. doi: 10.1111/j.1741-3737.2000.01052.x.

Patterson, C. J. (2006). Children of lesbian and gay parents. *Current Directions in Psychological Science, 15,* 241–244. doi: 10.1111/j.1467-8721.2006.00444.x.

Peplau, L. A., Cochran, S. D., and Mays, V. M. (1997). A national survey of the intimate relationships of African American lesbians and gay men: A look at commitment, satisfaction, sexual behavior, and HIV disease. In B. Greene (ed.), *Psychological perspectives on lesbian and gay issues: Ethnic and cultural diversity among lesbians and gay men* (pp. 11–38). Thousand Oaks, CA: Sage Publications.

Pinel, E. (1999). Stigma consciousness: The psychological legacy of social stereotypes. *Journal of Personality and Social Psychology, 76,* 114–128. doi:10.1037/0022-3514.76.1.114.

Powell, L. H., and Cassidy, D. (2007). *Family life education: Working with families across the life span.* Long Grove, IL: Waveland Press.

Rust, P. C. (2001). Two many and not enough. *Journal of Bisexuality, 1,* 31–68. doi: 10.1300/J159v01n01_04.

Sandfort, T. G. M., and Dodge, B. (2008). "… And then there was the down low": Introduction to Black and Latino male bisexualities. *Archives of Sexual Behavior, 37,* 675–682. doi: 10.1007/s10508-008-9359-4.

Savin-Williams, R. C. (1998). The disclosure of families of same-sex attractions by lesbian, gay, and bisexual youths. *Journal of Research on Adolescence, 8,* 49–68. doi: 10.1207/s15327795jra0801_3.

Schilt, K., and Westbrook, L. (2009). "Gender normals," transgender people, and the social maintenance of heterosexuality. *Gender and Society, 23,* 440–464.

Sears, B., and Mallory, C. (2011). *Documented evidence of employment discrimination and its effects on LGBT people.* Williams Institute, UCLA School of Law.

Selling, L. (1931). The pseudo family. *American Journal of Sociology, 37,* 247–253.

Stone, A. L. (2009). More than adding a T: American lesbian and gay activists' attitudes towards transgender inclusion. *Sexualities, 12,* 334–354, doi:10.1177/1363460709103894.

Swan, T., and Benack, S. (2012). Renegotiating identity in unscripted territory: The predicament of queer men in heterosexual marriages. *Journal of GLBT Family Studies*, 8, 46–66.

Tornello, S., and Patterson, C. (2012). Gay fathers in mixed-orientation relationships: Experiences of those who stay in their marriages and those who leave. *Journal of GLBT Family Studies*, 8, 85–98.

van Eeden-Moorefield, B., Martell, C., Williams, M., and Preston, M. (2011). Same-sex relationships and dissolution: The connection between heteronormativity and homonormativity. *Family Relations*, 60, 562–571.

Wainright, J. L., Russell, S. T., and Patterson, C. J. (2004). Psychosocial adjustment, school outcomes, and romantic relationships of adolescents with same-sex parents. *Child Development*, 75, 1886–1898. doi:10.1111/j.1467-8624.2004.00823.x.

Weed, E., and Schor, N. (1997). *Feminism meets queer theory*. Bloomington, IN: Indiana University Press.

Weston, K. (1991). *Families we choose: Lesbians, gays, kinship*. New York: Columbia University Press.

Windsor vs. The United States. Proceedings and Orders. Supreme Court of the United States. Retrieved January 7, 2013 from http://www.supremecourt.gov/opinions/09pdf/09a648.pdf.

3

The Stigma of Families with Mental Illness

Natalie R. Gela and Patrick W. Corrigan

In Chapter 3, Gela and Corrigan discuss how stigma and discrimination of people with mental illness contribute to their difficulty in accessing help, as well as the family's shame. Mental illness becomes a "secret" which can isolate affected individuals and their kin. We learn that although the stigma of mental illness has identifiable and persistent public and private dimensions, through education, advocacy, and contact with individuals and their families, public stigma can be combated.

Families with mental illness are confronted with many obstacles. Not only do people diagnosed with mental illness experience stigma, but family members face similar experiences through their association with the person who has been diagnosed with the illness. Erving Goffman (1963) called this courtesy stigma. We refer to "family stigma" as an efficient way to talk about the prejudice and discrimination experienced by people because of their relationship with relatives who have been diagnosed with mental illness. The family stigma process negatively impacts individuals in numerous ways. Family members may avoid social situations, spend energy and resources on hiding the secret of mental illness, and experience discrimination within employment and/or housing situations.

In this chapter, we first briefly review models of how mental illness stigma affects diagnosed individuals, and then extend this to how stigma impacts their families. The discussion includes a review of types of

stigma and constructs associated with the family; we base this in research conducted with the public as well as direct assessment of family members. The chapter ends with a discussion of strategies related to changing family stigma.

What is the Problem of the Stigma of Mental Illness?

As Ray's case on p. 34 illustrates, the stigma of mental illness is complex and multifaceted. Not only did the negative reactions of others to Ray's symptoms cause distress, but he also eventually internalized these negative thoughts and beliefs, causing himself further distress and harm. Figure 3.1 is a 2×4 grid incorporating cognitive and behavioral constructs involved in the stigma process (Corrigan and Sokol, 2012). Social-cognitive models have been especially useful as a way

Case Example: Ray

This case illustrates the various ways that stigma can impact the lives of those who have been diagnosed. Later, we will extend the types of stigma illustrated here to demonstrate stigma's impact on families.

Ray Goodman was diagnosed with "schizoaffective disorder" in his early twenties.[1] Schizoaffective disorder is characterized by a period of illness during which there is a mood episode concurrent with symptoms of schizophrenia. Delusions and hallucinations are also present during this period (American Psychological Association, 2013). People often say that the worst part of living with mental illness is not the disease itself as much as the negative attitudes that people have toward the disease. After Ray attempted suicide during his first psychotic break, some of Ray's friends never looked at him in the same way again. Ray felt sad and ashamed. As a result, he denied his problem, trying to hide it from everyone else that came along. During his second breakdown, Ray's symptoms

were so bad that he could no longer deny or hide his illness. As a result, Ray was socially isolated. Employers asked if he had a "nervous condition." Romantic relationships with women ended the moment they caught wind of Ray's illness. Members of Ray's family either pitied him, called him lazy, or blamed him for being ill. To most people, Ray was no longer just "Ray," but was a "mentally ill man," and all that was associated with that label. Ray also began to view himself differently. He believed he was broken and less capable of functioning in society.

With a lot of work, Ray has been able to remind himself and others that he is still just "Ray," who happens to have a psychiatric diagnosis. Think of your own attitudes toward mental illness and how that might affect those who are labeled with it. Have you thought about or reacted in a similar way to someone who you know or have encountered who has a mental illness?

to conceptualize the stigma of mental illness; these kinds of psychological models examine the structures and processes that comprise everyday thoughts and behaviors. Social-cognitive models include stereotypes, prejudice, and discrimination. *Stereotypes* are knowledge structures that evolve as part of "normal" development in a culture. They are ways in which humans categorize information about groups of people, often framed as seemingly fact-based beliefs with a negative evaluative component. Negative stereotypes often associated with mental illness include dangerousness or incompetence. Stereotypes become *prejudice* when people agree with the belief, leading to the development of negative emotions and evaluations of the group (Crocker, Major, and Steele, 1998; Eagly and Chaiken, 1993). *Discrimination* is the behavioral result of prejudice. Discrimination is typically punitive in form, and is experienced as taking away a rightful opportunity, or reacting to the target group aversively.

Research has identified a variety of prejudices and discriminatory behaviors reflecting the stigma of mental illness (Corrigan and O'Shaughnessy, 2007; Peluso and Blay, 2009; Pescosolido, Monahan, Link, Stueve, and Kikuzawa, 1999). The belief that people diagnosed with mental illness are dangerous is highly associated with fear (Corrigan *et al.*, 2002), and is exacerbated by the belief that people with mental illness are unpredictable. Fear leads directly to avoidance and withdrawal, the discriminatory result. The blame and shame that people with mental health problems often feel are the result of another important stereotype, that of being responsible for the illness; for example, people with these conditions somehow choose their illness. Another stereotype is incompetence, the idea that people diagnosed with mental illness are unable to achieve goals normally sought by peers in the same culture.

Three groups of discriminatory behaviors seem to ensue from the stigma of mental illness (Corrigan,

	Types of stigma experienced by the individual with mental illness constructs		
	Public stigma	**Self-stigma**	**Label avoidance**
Prejudice (stereotypes)	"He is dangerous."	"I am unreliable."	Diagnosis of mental illness means "crazy."
Discrimination	Employer refuses to hire person with mental illness.	Person with mental illness does not take on new tasks.	Individual refrains from going to the clinic to seek help.

Figure 3.1 A matrix for understanding stigma: typology by constructs to describe the "what" of stigma.

Markowitz, Watson, Rowan, and Kubiak, 2003): coercion (in terms of mandatory inpatient or outpatient treatment); segregation (or treating persons with mental illness away from their community, in institutions); and avoidance. Avoidance and withdrawal may be the most problematic of these (Corrigan and Miller, 2004). Members of the general public may avoid people diagnosed with mental illness in order to escape the perceived risks of associating with them. For example, prejudiced employers might not hire a person diagnosed with a serious mental illness because they fear that the person will harm co-workers (Tsang *et al.*, 2007).

Types of Stigma

A convergence of research has led to the conceptualization of *three types of stigma* known to be relevant to mental health disorders. These are summarized in the top row of Figure 3.1: public stigma, self-stigma, and label avoidance. Figure 3.1 also provides examples of prejudice and discrimination that might result from such stigma (Corrigan, Markowitz, and Watson, 2004).

Public stigma

Public stigma is the process by which members of the general population endorse stereotypes of mental illness and act in a discriminatory manner (Thornicroft, Rose, Kassam, and Sartorius, 2007). It represents the prejudice and discrimination directed at people known to have mental illness by the public. For example, prejudiced employers who believe that individuals with mental illness are dangerous (prejudice) will behave in a discriminatory manner, refusing to hire an individual with mental illness (discrimination). (See Box 3.1.)

Box 3.1   Population Research on the State of Mental Illness Stigma

How does the general public view mental illness? Schomerus and colleagues (2012) analyzed the results of long-term population studies focused on mental illness-related beliefs and attitudes toward mental illness. They found an increase over time in the biological causal beliefs related to depression and schizophrenia, as well as an increase in the belief that mental illness requires professional help. As for negative stereotypes about mental illness – for example, being dangerous or to blame for the problem – findings were mixed. Despite a greater acceptance of the neurobiological conception of mental illness and of seeking treatment, there was no evidence of a substantial increase in the public's social acceptance of people diagnosed with mental illness. In general, development over time of attitudes towards those with mental illness either demonstrated no change, inconsistent trends, or even trends towards the deterioration of public attitudes.

Self-stigma

Self-stigma occurs when people internalize the prejudice that they perceive to exist against them: "I have a mental illness so I must be incompetent." Applying or internalizing stereotypes has two harmful effects. (1) Cognitively and emotionally, internalizing stigma can hurt self-esteem ("I am not a good employee; I cannot keep up with the demands of my job because I have a mental illness.") and lessen self-efficacy ("I can't keep up with my job because I am an incompetent person with mental illness.") (Corrigan, Watson, and Barr, 2006; Link, Struening, Neese-Todd, Asmussen, and Phelan, 2001). (2) Behaviorally, self-stigma can lead to the "why try" effect (Corrigan, Larson, and Rüsch, 2009): a person diagnosed with mental illness may not seek out work thinking "someone like me is not worthy of real-world work". Self-discrimination may also exist in the form of self-isolation (Corrigan and Rao, 2012), which can result in decreased health care-service use, poor health outcomes, and poor quality of life (Sirey, Bruce, Alexopoulos, Perlick, Friedman, and Meyers, 2001; Sirey, Bruce, Alexopoulos, Perlick, Raue, Friedman, and Meyers, 2001).

Label avoidance

One way in which people are publicly labeled as "mentally ill" is by associating with a mental health program (Corrigan, 2004, 2007). To avoid labeling, some people refrain from seeking services that would be helpful, or do not continue to use services once initiated. Epidemiological research has shown that the majority of people who might benefit from mental health care either opt not to pursue it or do not fully adhere to treatment regimens once begun. Epidemiology is the science that seeks to define the depth and breadth of an illness in different populations. As an example, the National Comorbidity Survey (Kessler *et al.*, 2001) found that less than 40% of respondents with a serious mental illness, such as schizophrenia, had received medical treatment in the past year.

What is the Problem of Stigma and Families?

Types of Family Stigma

The Simpsons' case on page 37 illustrates types of family stigma that resemble the forms of stigma experienced by individuals diagnosed with mental illness (see Figure 3.2). First, we describe and define these types of family stigma. This general orientation is followed by a review of the research that supports our assertions related to these constructs.

Public stigma

Families may suffer the same kinds of negative attitudes and discrimination as their loved ones with mental illness, often in the context of encounters with individuals in the family's social network, or by other members of their community (Angermeyer, Schulze, and Dietrich, 2003). Public stigma can be expressed in various ways including derogatory language used to refer to the family, gossip and

Case Example: Gabby

Denise and Jay Simpson's 28-year-old daughter Gabby lives with bipolar disorder. Bipolar disorder is a clinical disorder characterized by one or more episodes of significant mood, energy, and activity changes consisting of symptoms of mania and/or depression (APA, 2013). Since the age of 17, Gabby has struggled to manage her symptoms while living as "normal" a life as possible. When Gabby first started showing symptoms of illness, the Simpson's family physician referred Gabby to a psychiatrist. This came as a shock, as no one in their family had ever seen a psychiatrist or had "mental problems." For several weeks, neither Gabby nor her parents scheduled the appointment with the psychiatrist. Her parents feared how others in their small town would react if they found out. They worried that friends and neighbors would assume there was something "wrong" with Gabby. They also worried that their son would be bullied at school because he was the brother of a "crazy person." They worried that people would think something was wrong with them; that they were "bad parents" for not doing anything to prevent Gabby from getting sick. They felt responsible for Gabby's condition, and were ashamed.

Types of family stigma				
	Public stigma	**Self-stigma**	**Label avoidance**	**Vicarious stigma**
Prejudice (stereotypes)	"They think I'm not trustworthy because my brother has a mental illness."	"I am a bad mother."	Taking my son to a therapist would mean he's "crazy."	"They see my spouse as dangerous."
Discrimination	Employer refuses to hire family member of person with mental illness.	Parent of person with mental illness avoids going out with friends.	Parent refrains from going to the clinic to seek help for their child.	Spouse feels ashamed.

Figure 3.2   A matrix for understanding family stigma: typology by constructs.

slander, remarks or questions that connote family blame for the condition or criticism, pity, unwelcomed and patronizing advice, stares in public, and social avoidance or exclusion (Larson and Corrigan, 2008; Norvilitis, Scime, and Lee, 2002). As the case example shows, Gabby's parents worried that others would blame them for her condition, and that their son would be bullied at school because of his sister's diagnosis.

Self-stigma

Self-stigma occurs when a family member internalizes stigmatizing views held by the general public related to the relative's association with an individual diagnosed with mental illness. This type of stigma is associated with shame and other various forms of psychological distress related to being a family member of an individual diagnosed with mental illness (Hasson-Ohayon, Levy, Kravetz, Vollanski-Narkis, and Roe, 2011; Tsang, Tam, Chan and Chang, 2003; Wahl and Harman, 1989). For example, in the case example, Gabby's parents worried that they were "bad parents" and were ashamed of having a child diagnosed with a mental illness.

Label avoidance

As described above, label avoidance occurs when an individual refrains from seeking mental health services in order to avoid a label and concomitant stigma (Corrigan, 2007). With respect to family stigma, a relative may fear being identified, or "labeled," as a family member of a person diagnosed with mental illness. In order to avoid labeling, the relative might discourage their mentally ill family member from pursuing activities that could result in that individual being labeled; or, they might not seek out services for the ill person. For example, label avoidance in family stigma could manifest as a parent not seeking treatment for their child in order to avoid the child being labeled, or to avoid potential blame for their child's problems. Gabby's parents waited to send Gabby to a psychiatrist for those reasons.

Vicarious impact

Research also shows that family members suffer from witnessing the negative impact of prejudice and discrimination on their relative with mental illness. As much as two-thirds of family members expressed concern about the stigma experienced by their relative (Angermeyer et al., 2003; Struening et al., 2001; Wahl and Harman, 1989). Family members widely agree that stigma hurts their relatives' self-esteem, ability to keep friends, success in finding and obtaining a job or place to live, acceptance by mental health professionals, and that it represents a major hurdle to the recovery of their relative. Stigma also likely exacerbates the burden of stress that family members who provide care to mentally ill individuals may experience (Avison and Comeau, 2013; Saunders, 2003). (See Box 3.2.)

Box 3.2   Mental Illness and Family Process

The interaction between serious mental illness and the family is complex and often a central focus in services meant to improve the goals of individuals with psychiatric illness and their relatives. In short, symptoms and disabilities of serious mental illnesses are typically disruptive on most roles and exchanges among both nuclear and extended families. Key issues for the family involve negative consequences to children in cases of parental mental illness, as well as caregiving burdens associated with the care of mentally ill individuals. Serious mental illness can be a source of chronic stress for families charged with the care of the mentally ill individual, who often have to deal with behavior management issues, worry about their family member's future, and experience emotional distress stemming from how mental illness may have restricted their own and their family member's life (Lefley, 1989). Despite these challenges, many families demonstrate resilience and overcome negative emotions, balance family needs, maintain supportive relationships and foster family stability (Saunders, 2003). The interested reader should examine Mueser and Gingrich's (2006) *Complete family guide to schizophrenia*.

Population Perspectives on Family Stigma

How does the public view family members of individuals who have been diagnosed with mental illness? Although the stigma associated with family members may be less than what the public assigns to the diagnosed individual (Corrigan, Watson, and Miller, 2006), studies have found evidence that the public perceives relatives of individuals diagnosed with mental illness in negative terms (Burk and Sher, 1990; Corrigan et al., 2006; Mehta and Farina, 1988). Studies suggest that members of the general public often view family members as responsible for the relative's mental illness (Corrigan and Miller, 2004; Corrigan et al., 2006). Moreover, these perceptions may have negative behavioral consequences. One study found that when members of the general public blame family members for the relative's mental illness, pity is also found to be decreased and, in turn, help for family members is withheld (Corrigan et al., 2006).

Family Perspectives on Stigma

Many studies have attempted to document the stigma experienced by family members of people with mental illness by surveying them directly (Arcia and Fernández, 1998; Drapalski et al., 2008; Fernández and Arcia, 2004; Phelan, Bromet, and Link, 1998; Phillips, Pearson, Li, Xu, and Yang, 2002; Thara and Srinivasan, 2000; Tsang et al., 2003; Wahl and Harman, 1989; Wong et al., 2009). The majority of family members in these studies reported that they were personally impacted by stigma. Family members have reported being blamed, feeling shame, and being discriminated against. Consequences of stigma reported by family members include disruption of social roles and relationships and psychological distress. Label avoidance and failed or discontinued treatment seeking may also be a consequence of this stigma.

Blame, shame and avoidance

Studies have demonstrated that between a quarter and a half of family members believe they should hide their relationship with a family member with mental illness in order to avoid bringing shame to the family (Angermeyer et al., 2003; Phelan et al., 1998; Phillips et al., 2002; Shibre et al., 2001; Wahl and Harman, 1989). Findings from a group of 178 family members showed that about 25% worried that other people might blame them for the relative's mental illness (Shibre et al., 2001). Struening and colleagues (2001) reported mixed findings on two independent samples related to relatives' perceptions of blame: almost half of one sample (n = 281) reported some concern about blame; whereas only about 10% of a second sample (n = 180) reported this kind of concern.

Disruption of social roles and relationships

Among the negative consequences of self stigma reported by participants in a study by Tsang and colleagues (2003), relatives reported that feelings of shame led them to conceal their relatives' illness, as well as to isolate themselves to avoid the family discrimination against mental illness that they perceived. In a cross-sectional study of caregivers of those diagnosed with Bipolar Disorder, Gonzalez and colleagues (2007) found that for both caregivers of patient-relatives who had been identified as having problems in the past year, as well as caregivers whose patient-relatives were identified as not having problems for more than three-fourths of the year, perceived stigma was associated with decreased social interactions.

Additional research has found less evidence of disruptions in social roles and relationships. Angermeyer and colleagues (2003) found that family members of people diagnosed with schizophrenia interviewed in a focus group study rarely mentioned their own perceived stigma experiences in the domain of "limited access to social roles" (such as exclusion from family, partnerships, or problems with integration at work); family members did, however, mention this as an area in which they perceived their relatives being stigmatized. Furthermore, another group of researchers found that as little as 10% of a sample reported occasional avoidance by others (Phelan et al., 1998). However, it is possible that this relatively low perceived avoidance by others result may actually be due, in part, to relatives' efforts to conceal their family member's mental illness diagnosis (Angermeyer et al., 2003) given that half of Phelan and colleagues' participants reported concealing the recent hospitalization of their relative at least to some degree.

Label avoidance and service/treatment seeking

Research on individuals diagnosed with mental illness has shown a significant relationship between shame and treatment avoidance. For example, Sirey and colleagues (2001) found that research participants who expressed a sense of shame from personal experiences with mental illness were less likely to be involved in treatment. Leaf, Bruce, and Tischler (1986) showed that respondents with psychiatric diagnoses were more likely to avoid services if they believed family members would have a negative reaction to these services – that is, if they learned from their family that being identified as mentally ill disgraced them and/or their family. Conversely, positive attitudes of family members were associated with greater service use in a sample of more than 1,000 (Greenley, Mechanic, and Cleary, 1987).

Despite the family members' reports of avoidance mentioned in the previous sections, the available literature has thus far not shown that family members' fear of labeling represents a direct obstacle to treatment seeking and service use. Labeling of children's behavioral problems has been associated with positive outcomes including treatment seeking. Klasen (2000) conducted semi-structured interviews with 29 parents of hyperactive children and 10 general practitioners and found that parents tended to experience medicalization and labeling as important aspects of the validation and legitimation of their experience. Furthermore, receiving a diagnosis, a clinical label, has been found to motivate parents to seek out professional assistance for their children (Arcia and Fernández, 1998), and perceiving stigma associated with having a child diagnosed with a mental illness has been found to be associated with earlier help-seeking (Fernández and Arcia, 2004). Drapalski and colleagues (2008) found that, although about a third (n = 108) of family members of individuals diagnosed with serious mental illness reported feeling stigmatized due to their family member's illness,

less than 10% said this stigma prevented them from seeking mental health services for themselves or their family member. Interestingly, however, feelings of stigma were strongly associated with family members' report of unmet family information and support needs, even when socio-demographic characteristics of the family member and the patient were controlled for. In sum, although family stigma research does not seem to support label avoidance at this point, Drapalski and colleagues' (2008) findings – as well as the evidence of label avoidance found in the research focused on individuals who carry the mental illness diagnosis – seem to indicate that label avoidance and other types of stigma still contribute to families' unmet support needs in some way, even if not related to interfering with treatment seeking.

Psychological distress and decreased social support

Family members have reported psychological distress associated with the family stigma of mental illness. Research has shown that relatives' self-stigma is linked to feelings of self-blame or guilt in relation to the family member who has been diagnosed with a mental illness (Tsang et al., 2003), to low self-esteem (Lefley, 1992; Shibre et al., 2001; Tsang et al., 2003; Wahl and Harman, 1989), and to feelings of grief or depression (Perlick et al., 2007; Thara and Srinivasan, 2000). Up to 50% of family members report these feelings (Angermeyer et al., 2003; Phelan et al., 1998; Wahl and Harman, 1989).

It is generally accepted that social support is protective against various forms of psychological distress (Kawachi and Berkman, 2001; Kessler, Price, and Wortman, 1985). Not surprisingly, then, some researchers have found a link between lower levels of social support and greater perceived stigma (Gonzalez et al., 2007; Perlick et al., 2007). Perlick and colleagues (2007) found a relationship between caregiver reports of depression and stigma that was explained by lower reported levels of social support, together with caregiver report of avoidance coping. Caregivers may retreat from social support, instead adopting avoidance coping in order to fend off anticipated rejection.

Factors that Affect Family Members' Perceptions of and Experience of Family Stigma

Here, we will review the literature on some of the other factors that may affect family members' experience of public stigma and self-stigma related to mental illness, such as type and severity of the family member's mental illness diagnosis and his or her role in the family.

Illness characteristics

Illness characteristics may be associated with reports of perceived stigma by family members and other caregivers (Gonzalez et al., 2007; Greenberg, Kim, and Greenley, 1997; Phillips et al., 2002; Sansone, Matheson, Gaither, and Logan, 2008). For example, some research has shown that younger age of illness onset is associated with caregivers' greater perceptions of mental illness stigma (Gonzalez et al., 2007; Phillips et al., 2002; Thara and Srinivasan, 2000). However, this has not been consistently observed (e.g., Phelan et al.,1998). There is also the question of whether relatives' and caregivers' perceptions of stigma change depend on whether or not the patient-relative is experiencing symptoms. Gonzalez and colleagues (2007) found no difference in perceived stigma between caregivers of patient-relatives who were identified as experiencing symptoms during the previous nine months, and those whose relatives were identified as not having problems in the previous year. Conversely, other researchers have found caregivers' perceptions of stigma differ depending on whether or not the diagnosed relative was experiencing symptoms (Phelan et al., 1998; Phillips et al., 2002). Finally, there is limited evidence demonstrating that caregivers may report higher levels of perceived stigma when their relatives have a greater number of hospitalizations, and a more severe diagnosis (i.e., Bipolar Disorder I rather than Bipolar Disorder II) (Gonzalez et al., 2007).

Family role

There is evidence that the specific family member role (i.e., parent, sibling, partner, or child) (Corrigan and Miller, 2004), as well as proximity to the diagnosed individual (e.g., living with the relative or not) (Phelan et al., 1998), affect the family stigma experience. Parents may blame themselves for causing their child's stigmatizing mental health condition. Struening and colleagues (2001) examined two independent samples of parents. Almost half of one sample (n = 281), comprising mostly mothers, reported some concern about being blamed for their children's mental illness. Results reported from their second sample (n = 180) demonstrated the same concerns though at a lower rate: about 10% of mothers experienced being blamed. Another qualitative study of mothers of young children with disruptive behaviors (n = 62) found that 83% of the mothers described narratives with references to feelings of stigma or blame (Fernández and Arcia, 2004). Mothers of children diagnosed with ADHD reported more frequent criticism of their parenting from those close to them, as well as from acquaintances and strangers (Norvilitis et al., 2002).

Siblings may also perceive blame and responsibility related to having a relative diagnosed with mental illness. A study of 164 siblings hinted at this stigma; survey participants were concerned about relatives with mental illness remaining adherent to treatment regimens and perceptions that relapse was somehow the siblings' fault (Greenberg et al., 1997).

Furthermore, family members' reports of avoidance by others may vary by proximity and the regularity of interactions between family members and the person with mental illness. In one study, compared to parents, spouses reported twice as much perceived avoidance (Phelan et al., 1989). In addition, parents not living with the family member with mental illness reported less perceived avoidance than parents who did, and family members who did not live with the relative with mental illness experienced reduced shame as compared to those who did.

Changing Stigma

In this section, we review research on changing public and self-stigma experienced by families, first by examining stigma-change for the person labeled mentally ill, then extrapolating these strategies to family stigma. We look separately at changing public and self-stigma.

Changing public stigma

Research has identified three approaches to erasing public stigma experienced by individuals diagnosed with mental illness: contact, education, and protest (Corrigan, 2004; Corrigan and Penn, 1999). Contact involves interaction between a member of the general public and someone who is diagnosed with a mental illness. Education entails challenging myths about mental illness with facts. Protest is a moral appeal for people to stop stigma.

Protest

Protest strategies highlight the injustices of various forms of stigma and chastise offenders for their stereotypes and discrimination. "Shame on us all for perpetuating the ideas that people with mental illness are just 'big kids' unable to care for themselves." As discussed previously, if family stigma is a "courtesy" passed on because of association with a marked person with mental illness, then it seems reasonable to expect less harm to families caused by stigma when the prejudice and discrimination directed towards people with the actual disease diminishes (Corrigan and Miller, 2004).

Although there is anecdotal evidence to suggest that protest can positively influence harmful behaviors (Wahl, 1995), in a recent meta-analysis of 79 studies that examined the effects of anti-stigma approaches including social activism (or protest), education of the public, and contact with persons with mental illness, no evidence was found to support the use of protest as a strategy for on improving attitudes and behavioral intentions toward people with mental illness (Corrigan, Morris, Michaels, Rafacz, and Rüsch, 2012). The approach also has its concerns. Protest campaigns that ask people to suppress their prejudice can produce an unintended "rebound" in which prejudices about a group remain unchanged or actually become worse (MacRae, Bondenhausen, Milne, and Jetten, 1994; Wegner, Erber, and Zanakos, 1993).

Education

Education programs contrast myths about a group (e.g., All mothers cause their child's mental illness) with facts (e.g., Most serious mental illnesses – especially schizophrenia and the affective disorders – are

biological illnesses. Neither parents, nor the person with the illness, are to blame). Educational strategies have included public service announcements, books, flyers, movies, videos, webpages, podcasts, virtual reality, and other audio-visual aids (Finkelstein, Lapshin, and Wasserman, 2008; SAMHSA, 2002). Some benefits of educational interventions include their low cost and broad reach. Research on education related to mental illness stigma has suggested that participation in these kinds of programs has led to improved attitudes about persons with these problems (Corrigan, Morris et al., 2012; Corrigan, Green, Lundin, Kubiak, and Penn, 2001; Holmes, Corrigan, Williams, Canar, and Kubiak, 1999; Penn et al.,1994). In Corrigan and colleagues' recent meta-analysis (2012), education was found to significantly improve attitudes and behavioral intentions toward people with mental illness.

Research on education as a public stigma change strategy is not always positive, however. Research suggests that education can lead to short-term improvements in prejudice, but that these improvements return to baseline soon after the education program ends (Corrigan et al., 2002). In addition, participants in education programs with a focus on the biological basis of mental illness may be more likely to believe that people with mental illnesses are less responsive to treatment and are unable to overcome their disabilities (Phelan, 2005; Phelan, Yang, and Rojas, 2006). As applied to family stigma, there is some evidence that education leads to less endorsement of stigmatizing attitudes (Penn et al., 1994; Penn et al., 1999). Families themselves seem to believe that educating the public is necessary. When asked about suggestions for reducing stigma related to schizophrenia, relatives of individuals diagnosed with schizophrenia suggested the following improvements and strategies related to educating the public: use the media to disseminate information about schizophrenia; create and release public presentations of research and public relations activities of mental health service institutions; and improve the education and training of mental health professionals, as well as all those who interact in a professional capacity with people diagnosed with mental illnesses (Angermeyer et al., 2003). Related to the idea of educating mental health professionals, the National Alliance on Mental Illness (NAMI) designed a 10-week course for mental health professionals: The Provider Education Program. The program is presented by two consumers, two Family-to-Family Education trainers, and one mental health professional who is either a family member or a consumer.[2] This program utilizes five presenters to provide viewpoints from various key stake-holders. Through personal stories, the course focuses on the courage needed to overcome hardships faced by consumers and family members. The course also reviews various types of mental health services. Anecdotal report from program participants has been that the course positively changed their approach toward consumers and family members (Mohr, Lafuze, and Mohr, 2000).

Contact

Research suggests that the best way to improve attitudes about people with mental illness is contact (Clement *et al.*, 2012; Corrigan *et al.*, 2012, 2001, 2002); people from the general population who interact with an individual with mental illness are likely to be less prejudicial than individuals without this kind of contact. Clement and colleagues (2012) compared contact-based approaches to changing stigma in the public with that of education. They found that both contact conditions (film-based contact and in-vivo contact) yielded significantly better effects on attitudes about mental illness compared to education. Similarly, the results of Corrigan and colleagues' meta-analysis (2012) demonstrated that contact yielded significantly greater effects on attitudes and behavioral intentions as compared to education.

Contact and stigma-change programs are most effective when targeting key groups of people, typically those in positions of power, like landlords and employers. These are people whose acknowledged authority yields some control over individuals with mental illness, and who can prevent people from obtaining fundamental life goals (Corrigan, 2004, 2012). It has also been suggested that contact is most effective as a stigma-reduction strategy when the contact program is local, the contact person is similar to the target group, and contact is continuous. Face-to-face contact between a person diagnosed with mental illness and a member of the public has also been found to have a greater effect on improving public stigma as compared to a story mediated by videotape (Corrigan *et al.*, 2012). One-time contact between a person with

mental illness and a targeted group may have some positive effects (Pettigrew and Tropp, 2006), but they are likely to be fleeting. Contact needs to be repeated over and over.

Given that research has shown that people from the general population who interact with an individual with mental illness are likely to be less prejudicial than individuals without this kind of contact, in like fashion, we would expect public stigma about family members would diminish as members of the public are put in contact with parents, spouses, siblings, etc. In qualitative interviews of family members of individuals diagnosed with schizophrenia, relatives believed that "the best and most efficient way" to challenge inaccurate information related to schizophrenia is to facilitate personal contact between the public, individuals diagnosed with schizophrenia, and their relatives (Angermeyer *et al.*, 2003). Note that accomplishing this goal requires an active decision on the part of family members to come out. Neighbors and co-workers typically do not know that a person is a relative of an individual with mental illness unless that person self-discloses. Research on contact suggests this kind of disclosure will ultimately lead to less stigma for family members (Corrigan and Miller, 2004). However, there are also costs for parents or siblings to publicly discuss their relative's mental illness (Ralph, 2002). For example, co-workers and neighbors who hear this information might react negatively, with the family member suffering some specific discriminatory results (e.g., the car pool does not want a father riding with them after hearing the story about his son).

Changing self-stigma

Several approaches may raise the diminished self-esteem and self-efficacy that result from self-stigma. One strategy is promoting personal empowerment (Corrigan and Rao, 2012; Rogers, Chamberlin, Ellison, and Crean, 1997) by participating in activities that promote a person's sense of agency and goal directedness. Investigators have shown empowerment to be associated with high self-esteem, better quality of life, increased social support, and increased satisfaction with mutual-help programs (Corrigan, Faber, Rashid, and Leary, 1999; Rogers *et al.*, 1997;

Rogers, Ralph, and Salzer, 2010). It should be kept in mind, however, that this kind of effort often requires disclosure of one's mental illness (Corrigan and Rao, 2012).

Alternatively, some researchers have proposed cognitive restructuring as a way to control the cognitive aspect of self-stigma. These researchers have framed self-stigma as self-statements that lead to depression, anxiety, or anger (Kingdon, Turkington, and John, 1994). Self-esteem replaces self-stigma through the judicious use of self-talk. For example, a person who has the thought "I am unreliable" (self-stigma), could instead shift that thought to, "I may have done something impulsive, but I usually am able to stop and think before I act." Participating in consumer advocacy and mutual help groups may also reduce self-stigma using a combination of empowerment and cognitive restructuring strategies. The mutual support and sense of positive identity promoted by these groups may help counter the negative self-statements that form the basis of self-stigma (Larson and Corrigan, 2008). Lending general support to these strategies, community involvement and positive in-group stereotyping (i.e., presenting the in-group as more authentic, sensitive, or intelligent) have been found to correlate with higher levels of self-esteem in people diagnosed with mental illness (Illic et al., 2012).

Programs focused on self-stigma reduction for people with mental illnesses are also a possibility on the horizon. One promising program is the Ending Self-Stigma Intervention (Lucksted et al., 2011), which uses a group approach to reduce self-stigmatization. This intervention covers education about mental health, cognitive-behavioral strategies to impact internalization of public stigmas, methods to strengthen family and community ties, and techniques for responding to public discrimination. A pilot study of the intervention demonstrated that self-stigma was reduced and perceived social support increased after participation in the nine-week intervention (Lucksted et al., 2011). Another program focused on self-stigma reduction is the Coming Out Proud program (COPp) (Corrigan and Lundin, 2012). COPp is a three-session group program run usually by pairs of trained leaders with lived experiences. The program is designed to aid in the facilitation of disclosure of certain aspects of

lived experience with the objective of reducing the self-stigma associated with mental illness. Coming Out Proud is now being used in beta research in the United States, Europe, Australia, and China.

NAMI has also developed two programs that may partially mitigate the family stigma associated with mental illness: the Family to Family Education Program, and the In Our Own Voice-Family Companion Program. The Family to Family Education Program (FFEP) is a 12-week course taught by family members that focuses on background knowledge about mental illness and treatments, teaching problem solving and communication skills, and helping improve coping skills. Dixon and colleagues' (2001) evaluation of FFEP demonstrated increased empowerment, improved attitudes, and reduced worry about relatives with mental illness (Dixon et al., 2001). A subsequent study by Dixon and colleagues (2004) also found that FFEP increased empowerment and reduced subjective burden in relatives of persons diagnosed with serious mental illness, without changes in objective burden (i.e., financial burden or caregiving time). Furthermore, knowledge about serious mental illness and the mental health system, as well as understanding of relatives' self-care, also improved. These changes were maintained at six-month follow-up (Dixon et al., 2004). However, other research involving a sample of family members, over half of whom had completed FFEP and were currently involved in support groups, demonstrated that participants nevertheless continued to report a significant amount of unmet support and informational needs across several domains (Drapalski et al., 2008). Specific reports of family stigma were also associated with greater unmet needs.

In Our Own Voice-Family Companion (IOOV-FC; Perlick et al., 2011) is a single-session intervention designed to reduce self-stigma among family members of individuals with serious mental illness. This intervention is modeled after NAMI's IOOV program. IOOV-FC trains family members who have a relative diagnosed with mental illness to describe their experiences and those of their families members related to coping with mental illness. The goal of the intervention is to leverage positive interactions with family member peers to disconfirm the negative, internalized stereotypes that may be held by family members. Family "peers" model their own methods of challenging self-stigma for their participant peers. Preliminary findings have demonstrated that family member participants reported significant reductions in self-stigma and secrecy as compared to those assigned to a family education control group (Perlick *et al.*, 2011). Caregivers who reported a low to moderate level of pretreatment anxiety reported larger decreases in self-stigma.

Summary

Both individuals diagnosed with mental illness and their families experience various forms of stigma, including: self-stigma, public stigma, label avoidance, and vicarious stigma. Research based on studies of the general public found that family members are often viewed as responsible for a relative's mental illness. These negative public perceptions lead to behavioral consequences such as withdrawal of instrumental support, social avoidance, and decreased pity.

The research based on direct assessment of family members has demonstrated that family members are aware of and often experience both public and self-stigma related to mental illness. Negative consequences of family stigma can include: feelings of blame, shame, and other forms of psychological distress; avoidance; and disruption of relationships and social roles. Although research has not yet demonstrated that family stigma is an obstacle to treatment and service seeking and use, label avoidance and other forms of family stigma may still contribute to families' unmet service needs. Perceptions of public stigma and self-stigma appear to vary by family member role and proximity to the relative diagnosed with mental illness. In addition, relatives' perception of family stigma may vary by factors such as socio-demographic characteristics of the family member diagnosed with mental illness and characteristics of the family member's specific mental illness experience (e.g., diagnosis and symptom severity and duration).

Many interventions now exist to combat the stigma of mental illness. Research has identified three approaches to erase public stigma: contact, education, and protest. Protest may have rebound effects that increase public stigma. Recently, these interventions have begun to be applied to family stigma. To combat self-stigma, NAMI developed the Family to Family Education Program, and the In Our Own Voice-Family Companion Program, both of which demonstrated initial, promising decreases in family and self-stigma. NAMI also developed a program to educate providers in an effort to reduce public stigma associated with families. Moving forward, more research is needed to help relatives cope with family stigma related to mental illness.

Critical Thinking Questions

1. Please compare and contrast family member public and self-stigma. Then, write out examples of each type of stigma as applied to family members.
2. According to available research, what are the benefits and problems of "labeling" mental illness?
3. Please describe how contact affects public stigma directed at family members. What are conditions that have been found to make contact more effective as a successful stigma-change strategy?
4. What are some stigma-change models and interventions that have been applied to reducing family self-stigma?

Notes

1. Diagnostic terminology used in this chapter is taken from the fifth edition of the *Diagnostic and statistical manual* (APA, 2013).
2. The Family-to-Family Education Program was developed by NAMI for family caregivers of individuals with mental illness. The 12-week course is taught by trained family members.

References

American Psychiatric Association (APA) (2013). *Diagnostic and statistical manual of mental disorders* (5th edn). Washington, DC: American Psychiatric Association.

Angermeyer, M. C., Schulze, B., and Dietrich, S. (2003). Courtesy stigma: a focus group study of relatives of schizophrenia patients. *Social Psychiatry and Psychiatric Epidemiology, 38*, 593–602. doi: 10.1007/s00127-003-0680-x.

Arcia, E., and Fernández, M. C. (1998). Cuban mothers' schemas of ADHD: development, characteristics, and help seeking behavior. *Journal of Child and Family Studies, 7*, 333–352.

Avison, W. R., and Comeau, J. (2013). The impact of mental illness on the family. In C. S. Aneshensel, J. Phelan, and A. Bierman (eds), *Handbook of the sociology of mental illness* (pp. 543–561). Dordrecht: Springer.

Burk, J. P., and Sher, K. J. (1990). Labeling the child of an alcoholic: negative stereotyping by mental health professionals and peers. *Journal of Studies on Alcohol, 51*, 156–163.

Clement, S., van Nieuwenhuizen, A., Kassam, A., Flach, C., Lazarus, A., de Castros, M., and Thornicroft, G. (2012). Filmed v. live social contact interventions to reduce stigma: randomized controlled trial. *British Journal of Psychiatry, 201*, 57–64.

Corrigan, P. W. (2004). How stigma interferes with mental health care. *American Psychologist, 59*, 614–625. doi: 10.1037/0003-066X.59.7.614.

Corrigan, P. W. (2007). How clinical diagnosis might exacerbate the stigma of mental illness. *Social Work, 52*, 31–39.

Corrigan, P. W. (2012). Research and the elimination of the stigma of mental illness. *British Journal of Psychiatry, 201*, 7–8. doi: 10.1192/bjp.bp.111.103382.

Corrigan, P. W., Faber, D., Rashid, F., and Leary, M. (1999). The construct validity of empowerment among consumers of mental health services. *Schizophrenia Research, 27*, 77–84.

Corrigan, P. W., Green, A., Lundin, R., Kubiak, M. A., and Penn, D. (2001). Familiarity with and social distance from people who have serious mental illness. *Psychiatric Services, 52*, 953–958.

Corrigan, P. W., Larson, J. E., and Rüsch, N. (2009). Self-stigma and the "why try" effect: impact on life goals and evidence-based practices. *World Psychiatry, 8*, 75–81.

Corrigan, P. W., and Lundin, R. K. (2012). *Coming Out Proud to Eliminate the Stigma of Mental Illness: Manual for program facilitators and participants*. Retrieved May 30, 2014 from www.ncse1.org.

Corrigan, P. W., Markowitz, F. E., and Watson, A. C. (2004). Structural levels of mental illness stigma and discrimination. *Schizophrenia Bulletin, 30*, 481–491.

Corrigan, P. W., Markowitz, F. E., Watson, A., Rowan, D., and Kubiak, M. A. (2003). An attribution model of public discrimination towards persons with mental illness. *Journal of Health and Social Behavior, 44*, 162–179.

Corrigan, P. W., and Miller, F. E. (2004). Shame, blame, and contamination: a review of the impact of mental illness stigma on family members. *Journal of Mental Health, 13*, 537–548.

Corrigan, P. W., Morris, S. B., Michaels, P. J., Rafacz, J. D., and Rüsch, N. (2012). Challenging the public stigma of mental illness: a meta-analysis of outcome studies. *Psychiatric Services, 63*, 963–973.

Corrigan, P. W., and O'Shaughnessy, J. R. (2007). Changing mental illness stigma as it exists in the real world. *Australian Psychologist, 42*, 90–97.

Corrigan, P. W., and Penn, D., (1999). Lessons from social psychology on discrediting psychiatric stigma. *American Psychologist, 54*, 765–776.

Corrigan, P. W., and Rao, D. (2012). On the self-stigma of mental illness: stages, disclosure, and strategies for change. *Canadian Journal of Psychiatry, 57*, 464–469.

Corrigan, P. W., Rowan, D., Green, A., Lundin, R., River, P., Uphoff-Wasowski, K., White, K., and Kubiak, M. A. (2002). Challenging two mental illness stigmas: personal responsibility and dangerousness. *Schizophrenia Bulletin, 28*, 293–309.

Corrigan, P. W., and Sokol, K. (2013). Erasing the stigma: where science meets advocacy. *Basic and Applied Social Psychology, 35*, 131–140.

Corrigan, P. W., Watson, A. C., and Barr, L. (2006). The self-stigma of mental illness: implications for self-esteem and self-efficacy. *Journal of Social and Clinical Psychology, 25*, 875–884.

Corrigan, P. W., Watson, A. C., and Miller, F. E. (2006). Blame, shame, and contamination: the impact of mental illness and drug dependence stigma on family members. *Journal of Family Psychology, 20*, 239–246. doi: 10.1037/0893-3200.20.2.239.

Crocker, J., Major, B., and Steele, C. (1998). Social stigma. In D. T. Gilbert, S. T. Fiske, and G. Lindzey (eds), *The handbook of social psychology*, vol 2 (4th edn) (pp. 504–553). New York: McGraw-Hill.

Dixon, L., Lucksted, A., Stewart, B., Burland, J., Brown, C. H., Postrado, L., and Hoffman, M. (2004). Outcomes of the peer-taught 12-week family-to-family education program for severe mental illness. *Acta Psychiatrica Scandinavica, 109*, 207–215.

Dixon, L., Stewart, B., Burland, J., Delahanty, J., Lucksted, A., and Hoffman, M. (2001). Pilot study of the effectiveness of the family-to-family education program. *Psychiatric Services, 52*, 965–967.

Drapalski, A. L., Marshall, T., Seybolt, D., Medoff, D., Peer, J., Leith, J., and Dixon, L. B. (2008). Unmet needs of families of adults with mental illness and preferences regarding family services. *Psychiatric Services, 59*, 655–662.

Eagly, A. H., and Chaiken, S. (1993). *The psychology of attitudes*. Fort Worth, TX: Harcourt Brace Jovanovich College Publishers.

Fernández, M. C., and Arcia, E. (2004). Disruptive behaviors and maternal responsibility: a complex portrait of stigma, self-blame, and other reactions. *Hispanic Journal of Behavioral Sciences, 26*, 356–372. doi: 10.1177/0739986304267208.

Finkelstein, J., Lapshin, O., and Wasserman, E. (2008). Randomized study of different anti-stigma media. *Patient Education and Counseling, 71*, 204–214.

Goffman, E. (1963). *Stigma: Notes on the management of spoiled identity*. Englewood Cliffs, NJ: Prentice Hall.

Gonzalez, J. M., Perlick, D. A., Miklowitz, D. J., Kaczynski, R., Hernandez, M., Rosenheck, R. A., and the STEP-BD Family Experience Study Group (2007). Factors associated with stigma among caregivers of patients with bipolar disorder in the STEP-BD Study. *Psychiatric Services, 58*, 41–48.

Greenberg, J. S., Kim, H. W., and Greenley, J. R. (1997). Factors associated with subjective burden in siblings of adults with severe mental illness. *American Journal of Orthopsychiatry, 6*, 231–241.

Greenley, J. R., Mechanic, D., and Cleary, P. (1987). Seeking help for psychological problems: a replication and extension. *Medical Care, 25*, 1113–1128.

Hasson-Ohayon, I., Levy, I., Kravetz, S., Vollanski-Narkis, A., and Roe, D. (2011). Insight into mental illness, self-stigma, and the family burden of parents of persons with a severe mental illness. *Comprehensive Psychiatry, 52*, 75–80. doi: 10.1016/j.comppsych.2010.04.008.

Holmes, E. P., Corrigan, P. W., Williams, P., Canar, J., and Kubiak, M. A. (1999). Changing attitudes about schizophrenia. *Schizophrenia Bulletin, 25*, 447–456.

Illic, M., Reinecke, J., Bohner, G., Hans-Onno, R., Beblo, T., Driessen, M., Frommberger, U., and Corrigan, P. W. (2012). Protecting self-esteem from stigma: a test of different strategies for coping with the stigma of mental illness. *International Journal of Social Psychiatry, 58*, 246–257.

Kawachi, I., and Berkman, L. F. (2001). Social ties and mental health. *Journal of Urban Health, 78*, 458–467.

Kessler, R. C., Berglund, P. A., Bruce, M. L., Koch, J. R., Laska, E. M., Leaf, P. J., and Wang, P. S. (2001). The prevalence and correlates of untreated serious mental illness. *Health Services Research, 36*, 987–1007.

Kessler, R. C., Price, R. H., and Wortman, C. B. (1985). Social factors in psychopathology: stress, social support, and coping processes. *Annual Review of Psychology, 36*, 531–572.

Kingdon, D., Turkington, D., and John, C. (1994). Cognitive behaviour therapy of schizophrenia: the amenability of delusions and hallucinations to reasoning. *British Journal of Psychiatry, 164*, 581–587.

Klasen, H. (2000). A name, what's in a name? The medicalization of hyperactivity, revisited. *Harvard Review of Psychiatry, 7*, 334–344.

Larson, J. E., and Corrigan, P. (2008). The stigma of families with mental illness. *Academic Psychiatry, 32*, 87–91.

Leaf, P. J., Bruce, M. L., and Tischler, G. L. (1986). The differential effect of attitudes on the use of mental health services. *Social Psychiatry, 21*, 187–192.

Lefley, H. P. (1989). Family burden and family stigma in major mental illness. *American Psychologist, 44*, 556–560.

Lefley, H. P. (1992). The stigmatized family. In P. Fink and A. Tasman (eds), *Stigma and mental illness* (pp. 127–138). Washington, DC: American Psychiatric Association.

Link, B. G., Struening, E. L., Neese-Todd, S., Asmussen, S., and Phelan, J. C. (2001). The consequences of stigma for the self-esteem of people with mental illnesses. *Psychiatric Services, 52*, 1621–1626.

Lucksted, A., Drapalski, A., Calmes, C., Forbes, C., DeForge, B., and Boyd, J. (2011). Ending self-stigma: pilot evaluation of a new intervention to reduce internalized stigma among people with mental illnesses. *Psychiatric Rehabilitation Journal, 35*, 51–54. doi: 10.2975/35.1.2011.51.54.

MacRae, C., Bondenhausen, G. V., Milne, A. B., and Jetten, J. (1994). Out of mind but back in sight: stereotypes on the rebound. *Journal of Personality and Social Psychology, 67*, 808–817.

Mehta, S. I., and Farina, A. (1988). Associative stigma: perceptions of the difficulties of college-aged children of stigmatized fathers. *Journal of Social and Clinical Psychology, 7*, 192–202.

Mohr, W. K., Lafuze, J. E., and Mohr, B. D. (2000). Opening caregiver minds: National Alliance for the Mentally Ill's (NAMI) Provider Education Program. *Archives of Psychiatric Nursing, 14*, 235–243.

Mueser, K. T., and Gingrich, S. (2006). *The complete family guide to schizophrenia*. New York: Guilford Press.

Norvilitis, J. M., Scime, M., and Lee, J. S. (2002). Courtesy stigma in mothers of children with Attention-Deficit/Hyperactivity Disorder: a preliminary investigation. *Journal of Attention Disorders, 6*, 61–68. doi: 10.1177/108705470200600202.

Peluso, E. T., and Blay, S. L. (2009). Public stigma in relation to individuals with depression. *Journal of Affective Disorders, 115*, 201–206.

Penn, D. L., Guynan, K., Daily, T., Spaulding, W. D., Garbin, C., and Sullivan, M. (1994). Dispelling the stigma of schizophrenia: what sort of information is best? *Schizophrenia Bulletin, 20*, 567–578.

Penn, D. L., Kommana, S., Mansfield, M., and Link, B. G. (1999). Dispelling the stigma of schizophrenia: II. The impact of information on dangerousness. *Schizophrenia Bulletin, 25*, 437–446.

Perlick, D. A., Miklowitz, D. J., Link, B. G., Struening, E., Kaczynski, R., Gonzalez, J., and Rosenheck, R. A. (2007). Perceived stigma and depression among caregivers of patients with bipolar disorder. *British Journal of Psychiatry, 190*, 535–536. doi: 10.1192/bjp.bp.105.020826.

Perlick, D. A., Nelson, A. H., Mattias, K., Selzer, J., Kalvin, C., Wilber, C. H., and Corrigan, P. W. (2011). In Our Own Voice – Family Companion: reducing self-stigma of family members of persons with serious mental illness. *Psychiatric Services, 62*, 1456–1462.

Pescosolido, B. A., Monahan, J., Link, B. G., Stueve, A., and Kikuzawa, S. (1999). The public's view of the competence, dangerousness, and need for legal coercion of persons with mental health problems. *American Journal of Public Health, 89*, 1339–1345.

Pettigrew, T. F., and Tropp, L. R. (2006). A meta-analytic test of intergroup contact theory. *Journal of Personality and Social Psychology, 90*, 751–783. doi: 10.1037/0022-3514.90.5.751.

Phelan, J. C. (2005). Geneticization of deviant behavior and consequences for stigma: the case of mental illness. *Journal of Health and Social Behavior, 46*, 307–322.

Phelan, J. C., Bromet, E. J., and Link, B. G. (1998). Psychiatric illness and family stigma. *Schizophrenia Bulletin, 24*, 115–126.

Phelan, J. C., Yang, L. H., and Rojas, R. C. (2006). Effects of attributing serious mental illnesses to genetic causes on orientations to treatment. *Psychiatric Services, 57*, 382–387. doi: 10.1176/appi.ps.57.3.382.

Phillips, M. R., Pearson, V., Li, F., Xu, M., and Yang, L. (2002). Stigma and expressed emotion: a study of people with schizophrenia and their family members in China. *British Journal of Psychiatry, 181*, 488–493. doi: 10.1192/bjp.181.6.488.

Ralph, R. O. (2002). The dynamics of disclosure: its impact on recovery and rehabilitation. *Psychiatric Rehabilitation Journal, 26*, 165–172.

Rogers, E. S., Chamberlin, J., Ellison, M. L., and Crean, T. (1997). A consumer-constructed scale to measure empowerment among users of mental health services. *Psychiatric Services, 48*, 1042–1047.

Rogers, E. S., Ralph, R. O., and Salzer, M. S. (2010). Validating the empowerment scale with a multisite sample of consumers of mental health services. *Psychiatric Services, 61*, 933–936.

Sansone, R. A., Matheson, M. V. G., Gaither, G. A., and Logan, N. (2008). Concerns about career stigma by military parents of children with psychiatric illness. *Military Medicine, 173*, 134–137.

Saunders, J. (2003). Families living with severe mental illness: a literature review. *Issues in Mental Health Nursing, 24*, 175–198.

Schomerus, G., Schwahn, C., Holzinger, A., Corrigan, P. W., Grabe, H. J., Carta, M. G., and Angermeyer, M. C. (2012). Evolution of public attitudes about mental illness: a systematic review and meta-analysis. *Acta Psychiatrica Scandinavica, 125*, 1–13. doi: 10.1111/j.1600-0447.2012.01826x.

Shibre, T., Negash, A., Kullgren, G., Kebede, D., Alem, A., Fekadu, A., and Jacobsson, L. (2001). Perception of stigma among family members of individuals with schizophrenia and major affective disorders in rural Ethiopia. *Social Psychiatry and Psychiatric Epidemiology, 36*, 299–303.

Sirey, J. A., Bruce, M. L., Alexopoulos, G. S., Perlick, D. A., Friedman, S. J., and Meyers, B. S. (2001). Stigma as a barrier to recovery: perceived stigma and patient-rated severity of illness as predictors of antidepressant drug adherence. *Psychiatric Services, 52*, 1615–1620.

Sirey, J. A., Bruce, M. L., Alexopoulos, G. S., Perlick, D. A., Raue, P., Friedman, S. J., and Meyers, B. S. (2001). Perceived sigma as a predictor of treatment discontinuation in young and older outpatients with depression. *American Journal of Psychiatry, 158*, 479–481.

Struening, E. L., Perlick, D. A., Link, B. G., Hellman, F., Herman, D., and Sirey, J. A. (2001). Stigma as a barrier to recovery: the extent to which caregivers believe most people devalue consumers and their families. *Psychiatric Services, 52*, 1633–1638. doi: 10.1176/appi.ps.52.12.1633.

Substance Abuse and Mental Health Services Administration (SAMHSA) (2002). *Results from the 2001 National Household Survey on Drug Abuse*, vol. 1, *Summary of national findings* (Office of Applied Studies, NHSDA Series H-17, DHHS Publication no. SMA02-3758). Rockville, MD: Department of Health and Human Services.

Thara, R., and Srinivasan, T. N. (2000). How stigmatising is schizophrenia in India? *International Journal of Social Psychiatry, 46*, 135–141.

Thornicroft, G., Rose, D., Kassam, A., and Sartorius, N. (2007). Stigma: ignorance, prejudice or discrimination? *British Journal of Psychiatry, 190*, 192–193. doi: 10.1192/bjp.bp.106.025791.

Tsang, H. W., Angell, B., Corrigan, P. W., Lee, Y. T., Shi, K., Lam, C. S., Jin, S., and Fung, K. M. T. (2007). A cross-cultural study of employers' concerns about hiring people with psychotic disorder: implications for recovery. *Social Psychiatry and Psychiatric Epidemiology, 42*, 723–733. doi: 10.1007/s00127-007-0208-x.

Tsang, H. W., Tam, P. K., Chan, F., and Chang, W. M. (2003). Sources of burdens on families of individuals with mental illness. *International Journal of Rehabilitation Research, 26*, 123–130.

Wahl, O. F. (1995). *Media madness: Public images of mental illness*. New Brunswick, NJ: Rutgers University Press.

Wahl, O. F., and Harman, C. R. (1989). Family views of stigma. *Schizophrenia Bulletin, 15*, 131–139.

Wegner, D. M., Erber, R., and Zanakos, S. (1993). Ironic processes in the mental control of mood and mood-related thought. *Journal of Personality and Social Psychology, 65*, 1093–1104.

Wong, C., Davidson, L., Anglin, D., Link, B., Gerson, R., Malaspina, D., McGlashan, T., and Corcoran, C. (2009). Stigma in families of individuals in early stages of psychotic illness: family stigma and early psychosis. *Early Intervention in Psychiatry, 3*, 108–115. doi: 10.1111/j.1751-7893.2009.00116.x.

4

Inside and Out
Family Life for Parents in Prison

Ann Booker Loper, Mathilde Whalen, and Joanna Will

> The incarcerated often come from the margins of society in that they dispropor-tionately have histories of cumulative disadvantage and difficult family back-grounds. Upon release, as a result of their imprisonment, incarcerated parents are subject to social stigma and many exclusionary practices bringing further troubles to their families. In Chapter 4, Ann Loper and colleagues explain that although families impacted by incarceration face many obstacles upon release, supportive family relationships can help justice-involved parents overcome key challenges and successfully reintegrate.

Family Life Prior to Incarceration

Case Example: Gloria

My name is Gloria and today is my fourteenth birthday. Doesn't feel all that great. My mama tried to make it a good day, gave me some money to spend. But when I got home from school, she and her new man, Donni, were at it with each other. I saw him hit her hard, and then he said I would get the same unless I shut up. Like that would be any different. I wonder whether it would be better if my dad were here. He's locked up, but I don't know why. I remember the day the police came and took him away. That was around my birthday, too. Long time ago and I was pretty little. He fought them off and my mama screamed. She doesn't want to talk about it. I think I will go see Jake. He loves me and we will get married one day. He and his friends do a little dope and sell some stuff. I help out some times. Mama says he's trouble, but she doesn't know that we've already had sex, and he is my man. It's no big deal helping him with his street business. And Mama doesn't really care anyway. When Donni gets rough, he storms out and she gets high. I can take care of myself on my own.

Family Problems: Stress, Risk, and Resilience, First Edition. Edited by Joyce A. Arditti.

Mothers and fathers in prison were once themselves children, like Gloria, and lived in a family. As we try to understand the family's role in the life of a prisoner, it makes sense to ask: "What was going on prior to prison?" One approach to understanding the life experiences and family contexts of those who come to be involved in the justice system is to examine differential risk factors for offending. In doing so, trends emerge that point to demographic characteristics, familial factors, and adverse youth experiences that are common to those who commit criminal acts.

Demographic characteristics

As of 2011, there are approximately 1.6 million adults incarcerated in state or federal prison (Glaze and Parks, 2012). The disproportionate demographic makeup of the United States prison system reflects four primary risk factors for incarceration – age, race, gender, and economic status. Young adults and teenagers are the most frequent offenders; over half of the state and federal arrests during 2011 were of individuals under the age of 30, and approximately one quarter of all arrests were of individuals under 21 years (FBI, 2012). In addition, the overwhelming majority of incarcerated adults in the United States are male, outnumbering incarcerated women by a ratio of about 14:1 (Guerino, Harrison, and Sabol, 2011).

Ethnicity is another strong risk-factor for incarceration. African Americans, and in particular African American males, are significantly overrepresented in prisons. Approximately 69% of incarcerated men and 54% of incarcerated women self-identify as African American, Hispanic, or another ethnic minority. When taken in comparison to the ethnic breakdown of the US population, African American men are over six times more likely to be incarcerated than Caucasian men, and African American women are almost three times more likely to be incarcerated than Caucasian women (Guerino et al., 2011). The disproportionate incarceration of poor males of ethnic minority status reflects a long history of marginalization and social disadvantage of these groups in the United States. During the Reagan and Bush administrations in the late 1980s and early 1990s, drug use became targeted as a major social issue, resulting in the increased criminalization of illegal drug activity (Humphreys and Rappaport, 1993).

This "War on Drugs" disproportionately affected low-income African Americans, particularly as a result of harsher sentencing for drugs more commonly used by these groups (e.g., crack cocaine) and increased police presence in 'high-crime', predominantly Black urban neighborhoods (Lynch, 2012; Pettit and Western, 2004). As these groups remain overrepresented in the US prison system, legal officials and the general public may hold skewed perceptions of young African American males. In turn, this may increase racial profiling by law enforcement and the ultimate risk that these individuals will become incarcerated (Pettit and Western, 2004). Examinations of legal outcomes provide strong evidence of sentencing disparities for males (Mustard, 2001) and African Americans (Blumstein, 1993).

Low economic status is also associated with criminal involvement (Mustard, 2001). Pettit and Western (2004) describe how the economic and industrialization shifts of the late 1900s and the corresponding lack of inner-city employment opportunities affected less-educated, lower-class males and contributed to increased criminal activity. There are also indirect ways that low socioeconomic status can contribute to criminal activity; for example, living in a poor neighborhood may result in exposure to criminal associates who involve other individuals in illegal activities (Agnew, Matthews, Bucher, Welcher, and Keyes, 2008; Bjerk, 2007). While the connection between low socioeconomic status and offending is complex, it is a strong predictor of who will end up in prison. In an analysis of arrest data from California, E. Brown and Males (2011) found that poverty was a more robust predictor of arrest than age or race.

Family characteristics and stressors

The childhood of an offender prior to incarceration is strongly influenced by the family structure and the dynamics of family relationships. In particular, parenting behaviors have a robust influence on various aspects of childhood development. For example, adolescents have more problematic conduct disorder and criminal problems if they have experienced inconsistent and harsh discipline from their parents. It is no surprise that when parents are not invested in their children's lives or fail to responsibly monitor child behavior, their children are more likely to become involved in criminal activities as they grow up (for review see Farrington, 2005; Racz and McMahon, 2011). Consistent with this picture of a stressed early family life, incarcerated and antisocial individuals are more likely to have young and single parents than do those who are not involved in the justice system (Henry, Caspi, Moffitt, and Silva, 1996; Nagin, Pogarsky, and Farrington, 1997). In most such cases, the single parent is the child's mother. While some single parents have strong external social and financial support, others are not as lucky; for example, it is more difficult for a single mother to supervise her children when she also has a full-time job if she has no additional help for child-rearing or other parenting responsibilities (Holmes, Slaughter, and Kashani, 2001).

The family instability that is often present in the histories of offenders can also take a more violent and traumatic form. Many offenders grew up with parents who abused alcohol and drugs, a context that is associated with conduct-disorder problems during adolescence (Ritter, Stewart, Bernet, Coe, and Brown, 2002). Like Gloria, individuals who are incarcerated disproportionately report that they witnessed family violence and conflict during childhood. Several studies converge on the conclusion that children who watch their parents engage in domestic violence are at higher risk for numerous life problems, including antisocial and criminal behavior, than children in the general population (Buehler *et al.*, 1997; Murrell, Christoff, and Henning, 2007). In particular, the trauma of witnessing violence that was initiated by one's father, often directed at the child's mother, can compound with other risks, leading to future criminal behavior (Fergusson and Horwood, 1998). Families experiencing domestic violence also have higher rates of parental substance abuse and mental health issues, unemployment, and residential instability (Holt, Buckley, and Whelan, 2008). Within these households, "the quality of parenting and ability of both parents to meet their child's needs are compromised" (Holt *et al.*, 2008, p. 800). As a result, children in these households are at greater risk for aggressive and delinquent behaviors (Wildeman, 2010) and internalizing and externalizing behaviors (Buehler *et al.*, 1997; Evans, Davies, and DeLillo, 2008).

In addition to witnessing violence between their parents, a large proportion of offenders have been directly victimized in the past, usually during early childhood (A. Brown, Miller, and Maguin, 1999; Weeks and Widom, 1998). This victimization can take the form of physical, sexual, or psychological abuse. Unfortunately, the traumatic experiences of household violence can be long-lasting. Children who have been abused are more likely to commit crimes and display antisocial tendencies (for review see Farrington *et al.*, 2012; see also Loper, Mahmoodzadegan, and Warren, 2008; Widom, 1989). In addition, children who are abused are at increased risk of being abused or otherwise victimized when they become adults (A. Brown *et al.*, 1999). To further complicate the picture, youth who have been so abused more frequently use drugs and alcohol, perhaps in an effort to block out their distress (Polusny and Follette, 1995). Underage alcohol use and mind-altering drug use can be a teen's 'medicine' for blocking out the pain of abuse. However, it then puts the youth squarely within the realm of criminal activity.

While childhood abuse increases the likelihood that a child will eventually become incarcerated, there is also evidence that protective factors can slow down this trend by buffering the effect of present risk factors (see Box 4.1). For example, children who are maltreated but who live in low-crime neighborhoods are less likely to become antisocial as adults. Possibly, by living in a low-crime neighborhood, the likelihood of contact with criminal peers is diminished, thereby slowing down the trajectory toward criminal behaviors. In addition, having higher cognitive skills may help protect abused (and other high-risk) children from later becoming incarcerated (for review see Farrington *et al.*, 2012). As previously mentioned, those who engage in criminal behavior often come from unstable homes in which parents provided little support and monitoring of their children's behavior. However, the converse is also true; positive, responsible parental monitoring can offer a protective effect for children who experienced victimization. In other words, when children are abused, they are less likely to engage in criminal activities in adulthood if they have had a positive relationship with their parents or other significant adults who have provided stable and responsible monitoring of their activities (Nash, Mujanovic, and Winfree, 2011). Regardless of whether the child has been exposed to violence, research consistently supports the same protective influence of the

Box 4.1 Women in the Criminal Justice System and Sexual Abuse

The percentage of incarcerated women who have been sexually abused prior to prison has been estimated to be between 59% and 78% (Briere and Elliot, 2003; A. Brown *et al.*, 1999; Finkelhor, 1994). However, the adverse effects of the abuse may be mitigated if there is intervention and support for the victim. When a woman first discloses an abuse incident, the initial reaction of friends, family, and authorities can have a major impact on her adjustment and coping. In a study comparing incarcerated and college women who had experienced sexual abuse in childhood, Asberg and Renk (2012) found that incarcerated women were more likely than non-incarcerated college women to have experienced negative reactions from the people they told about the abuse. In addition, the incarcerated women had more maladaptive coping strategies than the college women. In contrast, females in college reported experiencing more positive reactions to their disclosure of abuse. Even though an abused woman might be more likely to start down a path of criminal behavior than a woman who was not abused, results of this study suggest that receiving positive emotional and informational support when sharing the abuse incident to others may serve as a protective factor, in essence decreasing the likelihood that the woman will continue down the criminal path.

parent–child relationship in preventing criminality (W. Johnson, Giordano, Manning, and Longmore, 2011).

In sum, multiple aspects of a child's family life can increase the likelihood of the individual's eventual incarceration. Incarcerated individuals often have experienced adversities in their early lives related to their families. When children like Gloria are exposed to violence or are victims of violence themselves, or when they experience other types of home instability or parental incarceration, they become at heightened risk for engaging in deviant, criminal behavior that ultimately lends to the likelihood of incarceration. It is important to recognize that experiencing one or more of these risk factors in childhood does not definitively cause an individual to engage in criminal behaviors. Rather, these events can cause traumatic pain and difficulty to children who may then seek maladaptive means of coping. When taken as a whole picture, a constellation of overlapping risk factors emerges with an aggregating effect.

Social and contextual risk and resilience factors

In addition to the adverse family and individual experiences, social and environmental factors during childhood can contribute to criminal behavior. One such factor is the present lack of community mental health care. It is estimated that over half of incarcerated individuals suffer from mental illness (James and Glaze, 2006), and prisons currently house three to five times as many individuals with mental illness as mental hospitals (Côté, Lesage, Chawky, and Loyer, 1997). This overrepresentation of mentally ill individuals within prison is due, in part, to the deinstitutionalization of mental health treatment and increased criminalization of illegal drug activity. Starting in the 1960s, US mental hospitals engaged in a "community mental health" movement in which individuals who were formerly treated in mental hospitals were released with an assumption of community support for psychiatric service. The notion made sense at the time, as the redirection of funds from long-term hospitalization to treatment that was close to home and social support had both economic and health benefits. However, over time, as community resources dried up, so too did resources for mental health treatment (Dixon and Goldman, 2003). With fewer resources available, many individuals with mental illness have been unable to receive adequate psychiatric care. Mental illness, with associated problems of emotional regulation, can lead to clouded thinking and aggressive behaviors that, if untreated, can result in violent activities (Walters,

2011; Yang and Mulvey, 2012). In addition, the untreated mentally ill individual may seek the self-medication provided by the use of alcohol and illegal substances, ultimately increasing the risk of being arrested for drug-offending (Bradley-Engen, Cuddeback, Gayman, Morrissey, and Mancuso, 2010). After the community mental health movement, the "War on Drugs" continued to contribute to the large number of individuals incarcerated with mental illness. Due to the increase in support and funding for law enforcement officers to target drug use during the 1980s and 1990s, prison sizes substantially increased to accommodate these new arrests (Humphreys and Rappaport, 1993). The high prevalence of psychiatric illness in jails and prisons today is a residual effect of this drug movement.

Another extra-familial factor that is associated with offending concerns the characteristics of the youth's social network. Adolescents are influenced by the activities and characteristics of their peers, and those who interact with delinquent peers are at heightened risk of engaging in criminal acts themselves. In a study of 132 adolescents in California, Hart, O'Toole, Price-Sharps, and Shaffer (2007) examined how adolescents experienced different events or circumstances considered to be risk factors (e.g., drug use) or protective factors (e.g., having a caring community member in the child's life). They found that if adolescents used substances or engaged in substance use at an earlier age, or if they had more delinquent friends, they were more likely to become juvenile delinquents. On the other hand, youth were less likely to start engaging in deviant or criminal behavior if they had prosocial friends and participated in extracurricular activities. Interestingly, the researchers discovered that the violent delinquent adolescents and the non-delinquent adolescents experienced similar numbers of risk factors. However, the non-delinquent adolescents had many more protective, or positive, factors in their lives, while the violent delinquent teens had noticeably few protective factors. For example, if the teen had an unfavorable attitude toward violence or had a caring adult community member actively involved in his/her life, the teen was less likely to engage in violent delinquency. These results indicate that the risk factors children experience might not be as influential as

previously hypothesized; instead, it might be the positive and protective factors in a child's life that ultimately influence the likelihood that the child will grow up to carry out criminal behavior (Hart et al., 2007).

In addition, there is a link between children's and adolescents' experiences in school and their chances of future incarceration. Adolescents who drop out of high school prior to graduation are at increased risk for several negative outcomes, including incarceration (Heckman and LaFontaine, 2010). An adolescent's positive experiences in school can buffer the eventual likelihood of criminal behavior. In particular, those who may already be at increased risk of criminality – based on a history of many of the experiences previously described – are less likely to ultimately engage in criminal behaviors if they form a positive school bond, or feeling of cohesion to their school environment (Sprott, Jenkins, and Doob, 2005). Plausibly, positive engagement in school provides an alternative environment that affords a roadmap toward achievement, competence, and a prosocial self-image that contrasts with the negative messages that accompany adversity.

It is clear that incarcerated adults often come from difficult family backgrounds. These individuals are much more likely than the general population to experience numerous childhood adversities, particularly related to their families, such as abuse, low socioeconomic status, and mental illness. While not all offenders come from unstable families, the high proportion that are affected highlights the pivotal role of the family for many offenders. Adverse childhood experiences can play a compelling role in the lives of incarcerated offenders, particularly in terms of the child's access to the resources and support that could either compel the child into antisocial behavior or, conversely, assist him or her in making prosocial decisions. Likewise, there are many experiences and characteristics that can protect children at risk of incarceration. A family environment that provides responsible and supportive parental monitoring can build resilience despite the myriad risks associated with poverty and unsafe neighborhoods by encouraging positive peer supports, school connectedness, academic achievement, and adaptive coping strategies.

Impact on the Family: The Incarceration Years

Life for the imprisoned parent

Like Gloria, each year thousands of parents enter the US prison system. As previously described, prior to prison these mothers and fathers as a group have experienced numerous family problems, may suffer mental illness, have drug and alcohol addiction, and are often ill-equipped to handle stress. When they enter an environment that is specifically designed to restrict personal freedom and bring limits to previous sources of contact, the prisoner is challenged to come to grips with his or her past and make meaning of a present and future life. This can be a difficult hurdle.

For many mothers and fathers in prison, separation from children and the loss of identity as a primary parent is devastating (Celinska and Siegel, 2010). The majority of mothers in US prisons served as a primary caregiver prior to incarceration, typically as a single parent (Glaze and Maruschak, 2008). For many such women, their identities as mothers were central to their sense of themselves. As prisoners, they must shift notions about their mothering role and surrender control to caregivers. For women in prison, caregivers are typically their own mothers. However, in many cases this relationship itself is problematic (Loper and Novero, 2013). As discussed previously, most inmates come from troubled families. Yet it is these same families that are called upon to take up the responsibility for children left at home.

For a father in prison, the caregiver is typically the child's mother (Glaze and Maruschak, 2008). Much of a father's ability to stay connected to his children depends upon his pre-existing relationship with the child's mother. As many men in prison have pre-existing substance abuse, anger control, and other serious problems, it is not surprising that relationships

---

Case Example: Gloria

My name is Gloria and today is my twenty-fifth birthday. Not much to celebrate here in the state women's correctional and detention center. I call it prison. I have been here five years now. I was arrested when I was 16 for selling. Jake had me working for him. They charged me as an adult, but the judge was cool. Got me working with a probation lady. She was nice, but that didn't work out. Jake needed some more money and we figured a way of getting credit cards and charging stuff. I got caught and my probation was pulled and I went back for time at jail. Jake was waiting for me when I got out. At first, I didn't want to see him. I told him that, but he got mad and came after me. He beat me up. We made up, though, and I stayed with him. I wish I hadn't. I got into doing meth 'cause it just made things better. But when I was high, I was pretty mean. I caught Jake with that slut Destiny and I knew he was just playing me. Destiny and I got into a fight and I cut her pretty bad. That's what brought me here. I got 10 years. The only good thing that came

from me and Jake is my little Nevaeh. She's my little girl and I would die for her. She's eight years old now. Missing her is the worst part of being here. She lives with my mama and Mama's new man, Samuel. Jake's inside now, too. Samuel says that Nevaeh is just like me and needs more discipline. He uses the paddle and sometimes his belt to make her mind him. I worry that he is hurting her like Donni did to me. But I just don't know how to be a good mom from in here. I don't see her much. They only let her visit on weekends, and that is when Mama works. Mama has a hard time and she doesn't have much money. If they try to come see me, it costs too much because it's a day's drive to get here and gas is so high. And then I only get to see them for about an hour and the room is so noisy and they won't let me hold Nevaeh. She doesn't much like coming. Mama tries to call, but that costs too much, too. I write Nevaeh letters, though, and she writes me back. She keeps me from getting down. It's hard here.

with their partners are often tumultuous and unstable. Roy and Dyson (2005) described the "baby mama drama" experienced by many imprisoned fathers as they negotiate with ex-partners to stay in communication with children.

The ensuing parenting stress, experienced by both mothers and fathers, can itself be associated with feelings of depression and anger, and in some cases, acts of misconduct or rule-breaking (Houck and Loper, 2002; Loper, Carlson, Levitt, and Scheffel, 2009). Children's birthdays, graduations, holidays, and other important events can be particularly sad for imprisoned parents. To deal with such stress, mothers and fathers often look forward to seeing children and family members on visitation days. Visitation can be a positive experience for prisoners and may be key to positive outcomes after release (Bales and Mears, 2008). When visitation settings are child-friendly and geared toward positive contact, a visit can be healing and joyful (Poehlmann, Dallaire, Loper, and Shear, 2010). However, this positive picture of prison visits is often not the case. Most inmates in US prisons receive few visits with children (Glaze and Maruschak, 2008). Arranging visits can be difficult for family members who live great distances from the prison. Visitation settings can be noisy and uninviting. Additionally, security procedures, such as pat-downs, sniffing dogs, and imposing series of gates and locked entryways may be distressing for children. Long waits for short visits are common experiences for many prisoner families (Allard and Lu, 2006). Moreover, these visits are not necessarily helpful to children, particularly when the visitation set-up is uninviting. Shlafer and Poehlmann (2010) interviewed caregivers and children whose parents were incarcerated. Children reported largely negative visitation experiences that lacked meaningful contact and took place in child-unfriendly setting. Caregivers reported conflicted feelings of needing to 'gate-keep' or protect the child from the confusion and frustration of a visit while still promoting child contact with the parent.

As an alternate means of contact, many parents choose to phone home. Phoning can be less intrusive in the family members' lives. Phoning does not require long waits and awkward security features. However, in many prisons, phone calls are prohibitively expensive and time-limited, and the burden for the cost rests upon family members. For example, using interviews with family members of 247 Chicago prisoners, Naser and Visher (2006) found that families typically spent $50 each month for phone calls with the imprisoned family members. The financially strapped caregiver who tries to limit such expensive calls may provoke frustration and anger from the imprisoned parent. The ensuing resentment can, in turn, erode the alliance between the child, caregiver, and imprisoned parent.

Given this picture, one might imagine that Gloria and others like her would have no choice but to become depressed and dysfunctional as a result of separation from loved ones. However, this is not the case for resilient individuals who are able to take advantage of institutional programs that promote better child–parent contact. Many correctional agencies offer parenting training or support groups that can help parents learn to cope with the distress of being separated from children (Hoffmann, Byrd, and Kightlinger, 2010). When done carefully, parenting interventions offered to prisoners can make a difference. Loper and Novero (2010) reviewed 25 programs designed for incarcerated parents and identified multiple programs that were successful in reducing the parenting distress of the inmate parents, improving contact with children, and eliciting more positive parenting attitudes.

Life for families at home

The finding that prisoners are stressed by the separation from children is not surprising. Indeed, some might argue that this is part of the expected punishment for the crime and parents should have thought of their children before committing their crime. Regardless of the merits of this argument, there is an additional issue of the impact of incarceration on the children and families left at home who may share the parents' punishment through financial and emotional set-backs.

In some cases, parental incarceration can have positive family benefits, particularly when children and families enjoy more stability with the removal of the offender parent. For example, Eddy and Reid (2003) point out that the removal of a parent who involves the child with other dangerous individuals could be beneficial and afford more safety for the child.

Likewise, it is reasonable to assume that it would benefit a child if parental incarceration meant the removal of an abusive parent who exhibits violent behaviors toward the child or the child's other parent. Cho (2010) examined the impact of the frequency of incarceration and the length of incarceration on school outcomes for boys and girls. She found that girls had fewer school problems when their mothers were gone for the longer periods. Presumably the stability and routine offered by the longer separation helped the girls to stay focused on school goals. Boys whose mothers were incarcerated six or more times had fewer dropouts than those whose mothers had fewer prison admissions. Cho speculated that other family members and caregivers may be more likely to step up and assume stable guidance for vulnerable boys who experience such extreme frequencies of maternal incarceration. These results underscore the importance of avoiding a broad brush in making negative assumptions about incarceration-affected populations. To the degree that parental incarceration provides children with transition from a chaotic or dangerous home situation into one that is more stable and protective, the children are more likely to flourish.

However, more typically, parental imprisonment brings increased troubles to the family and to children. The economic challenges can be significant (Schwartz-Soicher, Geller, and Garfinkel, 2011). Schwartz-Soicher and colleagues used longitudinal data from a national survey of families in major urban areas and examined trajectories of financial hardship for families five years after a paternal incarceration. Families who experienced a paternal incarceration suffered significant loss of financial stability. The decline in the family's material stability was particularly evident if the father had previously lived in the home; when cohabiting fathers are sent to prison there is one less wage earner to carry financial burdens. The financial burdens can be complex and interwoven with collateral effects of the incarceration. For example, the increased financial strain can result in caregivers' greater substance abuse and mental distress, which further exacerbate the ability to effectively manage home finances.

While many family members wish to stay in close contact with their loved ones in prison, the costs can be prohibitive (Naser and Visher, 2006). Travel is expensive, often requiring costly overnight stays, gas, and restaurant meals for financially strapped family members. Many institutions require inmates to buy their own commodities including books, music, and hygiene items; prisoners may even be required to pay for medical care they receive. Although inmates may have work opportunities in prisons, the pay rate is intentionally low. With few resources to rely on, many inmates seek financial assistance from family members who are already suffering with the financial and emotional impact of the incarceration.

Consistent with the negative economic consequences, several studies converge on the conclusion that incarceration of a parent can negatively impact the children at home (Murray, Farrington, and Sekol, 2012). The most consistent finding is the greater likelihood that the children will follow in their parents' footsteps and engage in delinquent and criminal activity. For example, using a national longitudinal sample of adolescents, Swisher and Roettger (2012) found that adolescents who experienced paternal incarceration were more likely than youth who did not experience paternal incarceration to engage in delinquent activities. Moreover, this difference was apparent even when accounting for the many collateral adversities, such as low socioeconomic status and child abuse experiences within the parental incarceration cohort. Parental incarceration may also compound existing risks for youth who are already involved in the legal system, when the residential instability after incarceration increases the likelihood of further criminal activity (Taska, Rodriguez, and Zatz, 2011).

The growing and impressive body of information attesting to the impact of parental incarceration on children raises the question, "Why?" What is the specific mechanism or problem that fuels the negative outcomes? There are several related answers to this important question. One notion, grounded in attachment theory, argues that the disrupted attachment that comes from growing up with a parent who is unavailable or unpredictable can lead to difficulties in developing healthy interpersonal relationships (Poehlmann, 2010). As parents in prison, like most prisoners, typically have a pre-incarceration history of substance abuse, children of such parents may experience abandonment and uncertainty. In addition, the disruptions caused by the loss of the parent can be traumatic. Dallaire and Wilson (2010) interviewed parents, caregivers, and children about the impact on children of witnessing parental arrest. Both caregivers and parents reported high levels of emotional reactivity from children, including descriptions of "frantic" and "stunned" reactions (p. 411). Witnessing parental arrest was associated with increased child depression during the six months after separation.

Another theory that seeks to explain the poor outcomes for children of incarcerated parents is the bioecological theory as developed by Bronfenbrenner (1979). This theory situates the individual within a network of interrelated contexts. Poehlmann and colleagues (2010) point out how children with incarcerated parents have challenges in multiple ecological contexts. These include the child's microsystem, which consists of the child's immediate activities, personal characteristics, relationships, and roles (for example, the disrupted attachment pattern with the parent in prison). The child's mesosystem represents connections between microsystems, such as a disrupted relationship between the child's imprisoned parent and the child's caregiver. An exosystem includes settings that are external to the child, but yet have influence, such as the rules at the prison holding their parent. A macrosystem includes social and cultural contexts such as adverse judicial attitudes, racial attitudes, and correctional policies. These administrative and social systems often seem to stack the deck against families with an incarcerated parent. These families may not understand the legal system or procedures in which they find themselves, and frequently lack the knowledge or community support to express their concerns and needs in political arenas (Murray, 2007). Furthermore, families coping with incarceration are likely to have low income and social status, thereby restricting their access to helpful legal and political resources, farther limiting their ability to navigate these systems successfully (Murray). The chronosystem includes changes over time periods such as differences in sentencing policies during different time periods (Bronfenbrenner). As stressors within these varying contexts interact, the child's behavior can be understood as a method of dealing with his or her life through the perspective of these varying realms.

Closely related to a bioecological model are theories that emphasize the impact of multiple cumulative risks. Children of incarcerated parents are at risk not only because of the loss of their parent and associated attachment disruption, but also because of the myriad other risk factors they typically face, such as low socioeconomic status, limited education, criminal peers, dangerous neighborhood, etc. (E. Johnson and Easterling, 2012). Although a single risk factor may not lead to problem behaviors, parental incarceration may serve as a tipping point that potentiates the effects of the other accumulated risks. Other theories place the problem more squarely within the realm of weak social control mechanisms. Hirschi (1969) described how the family and community bonds that emphasize particular moral codes serve to discourage self-serving behavior and thereby promote a social awareness and conscience. Some children with incarcerated parents may fail to fully develop this moral awareness because of fractured social bonds, leading to eventual intergenerational patterns of offending. While these theories differ, they share a common attention to the cumulative effects of adversities that can "domino," with one adversity causing problems that in turn cause greater problems, or which can interact with one another to create a problem that is greater than the sum of the parts.

Despite these many challenges, the majority of children of incarcerated parents do not follow their parents in a criminal career, raising the question, "Why not?" What makes some children able to deal with such stress? Nesmith and Ruhland (2008) interviewed youth with incarcerated parents about their experiences and observed that youth coped with the difficulties of incarceration through positive support from caregivers and social networks. Positive family relationships, involvement in school and community groups, and strong faith affiliations can reduce the isolation, loneliness, and involvement with criminal peers that can lead a youth to criminal activity. A supportive relationship with the home caregiver who provides supervision and guidance is critical (Cecil, McHale, and Strozier, 2008).

There is a growing number of initiatives aimed at providing such support to children and families while parents are in prison (Zwiebach, Rhodes, and Rappaport, 2010). For example, Big Brothers Big Sisters supports a national mentoring program, Amachi, which matches adult volunteers with children of incarcerated parents. Consequent to the Second Chance Act of 2007, Congress authorized the Mentoring Children of Prisoners initiative that funded a number of community mentoring programs. However, emerging research cautions that simply providing a mentor for children is not enough (Zwiebach *et al.*, 2010). Rather, mentoring programs need to carefully select and monitor mentors, assess ongoing outcomes, provide support and training for mentors, encourage and provide structured positive activities, and involve key caregivers (DuBois, Holloway, Valentine, and Cooper, 2002). These fundamental ingredients for mentoring resonate with key features of successful parenting programs, child contact programs, and family support initiatives. To the degree that families and parents can be bolstered during the incarceration years with emotional and financial support, guidance on best parenting practices in this unique context, and encouragement to engage in positive prosocial activities, the resilient family can emerge through the crisis years of incarceration.

Family Life after Release

Tasks associated with release

Though release from prison or jail can be a joyful time, it can also trigger multiple stressors and road-blocks for the individual and their family. Upon release, the incarcerated parent has a long list of tasks to undertake in short order. Most immediately, the individual will need to seek employment, housing, medical care, educational opportunities, and mental health services (Alemagno, 2001). Despite their need, recently released offenders and their families are often reluctant to seek community resources or public assistance, as they feel suspicious of social institutions. Some ex-offenders particularly fear that they will be rejected or subject to additional surveillance if they seek formal assistance (M. Brown and Bloom, 2009). Staying sober is a particular concern for many offenders who may have experienced serious pre-incarceration substance problems (Smith, Krisman, Strozier, and Marley, 2004). The stress of resisting alcohol or drug use can be shared with family members, as the offender often requires additional family and parenting support while seeking substance abuse treatment (Alemagno, 2001). Transportation is also a frequent problem for offenders that likewise adds a burden to family and friends. Lack of transportation may limit access to community resources and childcare, as well as affecting the ability to sustain employment.

The individual's employment and income are often the primary contributing factors to his or her ability to accomplish the tasks associated with successful re-entry. However, a criminal record negatively affects the ex-offender's ability to get a good job (Arditti and Few, 2006). Recently released offenders are overwhelmed with financial obligations and have difficulty finding and sustaining employment (Arditti and Few, 2008). Lack of employment often results in increased strain on the family finances. With such precarious family financial situations (Arditti and Few, 2006), the ex-offender must find ways to deal with such economic inadequacies and their inability to provide for their children (Arditti and Few, 2008).

Case Example: Gloria

My name is Gloria and today is my twenty-ninth birthday. I go home today. Things got better my last few years inside. I got into some programs that helped me see things in a different way. I had a class on being a good parent. That really helped me. I was 17 years old when Nevaeh was born, and she was 3 years old when I finally landed here in prison. She calls Mama her mommy. That hurt at first, hearing her call my mama that name, but the class has helped and I am going to try to work with Mama so we can do what's right for Nevaeh. I got my GED and got some certificates for some job training I did. I have got to get a job. Mama is really having a hard time and I have to be there for her. Samuel left her years ago, but he hurt her pretty bad. She can't do much work, so it is up to me. And I have to pay my court costs. I got to stay straight. I don't want to go back.

Family and individual resources must be effectively garnered for the ex-offender to accomplish these tasks under such limits. However, as discussed in previous sections, families that have experienced incarceration are often both financially and socially strained, causing additional obstacles for the offender upon release. For example, shifting caregiving roles following release can be a major source of stress for both the ex-inmate and family. The financially strapped family may well need the returning inmate to find work as soon as possible. But doing so may mean finding new caregiving arrangements, or in many cases, calling on the existing caregiver to continue in the previous role. As a result, it may be difficult for the ex-inmate to work with the caregiver to allow for shared or transferred oversight of children. In addition, the nuts and bolts of providing effective parenting may be difficult, as the children are more likely to struggle with legal and behavioral issues (M. Brown and Bloom, 2009). In essence, many returning parents who are ill-equipped to carry on good parenting may find themselves needing and wishing to assume the role, but facing extraordinary challenges along the way. Necessary but complicated adjustments can impede alliance-building within the reuniting family (Smith *et al.*, 2004).

Most offenders leave prison with some form of conditional release by which they continue to be under the supervision of the judicial system. The components of this supervision can sometimes paradoxically add significant pressure to the re-entry period. Though maintaining and sustaining employment is difficult for most individuals with a criminal record, this task can be complicated for those under supervision, as they are subject to additional surveillance and control. Conditional release may require the individual to attend counseling at his or her own expense (Ferraro and Moe, 2003), and many ex-offenders struggle with payment of mandatory fees and charges throughout the re-entry process (Luther, Reichert, Holloway, Roth, and Aalsma, 2011). The additional responsibilities of supervision, such as substance abuse counseling or meetings with a parole officer may well benefit the inmate, but can complicate the logistics of finding employment. Required commitments may place the offender in a double bind, as failure to pay restitution may lead to a parole violation and re-arrest, but the employment needed to pay the restitution is difficult to attain if the offender has numerous required meetings or other mandated events (Ferraro and Moe, 2003). Despite the good intentions of such programs, families' perceptions of supervision requirements may lead to an increase in the family's feelings of instability and stress. However, many probation offices are currently working to deal with this challenge by training correctional staff to become more sensitive to these complications and more available and influential in the community they serve. For example, The Risk-Need-Responsivity (RNR) model for training probation officers is designed to help the officers effectively match the level and type of services to need and risks demonstrated by the offender and their family. Preliminary research on this method has demonstrated decreases in recidivism rates for offenders that were supervised by probation officers trained using the RNR model (Andrews and Bonta, 2010).

Individuals who are able to effectively utilize systems of external support are more likely to successfully overcome such obstacles and navigate the responsibilities of release. For example, employment is particularly influential in the re-entry process, as a job provides the offender with income and peer support and serves to limit involvement in criminal activity (Arditti and Parkman, 2011). The support offered by a regular workplace is thereby able to relieve much of the re-entry burden that is placed on the family. On the other hand, if such support is unavailable, the ex-offender's re-entry period is much less likely to be successful. It is at this point that offenders confront the social stigma that their families have faced throughout their incarceration and begin to experience discrimination associated with the lifetime label of ex-convict. Disclosure of ex-felon status is typically required for job and housing applications (Scanlon, 2001). With the consequent difficulties in finding a steady job or place to live, the ex-inmate faces further problems in adhering to parole or probation requirements for gainful employment and desisting from criminal contacts. The likelihood of offender recidivism is increased by the experience of racism and class discrimination, as well as any deficits in the areas of job opportunities, social support, marketable skills, and available housing (Bonhomme, Stephens, and Braithwaite, 2006).

Though drug treatment services are the most frequently used re-entry service, a large percentage of offenders do not receive any services when released (Arditti and Few, 2006; Lattimore and Visher, 2009). Confirming this need for support systems, when interviewed by researchers, offenders suggest that resources such as counseling, drug treatment, employment, halfway houses, a different town, or "better" parole officers might have helped them to stay out of prison (Harm and Phillips, 2001).

Unfortunately, this combination of high-pressure tasks and difficulty navigating community resources leads many individuals back into the correctional system. Approximately 15% of male offenders return to prison within a year of their release and most are rearrested due to a new charge. Approximately half of those under conditional release or supervision return to prison or jail for violating a condition of their parole (Visher and Courtney, 2007). These rates point to a stubborn problem in our justice system. Approximately 700,000 offenders were released from state and federal prisons in 2010 (Guerino et al., 2011). In 2011, approximately 800,000 individuals were confined to jails that typically hold individuals for less than 18 months (Minton, 2012). If these high numbers of released individuals follow the usual pattern of high rates of return, the need for massive allocation of public resources to maintain overcrowded correctional facilities will continue.

In addition to high rates of offender recidivism, the quick speeds with which offenders are rearrested also contribute to these growing problems. High rates of both volume and speed of rearrests demonstrate the immediate difficulties that offenders encounter following their long-awaited release. In a government report that followed 272,111 prisoners who were released in 1994, Langan and Levin (2002) found that 22.9% were rearrested within six months, 44.1% in the first year, and 59.2% within two years. This same sample of offenders had reconviction rates of 21.5% in the first year and 36.4% in the second year (Langan and Levin, 2002). In a 2001 survey study, Harm and Phillips (2001) found high numbers of multiple re-incarcerations in their sample. Of the women surveyed, 50% were serving a second prison sentence, 24% were serving a third prison sentence, 13% a fourth sentence, and 10% a fifth. Such high rates of recidivism demonstrate both the theme of instability

for the offender and their family as well as the need for programs and supportive resources to help offenders re-enter society in a constructive manner.

Successful re-entry

For most offenders, successful re-entry is built upon multiple systems of external support. Though offenders frequently turn to friends for support and help solving problems (Arditti and Few, 2008), successful ex-offenders must take care when choosing associates. Friends or family who engage in criminal or antisocial behaviors, use illegal drugs, or otherwise provide an unhealthy social network can lead the inmate right back through the revolving door of incarceration (Bahr, Armstrong, Gibbs, Harris, and Fisher, 2005). On the other hand, positive peer influences such as Narcotics Anonymous groups, religious and community support groups, or an intimate partner who does not tolerate drug use, can improve that chances that the released prisoner can stay home (Arditti and Few, 2008). The offender's own family of origin is a particularly important resource during the re-entry period. Family members, particularly the ex-offender's mother, frequently share resources linked to re-entry success such as housing, money, transportation, childcare, and networks for employment opportunities (Arditti and Few, 2006, 2008).

Just as relationships with their children have been found to help offenders reach goals while incarcerated, these relationships also help prevent recidivism following their release (Allard and Lu, 2006). The action of assuming a spouse or parenting role after release has been linked with more successful re-entry (Hairston, 2003). Positive relationships with their children provide ex-offenders with a sense of protective or caring companionship, thereby motivating the parents to abstain from drugs (Harm and Phillips, 2001). Formerly incarcerated parents often note guilt about the stress they have imposed on their children, as children will often encourage their released parents to attend rehabilitation or counseling programs, obey probation requirements, and stay clean in attempts to help their parents avoid re-incarceration (Arditti and Few, 2008). Accordingly, those inmates who maintain strong family ties throughout incarceration have greater release success than those who do not (Hairston, 2003).

For example, frequent in-prison family visits and visits that are near to the offender's release date are linked with reduced recidivism (Bales and Mears, 2008). Despite the stress placed on an offender's family throughout the course of their incarceration, close relationships with family, and children in particular, are a valuable support for offenders throughout the re-entry period.

Recent policy initiatives seek to incorporate these positive influences into pre- and post-release programming for offenders by assisting offenders in establishing housing, employment, and treatment arrangements that are stable and appropriate. The Serious and Violent Offender Reentry Initiative (SVORI) is one such policy that aims to improve the likelihood of successful re-entry for prisoners. Beginning in 2003, this initiative distributed $100 million dollars to 69 different agencies to improve re-entry services in the areas of criminal justice, employment, education, health, and housing. While there were few restrictions placed on programs receiving funding, all were required to provide services targeting offenders during their incarceration, the pre-release period, and several years following release (Lattimore and Visher, 2009). The Second Chance Act

of 2007 was designed to build upon the SVORI, and better address the issue of offenders who return to their communities and commit new crimes. The law specifically seeks to encourage successful re-entry by re-establishing family ties and supporting evidence-based programs. This law also established the National Re-Entry Resource Center in order to provide offenders and professionals with useful information regarding re-entry and recidivism.

Initial evaluation of SVORI programs indicated that the initiative primarily improved receipt of services rather than other targeted outcomes, such as reduced substance abuse and recidivism (Lattimore and Visher, 2009). However, a more recent evaluation has shown that SVORI programming decreased substance use and increased the likelihood that offenders would be supporting themselves 15 months following their release. While these outcomes are promising, three outcomes targeted by the original initiative (housing, family and peer relationships, and physical and mental health) did not show significant improvement (Garcia and Ritter, 2012). The important work of identifying programs and policies that effectively support the ex-offender and his or her family continues.

Case Example: Gloria

My name is Gloria and today is my thirty-fifth birthday. I am going to see Nevaeh graduate from high school. This is the happiest birthday I have ever had. Mama and I are going to have a party after and invite our friends who have helped me so much these last years. It hasn't been an easy road for Mama, Nevaeh, or me. Mama has been sick a lot. She has diabetes and needs to stay with her medicine. She can't work much, so it has been up to me to keep things going. When I came out, I was ready to get a job and work hard, but I had trouble finding one, even with my certificates. Money was hard, and I started doing some dope again. But my probation officer worked with me, got me into some counseling that helped me to think about what I really wanted for me, Mama, and, most of all, for Nevaeh. A few years ago, I got really scared when

Nevaeh got into some trouble with some rough kids. But some people at her school came through for us and got her with a college girl who became her big sister and helped her out. And folks from church really helped. Nevaeh turned around, got good grades, and got into the state university. I have a job as a secretary at a construction company. They are good about taking on people from inside, and I have been a good worker. I learned how to do spreadsheets and word processing when I was inside and that is what I do all the time now. My boss says I am the best secretary he has ever had. We may not live on 'easy street,' but I am clean and have a good job, Mama is doing OK, and Nevaeh is going to college. Most of the people I knew from inside are either still there or came back after they left. I am one of the lucky ones. I am home.

Summary

Incarceration affects not only the individual offender, but the family as well. The risks and adversities for these families resonate throughout the 'time-span' of the offender's justice-involvement trajectory. Both before, during, and after inmate imprisonment, the family is likely to be experiencing financial strain, marital and domestic problems, and involvement with criminal associates. Problems with mental illness, substance abuse, and other health problems complicate recovery and successful employment. But likewise, the remedies for the family and inmate are consistent and point to the pivotal role of support and services for family members. Mental health and substance abuse treatment, educational and rehabilitative programs, job training and educational opportunities, and other social support programs – whether applied during the life course of the inmate-to-be, the prisoner serving his or her term, or the ex-offender returning home – make a difference that affects not only the individual but the supporting family as well.

Critical Thinking Questions

1. What are the ecological system features that were involved in Gloria's life, before, during, and after prison?
2. What are some points for early intervention for children at risk for being incarcerated later in life? What sorts of programs might best reach these children?
3. What are the implications of attachment theory for children of an incarcerated mother or father?
4. What are some of the emotional and practical struggles that Gloria's mother and daughter might be coping with while she is incarcerated?
5. What are some ways to expand the reach of programming for ex-offenders and their families? Consider social stigma and the family's potential fear of supervision.

References

Agnew, R., Matthews, S. K., Bucher, J., Welcher, A. N., and Keyes, C. (2008). Socioeconomic status, economic problems, and delinquency. *Youth and Society, 40*, 159–181. doi: 10.1177/0044118X08318119.

Alemagno, S. A. (2001). Women in jail: Is substance abuse treatment enough? *American Journal of Public Health, 91*, 798–800. doi: 10.2105/AJPH.91.5.798.

Allard, P. E., and Lu, L. D. (2006). *Rebuilding families, reclaiming lives*. New York: Brennan Center for Justice at NYU School of Law.

Andrews, D. A., and Bonta, J. (2010). Rehabilitating criminal justice policy and practice. *Psychology, Public Policy, and Law, 16*, 39–5. doi: 10.1037/a0018362.

Arditti, J., and Few, A. (2006). Mothers' reentry into family life following incarceration. *Criminal Justice Policy Review, 17*, 103–123. doi:10.1177/0887403405282450.

Arditti, J., and Few, A. (2008). Maternal distress and women's reentry into family and community life. *Family Process, 47*, 303–321. doi:10.1111/j.1545-5300.2008.00255.x.

Arditti, J. A., and Parkman, T. (2011). Young men's reentry after incarceration: A developmental paradox. *Family Relations, 60*(2), 205–220. doi: 10.1111/j.1741-3729.2010.00643.x.

Asberg, K., and Renk, K. (2012). Comparing incarcerated and college student women with histories of childhood sexual abuse: The roles of abuse severity, support, and substance use. *Psychological Trauma: Theory, Research, Practice, and Policy* (advance online publication, February 13). doi: 10.1037/a0027162.

Bahr, S., Armstrong, A., Gibbs, B., Harris, P., and Fisher, J. (2005). The reentry process: How parolees adjust to release from prison. *Fathering, 3*, 243–265. doi: 10.3149/fth.0303.243.

Bales, W. D., and Mears, D. P. (2008). Inmate social ties and the transition to society: Does visitation reduce recidivism? *Journal of Research in Crime and Delinquency, 45*, 287–321. doi: 10.1177/0022427808317574.

Bjerk, D. (2007). Measuring the relationship between youth criminal participation and household economic resources. *Journal of Quantitative Criminology, 23*, 23–39. doi: 10.1007/s10940-006-9017-8.

Blumstein, A. (1993). Racial disproportionality in the U.S. prison population revisited. *University of Colorado Law Review, 64*, 743–760.

Bonhomme, J., Stephens, T., and Braithwaite, R. (2006). African-American males in the United States prison system: Impact on family and community. *Journal of Men's Health and Gender, 3*, 223–226. doi: 10.1016/j.jmhg.2006.06.003.

Bradley-Engen, M. S., Cuddeback, G. S., Gayman, M. D., Morrissey, J. P., and Mancuso, D. (2010). Trends in state prison admission of offenders with serious mental illness. *Psychiatric Services, 61*, 1263–1265. doi: 10.1176/appi.ps.61.12.1263.

Briere, J., and Elliot, D. M. (2003). Prevalence and psychological sequelae of self-reported childhood physical and sexual abuse in a general population sample of men and women. *Child Abuse and Neglect, 27*, 1205–1222. doi: 10.1016/j.chiabu.2003.09.008.

Bronfenbrenner, U. (1979). Contexts of child rearing: Problems and prospects. *American Psychologist, 34*, 844–850. doi: 10.1037/0003-066X.34.10.844.

Brown, A., Miller, B., and Maguin, E. (1999). Prevalence and severity of lifetime physical and sexual victimization among incarcerated women. *International Journal of Law and Psychiatry, 22*, 301–322. doi: 10.1016/S0160-2527(99)00011-4.

Brown, E., and Males, M. (2011). Does age or poverty level best predict criminal arrest and homicide rates? A preliminary investigation. *Justice Policy Journal, 8*, 1–30. Retrieved May 30, 2014 from http://www.cjcj.org/files/Does_age.pdf.

Brown, M., and Bloom, B. (2009). Reentry and renegotiating motherhood: Maternal identity and success on parole. *Crime and Delinquency, 55*, 313–336. doi: 10.1177/0011128708330627.

Buehler, C., Anthony, C., Krishnakumar, A., Stone, G., Gerard, J., and Pemberton, S. (1997). Interparental conflict and youth problem behaviors: A meta-analysis. *Journal of Child and Family Studies, 6*, 233–247. doi: 10.1023/A:1025006909538.

Cecil, D., McHale, J., and Strozier, A. (2008). Female inmates, family caregivers, and young children's adjustment: A research agenda and implications for corrections programming. *Journal of Criminal Justice, 36*, 513–521. doi: 10.1016/j.jcrimjus.2008.09.002.

Celinska, K., and Siegel, J. A. (2010). Mothers in trouble: Coping with actual or pending separation from children due to incarceration. *Prison Journal, 20*, 1–28. doi: 10.1177/0032885510382218.

Cho, R. M. (2010). Maternal incarceration and children's adolescent outcomes: Timing versus dosage. *Social Service Review, 84*, 257–282. doi: 10.1086/653456.

Côté, G., Lesage, A., Chawky, N., and Loyer, M. (1997). Clinical specificity of prison inmates with severe mental disorders: A case-control study. *British Journal of Psychiatry, 170*, 571–577. doi: 10.1192/bjp.170.6.571.

Dallaire, D. H., and Wilson, L. C. (2010). The relation of exposure to parental criminal activity, arrest, and sentencing to children's maladjustment. *Journal of Child and Family Studies, 19*, 404–418. doi: 10.1007/s10826-009-9311-9.

Dixon, L. B., and Goldman, H. H. (2003). Forty years of progress in community health: The role of evidence-based practices. *Australian and New Zealand Journal of Psychiatry, 37*, 668–673. doi: 10.1111/j.1440-1614.2003.01274.x.

DuBois, D. L., Holloway, B. E., Valentine, J. C., and Cooper, H. (2002). Effectiveness of mentoring programs for youth: A meta-analytic review. *American Journal of Community Psychology, 30*, 157–197. doi: 10.1023/A:1014628810714.

Eddy, J. M., and Reid, J. B. (2003). The adolescent children of incarcerated parents. In J. Travis and M. Waul (eds), *Prisoners once removed: The impact of incarceration and reentry on children, families, and communities* (pp. 233–258). Washington, DC: Urban Institute Press.

Evans, S. E., Davies, C., and DeLillo, D. (2008). Exposure to domestic violence: A meta-analysis of child and adolescent outcomes. *Aggression and Violent Behavior, 13*, 131–140. doi: 10.1016/j.avb.2008.02.005.

Farrington, D. P. (2005). Childhood origins of antisocial behavior. *Clinical Psychology and Psychotherapy, 12*, 177–190. doi: 10.1002/cpp.448.

Farrington, D. P., Lösel, F., Ttofi, M. M., and Theodorakis, N. (2012). *School bullying, depression and offending behaviour later in life: An updated systematic review of longitudinal studies.* Stockholm: Swedish National Council for Crime Prevention.

Federal Bureau of Investigation (FBI) (2012). *Crime in the United States, 2011.* Washington, DC: US Department of Justice, Federal Bureau of Investigation, Criminal Justice Information Services Division. Retrieved May 30, 2014 from http://www.fbi.gov/about-us/cjis/ucr/crime-in-the-u.s/2011/crime-in-the-u.s.-2011/persons-arrested/persons-arrested.

Fergusson, D. M., and Horwood, L. J. (1998). Exposure to interparental violence in childhood and psychosocial adjustment in young adulthood. *Child Abuse and Neglect, 22*, 339–357. doi: 10.1016/S0145-2134(98)00004-0.

Ferraro, K. J., and Moe, A. M. (2003). Mothering, crime and incarceration. *Journal of Contemporary Ethnography, 32*, 9–40. doi: 10.1177/0891241602238937.

Finkelhor, D. (1994). Current information on the scope and nature of child sexual abuse. *Future of Children, 4*, 31–53. doi: 10.2307/160252.

Garcia, M., and Ritter, N. (2012). Improving access to services for female offenders returning to the community. *National Institute of Justice Journal, 269*, 18–23.

Glaze, L. E., and Maruschak, L. (2008). Parents in prison and their minor children. Bureau of Justice Statistics, *Special Report.* Washington, DC: US Department of Justice.

Glaze, L. E., and Parks, E. (2012). Correctional populations in the United States, 2011. Bureau of Justice Statistics, *Bulletin.* Washington, DC: US Department of Justice.

Guerino, P., Harrison, P. M., and Sabol, W. J. (2011). Prisoners in 2010. Bureau of Justice Statistics, *Bulletin*. Washington, DC: US Department of Justice.

Hairston, C. (2003). Prisoners and their families: Parenting issues during incarceration. In J. Travis and M. Waul (eds), *Prisoners once removed: The impact of incarceration and reentry on children, families, and communities* (pp. 259–282). Washington, DC: Urban Institute Press.

Harm, N. J., and Phillips, S. D. (2001). You can't go home again: Women and criminal recidivism. *Journal of Offender Rehabilitation, 32*, 3–21. doi: 10.1300/J076v32n03_02.

Hart, J. L., O'Toole, S. K., Price-Sharps, J. L, and Shaffer, T. W. (2007). The risk and protective factors of juvenile offending: An examination of gender differences. *Youth Violence and Juvenile Justice, 5*, 367–384. doi: 10.1177/1541204006297367.

Heckman, J. J., and LaFontaine, P. A. (2010). The American high school graduate rate: Trends and levels. *Review of Economics and Statistics, 92*(2), 244–262. doi: 10.1162/rest.2010.12366.

Henry, B., Caspi, A., Moffitt, T. E., and Silva, P. A. (1996). Temperamental and familial predictors of violent and nonviolent criminal convictions: Age 3 to age 18. *Developmental Psychology, 32*, 614–623. doi: 10.1037/0012-1649.32.4.614.

Hirschi, T. (1969). *Causes of delinquency*. Berkeley and Los Angeles: University of California Press.

Hoffmann, H. C., Byrd, A. L., and Kightlinger, A. M. (2010). Prison programs and services for incarcerated parents and their underage children: Results from a national survey of correctional facilities. *Prison Journal, 90*, 397–416. doi: 10.1177/0032885510382087.

Holmes, S. E., Slaughter, J. R., and Kashani, J. (2001). Risk factors in childhood that lead to the development of conduct disorder and antisocial personality disorder. *Child Psychiatry and Human Development, 31*, 183–193. doi: 10.1023/A:1026425304480.

Holt, S., Buckley, H., and Whelan, S. (2008). The impact of exposure to domestic violence on children and young people: A review of the literature. *Child Abuse and Neglect, 32*, 797–810. doi: 10.1016/j.chiabu.2008.02.004.

Houck, K. D. F., and Loper, A. B. (2002). The relationship of parenting stress to adjustment among mothers in prison. *American Journal of Orthopsychiatry, 72*, 548–558. doi: 10.1037/0002-9432.72.4.548.

Humphreys, K., and Rappaport, J. (1993). From the community mental health movement to the war on drugs: A study in the definition of social problems. *American Psychologist, 48*, 892–901. doi: 10.1037/0003-066X.48.8.892.

James, D. J., and Glaze, L. E. (2006). Mental health problems of prison and jail inmates. Bureau of Justice Statistics, *Special Report*. Washington, DC: US Department of Justice.

Johnson, E., and Easterling, B. (2012). Understanding unique effects of parental incarceration on children: Challenges, progress, and recommendations. *Journal of Marriage and Family, 74*, 342–356. doi: 10.1111/j.1741-3737.2012.00957.x.

Johnson, W. L., Giordano, P. C., Manning, W. D., and Longmore, M. A. (2011). Parent–child relations and offending during young adulthood. *Journal of Youth and Adolescence, 40*, 786–799. doi: 10.1007/s10964-010-9591-9.

Langan, P. A., and Levin, D. J. (2002). Recidivism of prisoners released in 1994. Bureau of Justice Statistics, *Special Report*. Washington, DC: US Department of Justice.

Lattimore, P. K., and Visher, C. A. (2009). *Multi-site evaluation of SVORI: Summary and synthesis*. Raleigh, NC: RTI International.

Loper, A. B., Carlson, L. W., Levitt, L., and Scheffel, K. (2009). Parenting stress, alliance, child contact and adjustment of imprisoned mothers and fathers. *Journal of Offender Rehabilitation, 11*, 483–503. doi: 10.1080/10509670903081300.

Loper, A. B., Mahmoodzadegan, N., and Warren, J. L. (2008). Childhood maltreatment and cluster B personality pathology in female serious offenders. *Sexual Abuse: Journal of Research and Treatment, 2*, 139–160. doi: 10.1177/1079063208317463.

Loper, A. B., and Novero, C. (2010). Parenting programs for prisoners: Current research and new directions. In J. Poehlmann and M. Eddy (eds), *Children of incarcerated parents: A handbook for researchers and practitioners* (pp. 189–216). Washington, DC: Urban Institute Press.

Loper, A. B., and Novero, C. (2013). Attachment representations of imprisoned mothers as related to child contact and the caregiving alliance: The moderating effect of children's placement with maternal grandmothers. *Monographs of the Society for Research in Child Development, 78*, 41–56. doi: 10.1111/mono.12020.

Luther, J. B., Reichert, E. S., Holloway, E. D., Roth, A. M., and Aalsma, M. C. (2011). An exploration of community reentry needs and services for prisoners: A focus on care to limit return to high-risk behavior. *AIDS Patient Care and STDs, 25*, 475–481. doi: 10.1089/apc.2010.0372.

Lynch, M. (2012). Theorizing the role of the "war on drugs" in US punishment. *Theoretical Criminology, 16*, 175–199. doi: 10.1177/1362480612441700.

Minton, T. D. (2012). Jail inmates at midyear 2011. Bureau of Justice Statistics, Statistical Tables. Washington, DC: US Department of Justice.

Murray, J. (2007). The cycle of punishment: The social exclusion of prisoners and their children. *Criminology and Criminal Justice, 7*, 55–81. doi:10.1177/1748895807072476.

Murray, J., Farrington, D., Sekol, I. (2012). Children's antisocial behavior, mental health, drug use, and educational performance after parental incarceration: A systematic review and meta-analysis. *Psychological Bulletin, 138*, 175–210. doi: 10.1037/a00264071.

Murrell, A. R., Christoff, K. A., and Henning, K. R. (2007). Characteristics of domestic violence offenders: Associations with childhood exposure to violence. *Journal of Family Violence, 22*, 523–532. doi: 10.1007/s10896-007-9100-4.

Mustard, D. (2001). Racial, ethnic, and gender disparities in sentencing: Evidence from the U.S. Federal Courts. *Journal of Law and Economics, 44*, 285–314. doi: 10.1086/320276.

Nagin, D. S., Pogarsky, G., and Farrington, D. P. (1997). Adolescent mothers and the criminal behavior of their children. *Law and Society Review, 31*, 137–162. doi: 10.2307/3054097.

Naser, R. L., and Visher, C. A. (2006). Family members' experiences with incarceration and reentry. *Western Criminology Review, 7*, 20–31.

Nash, J. K., Mujanovic, E., and Winfree, L. T. (2011). Protective effects of parental monitoring on offending in victimized youth in Bosnia and Herzegovina. *Child and Youth Services, 32*, 224–242. doi: 10.1080/0145935X.2011.605313.

Nesmith, A., and Ruhland, E. (2008). Children of incarcerated parents: Challenges and resiliency, in their own words. *Children and Youth Services Review, 30*, 1119–1130. doi: 10.1016/j.childyouth.2008.02.006.

Pettit, B., and Western, B. (2004). Mass imprisonment and the life course: Race and class inequality in U.S. incarceration. *American Sociological Review, 69*, 151–169. doi: 10.1177/000312240406900201.

Poehlmann, J. (2010). Attachment in infants and children of incarcerated parents. In M. Eddy and J. Poehlmann (eds), *Children of incarcerated parents: A handbook for researchers and practitioners* (pp. 75–100). Washington, DC: Urban Institute Press.

Poehlmann, J., Dallaire, D., Loper, A. B., and Shear, L. D. (2010). Children's contact with their parents in prison: Research findings and recommendations. *American Psychologist, 65*, 575–598. doi: 10.1037/a0020279.

Polusny, M. A., and Follette, V. M. (1995). Long-term correlates of child sexual abuse: Theory and review of the empirical literature. *Applied and Preventative Psychology, 4*, 143–166. doi: 10.1016/S0962-1849(05)80055-1.

Racz, S. J., and McMahon, R. J. (2011). The relationship between parental knowledge and monitoring and child and adolescent conduct problems: A 10-year update. *Clinical Child and Family Psychology Review, 14*, 377–398. doi: 10.1007/s10567-011-0099-y.

Ritter, J., Stewart, M., Bernet, C., Coe, M., and Brown, S. A. (2002). Effects of childhood exposure to familial alcoholism and family violence on adolescent substance use, conduct problems, and self-esteem. *Journal of Traumatic Stress, 15*, 113–122. doi: 10.1023/A:1014803907234.

Roy, K. M., and Dyson, O. L. (2005). Gatekeeping in context: Babymama drama and the involvement of incarcerated fathers. *Fathering, 3*, 289–310. doi: 10.3149/fth.0303.289.

Scanlon, W. (2001). Ex-convicts: A workplace diversity issue. *Employee Assistance Quarterly, 16*, 35–51. doi: 10.1300/J022v16n04_03.

Schwartz-Soicher, O., Geller, A., and Garfinkel, I. (2011). The effect of paternal incarceration on material hardship. *Social Service Review, 85*, 447–473. doi: 10.1086/661925.

Shlafer, R. J., and Poehlmann, J. (2010). Attachment and caregiving relationships in families affected by parental incarceration. *Attachment and Human Development, 12*, 395–415. doi: 10.1080/14616730903417052.

Smith, A., Krisman, K., Strozier, A. L., and Marley, M. A. (2004). Breaking through the bars: Exploring the experiences of addicted parents in prison whose children are cared for by relatives. *Families in Society, 85*, 187–200.

Sprott, J. B., Jenkins, J. M., and Doob, A. N. (2005). The importance of school: Protecting at-risk youth from early offending. *Youth Violence and Juvenile Justice, 3*, 59–77. doi: 10.1177/1541204004270943.

Swisher, R. R., and Roettger, M. E. (2012). Father's incarceration and youth delinquency and depression: Examining differences by race and ethnicity. *Journal of Research on Adolescence, 22*, 597–603. doi: 10.1111/j.1532-7795.2012.00810.x.

Taska, M., Rodriguez, N., and Zatz, M. S. (2011). Family and residential instability in the context of paternal and maternal incarceration. *Criminal Justice and Behavior, 38*, 231–247. doi: 10.1177/0093854810391632.

Visher, C. A., and Courtney, S. M. E. (2007). *One year out: Experiences of prisoners returning to Cleveland.* Returning Home Policy Brief. Washington, DC: Urban Institute, Justice Policy Center.

Walters, G. D. (2011). Criminal thinking as a mediator of the mental illness–prison violence relationship: A path analytic study and causal mediation analysis. *Psychological Services, 8*, 189–199. doi: 10.1037/a0024684.

Weeks, R., and Widom, C. S. (1998). Self-reports of early childhood victimization among incarcerated adult male felons. *Journal of Interpersonal Violence, 13*, 346–361. doi: 10.1177/088626098013003003.

Widom, C. S. (1989). The cycle of violence. *Science, 244,* 160–166. doi: 10.1126/science.2704995.

Wildeman, C. (2010). Parental incarceration and children's physically aggressive behaviors: Evidence from the Fragile Families and Child Wellbeing Study. *Social Forces, 89,* 285–310. doi: 10.1353/sof.2010.0055.

Yang, S., and Mulvey, E. P. (2012). Violence risk: Re-defining variables from the first-person perspective. *Aggression and Violent Behavior, 17,* 198–207. doi: 10.1016/j.avb.2012.02.001.

Zwiebach, L., Rhodes, J. E., and Rappaport, C. D. (2010). Mentoring interventions for children of incarcerated parents. In M. Eddy and J. Poehlmann (eds), *Children of incarcerated parents: A handbook for researchers and practitioners* (pp. 217–236). Washington, DC: Urban Institute Press.

5

Social Disparities in Family Health

Jinette Comeau and William R. Avison

Chapter 5 highlights how the "second demographic transition" (i.e., increases in single parents) connects with health disparities among families whereby married households increasingly enjoy greater physical and mental health than families in which the parents either cohabit or remain single. Comeau and Avison point out that married families likely have greater social support, access to health care, and less exposure to adversity due to their more socioeconomically affluent position in society than families in which parents are not married. Social disparities in family health raise questions about the exclusion of unmarried families from important health resources and opportunity structures.

Increasingly, health psychologists and other social scientists have become interested in understanding how various social disadvantages translate into poorer physical and mental health for parents and children. We begin this chapter by describing how emerging trends in family formation and dissolution in Europe and North America have changed the composition of families over the past three decades. This "second demographic transition," as it is known, has contributed significantly to increased disparities between advantaged and disadvantaged families. Of course, family composition is not the only source of social disadvantage. It is well known that specific racial and ethnic minority groups are more disadvantaged than others as a result of lower levels of education, poor job opportunities, and discrimination in day-to-day life. These different sources of social disadvantage intersect with one another so that people often experience multiple disadvantages that threaten their health and well-being. It is therefore important to understand how these socioeconomic disparities translate into poorer health among parents and children in these disadvantaged families.

It is useful to have a conceptual model or framework to organize our thinking about disparities in family health. In this chapter, we use both Bronfenbrenner's bioecological model of human development and Pearlin's stress process model to understand how families experiencing social disadvantage have more health problems than do advantaged families. These models both emphasize the central role played by various stressors that individuals experience and individual differences in resilience to stress.

The chapter concludes with some thoughts about the implications of this research for health and social

Family Problems: Stress, Risk, and Resilience, First Edition. Edited by Joyce A. Arditti.
© 2015 John Wiley & Sons, Inc. Published 2015 by John Wiley & Sons, Inc.

Case Example: Elizabeth

The April 9 issue of the *New Yorker* magazine contains an account of single mother Elizabeth Jones (also known as "Cookie"), and her three children (Boo, 2001). Elizabeth's story describes the deep disadvantage in which she and her children are embedded, despite the fact that Elizabeth can be considered a welfare success story in that she is off public assistance. But working two jobs for $39,000 gives her little time to care for her children and their multiple needs, and the institutions she must interface with (such as schools, health care systems) are amazingly unresponsive. Here we use Elizabeth's story to illustrate how social disparities in income, education, and family life contribute to significant mental and physical health disadvantages for parents and their children. (See Boxes 5.2, 5.4, 5.5.)

policies regarding children and families. These ideas have the potential to reduce social disparities in child and family health.

The Second Demographic Transition

For many decades, research on family health tended to focus almost exclusively on "nuclear" families – family units comprising two parents and their children. In the majority of these families, the parents were legally married; relatively few were cohabiting. Since the 1990s, however, there has been a substantial increase in the number of different kinds of family structures. In addition to the increase in families headed by two cohabiting parents, there have also been increases in the proportions of single-parent families, blended or step-families, and same-sex families. How can we explain this increased diversity in family structures?

Many social demographers and family sociologists argue that a "second demographic transition" has occurred. During the eighteenth, nineteenth, and early twentieth centuries, the first demographic transition represented the change from high birth and death rates to lower birth and death rates. This was a result of the transition from largely agricultural to industrialized economic systems. In the latter part of the twentieth century and today, there is a second demographic transition in Western Europe and North America that has changed patterns of marriage, parenthood, and living arrangements.

In the second demographic transition, younger adults have postponed getting married and having children because of commitments to education and early career development. At the same time, there has been a marked increase in the number of new living arrangements. More adult children live with their parents than before; the number of same-sex couples (many of whom have children) has increased; and more women and men are raising children without partners. At the same time, there have been increases all across Europe and North America in the number of couples living together outside of marriage and an increasing proportion of births to unmarried persons. These patterns have occurred in the United States, Canada, and Europe (Le Bourdais and Lapierre-Adamcyk, 2004; Lesthaege and Neidert, 2006). These changes have dramatically altered the structure of families so that the family has become more diverse than ever before.

Box 5.1

In 2000, 358,390 of all US households were composed of same-sex partners (US Census Bureau, 2012). In 2010, this number jumped to 646,464, which represents an 80% increase in reported same-sex households over a 10-year period. It is estimated that 152,000 of these households were composed of same-sex spouses (US Census Bureau, 2011). Of all same-sex households, 115,064 report having their own children.

Two different trends in American family life have emerged from the second demographic transition. On the one hand, increases in mothers' employment and postponement of childbearing have resulted in economic gains for better educated couples. On the other hand, increases in the number of non-marital births and the number of divorces have resulted in financial challenges to many families. These two different trends have resulted in growing gaps between economically advantaged and disadvantaged families (McLanahan, 2004). These disparities are patterned by education and race/ethnicity so that increases in single-parent families have been more pronounced among more socially disadvantaged groups such as African Americans and Latinos (Ellwood and Jencks, 2004).

There are striking differences in education among unmarried mothers. Of mothers with less than a high school education, two-thirds are unmarried. In contrast, only 9% of college-educated mothers had non-marital births (Kennedy and Bumpass, 2007). Thus, social disadvantage is associated with family formation. Furthermore, patterns in family formation and dissolution have an important impact on parental resources, particularly income. For example, delays in childbearing are more common among women from advantaged backgrounds. Women who are older when they have their first child have more opportunities in the realms of education and work, both of which ultimately lead to higher income (McLanahan, 2009).

A large body of literature also points to important racial/ethnic differences in family structure. Over two-thirds of African American children and almost half of Hispanic children are born to unmarried parents. In contrast, only 24% of White children have unmarried parents at birth (McLanahan, 2009). Unmarried parents are typically younger and have a higher incidence of "multi-partnered fertility." For example, roughly 15% of married parents have children from multiple partners, compared to 35–40% of unmarried couples (Carlson and Furstenburg, 2006, 2007). Compared to married men with children, fathers who never marry or cohabit have greater rates of substance abuse, violence, and incarceration. They also have higher levels of unemployment and lower earnings. Thus, unmarried parents experience significant barriers to marriage and partnership stability.

All of this suggests that single parenthood may not be a choice that is made; rather, it may be the consequence of challenging social disadvantages. Indeed, single parenthood may be a "marker" or a "proxy" for an array of different social disadvantages. Gassman-Pines and Yoshikawa (2006) have identified economic barriers to marriage among socially disadvantaged people in the United States. Many low-income women prefer to delay marriage until they can be financially stable, but their economic challenges may be too great. Other researchers have noted that the exceptionally high rate of incarceration of young minority males also makes it less likely that minority couples will marry (Braman, 2004). As a consequence, marriage in the United States is driven to an important extent by economic adequacy.

Single parenthood has important consequences for children's outcomes. In particular, children living in a single-mother household are less likely to complete high school and obtain a post-secondary degree, and have lower socioeconomic status in adulthood (McLanahan and Percheski, 2008). Children raised by single mothers also have higher rates of early sexual initiation and teenage childbearing. Furthermore, young couples are at higher risk of dissolving their relationship than older couples. Thus, it appears that family structure is both a cause and consequence of social disadvantage (McLanahan, 2004, 2009; McLanahan and Percheski, 2008). Given that having a child outside of marriage occurs more frequently

Box 5.2

Elizabeth was raised in a single-parent household and never knew her father. Elizabeth had her first child, Wayne, when she was only 16 years old. All three of her children were born to separate fathers, all of whom are almost completely absent from their children's lives. Elizabeth worries that the cycle of poverty and single parenthood will continue with her children. She became particularly concerned when she heard that one of Drenika's peers at school was pregnant.

among minority and low-income groups, and that children raised in a single-parent household have lower socioeconomic attainment in adulthood, family structure is an important component in the reproduction of racial and socioeconomic inequalities across generations (McLanahan, 2008).

Although the impact of the second demographic transition has been a steady increase in births outside of marriage, non-marital childbearing is not the same as single parenthood (Musick, 2007). According to Raley (2001), as many as 50% of non-marital births are to cohabiting couples. Although cohabiting families with children may appear to be largely similar to married families, we know that cohabiting couples are more likely than married couples to dissolve their relationships. In addition, some researchers find that family structure is related to pregnancy outcomes. Luo, Wilkins, and Kramer (2004) analyzed data from over 720,000 births in the province of Quebec in Canada between 1990 and 1997. Over that time, the proportion of births to common-law couples grew from 20% to 44%. They found that common-law mothers had significantly poorer pregnancy outcomes than did married mothers in terms of the incidence of preterm births, low birth weight, being small for gestational age, and neonatal and postnatal mortality. These outcomes, however, were better than for single mothers living alone. Similar results have been reported in Europe (Raatikainen, Heiskanen, and Heinonen, 2005; Zeitlin, Saurel-Cubizolles, and Ancel, 2002).

Other demographic changes in North America have also contributed to substantial diversity in family structure. Increased rates of divorce (which peaked in the US in 1980 and then leveled off) as well as delays in marriage have led to a substantial decline in the proportion of two-parent families with children (Bianchi and Casper, 2000). Thus, family structure has become more diversified than ever before (Dupre and Meadows, 2007; Halpern-Meekin and Tach, 2008; Meadows, McLanahan, and Brooks-Gunn, 2008).

This diversity in family structure and composition means that the experiences of children are also likely to be more varied that ever before. This is likely to be even more pronounced as more individuals live in a wider number of different family structures during childhood and adolescence. Thus, it seems important to study how demographic trends play out in terms of the health of parents and children in different family structures (Avison, 2010a, 2010b).

The increasing variability in family structure may generate a broad array of stressors that are experienced by parents and their children. It seems likely that the second demographic transition may have exposed increasing numbers of parents and children to poverty, financial strain, and work–home strain (Avison, Ali, and Walters, 2007; Benzeval, 1998; G. Brown and Moran, 1997; Demo and Acock, 1996; Simons, Johnson, and Lorenz, 1996).

It is also possible that instability in family structures may be associated with greater exposure of children and adolescents to other life adversities or potentially traumatic experiences that affect their mental health (Hatch and Dohrenwend, 2007). Such experiences are likely to be associated later in the life course with higher probabilities of cohabitation or single parenthood and, among the married, less marital stability over the life course (Avison, Davies, Willson, and Shuey, 2008; Davies, Avison, and McAlpine, 1997).

It is important to recognize, however, that the relationship between family structure and health and well-being is complicated. For example, S. Brown (2004) finds that children living with their married biological parents have higher levels of well-being than children living with their cohabiting biological parents. These differences, however, seem to be a function of married parents' greater economic resources than cohabiting parents. It is also interesting that children in married stepfamilies, cohabiting stepfamilies, and single-mother families all have similar levels of well-being. This research suggests that parents' marital status alone is not especially important for children's health.

S. Brown (2006) has also studied the effects of transitions in family structures on children's well-being. She finds that moving out of a cohabiting stepfamily into a single-mother family had little impact on children's well-being and actually improved school engagement. The transition from a single-mother family to a cohabiting stepfamily decreased adolescents' well-being more than for those who moved into a married stepfamily.

Heiland and Liu (2006) suggest that differences in children's health have less to do with the actual marital status of their parents and more to do with parental

Box 5.3

We can measure several aspects of the health of families: physical or mental health, family functioning, and quality of life.

There are two distinctive approaches to the measurement of mental health problems. The first is a **diagnostic approach** that relies on patterns of psychiatric symptoms and decision rules to arrive at a specific diagnosis. The assessment is typically conducted by a psychiatrist or psychologist, and results in a specific diagnosis that is categorized as present or absent. A second approach is more **dimensional** in nature. This method involves a checklist of behavioral and emotional symptoms that is used to characterize an individual as exhibiting more or less of a particular mental health problem.

A major problem with the measurement of children's mental health is that parents' ratings do not always correspond to teachers' ratings or to children's self-reports. This may be because parents' own mental health affects their judgments or because parents and teachers base their assessments on different "time samples" of children's lives.

The challenge with measuring children's physical health is that most children are relatively healthy and the illnesses they experience are typically mild and transient. This makes it difficult to adequately assess the wide range of health issues that children may experience. Most studies of children's physical health examine specific chronic conditions that have been diagnosed by a health professional (asthma, epilepsy, cerebral palsy, etc.). Alternatively, parents may be asked about the number of days in a given time period that children's usual activities, like attending school, were limited. A global measure of general health, in which parents rate their child's health along a four- or five-point scale from poor to excellent, is also commonly used.

Measures of adult physical health are typically based on global self-report measures. More recently, health psychologists have also taken physiological measures such as cortisol levels from salivary samples, blood sugar levels and protein levels from blood samples, and blood pressure readings. These provide direct measures of health problems that are not biased by individuals' self-reports.

resources and background characteristics. This highlights the debate over whether family structure is a cause of social disadvantage or a consequence.

It is important to recognize that the relationships among social disadvantage, family structure, and family health are complex processes. To better understand these processes, we need to accurately measure parents' and children's health and develop conceptual models that enable us to make sense of these complexities.

Conceptual Models for Understanding Disparities in Family Health

A number of conceptual models have been developed to understand how family disadvantage is related to health disparities. We highlight two: the bioecological model of human development (Bronfenbrenner,

1979, 2005) and the stress process model (Pearlin, 1989). Both perspectives emphasize the interaction between individuals and their environment to show how social disparities translate into health disparities. These models provide the framework and research designs for testing the link between family disadvantage and health.

The bioecological model of human development consists of four interrelated principles: *process, person, context,* and *time*. Central to the model are *proximal processes,* which are the mechanisms that influence human development (Bronfenbrenner, 2005). These processes refer to the interaction between persons and their environment, which includes other people, symbols, and objects. The strength and direction of the relationship between proximal processes and developmental outcomes varies according to person characteristics, such as individual traits and attributes, the social context, and time frame in which these processes unfold.

Bronfenbrenner argues that the effect of proximal processes on developmental outcomes varies across different environmental contexts. Bronfenbrenner and Morris (2006) cite the unpublished research of Small and Luster (1990), who examined the relationship between parental involvement and children's educational achievement in three family contexts: children living with a single parent, two biological parents, and a mother and stepfather. Results indicate that disparities in children's educational achievement across different family structures are reduced at higher levels of parent involvement. In other words, parental involvement buffers the effects of living in a single-parent household on children's educational achievement. The relationship between parental involvement and school grades also differed as a function of person characteristics, particularly the child's gender. Parental involvement had a stronger influence on girls compared to boys. This gender difference was greater in families with two biological parents and less evident in households headed by a single mother.

The stress process model consists of three components: *sources of stress, mediators and moderators of stress,* and *manifestations of stress* (Pearlin, 1989). Life events such as the death of a loved one or loss of a job and chronic strains such as persistent poverty constitute important sources of stress. Conceptually, mediators are similar to proximal processes; they are the mechanisms or pathways through which stressful circumstances affect psychological well-being. For example, parents who experience financial problems (a chronic stressor) may experience more marital conflict and exhibit harsh and inconsistent parenting, which may have adverse consequences for children's psychological well-being (Conger and Donnellan, 2007). Thus, marital conflict and harsh parenting are mediators.

The effect of exposure to stressors on individuals' health varies a great deal. Two people can experience the same stressor, but its effects on their health may differ substantially, with some experiencing elevated health problems while others are only minimally affected. This happens because personal and social resources may moderate or buffer the effects of stress on health. For example, social support may function as a protective factor against the stressful consequences of divorce.

Manifestations of stress include all the potential physical and mental health outcomes that may result from stress exposure. One of the appealing aspects of the stress process model is that it can be applied to a wide range of health outcomes.

Bronfenbrenner distinguishes between proximal processes and environmental contexts, and argues that these processes influence developmental outcomes to a greater extent than the context in which they occur. In contrast, Pearlin emphasizes that the stress process does not occur in a vacuum, but rather is inextricably linked to the social context in which it unfolds. In particular, stress exposure is socially patterned so that the most disadvantaged individuals in society – the poor, the unemployed, racial and ethnic minority groups, and those who live in the most disadvantaged neighborhoods – are disproportionately exposed to stressors that undermine both their physical and mental health. Disadvantaged people may also have less access to financial, personal, and social resources that may reduce the effects of stress. An individual's location in the social structure is defined by the various status characteristics they may hold, which may include, for example, age, gender, marital status, socioeconomic status, and race/ethnicity. It is also defined by the roles they occupy, such as spouse or parent or worker.

The bioecological model of human development (Bronfenbrenner, 2005) stipulates that the association between proximal processes and developmental outcomes is bidirectional, with the environmental context influencing individuals and vice versa. For example, Bronfenbrenner describes three biopsychological characteristics of the person that influence the strength and direction of the relationship between proximal processes and human development: *dispositions, resources,* and *demand characteristics.* Dispositions refer to individual behaviors and characteristics, such as empathy, sociability, aggression, and withdrawnness, that may either initiate and maintain or restrict and delay proximal processes. Resources such as knowledge, skills, and capacities are required to participate in proximal processes, and for these processes to effectively influence developmental outcomes. Demand characteristics, such as children's temperament (e.g. fussy vs. happy), may encourage or inhibit responses from the environment and the individuals situated within it, thereby promoting or impeding the effect of proximal processes on development. It is in this way that individual traits and attributes moderate the effects of proximal processes on developmental outcomes.

Pearlin (1989) emphasizes that the effects of stress on one health outcome may not be generalizable to other outcomes because certain subgroups of the population may be affected by specific disorders to a greater or lesser extent than the general population. For example, studies consistently show that internalizing disorders, such as depression and anxiety, are more prevalent among women, whereas externalizing disorders, such as substance abuse and antisocial behavior, are more prevalent among men (Aneshensel, Rutter, and Lachenbruch, 1991).

Similarly, Bronfenbrenner notes that the effects of proximal processes may vary with the developmental outcomes under investigation. In particular, he distinguishes between positive outcomes such as intellectual and emotional growth (*developmental competence*) and negative outcomes such as behavioral and psychological problems (*development dysfunction*). In disadvantaged social contexts, proximal processes exert their greatest influence by minimizing developmental dysfunction; in advantaged social contexts, proximal process will have a more pronounced effect on developmental competence. Small and Luster (1990) show that the effects of parental involvement on academic achievement (an indicator of developmental competence) are stronger in households with two biological parents and where mothers have more than a high-school education.

More recently, the stress process and the bioecological model of human development have been expanded to incorporate a life course perspective (Bronfenbrenner and Morris, 2006; Elder, Johnson, and Crosnoe, 2003; Pearlin, Schieman, Fazio, and Meersman, 2005). In this context, both models highlight continuity and change in stress-related and developmental outcomes. Because social contexts are subject to change over time, so is the relationship between individuals and their environment. For example, research by McLeod and Shanahan (1996) demonstrates that children who are exposed to long-term poverty over the life course exhibit higher levels of psychological distress than children who experience short-term poverty. In other words, change or improvement in social circumstances, such

as movement out of poverty, has a positive impact on children's health and well-being.

Viewed from a stress process and life course framework, early experiences and status locations influence later stress exposure. Given that various life domains are interrelated, Pearlin emphasizes that stressors do not occur in isolation from other life circumstances. Thus, stress may generate additional stress, a process referred to as *stress proliferation*. Processes of stress proliferation are ideally examined within a life course perspective because they necessarily transpire over an extended period of time.

In demonstrating how the bioecological model of human development operates over time, Bronfenbrenner argues that proximal processes occurring earlier in the life course influence later proximal processes. For example, children exposed to positive parent–child relationships replicate this behavior in future interactions with others. Drawing upon research by Drillien (1957, 1964), Bronfenbrenner notes that children continuously exposed to negative parental interactions experience an exponential growth in behavioral problems over time, whereas children exposed to more positive parental interactions demonstrate only a minimal increase.

Age and developmental stage are central to the life course perspective, and may be important moderating factors in the stress process and bioecological model of human development. Childhood and adolescence represent critical periods of development, thus the negative effects of stress associated with family disadvantage may be particularly pronounced during this stage of the life course. For example, research indicates that effects of early economic deprivation on children's mental health persist over time despite increases in socioeconomic status later in life (McLeod and Shanahan, 1996).

The concept of *linked lives* is a core premise of the life course perspective and refers to the way in which individual lives are interconnected (Elder *et al.*, 2003). Stressors experienced by one individual can permeate the lives of others, particularly those who are in their immediate environment, such as family members. As Bronfenbrenner so clearly illustrates, parent–child interactions are one of the most important mechanisms linking the environment to developmental outcomes. Parents experiencing stress related to financial hardship may interact in negative ways with their children. Given that children share environments with their parents, and thus experience the same stressors associated with this environment, the concept of linked lives provides an important framework for understanding how family disadvantage translates into health disparities.

A life course perspective highlights the long-term impact of family disadvantage that operates through processes of cumulative disadvantage. Family disadvantage increases the risk for early onset of emotional and behavioral problems that may be exacerbated over time through exposure to additional stressors and adverse life events (Avison, 2010b; Grant et al., 2003). For example, children exposed to single parenthood before the age of 16 are at elevated risk for anxiety disorder, and are more likely to have lower educational attainment, to receive social assistance, and to be involved in criminal behavior between the ages of 21 and 25 (Fergusson, Boden, and Horwood, 2007). In this study, the long-term effects of single parenthood were explained by conditions in the family of origin, including socioeconomic status, exposure to violence, parental substance use, and mothers' age at birth. The risk for negative outcomes in adulthood increased in relation to the number of stressors experienced over the life course (Fergusson and Horwood, 2003).

The Central Role of Stressful Experiences

There is widespread agreement that disparities in family health are importantly related to differences among families in the stressors that they experience. In this context, it is important to recognize the wide range of stressful experiences that occur to individuals. Social scientists who study disparities in family health argue that socioeconomically disadvantaged families are likely to experience a greater number of these various stressors and that these ultimately erode the mental and physical health of parents and children alike. Wheaton (1994) has argued for the need to measure stressful experiences in a comprehensive manner. His idea is that the *stress universe* includes a wide range of different kinds of negative social experiences: stressful life events such as the death of a loved

one or the loss of a job; chronic role strains such as ongoing marital conflict or work stress; sudden traumas such as experiencing a natural disaster; daily hassles like long commutes to work; and ambient stressors such as living in noisy or run-down neighborhoods.

For most people, many of these stressors are ultimately experienced in the context of the family even if they initially occur on the job or at school or in the neighborhood. Thus, stressors that emerge out of socioeconomic disadvantage or that are the result of the experience of discrimination often play out among family members in the home.

Survey researchers have documented high levels of exposure to an array of different stressors among socially disadvantaged groups (Turner and Avison, 2003; Turner, Wheaton, and Lloyd, 1995). These studies found that younger people are more exposed to a variety of stressors than are older respondents. They also reported that members of racial/ethnic minority groups and individuals in lower compared to higher socioeconomic status positions in society encounter more stress in their daily lives. In their view, this clearly indicates that stressors are not experienced randomly in the population. Quite the contrary, results revealed that there is a *social distribution of stressors* characterized by greater exposure among members of disadvantaged social groups. This greater exposure to stressors among specific groups gives us clues to the sources of health disparities in families.

The growing awareness of the significance of multiple dimensions of stress for individuals' health has stimulated considerable research. The effects of adversities in childhood and adolescence on mental health problems in adulthood have attracted attention from a number of scientists (G. Brown and Moran, 1997; Davies et al., 1997; Hatch and Dohrenwend, 2007). This has generated a number of attempts to conceptualize and measure childhood adversities as a source of stress.

Burton (2007) has reported that children from disadvantaged families are at increased risk for *adultification*, which refers to ways in which children are required to assume adult roles and responsibilities to satisfy family needs (see also Chapter 11 in this volume). Adultification occurs most frequently among children with divorced, low-income, substance-dependent, and/or physically or mentally ill

Box 5.4

At age 7, Drenika began managing the household because Elizabeth stopped receiving day care subsidies. When many other children her age are out with their friends, Drenika is cooking meals and caring for her older brother, who is developmentally delayed. Elizabeth's children have also witnessed a tremendous amount of violence, including the drug-related shooting of a close family friend in their very own backyard.

parents. These children may take on primary responsibility for their siblings, provide health care to a sick parent, work to increase the household income, and provide emotional support to parents. Adultification also involves early exposure to adult knowledge and experiences, such as financial stress in low-income families, and violence and disorder in high-risk neighborhoods. Because adultified children take on roles and responsibilities that contradict normative behaviors for children in North American society, they often experience conflict between their roles at home and in other social spheres, such as school.

Other researchers have developed measures of perceived discrimination to add to inventories of stress. Kessler, Mickelson, and Williams (1999) have created measures of both lifetime discrimination and day-to-day perceived discrimination. These measures have effects on health that are comparable to other, more commonly studied stressors.

Still others have drawn attention to more ambient stressors that are characteristic of people's experiences in neighborhoods with high rates of crime and social disorder. Aneshensel and Sucoff (1996) and Ross and Mirowsky (2001) describe how the perception that one's neighborhood is dangerous is associated with higher levels of psychological distress.

With a steadily growing set of measures of stress, scientists are now better able than ever to describe how exposure to stressors varies by individuals' levels of social advantage or disadvantage in terms of their age, gender, race/ethnicity, and social class. The mapping of these social distributions of stress is extremely important, because it is now apparent that the negative impact of stressful experience on health is more substantial than had been estimated previously.

Protective Factors and Resilience

Throughout this chapter, we have emphasized the central role of stressful experiences to explain disparities in family health. Disadvantaged families encounter many more stressful experiences than do more affluent families and these stressors typically have adverse health effects. However, individuals demonstrate tremendous variation in their response to stressful experiences and the majority transcend the negative effects of family disadvantage (Fergusson and Horwood, 2003).

Resilience is defined as the capacity to overcome these aversive conditions. Some years ago, Luthar, Cicchetti, and Becker (2000) argued that individuals were resilient if they showed better than expected health outcomes, if they were able to adapt positively in the face of stressful experiences, or if they experienced good recovery from a traumatic event.

Much of the research on resilience focuses on how various protective factors interact with stressful conditions to produce positive outcomes. For example, protective factors may exert their strongest influence in the presence of adverse conditions. In other words, the positive effect of protective factors is more pronounced among individuals exposed to stress, but otherwise may have little to no effect independently of such exposure. This is consistent with Bronfenbrenner's (2005) model of development, which stipulates that proximal processes will have their greatest influence in disadvantaged contexts.

The effects of stress exposure may also vary across individuals. On the one hand, stressful family experiences may increase children's and adults' vulnerability to future stress and increase the likelihood of negative health outcomes (Rutter, 1985). This type of response to stress is referred to as a *sensitizing effect*. On the other hand, repeated exposure to stressors may serve to strengthen rather than weaken some individuals and may alter their response to subsequent stress, thereby decreasing the likelihood for a negative health outcome. This type of response to stress is referred to as a *steeling effect*.

Research on the dynamics of resilience typically focuses on *vulnerability* and *protective* factors that modify the impact of adversity on outcome. Vulnerability factors exacerbate the negative effects of adversity; protective factors ameliorate the negative effects.

Contemporary work on resilience has identified a number of circumstances in which the effects of vulnerability and protective factors vary by social context at the macro-level. So, for example, supportive relationships with teachers may positively affect the well-being of children living in urban poverty, but have lesser impact on more affluent children (DuBois, Felner, Meares, and Krier, 1994; Luthar, 1999).

At a more micro-level, contexts also condition the effects of vulnerability and protective factors. For example, Dumas and Wekerle (1995) have documented how disruptive child behaviors influence negative parenting reactions among most mothers, but not among those living in poverty. Presumably, the wide array of chronic strains experienced by mothers living in poverty makes disruptive child behaviors less salient.

With respect to personal resources that facilitate resilience, self-esteem and mastery are important protective factors that help children cope with early adversities. Fergusson and Horwood (2003), for example, find that high levels of self-esteem among children exposed to family disadvantage, including financial strain, conflict, and impaired parenting, decrease the likelihood of developing mental health problems. Furthermore, children who employ strategies to effectively deal with the stress associated with family disadvantage, particularly if these strategies involve building social support, demonstrate better adjustment (Sandler, Tein, and West, 1994).

Drawing upon Bronfenbrenner, Moen and Erickson (1995) offer a linked-lives approach to resilience. This approach emphasizes the connection between parents' and children's lives and the complex interaction between socialization and status attainment processes. It demonstrates how resilience is transmitted across generations. The socialization perspective stipulates that children learn how to be resilient by observing their parents' effective coping strategies. The status attainment perspective argues that children benefit from their parents' socioeconomic background. Parental socioeconomic status provides opportunities to acquire important social and economic resources

that influence children's development, particularly their self-esteem, mastery, and social integration. In addition, a life course framework highlights long-term processes that unfold over time. Resilience is dynamic and is shaped both by childhood and adult life experiences. For example, circumstances in adulthood, including educational, occupational, and marital status, may further contribute to the development of personal and social resources obtained in childhood, and may also moderate stressful childhood experiences that depleted these resources.

A life course perspective also illustrates the connection between childhood and adult experiences. Many children who experience family disadvantage grow up to be healthy and productive adults. According to Fergusson and Horwood (2003), it may be long-term processes of cumulative disadvantage that distinguish individuals at high risk for adult mental health problems from those who are not. In other words, individuals who experience a greater number of stressful experiences over the life course, ranging from divorce, compromised parenting, and abuse in childhood to later educational and occupational difficulties, are at greatest risk for health problems in adulthood. In contrast, individuals who overcome childhood disadvantage and exhibit resilience in adulthood are exposed to fewer stressors and are able to mobilize greater number of protective resources over the life course.

Contextual Influences

Disparities in family health do not occur in a vacuum. Differences in health outcomes between more and less advantaged families are also influenced by other social contexts. Perhaps the most noteworthy influences are the effects of neighborhoods and the effects of schools.

For some time, scientists have studied how neighborhoods affect individuals' well-being. Although much of this research has focused on adults, Aneshensel (2010) has conducted a program of research that documents the importance of the neighborhood context for the mental health of adolescents. She finds that the socioeconomic character of neighborhoods modifies the effect of social support on adolescent mental health. Among children living in disadvantaged neighborhoods, social support from friends and family made no difference on their psychological well-being. By contrast, the experience of social support had a more substantial, positive impact on the mental health of adolescents living in more affluent neighborhoods. Thus, the neighborhood context influences the way in which social support affects young people's psychological well-being.

In a very interesting study, Wheaton and Clarke (2003) show how the neighborhoods in which children grow up have important influences not only for mental health in childhood, but also for mental health in adulthood. They show how neighborhood disadvantages compromise parent–child relationships and childhood mental health, which, in turn, results in poorer mental health in adulthood.

In their study of adolescents in Chicago, Dupere, Leventhal, and Vitaro (2012) document how living in violent neighborhoods exposes adolescents to situations that are perceived as unsafe, unpredictable, and out of their control. These experiences erode these young persons' sense of self-efficacy, and this, in turn, increases their symptoms of depression and anxiety. Among those children who moved out of these neighborhoods to safer communities, self-efficacy increased and their symptoms decreased. This is a convincing example of how neighborhood context may influence adolescents' mental health.

Similar patterns have been well documented among adults. Research demonstrates how both actual and perceived neighborhood disorganization influence the mental health of persons of all ages (Ross and Mirowsky, 2001; Samson, Morenoff, and Gannon-Rowly, 2002; Samson, Raudenbush, and Earls, 1997). Thus, it seems clear that the kinds of neighborhoods in which families live can exacerbate or moderate the effects of social disparities on the health of children and their parents.

Closely related to this topic is the impact of schools on children's health. Because children spend significant portions of each day in school, it should not be surprising that this context is so important for their health. Foster and Brooks-Gunn (2009) point out that schools can provide the kinds of protective environments that emphasize positive role models, social support, and prosocial behavior. In schools that effectively foster this protective climate, the impact of disadvantage and adversity on children's health is

---

Box 5.5

Elizabeth's children go to schools that are plagued with problems. Drenika's school lacks resources, and although she would like to participate in extracurricular activities, there are none available. Students are not even allowed to bring books home to study. Dernard is in fourth grade. He reads at a seventh-grade level, but does not receive the intellectual stimulation needed to reach his academic potential. Perhaps the biggest challenge for Elizabeth is finding a good school for her learning-disabled son, Wayne. Thankfully, an attorney worked pro bono to help Elizabeth have Wayne removed from a school where the teachers could not meet his special needs.

---

moderated. By contrast, in schools that are poorly managed or where bullying occurs and safety is an issue, the effects of social disparities on children's health may be magnified.

Conclusions

Social disparities in health are pervasive in many if not most societies. There is substantial evidence that less well-educated and less affluent persons in our society, as well as members of racial/ethnic minority groups, are more likely to experience physical and mental health problems than are the more advantaged. Link and Phelan (1995) have argued that these socioeconomic disadvantages function as *fundamental causes* of health disparities. These operate at both the individual and family level. These disadvantages are "fundamental" because they have a massive array of social and psychological consequences, all of which contribute to disparities in both physical and mental health.

Both the stress process model and the bioecological model of human development identify consequences of socioeconomic disadvantage that contribute to poor health. In the stress process, the emphasis is on exposure to a wide range of stressors that challenge the mental and physical health of children and their parents. Stress exposure erodes individuals' sense of personal control and their levels of self-esteem. These experiences result in higher levels of psychological distress and other mental health problems. Over time, these processes also contribute to declining physical health. The bioecological model emphasizes how children's development and mental health are influenced by factors operating on many different levels: the individual, the family, the institutional, and the societal level.

It seems clear that social disadvantage exposes children and their parents to many more stressors than is the case within more advantaged families. This differential exposure seems to account for much of the observed disparities in health between poor and more affluent families. Nevertheless, there is also strong evidence that some families are more resilient to these stressors than others. This resilience in the face of adversity explains how some children and their parents withstand the effects of stress.

Implications for intervention programs and social policy

The research that has focused on socioeconomic disparities in family health clearly has a number of important implications for public policies that attempt to reduce these disparities. At the broadest level, some researchers have suggested that policies that reduce inequalities in resources will reduce disparities in health. Phelan, Link, and Tehranifar (2010) argue that initiatives such as low-income housing programs, increases in the minimum wage, parenting leaves, and head-start programs are all likely to reduce disparities between the poor and the more affluent. They believe that these reductions in economic disparities will reduce health disparities.

Other scientists have suggested a number of policies that focus directly on resilience and child well-being. Ager (2013) has presented a very comprehensive review of the public policy recommendations developed by researchers interested in studying resilience. Ager identifies six major themes that have emerged from this research:

1. increasing the capacity for counseling and mental health services;

2. developing curricula and teachers' skills that encourage supportive school environments;
3. promoting socioeconomic developments (similar to those suggested by Phelan *et al.*, 2010);
4. strengthening family dynamics and parenting skills;
5. developing community-based programs that integrate health, recreational, and after-school initiatives; and
6. adopting a comprehensive conception of resilience.

Two points seem important to emphasize about public policy aimed at reducing or eradicating social disparities in family health. First, it is clear that no single policy or intervention is likely to successfully address these problems. Just as the sources of socioeconomic disparities and their effects occur on many levels, so too do the strategies for reducing them. Second, attempts to reduce social disparities in family health will require the complementary efforts of multi-disciplinary teams from community health, social and psychological services, education, and other areas of expertise.

As we develop a stronger knowledge base for understanding how social disparities translate into disparities in family health, we are better positioned as a society to address these complex problems. Increasingly, the information that scientists have generated on social disparities in family health is influencing the policies and programs that our society implements to address this most important issue that affects the health of so many children and their parents.

Critical Thinking Questions

1. Drawing upon Elizabeth Jones's story presented at the beginning and throughout this chapter, answer the following questions using the information you have just learned.
   (a) How would you explain the cause of social disadvantage experienced by the Jones family?
   (b) What are some of the health and mental health consequences that Elizabeth and her children may experience as a result of their disadvantaged position?
   (c) Should Elizabeth be concerned that her children will experience similar disadvantage when they grow up? Why or why not?

2. Thinking about your own community and the people who live there, answer the following questions.
    (a) Can you identify any families experiencing social disadvantage? Who are they and what are the sources of their disadvantage?
    (b) Are these families at risk for health and mental health problems? Why or why not?
    (c) In what ways do the schools in your community reduce or increase disadvantages between families?

3. Imagine you are a policy analyst and your job is to reduce health disparities between advantage and disadvantaged families.
    (a) Despite all of her efforts, why are Elizabeth and her children still struggling financially?
    (b) In addition to helping single mothers find jobs, what other policy initiatives are needed to reduce poverty and help families gain self-sufficiency?
    (c) How can we promote resilience and reduce the risk of health problems among children and parents in disadvantaged families?

References

Ager, A. (2013). Annual research review. Resilience and child well-being: Public policy implications. *Journal of Child Psychology and Psychiatry, 54*, 488–500.

Aneshensel, C. S. (2010). Neighborhood as a social context of the stress process. In W. R. Avison, C. S. Aneshensel, S. Schieman, and B. Wheaton (eds), *Advances in the conceptualization of the stress process: Essays in honor of Leonard I. Pearlin* (pp. 35–52). New York: Springer.

Aneshensel, C. S., Rutter, C. M., and Lachenbruch, P. A. (1991). Social structure, stress, and mental health: Competing conceptual and analytic models. *American Sociological Review, 56*, 166–178.

Aneshensel, C. S., and Sucoff, C. A. (1996). The neighborhood context of adolescent mental health. *Journal of Health and Social Behavior, 37*, 293–310.

Avison, W. R. (2010a). Family structure and women's lives: A life course perspective. In W. R. Avison, C. S. Aneshensel, S. Schieman, and B. Wheaton (eds), *Advances in the conceptualization of the stress process: Essays in honor of Leonard I. Pearlin* (pp. 71–92). New York: Springer.

Avison, W. R. (2010b). Incorporating children's lives into the stress process model. *Journal of Health and Social Behavior, 51*, 361–375.

Avison, W. R., Ali, J., and Walters, D. (2007). Family structure, stress, and psychological distress: A demonstration of the impact of differential exposure. *Journal of Health and Social Behavior, 48*, 301–314.

Avison, W. R., Davies, L., Willson, A., and Shuey, K. (2008). Family structure and mothers' mental health: A life course perspective on stability and change. In H. A. Turner and S. Schieman (eds), *Stress processes across the life course: Advances in life course research*, vol. 13 (pp. 233–255). New York: Elsevier.

Benzeval, M. (1998). The self-reported health status of lone parents. *Social Science and Medicine, 46*, 1337–53.

Bianchi, S. M., and Casper, L. M. (2000). American families. *Population Bulletin, 55*, 3–43.

Boo, K. (2001). After welfare. *New Yorker,* April 9, 93–107.

Braman, D. (2004). *Doing time on the outside: Incarceration and family life in urban America.* Ann Arbor, MI: University of Michigan Press.

Bronfenbrenner, U. (1979). *The ecology of human development: Experiments by nature and design.* Cambridge, MA: Harvard University Press.

Bronfenbrenner, U. (2005). *Making human beings human: Bioecological perspectives on human development.* Thousand Oaks, CA: Sage Publications.

Bronfenbrenner, U., and Morris, P. A. (2006). The bioecological model of human development. In R. M. Lerner and W. Damon (eds), *Handbook of child psychology* (6th edn) (pp. 793–828). Hoboken, NJ: John Wiley & Sons, Inc.

Brown, G. W., and Moran, P. M. (1997). Single mothers, poverty, and depression. *Psychological Medicine, 27*, 21–33.

Brown, S. L. (2004). Family structure and child well-being: The significance of parental cohabitation. *Journal of Marriage and Family, 66*, 351–367.

Brown, S. L. (2006). Family structure transitions and adolescent well-being. *Demography, 43*, 447–461.

Burton, L. (2007). Childhood adultification in economically disadvantaged families: A conceptual model. *Family Relations, 56*, 329–345.

Carlson, M. J., and Furstenberg, F. F. (2006). Prevalence and correlates of multi-partnered fertility among urban U.S. parents. *Journal of Marriage and Family, 68*, 718–732.

Carlson, M. J., and Furstenberg, F. F. (2007). The consequences of multi-partnered fertility for parental involvement and relationships. Working Paper no. 2006–28–FF, Center for Research on Child Wellbeing, Princeton, NJ.

Conger, R. D., and Donnellan, B. M. (2007). An interactionist perspective on the socioeconomic context of human development. *Annual Review of Psychology, 58*, 175–199.

Davies, L., Avison, W. R., and McAlpine, D. D. (1997). Significant life experiences and depression among single and married mothers. *Journal of Marriage and the Family, 59*, 294–308.

Demo, D. H., and Acock, A. (1996). Singlehood, marriage, and remarriage: The effects of family structure and family relationships on mothers' well-being. *Journal of Family Issues, 17*, 388–407.

Drillien, C. M. (1957). The social and economic factors affecting the incidence of premature birth. *Journal of Obstetrical Gynecology, British Empire, 64*, 161–184.

Drillien, C. M. (1964). *Growth and development of the prematurely born infant.* Edinburgh, UK: Livingstone.

DuBois, D. L., Felner, R. D., Meares, H., and Krier, M. (1994). Prospective investigation of the effects of socioeconomic disadvantage, life stress, and social support on early adolescent adjustment. *Journal of Abnormal Psychology, 103*, 511–522.

Dumas, J. E., and Wekerle, C. (1995). Maternal reports and child behaviour problems and personal distress as predictors of dysfunctional parenting. *Development and Psychopathology, 7*, 465–479.

Dupere, V., Leventhal, T., and Vitaro, F. (2012). Neighborhood processes, self-efficacy, and adolescent mental health. *Journal of Health and Social Behavior, 53*, 183–198.

Dupre, M. E., and Meadows, S. O. (2007). Disaggregating the effects of marital trajectories on health. *Journal of Family Issues, 28*, 623–652.

Elder, G. H., Jr., Johnson, M. K., and Crosnoe, R. (2003). The emergence and development of life course theory. In J. Mortimer and M. Shanahan (eds), *Handbook of the life course* (pp. 3–19). New York: Kluwer.

Ellwood, D. T., and Jencks, C. (2004). The spread of single-parent families in the United States since 1960. In D. P. Moynihan, T. M. Smeeding, and L. Rainwater (eds), *The future of the family* (pp. 25–650). New York: Russell Sage Foundation.

Fergusson, D. M., Boden, J. M., and Horwood, L. J. (2007). Exposure to single parenthood in childhood and later mental health, educational, economic, and criminal behavior outcomes. *Archives of General Psychiatry, 64*, 1089–1095.

Fergusson, D. M., and Horwood, L. J. (2003). Resilience to childhood adversity: Results of a 21-year study. In S. S. Luthar (ed.), *Resilience and vulnerability: Adaptation in the context of childhood adversities* (pp. 130–155). Cambridge, UK: Cambridge University Press.

Foster, H., and Brooks-Gunn, J. (2009). Toward a stress process model of children's exposure to physical family and community violence. *Clinical Child and Family Psychology Review, 12*, 71–94.

Gassman-Pines, A., and Yoshikawa, H. (2006). Five-year effects of an anti-poverty program on marriage among never-married mothers. *Journal of Policy Analysis and Management, 25*, 11–30.

Grant, K. E., Compas, B. E., Stuhlmacher, A. F., Thurm, A. E., McMahon, S. D., and Halpert, J. A. (2003). Stressors and child and adolescent psychopathology: Moving from markers to mechanisms of risk. *Psychological Bulletin, 129*, 447–466.

Halpern-Meekin, S., and Tach, L. (2008). Heterogeneity in two-parent families and adolescent well-being. *Journal of Marriage and Family, 70*, 435–451.

Hatch, S. L., and Dohrenwend, B. P. (2007). Distribution of traumatic and other stressful life events by race/ethnicity, gender, SES and age: A review of the research. *American Journal of Community Psychology, 40*, 313–332.

Heiland, F., and Liu, S. H. (2006). Family structure and well-being of out-of-wedlock children: The significance of the biological parents' relationship. *Demographic Research, 15*, 61–104.

Kennedy, S., and Bumpass, L. (2007). Cohabitation and children's living arrangements: New estimates from the United States. *Demographic Research, 19*, 1663–1692.

Kessler, R. C., Mickelson, K. D., and Williams, D. R. (1999). The prevalence, distribution, and mental health correlates of perceived discrimination in the United States. *Journal of Health and Social Behavior, 40*, 208–230.

Le Bourdais, C., and Lapierre-Adamcyk, E. (2004). Changes in conjugal life in Canada: Is cohabitation progressively replacing marriage? *Journal of Marriage and Family, 66*, 929–942.

Lesthaege, R., and Neidert, L. (2006). The second demographic transition in the United States: Exception or textbook example? *Population and Development Review, 32*, 669–698.

Link, B. G., and Phelan, J. C. (1995). Social conditions as fundamental causes of disease. *Journal of Health and Social Behavior* Extra Issue, 80–94.

Luo, Z.-C., Wilkins, R., and Kramer, M. S. (2004). Effect of neighbourhood income and maternal education on birth outcomes: A population-based study. *Canadian Medical Association Journal, 174*, 1415–1421.

Luthar, S. S. (1999). *Poverty and children's adjustment.* Newbury Park, CA: Sage Publications.

Luthar, S. S., Cicchetti, D., and Becker, B. (2000). The construct of resilience: A critical evaluation and guideline for future work. *Child Development, 71*, 543–562

McLanahan, S. S. (2004). Diverging destinies: How children are faring under the second demographic transition. *Demography, 41*, 607–627.

McLanahan, S. S. (2009). Fragile families and the reproduction of poverty. *Annals of the American Academy of Political and Social Science, 621*, 111–131.

McLanahan, S. S., and Percheski, C. (2008). Family structure and the reproduction of inequalities. *Annual Review of Sociology, 34*, 257–276.

McLeod, J. D., and Shanahan, M. J. (1996). Trajectories of poverty and children's mental health. *Journal of Health and Social Behavior, 37*, 207–220.

Meadows, S. O., McLanahan, S. S., and Brooks-Gunn, J. (2008). Stability and change in family structure and maternal health trajectories. *American Sociological Review, 73*, 314–334.

Moen, P., and Erickson, M. A. (1995). Linked lives: A transgenerational approach to resilience. In P. Moen, G. H. Elder, Jr., and K. Luscher (eds), *Examining lives in context: Perspectives on the ecology of human development* (pp. 169–210). Washington, DC: American Sociological Association.

Musick, K. (2007). Cohabitation, nonmarital childbearing, and the marriage process. *Demographic Research, 16*, 249–286.

Pearlin, L. I. (1989). The sociological study of stress. *Journal of Health and Social Behavior, 30*, 241–256.

Pearlin, L. I., Schieman, S., Fazio, E. M., and Meersman, S. C. (2005). Stress, health, and the life course: Some conceptual perspectives. *Journal of Health and Social Behavior, 46*, 205–219.

Phelan, J. C., Link, B. G., and Tehranifar, P. (2010). Social conditions as fundamental causes of health inequalities: Theory, evidence, and policy implications. *Journal of Health and Social Behavior, 51*, S28–S40.

Raatikainen, K., Heiskanen, N., and Heinonen, S. (2005). Marriage still protects pregnancy. *BJOG: An International Journal of Obstetrics and Gynaecology, 112*, 1411–1416.

Raley, K. 2001. Increasing fertility in cohabiting unions: Evidence for the second demographic transition in the United States? *Demography, 38*, 59–66.

Ross, C. E., and Mirowsky, J. (2001). Neighborhood disadvantage, disorder, and health. *Journal of Health and Social Behavior, 42*, 258–276.

Rutter, M. (1985). Resilience in the face of adversity: Protective factors and resistance to psychiatric disorder. *British Journal of Psychiatry, 147*, 598–611.

Samson, R. J., Morenoff, J. D., and Gannon-Rowly, T. (2002). Assessing "neighborhood effects": Social processes and new directions in research. *Annual Review of Sociology, 28*, 442–478.

Samson, R. J., Raudenbush, S. W., and Earls, F. J. (1997). Neighborhoods and violent crime: A multilevel study of collective efficacy. *Science, 277*, 918–924.

Sandler, I. N., Tein, J. Y., and West, S. G. (1994). Coping, stress, and the psychological symptoms of children of divorce: A cross-sectional and longitudinal study. *Child Development, 65*, 1744–1763.

Simons, R. L., Johnson, C., and Lorenz, F. O. (1996). Family structure differences in stress and behavioral predispositions. In R. Simons and Associates (eds), *Understanding differences between divorced and intact families: Stress, interaction, and child outcome* (pp. 45–64). Thousand Oaks, CA: Sage Publications.

Small, S., and Luster, T. (1990, November). Youth at risk for parenthood. Paper presented at the Creating Caring Communities Conference, Michigan State University, East Lansing.

Turner, R. J., and Avison, W. R. (2003). Status variations in stress exposure among young adults: Implications for the interpretation of prior research. *Journal of Health and Social Behavior, 44*, 488–505.

Turner, R. J., Wheaton, B., and Lloyd, D. A. (1995). The epidemiology of social stress. *American Sociological Review, 60*, 104–124.

United States Census Bureau. (2011). Same-sex couple households. American Community Survey Briefs. Retrieved May 30, 2014 from http://www.census.gov/hhes/samesex/.

United States Census Bureau. (2012). Households and families 2010. 2010 Census Briefs. Retrieved May 30, 2014 from http://www.census.gov/prod/cen2010/briefs/c2010br-14.pdf.

Wheaton, B. (1994). The stress universe. In W. R. Avison and I. H. Gotlib (eds), *Stress and mental health: Contemporary issues and prospects for the future* (pp. 77–114). New York: Plenum.

Wheaton, B., and Clarke, P. (2003). Space meets time: Combining temporal and contextual influences. *American Sociological Review, 68*, 680–706.

Zeitlin, J. A., Saurel-Cubizolles, M.-J., and Ancel, P.-V. (2002). Marital status, cohabitation, and the risk of preterm birth in Europe: Where births outside marriage are common and uncommon. *Paediatric and Perinatal Epidemiology, 16*, 124–130.

6

Low-Income Fathers as Resilient Caregivers

Kevin M. Roy, Rob Palkovitz, and Damian Waters

Young disadvantaged men caught in an era of rising inequality are the focus of Chapter 6. Roy, Palkovitz, and Waters show how marginalization processes disconnect low-income men from mainstream fathering roles that are defined by the ability to "provide and reside." Though some young fathers drop out of their children's lives never to return, we learn here that resilient low-income fathers may walk a different fathering path that involves "being there," negotiating with children's mothers, and persisting in the face of economic adversity and social exclusion.

In the wake of economic recession across the globe, and after decades of critical shifts in how we work and live in communities and families, young disadvantaged men are perhaps the population most at risk for disconnection from work and family life that are the markers of successful adulthood. The number of low-income men (between the ages of 18 and 44 and living at twice the Federal Poverty Line) has grown 26%, from 13 million in 2000 to 16.5 million in 2010. This population accounts for 28% of all men living in the United States (McDaniel, Simms, Fortuny, and Monson, 2013).

Men may play a more significant role in family life as they take on normative roles as they age, and even many men who start out absent from their children's lives become more involved as they age. Townsend (2002) identified a set of normative roles – including marriage, home ownership, family-supportive employment, and fatherhood – as "the package deal." Under the best of circumstances, men's relationships require frequent adjustments and adaptations as men and family members change and develop and experience different circumstances, challenges, and resources (Palkovitz, 1987). However, achievement of a package deal is a challenge for many low-income men who are marginalized from their families and from mainstream employment. In effect, it was once common for poor fathers to be married and living with their children; in 2013, the large majority of poor fathers were unmarried and nonresidential, living very different lives and trying to maintain involvement as parents.

Poor fathers experience more critical transitions in and out of households, intimate relationships, father–child relationships, and employment than other fathers (Eggebeen and Uhlenberg, 1985; Mott, 1990). Men in these contexts report difficulties in overcoming

Family Problems: Stress, Risk, and Resilience, First Edition. Edited by Joyce A. Arditti.
© 2015 John Wiley & Sons, Inc. Published 2015 by John Wiley & Sons, Inc.

ecological factors, such as the lure of the street life, gang activity and police presence, drugs, and limited opportunity structures (Jarrett, Roy, and Burton, 2002; Roy, 2004). They may make positive life changes, but such gains can be tenuous, such as when a long-sought good job is lost, a cohabiting relationship with a partner falters, or depression sets in when money is tight. But in spite of unstable work engagement and low-quality relationships, some low-income men are not absent fathers. They "do for" their children through a range of financial, emotional, and physical support (Furstenberg, 1992; Hamer, 2001). How do some low-income men become resilient caregivers, even when facing a range of barriers?

In this chapter, we focus on the period of young men's lives from 18 to 30 years of age, and we explore the processes by which some fathers develop resilience, even in the face of prominent barriers to paternal involvement. We summarize findings on the marginalization of young, low-income men in urban communities and on caregiving and nurturance of children with extended kin and the mothers of their children. Further, we discuss how these fathers create strategies of resilience to stay involved with their children in challenging circumstances over time. We utilize life history interviews with 50 low-income fathers from Illinois and Indiana. Integrating life course and ecological approaches, we examine dimensions of three interrelated processes during this critical developmental period for young fathers: steeling and realistic adjustment of father role expectations; learning from past mistakes through maturation; and perseverance in "being there" consistently, often through reliance on stable support networks and resources.

Marginalization in an Era of Rising Inequality

Income inequality has grown substantially in the past three decades, and this era of rising inequality has reshaped the fortunes of young men who seek to establish themselves as good providers and family men. The economic fates of fathers have diverged dramatically since the 1970s, especially for young men without high-school degrees who do not live with

their children (Sum, Khatiwada, McLaughlin, and Palma, 2011). Recent economic crises have hit men in families hard, and what was once routine for many American men – a family-supportive wage, a lease on a house, a pension and health benefits – is no longer taken for granted. Changing labor markets and rising inequality have bifurcated populations of young fathers, not only by income, but by social class and across race (Furstenberg, 2011; Murray, 2012). It is important to note, in addition, that what is at issue is not the *status* of young men as "marginalized," but the *processes* of marginalization that move them repeatedly out of mainstream pathways to work and family life and into isolation (Roy and Jones, 2014).

Men's precarious position in the labor market threatens their ability to fulfill provider roles in traditional patterns (Johnson, 2010), particularly for younger fathers in a post-industrial workforce (Young, 2006). Stier and Tienda (1993) found that some non-residential fathers made great efforts to maintain regular contact with children and interact in ways that may positively contribute to their development, typically through in-kind contributions (also see Danziger and Radin, 1990; Mincy and Oliver, 2003). They often cannot contribute substantial fiscal child support (Amato and Gilbreth, 1999; McLanahan and Sandefur, 1994), which proves to be a deterrent to their continued involvement with their children (Roy, 2005). Lack of work and lack of access to good schools may lock these young adults into communities with few opportunities for advancement.

For low-income men who live in dangerous neighborhoods, navigation of gangs and police presence also present obstacles to free movement to be involved with their children. Dislocation and distance from children makes these fathers wary of commitment, in the midst of concern about intimate social relationships with peers (Roy, 2004). Daily life in low-income neighborhoods and disconnection from mainstream options put them at risk for incarceration, substance abuse, and domestic violence, each of which is negatively associated with men's involvement with mothers and children (Waller and Swisher, 2006).

However, fatherhood also presents low-income men in particular with an opportunity for "second chances" to rebuild their identities and daily routines around generative behavior, and to turn away from risky behavior (Roy and Lucas, 2007). Social institutions can also foster a context in which fathers can recover from risks. School attendance is a protective factor for young fathers who stayed in school (Weinman, Buzi, Smith, and Nevarez, 2007). For men who are unemployed and homeless, shelters provide behavioral and psychological boundaries within which fathers can build new parenting roles as well (Schindler and Coley, 2007).

As an integral aspect of the era of rising inequality, the mass incarceration of young men of color has undoubtedly deterred men's involvement with their children (Alexander, 2012). Many poor fathers spend the early years of their children's lives in and out of prison (Perry and Bright, 2012), and these men fared worse in employment, earning less and working fewer hours in underground and off-the-books jobs compared with never incarcerated fathers (Lewis, Garfinkel, and Gao, 2007). Incarceration forces men to confront starkly different expectations for being an inmate and being a father (Dyer, Pleck, and McBride, 2012). Fathering while doing prison time can be productive and generative, and men can be confident in their commitment to involvement and value of contact with their children (Roy, 2006). However, it is often not feasible to meet these expectations upon release, and the impacts of paternal incarceration are extensive. Children of incarcerated fathers show increased attention problems and aggressive behavior. Paternal incarceration has even stronger effects than father absence for children (Geller, Cooper, Garfinkel, Schwartz-Soicher, and Mincy, 2012). At the very least, the process of prisonization can lead fathers to experience stress and to practice more restrictive and harsh parenting upon release (Modecki and Wilson, 2009).

The real-life product of being marginalized may be that young fathers feel at risk for violence and isolation, while at the same time perceiving that their presence may be a risk to others close to them. The health effects of marginalization for these men may be most commonly expressed as depression, anger, and frustration. Although we may want to offer low-income fathers assistance with parenting and jobs, there is also an urgent need to offer mental health services (Fitzgerald, Roy, Anderson, and Letiecq, 2012). Depression is linked to parenting stress, and it decreases engagement with children, relationship quality with partners, and co-parenting support (Bronte-Tinkew, Moore, Matthews, and Carrano, 2007). One possible strategy to ameliorate depression for these men may be more active engagement with sons, including monitoring their safety and teaching them how to survive as young Black men in America, which increases personal mastery (Caldwell, Bell, Brooks, and Jennings, 2011). With the introduction of affordable health care in the United States, disadvantaged fathers may see more access, better resources, and potentially better health outcomes over time.

In sum, marginalization is not a simple process, and it has not resulted in clear distinctions between "good" and "bad" fathers. The different experiences of these men, as parents, partners, and workers, show how the heterogeneity of the population of disadvantaged fathers contradicts widely held assumptions that all have failed as fathers. For example, we have found that many low-income African American fathers integrate mainstream versions of manhood with street versions of manhood that emphasize independence, respect, and risk-taking that may run counter to what we associate with "good fathering" (Roy and Dyson, 2010). Through commitment to fathering that does not fit with mainstream expectations, these men reject stereotypes of the nonessential father, the deadbeat dad, and the "player" who runs in fear from commitment or marriage (Tamis-LeMonda and McFadden, 2010).

Caregiving and nurturance for low-income fathers

Much of what we know about father involvement has been based on the experience of White, middle- and working-class married men. Low-income fathers are more likely to show "complex" patterns of family formation and child-rearing that occur outside of marriage, across households, or within contexts of multiple-partner fertility (Furstenberg, 2011). For example, over a third of children in the United States live apart from their biological fathers, with higher proportions of poor children and children of color (DeBell, 2008). Some of these fathers also learned to care intensively for siblings and younger family members when they were adolescent "men of the house" (Roy, Messina, Smith, and Waters, 2014).

Lamb and colleagues' (1987) three-dimensional definition of father involvement (interaction, accessibility, responsibility) transformed how we think about what fathers do in families. Pleck (2010) recently highlighted men's positive engagement, warmth and responsiveness, and control – as well as indirect care and process responsibility, such as scheduling of doctor appointments or transportation. Similarly, father involvement can be framed as nurturance (Marsiglio and Roy, 2012), which moves us beyond a focus on "provide and reside," the popular notion of involved fathering that likely does not accurately describe the experiences of low-income fathers (Roy and Cabrera, 2009).

A key to increasing father involvement was quality relations with mothers (Ryan, Kalil, and Ziol-Guest, 2008). Despite the conflict between young parents that fathers often dub "babymama drama" (Roy and Dyson, 2005), mothers recruit biological fathers, as well as social fathers (usually non-biologically related boyfriends or male maternal kin), in search of an ideal model for their children, but are cautious about implications for intimacy and for the safety of their children (Roy and Burton, 2007). Relationship histories of young mothers can be important for understanding dynamics in subsequent partnering relationships. Moreover, fathers often respond and adjust their involvement in relation to mothers' decisions. Low-income nonresidential men are likely to end contact with their children if mothers find new partners (Guzzo, 2009), but not if fathers themselves find new partners.

Over many years, the commitment of low-income parents to raise children by remaining "together" as co-parents may take priority over a commitment to being "*together*" in a committed marital relationship (Roy, Buckmiller, and McDowell, 2008). Maternal support for father involvement in the first year after birth leads to more father engagement with children at age 3 (Fagan and Palkovitz, 2011). Regardless of the romantic status of these relationships, communication across households and co-parenting quality remains a strong predictor of future involvement for nonresidential fathers (Carlson, McLanahan, and Brooks-Gunn, 2008).

If men care for pregnant partners and provide resources and support prenatally, they are more likely to be engaged fathers up to three years later (Cabrera, Fagan, and Farrie, 2008). Bronte-Tinkew and colleagues (2007) also find that prenatal intentions are a vital aspect in predicting involvement for low-income fathers. Men who did not want their partners to carry pregnancies to term were less likely to show paternal warmth to their children. Cabrera, Cook, McFadden, and Bradley (2011) show that the quality of a father's relationship with his child in fifth grade predicted children's behavioral problems and peer relationship quality. Residence with children, however, had no long-term links to social development.

Disadvantaged urban men, men with depression, men with limited educational attainment, and unmarried or minority men are more likely to have children with multiple partners (Bronte-Tinkew, Ryan, Franzetta, Manlove, and Lilja, 2009), which presents another set of challenges for father involvement. About a third of men who have multiple children with multiple partners are involved in non-marital relationships, and that pattern is increasing. These men also tend to be younger at their first sexual activity or their first birth (Manlove, Logan, Ikramullah, and Holcombe, 2008). However, multiple-partner fertility is not primarily a problematic father behavior. Compared to unmarried fathers, mothers in low-income families are more likely to have a second child with a different partner (Guzzo and Hayford, 2010). For mothers or fathers, multiple-partner fertility is associated with negative child outcomes.

Young low-income fathers' involvement with their children is also shaped in important ways by an extended family network, including both maternal and paternal kin. In some ways, a father's involvement is secured most clearly by the investment of his own family members, such as his own mother (Roy and Smith, 2012; Roy and Vesely, 2009). The involvement of younger fathers in particular depends heavily on grandparent support, maternal gatekeeping efforts, and shifting romantic status of co-parents, even as it declines and stabilizes in the first few years of children's lives (Herzog, Umaña-Taylor, Madden-Derdich, and Leonard, 2007). But support from extended kin is not always beneficial for involvement. Support from paternal kin tends to increase men's involvement, whereas support from maternal kin may decrease involvement (Perry, 2009).

Transitions in low-income fathering across the life course

Men who experience changes in their fathering over time are often able to identify turning points (or transitions) in their relationships with their children. Transitions over the life course often occur in response to challenging circumstances (such as separation, divorce, eviction, job layoff, birth of a child with a disability, or serious illness) or as a result of events that tend to be viewed more positively (such as job promotion, birth of another child, or moving to a new home). Developmental psychologist Phillip Cowan identified that transitions must involve both a change in thinking and in behavior. He said:

> [T]ransitions a[re] long-term processes that result in qualitative reorganization of both inner life and external behavior … [I]t must involve a qualitative shift from the inside looking out (how the individual understands and feels about the self and the world) and from the outside looking in (reorganization of the individual or family's level of personal competence, role arrangements, and relationships with significant others). (Cowan, 1991, p.5)

In other words, transitions in fathering are processes and not just moment-in-time or short-lived events. Low-income fathers experience more frequent transitions in and out of households, intimate relationships, father–child relationships, and employment in comparison to fathers with more resources embedded in stable opportunity structures (Eggebeen and Uhlenberg, 1985; Mott, 1990). Many fathers, particularly African American men, are in flux, moving in and out of their families' lives (Eggebeen, 2002; Mott, 1990).

A life course approach allows us to take into account transitions in fathering, as well as the timing of such transitions for low-income men (Marsiglio and Roy, 2012). The life stage principle (Giele and Elder, 1998) suggests that becoming a father at a young age can push young men into different trajectories for family life and employment. In particular, transition to fatherhood between the ages of 18 and 30 results in specific developmental challenges for poor fathers. Moreover, taking into account specific historical contexts, this period of life for young poor men of color is marked by health risks, incarceration and foreclosed employment/educational opportunities, and an overall sense of being "targeted" by law enforcement, peers and gangs, media, and communities in general.

Given many transitions and multiple challenges in young low-income fathers' lives, how is it that they manage to maintain involvement with their children over time? If their relationships and living arrangements change, how do they adapt to maintain engagement with their children? What is the relationship between changes in their thinking, behavior, and adaptive fathering?

Resilient fathering and supports to stabilize involvement

A common approach to understanding development in multi-level ecological contexts is the risk and resilience framework (Rutter, 1985). Resilience is a dynamic process, or, as Cummings, Braungart-Reiker, and Du Rocher-Schundlich (2003) argue, resilience is "unstable." Maintaining tenuous protective factors may prove stressful over time, as some protective factors may erode or disappear, and risk factors may provide "steeling" effects to enhance coping and facilitate adjustment. Using a risk and resilience framework, we have begun to identify and explore the factors that support or deter men in paternal involvement (Fagan and Palkovitz, 2007; Fagan, Palkovitz, Roy, and Farrie, 2009; Roy, 2004, 2005). Risk factors comprise contexts, circumstances and events that reduce the likelihood of fathers' involvement with children. Resilience factors increase the likelihood of father involvement even when faced with barriers to paternal involvement (Harvey and Delfabbro, 2004).

Fagan and Palkovitz (2007) utilize the risk/resilience perspective to examine factors that correlate with high-risk fathers' involvement with young children. Using the Fragile Families data, they find that three resilience factors – the extent to which the young father's own father was involved in his life while growing up, attendance at religious services, and frequent contact with extended family members – are more significant for men with limited or no relationship with the mothers of their children. Conversely, the paternal involvement of men who maintain romantic involvement with the mothers of their children is more susceptible to risk factors. Roy (2005) found that changes in employment – job loss or underemployment in particular – were often turning points that led to the dissolution of tenuous family households, in which low-income fathers shared residence with their partners and children. Ecological factors, such as gang presence, police activity, and lack of resources, also inhibited men's involvement with children (Roy, 2004).

Studies also indicate that the meaning that men and families give to fatherhood may buffer them from risk factors. For example, Laub and Sampson (2004) examined the life trajectories of former offenders and found that they desisted from crime as they became married and found mainstream employment. Palkovitz (2002) found that fathers perceived that involvement with their children was operative in motivating them to reduce risky behaviors and deleterious lifestyles. Townsend (2002) identified a set of normative roles – including marriage, home ownership, family-supportive employment, and fatherhood – as "the package deal." However, achievement of a package deal is a challenge for many low-income men who are marginalized from their families and from mainstream employment. In short, low-income men may have a different "package deal" that facilitates adjustment – and resilience – through transitions within fathering.

In this chapter we illustrate how low-income men demonstrate risk and resilience by presenting findings from an original research study we conducted that examines the period of time between the ages of 18 to 30 for low-income fathers. This developmental period – in the context of poverty – required men to strategize actively to avoid risks (e.g., incarceration, gang activity, isolation, or depression) and to craft new resources for involvement (including spirituality, generativity, and a focus on "cleaning up [my] act"). We were interested in exploring the processes that allowed some fathers to maintain close relationships with their children despite formidable challenges. Their resilience emerged over time, with the right combination of maturation, social supports, and realistic assessment of fathering roles – often to result in fathers' description of "being there" as an alternative vision of successful involvement.

Methods

Few data sets document longitudinal changes in paternal involvement with multiple sets of children, and even fewer draw upon fathers' reports. This study, which received human subjects approval from our respective universities, analyzes retrospective life history interviews conducted with 146 low-income fathers in the Midwest. In the Life History Studies, we recruited low-income fathers in four different projects, linking eligibility to children's receipt of public assistance or attendance in Head Start programs. This pooled-sample of 146 men is diverse by race/ethnicity (62% African American (n = 84); 25% European American (n = 34); 11% Latino (n = 15); and 1% Asian or Native American (n = 2)) as well as age (40% 18–24 years (n = 60); 33% 25–35 years (n = 50); 26% 36 years and older (n = 40)). Almost three-quarters of all fathers across these studies had some history of incarceration, and another half had completed high school or a GED. Just over half of the participants were working at the time of the interview. To examine the emergence of paternal resilience more closely, a subsample of 50 fathers who have remained involved with their children over the course of multiple transitions were selected. Their demographics closely matched the overall sample in terms of race, ethnicity, age, and program source. We defined "involvement" as regular contact with children (at least once each week) as well as fathers' established knowledge of children's daily routines. Table 6.1 presents demographic data on an overall sample and a subsample of fathers for this study.

In each project, the research team conducted fieldwork and participant observation in community-based programs. Over the course of many months, team members served as case managers (projects 1 and 4) or classroom facilitators for life skills curricula (projects 2 and 3). For life history interviews, we used a calendar methodology (Freedman, Thornton, Camburn, Alwin, and Young-DeMarco, 1988). Men discussed significant transitions and related events in their lives. Participants were explicitly questioned regarding the timing of transition events in five key domains: residential change; involvement with family of origin; involvement with family of procreation, including partners and children; employment; education; and incarceration.

We used a *grounded theory approach* (LaRossa, 2005; Strauss and Corbin, 1998), in which theory is generated from systematic examination of data. Instead of beginning with a hypothesis, a grounded theory

Table 6.1 Demographics of total sample and subsamples of low-income fathers

	Total sample (n = 146)	Study subsample (n = 50)
Program		
Chicago fathers' program	n = 40	n = 12
Indiana work release facility	n = 40	n = 13
Indianapolis fathers' program	n = 35	n = 13
Chicago family programs	n = 31	n = 12
Race/ethnicity		
African American	62% (n = 84)	64% (n = 32)
European American	25% (n = 34)	18% (n = 9)
Latino	11% (n = 1 5)	16% (n = 8)
Asian or Native American	1% (n = 2)	2% (n = 1)
Age		
18–24 years	40% (n = 60)	32% (n = 16)
25–34 years	33% (n = 50)	36% (n = 18)
35 years and older	26% (n = 40)	32% (n = 16)

approach begins with coding of data by asking generally "what is going on (in this text)?" The result may be the development of hypotheses. We at first relied on the use of two concepts – resilience and, within the literature on resilience, the process of steeling – to frame our initial questions and analyses. Few studies have qualitatively explored the process of "steeling," which is a coping mechanism some men use in the face of disappointment. In the first wave of open coding, we coded relevant themes that emerged from each paragraph unit of text, with an emphasis on identifying salient transitions between families. In the second wave of axial coding, we compared and contrasted data across and within different participants' experiences, in order to capture different processes of resilient fathering. With the third wave of selective coding, we integrated these comparisons and patterns of transitions, to develop a theoretically based "narrative" to describe three linked processes of resilience: steeling; learning from past mistakes; and perseverance. Pseudonyms are used for all narrative data and cases included in the chapter.

We found that men became more consistently involved in their children's lives as they established alternative models of successful involvement. This process usually occurred over time, with many men reaching turning points in involvement by the age of 30. The period of the twenties, for these men, required

active strategizing to avoid risks (incarceration, gang activity, isolation, or depression) and to craft new resources for involvement (including spirituality, generativity, and a focus on "cleaning up [my] act"). When many fathers note that "being there" is their most important task as parents, it is often an ambiguous status. However, for fathers in fragile families, "being there" became an alternative vision of successful involvement with three related dimensions:

- *steeling* the self to cope with inevitable losses and settling for lower levels and types of involvement;
- *learning* from mistakes and offering lessons as basis for involvement with children; and
- *perseverance* – literally, surviving and being physically present – to offer consistent contact and support to children, even if it meant "less money and smaller joys."

"Be Real with Myself": Steeling for Inevitable Challenges

One strategy that resilient fathers employed to facilitate their engagement with their children could be labeled as "steeling." Although the connotations of steeling imply, according to *Webster's New World*

Dictionary, "making [oneself] hard, tough, relentless, unfeeling", in resilient families in challenging neighborhoods, it indicates a process by which contexts may be difficult, but still surmountable, similar to inoculation against disease (Cummings *et al.*, 2003).

We observed steeling to be a cognitive strategy whereby low-income fathers came to adjust their views about the realistic possibilities they had for engagement in their children's lives over time. In essence, steeling often required low-income men to set their sights lower. They adjusted their roles and fathering goals to be more realistic and to represent a better fit with the opportunity structures and changing circumstances of their lives.

When men continuously measured themselves against a standard of "good fathering" that is grounded in a larger culture including middle- and upper-class men with different opportunity structures and resources, low-income men became discouraged and viewed their failure to be all too certain. Men grew exhausted through constant confrontation with their shortcomings as parents. Without adjusting expectations to reflect more realistic levels given their opportunities and resources, the continual weight of falling short of unattainable goals often led to disengagement or despondency that yielded lack of resilience, absence, or dropping out of a child's life. Rather than face their

inevitable failure, some men, "cut and run fathers," chose to shorten the process by dropping out of fathering earlier as opposed to later.

In effect, steeling was a cognitive strategy that required a man to redefine successful fathering. As such, steeling represented an adaptive cognitive restructuring of roles and goals to reflect attainable levels of father involvement. In essence, men who envisioned an alternative to middle-class models of good fathering created a "good enough" model that allowed them to experience a level of satisfaction and dignity, given the challenges they faced in meeting provider roles and "being there" while frequently nonresidential.

Adaptive steeling required negotiating a balance between setting the sights high enough to motivate ongoing engagement, but not so high that failure was inevitable. At one end of the continuum was the need to set the role expectations and goals high enough to avoid learned helplessness or to enact an "opt out" of engagement because it was not expected (given the circumstances). Men who went overboard in revising their expectations and role prescriptions in a downward direction opted out of active fathering all together because they viewed father-absence as normative or justified in their circumstances. At the other end of the continuum were the high and

---

Case Example: Evan

Evan, a 38-year-old White father of three sons, was within a few weeks of leaving a work release program in Indiana, where he had been serving time for multiple DUI charges. He offered a definitive quote to illustrate steeling when he stated: "I'm already on a good track of blowing [my relationship with my boy, Nate the Great]. But I'm trying not to let the tire completely off the rim." He recognized that though he had performed in less than a stellar manner, he preferred to limp along on a deflated tire than to lose the opportunity to move ahead at all with his son. This quotation captures the ambivalence experienced when fathers engaged in steeling:

involvement with their kids was certainly not as good as it could be, but their fathering was not a total bust, either. Readjusting and lowering expectations as a father was better than not being a father at all.

When asked about his readiness to have a child at a young age, Evan said, "I wasn't done runnin' amuck yet … I'd say 30, late 20s is a good age to have a child … once you settle down, get a little older, start tirin' out." Although Evan was nominally a father during his twenties, he did not adjust his behavior to coincide with a social identity as a father, and only matured into a true recognition of his role as a father at a later age.

Box 6.1 The Concept of Steeling: An Illustration

The relationship between steeling and resilient fathering may be best represented by an inverted U-shaped curve where the y-axis represents involved role expectations (from low to high) and the x-axis paternal resilience over time (see Figure 6.1). Having moderately high expectations for paternal engagement was more adaptive over time than subscribing to unattainably high ideals or than setting the bar so low that disengagement was excused or expected.

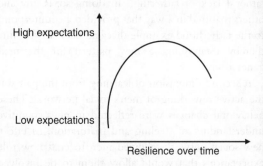

Figure 6.1 Steeling and resilient fathering.

---

unattainable expectations that shouted "failure" to men who attempted to attain them without adequate opportunities or resources.

Steeling also represented an awareness of a man's ability to cope with risk factors and how their current circumstances may be similar to or differ from past contexts that brought success or failure as a father. Amir was a 26-year-old African American father of a 2-year-old girl, and he tried to put distance between his current life and his past involvement with dealing drugs and incarceration in Indianapolis. He was transparent enough to acknowledge the difference between ways he presented himself to others and his less attractive reality. He said, "I can talk a good game, but when it comes to really applying it in my real life, there's some type of block

there. And I gotta be real with myself." Being real with the self was a central component to various aspects of steeling. Similarly, Bird, a 21-year-old former gangbanger with a 1-year-old daughter in Chicago, evaluated his ability to withstand the temptations faced in regard to substances in his neighborhood: "I know me and these projects, if I'm around too long, I'll get attracted to the same old mf shit." Having realistic expectations allowed him to move toward learning from past mistakes and to change his behavior.

"Gotta Change Play Groups": Maturation and Learning from Past Mistakes

Many men reported that the late teenage years through the mid-twenties were especially unstable periods in their lives that were marked by spells of incarceration, relationship volatility, drug and alcohol abuse, and inconsistent work histories. This instability often hindered men's active involvement with their children during this turbulent period. As men aged out of their twenties, however, the "lure of the streets" became less attractive and men began transitioning into behavioral patterns that were more conducive to involved parenthood.

Men began to see a range of different choices for their lives as they moved into their late twenties. Fathers in risky environments, in general, are more susceptible to significant effects of poor choices, compared to men in more safe environments. It is also likely that fathers without social supports stand to make "bigger mistakes" with poor choices, compared to men who are able to learn something from previous negative life experiences. While steeling represented a cognitive adaption, the process of learning from past mistakes, another coping strategy, represented the behavioral outcomes of cognitive adaption.

One dimension of learning from past mistakes was the noted maturation of fathers during their twenties. *Maturation* refers to the process of transformation whereby a man restructures his identity and changes his behavior to fulfill the roles required by his new identity (Palkovitz, 2002, p. 4). This new social identity as a father required men to "recognize that they had to de-center from their own interests and pursuits to become more oriented toward others, toward what was best for the children" (Palkovitz, 2002, p. 71). For example, Zach, a 22-year-old White father in a work-release program, said:

> I need to start thinking ahead about things. It's not just me, just a punk kid running around anymore you know. I got three kids, whatever happens to me happens to them too … I realize that I am not the only one that is being affected by this stuff anymore.

For many at-risk fathers, the process of prioritizing the lives of others above their own remained incomplete throughout their twenties as they continued to struggle with their own shortcomings as providers, partners, and parents.

Maturation often occurred at seminal moments during men's lives when circumstances allowed them to reflect on the meaning of being fathers. Incarceration during the later twenties and early thirties often provided the impetus for men to begin the process of identity redefinition and planning about how they would live up to challenging expectations as involved parents upon release. As Pat, a 35-year-old White father who recently completed a work release program remarked, "I guess getting re-incarcerated should have had [the] advantage to make me think about it the second time … but my challenge is putting my family back together. And, to where we could live happily ever after. The old fairy tale." Pat's sentiments highlighted how his experience in prison had led him to reassess his identity as a father. He accepted that a key dimension of his role was to care for the well-being of his 2-year-old daughter – not simply for his own.

Maturation also occurred when fathers recognized that someone had offered them a roadmap to resilience. In most cases, fathers began to identify with their biological, step, or "social" fathers (men outside of the family who the fathers in the study regarded as having taught them how to be fathers). While some men established social contact with their fathers, sometimes after many years of separation, such direct contact with their fathers was not necessary for men to identify themselves as similar to their fathers.

In both cases, men arrived at a cognitive realization when they remembered their own fathers at the age and phase of life where they currently found themselves. When resilient fathers had positive experiences of being fathered, they often chose to re-create the same parental patterns with their children. James, for example, recalled that his father spent time with him by teaching him how to work on cars and he – to varying degrees of success – "was trying to get him involved in working on his car" as a means to spend time with his son and impart knowledge to him. Not all resilient fathers, however, had positive experiences with their fathers or with men whom they regarded as surrogates. These men tended to follow the pattern of Remy, a 27-year-old African American father of three children, who "just based [his] fathering on [his father's] lack of fathering." In doing so, Remy and others matured in a way that provided a counterpoint to the fatherhood example that had been set for him, thereby establishing a new pattern for the next generation.

A second dimension of learning from the past was the active reworking of men's social networks. These behavioral changes were reflected in new cognitive understanding of steeling and maturation. In effect, new social networks allowed men to craft new role expectations that would allow them to be involved fathers. The environmental turbulence that men experienced during early adulthood (due to gang activity, unstable employment, and incarceration) inhibited their abilities to develop and enact active fatherhood roles.

When reflecting upon how he made the transition from a lifestyle that prevented him from interacting with his children to one of greater stability, Lionel, a 42-year-old father of four teens and a recovering alcoholic in Chicago, said, "I didn't go around where I used to do that type of stuff, I never went around. I mean I went around, but each time I would just flee cause I knew I didn't want to be around that stuff. I just stayed in the house."

Fathers' instability in their twenties also resulted in poor relationships with the mothers of their children. As resilient fathers aged, they tended to reorganize these relationships so as to improve their access to and relationships with their children. Although relationships with previous partners have

---

Case Example: Ben

Men often linked their negative behavior to the influence of negative peer groups and therefore sought to remove themselves from these groups as they worked towards being more involved with as father. The remarks of Ben, a 23-year-old African American father of four children in Indianapolis, embodied how men severed negative peer groups in favor of gaining positive relationships with their children:

> If you want to change the way you play you gotta change play groups is kinda how I go. The

people I used to hang around with and stuff, if I see 'em on the street or if I see them at the mall sure I will stop and talk to them. As to go to their house and hang out anymore, I'd just as soon get all new friends and stuff. So that is part of making this change. Um-huh. Yeah. I'm growing up.

In changing "play groups," men often withdrew completely from the groups they were involved with during their younger days.

---

the potential to be hostile and subsequently compromise fathers' opportunities to actively participate in their children's lives, resilient fathers learned to navigate this treacherous terrain for the benefit of their children through compromise and by showing respect. One father recounted having learned to "[suck] up to the mother and get in good graces with the mother [so] you can always see your son or daughter." This father, like many others, reorganized his interaction with the mother of his children as a means to see them and be a father to them. Whereas fathers may have been dissuaded by the negative patterns of interaction previously, many began forming new perceptions and gaining new skills that would help them interact with the mothers of their children so as to allow them to be involved in the lives of their children.

"Damn, I'm *Still* Around": Perseverance in "Being There" for Children

For fathers in the study who worked on redefining their roles as parents (the process of steeling) and changed their behavior as parents, partners, workers, and family members (the process of learning from past mistakes), their ability to remain involved with their children in the face of formidable barriers was striking.

If they maintained such resilient involvement over many months and years, they illustrated the final process of perseverance. In this way, these three processes represented an interactive system that yielded paternal resilience through adaptive life course changes.

As we suggest, these corrections are specific to the developmental time frame for low-income men, and particularly men of color. Although recognized changes, such as holding a stable job, earning a degree, or getting married, may occur later for many of these men, they are the end product of a long line of shifts in the life course. Each of these shifts requires a high level of engagement and work from low-income fathers. For example, it was uncommon to see many younger fathers "steel" themselves through lowered expectations – and then persevere in their involvement with their children. To an extent, the work of steeling was too intensive for young men who were primarily focused on their own shortcomings as parents and partners. A common expression for these men was that their mistakes or lack of involvement "is on me." Taking the sole blame for inability to live up to mainstream fathering expectations led many young men to curtail involvement with their children. In contrast, older men appeared to be better able to persevere through stepping outside of themselves. They compared their own involvement as parents to their own fathers' experiences, for example. The work of fathering for these men was less an issue of self-change and more an issue of recognizing how contextual

---

Case Example: Doc

This recognition of intergenerational patterns in part helped older fathers to grit through hard times with a basic strategy of persistence. Doc, a 35-year-old father of three boys, worked off-the-books as an auto detailer. He was pursued by Child Support Court to pay arrearages on a daughter who he had just been informed was born eight years earlier:

> You got to take whatever come your way. You can't back down. When pressure hits you, you can't panic. If you panic, you done lost. I got to be happy with myself. You still have to be there with the kids – that's my thing. I've always been a fighter, and I'm not going to let this beat me. I'm not going to let the system beat me. If I can't beat it, and it won't leave me alone, I am going to join it. I'll play the ball game, but I'm going to get something out of it myself. I'll earn it, I'll deserve it.

Doc's adaptation to make the most of difficult situations – and even gain from adverse events by adapting his daily routine – was a common strategy for low-income fathers.

---

barriers limited parental roles, and how patterns of intergenerational family relationships unfolded over time. Older men found continuity in the barriers to providing and care that they themselves and their fathers before them faced.

Younger men, like Otis, a 23-year old-father of a preschooler with another child on the way, had moved beyond what he described as "a pretty low period of depression." However, he also believed that hard times made him who he was, as a parent and partner, and he did not regret his past mistakes:

> If I could go back and change something, I probably would … but my life being how it is has made me the person that I am, and I'm kinda happy with myself. There's a whole lot I want to get better at, but I just take it one day at a time.

Resilience meant talking the talk and walking the walk in terms of fathering. These fathers had to come to grips with their own beliefs and valuation of being parents – in an environment that would usually not allow them to live up to the highest set of expectations of fathers as providers and caregivers. Resilient fathers had functional agency, in that they embraced parenting without access to what they perhaps wanted most. The term that perhaps described this status most accurately was "being there" for their children. "Being there" can appear to be a vague nod towards physical or emotional presence, but it did not necessarily mean

a round-the-clock, 24/7 presence, or even co-residence. Typically, low-income men who had come through many difficult challenges were surprised that they were still standing and could be active in their children's lives. "Being there" was a priority in terms of children exposed to men's lives and commitment, in spite of the barriers. Lombardo, a 30-year-old tree-cutter with a history of substance abuse and domestic violence, left work release to pursue relationships with his three biological and stepchildren. He recognized a complete change that came with his promise to "be there" for his children:

> I guess maybe I'm getting more responsibility and I know what I'm supposed to do. I don't depend so much on other stuff. I think I know what's right, it's just I chose not to do it. And now that I've been in trouble and don't want to be in this situation ever again, so not just changing the ways I do some things I'm just changing the ways I do everything.

However, with regard to perseverance, it was evident in the study that men could not sustain involvement on sheer force of will alone. Even if they invested in steeling and learning from past mistakes, and they returned daily to their children's lives, systemic barriers could inhibit these processes from resulting in resilient fathering. The contexts of men's lives – especially family supports, availability of work, and opportunity structures with ample resources – could permit them to attain and retain resilience. These environmental contexts also allowed men to "age out" of risky circumstances and behavior from their twenties. In this way, the process of perseverance was the most heavily contextualized of the three processes. Fathers could remain consistently involved in the face of barriers if their communities supported their continued involvement. The notion of "being there" becomes less ambiguous taking these factors into account. Understanding the barriers to men's involvement, especially for low-income men with little work history, a criminal record, or few successes as partners, students, or parents, "being there" is an accomplishment. As one father reflected, "Damn, I'm still around. You're still here, after years of expecting that you wouldn't be."

Summary

Young disadvantaged men are caught in the midst of historic social and economic shifts. In an era of rising inequality, they have become perhaps our most vulnerable population, at risk for separation from good jobs and stable family life. Although it was once common that poor fathers were married and living with children, in 2010 only about a third of these fathers were in that situation.

Moreover, the decade of the twenties (Arnett, 2000; Rindfuss, 1991) is packed with critical transitions, but developmental pathways for low-income men are clustered with unique risks. We stress that young men's ongoing disconnection from mainstream institutions, such as work, school, or family life, is not simply a status of being marginalized that stigmatizes and stereotypes them. In contrast, we see marginalization as a dynamic process that permeates everyday life and family interaction in many different ways. And, in spite of not being "provide and reside" fathers, we argue that many low-income fathers resist marginalization. They cultivate strategies to become resilient caregivers, through "steeling" themselves for challenges over time; through learning from mistakes and using those as the basis for continued involvement; and through perseverance, and simply being consistently present to witness the growth of their children.

Evidence from this chapter suggests that low-income fathers work to remake their involvement on a regular basis. However, it also suggests that it is not simply men who must "change their behavior." Social policies that can stabilize low-income men's lives – particularly their participation in the labor force and job training, correctional facilities, and the effects of drug economy, child support, and paternity establishment – can go a long way toward allowing the highest-risk poor fathers to engage positively with their children. Social policies and programs can benefit from noting which resources allow frustrated low-income fathers to "steady the boat" in the midst of rare accomplishments often beset by rapid setbacks. Policies and programs that help men to make positive life changes prior to becoming fathers may be the most effective in preventing low or decreasing patterns of paternal engagement in families in challenging circumstances across time.

Critical Thinking Questions

1. How have the processes of marginalization of young disadvantaged men shaped their efforts to be involved fathers?
2. How do low-income fathers develop resilience to keep involved with their children, in the face of substantial barriers?
3. Which policies and programs might promote resilience in father involvement for poor men?

References

Alexander, M. (2012). *The new Jim Crow: Mass incarceration in the age of color blindness*. New York: New Press.

Amato, P. R., and Gilbreth, J. G. (1999). Nonresident fathers and children's well-being: A meta-analysis. *Journal of Marriage and the Family, 61*, 557–573.

Arnett, J. (2000). Emerging adulthood: A theory of development from the late teens through the twenties. *American Psychologist, 55*, 469–480.

Bronte-Tinkew, J., Moore, K., Matthews, G., and Carrano, J. (2007). Symptoms of major depression in a sample of fathers of infants: Sociodemographic correlates and links to father involvement. *Journal of Family Issues, 28,* 61–99.

Bronte-Tinkew, J., Ryan, S., Franzetta, K., Manlove, J., and Lilja, E. (2009). Higher-order fertility among urban fathers. *Journal of Family Issues, 30,* 968–1000.

Cabrera, N., Cook, G., McFadden, K., and Bradley, R. (2011). Father residence and father–child relationship quality: Peer relationships and externalizing behavioral problems. *Family Science, 2,* 109–119

Cabrera, N., Fagan, J., and Farrie, D. (2008). Explaining the long reach of fathers' prenatal involvement on later paternal engagement. *Journal of Marriage and Family, 70,* 1094–1107.

Caldwell, C., Bell, L., Brooks, C., Ward, J., and Jennings, C. (2011). Engaging nonresident African American fathers in intervention research: What practitioners should know about parental monitoring in nonresident families. *Research on Social Work Practice, 21,* 298–307.

Carlson, M., McLanahan, S., and Brooks-Gunn, J. (2008). Coparenting and nonresident fathers' involvement with young children after a nonmarital birth. *Demography, 45,* 461–488.

Cowan, P. A. (1991). Individual and family life transitions: A proposal for a new definition. In P. A. Cowan and M. Hetherington (eds), *Family transitions* (pp. 3–30). Hillsdale, NJ: Lawrence Erlbaum Associates.

Cummings, E. M., Braungart-Reiker, J. M., and Du Rocher-Schundlich, T. (2003). Emotion and personality development in childhood. In R. M. Lerner, M. A. Easterbrooks, and J. Mistry (eds), *Handbook of psychology*, vol. 6, *Developmental psychology* (pp. 211–239).

Danzinger, S. K., and Radin, N. (1990). Absent does not equal uninvolved: Predictors of fathering in teen mother families. *Journal of Marriage and the Family, 52,* 636–642.

DeBell, M. (2008). Children living without their fathers: Population estimates and indicators of educational well-being. *Social Indicators Research, 87,* 427–443.

Dyer, J., Pleck, J., and McBride, B. (2012). Imprisoned fathers and their family relationships: A 40-year review from a multi-theory view. *Journal of Family Theory and Review, 4,* 20–47.

Eggebeen, D. (2002). The changing course of fatherhood: Men's experiences with children in demographic perspective. *Journal of Family Issues, 23,* 486–506.

Eggebeen, D., and Uhlenberg, P. (1985). Changes in the organization of men's lives: 1960–1980. *Family Relations, 34,* 251–257.

Fagan, J., and Palkovitz, R. (2007). Nonresident, not-married fathers' involvement with their infants: A risk and resilience perspective. *Journal of Family Psychology, 21,* 479–489.

Fagan, J., and Palkovitz, R. (2011). Coparenting and relationship quality effects on father engagement: Variations by residence, romance. *Journal of Marriage and Family, 73,* 637–653.

Fagan, J., Palkovitz, R., Roy, K., and Farrie, D. (2009). Pathways to paternal engagement: Longitudinal effects of risk and resilience on nonresident fathers. *Developmental Psychology, 45,* 1389–1405.

Fitzgerald, M., Roy, K., Anderson, E., and Letiecq, B. (2012). The effect of depressive symptoms on low-income men in responsible fathering programs. *Fathering, 10,* 47–65.

Freedman, D., Thornton, A., Camburn, D., Alwin, D., and Young-DeMarco, L. (1988). The life history calendar: A technique for collecting retrospective data. *Sociological Methodology, 18,* 37–68.

Furstenberg, F. F., Jr. (1992). Daddies and fathers: Men who do for their children and men who don't. In F. F. Furstenberg, Jr., K. E. Sherwood, and M. L. Sullivan (eds), *Caring and paying: What fathers and mothers say about child support* (pp. 34–56). New York: Manpower Demonstration Research Corporation.

Furstenberg, F. F., Jr. (2011). Comment: How do low-income men and fathers matter for children and family life? *Annals of the American Academy of Political and Social Science, 635,* 131–139.

Geller, A., Cooper, C., Garfinkel, I., Schwartz-Soicher, O., and Mincy, R. (2012). Beyond absenteeism: Father incarceration and child development. *Demography, 49,* 49–76.

Giele, J., and Elder, G. H. (1998). Life course research: Development of a field. In J. Giele and G. H. Elder (eds), *Methods of life course research: Qualitative and quantitative approaches* (pp. 5–27). Thousand Oaks, CA: Sage Publications.

Guzzo, K. (2009). Maternal relationships and nonresidential father visitation of children born outside of marriage. *Journal of Marriage and Family, 76,* 632–649.

Guzzo, K., and Hayford, S. (2010). Single mothers, single fathers: Gender differences in fertility after a nonmarital birth. *Journal of Family Issues, 31,* 906–933.

Hamer, J. (2001). *What it means to be Daddy: Fatherhood for Black men living away from their children.* New York: Columbia University Press.

Harvey, J., and Delfabbro, P. H. (2004). Resilience in disadvantaged youth: A critical overview. *Australian Psychologist, 39,* 3–13.

Herzog, M., Umaña-Taylor, A., Madden-Derdich, D., and Leonard, S. (2007). Adolescent mothers' perceptions of fathers' parental involvement: Satisfaction and desire for involvement. *Family Relations, 56,* 244–257.

Jarrett, R., Roy, K., and Burton, L. (2002). Fathers in the 'hood: Qualitative research on African American men.

In C. Tamis-LeMonda and N. Cabrera (eds), *Handbook of father involvement: Multidisciplinary perspectives* (pp. 211–248). Hillsdale, NJ: Lawrence Erlbaum Associates.

Johnson, W. (ed.). (2010). *Social work with African American males: Health, mental health, and social policy.* New York: Oxford University Press.

Lamb, M. E., Pleck, J. H., Charnov, E. L., and Levine, J. A. (1987). Paternal behavior in humans. *American Zoologist, 25,* 883–894.

LaRossa, R. (2005). Grounded theory methods and qualitative family research. *Journal of Marriage and Family, 67,* 837–857.

Laub, J., and Sampson, R. (2004). *Shared beginnings, divergent lives: Delinquent boys until age 70.* Cambridge, MA: Harvard University Press.

Lewis, C., Jr., Garfinkel, I., and Gao, Q. (2007). Incarceration and unwed fathers in fragile families. *Journal of Sociology and Social Welfare, 34,* 77–94.

Manlove, J., Logan, C., Ikramullah, E., and Holcombe, E. (2008). Factors associated with multiple-partner fertility among fathers. *Journal of Marriage and Family, 70,* 536–548.

Marsiglio, W., and Roy, K. (2012). Fathers' nurturance of children over the life course. In G. Petersen and K. Bush (eds), *Handbook of marriage and the family* (3rd edn) (pp. 353–376). New York: Springer.

McDaniel, M., Simms, M., Fortuny, K., and Monson, W. (2013). *A demographic snapshot of disconnected low-income men.* Race, Place, and Poverty: An Urban Ethnographers Symposium on Low Income Men. US Department of Health and Human Services, ASPE/Human Services Policy, Issue Brief 1, August 2013. Washington, DC: Urban Institute.

McLanahan, S. S., and Sandefur, G. D. (1994). *Growing up with a single parent: What hurts, what helps?* Cambridge, MA: Harvard University Press.

Mincy, R. B., and Oliver, H. (2003). Age, race, and children's living arrangements: Implications for TANF reauthorization. Washington, DC: Urban Institute.

Modecki, K, and Wilson, M. (2009). Associations between individual and family level characteristics and parenting practices in incarcerated African American fathers. *Journal of Child and Family Studies, 18,* 530–540.

Mott, F. (1990). When is father really gone? Paternal-child contact in father-absent families. *Demography, 27,* 399–518.

Murray, C. (2012). *Coming apart: The state of White America, 1960–2010.* New York: Crown Forum.

Palkovitz, R. (1987). Consistency and stability in the family microsystem environment. In D. L. Peters and S. Kontos (eds), *Annual advances in applied developmental psychology,* vol. 2 (pp. 40–67). New York: Ablex.

Palkovitz, R. (2002). *Involved father and men's adult development.* Mahwah, NJ: Lawrence Erlbaum Associates.

Perry, A. (2009). The influence of the extended family on the involvement of nonresident African American fathers. *Journal of Family Social Work, 12,* 211–226.

Perry, A., and Bright, M. (2012). African American fathers and incarceration: Paternal involvement and child outcomes. *Social Work in Public Health, 27,* 187–203.

Pleck, J. (2010). Paternal involvement: Revised conceptualization and theoretical linkages with child outcomes. In M. Lamb (ed.), *The role of the father in child development* (5th edn) (pp. 59–93). Hoboken, NJ: John Wiley & Sons, Inc.

Rindfuss, R. (1991). The young adult years: Diversity, structural change, and fertility. *Demography, 28,* 493–512.

Roy, K. (2004). Three-block fathers: Spatial perceptions and kin-work in low-income neighborhoods. *Social Problems, 51,* 528–548.

Roy, K. (2005). Transitions on the margins of work and family for low-income African American fathers. *Journal of Family and Economic Issues, 26,* 77–100.

Roy, K. (2006). Father stories: A life course examination of paternal identity among low-income African American men. *Journal of Family Issues, 27,* 31–54.

Roy, K., Buckmiller, N., and McDowell, A. (2008). Together but not "together": Trajectories of relationship suspension for low-income unmarried parents. *Family Relations, 57,* 197–209.

Roy, K., and Burton, L. (2007). Mothering through recruitment: Kinscription of non-residential fathers and father figures in low-income families. *Family Relations, 56,* 24–39.

Roy, K., and Cabrera, N. (2009). Father involvement and children-at risk in low-income families. In B. Risman (ed.), *Families as they really are* (pp. 301–306). New York: W. W. Norton.

Roy, K., and Dyson, O. (2005). Gatekeeping in context: Babymama drama and the involvement of incarcerated fathers. *Fathering: A Journal of Theory, Research, and Practice about Men as Fathers, 3,* 289–310.

Roy, K., and Dyson, O. (2010). Making daddies into fathers: Community-based fatherhood programs and the construction of masculinity for low-income African American men. *American Journal of Community Psychology, 45,* 139–154.

Roy, K., and Jones, N. (2014). Theorizing alternative pathways through adulthood: The experiences of low-income disconnected young men. *New Directions for Child and Adolescent Development, 143,* 1–9.

Roy, K., and Lucas, K. (2006). Generativity as second chance: Low-income fathers and transformation of the difficult past. *Research on Human Development, 3,* 139–159.

Roy, K., Messina, L., Smith, J., and Waters, D. (2014). Growing up as "man of the house": Adultification and transition into adulthood for young men in economically disadvantaged families. *New Directions for Child and Adolescent Development*, *143*, 55–72.

Roy, K., and Smith, J. (2012). Nonresident fathers and inter-generational parenting in kin networks. In N. Cabrera and C. Tamis-LeMonda (eds), *Handbook of father involvement: Multidisciplinary perspectives* (2nd edn) (pp. 320–337). New York: Routledge.

Roy, K., and Vesely, C. (2009). Caring for "the family's child": Social capital and kin networks of young low-income African American fathers. In R. Coles and C. Green (eds), *The myth of the missing Black father* (pp. 215–240). New York: Columbia University Press.

Rutter, M. (1985). Resilience in the face of adversity: Protective factors and resistance to psychiatric disorder. *British Journal of Psychiatry*, *147*, 598–611.

Ryan, R., Kalil, A., and Ziol-Guest, K. (2008). Longitudinal patterns of nonresident fathers' involvement: The role of resources and relations. *Journal of Marriage and Family*, *70*, 962–977.

Schindler, H., and Coley, R. (2007). A qualitative study of homeless fathers: Exploring parenting and gender role transitions. *Family Relations*, *56*, 40–56.

Stier, H., and Tienda, M. (1993.) Are men marginal to their families? In Jane Hood (ed.), *Men, work, and family* (pp. 23–44). Newbury Park, CA: Sage Publication.

Strauss, A., and Corbin, J. (1998). *Basics of qualitative research: Techniques and procedures for developing grounded theory* (2nd edn). Thousand Oaks, CA: Sage Publications.

Sum, A., Khatiwada, I., McLaughlin, J., and Palma, S. (2011). No country for young men: Deteriorating labor market prospects for low-skilled men in the United States. *Annals of the American Academy of Political and Social Science*, *635*, 24–55.

Tamis-LeMonda, C., and McFadden, K. (2010). Fathers from low-income backgrounds: Myths and evidence. In M. Lamb (ed.), *The role of the father in child development* (5th edn) (pp. 296–318). Hoboken, NJ: John Wiley & Sons, Inc.

Townsend, N. (2002). *The package deal: Marriage, work and fatherhood in men's lives.* Philadelphia: Temple University Press.

Waller, M., and Swisher, R. (2006). Fathers' risk factors in fragile families: Implications for "healthy" relationships and father involvement. *Social Problems*, *53*, 392–420.

Weinman, M., Buzi, R., Smith, P., and Nevarez, L. (2007). A comparison of three groups of young fathers and program outcomes. *School Social Work Journal*, *13*, 1–13.

Young, A. (2006). *The minds of marginalized men: Making sense of mobility, opportunity, and future life opportunities.* Princeton series in cultural sociology. Princeton, NJ: Princeton University Press.

Part II

Parenting and Caregiving in Diverse Contexts

Part II

Parenting and Caregiving in Diverse Contexts

7

"Do What You Gotta' Do"

How Low-Income African American Mothers Manage Food Insecurity

Robin L. Jarrett, Ozge Sensoy Bahar, and Ezella McPherson

Unfortunately, food insecurity is an all too common experience in the lives of female-headed African American households with children. Jarrett, Sensoy Bahar, and McPherson's qualitative study of low-income mothers provides evidence of resilient parenting in the face of economic hardship and food shortages. Despite the great potential for despair, in Chapter 7 we learn how mothers actively cope with food insecurity and provide care for their children using innovative strategies in the face of extreme material deprivation.

Introduction

For many low-income African American women with children who live in inner-city neighborhoods, food shortages are all too common. Research identifies the disproportionate burden of food insecurity among low-income African American households with children that are located in urban neighborhoods (Coleman-Jensen, Nord, Andrews, and Carlson, 2012; Congressional Digest, 2010). According to the most recent United States Department of Agriculture (USDA) report, 17.9 million households (14.9%) in the United States were food insecure, or had limited access to adequate food supplies in 2011 (Coleman-Jensen et al., 2012). Moreover, 5.7% (6.8 million) of households experienced very low food security, where food intake of one or more household members was reduced and their eating patterns were disrupted because of limitations in resources (Coleman-Jensen et al., 2012). Food insecurity is most closely associated with the demographic correlates of social class (poverty), race, place, and family composition (Tarasuk, 2001). Compared to non-Hispanic Whites, and higher-income households, low-income urban African American households with children have higher rates of food insecurity (Coleman-Jensen et al., 2012). Food insecurity is also higher, relative to two-parent households, in female-headed households with children (Coleman-Jensen et al., 2012; Congressional Digest, 2010). Quantitative studies further report that food insecurity is correlated with negative health and developmental consequences for both adults and children. Among adults, food insecurity has been associated with depression and obesity-related diseases (Cook and Frank, 2008; Laraia, Borja, and Bentley, 2009; Larson and Story, 2011), and it has been

Family Problems: Stress, Risk, and Resilience, First Edition. Edited by Joyce A. Arditti.
© 2015 John Wiley & Sons, Inc. Published 2015 by John Wiley & Sons, Inc.

associated with cognitive, behavioral, and physiological delays among children (Cook and Frank, 2008; Larson and Story, 2011; Mammen, Bauer, and Richards, 2009).

A smaller body of qualitative research describes how low-income households manage food insecurity (Ahluwalia, Dodds, and Baligh, 1998; Hoisington, Shultz, and Butkus, 2002; Monroe, O'Nell, Tiller, and Smith, 2002; Quandt, Arcury, Early, Tapia, and Davis, 2004). In contrast to quantitative studies of food insecurity that primarily examine the demographic characteristics of food insecurity and the consequences of food insecurity, qualitative research more directly examines the firsthand experiences of food insecurity (Hoisington et al., 2002; Seefeldt and Castelli, 2009). Qualitative studies consider food insecurity as a "managed process" that entails active coping efforts on the part of households in response to food shortages (Radimer, Olson, and Campbell, 1990). Based on racially/ethnically diverse low-income samples, including African Americans in urban and rural settings (Ahluwalia et al., 1998; Monroe et al., 2002; Radimer et al., 1990), Hispanics in urban and rural settings (Mammen et al., 2009; Olson, Anderson, Kiss, Lawrence, and Seiling, 2004; Quandt et al., 2004), and non-Hispanic Whites in urban and rural settings (De Marco, Thorburn, and Kue, 2009; Hoisington et al., 2002; Mammen et al., 2009; Olson et al., 2004; Radimer et al., 1990), researchers elicited narrative accounts from household members experiencing food insecurity and examined how they coped with inadequate food supplies. Most studies of food insecurity focused on women because they bear the primary responsibility for "feeding the family."

Researchers found that households used four types of coping strategies to avoid or delay food shortages: (1) food provisioning strategies that included strategies for procuring food, such as shopping activities; (2) food consumption strategies that involved cooking and meal preparation techniques, and eating practices; (3) social network strategies which entailed food assistance from family and non-family members (e.g., friends, neighbors, significant others); and (4) institutional strategies that relied on food assistance from governmental food programs and community-based organizations (Ahluwalia et al., 1998; Hoisington et al.,

2002; Monroe et al., 2002; Quandt et al., 2004). Low-income households typically used multiple strategies to cope with food insecurity as they cycled between periods of adequate food supplies and food shortages (Ahluwalia et al., 1998; Radimer et al., 1990).

In this chapter, we explore the experience of food insecurity with a sample of low-income, African American female caregivers of preschoolers who live in one inner-city neighborhood and who fit the demographic profile of households at extreme risk for food insecurity. We conducted qualitative interviews with eight caregivers (see Box 7.1), drawing upon women's firsthand accounts to better understand the lived experience of food insecurity and the related coping strategies that caregivers use to manage food insecurity. Most of the knowledge that informs social policy, especially policies that target marginalized populations such as welfare recipients, comes from statistical and 'objective' studies (Krumer-Nevo, 2005). Yet, the lived reality as expressed by the people themselves is often different from the dry statistical data (Edin and Lein, 1997). While quantitative data from the USDA can identify the existence and/or severity of food insecurity within households and tell us which groups are most at risk for food insecurity, it is limited in its ability to document the experiences, meaning-making processes, and the full range of coping strategies households use in response to food insecurity.

In this chapter, we elaborate on quantitatively derived demographic profiles by privileging women's accounts. Qualitative research on the firsthand experiences of low-income African American households can provide a full contextual picture of the daily lives of households experiencing food shortages (Stevens, 2010). Qualitative data also allow us to highlight the dynamic and complex processes "behind the numbers" that are missed in quantitative studies of food security that focus on correlates and prevalence rates (Hamelin, Habicht, and Beaudry, 1999; Pinstrup-Andersen, 2009).

We also use a strengths-based approach to understand the experience of food insecurity (see Box 7.2). Moving away from a social problems perspective that largely frames food insecurity in deficit terms, our research is informed by a family resilience framework that concentrates on caregivers' coping activities in

Box 7.1   Study Design

Study Setting: The Lincoln Heights Neighborhood

Low-income female-headed African American households with children and that live in inner-city settings are particularly vulnerable to food insecurity (Congressional Digest, 2010; Nord, Coleman-Jensen, Andrews, and Carlson, 2010). Such households predominated in Lincoln Heights (pseudonym), the targeted community. 2010 Census data revealed this predominantly (97.8%) African American and/or Black community to be an extremely impoverished one (US Census Bureau, 2010a). The median household income was $25,583.00 (US Census Bureau, 2010b). The percentage of community residents living below the poverty line was 43.23%, with an unemployment rate of 29.8% for the population sixteen years of age and older (US Census Bureau, 2010b). The percentage of impoverished female-headed households constituted 71% of households with children under age 18 in this community (US Census Bureau, 2010a). In 2012, the food insecurity rate for individuals in Lincoln Heights was 44.2% (Greater Chicago Food Depository, 2012b).

The Sample

Our sample included eight women (pseudonyms used throughout) who met the following criteria:

(1) self-identified as African American; (2) were at least 18 years of age; (3) had a household income at or lower than 185% of the Federal Poverty Level; (4) had at least one child enrolled in one targeted preschool program; and (5) resided in the targeted high-poverty neighborhood in Chicago. We selected this population because they were at particular risk for food insecurity (Coleman-Jensen et al., 2012).

Participants' ages ranged from 18 to 52 (mean = 33). The oldest participants were grandmothers (n = 2) in their early and late fifties and the youngest participant, age 18, was a sibling caregiver. In five households, caregivers were never-married. One mother was divorced, one grandmother was widowed, and one caregiver was married. Households included two to nine children. Three caregivers were formally employed. One caregiver had a bachelor's degree, two had some college education, and four had a high-school degree or equivalent (see Table 7.1).

Data Collection and Analysis

Between January 2008 and May 2009, an African American female research assistant conducted open-ended interviews with participants. Instead of using the more structured USDA questions to assess food insecurity, we used open-ended questions that helped us to understand caregivers' personal

Table 7.1   Demographics

	Age	Marital status	Household size	Adults/children	Education
Aisha	26	Single	4	2/2	High school or GED graduate
Ayana	32	Divorced	3	1/2	Some college
Candice	58	Married	9	3/6	High school or GED graduate
Claudia	24	Single	5	3/2	Some high school
Dominique	26	Single	9	3/6	High school or GED graduate
Latoya	18	Single	12	3/9	8th grade graduate
Shawna	28	Single	6	4/2	Some college
Tracy	52	Widowed	4	1/3	Bachelor's degree

perspectives on food insecurity. Each interview ranged from one and a half to two hours in length and was conducted in caregivers' homes or at the preschool site. The interviews were audio-taped and transcribed verbatim. We began with an initial set of a-priori codes related to coping strategies in response to food shortages. Other newly developed codes emerged from repeated readings of the interviews. We used visual data displays (e.g., graphs, charts, tables) to identify patterns within the data, including similarities and differences between caregivers (Miles and Huberman, 1994).

Box 7.2   A Family Resilience Perspective

We used a family resilience perspective (McCubbin, Thompson, Thompson, and Fromer, 1998; Walsh, 2002) to consider how families actively cope with the adversity of food insecurity. Family strengths, as opposed to deficits, are highlighted, with particular emphasis on families' agency in using existing resources to promote collective well-being (Logan, 2000; Hill, 1998; Walsh, 2002). Studies of low-income African American families, often characterized by networks of female kin, have focused on family coping and "survival" strategies that allow households to survive and thrive despite adversity (Dickerson, 1995; Dominguez and Watkins, 2003; E. Martin and Martin, 1978; Stack, 1974; Zollar, 1985). In particular, studies of Black family strengths have documented the prominent role of female caregivers in maintaining families and nurturing children (Jarrett, Sensoy Bahar, and Taylor, 2011; Jarrett, Jefferson, and Kelly, 2010; Jarrett and Jefferson, 2003).

---

response to the adversity of food insecurity. The use of a family resilience framework allowed us to uncover coping strategies that reflect agency and strength in the face of economic constraints. Caregivers demonstrated skill and competence in managing limited food resources, and expressed pride in their coping efforts. Contrary to a deficit approach, women's coping efforts around inadequate food supplies were life-affirming, despite the potential for despair. A family resilience perspective also provides direction for intervention and prevention policies and programs that are collaborative in nature and, taking into account women's agency, seek to empower the people for whom policies and programs are developed.

Given its emphasis on active coping and survival strategies, a resilience framework is particularly appropriate to highlight household assets and agency, with a focus on how caregivers utilize their resources to deal with food shortages.

Defining Food Insecurity

The United States Department of Agriculture (USDA) defines *food security* as "access by all people at all times to enough food for an active, healthy life" (USDA, 2012, para. 1). The USDA differentiates between *high food security*, which is characterized by no reported indications of problems with food access, and *marginal food security*, which entails only one or two reported indications of problems with access to food and some anxiety over food sufficiency or food shortages in the house (USDA, 2012). Relatedly, the USDA defines *food insecurity* as "limited access to adequate food due to lack of money and other resources" (Coleman-Jensen *et al.*, 2012, p. 2), classifying households that report "reduced quality, variety, or desirability of diet" as *low food insecure* and those that report "multiple indications of disrupted eating patterns and reduced

---

Case Example: Experiencing Food Insecurity: "They just want to keep eatin'"

All of our participants said that there were times when household members had experienced inadequate food supplies. For example, when asked if her household had experienced food shortages, Ayana, a 32-year-old single mother of a preschooler, Felicia, and a teenager, loudly exclaimed, "Yes." She said that she had experienced a bout of food insecurity when she was pregnant with her youngest daughter.

Eighteen-year-old, Latoya, one of the 9 siblings in a household of 12 and the caregiver of her sibling Rachel, the target child, also reported that her family experienced food shortages because of limited money. Commenting on the situation,

Latoya said not having enough food was "bad" because her family "loved" to eat.

Twenty-six-year-old Dominique and her preschooler Patrice live in a household of nine, including her parents, siblings, and her siblings' children. She said there had been times when the family did not have enough to eat. Although Dominique pointedly asserted that Patrice did not engage in extreme forms of eating behavior in response to food insecurity, she described the behaviors of other children experiencing fluctuations in food access: "[Some kids] go crazy when [they] see a lot of food. Like most kids they see a lot of stuff and they just want to keep eatin', keep eatin', sneaks through it durin' the night."

---

food intake" as *very low food insecure* (USDA, 2012, para. 2). These definitions were operationalized by the Working Group of the American Institute of Nutrition and used to develop the 18-item USDA Food Security Scale (FSS), which is administered annually and upon which the USDA bases its reports and statistics (Cook and Frank, 2008).

Demographic Correlates of Food Insecurity: Income, Race, Household Composition, and Context

Food insecurity is inextricably related to income (social class), race, household composition (one-parent, two-parent), and locational context (urban–rural; Coleman-Jensen *et al.*, 2012).

Income/social class

Food insecurity is strongly related to financial insecurity (Khan, Pinckney, Keeney, Frankowski, and Carney, 2011; Mammen *et al.*, 2009), especially to persistently inadequate incomes that are insufficient to cover households' expenses, including rent, utilities,

and food (Tarasuk, 2001). USDA statistics revealed that rates of food insecurity were significantly higher than the national average among households with incomes near or below poverty levels. More specifically, 41.1% of low-income households with incomes below 185% of the poverty threshold were food insecure, compared to 7% of those above 185% of the poverty line (Coleman-Jensen *et al.*, 2012). In 2011, 5.7% of the households had very low food insecurity, which meant that their access to adequate food was limited to the extent that some household members' food intake was reduced and their normal eating patterns were disrupted at times during the year (Coleman-Jensen *et al.*, 2012). This rate was higher than that in 2010 (5.4%). Increases in the level of very low food insecurity were highest among households below the 185% poverty line, along with women living alone and Black households (Coleman-Jensen *et al.*, 2012).

Many quantitative studies do not tap informal sources of income. Because these activities are often at odds with formal public assistance regulations, participants are reluctant to share this information (Edin and Lein, 1997). More typically, such information is better accessed in qualitative research where rapport and trust has developed between participants and researchers (Stack, 1974; Valentine, 1978).

Case Example: Employment: "Food is so expensive"

Tracy is a 52-year-old grandmother and her household includes her adult daughter, two grandchildren, and teen daughter. Although Tracy has a college degree, she experienced a food crisis when a medical emergency caused her to lose her job at a community center.

Tracy spoke of living on unemployment income, where her monthly income dropped from $1,500.00 to $600.00. While she greatly appreciated this income, Tracy found that unemployment income was not enough to cover family expenses. She said maintaining food supplies during this time was particularly difficult because "food is so expensive."

Twenty-eight-year-old Shawna is a single mother of two who lives in a three-generational household with a total of six people, her two children and three other adults, including her grandmother. Shawna has lived in her grandmother's home all her life. Shawna is currently attending a technical college. She works part-time at a local currency exchange and relies on school loans to make ends meet.

When Shawna talked about not having enough food for her household, she noted the importance of full-time employment. She currently works part-time and asserted: "I need more money. Yeah, that's what I need, and a better job." However, when she was employed full-time at a trucking company, a job that she spoke about with affection – "I loved it when I had my other job" – Shawna said it was easier to maintain adequate food supplies.

Case Example: Other Forms of Work: "I do hair …"

In the absence of full-time and stable employment, several of our participants used informal work to bolster their limited incomes and food budgets. Candice is a married 58-year-old grandmother caring for her granddaughter, Kelly. Candice completed high school and lives in a household of nine, including three adults and six children. The household income includes TANF. In the face of inadequate income, Candice, who liked children, provided babysitting services to mothers in the neighborhood:

> I do babysitting, two children, three days a week for all three children [for a total of] $125.00 a week … I like dealin' with kids, like I say. And I like the fact that their parents pick 'em up on time and they pay me on time.

Twenty-four-year-old Claudia is a single mother of two young children and she shares a home with her mother and sister. Claudia has some high school education and receives Medicaid resources. Braiding hair was a source of income to supplement her limited budget. Informal work allowed Claudia to work around her children's schedule. Yet Claudia recognized that this work activity was unstable:

> I also do hair … I can't really say like I do it every week or every month. It's basically if somebody comes to me and say they need their hair done. I always have an open space, other than the time between droppin' my kids off at school and pickin' 'em up. So I do it whenever somebody needs their hair done … Different styles is different money. But I had one other client. She paid $50.00 … So I really don't count that 'cause it comes when it wants.

In Latoya's household of twelve, the family relies on multiple income streams. They receive governmental assistance from TANF and Supplemental Security Income (SSI). Latoya's siblings' informal side jobs, which entailed selling CDs and braiding hair, stretched the family's income and food budgets. According to Latoya:

> Now that my brother Jerime … is helpin', [my mother] can get all the food that she wants … Jerime, he sells CDs. He does that every day. The CDs that he makes, he charge $5.00. But if somebody wants to buy two, that's $10.00 … My big sister NeNe braids hair. Out of a week she'll braid like three hairs [heads] and she'll get $50.00.

Race

According to USDA statistics (Coleman-Jensen *et al.*, 2012), the prevalence of food insecurity was lower than the national average for White non-Hispanic households (11.4%). Conversely, the rates of food insecurity were higher than the national average for Black non-Hispanic households (25.1%) and Hispanic households (26.2%). Very low food insecurity also showed similar patterns. While the percentage of very low food-insecure, White non-Hispanic households (4.6%) were below the national average of 5.7%, the rates of very low food insecurity were higher for Black non-Hispanic (10.5%) and Hispanic households (8.3%).

Household composition

Households with children are at a high risk for food insecurity (Metallinos-Katsaras, Gorman, Wilde, and Kallio, 2010; Swanson, Olson, Miller, and Lawrence, 2008). In 2011, households with children had higher rates of food insecurity (20.6%) compared to the national average (14.9%) (Coleman-Jensen *et al.*, 2012). Households with children younger than age 6 had even higher rates of food insecurity (21.9%), when compared to the national average

(Coleman-Jensen *et al.*, 2012). Female-headed households with children were the most vulnerable, with 36.8% experiencing food insecurity (Coleman-Jensen *et al.*, 2012; Congressional Digest, 2010; Nord *et al.*, 2010). Very low food insecurity was also more prevalent in households with children headed by single women (11.5%), compared to the national average of 5.7%.

Location

Households located in principal cities of metropolitan areas had the highest prevalence of food insecurity at 17.7%, followed by cities in nonmetropolitan areas (15.4%), and suburban and other metropolitan areas outside of principal cities (13.2%) (Coleman-Jensen *et al.*, 2012). Rural–urban comparisons revealed that 22% of food-insecure households were located in largely rural areas, whereas 24.2% of food-insecure households were located in major cities in metropolitan areas (Coleman-Jensen *et al.*, 2012). According to 2010 Census data, Chicago is the third largest city in the nation and food insecurity rates reflected this status (City-data.com, n.d.).

In Cook County, where Chicago is located, data released by Feeding America in 2012 showed that one in six individuals was food insecure, or did not know

---

Case Example: Single Mothers: "I don't have nobody helpin' me"

Dominique, who has a high school education, is unemployed and receives Medicaid income. She described the particular economic concerns, including providing food, of unmarried women raising children without a partner:

> We need a lot of help. A little bit more lift up for womens [sic] out here. Mens [sic] could always survive. Womens always can't really too much survive 'cause you have to take care of a child; you have to take care of your mother or you have to take care of your daddy. Sometime people don't have it and if y'all have programs out here for womens to give out food and stuff like that, pronounce [announce] it. Let it be known that it's

out here 'cause some people will accept the help, 'cause I know I would. I wouldn't turn down nothin'. 'Cause I need help. I don't have a baby daddy. I don't have nobody helpin' me and my daughter Patrice.

Claudia, also a single mother of two young children, identified the unique issue of managing food supplies without a partner. As a lone parent, Claudia worried about not being able to provide adequate food for her children from month to month. So she was careful in her shopping habits: "I'm doin' this by myself. I have to provide food for them myself. So I'm not finna' go out there and just buy a whole lot of junk."

when or where their next meal would be (Greater Chicago Food Depository, 2012a). Overall, the rate of food insecurity was 18.3% in Chicago in 2012 (Greater Chicago Food Repository, 2012b). Neighborhoods on the south and west sides of Chicago that were mainly populated by African Americans had high concentrations of food insecurity (Center for Healthcare Equity, 2011; City of Chicago, 2011; Greater Chicago Food Depository, 2012b). For example, the top food-insecure communities had rates of food-insecure individuals ranging from 40% to 53%. These individuals lived in communities that were overwhelmingly African American (97–98%) and impoverished. The percentage of households below the poverty level ranged from 42% to 61% (Center for Healthcare Equity, 2011; City of Chicago, 2011; Greater Chicago Food Depository, 2012b). As previously mentioned, in 2010, Lincoln Heights reflected a similar pattern: over 44% of residents were food insecure and the poverty rate was over 43% in this almost exclusively African American community (97.8%) (Greater Chicago Food Depository, 2012b; US Census Bureau, 2010a, 2010b).

The Consequences of Food Insecurity

Food insecurity poses health risks to adults and children. Food insecurity influences health through its impact on overall family stress, especially for mothers, who are the primary food managers. Food insecurity, as a form of economic insecurity, has been related to protracted stress that suppresses the immune system and is related to major diseases such as cancer (Cook and Frank, 2008; Whiting and Ward, 2010). Food insecurity has been associated with low levels of energy, maternal depression, and obesity (Cook and Frank, 2008; Laraia *et al.*, 2009; Larson and Story, 2010; Stevens, 2010). In her study with young mothers aged 15–24 who were single heads of households with children, Stevens (2010) found that food insecurity correlated positively with depression and was also associated with obesity, a precursor for diabetes, heart disease and early mortality. Researchers have found an association between food insecurity and obesity, especially among low-income African American women

---

Case Example: Family Stress: "It hurts a lot"

Caregivers discussed the stress of managing their households with inadequate food supplies. For example, Claudia described feeling overwhelmed as she pondered how she would secure more food for her children. Candice detailed increased family tensions when food was scarce, but that subsided when there was enough food.

Ayana offered a particularly painful account of how inadequate food supplies impacted parents and children. She said that not having enough food "really hurts. It hurts a lot." Perhaps what was most painful was the fact that Ayana's children were aware of the stress that she faced in dealing with food shortages. She said: "I mean kids sense everything a parent is goin' through, when you're depressed, when you're happy."

Aisha is 26 years old, and the single mother of one child, Tiara. Aisha shares a household with her sister, Alayah and her preschool-age daughter, Malika. Aisha has completed her GED and receives TANF, SSI and food stamps (LINK). Aisha described a roller-coaster ride of fluctuations in LINK allocations. One month the amount she had for food increased, but then decreased shortly afterwards. Here she details the physical toll that resulted from changes in her LINK allocation:

> If I get stressed, my whole body hurt. My hair fall out, and then I start bleedin', like spottin', and I have a big knot in my stomach and I won't be able to stand up straight. So I try not to get upset, and then my chest be hurtin' and then I won't be able to move or nothin'. So I try to be calm and relax and don't take it so personal that it messes with me. So I'm workin' on that.

(Laraia *et al.*, 2009). In their review of food insecurity and health consequences, Larson and Story (2010) reported that multiple studies documented that food-insecure women were more likely to be obese, relative to their food-secure peers.

Researchers have also documented that food insecurity among low-income children poses considerable risks, including negative effects on physical and mental health, and adverse growth and developmental outcomes (Mammen *et al.*, 2009). For example, negative academic outcomes, such as lower arithmetic scores and poorer concentration related to cognitive, behavioral, and physiological delays are associated with child nutritional deficits caused by food insecurity (De Marco *et al.*, 2009; Khan *et al.*, 2011). Food-insecure children, relative to food-secure peers, have a greater prevalence of iron deficiencies and stomach-aches and colds (Cook and Frank, 2008;

Khan *et al.*, 2011). Moreover, there is some evidence that food insecurity is linked to childhood obesity (Larson and Story, 2011). The effects of childhood food insecurity are long-term and can lead to compromised health across the life cycle (Cook and Frank, 2008; Khan *et al.*, 2011).

Qualitative Studies of Coping Strategies against Food Insecurity

A small number of qualitative studies identified four categories of coping strategies households use to avoid or delay running out of food or going hungry (Radimer *et al.*, 1990). These categories include food provisioning, food consumption, social network, and institutional strategies (Hoisington *et al.*, 2002; Quandt *et al.*, 2004; Swanson *et al.*, 2008). Households at risk

---

Case Example: Provisioning Strategies: "Smart shopper"

Despite experiencing stress, caregivers actively responded to the adversity of possible food shortages. Ayana's account highlights preventive strategies that some caregivers used. Ayana viewed herself as a particularly competent manager of scarce resources. She asserted that she was a "smart shopper" who handled her food monies wisely, thereby avoiding the "predicament" of food shortages.

As a savvy shopper, Ayana had a repertoire of shopping strategies that she used. She monitored prices and was knowledgeable about the various grocery stores. For example, Ayana declared: "Moo and Oink [meat store] is too high! It's not worth it. It's the highest store out here if you want me to tell it. And I don't see why people go." Instead of shopping at Moo and Oink, she shopped at the Meat House.

Ayana went on to describe how she compared prices across stores:

> You get your ground beef [for] 99 cents a pound at the Meat House. So everything is fresh. I buy my

smoked turkey tails from the Meat House. At Fair Play I [would be] payin' about $5.00, three in a six-pack. At the Meat House, 99 cents a pound and it got me a bag-full.

Ayana shopped at multiple stores to secure the best prices for specific items. She chuckled as she shared this information about her shopping routine:

> I get my juices and my milk at Food for Less. But I get mainly my juice from Fair Play 'cause I be gettin' a good deal. Dean's be havin' a juice sale for 99 cents. So I get the assorted juices. My coffee, I get from Fair Play or Food for Less dependin' on which one got it on sale. I buy a big thing of Maxwell [coffee], but I don't make too much coffee in the house, it's just there in case I'm broke.

To round out her proactive repertoire of food management strategies, Ayana said she stocked up on extra food supplies each month just in case her food stamps were cut.

for food insecurity typically combine various strategies from the food-based, network-based, and institution-based categories (De Marco *et al.*, 2009; Seefeldt and Castelli, 2009).

Food provisioning strategies were mainly acquisition strategies that included shopping for low-priced food, purchasing store or generic brands, purchasing in large quantities, utilizing coupons, shopping at discount stores, and shopping at multiple stores to secure the best prices (Ahluwalia *et al.*, 1998; De Marco *et al.*, 2009; Mammen *et al.*, 2009; Quandt *et al.*, 2004). Households also reduced food items that were purchased and made lower-cost food substitutions by purchasing canned foods as opposed to fresh fruits and vegetables (Hoisington *et al.*, 2002; Stevens, 2010). Food provisioning strategies relied upon caregivers' human capital skills and represented proactive strategies designed to forestall food shortages.

Food consumption strategies included using leftovers to cook meals, storing extra foods in freezers for later, serving smaller amounts of food, and preparing large-pot meals that allowed households to stretch low-cost ingredients (De Marco *et al.*, 2009; Mammen *et al.*, 2009; Olson *et al.*, 2004). Household members ate what was available, ate smaller meal portions or leftovers from others, and skipped meals altogether when food was not available (Hoisington *et al.*, 2002). Some households used riskier strategies such as the consumption of spoiled and unsafe foods (Hoisington *et al.*, 2002). Households typically used food consumption strategies when they anticipated or experienced food shortages. While food insecurity could not be prevented, caregiver efforts were used to stretch existing food supplies longer and to limit the duration of food shortages.

Social network strategies entailed reliance on kin, significant-other males, and friends and neighbors. Kin were the most frequently used source for food-insecure households (De Marco *et al.*, 2009; Mammen *et al.*, 2009). Friends and neighbors were used either to supplement kin aid or when kin support was unavailable (Campbell and Desjardins, 1989; De Marco *et al.*, 2009; Mammen *et al.*, 2009). Significant-other males included romantic partners and children's fathers (Edin and Lein, 1997). Network members contributed to household food budgets by giving money, purchasing food items for households, and sharing meals (De Marco *et al.*, 2009; Mammen *et al.*, 2009). As a form of social capital, network strategies reflected caregivers' ability to develop, maintain, and

Case Example: Food Consumption Strategies: "Eating less"

When families experienced food shortages they used the consumption strategies of eating less and skipping meals. In Dominique's and Latoya's households both adults and children ate less. These households developed a pattern of eating more when food was available and eating less when food was scarce.

In response to food shortages Candice's household skipped meals, cutting the number of mealtimes from three to two a day. Like Dominique's and Latoya's households, children were not spared and ate fewer meals as well. The inclusion of children was not surprising given

that these were the largest households in the study. Candice was philosophical about her family's food management strategy. Despite the family's best efforts to maintain food supplies, at this point, there was nothing else the family could do but to accept their diminished food supplies.

Ayana's smaller household also experienced food shortages. However, Ayana managed to spare her children. While she ate less during periods of inadequate food supplies, Ayana made sure her children were not deprived of food. She was adamant that her children's needs would be given priority over hers.

Case Example: Social Network Strategies: "I'm glad I got they help"

Aisha relied on extended kin to manage her inadequate food budget. When her food stamps were cut by $70.00, Aisha had help from her uncles and grandmother. Here she describes her gratefulness for their unwavering support:

> I'm OK. I'm glad I got they help. So if I didn't have they help, then I'll probably be upset … So, if I didn't have they help, if I was just gettin' that TANF, I'd be upset 'cause it wouldn't be the same … I can call my grandma even if she just helped me. I can call her and she'll still help me.

Shawna relied on her partner Andre for money and food assistance. Although Andre could not provide full economic support, Shawna said he gave her money when she was "short" on cash. Andre also helped Shawna manage household food shortages by buying food from fast-food restaurants. Kenya's partner Malik similarly eased food shortages by giving Kenya money to purchase prepared meals outside the home.

Shawna also addressed her food needs through the inclusion of close friends who were also neighbors. When she experienced inadequate food supplies, Shawna said that her daughter Nikki remained unaffected because she ate next door at Lisa's house. The two women had grown up together and Shawna saw Lisa as a family member. As an example of their friendship, Lisa and her family also stepped in to help Shawna when she could no longer rely upon her grandmother to properly feed Nikki: "The thing is my grandmother is getting kind of old. So she mostly does not cook a lot … So I rather prefer Nikki to go next door because they always feed her … I just would rather her go next door."

mobilize social ties in response to inadequate food supplies.

Institutional strategies were identified as resources beyond the household level. Governmental programs such as the Special Supplementary Nutrition Program for Women, Infants, and Children (WIC) and the Supplemental Nutrition Assistance Program (SNAP) (called LINK in Illinois) were frequently utilized by low-income, food-insecure households (Mammen *et al.*, 2009; Swanson *et al.*, 2008; Seefeldt and Castelli, 2009).

Research also demonstrates that Federal food and nutrition assistance programs reduced food insecurity. For example, using national data from the Current Population Survey Food Security Supplements from 2001 to 2006, researchers reported that while the most needy families utilized SNAP, participation in the program reduced the prevalence of very low food security by nearly a third (Nord and Golla, 2009). Data from the Current Population Survey Food Security Supplements from 2001 to 2009, Nord (2012) also indicated that SNAP had an ameliorative effect on very low food security, with a reduction in the 20–50% range. Using national Census data from the Survey of Income and Program Participation (SIPP), Ratcliffe and McKernan (2009) estimated that SNAP decreased food insecurity by 30% and very low food insecurity by 20%.

Households experiencing food insecurity made use of community resources, in addition to governmental resources. At the community level, food-insecure households used day care settings, food pantries, church food give-aways, and food banks (Campbell and Desjardins, 1989; De Marco *et al.*, 2009; Hamelin *et al.*, 1999). Local organizations were another institutional resource for households experiencing food shortages.

Caregivers' ability to access food programs and overcome food program limitations was critical in the use of this type of strategy.

Case Example: Institutional Strategies: "Do what you gotta' do"

Caregivers said that LINK was essential to their ability to manage food shortages and highly praised the program. Dominique believed that her family would experience more extreme bouts of hunger without LINK. Latoya highlighted how having access to LINK ensured that there were times when there was enough food on the table. Claudia explained that without LINK she would not be able to adequately feed her children.

Like other low-income caregivers, LINK was a critical component of Ayana's food budget and primary strategy to manage food insecurity. Yet, as her story reveals, LINK income was inadequate. Consequently, Ayana had to be creative with her LINK card:

> I get $400.00 from LINK. Nowadays, no matter how much your income, it's not gonna' add up to what you [need] … Then bein' a woman with kids, you gotta' do what you gotta' do. That mean you have to find someone who's tryin' to sell a LINK card. I get a LINK card and I buys a LINK card [each] month if I have to, and I'll sell a LINK card if I have to. I might have a $100.00 [card], and I know this $100.00 goin'

to give me $150.00. It's goin' to give me an extra $50.00, OK, I'll buy it … You know, it has to be like that nowadays. You don't have a choice.

Other caregivers used local resources. Both Tracy and Dominique relied on neighborhood organizations when food supplies were short, but they used local resources differently. Tracy used "food baskets" at her church and "food giveaways" at community centers only during extreme emergencies. For Tracy, a period of unemployment motivated her to seek food for her family at local community resources.

Caregivers like Dominique used local institutional resources regularly as an extension of their LINK resources. Dominique was familiar with local food venues that provided food to families with few eligibility restrictions. Each month when her food stamps ran out, Dominique supplemented her food supplies with food from various community organizations, including churches and the Salvation Army. She found that she was able to prepare entire meals with the provisions provided: "You can still cook a meal with that box of food that God done gave you from the church."

Discussion

We used qualitative data and a family resilience perspective to explore the experience of food insecurity among a sample of African American female caregivers with young children and who live in an inner-city neighborhood. People living in poverty are often perceived to have poor learning and abstraction skills, and thus only incomplete knowledge (Krumer-Nevo, 2005). Yet, as pointed out by Krumer-Nevo, low-income populations have valuable life knowledge that can provide a full contextual picture of the realities of life in poverty. These qualitative data allowed us to elaborate on quantitative profiles of food-insecure households that identified the demographic risk factors of social class, race, household composition, and

location and the prevalence and severity of food insecurity. Based on women's firsthand accounts we highlighted coping behaviors that reflected family strengths. As found in other studies that report on food insecurity coping strategies (Ahluwalia et al., 1998; Hoisington et al., 2002; Monroe et al., 2002; Quandt et al., 2004), participants in our study used food provisioning, food consumption, social network, and institutional strategies.

Participants exhibited great agency despite the adversity of inadequate food supplies. As an example of human capital, caregivers were proud of their coping efforts that required active planning, budgeting, decision-making, and resource seeking. Caregivers also relied upon social connections. Social ties to kin, significant others, and friends and neighbors represented an important source of social capital that buffered women from a sense of despair and engendered a sense of hopefulness. To be sure, caregivers' coping strategies did not always prevent food shortages, but it is likely that women's efforts lessened the severity and frequency of food insecurity.

Implications

Our study findings have relevance for nutrition educators as they design programs for low-income families. For instance, the Expanded Food and Nutrition Education Program (EFNEP) curriculum focuses on shopping on a budget, effective shopping skills, and stretching food dollars. Nutrition educators can work to promote the full range of proactive and preventive skills to those household managers that may not be making use of them, while reinforcing these strategies for the most skilled household managers. Nutrition educators would be wise to include the most knowledgeable home managers as peer advisors to other women. Women who are skillful in managing food resources on a limited income can share their strategies with other women who also struggle with food insecurity. This will not only provide social support to women, but also strengthen the sense of community.

Firsthand insights from caregivers can provide directions for food and nutrition assistance programs such as SNAP (LINK), WIC, and non-profit food banks. Because SNAP is a critical component of household food budgets and participants' strategies to manage food insecurity, efforts are needed to reduce barriers that interfere with food stamp receipt, such as longer recertification periods, and to reduce the length of the application process (K. Martin, Cook, Rogers, and Joseph, 2003; Metallinos-Katsaras et al., 2010).

WIC, another nutrition program, can be a vital component of women's efforts to prevent food insecurity. Findings from our study support the need to encourage greater utilization of WIC resources. Four of the households had children under 5 years of age who were eligible for WIC. The other four households had children who were 5 years of age and not eligible for WIC. None of the four eligible households was using WIC during the study period,

despite the known benefits of WIC in enhancing child nutrition and reducing maternal depression that has been associated with food insecurity (Black et al., 2012; Herman, Harrison, Afifi, and Jenks, 2004). WIC has been found to reduce household food insecurity among vulnerable populations, particularly if WIC participation begins early and is long-term (Metallinos-Katsaras et al., 2010). Attention to barriers that discourage use, such as transportation and access, office waiting times, and frequent recertification requirements, is necessary to expand the usage of the WIC program (Bhattarai, Duffy, and Raymond, 2005).

At the community level, other institution-based sources should be more widely used, including food pantries, the Salvation Army, and churches. In particular, food-insecure households should be made aware of the locations of these resources as a way of supplementing food reserves and discouraging crisis-oriented strategies such as eating less (McIntyre et al., 2003).

As part of TANF, LINK assistance, an institution-based strategy, was the cornerstone of women's management efforts. Without this assistance it is likely that our households would have experienced even higher levels of food insecurity (Nord, 2012; Ratcliffe and McKernan, 2009). Yet, LINK assistance, along with other careful management strategies, including low-wage and informal employment, was not enough. Non-food interventions are needed to help families move out of poverty, as inadequate income was inextricably related to food insecurity (Tarasuk, 2001). Interventions should continue to help families become economically independent through employment options that increase income and allow participants to become less reliant on social assistance programs (McIntyre et al., 2003).

More fundamentally, our research supports collaborative prevention and intervention efforts that are empowering in nature and build upon caregivers' drive and agency. Household food providers should be included in discussions of food insecurity, and encouraged to take an active stance against the economic and political conditions that undergird food insecurity (Hoisington et al., 2002; Ramadurai, Sharf, and Sharkey, 2012). At the community level, nutrition educators and social workers should focus on empowerment efforts that encourage household managers to collaborate with community organizations, including membership on advisory boards, to develop a local food environment that better addresses food insecurity among adults and children (Hoisington *et al.*, 2002). Other local interventions can include encouraging community gardens that provide fruits and vegetables to local food banks (Armstrong, 2002; Wakefield, Yeudall, Taron, and Reynolds, 2007).

Critical Thinking Questions

1. Based on resilience theory, what are the risk factors for food insecurity?
2. What is the relationship between, race, social class, and food insecurity?
3. What are the strategies that women use to address food insecurity? How do these strategies reflect resilience?
4. How do qualitative research methods uniquely contribute to our understanding of food insecurity?

5. What family policies and interventions would you recommend to address food insecurity for low-income, African American families living in inner-city neighborhoods?

Acknowledgments

This research was funded by awards from the Pampered Chef and Christopher Family Foundation through the Family Resiliency Center at the University of Illinois at Urbana-Champaign. Additionally, this project was supported by a USDA Institute of Food and Agriculture, Hatch Award # 600111 793 000 793369. Maria Greaves-Barnes assisted with data collection and Kimberly Crossman assisted with data analyses for the study. Tolu Olorode, Ngozi Emuchay, Joe Whatoff, and Khara Harper, undergraduate members of the Ethnographic Research Lab team in the Department of Human and Community Development at UIUC, also contributed to the research project. We gratefully acknowledge the enthusiastic involvement of our participants, who made this study possible.

References

Ahluwalia, I. B., Dodds, J. M., and Baligh, M. (1998). Social support and coping behaviors of low-income families experiencing food insufficiency in North Carolina. *Health Education and Behavior, 25*, 599–612.

Armstrong, D. (2002). A survey of community gardens in upstate New York: Implications for health promotion and community development. *Health and Place, 6*, 319–327.

Bhattarai, G. R., Duffy, P. A., and Raymond, J. (2005). Use of food pantries and food stamps in low-income households in the United States. *Journal of Consumer Affairs, 39*, 276–298.

Black, M. M., Quigg, A. M., Cook, J., Casey, P. H., Cutts, D. B., Chilton, M., and Frank, D. (2012). WIC participation and attenuation of stress-related child health risks of household food insecurity and caregiver depressive symptoms. *Archives of Pediatrics and Adolescent Medicine, 166*, 444–451.

Campbell, C. C., and Desjardins, E. (1989). A model and research approach for studying the management of limited resources by low income families. *Journal of Nutritional Education, 21*, 162–171.

Center for Healthcare Equity. (2011). Chicago's people and neighborhoods: Demographic and socioeconomic characteristics. Retrieved May 20, 2014 from http://chicagohealth77.org/characteristics/demographics/.

City-data.com (n.d.). Top 100 biggest cities. Retrieved May 30, 2014 from www.city-data.com/top1.html.

City of Chicago. (2011). Census data: Selected socioeconomic indicators in Chicago, 2006–2010. Retrieved May 30, 2014 from https://data.cityofchicago.org/Health-Human-Services/Census-Data-Selected-socioeconomic-indicators-in-C/kn9c-c2s2.

Coleman-Jensen, A., Nord, M., Andrews, M., and Carlson, S. (2012). *Household food security in the U.S. in 2011.* Economic research report 141. Washington, DC: United States Department of Agriculture, Economic Research Service. Retrieved October 10, 2012 from http://ers.usda.gov/publications/err-economic-research-report/err141.aspx.

Congressional Digest. (2010, December). Food insecurity in the United States: Impact on households with children. *Congressional Digest, 89*, 301–306.

Cook, J. T., and Frank, D. A. (2008). Food security, poverty, and human development in the United States. *Annals of the New York Academy of Sciences, 1136*, 193–209.

De Marco, M. D., Thorburn, S., and Kue, J. (2009). "In a country as affluent as America, people should be eating": Experiences with and perceptions of food insecurity among rural and urban Oregonians. *Qualitative Health Research, 19*, 1010–1024.

Dickerson, B. J. (1995). *African American single mothers: Understanding their lives and families.* Thousand Oaks, CA: Sage Publications.

Dominguez, S., and Watkins, C. (2003). Creating networks for survival and mobility: Social capital among African American and Latin American low-income mothers. *Social Problems, 50*, 111–135.

Edin, K., and Lein, L. (1997). *Making ends meet: How single mothers survive welfare.* New York: Russell Sage Foundation.

Greater Chicago Food Depository. (2012a). Food insecurity. Retrieved May 30, 2014 from http://www.chicagos-foodbank.org/site/PageServer?pagename=hunger_research.

Greater Chicago Food Depository. (2012b). Food insecurity data. Retrieved May 30, 2014 from http://www.chica-gosfoodbank.org/site/DocServer/Food_Insecurity_Data_2012.pdf?docID=8363.

Hamelin, A. M., Habicht, J. P., and Beaudry, M. (1999). Food insecurity: Consequences for the household and broader social implications. *Journal of Nutrition, 129*, 552S–558S.

Herman, D. R., Harrison, G. G., Afifi, A. A., and Jenks, E. (2004). The effect of WIC programs on food security status of pregnant, first-time participants. *Family Economics and Nutrition Review, 16*, 21–30.

Hill, R. B. (1998). *The strengths of African American families: Twenty-five years later.* Washington, DC: R & B Publishers.

Hoisington, A., Shultz, J. A., and Butkus, S. (2002). Coping strategies and nutrition education needs among food pantry users. *Journal of Nutrition Education and Behavior, 34*, 326–333.

Jarrett, R. L., and Jefferson, S. (2003). "A good mother got to fight for her children": Maternal strategies in a housing project. *Journal of Children and Poverty, 9*, 21–39.

Jarrett, R. L., Jefferson, S. R., and Kelly, J. N. (2010). Finding community in family: Neighborhood effects and African American extended kinship networks. *Journal of Comparative Family Studies, 30*, 177–187.

Jarrett, R. L., Sensoy Bahar, O., and Taylor, M. A. (2011). "Holler, run, be loud": Management strategies to promote child physical activity in a low-income, African American neighborhood. *Journal of Family Psychology, 25*, 825–836.

Khan, S., Pinckney, R. G., Keeney, D., Frankowski, B., and Carney, J. K. (2011). Prevalence of food insecurity and utilization of food assistance program: An exploratory survey of a Vermont middle school. *Journal of School Health, 81*, 15–20.

Krumer-Nevo, M. (2005). Listening to "life knowledge": A new direction in poverty studies. *International Journal of Social Welfare, 19*, 99–106. doi: 10.1111/j.1369-6866.2005.00346.x.

Laraia, B. A., Borja, J. B., and Bentley, M. E. (2009). Grandmothers, fathers, and depressive symptoms are associated with food insecurity among low-income first-time African-American mothers in North Carolina. *American Dietetic Association, 109*, 1042–1047.

Larson, N. I., and Story, M. T. (2010). Food insecurity and weight status among U.S. children and families. *American Journal of Preventive Medicine, 40*, 166–173.

Logan, S. L. M. (2000). *The Black family: Strengths, self-help, and positive change.* Boulder, CO: Westview Press.

Mammen, S., Bauer, J. W., and Richards, L. (2009). Understanding persistent food insecurity: A paradox of place and circumstance. *Social Indices Research, 92*, 151–168.

Martin, E. P., and Martin, J. (1978). *The Black extended family.* Chicago: University of Chicago Press.

Martin, K. S., Cook, J. T., Rogers, B. L., and Joseph, H. M. (2003). Public vs. private food assistance: Barriers to participation differ by age and ethnicity. *Journal of Nutrition Education and Behavior, 35*, 249–254.

McCubbin, H. I., Thompson, E. A., Thompson, A. I., and Fromer, J. E. (1998). *Resiliency in African-American families.* Thousand Oaks, CA: Sage Publications.

McIntyre, L., Glanville, N. T., Raine, K. D., Dayle, J. B., Anderson, B., and Battaglia, N. (2003). Do low-income lone mothers compromise their nutrition to feed their children? *Canadian Medical Association Journal, 168*, 686–691.

Metallinos-Katsaras, E., Gorman, K. S., Wilde, P., and Kallio, J. (2010). A longitudinal study of WIC participation on household food insecurity. *Maternal and Child Health Journal, 15*, 627–633.

Miles, M. B., and Huberman, A. M. (1994). *Qualitative data analysis: A source book of new methods.* Beverly Hills, CA: Sage Publications.

Monroe, P. A., O'Nell, C., Tiller, V. V., and Smith, J. (2002). *The challenge of compliance: Food security in rural households affected by welfare reform.* Food assistance needs of the South's vulnerable populations 5. Mississippi State, MS: Southern Rural Development Center.

Nord, M. (2012). How much does the Supplemental Nutrition Assistance Program alleviate food insecurity?

Evidence from recent programme leavers. *Public Health Nutrition, 15*, 811–817.

Nord, M., Coleman-Jensen, A., Andrews, M., and Carlson, S. (2010). *Household food security in the United States, 2009.* Economic research report 108. Washington, DC: United States Department of Agriculture, Economic Research Service. Retrieved May 30, 2014 from http://www.ers.usda.gov/Publications/err108/err108.pdf.

Nord, M., and Golla, M. (2009). *Does SNAP decrease food insecurity? Untangling the self-selection effect.* Economic research report 85. Washington, DC: United States Department of Agriculture, Economic Research Service. Retrieved May 30, 2014 from http://www.ers.usda.gov/media/184824/err85_1_.pdf.

Olson, C. M., Anderson, K., Kiss, E., Lawrence, F. C., and Seiling, S. B. (2004). Factors protecting against and contributing to food insecurity among rural families. *Family Economics and Nutrition Review, 16*, 12–20.

Pinstrup-Andersen, P. (2009). Food security: Definition and measurement. *Food Security, 1*, 5–7.

Quandt, S. A., Arcury, T. A., Early, J., Tapia, J., and Davis, J. D. (2004). Household food security among migrant and seasonal Latino farmworkers in North Carolina. *Public Health Reports, 119*, 568–576.

Radimer, K. L., Olson, C. M., and Campbell, C. C. (1990). Development of indicators to assess hunger. *Journal of Nutrition, 120*, 1544–1548.

Ramadurai, V., Sharf, B., and Sharkey, J. R. (2012). Rural food insecurity in the United States as an overlooked site of struggle in health communication. *Health Communication, 27*, 794–805.

Ratcliffe, C., and McKernan, S. M. (2009). *How much does SNAP reduce food insecurity?* Report for the Urban Institute. Retrieved May 30, 2014 from http://www.urban.org/url.cfm?ID=412065.

Seefeldt, K. S., and Castelli, T. (2009). Low-income women's experiences with food programs, food spending, and food-related hardships. USDA Economic Research Services Food and Nutrition Assistance Research Program, contractor and cooperator report 52. Washington, DC: United States Department of Agriculture, Economic Research Service.

Stack, C. B. (1974). *All our kin: Strategies for survival in a Black neighborhood.* New York: Harper and Row.

Stevens, C. A. (2010). Exploring food insecurity among young mothers (15–24 years). *Journal for Specialists in Pediatric Nursing, 15*, 163–171.

Swanson, J. A., Olson, C. M., Miller, E. O., and Lawrence, F. C. (2008). Rural mothers' use of formal programs and informal social supports to meet family food needs: A mixed methods study. *Journal of Family Economic Issues, 29*, 674–690.

Tarasuk, V. S. (2001). Household food insecurity with hunger is associated with women's food intakes, health and household circumstances. *American Society for Nutritional Sciences, 131*, 2670–2676.

United States Census Bureau. (2010a). Profile of general population and housing characteristics: 2010 Census demographic profile [data file]. Washington, DC: United States Census Bureau. Retrieved March 31, 2012 from http://factfinder2.census.gov/faces/tableservices/jsf/pages/productview.xhtml?pid=DEC_10_DP_DPDP1&prodType=table.

United States Census Bureau. (2010b). Median income in the past 12 months: 2006–2010 American Community Survey 5-year estimates [data file]. Washington, DC: United States Census Bureau. Retrieved March 31, 2012 from http://factfinder2.census.gov/faces/nav/jsf/pages/searchresults.xhtml?ref=geo&refresh=t#.

United States Department of Agriculture. (2012). Definitions of food insecurity. Washington, DC: United States Department of Agriculture, Economic Research Service. Retrieved October 1, 2012 from http://www.ers.usda.gov/topics/food-nutrition-assistance/food-security-in-the-us/definitions-of-food-security.aspx#.U3M4QYFdV8E.

Valentine, B. (1978). *Hustling and other hard work: Life styles in the ghetto.* New York: Free Press.

Wakefield, S., Yeudall, F., Taron, C., and Reynolds, J. (2007). Growing urban health: Community gardening in southeast Toronto. *Health Promotion International, 22*, 92–102.

Walsh, F. A. (2002). Family resilience framework: Innovative practice applications. *Family Relations, 51*, 130–137.

Whiting, E. F., and Ward, C. (2010). Food provisioning strategies, food insecurity, and stress in an economically vulnerable community: The Northern Cheyenne case. *Agriculture and Human Values, 27*, 489–504.

Zollar, A. C. (1985). *A member of the family: Strategies for Black family continuity.* Chicago: Nelson-Hall.

8

The Diverse Family Contexts
of Youth in Foster Care

Lenore M. McWey and Armeda Stevenson Wojciak

In Chapter 8, McWey and Stevenson Wojciak tackle the issue of children who cannot be cared for by their parent(s) due to maltreatment or other reasons that contribute to their need for foster care. Out-of-home placements vary in their structure (e.g., relative versus nonrelative care, temporary or long-term group care) and are diverse contexts of care for youth – with some children doing better than others. The effects of foster care depend on placement type, stability, duration, and most importantly the quality of care by the adults in children's lives.

Case Example: Robin

"What happens under this roof – stays under this roof." That was the cardinal rule of our household. I hope my family forgives me for sharing a little about our story.

My name is Robin.[1] I am 16 and the oldest of four siblings. My siblings and I are very close – I think it is because we have to be. You see, my parents never really got along. Sometimes their fighting got pretty scary. Even the kid next door once said, at the bus stop of all places, that she could hear my mom and dad fighting all the way from inside her bedroom. I never did like that kid. So, when my parents finally told us they were getting a divorce, I was actually excited. I thought things would get better, but things just seemed to get worse …

There are over 400,000 children currently in foster care (Adoption and Foster Care Analysis and Reporting System (AFCARS), 2012). Children and adolescents are placed in foster care when courts have deemed it too dangerous for them to continue to live in their homes (Lawrence, Carlson, and Egeland, 2006). The average age of a child in foster care is 9 years old, and the age of youth in foster care ranges from infants to adolescents (AFCARS, 2012). Foster care is a complicated system. In this chapter we discuss precipitating factors associated with foster care placement, the process once involved with foster care, foster care policy, and diverse family contexts associated with foster care.

The foster care system falls under the umbrella of the child welfare system (CWS). The mission of the CWS is to respond to the needs of children who have been reported to child protective services because of abuse and/or neglect (Pecora, Whittaker, Maluccio, and Barth, 2000). The primary goal of the CWS is to protect children from harm; the secondary goals are to preserve existing family units and encourage the children's development into independent adults who contribute to their communities (Pecora *et al.*, 2000). The mission and functionality of the CWS are particularly important given the estimated 3.3 million reports annually to child protective services agencies across the country (US Department of Health and Human Services (USDHHS), 2010). Fortunately, once a family becomes involved with the CWS most children do not experience further maltreatment (US Department of Health and Human Services, 2013). Yet because of the negative outcomes associated with CWS involvement, it is not uncommon to hear skepticism about the foster care system (Jonson-Reid and Barth, 2000; Lawrence *et al.*, 2006).

Factors that Precipitate Foster Care Placement

Case Example: Robin

Mom didn't come out of her bedroom much after dad moved out. She started drinking even more than she used to and things started to slip through the cracks. Sometimes she'd forget to pay the electric bill and our electricity would get turned off (we'd always get it turned back on though) or she'd forget to go grocery shopping – things like that. Oh, and the plumbing in our house wasn't working right. I don't know why but the kitchen sink wouldn't drain and the toilets were always backing up. Money was tight, so we just made the best of it.

Children and adolescents are often placed in foster care due to substantiated cases of abuse and/or neglect. Definitions of child abuse and neglect differ from state to state. Most states, however, classify child maltreatment into four general types: neglect, physical abuse, psychological maltreatment, and sexual abuse (USDHHS, 2010). Cases are classified as "other" if they do not fall under one of the main categories. "Other" forms of maltreatment may include things such as abandonment or lack of supervision.

Neglect is the leading form of maltreatment of children involved in the CWS. Approximately 78% of children in foster care experience neglect, followed by physical abuse (18%), sexual abuse (9%), and psychological maltreatment (8%; USDHHS, 2010). Approximately 10% of children suffer "other" types of maltreatment. These percentages do not total 100% because it is possible for children to have suffered multiple types of maltreatment.

A complex combination of risk factors may be associated with increased risk for child maltreatment and subsequent CWS involvement (Benjet, Azar, and Kuersten-Hogan, 2003; Rittner and Dozier, 2000). Specific parental risk factors include poverty, domestic violence, incarceration, mental health issues, and substance use. Although these risk factors in and of themselves often do not provide sufficient grounds for removal of children from the homes, they often place families at increased risk for foster care placement. For example, lower-income and working-poor families are exposed to additional stressors and have fewer resources, which may obstruct parents' ability to care for their children (Dyk, 2004). Although poverty does not necessarily constitute neglect, it often can be hard to distinguish between the two. In fact, the connection between maltreatment, poverty, and foster care has long been established (e.g., Jones, 1998; Ondersma, 2002), and as already stated, neglect is the leading reason for the removal of children from their homes.

The presence of parental domestic violence also places children at greater risk for child abuse and neglect (Stover, 2005). For instance, Kohl, Edleson, English, and Barth (2005) found that families with active domestic violence were more likely to have substantiated cases of child maltreatment. The same study also found that domestic violence, along with other cumulative risk factors, was associated with increased likelihood of placement in out-of-home care.

In addition, children of incarcerated parents have become increasingly involved in the foster care system (Johnson and Waldfogel, 2002). As with other risk factors, although incarceration cannot be the sole reason for termination of parental rights (Seymour and Finney-Hairston, 2001), those who are incarcerated often lose parental rights due to deficiencies in permanency planning procedures (Johnson and Waldfogel, 2002).

Parental mental health issues pose another risk factor associated with increased likelihood for involvement with the CWS. While severe mental health issues could indeed affect one's ability to parent, mental health issues alone do not equate with potentially problematic parenting (Benjet et al., 2003). Even adults with severe mental health issues can be effective parents with the proper medications and treatment (Mullick, Miller, and Jacobsen, 2001; Risley-Curtiss, Stromwall, Hunt, and Teska, 2004). In fact, courts are to avoid making universal decisions regarding mental health and foster care, but are instead mandated to consider whether or not a parent's mental health concerns are "significantly detrimental" to parenting (Azar, Benjet, Fuhrmann, and Cavallero, 1995, p. 601; Benjet et al., 2003). Yet, some have found parental mental health to be associated with an increased risk for maltreatment (Sidebotham, Golding, and the ALSPAC Study Team, 2001), and foster care placement outcomes (Azar et al., 1995; Zuravin and DePanfilis, 1997).

Many parents of children in foster care also struggle with alcohol or other drug use (AOD) issues. For example, Famularo, Kinscherff, and Fenton (1992) estimated that approximately two-thirds of abuse and neglect cases involved parental AOD. As with other presenting problems, parents with AOD are frequently facing a number of risk factors, such as mental health issues (Young, Gardner, and Dennis, 1998). In fact, the specific combination of parental AOD and parental mental health issues is particularly concerning because such parents are at greater risk for termination of parental rights (Azar et al., 1995; Zuravin and DePanfilis, 1997).

The notion of "cumulative risk" of families is important. The cumulative risk hypothesis suggests that the buildup of risk factors affects family outcomes, such that the more risk factors a family has, the higher the prevalence of problems (Appleyard, Egeland, van Dulmen, and Sroufe, 2005). While one risk factor alone may or may not elevate propensity for child maltreatment and foster care placement, the culmination of a number of risk factors may place families at heightened risk for CWS involvement. For example, scholars examined the impact of cumulative risk factors including family size, negative life events, mental health issues, substance use, history of abuse, and incarceration among a high risk sample of mothers with substance use concerns. They found that mothers with more cumulative risk demonstrated parental attitudes associated with a greater propensity for child abuse (Nair, Schuler, Black, Kettinger, and Harrington, 2003). Additionally, other researchers reported children in families with the highest level of cumulative risk were 10 times more likely to be placed in foster care compared to families with lower levels of cumulative risk (Kohl et al., 2005). As such, it is often a combination of factors that places families at increased risk.

The Foster Care Process

As Robin's case illustrates, children and families become involved with the foster care system when reports of suspected abuse or neglect are made to the CWS. Most recent data suggest that in one year an estimated 3.3 million reports were made to the CWS, representing approximately 5.9 million children across the country (USDHHS, 2010). Whereas some states require all citizens to report child abuse and neglect, other states identify members of specific professions as "*mandated reporters*." Such professionals are often social workers, teachers, day care providers, police officers, and mental and physical health professionals (Child Welfare Information Gateway, 2010a). It is important to know your state laws about mandated reporting because failure to report suspected abuse may not only maintain a child's risk, but may also result in a fine or imprisonment. You can visit this website to search for your state statute regarding mandated

Case Example: Robin

I knew I shouldn't have gone to basketball practice!

It didn't happen often, but sometimes mom would get so mad she'd go a little crazy.

My bruises weren't too bad when I left for school in the morning and I was careful to bring makeup to put on before basketball practice that afternoon. But I forgot it was report card day. Coach always made our whole team run a mile for every D or F any girl on the team made. So, of course, by the end of practice my makeup strategy failed miserably. Coach asked me about it and I thought he believed my excuse. But when the stranger with a Child Protective Services name tag showed up at our house the next night, I knew I was wrong.

Maybe if this were the first time Child Protective Services had come to our home, my basketball mistake wouldn't have been so bad. But I overheard them saying they already knew about my parents' fights and how mom sometimes forgot to pay the electric bill. They looked inside our kitchen cabinets and all throughout our home. I guess my bruises sealed the deal. They decided to put us in foster care. They removed the four of us that night.

reporting: https://www.childwelfare.gov/systemwide/laws_policies/state/.

Once the CWS receives a report about suspected maltreatment, a two-stage process is initiated: (1) screening and (2) response (USDHHS, 2010). In the screening phase, the information provided is evaluated to determine whether the report requires CWS action. Referrals that do not meet specific state and agency defined criteria are "screened out." Estimates suggest, however, that approximately 61% of reports are "screened in." If a referral is "screened in," the CWS must respond (Child Welfare Information Gateway, 2010a). The response usually begins with an investigation and concludes with a determination: either a case is "unsubstantiated," meaning there was insufficient evidence to suspect the child was at risk for or was being maltreated; or "substantiated," which means the allegation was supported (USDHHS, 2010).

Recent data suggest that 81% of child victims were maltreated by a parent, with mothers more often than fathers perpetrating the maltreatment (USDHHS, 2010). Among child victims, 34% were younger than 4 years old and 23% were between the ages of 4 and 7. Substantiated cases involved a nearly even number of boys and girls, and the race or ethnicities of child victims were: 45% White, 22% African American, and 21% Hispanic (USDHHS, 2010).

Reponses to substantiated cases vary and are based on an evaluation of a family's needs and strengths. In most instances, children remain in their homes and "in-home services" are offered to families. In cases where it is deemed unsafe for children to remain in the home, foster care services are provided. An estimated 254,375 children entered foster care in the most recent fiscal year (Child Welfare Information Gateway, 2012a). Once a child is removed from the home, states are required to develop a case plan. In most cases, reunification with biological parents is the primary objective (52%; AFCARS, 2012). Case plans often include goals that the parents must meet in order to regain custody of their children and a time frame for accomplishing those goals (Child Welfare Information Gateway, 2011). In essence, case plans are developed to help parents remedy the conditions that led to the removal of the child from the home.

Given the complexity of the issues frequently associated with child removal (e.g., domestic violence, physical abuse, neglect, parental mental health and/or substance use issues), there may be many case plan requirements. For example, in a study of families involved with the foster care system, parental substance abuse was a problem for 75% of the sample (D'Andrade and Chambers,

2012). Furthermore, 30% of the parents in the sample experienced domestic violence, 26% had mental health problems, 40% experienced incarceration, 30% had housing issues, 20% were unemployed, and 16% had physical health problems. On average, parents had 2.5 problems, and substance use and domestic violence were the most common combination, followed by mental health and substance abuse (D'Andrade and Chambers, 2012). As such, case plans may require parents to complete services such as domestic violence psychoeducation, mental health and substance use treatment, parent education, and attend scheduled visitation with their children, all while gaining or maintaining employment. Completing numerous case plan requirements and remedying these conditions can be a formidable challenge for some parents.

To illustrate, consider Robin's mother. She is struggling with depression and self-medicates her feelings of depression with alcohol. The CWS removed her four children from the home because of concerns about potential neglect and physical abuse. The house is in shambles; there is no food in the refrigerator, major repairs are needed to the home, and money is scarce. According to the case plan, Robin's mother must successfully complete a number of services in order to regain custody of her children. She has to complete: (a) substance use treatment for her use of alcohol; (b) individual counseling to address her depression; and (c) parent education classes due to the alleged physical abuse. In addition, she has to maintain employment and make repairs to the home so that conditions are suitable for family living. Unfortunately, however, her depression has only worsened now that her children have been removed, and she can't seem to do all the things she is required to do in order to get them back. This can perpetuate a cycle, one that would make it difficult for parents to meet all the requirements of their case plans in order to successfully remedy the conditions that led to the removal of their children from their homes. This illustration is just one example of the many difficulties parents may experience while working toward reunification, particularly if there are multiple risk factors present.

Types of Placement for Children in Out-of-Home Care

Case Example: Robin

They said they'd try to place us with relatives, but our closest relative lived seven states away so I wasn't too hopeful about that. They also said they'd try to keep me and my siblings together, but they warned that it was harder to find a home for older kids.

My baby sister and brother got to stay together. They were placed with a nice family who had two kids of their own. My other sister and I were placed in what they call "group" homes. My group home was basically a place where a bunch of other teenaged girls stayed who also weren't allowed to live at home.

While case plans are developed for parents, an out-of-home placement is secured for the children. Generally speaking there are three different types of out-of-home placements for children who are removed from their homes: (1) traditional foster care; (2) kinship care; and (3) residential care. Each type of treatment has strengths and weaknesses and the empirical knowledge associated with each placement type is still growing.

Traditional foster care

Traditional foster care typically involves a child placed with a family that he or she does not have a prior relationship with/does not know. Another term for this type of placement is "non-relative family foster care" and 47% of youth in out-of-home care live in these settings (AFCARS, 2012). The transition to these placements often involves important changes for the child, including obvious changes to who they live with, changes to their community, and changes in schools. These placement types also are characterized as having a larger number of children residing in

them compared to non-foster care placements
(O'Hare, 2008). There also is a greater likelihood that
the placement involves a single parent or cohabitating family with a lower than average household
income (O'Hare, 2008).

The quality of foster parent–child relationships
varies widely, and is known to be associated with
child mental health outcomes. For example, children
who have poor quality relationships with foster parents are more likely to display specific mental health
problems and low self-esteem (Dore and Eisner,
1993), whereas greater cohesion with foster parents
is associated with fewer mental health problems
(Fernandez, 2009). Orme and Buehler (2001) conducted a review of literature of foster family characteristics and the impact of this placement type
on the child's emotional and behavioral problems.
Although extant research was limited, their review
included 34 studies of non-relative foster homes.
Unfortunately, much of the research had limitations
such as small sample sizes and cross-sectional research
designs leaving many important questions unanswered. Based on the research available, however, the
authors concluded that an association indeed exists
between foster family characteristics and the child's
emotional and behavioral problems. It is important
to consider, though, that the children may have
already had emotional and behavioral problems prior
to placement in foster care.

Children's emotional or behavioral problems
prior to placement and those that are demonstrated
while in care often have negative influences on the
child's placement stability. For instance, children
with emotional and/or behavior problems have a
2.5 greater likelihood to experience more placement moves than those without emotional or
behavioral problems (Barth et al., 2007). Placement
instability is an important concern for youth in foster care because placement instability has been
associated with negative outcomes for the child
(Thorpe and Swart, 1992). For instance, children
who experienced more changes in their placement
were associated with declines in their academic
performance (Thorpe and Swart, 1992), whereas
those with fewer placement changes or school
changes had lower levels of depression (White
et al., 2009).

Kinship foster care

Kinship foster care is the second largest type of out-
of-home placement, with 27% of youth in foster
care residing in these placements. Kinship care can
include formal and informal arrangements with the
children's relatives, godparents, stepparents, or close
family friends where full-time care is provided to
the child (Child Welfare Information Gateway,
2010b). The number of children in kinship care has
grown dramatically over the past two decades. The
increased use of kinship placements may be related
to a lack of non-family foster care homes, and shifts
in federal policy prioritizing kin as caregivers (Leos-
Urbel, Bess, and Green, 2002). A more detailed discussion of foster care policies is provided later in
this chapter.

In a synthesis of a decade and a half of literature on
kinship care, results indicated that kinship caregivers
were more likely to be African American, had a lower
socioeconomic status, were less educated, unemployed, and received less support, services, and training compared to non-relative foster care providers
(Cuddeback, 2004). Results of the review also indicated that child welfare professionals often applied
different standards to kinship care providers compared
to non-relative care providers.

A recent study compared differences in youth's
reported closeness to their caregivers across different
out-of-home placement types (Helfrich, Stevenson-
Wojciak, and McWey, in press). Results indicated that
youth in kinship placements reported the highest levels of closeness to their caregivers compared to other
types of placements. Further, youth in kinship care
demonstrated the lowest levels of mental health problems compared to those in foster and residential care.
This may be because there is a continuity of family
relationships.

Another concern associated with foster care is the
number of times children move from home to
home. An added benefit of kinship placements,
however, is that children in this type of setting tend
to stay in the same kinship home – a concept called
placement stability. In a comparative study of 270
youth in non-relative foster homes and kinship care,
no differences were found between the two groups
on outcome variables such as school attendance,

with one exception – those in kinship care had greater placement stability than those in non–relative foster care (Farmer, 2009). This finding is important because placement stability has been associated with more positive outcomes for youth in foster care (White *et al.*, 2009).

Residential care

Although traditional foster care and kinship care placements are preferred, approximately 20% of youth in foster care are placed in "residential" or group homes (Child Welfare Information Gateway, 2012a). Defining residential care is more difficult, because this placement type encompasses a wide range of environments including smaller group homes serving up to 10 youth to institutional programs with up to 100 youth in very structured and restrictive environments (Frensch and Cameron, 2002). Residential care is often referred to as the "last resort" for children for multiple reasons: (a) it is considered an invasive intervention; (b) the youth often have not been successful in other placement types; (c) the youth placed in residential treatment are considered the most difficult to treat; and lastly (d) it is the most costly of all placement options (Frensch and Cameron, 2002; Sunseri, 2005). A review of the residential care literature indicated that better outcomes have been documented for youth with higher self-esteem, less involvement with substance use, and more familial support (Frensch and Cameron, 2002).

In our example, Robin was placed in a group home not because of acute mental health concerns or a failed placement history, but instead because there were no nearby relatives able to serve as her caregiver and no foster home openings specifically for older youth. According to research, her success in this type of setting will depend on her ability to maintain a high level of self-esteem, resist peer pressure to engage in substance use, and her capability to sustain contentions with biological family members.

Common Challenges Associated with the Foster Care Context

Placement instability

The longer it takes for parents to remedy the conditions that led to the removal of the children from their homes, the longer children remain in foster care. The longer the children are in foster care, the higher the likelihood for placement disruption and the higher the number of out-of-home placements (Children's Bureau, 2010). Placement instability and increased number of placements, in turn, are associated with negative outcomes such as poorer academic achievements (Pecora *et al.*, 2006), greater instances of

---

Case Example: Robin

I am so thankful that my baby brother and sister are together and with a nice family. My other sister, though, is having a really hard time. She is acting out at her group home and they are threatening to move her to yet another placement. Plus, she never did like school much and is doing even worse now. She secretly told me she even tried to break her own finger to avoid having to go to school. Of course, that didn't work and that very day she was beat up by a bully in the school bathroom. I'm really worried about her.

It seems the four of us siblings rarely get to see each other anymore. I miss them very much.

Mom keeps saying she is doing everything thing she can to get us back. "Not much longer," she keeps telling us. Every time I see her, though, it looks like she has been crying. I know that can't be a good sign.

I'm just so thankful that I'll be 18 soon. Then I can do whatever I want.

depression (White et al., 2009), and a higher propensity for delinquency (Ryan and Testa, 2005).

Whereas some suggest that having more placements causes these negative outcomes (e.g., Lewis, Dozier, Ackerman, and Sepulveda-Kozakowski, 2007), other suggest that perhaps those with more emotional and behavioral problems are more likely to experience placement instability (Barth et al., 2007). Regardless of cause and effect, the experience can be difficult for youth, and scholars have studied this phenomenon. For example, one researcher found that children's inability to form relationships with foster families was predictive of placement disruptions, positing a bidirectional effect (Leathers, 2002). Perhaps a foster parent was not displaying warmth to the child, and over time the child had learned not to attach to others. In a qualitative investigation of this experience, a youth who experienced multiple moves shared: "I never attached ... I learned not to trust anybody but myself. You know I was extremely detached from any caretaker that I ever had purposefully 'cause that was my survival technique" (Unrau, Seita, and Putney, 2008, p. 1261).

Separation from siblings

Children in foster care also may experience separation from siblings. Although policies and practices often state that reasonable efforts should be made to place siblings together, this may not happen for a number of reasons. Such reasons include a lack of placements that can accommodate larger sibling sets, and placements lacking the necessary certifications to care for children with special needs (Shlonsky, Bellamy, Elkins, and Ashare, 2005; Whelan, 2003). Other reasons for not placing siblings together may involve the relationship between the siblings themselves. For instance, siblings may be separated in cases involving abuse between siblings or acute sibling rivalry (Leathers, 2005). Furthermore, foster parents may request a child in a sibling set who has emotional or behavioral problems be removed from the home, while asking for the other siblings to stay (Leathers, 2005).

Among families involved with the CWS, the sibling relationship may be the most important familial relationship prior to foster care placement and while in care; the presence of a sibling can help provide stability, love, be a permanent relationship, and help lessen some of the trauma and loss experienced due to foster care placement (Herrik and Piccus, 2005). A growing body of research has examined the potential benefits of siblings of youth in foster care, primarily when siblings are in the same placement. For example, youth who were placed with all their siblings had higher academic achievement and lower reports of internalizing behaviors than those placed with a few of or none of their siblings (Hegar and Rosenthal, 2009). Further, children who were placed with their siblings tended to be better integrated into their foster homes (Leathers, 2005). Unfortunately, most of the research focused on siblings in foster care has to do with whether they are placed together, rather than outcomes of such placements. Thus more needs to be done to better understand relationship quality among siblings and how to maintain these important relationships for youth in foster care.

Runaways

Running away from foster placements places youth at risk for serious adverse outcomes (Courtney and Zinn, 2009). For instance, youth who run away are at a greater risk of being physically assaulted and sexually exploited (Biehal and Wade, 1999). Estimates vary widely; however, one study reported that anything from 21% to 71% of youth run away from their foster placement (Biehal and Wade, 1999). Researchers have identified two groups of runaways within the foster care system: those who run away to be with their friends and family, and those that run away to get away from their current living environment (Biehal and Wade, 1999). As with those who ran away from their current living arrangement, those who ran away to stay with friends also tended to have difficulty with their placements, but were not often exposed to victimization like the other group was. Building upon this understanding, studies have investigated predictors of running away. In a sample of 352 cases, the greatest predictors of running away were longer periods of time in foster care, being older, having a prior history of running away, as well as having "other" listed as your permanency goal rather than reunification or adoption (Nesmith, 2006). In a larger study, predictors of running away were investigated with a sample of 14,282 youth who had run away between 1993 and 2003, and who were between the ages of 12 and 18 at first run (Courtney and Zinn, 2009). Findings were similar to prior research. Those who were older, as well as those who entered foster care as an adolescent, were more likely to run away. Girls were more likely to run away than boys. Type of placement was also a predictor: those with the least likelihood of running away were in kinship placements, followed by non-relative placement, with more youth running away from residential facilities. African American or Hispanic youth were more likely to have a first-time run compared to Caucasian youth; however, race was not predictive of subsequent runs. Further, the presence of mental health or behavioral problems and substance use were associated with a higher likelihood of running away. However, if a youth had a more serious mental health diagnosis like schizophrenia or if they had anxiety or a somatoform disorder, they were less likely to run away. Lastly, those placed with their sibling also were less likely to run away.

Aging-out

In 2010, 27,000 adolescents "aged out" of the foster care system (USDHHS, 2010). These adolescents were neither successfully reunified with their biological families nor adopted by a new family. The average age of exit from the foster care system is around 18.5 years old. While in foster care, the average number of placements for youth who aged out was 6.5 and the average length of time in care was approximately six years.

Approximately a third of youth who aged out had 10 or more school changes between elementary and high school (Pecora *et al.*, 2006).

Although this sub-population of youth in foster care is now gaining specialized attention and services (see Box 8.1), until the mid-1980s adolescents were aging out of the foster care system without permanency plans and were experiencing adverse outcomes as a result (Scannapieco, Connell-Carrick, and Painter, 2007). Youth in foster care may not have been as well prepared to transition into adulthood and often lose access to services as they age out of the system (Osgood, Foster, and Courtney, 2010). Perhaps not surprisingly, youth who age out of foster care are at risk for experiencing many negative outcomes, including homelessness, (Massinga and Pecora, 2004; Pecora *et al.*, 2003), poorer access to health care (Kushel, Yen, Gee, and Courtney, 2007), educational shortcomings (Greeson, Usher, and Grinstein-Weiss, 2010; Pecora *et al.*, 2003), greater likelihood of early pregnancy (Love, McIntosh, Rosst, and Tertzakian, 2005), increased likelihood of involvement with the criminal justice system (Massinga and Pecora, 2004), and greater reliance on public assistance (Pecora *et al.*, 2006).

It is important to identify patterns of risk and resilience among adolescents who aged out of the foster care system (Yates and Grey, 2012). For example, one study found that approximately half of a sample of youth in foster care was categorized as *resilient*. These youth experienced hardships, but were able to score reasonably well on measures of self-esteem, depression, and educational, occupational, and relational

---

Box 8.1   Independent Living Programs Help Youth who "Age Out"

Across the country there are "independent living programs" aimed to help youth who are aging out of foster care; however, researchers suggest major changes to such programs in order to ensure children aging-out have the same advantages as others (e.g., Pecora *et al.*, 2006). These suggested changes include working with youth to develop a transition plan six months prior to them aging out, and participating in life skills training. Other suggestions include extending foster care services until the age of 21 and ensuring independent living services until the age of 25. Interestingly, the suggestions are not all financial or educational; another recommendation was to encourage youth to build and maintain lifelong relationships with foster parents or other supportive people in their life so they have someone to turn to in times of difficulty.

competence. There were also two other forms of resilient groups, those with internal resilience and those with external forms of resilience. Those with internal resilience were characterized as having healthy self-esteem and lower levels of depression, whereas those with external resilience were doing better with educational and occupational adjustment. The last group was categorized as *maladapted*. These youth were reportedly struggling with adjustment in all areas of their lives. Results of these studies, however, are based on samples representing specific areas of the United States, and therefore may not be generalizable to the entire population of youth in foster care.

Factors Associated with Resilience

Despite the fact that youth in foster care have a heightened risk for many adverse outcomes compared to youth not involved in the foster care system, many of these children and adolescents demonstrate *resilience*. Resilience is a term that signifies that one was able to overcome a difficult time and demonstrate successful outcomes (Cicchetti and Garmezy, 1993). In other words, resilience is the ability to thrive in the midst of adversity and stress (Connor and Davidson, 2003). The body of research examining factors associated with resilience of youth in foster care is growing. For example, researchers studying a sample of 1,087 youth who aged out of foster care examined factors associated with risk and resilience, finding that youth had significantly higher self-esteem if they received mental health services and perceived their foster

parents as helpful (Anctil, McCubbin, O'Brien, and Pecora, 2007). In another study, social support was a contributing factor associated with youth who aged out and were "successful" (Hass and Graydon, 2009). In these cases, youth were successful if they completed post-secondary education, vocational training, or were in at least their junior year in a university. Social support not only came from individuals such as family and friends, but also from therapists, or community centers or programs. Findings also suggested that youth enjoyed being in school and felt that they had someone at school who believed that they could be successful. These youth also expressed a strong desire to help others and to be part of community activities such as sport teams, clubs, and church. The majority of these youth specified having long-term goals, as well as a sense of confidence in achieving those goals. Lastly, results indicated that these youth also had self-awareness about their behaviors and a sense of purpose in life. The authors of this study cautioned, however, that the sub-sample of "successful" youth in their sample may have importantly differed from youth in the foster care population in that they had few instances of mental health treatment, involvement with the criminal justice system, and educational challenges, each of which is common for youth in foster care.

Potential Benefits of Foster Care Placement

The goal of reducing the number of children who are abused or neglected once in foster care is a national priority, and the rates of maltreatment indicate improvement toward this goal, with a median rate of 0.35% of youth in out-of-home care experiencing maltreatment while in foster care (Children's Bureau, 2010). Protection from harm and child well-being, however, are not synonymous. Understanding the well-being of youth in foster care is complex, because children often enter care with more challenges than children not involved with the CWS. In fact, studies indicate that behavior problems of children in foster care are 2.5–3.5 times higher than the general population (Dubowitz, Zuravin, Starr, Feigelman, and Harington, 1993).

Case Example: Robin

I am certain college is my ticket out of this. Thank God I've always done well in school. My SAT scores just came back and I think they are good enough to get me into a four-year college. I just want to move away from here and start all over again. Maybe they'll even let me get custody of my siblings when I turn 18.

Researchers have concluded that not only do children in foster care have high rates of emotional and behavioral problems when compared to children not in foster care but they also have "exceptionally high" rates in absolute terms (Tarren-Sweeney, 2008, p. 7). Specifically, research suggests that youth in out-of-home care exhibit higher levels of both internalizing and externalizing behavior problems (Heflinger, Simpkins, and Combs-Orme, 2000). Internalizing behaviors include depression, withdrawal, and anxiety; externalizing behaviors include school problems, aggression, and oppositional disorders (Achenbach, 1991; Leadbeater, Kuperminc, Blatt, and Hertzog, 1999).

Indeed, the contextual consequences of removing children from their homes and placing them in new, unfamiliar environments may lead to initial heightened problem behaviors. Protective factors, however, may be associated with decreases in problem behaviors over time (Leon, Ragsdale, Miller, and Spacarelli, 2008) since protective factors are thought of as a buffer or a way to lessen the effects of risk factors (Legault, Anawati, and Flynn, 2006). If youth are placed in settings that promote healthy development, and as they adjust to the transition to foster care (McDonald, Allen, Westerfelt, and Piliavin, 1996), one may expect externalizing and internalizing problems to decrease. Although nationally representative longitudinal research on changes in mental health of youth in foster care is limited, researchers have found adolescents in long-term foster care demonstrated decreases in both externalizing and internalizing problems over time (McWey, Cui, and Pazdera, 2010). Unfortunately, much more remains to be learned about this population so that the children and families can be better served through practice and policy.

Foster Care Policy in the United States

There have been two major changes in federal policy related to foster care in the last two decades. The first is the Adoption and Safe Families Act (ASFA, PL 105-89). Before 1997, family preservation was the primary goal of foster care policy. Some suggested, however, that the consequence of prolonged attempts to reunify children with their parents was

that youth were languishing in foster care for long periods of time without a sense of permanency – not knowing when or if they would return home, or who their permanent caregiver would be if they did not. The goals in enacting ASFA were to promote stable homes for youth in out-of-home care and to make decisions in their best interests "without delay" (Festinger and Pratt, 2002, p. 218).

The enactment of ASFA marked a shift away from family preservation toward "concurrent planning" and adoption. The aim of concurrent planning is to consider all reasonable options for a youth's permanency as soon as possible following a youth's placement in foster care (Child Welfare Information Gateway, 2012b). In essence, concurrent planning means that at least two plans are simultaneously developed for youth in foster care. One plan outlines provisions for what parents must do in order to regain custody of their children, whereas the other plan identifies steps that will be taken to terminate parental rights (TPR) and promote the identification of alternate permanent placements and/or the adoption of children in foster care.

ASFA also mandates that foster care decisions be made in the best interests of the child (Stein, 2000). Also under ASFA, the amount of time parents have to regain custody of their children before judicial hearings are initiated to TPR was reduced to the first year of a youth's placement in foster care unless parents effectively demonstrate that they are working to substantially improve the situations that lead to the removal of their children from the home.

Ultimately, a judicial decision is made regarding parental rights, and these decisions generally involve one of two outcomes: TPR, or family reunification (McWey, Henderson, and Burroughs, 2008). A verdict of TPR is "an extreme action initiated by the state to irrevocably sever the legal bond between parent and child" (Wattenberg, Kelley, and Kim, 2001, p. 406). When considering termination of parental rights in foster care cases, judges must reflect on both "clear and convincing evidence" as well as what is in the "best interests of the child" (Benjet et al., 2003; McWey et al., 2008). Finding the balance between parental rights and best interests of children can be complicated (Coulton, Korbin, and Chow, 1995). In order to TPR, however, there must be "clear and convincing" evidence that the consequences of allowing the parent–child relationship to continue are more severe than the consequences of TPR (Stein, 2000).

The second major change in policy came a decade later with the Fostering Connections to Success and Increasing Adoptions Act (PL 110-351) in 2008. This policy continued the goal set forth by ASFA by promoting permanent living arrangements, and also aimed to improve educational, health, and long-term outcomes of youth in care. In order to promote greater permanency for youth, this act declared that all adult family members should be notified within 30 days of children's removal from their parents' homes to determine if a relative could be their care provider. This act increased financial support available to those that offer kinship care as well as increased incentives for states to find more permanent placements through adoption. Further, this act required that reasonable efforts be made to keep siblings together if it is deemed safe and in the well-being of the children to do so, and if not, required efforts be made to promote frequent visitation so that siblings may have ongoing interactions.

The Fostering Connections to Success and Increasing Adoptions Act also was designed to help the outcomes of youth who are aging out of the foster care system, by giving US states the option of allowing youth to remain in foster care up to the age of 21, and be afforded independent living assistance throughout that time provided they meet certain criteria. These criteria include: being enrolled in and completing education; participating in a program aimed to enhance employment; currently working; or unable to complete any of the criteria due to a medical condition. Further, with the aim of improving educational outcomes, this policy specified that children should remain at their school of origin whenever possible, and if moves are necessary that they be done in a timely manner while also warranting the child's academic records be accurately kept and provided to the new school. Additionally, this act aimed to promote continuity in health care services and appropriate record keeping so that health needs could be identified, monitored, and treated. Lastly, this act enabled tribes to directly access and administer federal funding for youth in foster care. Advocates suggest these acts have helped improve the lives of youth in care; however, others ague much more remains to be done.

Unfortunately, not much is known about how the United States CWS compares to systems in other countries. It is a challenge to make comparisons, because different countries have different definitions, policies, aims, and outcomes. Additionally, the term "family" and the norms associated with what is acceptable within families differ internationally. Furthermore, some developed countries may not have "formalized" foster care systems but rather rely on informal family networks to take care of the needs of children (George, Van Oudenhoven, and Wazir, 2003). Ultimately, international cooperation has the potential to broaden strategies aimed to promote child welfare globally.

Conclusion

In sum, children in foster care experience diverse family contexts. They have biological parents, foster parents, biological siblings, foster siblings, and a host of other potential short- and long-term family members. Their living situations may differ; some may be placed with strangers, others with kin, and still others in group homes with other youth. The stability of their placements is not guaranteed, and the longer they are in foster care, the higher the risk for negative outcomes. Responding to the concern about the length of time youth were spending in foster care, recent federal policy shortened the amount of time parents have to regain custody of their children and mandated concurrent planning in order to help achieve permanency. Despite these efforts, approximately 107,000 children were waiting for adoption in 2010 (Children's Bureau, 2010). Youth in foster care are at risk for a number of negative outcomes, including mental health concerns, educational shortcomings, and involvement with the criminal justice system. Despite these risks, however, many youth demonstrate resilience. Support from individuals, families, and communities may help promote this resilience. Given the complexities of the foster care context and the potential for negative outcomes, it is important to offer effective services and evaluate the longitudinal outcomes of such services for children and families involved with the foster care system.

Critical Thinking Questions

1. What are your thoughts about Robin's situation? What concerns do you have? What factors do you think are important to consider for Robin and her siblings?

2. What factors are associated with placement in foster care? What risk factors are associated with an increased risk for foster care placement?

3. What are some of the benefits of placing a child in foster care? What are some of the challenges?

4. What factors are associated with resilience of youth in foster care?

5. What recommendations would you make to officials of the child welfare system in your state in order to promote child well-being?

Note

1. Name changed to protect confidentiality.

References

Achenbach, T. M. (1991). *Manual for the youth self-report and the 1991 profile*. Burlington, VT: Department of Psychiatry, University of Vermont.

Adoption and Foster Care Analysis and Reporting System (AFCARS). (2012). The AFCARS report, preliminary FY 2011. Retrieved May 30, 2014 from http://www.acf. hhs.gov/programs/cb/resource/afcars-report-19.

Anctil, T. M., McCubbin, L. D., O'Brien, K., and Pecora, P. (2007). An evaluation of recovery factors for foster care alumni with physical or psychiatric impairments: Predictors of psychological outcomes. *Children and Youth Services Review, 29*, 1021–1034.

Appleyard, K., Egeland, B., van Dulmen, M. H. M., and Sroufe, L. A. (2005). When more is not better: The role of cumulative risk in child behavior outcomes. *Journal of Child Psychology and Psychiatry, 46*, 235–245.

Azar, S. T., Benjet, C. L., Fuhrmann, G. S., and Cavallero, L. (1995). Child maltreatment and termination of parental rights: Can behavioral research help Solomon? *Behavior Therapy, 26*, 599–623.

Barth, R. P., Lloyd, E. C., Green, R. L., James, S., Leslie, L. K., and Landsverk, J. (2007). Predictors of placement moves among children with and without emotional and behavioral disorders. *Journal of Emotional and Behavioral Disorders, 15*, 45–55.

Benjet, C., Azar, S. T., and Kuersten-Hogan, R. (2003). Evaluating the parental fitness of psychiatrically diagnosed individuals: Advocating a functional-contextual analysis of parenting. *Journal of Family Psychology, 17*, 238–251.

Biehal, N., and Wade, J. (1999). Taking a chance? The risks associated with going missing from substitute care. *Child Abuse Review, 8*, 366–376.

Child Welfare Information Gateway. (2010a). Mandatory reporters of child abuse and neglect: Summary of State Laws. Retrieved May 30, 2014 from: https://www. childwelfare.gov/responding/mandated.cfm.

Child Welfare Information Gateway. (2010b). Placement of children with relatives. Washington, DC: US Department of Health and Human Services, Administration for Children and Families.

Child Welfare Information Gateway. (2011). Case planning for families involved with child welfare agencies. Washington, DC: US Department of Health and Human Services, Children's Bureau.

Child Welfare Information Gateway. (2012a). Foster care statistics 2010. Washington, DC: US Department of Health and Human Services, Children's Bureau. Retrieved May 30, 2014 from: https://www.childwelfare. gov/pubs/factsheets/foster.pdf#Page=1&view=Fit.

Child Welfare Information Gateway. (2012b). Concurrent planning: What the evidence shows. Washington, DC: US Department of Health and Human Services, Children's Bureau.

Children's Bureau. (2010). Child welfare outcomes 2007–2010. Retrieved May 30, 2014 from: http://archive.acf. hhs.gov/programs/cb/pubs/cwo07-10/cwo07-10.pdf.

Cicchetti, D., and Garmezy, N. (1993). Prospects and promise in the study of resilience. *Development and Psychopathology, 5*, 497–502.

Conner, K. M., and Davidson, J. R. T. (2003). Development of a new resilience scale: The Connor-Davidson Resilience Scale (CD-RISC). *Depression and Anxiety, 18*, 76–82.

Coulton, C. J., Korbin, M. S., and Chow, J. (1995). Community-level factors and child maltreatment rates. *Child Development, 66*, 1262–1276.

Courtney, M. E., and Zinn, A. (2009). Predictors of running away from out-of-home care. *Children and Youth Services Review, 31,* 1298–1306.

Cuddeback, G. S. (2004). Kinship family foster care: A methodological and substantive synthesis of research. *Children and Youth Services Review, 26,* 623–639. doi:10.1016/j.childyouth.2004.01.014.

D'Andrade, A. C., and Chambers, R. M. (2012). Parental problems, case plan requirements, and service targeting in child welfare reunification. *Children and Youth Services Review, 34,* 2131–2138.

Dore, M., and Eisner, E. (1993). Child-related dimensions of placement stability in treatment foster care. *Child and Adolescent Social Work Journal, 10,* 301–317.

Dubowitz, H., Zuravin, S., Starr, R., Feigelman, S., and Harrington, D. (1993). Behavior problems of children in kinship care. *Developmental and Behavioural Pediatrics, 14,* 386–393.

Dyk, P. (2004). Complexity of family life among the low-income and working poor: Introduction to the special issue. *Family Relations, 53,* 122–126.

Famularo, R., Kinscherff, R., and Fenton, T. (1992). Parental substance abuse and the nature of child maltreatment. *Child Abuse and Neglect, 16,* 475–483.

Farmer, E. (2009). How do placements in kinship care compare with those in non-kin foster care: Placement patterns, progress and outcomes? *Child and Family Social Work, 14,* 331–342. doi:10.1111/j.1365-2206.2008.00600.x.

Fernandez, E. (2009). Children's wellbeing in care: Evidence from a longitudinal study of outcomes. *Children and Youth Services Review, 31,* 1092–1100.

Festinger, T., and Pratt, R. (2002). Speeding adoptions: An evaluation of the effects of judicial continuity. *Social Work Research, 26,* 217–224.

Frensch, K. M., and Cameron, G. (2002). Treatment of choice or a last resort? A review of residential mental health placements for children and youth. *Children and Youth Care Forum, 31,* 307–339.

George, S., Van Oudenhoven, N., and Wazir, E. (2003). Foster care beyond the crossroads: Lessons from an International comparative analysis. *Childhood, 10,* 343–361.

Greeson, J., Usher, L., and Grinstein-Weiss, M. (2010). One adult who is crazy about you: Can natural mentoring relationships increase assets among young adults with and without foster care experience? *Children and Youth Services Review, 32,* 565–577.

Hass, M., and Graydon, K. (2009). Sources of resiliency among successful foster youth. *Children and Youth Services Review, 31,* 457–463.

Heflinger, C. A., Simpkins, C. G., and Combs-Orme, T. (2000). Using the CBCL to determine the clinical status of children in state custody. *Children and Youth Services Review, 22,* 55–73.

Hegar, R. L., and Rosenthal, J. A. (2009). Kinship care and sibling placement: Child behavior, family relationships, and school outcomes. *Children and Youth Services Review, 31,* 670–679.

Helfrich, C., Stevenson Wojciak, A., and McWey, L. M. (in press). Closeness to caregivers and externalizing and internalizing behaviors of youth in out-of-home placement. *American Journal of Family Therapy.*

Herrick, M. A., and Piccus, W. (2005). Sibling connections: The importance of nurturing sibling bonds in the foster care system. *Children and Youth Services Review, 27,* 845–861.

Johnson, E. I., and Waldfogel, J. (2002). Parental incarceration: Recent trends and implications for child welfare. *Social Service Review, 76,* 460–479.

Jones, L. (1998). The social and family correlates of successful reunification of children in foster care. *Children and Youth Services Review, 20,* 305–232.

Jonson-Reid, M., and Barth, R. P. (2000). From placement to prison: The path to adolescent incarceration from child welfare supervised foster or group care. *Children and Youth Services Review, 22,* 493–516.

Kohl, P. L., Edleson, J. F., English, D. J., and Barth, R. P. (2005). Domestic violence and pathways into child welfare services: Findings from the National Survey of Child and Adolescent Well-Being. *Children and Youth Services Review, 27,* 1167–1182.

Kushel, M. G., Yen, I. H., Gee, G., and Courtney, M. E. (2007). Homelessness and health care access after emancipation. *Achieve of Pediatric and Adolescent Medicine, 16,* 986–993.

Lawrence, C. R., Carlson, E. A., and Egeland, B. (2006). The impact of foster care on development. *Development and Psychopathology, 18,* 57–76.

Leadbeater, B. J., Kuperminc, G. P., Blatt, S. J., and Hertzog, C. (1999). A multivariate model of gender differences in adolescents' internalizing and externalizing problems. *Developmental Psychopathology, 35,* 1268–1282.

Leathers, S. J. (2002). Foster children's behavioral disturbance and detachment from caregivers and community institutions. *Children and Youth Services Review, 24,* 239–268.

Leathers, S. J. (2005). Separation from siblings: Associations with placement adaptation and outcomes among adolescents in long-term foster care. *Children and Youth Services Review, 27,* 793–819.

Legault, L., Anawati, M., and Flynn, R. (2006). Factors favoring psychological resilience among fostered young people. *Children and Youth Services Review, 28,* 1024–1038.

Leon, S. C., Ragsdale, B., Miller, S. A., and Spacarelli, S. (2008). Trauma resilience among youth in substitute care demonstrating sexual behavior problems. *Child Abuse and Neglect, 32,* 67–81.

Leos-Urbel, J., Bess, R., and Green, R. (2002). The evolution of federal and state policies for assessing and supporting kinship caregivers. *Children and Youth Services Review, 24,* 37–52.

Lewis, E. E., Dozier, M., Ackerman, J., and Sepulveda-Kozakowski, S. (2007). The effect of placement instability on adopted children's inhibitory control abilities and oppositional behavior. *Developmental Psychology, 43,* 1415–1427.

Love, L. T., McIntosh, J., Rosst, M., and Tertzakian, K. (2005). *Fostering hope: Preventing teen pregnancy among youth in foster care.* Washington, DC: National Campaign to Prevent Teen and Unplanned Pregnancy.

Massinga, R., and Pecora, P. J. (2004). Providing better opportunities for older children in the child welfare system. *Future of Children, 14,* 150–173.

McDonald, T., Allen, R., Westerfelt, A., and Piliavin, I. (1996). *Assessing the long-term effects of foster care: A research synthesis.* Washington, DC: Child Welfare League of America.

McWey, L. M., Cui, M., and Pazdera, A. L. (2010). Changes in externalizing and internalizing problems of adolescents in foster care. *Journal of Marriage and Family, 72,* 1128–1140.

McWey, L. M., Henderson, T. L., and Burroughs, J. (2008). Parental rights and the foster care system: A glimpse of decision-making in Virginia. *Journal of Family Issues, 29,* 1031–1050.

Mullick, M., Miller, L. J., and Jacobsen, T. (2001). Insight into mental illness and child maltreatment risk among mothers with major psychiatric disorders. *Psychiatric Services, 52,* 488–492.

Nair, P., Schuler, M. E., Black, M. M., Kettinger, L., and Harrington, D. (2003). Cumulative environmental risk in substance abusing women: Early intervention, parenting stress, child abuse potential and child development. *Child Abuse and Neglect, 27,* 997–1017. doi:10.1016/S0145-2134(03)00169-8.

Nesmith, A. (2006). Predictors of running away from family foster care. *Child Welfare, 85,* 585–609.

O'Hare, W. P. (2008). Data on children in foster care from the Census Bureau. Baltimore, MD: The Annie E. Casey Foundation.

Ondersma, S. J. (2002). Predictors of neglect within low-SES families: The importance of substance abuse. *American Journal of Orthopsychiatry, 72,* 383–391.

Orme, J. G., and Buehler, C. (2001). Foster family characteristics and behavioral and emotional problems of foster children: A narrative review. *Family Relations, 50,* 3–15.

Osgood, D. W., Foster, E. M., and Courtney, M. E. (2010). Vulnerable populations and the transition to adulthood. *Future of Children, 20,* 209–229.

Pecora, P. J., Kessler, R. C., O'Brien, K. O., White, C. R., Williams, J., Hiripi, E., English, D., White, J., and Herrick, M. A. (2006). Educational and employment outcomes of adults formerly placed in foster care: Results from the Northwest Foster Care Alumni study. *Children and Youth Services Review, 28,* 1459–1481.

Pecora, P. J., Whittaker, J. K., Maluccio, A. N., and Barth, R. P. (2000). *The child welfare challenge: Policy, practice, and research* (2nd edn). New York: Aldine-De Gruyter.

Pecora, P. J., Williams, J., Kessler, R. C., Downs, A. C., O'Brien, K., Hiripi, E., and Morello, S. (2003). *Assessing the effects of foster care: Early results from the Casey National Alumni study.* Seattle, WA: Casey Family Program.

Risley-Curtiss, C., Stromwall, L. K., Hunt, D., and Teska, J. (2004). Identifying and reducing barriers to reunification for seriously mentally ill parents involved in child welfare cases. *Families in Society: The Journal of Contemporary Social Services, 85,* 107–118.

Rittner, B., and Dozier, C. D. (2000). Effects of court-ordered substance abuse treatment in child protective services cases. *Social Work, 45,* 131–140.

Ryan, J. P., and Testa, M. (2005). Child maltreatment and juvenile delinquency: Investigating the role of placement and placement instability. *Children and Youth Services Review, 27,* 227–249.

Scannapieco, M., Connell-Carrick, K., and Painter, K. (2007). In their own words: Challenges facing youth aging out of foster care. *Child and Adolescence Social Work Journal, 24,* 423–435.

Shlonsky, A., Bellamy, J., Elkins, J., and Ashare, C. J. (2005). The other kin: Setting the course for research, policy, and practice with siblings in foster care. *Children and Youth Services Review, 27,* 697–716.

Seymour, C., and Finney-Hairston, C. (2001). *Children with parents in prison: Child welfare policy, program, and practice issues.* Piscataway, NJ: Transaction Publishers.

Sidebotham, P., Golding, J., and the ALSPAC Study Team (2001). Child maltreatment in the "Children of the Nineties": A longitudinal study of parental risk factors. *Child Abuse and Neglect, 25,* 1177–1200.

Stein, T. J. (2000). The Adoption and Safe Families Act: Creating a false dichotomy between parents' and children's rights. *Families in Society: The Journal of Contemporary Human Services, 81,* 586–590.

Stover, C. S. (2005). Domestic violence research. What have we learned and where do we go from here? *Journal of Interpersonal Violence, 20,* 448–454.

Sunseri, P. A. (2005). Children referred to residential care: Reducing multiple placements, managing costs, and improving treatment outcomes. *Residential Treatment for Children and Youth, 22,* 55–66. doi:10.1300/J007v22n03_4.

Tarren-Sweeney, M. (2008). Retrospective and concurrent predictors of the mental health of children in care. *Children and Youth Services Review, 30,* 1–25.

Thorpe, M. B., and Swart, G. T. (1992). Risk and protective factors affecting children in foster care: A pilot study of the role of siblings. *Canadian Journal of Psychiatry, 37,* 616–622.

Unrau, Y. A., Seita, J. R., and Putney, K. S. (2008). Former foster youth remember multiple placement moves: A journey of loss and hope. *Children and Youth Services Review, 30,* 1256–1266.

US Department of Health and Human Services, Administration on Children, Youth, and Families. (2010). *Child maltreatment 2010.* Washington, DC: Government Printing Office.

US Department of Health and Human Services, Administration for Children and Families, Administration on Children, and Youth and Families Children's Bureau. (2013). *Child Welfare Outcomes 2008–2011: Report to Congress Executive Summary.* Retrieved May 30, 2014 from http://www.acf.hhs.gov/sites/default/files/cb/cwo08_11_exesum.pdf.

Wattenberg, E., Kelley, M., and Kim, H. (2001). When the rehabilitation ideal fails: A study of parental rights termination. *Child Welfare, 80,* 405–431.

Whelan, D. J. (2003). Using attachment theory when placing siblings in foster care. *Child and Adolescent Social Work Journal, 20,* 21–36.

White, C. R., O'Brien, K., Pecora, P. J., English, D., Williams, J. R., and Phillips, C. M. (2009). Depression among alumni of foster care: Decreasing rates through improvement of experiences in care. *Journal of Emotional and Behavioral Disorders, 17,* 38–48.

Yates, T. M., and Grey, I. K. (2012). Adapting to aging out: Profiles of risk and resilience among emancipated foster youth. *Development and Psychopathology, 24,* 475–492.

Young, N. K., Gardner, S., and Dennis, K. (1998). *Responding to alcohol and other drug problems in child welfare: Weaving together practice and policy.* Washington, DC: CWLA Press.

Zuravin, S. J., and DePanfilis, D. (1997). Factors affecting foster care placement of children receiving child protective services. *Social Work Research, 21,* 34–42.

9

Grandparents Raising Grandchildren

Megan L. Dolbin-MacNab and Bert Hayslip, Jr.

Increasing numbers of grandparents are raising their grandchildren. In Chapter 6, Dolbin-MacNab and Hayslip explain how, while the reasons grandparents may assume the care of their grandchildren are varied, this caregiving constellation most often arises due to disruptive and stigmatizing family events such as child maltreatment, incarceration, teen pregnancy, or parental absence due to divorce or death. The fact that grandparent caregivers are disproportionately poor, female, African American or Latino, and isolated from important resources suggests that the well-being of grandparent-headed households is impacted by "intersectionality" – a cultural pattern of oppression. At the same time, however, a growing body of work on resilience suggests that grandparents may be supported in successfully coping with the challenges associated with raising their grandchildren.

What do United States President Barack Obama, actor Jack Nicholson, musician Eric Clapton, and media figure Oprah Winfrey share in common? Each of these individuals was raised, at least in part, by a grandparent. Grandparent-headed families have also been referenced or depicted in films (e.g., Neville Longbottom in the *Harry Potter* films), television programming (e.g., Sookie and Jason Stackhouse in *True Blood*), and popular fiction (e.g., James Patterson's character Detective Alex Cross). As these examples illustrate, grandparent-headed families have become increasingly prominent within mainstream culture, both in the United States and around the world. Government officials and service providers have also

given greater attention to these families by developing legislation and programs to help support their needs (Generations United, 2011; Pew Charitable Trusts, 2007).

In the United States, approximately 7.8 million or 1 in 10 children live with a grandparent and approximately 40% of these children are being raised by their grandparents (AARP, 2010). Over the last several decades, there has been a significant increase in the number of children being raised by grandparents (Kreider and Ellis, 2011). According to the most recent US Census data, there are approximately 2.7 million grandparents raising 2.9 million grandchildren, which represents a 16% increase since 2000 alone (Livingston and Parker, 2010; Murphey, Cooper, and

Moore, 2012). Globally, grandparents raising grandchildren is also common, especially in countries that have experienced devastating natural disasters or disease epidemics such as HIV/AIDS (International Social Service and UNICEF, 2004).

Structurally, grandparent-headed families in the United States are extremely diverse. Some grandparents live with their grandchildren and their adult children (i.e., the grandchild's parent). These grandparents are often referred to as "co-resident" or "co-parenting" grandparents. In these households, grandparents may have significant caregiving responsibilities for their grandchildren, or their role may be more similar to that of a babysitter. In contrast to co-resident or co-parenting households, the phrase "skipped-generation households" signifies situations where the grandchild's parents are not present in the home. Grandparents in skipped-generation households typically have the sole or major responsibility for all aspects of their grandchildren's care. Beyond these variations in household configuration, some grandparents are raising their grandchildren formally, in that they have obtained the legal authority (e.g., guardianship, legal custody) to act as parents for their grandchildren. However, many grandparents are raising their grandchildren informally, which means that they have made some type of informal, non-legal arrangement with their grandchildren's parents to care for their grandchildren. Finally, in terms of timing, there are grandparents who assume the care of their grandchildren very suddenly, often in response to a crisis situation (e.g., the grandchild being abandoned by a parent). Other grandparents find that their responsibility for their grandchildren increases gradually over time. Additionally, some grandchildren begin being raised by their grandparents soon after birth, while others are older when their grandparents become their primary caregivers. The diversity that is present in all of these elements of grandparent-headed families means that their experiences and needs are extremely diverse as well.

Besides the fact that grandparent-headed families are becoming increasingly common, these families are worthy of attention for a number of other reasons. First, as will be discussed in more detail later, both grandparents and grandchildren are at increased risk for various negative physical and psychological outcomes (Hayslip and Kaminski, 2005). Therefore,

understanding these families and their experiences is important for developing interventions to prevent negative outcomes. Second, grandparents raising grandchildren provide an invaluable service to society. They offer safety and stability to children who might otherwise be in the juvenile justice system or the foster care system (Kreider, 2008). In addition, some have estimated that grandparent caregivers save US taxpayers more than $6.5 billion per year in federal foster care costs (Dervarics, 2004). Beyond these financial benefits to society, grandparent caregivers also preserve community connections, promote continuity within family relationships, and uphold cultural traditions (Kopera-Frye and Wiscott, 2000). Given all of these important contributions, understanding and supporting grandparent-headed families is essential to promoting the successful development of millions of children.

In this chapter, we provide an overview of issues salient to grandparent-headed families, including a discussion of factors that have contributed to the development of these families and a profile of their demographic characteristics. Next, we examine the unique experiences and needs of grandparent caregivers and their grandchildren. Following this discussion, we shift our attention to factors that have been associated with resilience or successful outcomes for grandparents and grandchildren, and address intervention strategies that can be utilized to help promote resilience. Although this chapter focuses on the experiences of grandparent-headed families in the United States, we conclude the chapter with a brief discussion of grandparent caregiving in other countries around the world. Together, the material in this chapter should provide a comprehensive overview of grandparent-headed families and highlight the unique strengths and challenges of this growing family form.

Influences on the Development of Grandparent-Headed Families

As the case example on the next page suggests, grandparents assume the care of their grandchildren for varied reasons, and multiple factors have influenced the emergence of this particular family caregiving arrangement. Hayslip and Kaminski (2005) note that grandparents usually assume responsibility for their

Case Example: Martha

When her 16-year-old daughter, Jessie, gave birth, Martha Willis[1] agreed to help take care of her grandson. Martha wanted Jessie to finish school, get a good job, and support her child. However, Jessie started spending more time with friends, leaving Martha to provide most of her grandson's care. Soon, Jessie moved out and started using drugs. Because of her drug binges, Jessie would disappear for long periods of time. Sometimes Jessie would show up at Martha's home, clearly intoxicated, and demand that Martha let her take her son to live with her. Fearing for his safety, Martha went to court to obtain guardianship of her grandson.

grandchildren due to a variety of disruptive and often stigmatizing family events including the death of a parent, parental divorce, incarceration, substance abuse, child abuse and neglect, teen pregnancy, or HIV/AIDS (Cox, 2000; Hayslip and Kaminski, 2005; Park and Greenberg, 2007). Some of these factors arise unexpectedly (e.g., the sudden death of a parent), while others reflect an accumulation of stressors and disadvantage over time (e.g., parental incarceration). In most situations, multiple factors tend to be at work at once (e.g., parental substance abuse leading to child neglect and parental incarceration).

Despite the fact that most grandparents begin raising their grandchildren due to difficulties experienced by the grandchildren's parents, the reasons that grandparents take on the role of caregiver have been shown to vary by ethnicity and household structure. Regarding ethnicity, Caucasian grandparents commonly report that the grandchild's parents are dysfunctional, while African American grandparents tend to note unemployment and teenage pregnancy as contributing to the caregiving arrangement (Pebley and Rudkin, 1999). In terms of household structure, co-resident or co-parenting grandparents typically mention that they are helping out financially, assisting because of the adult child's divorce, or supporting a young (teenage) parent (Goodman and Silverstein, 2002; Pebley and

Rudkin, 1999). For grandparents in skipped-generation households, parental substance abuse, child abuse and neglect, parental mental or emotional distress, and parental criminal behavior were commonly cited as reasons for the caregiving arrangement (Goodman and Silverstein, 2002).

Beyond these factors, grandparents themselves often have reasons for wanting to assume the care of their grandchildren. For instance, grandparents may take responsibility for their grandchildren in order to keep the grandchildren from being separated from their siblings or extended family members due to foster care placements (Hayslip and Kaminski, 2005). Grandparents may also assume responsibility for their grandchildren out of fear of involvement of social services in their lives or a distrust of the foster care system (Dolbin-MacNab, Johnson, Sudano, Serrano, and Roberto, 2011). In addition to these reasons, for reasons of love and loyalty, grandparents may be reluctant to report their adult child's problematic behavior (e.g., substance abuse) to the authorities because they do not want to risk legal action or other negative consequences for their grandchild's parent(s) (Dolbin-MacNab et al., 2011). Also, a proportion of grandparents choose to care for their grandchildren out of love, affection, and a desire to be involved in their lives (Dolbin-MacNab and Keiley, 2006).

Finally, there are also cultural, policy, and economic factors that influence the development of grandparent-headed families. Culturally, grandmother involvement in child-rearing is normative in many cultures globally and within the United States, as are traditions of familism, particularly among African American and Latino grandparents (Burnette, 1999; Fuller-Thomson and Minkler, 2007; Goodman and Silverstein, 2006; Hunter and Taylor, 1998). From a policy perspective, federal legislation and most states require or encourage a child who needs foster care to be placed with relatives, such as grandparents, if at all possible (Generations United, 2011; Pew Charitable Trusts, 2007). This arrangement is known as kinship care, and tends to be preferred because of evidence of its benefits for children (Pew Charitable Trusts, 2007). Additionally, if parents are unable to obtain social service benefits or lose those benefits, grandparents are increasingly needed to serve as financial "safety nets" for their families. That is, when families are struggling financially, grandparents may become key sources of financial and practical (e.g., housing, food) assistance (Hayslip and Page, 2012).

A Demographic Profile of Grandparent-Headed Families

While grandparent-headed families share a number of similarities in terms of their structure and development, in reality, they are a demographically diverse group (Kropf and Kolomer, 2004). This demographic diversity contributes to variations in grandparent's experiences of raising their grandchildren and highlights how grandparents define and experience their roles in idiosyncratic ways. An acknowledgement of the demographic diversity of grandparent-headed families also implies that grandparents and grandchildren, depending on their demographic characteristics, are likely to experience diverse outcomes.

Why is this the case? One explanation for the variations in the experiences and outcomes among grandparent-headed families is intersectionality, which emphasizes that "cultural patterns of oppression are not only interrelated but are bound together and influenced by the intersectional systems of society, such as race, gender, class, and ethnicity" (Collins, 2000, p. 42). As such, the variation observed in grandfamilies' experiences and outcomes would stem from the fact that some grandparents and grandchildren have social identities that increase their vulnerability to negative outcomes, as well as their risk of marginalization, discrimination, and oppression. For example, a poor, African American, single grandmother might have a very different experience of raising a grandchild than a middle-class, White, married grandfather. Thus, to understand grandparent-headed families, it is necessary to attend to the historical, cultural, and economic factors (e.g., racism, poverty) that contribute to the existence of these families (Keene and Batson, 2010) as well as their experiences of marginalization and oppression.

Demographics of grandparents raising grandchildren

Census data suggest that the prevalence of grandparent caregiving varies based on grandparents' gender, marital status, age, and income (Livingston and Parker, 2010). These demographic variations further

demonstrate intersectionality (Collins, 2000) and how some grandparents and grandchildren may be at greater risk for marginalization and negative outcomes than others. Numerically, most grandparent caregivers are women (62%), married (66%), and younger than age 60 (67%; Livingston and Parker, 2010). However, grandparent caregivers "are more likely to be poor, single, older, less educated, and unemployed than families in which at least one parent is present" (Annie E. Casey Foundation, 2012, pp. 5–6). Regarding income, approximately 1 in 5 custodial grandparents live in poverty, and nearly half have incomes between one and three times the poverty line (Livingston and Parker, 2010). Additionally, data indicate that caregiving is typically a long-term arrangement, with many grandparents having provided care for their grandchildren for at least two years (Livingston and Parker, 2010; Luo, La Pierre, Hughes, and Waite, 2012).

Demographics of children being raised by grandparents

With regard to the grandchildren, approximately half of the children being raised by grandparents are under the age of six (Murphey et al., 2012). There are no clear patterns in terms of grandchild gender and, as mentioned previously, a substantial portion of children being raised by grandparents are living in poverty (Livingston and Parker, 2010). In fact, Census data reveal that children who lived in a home with neither parent present were more likely to be in poverty when they were living with a grandparent (31%) than when they did not (23%; Kreider and Ellis, 2011). Data also indicate that, when compared to other children, children living with custodial grandparents are less likely to have health insurance and more likely to be living in a household receiving public assistance (Bryson and Casper, 1999). All of these factors, in combination, may increase grandchildren's risk of negative outcomes.

Ethnicity: A Key Demographic Characteristic

Of all the demographic characteristics associated with grandparent-headed families, ethnicity emerges as a key consideration. Ethnicity has been linked to the prevalence of grandparents raising grandchildren (Livingston and Parker, 2010; Luo et al., 2012; Mutchler, Lee, and Baker, 2006). It also has been associated with grandparents' circumstances, needs, and overall well-being (Burnette, 1999; Goodman and Silverstein, 2002; Musil, Schrader, and Mutikani, 2000; Pruchno, 1999; Shakya, Usita, Eisenberg, Weston, and Liles, 2012).

Regarding prevalence, in terms of shear numbers, most grandparent caregivers are Caucasian (51%). Significant numbers of African American (38%), and Hispanic (13%) grandparents also care for their grandchildren (Fuller-Thomson and Minkler, 2001). Proportionally, however, African Americans (4.3%) and Hispanics (2.9%) are more likely to be caring for grandchildren than Caucasians (1%; US Bureau of the Census, 2000). There is also ethnic variation in the recent growth of grandparent-headed families. For instance, between 2007 and 2008, there was a 9% increase among White, a 2% increase among African American, no increase among Hispanic, and 3% decline among Asian grandparents (Livingston and Parker, 2010). Generally, available data suggest that the likelihood of co-residing with or caring for a grandchild increases greatly if a grandparent is African American or Hispanic (Luo et al., 2012). American Indian and Asian American grandparents are also more likely to co-reside and care for grandchildren than their White counterparts (Mutchler et al., 2006).

Beyond variations in prevalence, attending to ethnic and associated cultural variations among grandparent-headed families is also vital to a nuanced understanding of their circumstances and needs. For instance, household composition varies according to ethnicity (Keene and Batson, 2010); Pruchno (1999) found that Black (compared to White) custodial grandmothers were more likely to be co-residing with their grandchildren, to have been raised in multigenerational households themselves, and to be receiving formal social services. Similarly, research suggests that Hispanic and African American grandparents are more likely than Caucasian grandparents to be co-parenting with one of their grandchild's parents, which is culturally consistent with an emphasis on multigenerational households and intergenerational assistance (Burnette, 1999; Cox, Brooks, and Valcarcel, 2000, Fuller-Thomson and Minkler, 2007; Goodman and Silverstein, 2006; Hunter and Taylor, 1998; Pebley and Rudkin, 1999).

Finally, while co-parenting grandparents tend to have more positive outcomes than grandparents raising grandchildren in skipped-generation households (Musil et al., 2000; Shakya et al., 2012), even this relationship varies by ethnicity. For example, Goodman and Silverstein (2002) found that Latino grandmothers' well-being was positively related to being in a co-parenting situation, whereas African American grandmothers' well-being was higher in custodial (skipped-generation) families. These variations may stem from variations in cultural expectations associated with grandparents and childcare, as well as other related social factors.

As the foregoing discussion has illustrated, ethnicity has a significant impact on the prevalence of grandparents raising grandchildren, the composition of grandparent-headed households, and even grandparents' well-being. Moreover, given the linkages between ethnicity, gender, socioeconomic status, and the history of racism and discrimination in the United States, ethnicity may be one key to understanding why some grandparent-headed families are more vulnerable than others. In the next section, we further examine the experiences of grandparent-headed families and highlight how some grandparent-headed families may be at increased risk.

Experiences of Grandparent-Headed Families

Grandparent-headed families experience a number of challenges. As a result of these challenges, grandparents and grandchildren may be at risk for a variety of negative outcomes. Grandparents may be at risk for physical health problems (Hughes, Waite, LaPierre, and Luo, 2007; Minkler and Fuller-Thomson, 1999) and psychological difficulties such as anxiety and depression (Hayslip, Shore, Henderson, and Lambert, 1998; Minkler, Fuller-Thomson, Miller, and Driver, 1997). Grandchildren may be at risk for emotional and behavioral problems, as well as difficulties in school (Billing, Ehrle, and Kortenkamp, 2002; Smith and Palmieri, 2007).

In addition to the explanation provided by intersectionality (Collins, 2000), ecological systems theory (Bronfenbrenner, 1979) also provides insight as to why some grandparent-headed families might be especially at risk for negative outcomes. This theory argues that individuals and their environments are interdependent (Bronfenbrenner, 1979). Additionally, environments are conceptualized as being nested within one another and range from more proximal to more distal environments (Bronfenbrenner, 1979). The proximal environments are those environments with which grandparents and grandchildren have frequent and direct contact. These would include family members, friends, co-workers, schools, etc. More distal environments, which are still influential, are those environments with which grandparents and grandchildren do not have frequent or direct contact. Examples of these environments are the larger community, laws, government agencies, as well as sociocultural traditions and values.

From an ecological perspective, grandparent-headed families are impacted by the quality of the proximal and distal environments within which they are embedded (Bronfenbrenner, 1979). Higher-quality environments provide grandparents and grandchildren with more opportunities, while poorer-quality environments create limitations that can ultimately compromise the well-being of the family system and its individual family members (Bronfenbrenner, 1979). Thus, according to ecological systems theory, having more opportunities is important to the overall well-being of grandparents and grandchildren in the sense that these families have more control over their situations and more resources available to them in terms of responding and adapting to stressors and other challenges (Bronfenbrenner, 1979). For example, a grandparent who is poor, has few friends, is in conflict with her family members, and lives in a dangerous urban community may have a more difficult time dealing with a grandchild's developmental disability than a grandparent in a higher-quality environment.

Grandparents raising grandchildren experience challenges at all levels (i.e., proximal and distal) of their environments. For instance, as noted previously, many grandparents experience significant financial strain. More specifically, grandparents often live in poverty or on fixed incomes, and may have difficulty providing for their families' needs (Generations United, 2011; Henderson and Cook, 2006). Financial assistance from a variety of government programs

(e.g., TANF) is an essential lifeline for many grandparent-headed families, but may be difficult to obtain due to a lack of eligibility or other barriers (Dolbin-MacNab, Roberto, and Finney, 2013). In addition to financial difficulties, many grandparents also experience legal challenges. This is because it can be difficult for grandparents to obtain custody of their children for financial reasons or for fear of a confrontation with the grandchild's parents (Generations United, 2011). When grandparents do not have a legal relationship (e.g., custody or guardianship) to their grandchildren, it can be difficult for them to obtain services (e.g., medical care) for their grandchildren or enroll them in school (Hayslip and Kaminski, 2005). Additionally, the lack of a legal relationship can make the family situation unstable – adult parents could reclaim custody of the grandchild at any time, even if it is not in the grandchild's best interests. Finally, grandparents may have difficulty obtaining adequate housing (Dolbin-MacNab et al., 2011). In these situations, grandparents may live in communities that do not allow children, or their homes may not be appropriate (e.g., not large enough) for their expanded family system.

Beyond these challenges, grandparent-headed families also experience a variety of relational challenges. For instance, as a result of the demands associated with caring for their grandchildren, grandparents may lose connection with their social networks of friends (Gerard, Landry-Meyer, and Roe, 2006; Jendrek, 1993). Not having the emotional and instrumental support of friends can be very stressful for grandparents and can make it difficult for them to cope with their caregiving responsibilities. Additionally, grandparents often experience relational challenges with other members of their families (Dolbin-MacNab and Traylor, 2008; Weber and Waldrop, 2000). For example, other adult children might be angry about the investment the grandparent is making in part of the family, or may feel that the grandparent is being taken advantage of or mistreated. Grandparents may struggle in their relationships with their grandchildren's parent(s). While the grandparent may want to help the adult child address his or her problems, at the same time grandparents also need to protect themselves and their grandchildren from parents' sometimes erratic or unsafe behavior. Grandchildren, too, may struggle with their relationships with their parents – they may want to maintain a relationship with their parents but find it difficult because their parents may be unpredictable, unstable, or otherwise unavailable to them (Dolbin-MacNab and Keiley, 2009).

The grandparent–grandchild relationship also poses challenges for grandparents and grandchildren. Grandchildren describe difficulties with a "generation gap," and may feel that their grandparents are out of touch with issues (e.g., dating, leisure activities, technology) that are significant in their lives (Dolbin-MacNab and Keiley, 2009). For their part, grandparents often describe a number of difficulties related to parenting. Many grandparents raising grandchildren are not up to date with the most recent information about child development and appropriate strategies for child discipline (Hayslip and Kaminski, 2005). Additionally, grandparents often find the time and energy demands of parenting to be stressful, particularly as grandparents themselves may be dealing with their own health and aging issues (Dolbin-MacNab, 2006). Parenting stress is a significant issue for many grandparents and may contribute to a number of their negative outcomes, including depression and anxiety (Hayslip et al., 1998; Pruchno and McKenney, 2002; Rodgers-Farmer, 1999; Sands and Goldberg-Glen, 2000; Smith, Palmieri, Hancock, and Richardson, 2008; Smith and Richardson, 2008; Young and Dawson, 2003). Grandparents' parenting stress is often exacerbated by the fact that, due to their histories (i.e., abuse/neglect, prenatal exposure to drugs or alcohol), grandchildren frequently experience developmental, emotional, and behavior issues that make parenting them even more challenging (Hayslip et al., 1998; Sands and Goldberg-Glen, 2000; Smith et al., 2008; Young and Dawson, 2003).

A final challenge experienced by grandparent-headed families is social stigma from peers as well as human service professionals (Gibson, 2002; Gladstone, Brown, and Fitzgerald, 2009; Hayslip and Glover, 2008). Many grandparents describe feeling judged or disrespected by service providers (Dolbin-MacNab et al., 2011; Gibson, 2002). This judgment may stem from a larger sociocultural assumption that, if they are raising their grandchildren, grandparents must have failed in raising their own children (i.e., the grandchild's parent; Dolbin-MacNab et al., 2011; Hayslip and Glover, 2008). When compounded with cultural expectations about caregiving, racism, and other forms of discrimination, these societal attitudes can leave grandparents feeling ashamed about their family situation, and further isolated from sources of support.

Despite all of these challenges with their proximal and distal environments, grandparents and their grandchildren still describe a number of positive aspects of their caregiving arrangement. For grandparents, there are rewards associated with having a second chance at parenting and seeing their grandchildren develop into successful adults (Dolbin-MacNab, 2006; Waldrop and Weber, 2001). The emotional bond that forms between grandparents and their grandchildren is also emotionally rewarding to grandparents (Dolbin-MacNab and Keiley, 2006). Similarly, grandchildren note the benefits of a close relationship with a loving, responsive caregiver (Dolbin-MacNab and Keiley, 2009). Grandchildren also describe the rewards of living in a safe and stable environment and knowing they are on a better life trajectory due to their grandparents' involvement in their lives (Dolbin-MacNab and Keiley, 2009). Thus, for both grandparents and grandchildren, any challenges associated with their family constellation must also be viewed in light of a number of specific rewards and benefits.

In sum, from an ecological perspective (Bronfenbrenner, 1979), when considering the experiences of grandparent caregivers and their grandchildren, it is important to remember that all of these rewards and challenges interact with and influence one another. They also intersect with a family's demographic characteristics. Thus, the specific combination of demographic characteristics, rewards, and challenges is likely to have a significant impact on the overall experiences and well-being of grandparent caregivers as well as their grandchildren.

A Resilience Perspective on Grandparent-Headed Families

Imagine two single-grandmother-headed families. Both grandmothers are African American and raising 10-year-old grandsons. Due to prenatal drug exposure, both grandsons have developmental disabilities and behavioral problems. Both grandmothers have financial difficulties. One grandmother describes raising her grandchild as being very rewarding, and explains all of the ways that her grandson's behavior has been improving in school and at home. The other grandmother is completely overwhelmed by her caregiving responsibilities, and describes herself as being very depressed. Her grandson is struggling in school.

Why would these two grandparents, with their similar experiences and backgrounds, show such differences in terms of their outcomes? What factors contribute to the one grandmother's success? These types of questions, posed by Rutter (2010), have been associated with the resilience perspective. Resilience (Rutter, 2007; Wright and Masten, 2005), which has gained prominence in the contemporary scholarship on grandparent-headed families, is a valuable perspective for several reasons. First, a resilience perspective allows for a more comprehensive understanding of grandparent caregivers that goes beyond the previous focus on the challenges confronting these families and the associated negative outcomes. By taking a more comprehensive perspective, practitioners can develop interventions and support programs that address the challenges experienced by grandparents and grandchildren, but that also build on and further develop their strengths and resources (Hayslip and Smith, 2013). Policy makers can also use a resilience perspective to guide the development of state and federal policies and programs, with the goal of improving grandparent and grandchildren's overall physical and psychosocial health (Hayslip and Smith, 2013).

Defining resilience in grandparent-headed families

The assumption that grandparent caregivers are overwhelmed with their parenting responsibilities and are experiencing a great deal of stress reflects, in many ways, an underestimation of them – grandparents raising grandchildren can be quite resilient in the face of the many challenges they confront. "Resilience has typically been defined as a pattern of positive (or the avoidance of negative) adaptation in the context of past or present adversity or risk that poses a substantial threat to healthy adjustment" (Hayslip and Smith, 2013, p. 252). When thinking about resilience

among grandparent-headed families, it is important to note that many factors influence grandparents and grandchildren's resilience and that some grandparent-headed families will be more resilient than others.

Resilience in grandparent-headed families is a direct result of the *interactions* between the resilient personal characteristics of grandparents and grandchildren and aspects of their larger environments (Vanderbilt-Adriance and Shaw, 2008; Wright and Masten, 2005). This means that grandparent and grandchild resilience stems, in part, from the quality and nature of their personal interactions with their immediate (proximal; e.g., friends, family members) and larger societal or cultural (distal; e.g., social service agencies, policies, cultural norms, mores) environments (Bronfenbrenner, 1979). In addition, resilience in grandparent-headed families can be thought of as being *dynamic* in that it often varies over time and with changes in a family's environments and circumstances. Thus, when applying a resilience perspective to grandparent-headed families, it must be remembered that differences in grandparent and grandchild well-being are largely influenced by how they personally respond, over time, to the challenges of their particular contexts or environments (Baltes, Reese, and Nesselroade, 1988).

Flowing from this conceptualization of resilience, grandparents and grandchildren can be thought of as having a certain amount of adaptive (or resilient) *personal attributes* (Hayslip and Smith, 2013). An example of a resilient personal attribute would be having an optimistic outlook on life. As grandparents and grandchildren interact with their environments, their resilient personal attributes result in the development and expression of *adaptive processes* or behaviors that help them successfully cope with everyday stressors, acute crises, and normative life changes (Leipold and Greve, 2009). Problem-solving or coping skills would be examples of resilient adaptive processes. It should be noted, however, that resilience could also be an *outcome* or result of a grandparent's or grandchild's success in addressing challenges. Thus, while a grandparent caregiver or grandchildren may not have been initially resilient (e.g., lacking in resilient attributes or processes), life events and experiences may uncover and promote hidden resilience. This illustrates what Allport (see Hall and Lindzey, 1978) has termed *functional autonomy*, which refers to new skills and behaviors that were not present before, but evolve out of the need to use them to address a challenge or stressor.

Whether the focus is on personal attributes, processes, or outcomes, as suggested previously, resilience among grandparent-headed families is best viewed as existing along a *continuum* (Smith, Dannison, and James, 2013). This means that some grandparents may be highly resilient and experience few difficulties in raising their grandchildren. In turn, there may also be grandparents who are somewhat resilient, but become overwhelmed by stressors or a family crisis. Finally, there may be grandparents whose resilience is limited; these grandparents may be unable to provide adequate care to themselves or their grandchildren. Similarly, grandchildren would also vary in terms of their resilience; some are likely to be experiencing significant psychological, academic, or physical difficulties (Billing *et al.*, 2002; Smith and Palmieri, 2007), while others may experience few difficulties or actually improve their well-being as a result of living with their grandparents (Dolbin-MacNab and Keiley, 2009).

What influences where a grandparent-headed family falls on the continuum of resilience? As suggested by Bronfenbrenner (1979), it depends on the interactions among several specific aspects of the family's larger environment, namely *risk/adversity, vulnerability, resources,* and *protective factors* (Hayslip and Smith, 2013). *Risk/adversity* factors, as they accumulate, increase the chances that a grandparent or grandchild will experience an undesirable outcome like depression or health problems. For example, having a history of health problems, experiencing marital conflict, being economically deprived, and being socially isolated might predispose a grandparent to greater difficulty in adjusting to the demands of raising a grandchild. When grandparent-headed families experience a high degree of risk/adversity factors, they then experience increased *vulnerability* and a potential failure of resilience (Hayslip and Smith, 2013). Greater vulnerability also further increases the probability of negative outcomes. Ultimately, the impact of vulnerability on resilience and negative outcomes is determined by how grandparents' and grandchildren's personal attributes combine with the risk/adversity factors in their environments to determine the *resources* they have to use when responding to stressors and challenges (Cohler,

Stott, and Musick, 1995). For instance, grandparents with greater resources (e.g., being happily married, being highly educated, or having greater social support) would likely be less vulnerable personally, socially, or physically and demonstrate greater resilience. Finally, *protective factors* are those individual or environmental characteristics associated with positive outcomes. These factors counteract the impact of risk/adversity and vulnerability such that grandparents and grandchildren can be more effective (than they would be without the presence of the protective factors) in responding to stressors, crises, and other challenges (Cohler *et al.*, 1995). Example of protective factors that are relevant to grandparents raising grandchildren include being able to accurately and positively interpret life events (Pearlin, Mullan, Semple, and Skaff, 1990), having support and assistance from others (Dolbin-MacNab *et al.*, 2013), and assuming an optimistic attitude towards life and the caregiving situation (Castillo, Henderson, and North, 2013). For some grandparents, the act of providing care to their grandchild can also be protective, due to the associated rewards addressed previously (Dolbin-MacNab, 2006; Hayslip and Smith, 2013; Waldrop and Weber, 2001).

Factors associated with grandparent resilience

Though there have been very few studies of grandchild resilience, numerous factors have been associated with grandparent resilience. While space limitations preclude a full discussion of all of these factors, some key factors associated with grandparent resilience include resourcefulness (Zauszniewski and Musil, 2013), being able to judge or appraise a situation positively (Smith and Dolbin-MacNab, 2013), and feeling empowered within the caregiving role (Cox, 2000; Hayslip and Smith, 2013). Of these factors, how a grandparent views her caregiving situation may be particularly important; grandparents who view the role negatively or see it as conflicting with their other roles (e.g., spouse, friend, etc.) have been shown to experience more stress, feelings of ambivalence about their caregiving role, and compromised mental health (Hayslip *et al.*, 1998; Hayslip and Kaminski, 2005; Park and Greenberg, 2007). Additionally, grandparents' ability to cope with stressors has also been linked to their resilience, in that active problem solving (versus avoiding a problem or reacting to it emotionally) has been associated with better grandparent physical and mental health (Castillo *et al.*, 2013; Hayslip *et al.*, 2013). Finally, grandparents' psychological well-being is also related to their resilience. Specifically, grandparent depression has been linked to greater parenting stress and poorer parenting behaviors (Smith and Dolbin-MacNab, 2013). When grandparents have difficulty with parenting, this can further exacerbate their stress and depression and erode their overall resilience.

Consistent with the view that resilience should be seen as contextual in nature (Vanderbilt-Adriance and Shaw, 2008; Wright and Masten, 2005), it is not surprising that factors outside themselves and their immediate family relationships (e.g., the grandparent–grandchild and grandparent–spouse relationship) also influence grandparents' resilience. For instance, grandparents who have strong social support networks have been shown to be more resilient and have better psychological well-being (Gerard *et al.*, 2006). Similarly, feeling supported and encouraged (versus judged) by grandparent peers and professionals can also promote grandparent resilience (Dolbin-MacNab *et al.*, 2011; Hayslip and Glover, 2008; Gibson, 2002). Even living in a supportive neighborhood or community can help grandparents better manage the challenges of raising their grandchildren.

Grandparents who possess a number of resilient personal attributes and processes may find that, despite the challenges associated with raising their grandchildren, they actually *grow* and *prosper* (Hayslip and Smith, 2013). In fact, despite enormous odds, many grandparents raising grandchildren display astounding strength, responsibility, hope, faith, and commitment (Hayslip and Smith, 2013). When grandparents are able to successfully navigate the challenges of caregiving, they may be more available and responsive to their grandchildren, engage in better parenting behavior, and provide stability and support, thus positively impacting their grandchildren's adjustment (Hayslip *et al.*, 2013). This, in turn, could further contribute to the resilience and well-being of the grandparent, reflecting the interconnected and systemic nature of grandparent-headed families (Goodman and Hayslip, 2008; Smith and Dolbin-MacNab, 2013).

Promoting resilience in grandparent-headed families

Given the link between caregiving stressors and grandparents' overall well-being (Hayslip and Kaminski, 2005; Park and Greenberg, 2007), it becomes clear that helping grandparents learn how to manage stress and respond to the challenges of raising their grandchildren is a key means of building resilience and preventing negative outcomes. Thus, for practitioners, a valuable focus for intervention is developing grandparents' resilience. Building grandparents' resilience can help protect them from physical and psychological health problems, especially since they may become more vulnerable over time (Goodman, 2006; Hayslip, Patrick, and Panek, 2011). Promoting grandparent resilience may also be beneficial for the grandchildren, as discussed previously. Practitioners can even target grandchildren and create interventions that would help grandchildren develop their own resilience.

The complexity of resilience works to the advantage of practitioners interested in promoting the well-being of grandparent-headed families. That is, practitioners can work to address risk/adversity factors, vulnerabilities, resources, and/or protective factors. To be most effective, Hildon and colleagues (2010) suggest that practitioners assist grandparents in building their resources and protective factors, while also reducing the impact of risk factors and vulnerability (Hayslip and Smith, 2013). This means intervening at the level of individual characteristics and attributes *as well as* intervening with aspects of the larger environment in which the family is embedded (Danish, 1981). Assuming this type of comprehensive approach to building resilience among grandparent caregivers and grandchildren is aligned with an ecological perspective (Bronfenbrenner, 1979), which would suggest improving aspects of the environment that are negatively impacting the grandparent-headed family, it is possible to increase the opportunities available to the family and, in turn, their resilience and well-being.

By taking an ecological perspective (Bronfenbrenner, 1979) on promoting resilience in grandparent-headed families, it is possible to see how practitioners could intervene in multiple ways and with both proximal and distal environments. For instance, as suggested by Hayslip and Smith (2013), practitioners could direct

---

Box 9.1 Grandparent Skill Training

Practitioners can promote resilience within grandparent-headed families by developing grandparents' protective attributes, skills, and processes (Rutter, 2010). For instance, grandparents can learn to reframe challenges (i.e., seeing something negative in a more positive way), take an optimistic or positive outlook (i.e., making positive appraisals), be more flexible in the face of challenges and change, and identify the benefits of their situations (Hayslip and Smith, 2013). Grandparents can also develop their coping skills, such as their ability to respond to stressors by taking action to resolve or address the issue (Castillo *et al.*, 2013). Beyond these skills, practitioners can teach assertive communication skills, stress management techniques, and physical and emotional self-care (Hayslip and Smith, 2013). Resilience can even be promoted by teaching grandparents where to go for help, how to ask for help, and how to advocate for themselves and their families (Dolbin-MacNab *et al.*, 2013). Finally, doing volunteer work or becoming involved in the community can help promote grandparent resilience (Park and Greenberg, 2007).

If grandparents are able to develop these types of protective skills, they and their grandchildren are likely to be buffered against stressors and negative outcomes (Hayslip and Smith, 2013). This is because resilience plays a key role in diminishing the impact of the stress associated with raising grandchildren on grandparents' emotional, physical, social, or behavioral outcomes (Hayslip and Smith, 2013). Thus, by teaching grandparents skills that are resource- or solution-based (Smith and Dolbin-MacNab, 2013), practitioners can provide grandparents with the tools they need to be proactive in addressing stressors, overcoming challenges, and building their overall resilience.

---

their interventions to grandparents, grandchildren, service providers, and even the general public. Interventions for grandparents might focus on building a variety of resilient characteristics or skills (see Box 9.1) and could be delivered via support groups, psychotherapy, mentoring programs, or psychoeducational workshops (Hayslip, 2003; Smith, 2003). Building a "resilience narrative" (i.e., developing a grandparent's personal story (or belief) that she is resilient and can overcome her challenges) might be especially valuable for at-risk grandparents (Bailey, Letiecq, Erickson, and Koltz, 2013). Resilience in grandchildren could be developed by addressing the challenges in their relationships with their grandparents and parents (Dolbin-MacNab and Keiley, 2009; Hayslip and Kaminski, 2006), helping them connect with other children being raised by grandparents, and by addressing underlying issues (e.g., trauma) impacting their current well-being. Practitioners interested in working with grandchildren might consider psychotherapy, support groups, workshops, and online communities as means of intervention. With regard to service providers, intervention efforts could be targeted toward removing barriers to grandparents' accessing services (e.g., lack of transportation, restrictive eligibility requirements, confusing policies) and curtailing judgmental attitudes (Dolbin-MacNab *et al.*, 2013; Dolbin-MacNab *et al.*, 2011). As illustrated by all of these examples, by assuming an ecological perspective (Bronfenbrenner, 1979) on promoting resilience among grandparent-headed families, practitioners have the ability to support and benefit grandparents and their grandchildren in numerous ways.

Regardless of the exact approach to building resilience, practitioners would do well to remember that every grandparent-headed family has a unique constellation of risk factors, vulnerability, resources, and protective factors that interact to influence their resilience and overall functioning and well-being. Furthermore, families will enter interventions with varying levels of resilience and the exact nature of their resilience will vary (Hayslip and Smith, 2013). This diversity means that some interventions will not be beneficial to particular families and, even when interventions are generally effective, there will be variation in how well grandparents and grandchildren respond to them (Hayslip and Smith, 2013). In fact, it is also possible that some intervention programs could negatively impact resilience. For instance, in a study of a six-week intervention designed to promote positive grandparent functioning through the acquisition of new skills and knowledge, Hayslip (2003) found that grandparents reported better relationships with their grandchildren and improved parental efficacy. However, grandparents' parental role strain, financial stress, and depression also increased over the course of the intervention. As this example illustrates, interventions may help promote resilience, but they can also sensitize grandparents to the challenges in their lives and their lack of control over these issues. Thus, practitioners should make special efforts to ensure that their interventions are having their intended effects and actually promoting resilience within grandparent-headed families.

Intervention programs

There are several examples of intervention programs that are currently being used to promote resilience among grandparent-headed families (Hayslip and Smith, 2013). Most of these programs incorporate skill training (see Box 9.1), in which grandparents are taught a variety of skills that have been associated with resilience. Many of these programs also take an ecological perspective (Bronfenbrenner, 1979), in that they target other aspects of the grandparent-headed family ecology, including grandparent and children physical and mental health, instrumental needs (e.g., housing, legal assistance, food), and even the quality of their larger communities. Example programs address these needs through a variety of services including educational workshops, medical care, advocacy, developmental assessments (for grandchildren), support groups, and psychotherapy.

Project Healthy Grandparents (Whitley, Kelley, and Campos, 2013) is a comprehensive program that builds resilience by empowering grandparents to advocate for themselves and their grandchildren by connecting them with community resources and by caring for their physical and psychological health. Similarly, the Skip Generation program (James and Ferrante, 2013) targets resilience by providing grandparents with mentors who are also grandparents raising grandchildren. These mentors visit grandparents' homes and provide them with resources, education, and support. Besides the resilience that is built through these services, grandparents can further develop

their resilience by becoming mentors themselves. A final example of a program targeting grandparent resilience is the multi-site Grandparent Resource Site program (Smith *et al.*, 2013). Grandparents within the program's sites participate in support groups, educational trainings, and in-home services. Depending on the needs of the specific site, there are also services available for grandchildren and professionals within the communities (Smith *et al.*, 2013). Participants in this program report a variety of resilient personal attributes and processes: a sense of pride, problem-solving skills, a willingness to be persistent, and an optimistic outlook (Hayslip and Smith, 2013; Smith *et al.*, 2013). Together, all of these programs highlight the need to address individual characteristics as well as multiple aspects of families' larger environments when attempting to promote resilience.

Global Perspectives on Grandparents Raising Grandchildren

While this chapter has focused on grandparents raising grandchildren in the United States, this phenomenon exists worldwide. Globally, grandparents or other extended family members are the people primarily responsible for providing care for children who cannot be cared for by their parents (International Social Service and UNICEF, 2004). High rates of grandparent caregivers have been noted around the world, in both developing and industrialized nations (Save the Children, 2007). Asia and sub-Saharan Africa have particularly high rates of grandparents raising grandchildren (Save the Children, 2007). However, depending on the particular cultural and socioeconomic context, the experiences and needs of grandparent caregivers and their grandchildren vary widely. The reasons underlying the caregiving arrangement also vary.

Globally, the reasons that grandparents provide care for their grandchildren are as diverse and unique as their sociopolitical contexts. For instance, in Africa and parts of Asia, the HIV/AIDs epidemic has resulted in millions of children being orphaned and needing to be cared for by grandparents or other relatives (UNICEF, 2008). Additionally, natural disasters (e.g., the 2004 tsunami in Indonesia) and human conflicts (e.g., the Kosovo War) have resulted in many children requiring care (Save the Children, 2007). Parental migration is another significant reason that grandparents assume responsibility for the care of their grandchildren; in many countries, parents leave their towns and villages to seek education and/or employment in other cities or abroad – leaving their children behind with relatives. This is increasingly common in China (Chen, Liu, and Mair, 2011) and very common in parts of Africa. The reasons for grandparents assuming care of their grandchildren have significant implications for their needs and well-being – for example, grandparents raising grandchildren infected with HIV may be at high risk for contracting the virus.

Throughout the world, most grandparents are providing informal care to multiple grandchildren, particularly within developing nations (Save the Children, 2007). These grandparents often have limited access to services, or there are no available services (Chazan, 2008). As such, grandparent caregivers may struggle to provide basic necessities such as food, housing, and clothing (Chazan, 2008). Grandparents also experience high levels of burden, the stigma of HIV/AIDs, lack of housing, limited or no financial resources, and difficulties with their own health (Chazan, 2008; Save the Children, 2007). Given the lack of resources and limited support services, grandchildren in these family arrangements may be at risk for abuse and child exploitation (Save the Children, 2007). There are numerous examples of grandchildren being made to work as domestic servants, or being forced into prostitution. There can also be family conflicts over any small grants that the grandchild receives from the government, arguments about parenting and child discipline, and disagreements about family roles and responsibilities (Save the Children, 2007). With limited or no monitoring of informal grandparent caregivers in many developing nations (Save the Children, 2007), children in these caregiving arrangements can be at substantial risk for a variety of devastating outcomes.

Due to cultural traditions of familism and grandparent caregiving, in many countries, grandparents are a major source of care for needy grandchildren. While a significant proportion of grandparents are able to provide their grandchildren with loving homes and basic necessities, poverty and limited supports and resources means that many grandparent-headed families around the world are extremely vulnerable. More research, supports, and services are needed in order to better understand and assist these families.

Summary

Although grandparents all over the world have been responsible for the care of their grandchildren for centuries, in recent decades there has been significant growth in the number of grandparent-headed families, particularly within the United States (Kreider and Ellis, 2011). Grandparent-headed families are extremely diverse and, when viewed from an ecological perspective (Bronfenbrenner, 1979), have a variety of interrelated needs and challenges. Research suggests that, while some grandparents and grandchildren experience negative outcomes, many grandparent-headed families are resilient in the face of their challenges. A number of interventions have been developed to help address the needs of grandparent-headed families and promote their resilience. Given the likelihood that grandparent-headed families will continue to be a common family form, future work in this area should continue to focus on understanding the factors that promote resilience, as well as interventions that can help these families succeed.

Critical Thinking Questions

1. Do you know someone who has lived in a grandparent-headed family? How do their experiences compare to those presented in this chapter?
2. What policy and practice initiatives should be developed in order to support grandparent caregivers and their grandchildren?
3. How can practitioners promote resilience among grandparents raising grandchildren?
4. If you were studying grandparent-headed families, what questions would you investigate? Why do you think these are important areas of investigation?

Note

1. All case scenarios in this chapter are based on fictional families. Names and details have been developed expressly for the purpose of this chapter.

References

AARP. (2010). More grandparents raising grandkids: New census data shows increase in children being raised by extended family. Retrieved May 30, 2014 from www.aarp.org/relationships/grandparenting/info.

Annie E. Casey Foundation (2012). *Stepping up for kids: What government and communities should do to support kinship families.* Baltimore, MD: The Annie E. Casey Foundation. Retrieved May 30, 2014 from http://www.aecf.org/KnowledgeCenter/Publications.aspx?pubguid={642BF3F2-9A85-4C6B-83C8-A30F5D928E4D}.

Bailey, S., Letiecq, B., Erickson, M., and Koltz, R. (2013). Resilient grandparent caregivers: Pathways to positive adaptation. In B. Hayslip and G. Smith (eds), *Resilient grandparent caregivers: A strengths-based perspective* (pp. 70–88). New York: Routledge.

Baltes, P., Reese, H., and Nesselroade, J. (1988). *Life span developmental psychology: Introduction to research methods.* Hillsdale, NJ: Erlbaum.

Billing, A., Ehrle, J., and Kortenkamp, K. (2002). Children cared for by relatives: What do we know about their well-being? New Federalism: National Survey of America's Families, Policy Brief B-46. Washington, DC: Urban Institute.

Bronfenbrenner, U. (1979). *The ecology of human development: Experiments by nature and design.* Cambridge, MA: Harvard University Press.

Bryson, K., and Casper, L. M. (1999). Coresident grandparents and grandchildren. Current Population Reports, Special Studies, P23-198. Washington, DC: US Census Bureau.

Burnette, D. (1999). Physical and emotional well-being of custodial grandparents in Latino families. *American Journal of Orthopsychiatry, 69,* 305–317.

Castillo, K., Henderson, C., and North, L. (2013). The relation between caregiving style, coping, benefit finding, grandchild symptoms, and caregiver adjustment among custodial grandparents. In B. Hayslip and G. Smith (eds), *Resilient grandparent caregivers: A strengths-based perspective* (pp. 25–37). New York: Routledge.

Chazan, M. (2008). Seven 'deadly' assumptions: Unravelling the implications of HIV/AIDS among grandmothers in South Africa and beyond. *Aging and Society, 28,* 935–958.

Chen, F., Liu, G., and Mair, C. (2011). Intergenerational ties in context: Grandparents caring for grandchildren in China. *Social Forces, 90,* 571–594.

Cohler, B. J., Stott, F. M., and Musick, J. S. (1995). Adversity, vulnerability, and resilience: Cultural and developmental perspectives. In D. Cicchetti and D. J. Cohen (eds),

Developmental psychopathology, vol. 2, *Risk, disorder, and adaptation* (pp. 753–800). New York: John Wiley & Sons, Inc.

Collins, P. H. (2000). *Black feminist thought: Knowledge, consciousness, and the politics of empowerment* (2nd edn). New York: Routledge.

Cox, C. B. (2000). Why grandchildren are going to and staying at grandmother's house and what happens when they get there? In C. B. Cox (ed.), *To grandmother's house we go and stay: Perspectives on custodial grandparents* (pp. 3–19). New York: Springer.

Cox, C. B., Brooks, L. R., and Valcarcel, C. (2000). Culture and caregiving: A study of Latino grandparents. In C. B. Cox (ed.), *To grandmother's house we go and stay: Perspectives on custodial grandparents* (pp. 215–233). New York: Springer.

Danish, S. (1981). Life-span development and intervention: A necessary link. *Counseling Psychologist, 9,* 40–43.

Dervarics, C. (2004). American grandparent responsibilities on the rise. Washington, DC: Population Reference Bureau. Retrieved May 30, 2014 from http://www.prb.org/Articles/2004/AmericanGrandparentResponsibilitiesontheRise.aspx.

Dolbin-MacNab, M. L. (2006). Just like raising your own? Grandmothers' perceptions of parenting a second time around. *Family Relations, 55,* 564–575.

Dolbin-MacNab, M. L., and Keiley, M. K. (2006). A systemic examination of grandparents' emotional closeness with their custodial grandchildren. *Research in Human Development, 3,* 59–71.

Dolbin-MacNab, M. L., and Keiley, M. K. (2009). Navigating interdependence: How adolescents raised solely by grandparents experience their family relationships. *Family Relations, 58,* 162–175.

Dolbin-MacNab, M. L., Johnson, J., Sudano, L., Serrano, E., and Roberto, K. (2011). *Focus groups: Professionals serving grandparent-headed families.* Blacksburg, VA: Department of Human Development, Virginia Tech.

Dolbin-MacNab, M. L., Roberto, K. A., and Finney, J. W. (2013). Formal social support: Promoting resilience in grandparents parenting grandchildren. In B. Hayslip and G. Smith (eds), *Resilient grandparent caregivers: A strengths-based perspective* (pp. 134–151). New York: Routledge.

Dolbin-MacNab, M. L., and Traylor, R. M. (2008). Clinical update: Grandparents raising grandchildren. *Family Therapy Magazine, 7,* 40–46.

Fuller-Thomson, E., and Minkler, M. (2001). American grandparents providing extensive childcare to their grandchildren: Prevalence and profile. *The Gerontologist, 41,* 201–209.

Fuller-Thomson, E., and Minkler, M. (2007). Central American grandparents raising grandchildren. *Hispanic Journal of Behavioral Sciences, 29*, 5–18.

Generations United. (2011). *Grandfamilies: Challenges of caring for a second family.* Washington, DC: Generations United.

Gerard, J. M., Landry-Meyer, L., and Roe, J. G. (2006). Grandparents raising grandchildren: The role of social support in coping with caregiving challenges. *International Journal of Aging and Human Development, 62*, 359–383.

Gibson, P. (2002). Barriers, lessons learned, and helpful hints: Grandmother caregivers talk about service utilization. *Journal of Gerontological Social Work, 39*, 55–74.

Gladstone, J. W., Brown, R. A., and Fitzgerald, K. J. (2009). Grandparents raising grandchildren: Tensions, service needs and involvement with child welfare agencies. *International Journal of Aging and Human Development, 69*, 55–78.

Goodman, C. C. (2006). Grandmothers raising grandchildren: The vulnerability of advancing age. In B. Hayslip and J. Patrick (eds), *Custodial grandparenting: Individual, cultural, and ethnic diversity* (pp. 133–150). New York: Springer.

Goodman, C. C., and Hayslip, B. (2008). Mentally healthy grandparents' impact on their grandchildren's behavior. In B. Hayslip and P. Kaminski (eds), *Parenting the custodial grandchild: Implications for clinical practice* (pp. 41–52). New York: Springer.

Goodman, C. C., and Silverstein, M. (2002). Grandparents raising grandchildren: Family structure and well-being in culturally diverse families. *The Gerontologist, 42*, 676–689.

Goodman, C. C., and Silverstein, M. (2006). Grandmothers raising grandchildren: Ethnic and racial differences in well-being among custodial and coparenting families. *Journal of Family Issues, 27*, 1605–1626.

Hall, C., and Lindzey, G. (1978). *Theories of personality.* New York: John Wiley & Sons, Inc.

Hayslip, B. (2003). The impact of a psychosocial intervention on parental efficacy, grandchild relationship quality and well being among grandparents raising grandchildren. In B. Hayslip and J. Hicks Patrick (eds), *Working with custodial grandparents* (pp. 163–178). New York: Springer.

Hayslip, B., Davis, S., Neumann, C., Goodman, C., Smith, G., Maiden. R., and Carr, G. (2013). The role of resilience in mediating stressor-outcome relationships among grandparents raising grandchildren. In B. Hayslip and G. Smith (eds), *Resilient grandparent caregivers: A strengths-based perspective* (pp. 48–69). New York: Routledge.

Hayslip, B., and Glover, R. (2008). Traditional grandparents' views of their caregiving peers' parenting skills: Complimentary or critical? In B. Hayslip and P. Kaminski (eds), *Parenting the custodial grandchild: Implications for clinical practice* (pp. 149–164). New York: Springer.

Hayslip, B., and Kaminski, P. L. (2005). Grandparents raising their grandchildren: A review of the literature and suggestions for practice. *The Gerontologist, 45*, 262–269.

Hayslip, B., and Kaminski, P. (2006). Custodial grandchildren. In G. Bear and K. Minke (eds), *Children's needs III: Understanding and addressing the needs of children* (pp. 771–782). Washington, DC: National Association of School Psychologists.

Hayslip, B., and Page, K. (2012). Grandparent–grandchild/great-grandchild relationships. In R. Blieszner and V. H. Bedford (eds), *Handbook of aging and the family* (pp. 183–212). New York: Praeger.

Hayslip, B., Patrick, J., and Panek, P. (2011). *Adult development and aging* (5th edn). Malabar, FL: Krieger.

Hayslip, B., Shore, R. J., Henderson, C. E., and Lambert, P. L. (1998). Custodial grandparenting and the impact of grandchildren with problems on role satisfaction and role meaning. *Journal of Gerontology: Social Sciences, 53B*, S164–S173.

Hayslip, B., and Smith, G. C. (2013). Epilogue. In B. Hayslip and G. Smith (eds), *Resilient grandparent caregivers: A strengths-based perspective* (pp. 251–257). New York: Routledge.

Henderson, T., and Cook, J. L. (2006). The voices of Black grandmothers parenting grandchildren with TANF assistance. In B. Hayslip and J. Patrick (eds), *Custodial grandparenting: Individual, cultural, and ethnic diversity* (pp. 303–320). New York: Springer.

Hildon, Z., Montgomery, S. M., Blane, D., Wiggins, R. D., and Netuveli, G. (2010). Examining resilience of quality of life in the face of health-related and psychosocial adversity at older ages: What is "right" about the way we age? *The Gerontologist, 50*, 36–47.

Hughes, M. E., Waite, L. J., LaPierre, T. A., and Luo, Y. (2007). All in the family: The impact of caring for grandchildren on grandparents' health. *Journal of Gerontology: Social Sciences, 62B*, S108–S119.

Hunter, A. G., and Taylor, R. J. (1998). Grandparenthood in African American families. In M. Szinovacz (ed.), *Handbook on grandparenthood* (pp. 70–86). Westport, CT: Greenwood Press.

International Social Service and UNICEF. (2004). *Kinship care: An issue for international standards.* New York: UNICEF.

James, L., and Ferrante, C. (2013). Skip generations: A strength-based mentoring program for resilience grandparent caregivers. In B. Hayslip and G. Smith (eds), *Resilient grandparent caregivers: A strengths-based perspective* (pp. 167–183). New York: Routledge.

Jendrek, M. P. (1993). Grandparents who parent their grandchildren: Effects on lifestyle. *Journal of Marriage and the Family, 55*, 609–621.

Keene, J. R., and Batson, C. D. (2010). Under one roof: A review of research on intergenerational coresidence and multigenerational households in the United States. *Sociology Compass, 4*, 642–657.

Kopera-Frye, K., and Wiscott, R. (2000). Intergenerational continuity: Transmissions of beliefs and culture. In B. Hayslip and R. Goldberg-Glen (eds), *Grandparents raising grandchildren: Theoretical, empirical, and clinical perspectives* (pp. 65–84). New York: Springer.

Kreider, R. M. (2008). Living arrangements of children: 2004. Current Population Reports, P70-114. Washington, DC: US Census Bureau. Retrieved May 30, 2014 from http://www.census.gov/prod/ 2008pubs/p70-114.pdf1.

Kreider, R. M., and Ellis, R. (2011). Living arrangements of children: 2009. Current Population Reports, P70-126. Washington, DC: US Census Bureau. Retrieved May 30, 2014 from http://www.census.gov/prod/2011pubs/ p70-126.pdf.

Kropf, N. P., and Kolomer, S. (2004). Grandparents raising grandchildren: A diverse population. *Journal of Human Behavior in the Social Environment, 9*, 65–83.

Leipold, B., and Greve, W. (2009). Resilience: A conceptual bridge between coping and development. *European Psychologist, 14*, 40–50.

Livingston, G., and Parker, K. (2010). Since the start of the Great Recession, more children raised by grandparents. Washington, DC: Pew Research Center. Retrieved May 30, 2014 from http://pewsocialtrends.org/2010/09/09/ since-the-start-of-the-great-recession-more-children-raised-by-grandparents/#prc-jump.

Luo, Y., LaPierre, T., Hughes, M., and Waite, L. (2012). Grandparents providing care to grandchildren: A population-based study of continuity and change. *Journal of Family Issues, 33*, 1143–1167.

Minkler, M., and Fuller-Thomson, E. (1999). The health of grandparents raising grandchildren: Results of a national study. *American Journal of Public Health, 89*, 1384–1389.

Minkler, M., Fuller-Thomson, E., Miller, D., and Driver, D. (1997). Depression in grandparents raising grandchildren: Results of a national longitudinal study. *Archives of Family Medicine, 6*, 445–452.

Murphey, D., Cooper, M., and Moore, K. A. (2012). Grandparents living with children: State-level data from the American Community Survey. Bethesda, MD: Child Trends. Retrieved May 30, 2014 from childtrends.org/ wp-content/uploads/2012/10/2012-30Grandparents.pdf.

Musil, C. M., Schrader, S., and Mutikani, J. (2000). Social support, stress, and special coping tasks of grandmother caregivers. In C. B. Cox (ed.), *To grandmother's house we go and stay: Perspectives on custodial grandparents* (pp. 56–70). New York: Springer.

Mutchler, J., Lee, W., and Baker, L. (2006). Grandparent care in the United States: Comparisons by race and ethnicity. Boston, MA: Institute of Gerontology, University of Massachusetts. Retrieved May 30, 2014 from http://www.geront.umb. edu/inst/pubAndStudies/DiversityinGrandparent CareHouseholds.pdf.

Park, H., and Greenberg, J. (2007). Parenting grandchildren. In J. Blackburn and C. Dumus (eds), *Handbook of gerontology: Evidence-based approaches to theory, practice, and policy* (pp. 397–425). Hoboken, NJ: John Wiley & Sons, Inc.

Pearlin, L., Mullan, J., Semple, S., and Skaff, M. (1990). Caregiving and the stress process: An overview of concepts and their measures. *The Gerontologist, 30*, 583–594.

Pebley, A. R., and Rudkin, L. L. (1999). Grandparents raising grandchildren: What do we know? *Journal of Family Issues, 20*, 218–242.

Pew Charitable Trusts. (2007). *Time for reform: Support relatives in providing foster care and permanent families for children.* Washington, DC: Pew Charitable Trusts. Retrieved May 30, 2014 from http://www.pewtrusts.org/our_ work_report_detail.aspx?id=48986.

Pruchno, R. (1999). Raising grandchildren: The experiences of Black and White grandmothers. *The Gerontologist, 39*, 209–221.

Pruchno, R., and McKenney, D. (2002). Psychological well-being of Black and White grandmothers raising grandchildren: Examination of a two-factor model. *Journals of Gerontology: Psychological Sciences and Social Sciences, 57B*, P444–P452.

Rodgers-Farmer, A. Y. (1999). Parenting stress, depression, and parenting in grandmothers raising their grandchildren. *Children and Youth Services Review, 21*, 377–388.

Rutter, M. (2007). Resilience, competence, and coping. *Child Abuse and Neglect, 31*, 205–209.

Rutter, M. (2010). From individual differences to resilience: From traits to processes. Presented at the 118th Convention of the American Psychological Association. August 12–15, San Diego, CA.

Sands, R. G., and Goldberg-Glen, R. S. (2000). Factors associated with stress among grandparents raising their grandchildren. *Family Relations, 49*, 97–105.

Save the Children. (2007). *Kinship care: Providing positive and safe care for children living away from home.* London: Save the Children UK. Retrieved May 30, 2014 from http:// www.savethechildren.org.uk/sites/default/files/docs/ kinship_care_1.pdf.

Shakya, H., Usita, P., Eisenberg, C., Weston, J., and Liles, S. (2012). Family well-being and concerns of grandparents in skipped generation families. *Journal of Gerontological Social Work, 55*, 39–54.

Smith, A., Dannison, L., and James, M. (2013). Resiliency and custodial grandparents: Recognizing and supporting strengths. In B. Hayslip and G. Smith (eds),

Resilient grandparent caregivers: A strengths-based perspective (pp. 222–234). New York: Routledge.

Smith, G. C. (2003). How grandparents view support groups: An exploratory study. In B. Hayslip and J. Patrick (eds), *Working with custodial grandparents* (pp. 69–92). New York: Springer.

Smith, G. C., and Dolbin-MacNab, M. L. (2013). The role of negative and positive caregiving appraisals in key outcomes for custodial grandmothers and grandchildren. In B. Hayslip and G. Smith (eds), *Resilient grandparent caregivers: A strengths-based perspective* (pp. 3–24). New York: Routledge.

Smith, G. C., and Palmieri, P. A. (2007). Risk of psychological difficulties among children raised by custodial grandparents. *Psychiatric Services, 58*, 1303–1310.

Smith, G. C., Palmieri, P. A., Hancock, G. R., and Richardson, R. A. (2008). Custodial grandmothers' psychological distress, dysfunctional parenting, and grandchildren's adjustment. *International Journal of Aging and Human Development, 67*, 327–357.

Smith, G. C., and Richardson, R. A. (2008). Understanding the parenting practices of custodial grandmothers: Overcompensating, underserving, or overwhelmed? In B. Hayslip and P. Kaminski (eds), *Parenting the custodial grandchild* (pp. 131–147). New York: Springer.

UNICEF. (2008). *State of the world's children: Child survival.* New York: UNICEF. Retrieved May 30, 2014 from http://www.unicef.org/sowc08/report/report.php.

US Bureau of the Census. (2000). *Current population survey.* Washington, DC: US Government Printing Office.

Vanderbilt-Adriance, E., and Shaw, D. S. (2008). Conceptualizing and re-evaluating resilience across levels of risk, time, and domains of competence. *Clinical Child and Family Review, 11*, 30–58.

Waldrop, D. P., and Weber, J. A. (2001). From grandparent to caregiver: The stress and satisfaction of raising grandchildren. *Families in Society, 82*, 461–472.

Weber, J. A., and Waldrop, D. P. (2000). Grandparents raising grandchildren: Families in transition. *Journal of Gerontological Social Work, 33*, 27–46.

Whitley, D. H., Kelley, S., and Campos, P. E. (2013). Promoting family empowerment among African American grandmothers raising grandchildren. In B. Hayslip and G. Smith (eds), *Resilient grandparent caregivers: A strengths-based perspective* (pp. 235–250). New York: Routledge.

Wright, M. O., and Masten, A. S. (2005). Resilience processes in development: Fostering positive adaptation in the context of adversity. In S. Goldstein and R. B. Brooks (eds), *Handbook of resilience in children* (pp. 17–37). New York: Springer.

Young, M., and Dawson, T. (2003). Perception of child difficulty and levels of depression in caregiving grandmothers. *Journal of Mental Health and Aging, 9*, 111–122.

Zauszniewski, J., and Musil, C. (2013). Resourcefulness in grandmothers raising grandchildren. In B. Hayslip and G. Smith (eds), *Resilient grandparent caregivers: A strengths-based perspective* (pp. 38–47). New York: Routledge.

10

Caring for Older Adults
Challenges for Families

Kathleen W. Piercy

In Chapter 10, Piercy turns our attention from the care that elders may provide to their families, to the caregiving that they increasingly need from them. Using a family systems perspective, we see how all members of the family are connected, and when a family member can no longer care for him- or herself, everyone in the family is affected. The fact that most eldercare responsibilities fall to the women in families has implications for their mental and physical health, and their ability to carry out other care responsibilities (e.g., their children).

Introduction

Situations like Terrence and Louise's (see page 151) occur every day. Though people become caregivers to older adults for many reasons, those who care for persons with dementia face a plethora of daily challenges. In addition to providing help with basic tasks of everyday life, dementia caregivers must deal with the loss of the person they have known as the disease progresses. This loss strikes families equally hard regardless of their financial and social circumstances. The actor David Hyde Pierce, author and reporter Maria Shriver, and former first lady Rosalynn Carter have dedicated considerable time and resources to raising funds and awareness for those with Alzheimer's disease and their caregivers. Mrs. Carter founded The Rosalynn Carter Institute for Caregiving for the express purpose of "building support for caregivers throughout the world"

(www.rosalynncarter.org/). My recent search of elder-care books listed on Amazon.com yielded 919 published entries, reflecting the keen public interest in how to deal with their aging relatives and friends.

What is Caregiving?

Pearlin, Mullan, Semple, and Skaff (1990) made a distinction between caring and caregiving that is useful for our discussion. They defined *caring* as the affective (feeling) part of a person's commitment to the welfare of another person. *Caregiving*, then, is the "behavioral expression of this commitment" (pp. 583). Caring feelings towards an elder in need may contribute to decisions to provide assistance, though there are usually additional reasons why people become caregivers.

Family Problems: Stress, Risk, and Resilience, First Edition. Edited by Joyce A. Arditti.
© 2015 John Wiley & Sons, Inc. Published 2015 by John Wiley & Sons, Inc.

Case Example: Terrence and Louise

Six months ago, 70-year-old Terrence Jones was diagnosed with Alzheimer's disease. He and his wife of 48 years, Louise, live in a small house just outside of Baton Rouge. Though Louise knew that Terrence's memory "wasn't quite right," she was stunned by the doctor's diagnosis. The couple have three children, but only a son lives nearby, and he works days and some evenings, so he is unable to help his parents much. His wife works full-time, too, but has Wednesdays off, so she helps Louise with household chores when her children are in school.

It seems that Terrence's dementia is progressing rapidly; he cannot drive, needs Louise's help remembering to take his medications, and takes forever to dress himself. Last night, he fell and broke his hip. He will need surgery and physical therapy if he is to walk on his own again. Louise's blood pressure has skyrocketed lately. Terrence was her "rock," and she is still grieving the loss of the man she relied on. She feels worn out from the work of caring for him.

For our discussion here, we adopt the following definition, which is "unpaid care to a relative or friend 18 years or older to help them take care of themselves" (National Alliance for Caregiving (NAC) and AARP, 2009, p. 2). Care activities can include help with or completing household chores, managing the person's money, arranging paid assistance for them, or providing hands-on assistance with activities of daily living, such as grooming or bathing.

Prevalence of Caregiving

In 2008, an estimated 65.7 million individuals in the United States have cared for an adult or child. This represents about 36.5 million households. Most primary caregivers are women who average 48 years of age. Over a third of them assist a parent; while one in seven adults care for their own child. However, the average age of a care receiver is 61, reflecting the fact that the preponderance of caregiving is to old persons (NAC and AARP, 2009).

Caregiving and caregivers are worthy of our attention for several reasons. First, with the aging of baby boomers (see Box 10.1) and their relatively small and mobile families, there is concern about whether enough family caregivers will be available to all boomers who need assistance. If not, then other solutions are needed. However, recently, both federal and state governments in the United States and elsewhere have either frozen or cut funding for caregiver-related services. If this trend continues, how will aging boomers get the help they need? Second, unpaid caregiving is a valuable contribution to society. The estimated worth of unpaid care to elderly persons was $450 billion in 2009, more than the total sales of the world's largest companies, including Wal-Mart (Feinberg, Reinhard, Houser, and Choula, 2012). However, many caregivers, especially women (the majority of caregivers), pay a price for their unpaid labor in lost wages, forgone promotions, and less retirement income. Finally, many caregivers experience health and/or mental health problems, such as anxiety and depression, that are directly related to care provision. They themselves may need help.

The rest of this chapter covers the following topics: who provides care and the differences between paid and unpaid care; the demands of providing dementia care vs. care for other problems; and several theoretical perspectives that inform caregiving patterns and are useful in conceptualizing caregiving problems and solutions. Next I discuss important issues that caregivers face: deciding how to structure care provision (including family dynamics among those families providing care); stress, coping, burden, and benefits; obtaining supportive services; and looking ahead to future programs and policies that are friendly to caregivers.

Box 10.1   Population Aging

Life expectancy, which is "the average number of years of life remaining to a person at a given age," increased dramatically during the twentieth century (Federal Interagency Forum on Aging-Related Statistics (FIFARS), 2010, p. 25). In the United States today, a person who reaches age 65 lives, on average, 18.5 additional years. This number differs slightly for persons of minority race or ethnic status, with Caucasians living longest (FIFARS, 2010).

In addition, we tend to live longer in *better health* than our predecessors. The number of older persons with functional limitations; that is, difficulty or inability to perform activities needed for independent living, has declined in recent years, as has the number of people with dentures. Medical and technological advances have increased the ability to detect and treat progressive diseases (FIFARS, 2010). Because of a combination of lifestyle behaviors, environmental

exposures, and genes, women outlive men by 5–10 years (Blue, 2008).

One's resources also contribute to longevity. In the United States, persons with high socioeconomic status (SES) fare better health-wise than those with lower SES and impoverished persons, somewhat because of better access to health care services. Because higher percentages of racial minorities like African Americans and ethnic minorities like Hispanics have lower average levels of income and education, they are more likely than their Caucasians counterparts to enter old age with greater functional limitations and diseases, such as diabetes or hypertension (FIFARS, 2010). Chronic diseases that limit one's ability to function without assistance are what often lead to the need for caregivers. These diseases are often physical in nature, such as arthritis or stroke-related impairments, but as people live to advanced old age, they may develop cognitive disorders, such as Alzheimer's disease or other dementia.

Who Provides Care and Why?

Studies of caregivers show that the majority are women, most often daughters, wives, or daughters-in-law. Among the reasons that women are more often caregivers than men include greater availability, norms and cultural values that assign kin-keeping to women and promote a greater felt obligation, which is then reinforced by women's socialization patterns. However, there are husbands who provide daily care to their wives, and sons are caregivers as well. However, sons are more likely to manage money, maintain the home, and hire help for personal-care tasks than to do personal care or homemaker chores themselves (NAC and AARP, 2009).

The top two reasons for providing care are a person's old age or the presence of dementia or Alzheimer's disease. Less often mentioned are emotional illness, cancer, heart disease, and stroke. However, it is not unusual for older adults to have multiple health problems that chip away at their ability to

remain independent. Some persons with Alzheimer's disease also have heart disease, arthritis, or diabetes, which can lead to limitations in physical abilities. In total, 69% of older adults receiving care have long-term physical conditions (NAC and AARP, 2009). The simultaneous presence of memory and physical impairment presents caregivers with very demanding situations. On average, caregivers spend nearly 21 hours each week providing assistance. For those who co-reside with the person for whom they care, that figure averages over 39 hours per week, the equivalent of full-time, paid employment (FIFARS, 2010).

Informal and formal care provision

What we have been discussing thus far is labeled *informal care*; that is, tasks that are done by family members or friends to assist the person who can't carry out all the activities of daily living. Informal care can be as simple as mowing a parent's lawn and paying his bills, or as complex as bathing, grooming, and toileting a bedridden elder living at home. But what happens when the needs of the older adult exceed the abilities of the unpaid caregiver? To keep care receivers in their own homes, some services are available, such as home-delivered meals, housekeeper services, home health care, and adult day centers. These programs, as well as assisted living and nursing facilities, make up the range of formal (paid), long-term care services, and are discussed in detail near the end of this chapter. The various ways to pay for such services are complex and depend on the older adult's financial resources, family financial resources, or medical needs of the elder. For persons with dementia who live until the disease has reached severe disablement, nursing home placement may be inevitable. Persons with dementia are far more likely than those without dementia to be placed in nursing homes or to receive home health care (Alzheimer's Association, 2012). Although formal care is increasingly used, there are many families who provide all care on their own (P. Jones, Zhang, Jaceldo-Siegl, and Meleis, 2002).

Care for persons with dementia

A report on dementia caregivers offers more insight into caregiver characteristics and intensity of care provision when a loved one has dementia. For example, among dementia caregivers, most are age 55 and over, half live with the person with dementia, and almost half of them are employed in the paid labor force. However, between 1.4 and 2.3 million caregivers live at a distance of at least two hours' drive from the person with dementia. Providing care at a distance is quite challenging (Alzheimer's Association, 2012).

Moreover, dementia care intensity varies by race and ethnicity. Hispanic and African American dementia caregivers spend an average of 30 hours a week assisting persons with dementia, compared with 20 hours per week for Caucasian caregivers. Hispanic and African American caregivers also report more feelings of burden from caregiving than do their Caucasian and Asian American counterparts (Alzheimer's Association, 2012). Additionally, dementia caregivers provide help for longer durations than caregivers who help those elders without cognitive or memory impairment.

For some caregivers, providing assistance is done happily, with a sense of purpose and reward. For other caregivers, the role is an obligation, with few rewards. Many caregivers describe a combination of rewards and hassles. These caregivers often describe their help as reciprocity for the care they were given as spouses or children (Piercy, 1998). Other benefits of caregiving include assuming a meaningful role, feeling a sense of accomplishment, and enhancing relationship quality with the care recipient (Carbonneau, Caron, and Desrosiers, 2010). Caregivers whose personalities are high in agreeableness and extroversion, and who experience high levels of spouse/partner support, are most likely to report benefits or gains from care provision (Koerner, Kenyon, and Shirai, 2009).

Whatever the trajectory of illness(es) for an older adult, who cares for them and how that care is provided can best be understood by the following perspectives: familism, intergenerational solidarity and ambivalence, and family systems and ecological systems.

Familism

Familism, or strong identification with and attachment to one's family, both nuclear and extended, is a cultural value that may influence or shape behavior in family crises. For example, high levels of belief in familism may prompt a family to rely on its own resources, rather than turn to professional help, in a crisis. In the United States, it is believed that members of racial and ethnic minority families are higher in familism, on average, than Caucasian families. However, there is variability within racial groups, as Rozario and DeRienzis (2008) found in their study of over 500 African American women who were caregivers to elderly family members.

For family caregivers, having high levels of familism, or traditional beliefs about family care to older adults, has potential positive and negative outcomes. Studies of African American and Spanish caregivers found that caregivers who endorsed higher levels of familism perceived higher levels of family support for their care activities (Losada et al., 2010). However, these caregivers were more likely to be depressed than caregivers who endorsed lower levels of familism (Losada *et al.,* 2010; Rozario and DeRienzis, 2008). Losada and associates established a link between familism and dysfunctional thoughts (irrational thoughts; e.g., "I should be with my spouse 24/7"; "a break isn't necessary"), and in turn, between dysfunctional thinking and high levels of depressive symptoms. Thus, some expressions of familism may come at a cost to caregiver well-being when those beliefs are practiced to an extreme.

Intergenerational solidarity and ambivalence in families

Bengtson and Roberts (1991) developed a theory of how family members interact with one another that they called *intergenerational solidarity*. It has six component parts, defined as associational (frequency and patterns of interaction); affectional (positive feelings); functional (exchange of assistance between generations); normative (degree of agreement with notion of familial obligations; similar to the idea of familism); consensual (degree of agreement on values and beliefs); and structural (proximity and availability of family members to one another) solidarity. Taken as a whole, to the degree a family exhibits these types of solidarity, they are more likely to have positive relationships and to care for one another as needs arise.

Other scholars felt that the notion of solidarity presented a somewhat rosy picture of family relationships, and proposed that ambivalence might better characterize relationships between generations in families (Connidis and McMullin, 2002; Luescher and Pillemer, 1998). Both sets of scholars have found support for their theories, but until recently, no one had conducted a test of the competing theories in a longitudinal study with a national population sample. Hogerbrugge and Komter (2012) examined five of the six dimensions of intergenerational solidarity, using a sample of Dutch adults diverse in age. The participants rated the relationship between them and one of their parents. They found fairly high levels of solidarity and low levels of ambivalence. In addition, the researchers found that having more solidarity to begin with *increased* solidarity later. As expected, the proximity of parent and child to each other influenced their levels of association.

These theoretical ideas – familism, and intergenerational solidarity and ambivalence – have shaped thinking about how people get into a caregiver role, as well as how committed they become to that role. These notions are also used to make sense of

caregiving decisions; for example, why one family teams up to provide help to an elderly parent in an effort to keep him at home, while faced with similar circumstances, another family decides to put their relative into a nursing home.

Families as dynamic systems

Feelings of obligation or desire to care for an older family member cannot explain every care decision that is made or how caring is carried out. Understanding the mutually dependent interactions of family members, along with how larger environments like workplaces and policies shape care decisions, is important to assisting a given elder and family with care challenges.

A family systems perspective is a useful way to understand caregiving issues in families. Although only one or two family members (in the case of dependent parents, or a child with disabilities and an aging parent) may need assistance at a given time, all members of the immediate and/or extended family are affected by their needs for help. To think of families as systems, one accepts the notions that all parts of a system are interconnected, understanding a situation is possible only by viewing the whole system, and a system's behavior affects its environment, just as the larger environment affects the family system. It is important to recognize that viewing a family as a dynamic system is a way of *thinking about* families; family systems are not concrete objects (White and Klein, 2008).

Some important concepts in viewing families as systems include *boundaries, variety, and subsystems*. A system's *boundaries* represent the borders between a given family system and its environment. System *boundaries* affect the flow of information in and out of a system, and are more or less permeable by others (White and Klein, 2008). With respect to family care, for example, an Asian American immigrant family may decide to provide all assistance to a respected elder within the family, never contacting professional (formal) care providers regardless of how intense the elder's care needs become. This family's boundaries would be labeled as closed or non-permeable. Another family, Caucasian and well-off financially, may enlist the support of around-the-clock hired help to provide personal care and housekeeping services to the elderly family member while family members preserve their current lifestyles. Several family members may supervise the formal care providers and make decisions about care. These choices indicate an extended family system with permeable boundaries.

When a family system possesses the resources, whether financial, emotional, or task-oriented, to adapt to changes, it possesses *variety* (White and Klein, 2008). Family rules may enhance or inhibit its ability to adapt to changes. For example, an aging couple with a grown child who has Down's syndrome faces a series of decisions regarding the care of that child as they become less able to look after the child themselves. If the couple has always cared for the child at home, and rejected all state or private services to assist the adult child with developing independence, the family lacks the *variety* it needs to adjust to changing circumstances. This family may experience a crisis when one or both members of the older couple cannot care for the child with Down's syndrome and future plans are not in place.

A *subsystem* is a part of a larger system. All family systems are composed of two or more subsystems, such as parent–child, marital, and sibling subsystems (White and Klein, 2008). Sometimes subsystems may vie for control of the family system, especially as the oldest generation ages and becomes more reliant on the children or grandchildren in the family. When a sibling subsystem is presented with the challenge of caring for a widowed parent with dementia, decisions often are made based on sibling cohesion and flexibility. Siblings may work collaboratively to see that their parent receives good care, or some siblings may collaborate, while the other siblings stay out of care provision (Matthews and Rosner, 1988). How the sibling subsystem handles such a transition in their family may affect their relationships with each other for the duration of caregiving, or for the rest of their lives.

Ecological systems

Families are assisted or constrained in how they can be helped by the resources available to them (Piercy and Dunkley, 2004). An ecological systems perspective developed by Bronfenbrenner (1979) described families as microsystems that interact with multiple layers of larger systems to determine developmental outcomes for individuals within families. Other microsystems such as caregivers' employers may affect how much care can be provided, or whether caregivers keep their jobs. Likewise, local agencies may provide programs that can supplement a family caregiver's labor, such as home health care or a senior companion. These agencies make up part of the exosystem. Finally, the macrosystem, which includes governmental family leave policies and financial support for paid care, may help or hinder a caregiver's ability to continue her own paid employment.

The next sections of this chapter address how families create systems of care. The degree of anxiety these issues provoke depend on the strengths and resources of individual family members, existing family relationships (degree of solidarity and ambivalence), family communication patterns, health and social welfare system resources available to the family, and the ability of family caregivers to find meaning in the tasks they perform for dependent relatives.

How do Families Decide on who Provides Elder Care?

All eldercare research shows that women predominate as caregivers, whether they are wives, daughters, daughters-in-law, or granddaughters. As previously noted, a combination of cultural values, socialization patterns and societal expectations encourages women

---

Case Example: Family 1

Ellen is 72, African American, divorced, and living alone. She forgets people's names, and recently drove herself to the store, only to forget the way home. Her daughter Millie went looking for her after she failed to show for their weekly dinner date. After assessing Ellen, her family doctor suggests that Ellen has dementia, most likely of the Alzheimer's type. She is in good health otherwise, so she wants to remain at home as long as possible. Millie is one of three children; she has two brothers, but only one of them lives in town and is married.

Case Example: Family 2

Masao is 78, widowed, and an Asian immigrant. He lives alone, but has three sons nearby. He recently suffered a stroke and is in a rehabilitation facility to regain his speech and mobility. He will be discharged in two weeks. His apartment has two floors, with the only bathroom upstairs. His sons don't think he should return to his apartment, but they cannot agree on who should take him into their home. Masao and his eldest son Hideki are estranged since Hideki's marriage to an American woman, Tracy. The other sons are single and work full-time.

to fulfill caregiver roles repeatedly throughout their lives. Generally, in most families, if a husband or wife is available, he or she becomes the primary caregiver to the spouse. An exception to this norm occurs in traditional Asian families. Asian cultural norms dictate that a son, usually the eldest, and his wife look after his aging parents. Even with acculturation, many Asian American-born daughters and daughters-in-law take on the caregiver role (P. Jones *et al.*, 2002).

In other families, many elderly men and women provide extensive help to their spouses, often without much assistance from either family or paid providers. But exceptions to this pattern of spousal care occur when the second spouse is also dependent on others for assistance. In other families, spouses with minimal health problems of their own may provide hands-on care, while one or more children (or grandchildren) perform other tasks, such as home and lawn maintenance, bill-paying, grocery shopping, and transportation to doctor visits (Piercy, 1998).

When no spouse is available, one or more adult children are called on to provide assistance, with daughters heavily relied upon. Sarah Matthews and her colleagues have examined family caregiving patterns among families with multiple siblings of both sexes, siblings with sons and a lone daughter, and sibling groups composed of sons only (Matthews, 1995; Matthews and Heidorn, 1998; Matthews and Rosner, 1988). These studies determined that family structure,

family history, and extra-familial ties affect the style of care that siblings provide to their parents. When there is one or more brothers, but only one sister in families, sisters usually provide parent care (Matthews, 1995). When there are only sons, parents are treated as independent, and assistance is usually limited to typically male tasks, such as home and lawn maintenance, financial management, and checking up on parents (Matthews and Heidorn, 1998). When there are multiple sons and daughters, adult children within families adopt one of five styles, called routine, backup, circumscribed, sporadic, and dissociation. Routine providers incorporate regular help into their ongoing activities and often become primary caregivers to their parent(s). Adult children with backup, circumscribed, and sporadic caregiving styles offer varying but limited amounts of help to aging parents. A dissociated sibling could not be depended on to provide any assistance (Matthews and Rosner, 1988). Taken together, these studies provide powerful evidence of the gendered nature of care provided by adult children.

Examining multiple generations of families involved in elder care, Piercy (1998) found that often several members of intergenerational family systems mobilized to provide assistance to an elderly member, including daughters and sons-in-law, grandchildren, and close friends who were considered to be "one of the family" or fictive kin. Family history, values, and the modeling of elder care behaviors by family members or friends were influential in who took on responsibility for care, and how many others assisted in that endeavor. In some, but not all families, male adult grandchildren were exempted from hands-on care activities, having either no role or a supervisory (care management) role.

There are, however, families in which there is only one child, and elderly parents who outlive or are estranged from their children. Only-children carry alone the responsibility for hands-on care, making care decisions, and responding to parent health crises. Help from a spouse or others may or may not be available. Very old adults often outlive one or more of their children, so they may rely on nieces, nephews, grandchildren, or paid help to assist them. Some of today's elders never married, and may have more limited family networks to access when help is needed. For them, extended family, paid help, or a multigenerational friendship network cultivated during their lifetimes, may be crucial to getting the help they need (Wenger, 2009).

Family Dynamics that Impact Elder Care Provision

Despite the fact that many older adults with difficulties living independently have a family member to assist them, family interaction patterns may lead to conflict in decisions about care provision. Connidis and Kemp's (2008) study of three-generation families showed that many families do not discuss care needs and preferences in advance of care provision, and when they do discuss this issue, family members do not necessarily agree on who should provide assistance or how much assistance should be given. Likewise, among families currently providing care to an elderly parent, care arrangements may change over time as the circumstances of adult children's lives change. Deciding who should take over primary care when a sibling can no longer serve in that role can create additional conflict in families.

Family conflict has negative effects on caregivers, regardless of gender, race, or ethnicity. Observed conflict in family discussions was associated with caregiver distress and was an important influence on the relationship between a caregiver's objective level of burden and her felt stress (Mitrani *et al.*, 2006). Likewise, perceived family conflict was also a strong influence on the relationship between older adult impairment and caregiver stress, with family conflict playing a stronger role in stress felt by caregiving sons than daughters (Kwak, Ingersoll-Dayton, and Kim, 2012). These studies demonstrate that family conflict over how to provide elder care affects not only families, but the well-being of the primary caregiver. However, when families exhibit adaptability, caregivers reported lower levels of depressive symptoms, suggesting a focal area for interventions with families who struggle to make good care decisions.

Assessment and application

It would appear that the African American family may have an easier time than the Japanese American family when deciding on how to care for Ellen. There is reasonably close mother-daughter solidarity, so Millie is likely to assume initial care responsibilities for her mother. If her in-town brother is married, then her sister-in-law might be willing to pick up a few responsibilities that Millie cannot handle because of her part-time job. Millie's brother may be involved as a backup or circumscribed caregiver (Matthews and Rosner, 1988).

By contrast, the Japanese American family has been thrown into crisis by Masao's stroke. The family has a strong sense of filial responsibility, but Masao's estrangement from his eldest son Hideki (who culturally is most likely to assume a caregiver role) means that Masao and Hideki must deal with their ambivalence towards each other, or one of the two single sons will be forced to assume the role of caregiver. The desire to hire help for Masao may be tempered by cultural norms of familism and filial piety that push the sons to find ways to provide help themselves.

Stress, Coping, Burden, and Burnout among Family Caregivers

Despite the varied care configurations discussed in earlier sections, many spouses, children, or children-in-law find that the primary responsibility for care provision falls mostly to them alone. When the adult receiving care has dementia, the care becomes more intense, leading to significant stress and burden for many caregivers. No matter how committed they are, and how much they enjoy care provision, all caregivers experience stress. These concepts and their effects on caregivers are addressed next.

Providing care to dependent adults often is stressful. As they age and develop impairments that threaten their independence, many adults are uncomfortable with relying on others for aid and many Western cultures have promoted values of personal autonomy and independence as hallmarks of full adulthood. Thus, those who need help may resist it, a process that creates stress for both them and their family members. Frustrated elders may be feeling useless and trapped in a cycle of dependence, but are unable to articulate those feelings to caregivers. Instead, they resist changes or lash out at other things, like the daughter-in-law's cooking.

Case Example: Family 1

Millie has been looking after her mother for two years. Though Ellen has stayed in her own apartment, it is clear to Millie that Ellen can no longer live alone. She moves her mother in with her and asks a neighbor to take Ellen to the senior center while Millie works part-time. She has reduced her work hours to be with her mother four days a week. One day, about two months after Ellen's arrival, Millie gets home from work 30 minutes late to find her apartment torn up, Ellen packed, and a pot burned on her stove. Ellen says she's moving home and was boiling water for tea. Millie feels a migraine headache beginning to form.

Case Example: Family 2

Hideki and Masao reconciled so that Masao could move to Hideki and Tracy's home while recovering from his stroke. Masao is recovering physically, but with a considerable loss of strength. He walks unsteadily with a cane. He berates Tracy's cooking because it is not familiar to him. He does not clean up after himself. Hideki comes home from work and Tracy calls a family conference. She is fed up, and wants Masao out of the house in two weeks.

Likewise, getting a parent to stop driving or a spouse or parent to make a living will, appoint a health care power of attorney, or make funeral plans can be very difficult tasks. Studies show that the majority of older adults do not have advanced directives in place to guide family and health care providers in respecting their end of life preferences (Wilkinson, Wenger, and Shugarman, 2007).

Although any kind of care provision can be stressful, in general, caring for someone with dementia is more intensive in terms of hours and stress than caring for someone with only physical impairments (Ory, Hoffman, Yee, Tennstedt, and Schulz, 1999). Persons with dementia may exhibit behaviors such as wandering, emotional outbursts, and inappropriate behavior that present challenges to caregivers. Communication with persons with dementia becomes more difficult as the disease progresses. Research has established that giving assistance to persons with dementia can have negative physical and psychological effects (Sörensen and Conwell, 2011), and of these two types of effects, understanding the psychological effects of depression is more studied. Researchers and clinicians alike have examined dementia caregiver stress, coping strategies, and levels of burden, burnout, depression, and anxiety to better understand the dementia caregiver experience and to design caregiver interventions.

Keep in mind, though, that not all caregivers experience burden, burnout, anxiety, and depression, including dementia caregivers who provide daily care (Piercy et al., 2012). Some caregivers view their efforts as an opportunity to reciprocate for a spouse's or parent's care in earlier times, and others see themselves as fulfilling cultural expectations of respect for parents (called filial piety in Asian cultures; P. Jones et al., 2002). Still other caregivers find existential or spiritual meaning in the care experience, which enables them to persevere in providing care under challenging circumstances (Farran, Kean-Hagerty, Salloway, Kupferer, and Wilken, 1991; McLennon, Habermann, and Rice, 2011). When compared with Caucasian dementia caregivers, African American dementia caregivers report more positive aspects of care, with the latter group's higher levels of religiosity influencing their positive perceptions of care (Roff et al., 2004).

Caregiver Coping Strategies and their Relationship to Depression and Anxiety

The stress process model is the framework most often used to understand how caregiver stress leads to outcomes such as depression (Pearlin et al., 1990). This model incorporates caregiver characteristics, primary and secondary stressors, and mediating factors (such as coping and social support) as contributors to individual caregiver outcomes like depression or physical health. In this type of research, important aspects of care provision, such as the degree of family conflict, are viewed as one component that contributes directly or indirectly to caregiver well-being, with the focus on individual caregivers rather than outcomes for the whole family. Thus we know relatively little about *family outcomes* as a result of care provision to an older family member. We next discuss caregiver coping and its outcomes in the context of providing care.

In their transactional model of stress, Lazarus and Folkman (1984) conceptualized stress as a transaction between a person and his or her environment. Building on the transactional model, Pearlin and associates (1990) defined coping as the *personal management of a stressful situation that changes the meaning and reduces threat*. Lazarus and Folkman (1984) characterized coping strategies or behaviors as problem-focused or emotion-focused. A problem-focused coping strategy includes behaviors such as making a plan to resolve a problem, or seeking the support of others to face problems. An emotion-focused coping strategy might be to avoid or deny the problem, or to blame oneself or others for the problem. In general, among dementia caregivers, when caregivers use more problem-focused strategies they experience fewer depressive symptoms and when they use certain emotion-focused strategies, they report more depressive symptoms (Li, Cooper, Bradley, Shulman, and Livingston, 2012; Piercy *et al.*, 2012). Because coping strategies can be modified, some interventions with caregivers attempt to change their ways of appraising stressors and coping with challenges.

Caregiver Burden and Influences on Burden

Application

Caregiver burden is defined as "a multidimensional response to the negative appraisal and perceived stress resulting from taking care of an ill individual. Burden threatens the physical, psychological, emotional and functional health of caregivers" (Kim, Chang, Rose, and Kim, 2011, p. 846). Women, spouses, and caregivers

---

Case Example: Family 1

Millie is experiencing more burden as her mother's dementia progresses. The incident that precipitated the headache occurred as Millie realized that the care arrangements she has made for Ellen will not be enough as Ellen's dementia progresses. She is at a crossroads in her decision-making. Because her family has good solidarity, she is able to call a meeting with her brothers and sister-in-law to discuss what to do next.

Case Example: Family 2

Hideki has done what his cultural values suggest he should do, but his wife Tracy is bearing the responsibility for daily care with a father-in-law who does not respect her. Tracy would like to see her brothers-in-law take more responsibility for their father, even if it means paying a care provider to take Masao out of the house or coming up with money for adult day services. Tracy wonders why she must carry the responsibility for a man who does not seemingly appreciate her or her husband.

---

with fewer socio-economic resources are more vulnerable to burden and its negative outcomes of depression or anxiety (Sörensen and Conwell, 2011). Women in racial and ethnic minority groups are often at increased risk of financial or emotional burden and hardship because of caregiving responsibilities (Feinberg *et al.*, 2012), lending validity to the notion of *intersectionality*. Intersectionality is "the active interaction of the various relations of inequality such as race, class, sexuality, gender and age within and across all of the institutions of society" (Ferree, 2010, p. 425). Thus, female gender interacts with minority group and low-income statuses to put women minority caregivers at greater risk than their Caucasian counterparts of financial difficulties, or stress and poor mental health.

Fewer financial resources on the part of elders and/or their caregivers often means less access to long-term care services, which, in turn, may force the caregiver to reduce her work hours or forgo paid employment altogether to provide help herself. When they change their work conditions, caregivers may lose health benefits or be unable to access affordable health care, thus putting themselves at increased risk of untreated health-related difficulties.

However, some factors may lessen or increase the impact of stress on a caregiver's felt burden. Cultural background matters: in general, ethnic minority caregivers report a lower socioeconomic status than Caucasian caregivers; they are younger, less likely to be a spouse, and more likely than their Caucasian counterparts to receive informal (non-paid) support (Pinquart and Sörensen, 2005). African American and Hispanic caregivers are more likely than Caucasian caregivers to report more personal benefits of care provision (Pinquart and Sörensen, 2005). In general, ethnic minority caregivers report fewer burdens, but more physical health problems than their Caucasian counterparts. However, Hispanic and Asian American caregivers are more depressed than their Caucasian peers (Pinquart and Sörensen, 2005). Findings regarding depression and poorer physical health could be explained by less minority group access to culturally appropriate services for care recipients, which would mean fewer breaks from care provision for these caregivers. Lifetime health disparities (discussed in Chapter 5 of this volume) may also leave caregivers from ethnic or racial minority groups with poorer health at the onset of caregiving, thereby leading to increased health problems during the care process.

Caregiver gender also matters: Women caregivers tend to report more depression than their male counterparts (Sörensen and Conwell, 2011), although when resources and stressors are similar, gender differences are small (Pinquart and Sörensen, 2006). The reasons for this finding could be several: women tend to provide more hands-on care in similar care situations than men, while men are more likely to enlist other family members or paid providers to assist with care; some women caregivers report that caregiving strains their household finances (Feinberg et al., 2012); and women are more likely than men to make workplace accommodations, especially as

caregiving demands intensify beyond 20 hours per week (NAC and AARP, 2009). Caregivers can protect themselves from excessive burden and depression by utilizing their social networks, and enlisting members of their social networks to assist with care provision (Sörensen and Conwell, 2011). Caregiver isolation is a strong contributing factor to burden and depression, and a "go it alone" mentality, especially in circumstances where long-term care is needed, can be a prescription for caregiver burden and eventual burn out.

The Consequences of Caregiver Burnout

Burnout is a concept that was developed in the context of research on work and employment, but has been applied to caregivers. Burnout is characterized by feelings of being emotionally overextended and exhausted by care provision, and may result in an "unfeeling and impersonal response" to the care recipient (Maslach, Jackson, Leiter, Schaufeli, and Schwab, 2012). Caregiver burnout may lead to a change in family caregiver, institutionalization (Gaugler et al., 2011) or neglect of the care recipient. A recent Canadian study showed that dementia family caregivers who could not obtain home care or respite services were likely to place their relatives in an institution because they felt overwhelmed with care responsibilities and were unable to preserve their own emotional health (Lilly, Robinson, Holtzman, and Bottorff, 2012).

Help for Caregivers: Supportive Services

For family caregivers who need assistance in their care provision, several options are available. Some caregivers prefer using volunteer resources to help them, such as neighbors, friends, or church members. They may be reluctant to allow unknown persons, even professionals, into their homes. There are also national organizations, such as Interfaith Caregivers, who with a volunteer network provide transportation, telephone reassurance, and other supportive services through

Case Example: Family 1

Millie has met with her brothers. They have decided to keep Ellen in Millie's home, but to use supportive services to the maximum extent possible. Millie contacts the local area agency on aging, whose caseworker assesses their situation. She gets Ellen a "scholarship" to attend an adult day center three days a week, and puts her on a waitlist for a "senior companion," who will take Ellen to appointments and spend some time with her in Millie's home. After a three months wait, Ellen is assigned a companion, Merle, a 60-year-old African American woman who gets along well with everyone.

Case Example: Family 2

Masao still lives with Hideki and Tracy, but his condition is worsening. The three sons have pooled their money and hired a middle-aged Japanese American woman, Nori, to be Masao's companion during daytime hours. Tracy happily returned to work. Nori cooks some of Masao's favorite meals and takes him to the Japanese Senior Center in town each week.

local affiliate chapters located around the United States. There are also national organizations such as the Alzheimer's Association that offer caregiver support groups and other services through their local chapters.

But for most dependent elders and their caregivers, supportive services come from local, state, or federal programs. For example, the Older Americans Act established the nutrition programs for older adults known as congregate dining in local senior centers and home-delivered meals for homebound persons. The National Family Caregiver Support Program of 2000 (Administration on Aging, 2012) established a funding mechanism for programs that assist families in providing long-term care at home. Programs provide information to caregivers about locally available services and offer help in accessing these services, offer counseling and training services for caregivers, and respite care. These programs are available to elder caregivers, grandparents caring for grandchildren, and relatives caring for adults aged 18–59 with disabilities.

For those giving long-term care in a home setting, there are several types of services that can be beneficial for at least some of the time of need. Each major type of service, along with who is most likely to be eligible for the service, is described next. For people who have no idea of where to begin a search for services, the local Area Agency on Aging is a good start. The staff is familiar with all services provided to elders in their jurisdiction. All counties in the United States have such an agency, although the agency might be located in an adjacent county. Another good resource is the Eldercare Locator service, reachable by phone in the US at 1-800-677-1116 or online at http://www.eldercare.gov/Eldercare.NET/Public/Index.aspx.

Home care services

Home care refers to a variety of services performed by both professional and paraprofessional providers, including nurses, occupational and physical therapists, social workers, and certified nursing assistants. Those persons with acute illnesses recently discharged from hospitals, or with long-term health conditions, permanent disability, or terminal illnesses may benefit from home care. The Medicare home health benefit provides skilled nursing care, personal care, physical and occupational therapy, and social work services for up to 60 days per episode. This service must be authorized by a doctor. For persons with long-term health conditions or permanent disability, state, private pay, or Medicaid waiver programs may provide personal care and housekeeping or chore services. For persons able to live at home with terminal illnesses, hospice care, usually paid for by Medicare, can provide palliative care services, such as nursing care and spiritual services, as well as family counseling during bereavement. These services are among the most popular for older adults and their caregivers.

When of good quality, home care offers specific benefits to older adults and their family caregivers. Older adults often form friendship or family-like relationships with their home care aides, thereby decreasing their social isolation (Piercy, 2000). Family caregivers benefit from good-quality home care in two ways: they feel that their relatives receive enhanced quality of life, and the paid care providers help caregivers to improve their own competence by teaching them important skills and giving them opportunities for brief respite from caregiving duties (Piercy and Dunkley, 2004). Other research has shown that use of home care services such as medical and personal care is associated with lower levels of caregiver depression (Bass, Noelker, and Rechlin, 1996).

Adult day centers

Adult day centers provide part- or full-time care to older adults who are too impaired physically or cognitively to be left alone by their caregivers. They can be used one or more days per week by working caregivers or those who would like cognitive stimulation for their relatives or respite from care for themselves. Nearly all centers offer social activities, transportation to and from the center, nutritious meals and snacks, personal care (help with activities of daily living), and therapeutic activities, including exercise and cognitively stimulating interactions (National Adult Day Services Association, 2009). On average in the United States, adult day centers cost $67 per day (Metropolitan Life, Inc., 2009), and may be paid by Medicaid (if eligible), long-term care insurance, scholarship, or a sliding-scale fee, based on a client's means.

When home-based care is no longer feasible, assisted living facilities and nursing homes are available. There is also hospice care for persons nearing the end of their lives.

Assisted Living Facilities (ALF)

These are group residential long-term care facilities that help an older or disabled adult maintain as much independence as possible while receiving needed assistance. The philosophy of assisted living facilities is to deliver services that maximize individual choice, dignity, autonomy, independence, and quality of life.

However, most ALF do not offer skilled nursing care to frail persons. A resident's needs are assessed upon admission, and a care plan is written into the resident's contract, which can be modified with changing needs. By law, all ALF must offer the following services: 24-hour-awake staff to provide oversight and meet needs, scheduled or unscheduled, provision and oversight of personal care and supportive services, health-related services, such as medication management; meals, laundry, and housekeeping; recreational activities, transportation and social services. Services are not necessarily limited to those listed here (Mollica, Sims-Kastelein, and O'Keeffe, 2007). These facilities are increasingly popular, but are rarely funded by government programs. Thus, most residents in ALF are relatively affluent or have bought long-term care insurance that funds assisted living.

Nursing home care

The decision to place a loved one in a nursing home is among the most difficult care decisions families make. Most elders do not want to go there, and family conflicts about it often occur. Cultural prohibitions may discourage some families from considering nursing home placement, even when it is warranted, and African Americans and Hispanic caregivers are less likely to institutionalize their relatives than Caucasians (Gaugler, Kane, Kane, Clay, and Newcomer, 2003).

Case Example: Family 1

Millie has cared for Ellen in her home for six years. Ellen can no longer feed herself, and she cannot get from bed to toilet without help. More often than not, Ellen no longer recognizes Millie, who has hung on to her part-time job, but is often exhausted. Millie prays about her next decision, talks to her siblings, and reluctantly agrees with her home health nurse that a nursing home is the best option for all concerned. There are no funds beyond Ellen's meager social security check, so Ellen will go in as a Medicaid patient.

However, balancing the care needs of a frail or demented elderly relative with a caregiver's needs and/or that of the caregiver's immediate family is a crucial task that may be made more difficult to achieve when the care recipient's requests for continuing home care become unrealistic. Nursing homes are designed to meet the needs of persons whose cognitive and/or functional limitations require that they receive medical care and supervision 24 hours per day, seven days a week.

Families should visit several nursing homes before deciding on which one to use. Many facilities have waiting lists. Most homes are operated for profit (A. Jones, Dwyer, Bercovitz, and Strahan, 2009), and a majority of the staff in nursing homes consist of nursing assistants. Turnover of staff is problematic for many nursing facilities.

Placing a relative in a nursing home begins a transition period in which family members may experience stress, guilt, and anger. Over time, families develop different roles with nursing home residents and staff. Caron (1997) characterized those relationships as disengaged (rare visits), consultants (attend care conferences but don't maintain a relationship with their resident), competitive (try to gain control over staff in how care is delivered), and collaborating (support the staff and act as partners in care). These roles and behaviors have tradeoffs. Those who have disengaged and consultant roles minimize boundary ambiguity by eliminating the older adult from the family system (Caron, 1997). However, their relatives may not receive optimal care. By establishing respectful relationships with key staff members from the outset of care, and by visiting frequently to observe care provision, family caregivers promote the best possible care for their relative by engaging with both the elderly relative and the nursing home staff (Julie Seefeldt, personal communication, November 15, 2009).

Hospice care

Hospice care is available to persons with terminal illnesses and their families, and offers pain management, medical, emotional and spiritual care provided by an interdisciplinary team of medical professionals, social workers, clergy, and volunteers (National Hospice and Palliative Care Organization, 2009). As part of the

Case Example: Family 2

Masao has suffered a massive stroke that has left him paralyzed on one side. He can no longer leave his home to attend senior center activities, and he cannot communicate verbally with Hideki, Tracy, or Nori. Masao's doctor says he has less than two months to live, and suggests hospice care. This choice is more palatable to Hideki and his brothers than nursing home placement. They engage hospice services and keep Masao in Hideki's home. The social worker helps this family deal with their feelings about Masao's impending death, and a volunteer stays at Masao's side part of every work day.

Medicare benefits package, hospice care must be ordered by a physician.

Although Caucasian families are more likely to use hospice care than members of minority groups, hospice care is growing in popularity. It has benefits for both patients and families who use it. Patients receive intense medical services, with closely monitored pain management strategies. Home care aides perform personal care tasks that are difficult for caregivers to undertake. Hospice volunteers are trained to provide compassionate care, and their willingness to sit with the dying person offers the caregiver an opportunity to attend to other matters. Volunteers may also reduce the isolation that comes with being homebound, whether a patient or caregiver. Clergy provide the spiritual nurturing so important to many dying persons and their families. Finally, hospice services include bereavement counseling for family members that extend well beyond the patient's death.

Looking Ahead: The Costs and Needs of Current Caregiver Policies

World-wide, families are expected to provide help to their aged or disabled members. Few services are structured to exempt family caregivers from responsibilities; even residential facilities expect end-of-life and emergency medical decisions to be made with family member input. As a result, providing care is often lengthy and taxing to those who undertake it. Families, especially women in families, are under unyielding pressure to assume caregiving duties, given that governments' presumption that paid care should supplement and not substitute for family care, that recent policies have shifted to increased self-reliance and privatization, and because of beliefs in many cultures that women are "natural" caregivers (Hooyman and Gonyea, 1999). But in societies like the United States, the idea that women can just quit or scale back their jobs and offer care to aged relatives is outdated, given that women are now sole or primary breadwinners in 40% of all American families with children (Pew Research Center, 2013). On the basis of the material reviewed here, I make the following observations regarding US policy.

Elder care services are expensive, and only those covered by Medicare are available to anyone who needs them. Medicaid offers home care and nursing home care, but only to very poor persons. When states offer their own home care programs, they usually cover only those who just make above the Medicaid eligibility criteria. Whether state- or Medicaid-funded, there are long waiting lists; thus, these vital services are chronically underfunded. This state of affairs is tragic, because those caregivers who cannot provide care without them usually place their relatives in nursing homes, which cost governments (and therefore taxpayers) more money than home care, and fail to honor family preferences for home care.

At the other end of the financial spectrum, wealthy and upper-middle-class families can purchase home care, adult day care, assisted living, or nursing home care, or insurance that covers these services, which gives them more resources for long-term care. For these families, such purchasing power may lead to less burden or burnout among family caregivers. Working

caregivers to affluent elders can usually continue paid employment with minimal disruption.

Persons in the middle class are least well served by the current American "system"; generally they must creatively construct elder care provision from whatever resources, financial or otherwise, they can muster. Thus, in America, only well-to-do elders and their families enter old age knowing that they can access whatever services they might need in late life; everyone else lives with some uncertainty about their future help options. With women's greater participation in the paid labor force and smaller family sizes among our current demographic trends (Kreider and Elliott, 2009), it is legitimate to ask who will be available to provide elder care to many older adults. While most families can and do look after their older members, many middle-aged and older family members pay a high price for caring labors in terms of reduced lifetime earnings, increased stress, and strained family relationships. Advocacy for a better-funded network of services to older adults and their caregivers is an urgent priority, one from which all citizens, old and young alike, may benefit.

Critical Thinking Questions

1. How can we encourage more men, especially sons, to take a larger role in providing care to aging relatives?
2. What are some ways to help families who struggle to communicate effectively with one another about care decisions for their elderly relatives?
3. What are some ways that ordinary citizens can advocate for changes in service availability with state and local policymakers?
4. How can we make eldercare services more culturally appropriate for elders in minority groups and their families so that they will feel more comfortable using them?

References

Administration on Aging. (2012). National family caregiver support program (OAA Title IIIE). Washington, DC: Department of Health and Human Services, Administration on Aging. Retrieved May 30, 2014 from http://www.aoa.gov/AoA_programs/HCLTC/Caregiver/index.aspx.

Alzheimer's Association. (2012). *2012 Alzheimer's disease facts and figures*. Chicago: Alzheimer's Association. Retrieved May 30, 2014 from http://www.alz.org/downloads/facts_figures_2012.pdf.

Bass, D. M., Noelker, L. S., and Rechlin, L. R. (1996). The moderating influence of service use on negative caregiving consequences. *Journals of Gerontology: Social Sciences, 51B*, S121–S131.

Bengtson,V.L.,and Roberts,R.E.L.(1991).Intergenerational solidarity in aging families: An example of formal theory construction. *Journal of Marriage and the Family, 53*, 856–870.

Blue, L. (2008).Why do women live longer than men? *Time*, August 6. Retrieved May 30, 2014 from http://www.time.com/time/printout/0,8816,1827162,00.html.

Bronfenbrenner, U. (1979). *The ecology of human development: Experiments by nature and design*. Cambridge, MA: Harvard University Press.

Carbonneau, H., Caron, C., and Desrosiers, J. (2010). Development of a conceptual framework of positive aspects of caregiving in dementia. *Dementia, 9*, 327–353.

Caron, W. A. (1997). Family systems and nursing home systems: An ecosystemic perspective for the systems practitioner. In T. D. Hargrave and S. M. Hanna (eds), *The aging family: New visions in theory, practice, and reality* (pp. 235–258). Philadelphia, PA: Brunner/Mazel.

Connidis, I. A., and Kemp, C. L. (2008). Negotiating actual and anticipated parental support: Multiple sibling voices in three-generation families. *Journal of Aging Studies, 22*, 229–238.

Connidis, I. A., and McMullin, J. A. (2002). Sociological ambivalence and family ties: A critical perspective. *Journal of Marriage and Family, 64*, 558–567.

Farran, C. J., Kean-Hagerty, E., Salloway, S., Kupferer, S., and Wilken, C. S. (1991). Finding meaning: An alternative paradigm for Alzheimer's disease family caregivers. *The Gerontologist, 31*, 483–489.

Federal Interagency Forum on Aging-Related Statistics (FIFARS). (July, 2010). *Older Americans 2010: Key indicators of well-being*. Washington, DC: US Government Printing Office.

Feinberg, L., Reinhard, S. C., Houser, A., and Choula, R. (2012). *Valuing the invaluable: 2011 update: The growing contributions and costs of family caregiving*. Washington, DC: AARP Public Policy Institute. Retrieved May 30, 2014 from http://assets.aarp.org/rgcenter/ppi/ltc/i51-caregiving.pdf.

Ferree, M. M. (2010). Filling the glass: Gender perspectives on families. *Journal of Marriage and Family, 72*, 420–439.

Gaugler, J. E., Kane, R. L., Kane, R. A., Clay, T., and Newcomer, R. (2003). Caregiving and institutionalization of cognitively impaired older people: Utilizing dynamic predictors of change. *The Gerontologist, 43*, 219–229.

Gaugler, J. E., Wall, M. M., Kane, R. L., Menk, J. S., Sarsour, K., Johnston, J. A., … and Newcomer, R. (2011). Does caregiver burden mediate the effects of behavioral disturbances on nursing home admission? *American Journal of Geriatric Psychiatry, 19*, 497–506.

Hogerbrugge, M. J. A., and Komter, A. E. (2012). Solidarity and ambivalence: Comparing two perspectives on intergenerational relations using longitudinal panel data. *Journals of Gerontology Series B: Social Sciences, 67B*, 372–383.

Hooyman, N. R., and Gonyea, J. G. (1999). A feminist model of family care: Practice and policy directions. *Journal of Women and Aging, 11*(2/3), 149–169.

Jones, A. L., Dwyer, L. L., Bercovitz, A. R., and Strahan, G. W. (2009). The National Nursing Home Survey: 2004 overview. *National Center for Health Statistics. Vital Health Statistics, 13*, 1–164.

Jones, P. S., Zhang, X. E., Jaceldo-Siegl, K., and Meleis, A. I. (2002). Caregiving between two cultures: An integrative experience. *Journal of Transcultural Nursing, 13*, 202–209.

Kim, H., Chang, M., Rose, K., and Kim, S. (2011). Predictors of caregiver burden in caregivers of individuals with dementia. *Journal of Advanced Nursing, 68*, 846–855. doi: 10.1111/j.1365-2648.2011.05787.x.

Koerner, S. S., Kenyon, D. B., and Shirai, Y. (2009). Caregiving for elder relatives: Which caregivers experience personal benefits/gains? *Archives of Gerontology and Geriatrics, 48*, 238–245.

Kreider, R. M., and Elliott, D. B. (2009). America's families and living arrangements: 2007. Current Population Reports, P20-561. Washington, DC: US Census Bureau.

Kwak, M., Ingersoll-Dayton, B., and Kim, J. (2012). Family conflict from the perspective of adult child caregivers: The influence of gender. *Journal of Social and Personal Relationships, 29*, 470–487. doi: 10.1177/0265407511431188.

Lazarus, R. S., and Folkman, S. (1984). *Stress, appraisal, and coping*. New York: Springer.

Li, R., Cooper, C., Bradley, J., Shulman, A., and Livingston, G. (2012). Coping strategies and psychological morbidity in family careers of people with dementia: A systematic review and meta-analysis. *Journal of Affective Disorders, 139*, 1–11. doi 10.1016/j.jad.2011.05.055.

Lilly, M. B., Robinson, C. A., Holtzman, S., and Bottorff, J. L. (2012). Can we move beyond burden and burnout to support the health and wellness of family caregivers to persons with dementia? Evidence from British Columbia, Canada. *Health and Social Care in the Community, 20*, 103–112.

Losada, A., Marquez-Gonzalez, M., Knight, B. G., Yanguas, J., Sayegh, P., and Romero-Moreno, R. (2010). Psychosocial factors and caregivers' distress: Effects of familism and dysfunctional thoughts. *Aging and Mental Health, 14,* 193–202.

Luescher, K., and Pillemer, K. (1998). Intergenerational ambivalence: A new approach to the study of parent–child relations in late life. *Journal of Marriage and the Family, 60,* 413–425.

Maslach, C., Jackson, S. E., Leiter, M. P., Schaufeli, W. B., and Schwab, R. L. (2012). *Maslach burnout inventory (MBI).* Retrieved May 30, 2014 from http://www.mindgarden.com/products/mbi.htm.

Matthews, S. H. (1995). Gender and the division of filial responsibility between lone sisters and their brothers. *Journals of Gerontology: Social Sciences, 50B,* S312–S320.

Matthews, S. H., and Heidorn, J. (1998). Meeting filial responsibilities in brothers-only sibling groups. *Journals of Gerontology: Social Sciences, 53B,* S278–S286.

Matthews, S. H., and Rosner, T. T. (1988). Shared filial responsibility: The family as the primary caregiver. *Journal of Marriage and the Family, 50,* 185–195.

McLennon, S. M., Habermann, B., and Rice, M. (2011). Finding meaning as a mediator of burden on the health of caregivers of spouses with dementia. *Aging and Mental Health, 15,* 522–530.

Metropolitan Life, Inc. (2009, October). *MetLife market survey of long-term care costs.* Retrieved May 30, 2014 from http://www.MatureMarketInstitute.com.

Mitrani, V. B., Lewis, J. E., Feaster, D. J., Czaja, S. J., Eisdorfer, C., Schulz, R., and Szapocznik, J. (2006). The role of family functioning in the stress process of dementia caregivers: a structural family framework. *The Gerontologist, 46,* 97–105.

Mollica, R., Sims-Kastelein, K., and O'Keeffe, J. (2007). *Residential care and assisted living compendium: 2007.* Washington, DC: US Department of Health and Human Services, Office of Disability, Aging, and Long-Term Care Policy.

National Adult Day Services Association. (2009). Adult day services: Overview and facts, November 29. Retrieved May 30, 2014 from http://www.nadsa.org/adsfacts/default.asp.

National Alliance for Caregiving and American Association of Retired Persons. (2009). *Caregiving in the U.S. 2009.* Retrieved May 30, 2014 from http://www.caregiving.org/data/Caregiving_in_the_US_2009_full_report.pdf.

National Hospice and Palliative Care Organization. (2009). *Facts and figures: Hospice care in America.* Alexandria, VA. Retrieved May 30, 2014 from http://www.nhpco.org.

Ory, M., Hoffman, R. R., Yee, J. L., Tennstedt, S., and Schulz, R. (1999). Prevalence and impact of caregiving: A detailed comparison between dementia and nondementia caregivers. *The Gerontologist, 39,* 177–185.

Pearlin, L. I., Mullan, J. T., Semple, S. J., and Skaff, M. M. (1990). Caregiving and the stress process: An overview of concepts and their measures. *The Gerontologist, 30,* 583–594.

Pew Research Center. (2013). Breadwinner moms. Washington, DC: Pew Research Center. Retrieved May 30, 2014 from http://www.pewsocialtrends.org/files/2013/05/Breadwinner_moms_final.pdf.

Piercy, K. W. (1998). Theorizing about family caregiving: The role of responsibility. *Journal of Marriage and the Family, 60,* 109–118.

Piercy, K. W. (2000). When it's more than a job: Relationships between home health workers and their older clients. *Journal of Aging and Health, 12,* 362–387.

Piercy, K. W., and Dunkley, G. J. (2004). What quality paid home care means to family caregivers. *Journal of Applied Gerontology, 23,* 175–192.

Piercy, K. W., Fauth, E. B., Norton, M. C., Pfister, R., Corcoran, C. D., Rabins, P. V., ... and Tschanz, J. T. (2012). Predictors of dementia caregiver depressive symptoms in a population: The Cache County dementia progression study. *Journals of Gerontology Series B: Psychological Sciences and Social Sciences.* doi: 10.1093/geronb/gbs116.

Pinquart, M., and Sörensen, S. (2005). Ethnic differences in stressors, resources, and psychological outcomes of family caregiving: A meta-analysis. *The Gerontologist, 45,* 90–106.

Pinquart, M., and Sörensen, S. (2006). Gender differences in caregiver stressors, social resources, and health: An undated meta-analysis. *Journals of Gerontology: Psychological Sciences, 61B,* P33–P45.

Roff, L. L., Burgio, L. D., Gitlin, L., Nichols, L., Chaplin, W., and Hardin, J. M. (2004). Positive aspects of Alzheimer's caregiving: The role of race. *Journals of Gerontology: Psychological Sciences, 59,* 185–190.

Rozario, P. A., and DeRienzis, D. (2008). Familism beliefs and psychological distress among African American women caregivers. *The Gerontologist, 48,* 772–780.

Sörensen, S., and Conwell, Y. (2011). Issues in dementia caregiving: Effects on mental and physical health, intervention strategies, and research needs. *American Journal of Geriatric Psychiatry, 19,* 491–496. doi: 10: 1097/JGP:0b013e31821c0e6e.

Wenger, G. C. (2009). Childlessness at the end of life: Evidence from rural Wales. *Ageing and Society, 29,* 1243–1259.

White, J. M., and Klein, D. M. (2008). *Family theories* (3rd edn). Thousand Oaks, CA: Sage Publications.

Wilkinson, A., Wenger, N., and Shugarman, L. R. (2007). Literature review on advance directives (contract #HHS-100-03-0023). Retrieved May 30, 2014 from http://aspe.hhs.gov/daltcp/reports/2007/advdirlr.htm.

11

Childhood Adultification and the Paradox of Parenting

Perspectives on African American Boys in Economically Disadvantaged Families

Linda M. Burton, Donna-Marie Winn, Howard Stevenson, and Marvin McKinney

Family contexts of economic disadvantage are often fertile ground for childhood adultification – a process by which children and adolescents in families are required to take on family responsibilities that are typically reserved for parents. In Chapter 11, Burton and colleagues draw attention to the all too common circumstances of African American boys in hard-pressed families. Adultification is a parenting "paradox" because it poses a developmental conflict between children's need for adult guidance and care, and the requirement that these needs be suppressed or ignored as boys do the "heavy lifting" for their parent(s) as family providers and caregivers. Despite the intense difficulties adultified children may face, we see evidence of resilience as African American boys enact family roles that involve a great deal of effort and maturity.

DeVaughn's life story (see p. 168) is one of many we followed for over a decade in a longitudinal ethnographic study of low-income families residing in a small city in central Pennsylvania. Ethnography is a well–established naturalistic method for gathering data about the thoughts, behaviors, and everyday life experiences of families and individuals in the contexts in which they develop and spend time (Abbott, 2004; Burton, Garrett-Peters, and Eaton, 2009; see also Box 11.1). In this ethnography as well as others we have conducted, we discerned that DeVaughn's situation was

not an uncommon one among low-income African American boys and teens. Throughout our careers as ethnographic and clinical researchers specializing in the study of African American families, we have become well acquainted with adultified boys like DeVaughn who take on various forms of adult roles (e.g., becoming the de-facto financial head-of-household) to meet the economic, social, and psychological needs of their families.

Adultification comprises contextual, social, and developmental processes in which youth are prematurely, and

Family Problems: Stress, Risk, and Resilience, First Edition. Edited by Joyce A. Arditti.
© 2015 John Wiley & Sons, Inc. Published 2015 by John Wiley & Sons, Inc.

Case Example: DeVaughn

Fifteen-year-old DeVaughn entered the room as his mostly absent father, Eli, laid a twenty-dollar bill on the kitchen table within reach of Vanessa, the woman Eli calls both his "occasional wife" and DeVaughn's "devoted mother." "What are you doing here?" DeVaughn yelled at his father. "You don't belong here, cuz I'm the man of this house! Get the hell outta here!" DeVaughn then reached deep into his right pants pocket and pulled out a wad of ones and tens, slamming them on the table atop his father's twenty. Eli reprised, "Boy, you think you a man, showing out, acting gangsta … I will knock the black off you talkin' to me that way! You respect me, you hear!" DeVaughn leaned back, ratcheting his arm and tightly balled fist to punch "the shit" out of Eli. Vanessa quickly jumped between the two "men," screaming at the top of her lungs, "Dee, don't hurt your daddy …

Eli just get out!" Eli retreated, bumping up against DeVaughn's shoulder as he stomped past him, slamming the door on his exit, and leaving in his wake a temporarily emotionally paralyzed wife and son. When the dust from the incident cleared, Vanessa asked DeVaughn to sit with her as she sheepishly wept about the family's financial woes and her lost youth as a result of loving, marrying, and bearing children with Eli. She never asked DeVaughn about how he was feeling, whether his shoulder was hurt, where he got the wad of money from, or where and who he had been with for the last 14 hours. DeVaughn listened quietly to his mother and eventually interjected his patented phrase: "Don't worry momma, I will take care of you and everybody [meaning his five brothers and sisters] like I always do. I got this. I'm the man of the house like you say."

Box 11.1　What is Ethnography?

As typically practiced, ethnography refers to some combination of participant observation and interviewing (structured or unstructured, formal or informal) as the primary modes of data collection. Participant observation, the close-up and intensive study of some social group or social world through human group activities, is the hallmark of ethnographic research. One of the primary aims of ethnographic researchers is to describe a particular social-cultural world in detail. This means to record and re-create, typically through written narrative, as accurate a picture as possible of the social setting(s) being studied and the cultural meanings, practices, and analytic categories humans employ there.

Ethnographic research is descriptive and analytical, aimed at re-creating a more or less comprehensive picture of some setting or behaviors of some group of social actors. One way in which ethnographers achieve description and analysis is by highlighting social processes, for example, focusing on what children, adolescents, and parents actually do with one another as they respond to situations and simultaneously adapt and develop as human beings in socially circumscribed worlds. Quality ethnographic description and analysis vividly recreate social and cultural worlds for readers and provide the opportunity to move readers to take the perspective of the actors in question, to see their social worlds, and to realize the attendant pressures, joys, and dangers that impinge on their actions (Burton et al., 2009).

often inappropriately, exposed to adult knowledge and assume extensive adult roles and responsibilities, principally in response to unmet family needs (Burton, 2007; Jurkovic, 1997; Jurkovic, Thirkield, and Morrell; 2001, Minuchin, Colapinto, and Minuchin, 1998). In the situation described above, DeVaughn's manifestations of adultified behaviors are striking. It is clear that because DeVaughn financially supports the household, his mother, Vanessa, has cast him in the role of "man of the house" regardless of his father Eli's sporadic appearances in their home. What is more, DeVaughn feels justified in calling Eli out in ways that suggest he has also assumed the principal role of family protector. Vanessa does very little in the way of decreasing her son's adultification when she relies on him heavily, and quite inappropriately, as her primary source of emotional support to cope with her own disappointments in life, and when she involves him in conversations and decision-making about complex family matters. Indeed, DeVaughn's behaviors and circumstances raise important issues about the challenges some low-income mothers and fathers may face in parenting children whom they, or the situations in which they find themselves, have positioned to prematurely assume and continually perform adult-like roles.

As the current parenting literature suggests, an optimal parenting situation for DeVaughn would involve his mother *and* father investing great swaths of time, resources, energy, and emotional labor in raising him with the expectations about their respective roles as child and parents being hierarchically distinct and developmentally in sync with their stations in the life course (Azar, Reitz, and Goslin, 2008; Crosnoe and Cavanagh, 2010; Elder and Shanahan, 2006; McLoyd, 1990; Roopnarine and Hossain, 2013). On occasion, DeVaughn's parents have marginally exercised these parenting behaviors, particularly when the couple experienced short episodes of financial stability early in DeVaughn's life. Nonetheless, because Eli and Vanessa have lived most of their adult lives in the throes of poverty, uncertainty, partner discord, and the inability to meet basic family needs, neither parent consistently shields their son from their emotionally and physically charged "grown-folks" tête-à-têtes about money, and their disappointments about their own romantic relationship.

During the ethnographic study DeVaughn's family participated in, Eli and Vanessa were rarely observed providing DeVaughn with parental affection and a sense of being nurtured, nor were they seen administering the necessary forms of correction or discipline that DeVaughn's behavior occasionally warranted. Overall, DeVaughn's parents had yet to establish appropriate parent–child connections with him, and they did not seem to be in the position to foster positive connections to others for him so that he might garner healthy support, guidance, and access to viable vocational and social opportunities elsewhere.

What is more, Vanessa and Eli did not effectively monitor DeVaughn's shady connections with "his boys" who provided him with the type of work that gave him the ability to usurp Eli's power with his wad of ones and tens. For the most part, DeVaughn was left on his own to navigate and make sense of the paradoxical world of his mother's and father's parenting and his role as man-in-charge at a mere 15 years of age. The paradox is reflected in how Vanessa and Eli try to parent DeVaughn as an adolescent and expect him to behave like one by "staying in a child's place" (e.g., "DeVaughn, you respect your daddy and don't hit him either"), while they simultaneously anoint him an adult with rights and privileges. The contradictory nature of this parent–child relationship is explicit in this family's everyday life. When parents adultify a child to the extent DeVaughn has been adultified, it is difficult to expect that child to assume a child's role at the parents' convenience. Sometimes that child will rebel as he or she realizes that their parents can't have it both ways.

In this chapter, our goal is to draw attention to the paradoxical circumstances that characterize childhood adultification and parenting in some low-income African American families, particularly those with sons. We acknowledge that many of the insights we share in this chapter are similarly experienced by girls, by children from different ethnic and racial backgrounds, and by youth whose adultification behaviors were initiated by circumstances other than poverty such as immigration, single-parenthood, parental deployment for military duties, parental incarceration, families with adult parents with a disability (e.g., deaf), or families with adult parents with addictions (e.g., alcohol, illicit drugs; see

Burton *et al.*, 2009). Here, however, we focus on low-income African American boys because reality and empirical research indicate that the circumstances related to the poverty in which many of them live, go to school, play, and work all too frequently shape their propensity for being adultified children or adolescents (Burton and Stack, 2014).

For example, based on a study of a nationally representative sample of children born in the United States, 46% of African American boys are likely to experience the first five years of life in poverty compared to 13% of White boys (Aratani, Wight, and Cooper, 2011). Seventy-two percent of these boys are born in households headed by a single or occasionally single mother who may unwittingly position her son, as the eldest, most consistent male in the household, to take on adult-like responsibilities. These boys' fathers, who are predominately African Americans, are among the most under- and unemployed populations in the US workforce (Roopnarine and Hossain, 2013). Moreover, as Davis, Kilburn, and Schultz (2009) report, many of these boys grow up in families that live in dangerous, violent neighborhoods where they are overexposed to stress, violence, and trauma. All these factors have been identified as influencing a boy's propensity for adultification (Burton, 2007).

In addition, ethnographies such as Sullivan's (1989) *Getting paid: Youth crime and work in the inner city*, Anderson's (1990) *Streetwise*, MacLeod's (1987) *Ain't no making it*, Ferguson's (2001) *Bad boys: Public schools in the making of Black masculinity*, Bourgois's (2002) *In search of respect: Selling crack in El Barrio*, Venkatesh's (2008) *Gang leader for a day*, Bergmann's (2008) *Getting ghost: Two young lives and the struggle for the soul of an American city*, and Harding's (2010) *Living the drama: Community, conflict, and culture among inner-city boys* have dominated the academic and public policy literature with constant reminders that low-income African American boys are one of the most vulnerable populations in the United States. This literature provides thick descriptions of the lives of African American boys who "grow up a little faster," like DeVaughn, and are parented in counterintuitive ways (Foster, Hagan, and Brooks-Gunn, 2008; Johnson and Mollborn, 2009; Winn *et al.*, 2012). It is important to qualify these descriptions, however, as not all economically poor, African American male youth have

these experiences, and even for some who do, the adultification processes that ensue, depending on the circumstances, can be the basis on which some boys develop profound resilience rather than risky behaviors (Burton, 2007; Stack, 1974).

We begin our discussion with an overview of how economic disadvantage shapes the emergence of adultification for children in families with special needs. Next, we describe relevant elements of a conceptual model of adultification (see Burton, 2007) focusing on how four forms – precocious knowledge, mentored adultification, peerification/spousification, and parentification – differentially emerge in the lives of low-income African American boys, in particular. We then discuss the role of parenting relative to adultified male children using a model of parenting developed by Stevenson, Davis, and Abdul-Kabir (2001) and Winn *et al.* (2012) and referred to herein at PACC (for protection, affection, connection, and correction). We frame our discussion using this model because it offers the best conceptual fit for assessing adultification and parenting for African American boys. This model originally comprised three dimensions of parenting – protection, affection, and correction – and was developed to address the specific parenting practices used in raising African American children and adolescents who were growing up under adverse and uncertain conditions (Hughes *et al.*, 2006; Stevenson, 2003). In 2012, Winn *et al.* added a fourth dimension, connection, to the model to highlight the role that parents take on in deliberately connecting their children to social capital (e.g., human resources, access to opportunities, exposure to novel situations and situations to grow and develop interests and hobbies). This model focuses on parenting domains that we have already highlighted in DeVaughn's case study – how parents protect their sons, provide affection for them, correct or appropriately discipline them, and connect them to meaningful, affirming networks of people.

As we address this topic, we will incorporate representative exemplar case studies from our ethnographic and clinical research with low-income African American males and their families to illustrate relevant links between aspects of adultification and parenting. The use of exemplars or illustrative cases is a valid and well-established process for integrating empirical findings into conceptual discussions as a way of giving the reader a sense of the reality of particular experiences and a viewpoint of the actors, as well as a way to provide empirical verification of the pattern of behaviors that are discussed (Abbott, 2004; Strauss and Corbin, 1998). We conclude the chapter by raising critical questions to consider in thinking about the relationship between adultification and parenting among low-income African American boys.

Economic Disadvantage and Childhood Adultification

By its very definition, adultification circumscribes children to precociously take on adult-like "heavy lifting" in their families with the intent of meeting specific family needs. Given the uncertainty and considerable range of needs that usually accompany poverty, families who experience economic hardship are often prime contexts for children's adultification, particularly boys (Wood, 2001, 2003). However, as we consider the relationship between a family's financial resources and childhood adultification, it is important to acknowledge that all economic disadvantage and its effects are not created equal. Factors associated with economic disadvantage, and the forms of adultification it encourages, can vary according to the characteristics of the disadvantage. There are important differences between rural and urban poverty; between transitory and persistent poverty; and between poverty caused by a broad-based economic restructuring (e.g., the 1980s farm crisis) and that caused by an individual's lifelong disadvantage (Burton, Lichter, Baker, and Eason, 2013; Davidson, 1996; V. McLoyd, 1998; Wilson, 1987, 1996). Moreover, as noted earlier, several factors associated with poverty (i.e., single-parent household, parents with severe chronic illnesses, disabilities, or substance abuse) may lead to certain forms of adultification (Deutsch, 1982; Preston, 1994; Stein, Riedel, and Rotheram-Borus, 1999).

Beyond the difficulty that it creates in obtaining the basic necessities of life, economic disadvantage shapes additional characteristics of families' everyday lives that may lead to adultification. For example, families may have limited access to formal childcare

or other social services and require older children in the family to provide extensive care for younger ones. Ten-year-old Reggie found himself in such a situation as he provided primary care for his four younger siblings for long stretches of time while his mother worked three jobs to support her children. To boot, family members may lack privacy at home because of poorly constructed, confined, inadequately sound-proofed, shared spaces and, by default, expose children to sensitive adult conversations and romantic sexual behaviors (Burton and Clark, 2005). What is more, in neighborhoods characterized by severe economic deprivation, physical segregation from the mainstream, and high levels of violence, a perceived foreshortening of the life course with consequent accelerated developmental trajectories is also common (Burton, 1990; Foster et al., 2008; Harding, 2010).

Sociologist Glen Elder (1974) eloquently described what he terms the "downward extension of adult responsibilities to children" that occurs in families in response to economic deprivation. He suggests that families experiencing economic hardship are required to both increase their production and reduce their consumption of market goods and services. They do this by increasing their members' participation in the labor market, relying on family members to supply goods and services that might typically be purchased from the market (e.g., childcare), and cutting back on the family's spending. As a result, children in these families are more likely to be involved in household labor than their economically better-off peers. As parents are required to put more hours into work to improve the family's financial situation, the children are expected to assume responsibilities that the parents might otherwise have taken on were they not constantly working.

The stress and strain felt by families experiencing economic hardship also increase the likelihood that children in these contexts will become adultified. Parents in these families experience greater levels of emotional distress than more financially stable families (V. McLoyd, 1990; Luthar, 2003). Children like DeVaughn may implicitly feel pressure to comfort their parents and reduce their feelings of stress or depression. The emotional burden parents feel in the context of economic hardship might also take a toll on their availability to their children, a situation that may lead older children to act in a parenting role toward their siblings. Further, the marital difficulties experienced by many couples in the face of economic hardship increase the likelihood of children acting in the role of a peer or a parent in their family, as their parents may pressure them to take sides between them or act in a quasi-spousal role to one or the other (Weiss, 1979).

Another source of potential childhood adultification in poor families, especially families residing in communities with blighted labor markets, concerns the employment opportunities available for adolescents and adults (Wilson, 1987, 1996). In some families, the work world of parents and their adolescent children overlap as a direct consequence of limited neighborhood job opportunities (Burton, Obeidallah, and Allison, 1996). Teenage daughters and sons and their adult mothers and fathers can sometimes be put in a situation in which they compete for the same low-wage labor jobs. Devon, a 17-year-old eleventh-grader, once said, "I can get a job when my father can't. We fight about it sometimes. He gets mad because they will hire me and not him. One man told him he was too old and beat up [at age 35] to get a job and that he wanted a young guy like me to work for him." Sixteen-year-old Michael shared a similar sentiment, "It's hard for a man to get a job when our fathers and grandfathers are trying for the same jobs we are."

Although economic disadvantage can contribute to the emergence of childhood adultification, it is likely that most children in low-income families do not experience the most extreme forms of adultification, or if they do, do not necessarily experience them for prolonged periods of time. It is reasonable to assume that many poor families do not intentionally enlist their children as adults in family labor, and to the best of their abilities work to keep their children free from adult concerns. Particularly in the case of temporary poverty, such as that experienced by families as a result of a parent's short-term job lay-off, the effects of adultification on children and families may be short-term and somewhat benign. However, in the case of long-term sustained poverty, the effects of childhood adultification are readily discernible and can create considerable developmental costs and lost opportunities for children, particularly boys.

Forms of Childhood Adultification

Figure 11.1 presents the model of childhood adultification that guides our discussion. (For a detailed overview of the model, see Burton, 2007.) In this chapter, we draw attention to the forms of adultification and how they have been experienced by low-income African American boys we have seen in our ethnographic research projects and clinical practices. Four forms of adultification are featured in the model – precocious knowledge, mentored adultification, peerification/spousification, and parentification. The array of forms represents a gradient or levels approach to defining adultification, with precocious knowledge being the most basic and simplest form and parentification being the most complex and specialized form. This model does not imply that adultified children experience only one form consistently. Rather, the real-life experiences of adultified children that we have observed in working with low-income African American youth suggest that they all have some experience with precocious knowledge, but those who advance to higher levels of adultification (e.g., parentification) move back and forth across all levels as family situations demand.

Precocious knowledge

Precocious knowledge is perhaps the most amorphous and prevalent form of childhood adultification. It involves witnessing situations and acquiring knowledge that are advanced for the child's age. With precocious knowledge, children are often privy to adult conversations and transactions, visually exposed to types of behaviors from which other children are often shielded (e.g., parents' frustrations with financial hardships), or consistent witnesses to the harsh realities of life in high-risk environments.

Young children and adolescents in economically disadvantaged families are exposed to precocious knowledge through a variety of means. Although many parents may try to protect their children from knowledge about adults' financial problems, children can easily learn a great deal about this topic because of their access to adult conversations in public places. For instance, the lack of privacy in poorly constructed and

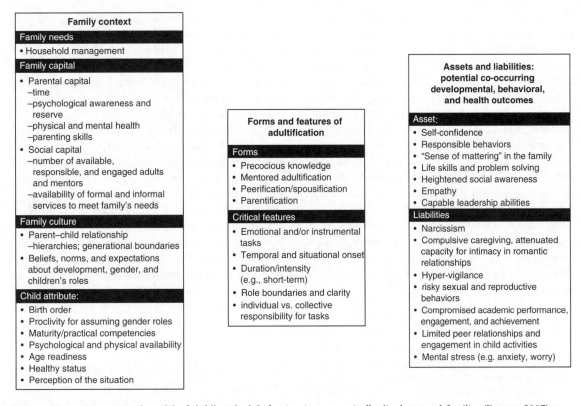

Family context

Family needs
• Household management

Family capital
• Parental capital
   –time
   –psychological awareness and reserve
   –physical and mental health
   –parenting skills
• Social capital
   –number of available, responsible, and engaged adults and mentors
   –availability of formal and informal services to meet family's needs

Family culture
• Parent–child relationship
   –hierarchies; generational boundaries
• Beliefs, norms, and expectations about development, gender, and children's roles

Child attribute:
• Birth order
• Proclivity for assuming gender roles
• Maturity/practical competencies
• Psychological and physical availability
• Age readiness
• Healthy status
• Perception of the situation

Forms and features of adultification

Forms
• Precocious knowledge
• Mentored adultification
• Peerification/spousification
• Parentification

Critical features
• Emotional and/or instrumental tasks
• Temporal and situational onset
• Duration/intensity (e.g., short-term)
• Role boundaries and clarity
• individual vs. collective responsibility for tasks

Assets and liabilities: potential co-occurring developmental, behavioral, and health outcomes

Asset:
• Self-confidence
• Responsible behaviors
• "Sense of mattering" in the family
• Life skills and problem solving
• Heightened social awareness
• Empathy
• Capable leadership abilities

Liabilities
• Narcissism
• Compulsive caregiving, attenuated capacity for intimacy in romantic relationships
• Hyper-vigilance
• risky sexual and reproductive behaviors
• Compromised academic performance, engagement, and achievement
• Limited peer relationships and engagement in child activities
• Mental stress (e.g. anxiety, worry)

Figure 11.1 A conceptual model of childhood adultification in economically disadvantaged families (Burton, 2007).

spatially inadequate low-income housing makes it difficult to shield children from overhearing such exchanges. In neighborhoods where it is common to find families doubled- and even tripled-up in single-family houses and one- or two-bedroom apartments, there is little opportunity for adults to conceal financial problems from their children. Moreover, when children accompany their parents to social service agencies to secure resources such as money, food, housing, or health care, details of the families' economic situations and personal tragedies are openly discussed by social service workers in front of them and often within earshot of others.

Despite parents' best efforts, many economically disadvantaged children can thus become acutely aware of their parents' financial concerns and stresses. Weiss (1979) discussed this flow of information from parent to child, suggesting that children in economically disadvantaged families are not freed from the adult concerns and worries in the manner that many

children are in families with modest to substantial resources. In many of Weiss's families (1979, p. 104), the children were made aware of their family's economic circumstances and the limitations that these put on their lives. One mother recalled how she found herself making the children aware of how financially pressed they were, "And every so often, if they're bugging me for something that costs too much money, that's out of proportion to what I can afford, I take the bills out and show them the bills, what we get in monthly, and say, 'Now you make sense of it.'"

We have observed heightened awareness and anxiety about their families' financial woes in children as young as age 3. Three-year-old Josiah, for example, emptied his piggy bank of the ninety cents he had been saving for months. He told his financially distressed mother, "I take care of you, mama. I got all the money you need. You can have it all!"

Thomas, a precocious 4-year-old, revealed his awareness of his family's financial problems in another setting. As part of our research, one of our staff members took Thomas and his family to a local restaurant to celebrate his mother's birthday. At the end of the meal, the staff member invited Thomas to accompany her to the cashier to pay the bill. The cashier jokingly asked Thomas if he had the money to pay for the bill. Thomas reached into his pockets and then a painfully apparent sadness reconfigured his facial expression. The staff member quickly noted the change, but before she could assure Thomas that she would be paying the bill, Thomas woefully declared, "We ain't got no money. We can't pay. What you gonna make us do to pay the bill?"

Precocious knowledge also may follow from extraordinary stresses in high-risk environments, such as the grasp of environmentally appropriate battlefield conduct of 12-year-old Lafeyette and his 4-year-old brother described by Kotlowitz (1991, p. 9):

> Suddenly, gunfire erupted. The frightened children fell to the ground. "Hold your head down!" Lafeyette snapped, as he covered Dede's head with her pink nylon jacket. If he hadn't physically restrained her, she might have sprinted for home, a dangerous action when the gangs started warring. "Stay down," he ordered the trembling girl. The two lay pressed to the beaten grass for half a minute, until the shooting subsided. Lafeyette held Dede's hand as they cautiously crawled through the dirt toward home.

A 4-year-old, in the same family, showed the beginning of insight into the stresses of his environment when he imitated his older brother and comforted their mother by saying, "Your head be hurting all the time. Lemme worry for you."

It is important to note that "battlefield environments" and children's exposure to them are not restricted to poor urban neighborhoods. For instance, 3-year-old Jarrett's exposure to violence in an isolated rural hamlet was extensive. Jarrett, his two younger sisters, and 23-year-old mother and father resided in a double-wide trailer situated on Jarrett's grandparents' land. Jarrett and his sisters' housing arrangement was not one desired by his parents. They simply did not have the financial resources to live anywhere else.

During our staff member's fifth visit to Jarrett's home, she arrived to find several police cars leaving the property. Jarrett's uncle was handcuffed in the back seat of one of the cars. Jarrett's mother explained that her brother-in-law had just had a shoot-out with the police. She protected her children from the bullets by telling them to lie on the couch and cover themselves with a blanket. Several weeks later, young Jarrett asked his mother to paint his bedroom to make it look like someone had been shot there.

Some children act on exposure to precocious knowledge by emulating adult perpetrator behaviors, whereas others worry about what they have witnessed and long for the resources and skills to solve the problem. Some children do both. What differentiates this very basic form of adultification from others is that children are not called upon to assume adult-like roles in their families at this point. Rather, children gather and store the information they observe and hear, often seeking explanations about what they do not understand from adults and, more often than not, from other children.

Mentored adultification

Mentored adultification involves children's moving beyond precocious knowledge to the assumption of adult-like roles with limited adult supervision. Not uncommonly, economically disadvantaged children exhibit adultification that is intentionally developed or mentored, having learned to carry out tasks at precociously young ages. Such is the case of 12-year-old Jeffrey.

Jeffrey is described by his mother as her most reliable helper. When Jeffrey was 8 years old, his parents divorced and his father remarried, moved far away, and had three additional children. Jeffrey's newly configured family (himself, his brother, and his mother) was left with severe economic hardship that required his mother to work. Jeffrey helped out his mother by taking care of his younger brother, and occasionally cleaning the house. At one point, his grandparents moved in to help, but they both were in extremely poor health, so Jeffrey ended up caring for them, too. Through all of this, Jeffrey's mother never relinquished her parental authority, even though she assigned him extensive family responsibilities that he was expected to carry out with minimal supervision from her.

Jeffrey's circumstance is a very common form of adultification among African American boys. Unlike the two forms of adultification we will discuss shortly, children who bear heavy, but quasi-mentored family roles and responsibilities, like Jeffrey, are usually made to feel needed and appreciated by their parents. Moreover these children may value and gain confidence from the useful domestic and social skills they develop carrying out their assigned tasks. The key issue here is that the parent retains authority over the child and as such may be in a much better position than DeVaughn's parents to exercise necessary and appropriate parenting behaviors. Jeffery always said of his tasks and his mother, "I have a lot of jobs to do, but I know who the boss is … Mama! She will never let me forget that, no matter how much I have to do. And, even though things are hard and we don't have much money, I am happy that I can help her."

Peerification/spousification

As noted above, with mentored adultification, although children take on adult-like responsibilities, the usual parent–child authority hierarchy remains in place and the generational boundaries are somewhat clear, as parents occasionally remind their child about "who's really in charge." Adultification takes the form of peerification when the child behaves more like a parent's peer than like a parent's subordinate. Essentially, the parent–child authority hierarchy and generational boundaries are leveled, with children having power and status equal to that of their parents. Kindred constructs to peerification in the family therapy literature are spousification and child-as-mate (Sroufe and Ward, 1980). This form is apparent when children assume the role of quasi-wife, -husband, -partner, or confidante to their parents.

Telltale signs of children being peerified may be noted when parents routinely confide in their children in much the same way Vanessa confided in DeVaughn. Weiss (1979, p.103) wrote that parents often turn to their peerified children because "there may be no one other than the children for the parent to confide in or turn to for advice or company, especially about household or family problems." He further suggested that the responsibility borne by children in sustaining the household may justify parents' decision to share their worries with the children. This behavior is quite pronounced in some single-parent family structures (see Arditti, 1999).

In economically hard-pressed families, children may also seem like their parents' peers in the way they contribute materially. Dei (1997, p. 303), describing one of his ethnographic respondents, characterizes this behavior thus: "Even though he did not watch television often, Gerald [aged 16 years] had cable installed (and paid the monthly fees) because his mother, sister, and niece liked to watch television." This form of peerification is especially evident when it involves money that we would expect children to feel strongly possessive about: "When one woman lost the support of her family, her high school-aged son took an after-school job at McDonald's and gave virtually all his earnings to his mother" (Edin and Lein, 1997, p. 153).

Peerification of children slides into spousification when a child's instrumental duties and responsibilities model those of a spouse or partner. We have witnessed powerful exemplars of spousification in our work when young sons assume the role of the man of the house. Fifteen-year-old Antoine took on this role at age 13 when his mother, Sandra, started a job as a cafeteria worker in compliance with welfare-to-work regulations. Sandra's job required an hour-long commute by bus both ways, long work hours, and very low pay. The considerable time Sandra spent being at and getting to and from work greatly decreased the amount of time she had to parent her eight sons (Antoine is the second oldest) and sustain relationships with a partner and her friends. As her partner and friend relationships dwindled, and her availability for parenting her sons all but disappeared, Antoine increasingly became her "spouse-apparent," serving as her confidante, consultant, and co-parent to his younger siblings. Antoine's fate as child-as-mate was sealed when his older brother, Kerrick, was arrested and jailed for attempting to contribute to the family economy by selling drugs.

Long-term observations of and interviews with Antoine and Sandra indicated that Antoine more than carried his weight as man of the house for several years, until at 15 years of age he grew weary of his responsibilities. He had been responsible for getting his younger brothers and himself off to school every morning. One day, according to him, he just decided to stop. He and his brothers stayed home from school for almost two months before his mother was alerted to their truancy by school officials and was forced to quit her job and stay at home to ensure that her sons went to school every day. While Antoine's parenting responsibilities diminished somewhat because of the truancy incident and his mother's displeasure with his failure as a co-parent, Sandra seemed to need him more than ever as an emotional confidante after she quit her job. She became increasingly depressed and anxious about the family's financial situation and struggled not to turn to drugs as an option to settle her nerves.

Like Antoine, 16-year-old Alex served as the man of the house, providing solace and financial support to his mother and parenting for his 15-year-old sister and her 1-year-old son. Alex's mother, however, was very ambivalent about his role and often sent him mixed messages about the importance of his contributions to the family. Whenever his mother started a relationship with a new boyfriend, she would demote Alex, requiring that he cease being her peer and act like a child in the presence of her boyfriend. On one occasion, his mother's boyfriend demanded that Alex take out the trash "like a good boy." Alex threw the trashcan at the boyfriend and demanded that he leave *his* house "because he was the man of the house and helped his mother to pay the bills and raise his nephew." Alex's mother responded by telling him to go to his room. Instead, Alex left the house and moved in with a 25-year-old woman down the street. He said, "Now, I am really the man of the house."

Spousification and peerification can take a heavy internal toll on a child or adolescent: Kotlowitz (1991, p.15) said of 12-year-old Lafeyette, "Sometimes the strain of responsibility showed in his thin, handsome face; it would tighten, like a fist, and it seemed as if he would never smile again." Moreover, if a child is contributing substantial material resources, he or she may be implicitly reinforced for engaging in risky enterprises:

> If they [adolescents] need or want immediate cash ... they may try their hand at street drug hustles. And if they are competent in small business transactions, the cash flows into the home. Suddenly the teenager can help pay for the family's groceries, rent, and clothing. In return, the stressed and often distraught parent may not ask too many questions. (Williams and Kornblum, 1994, p. 58)

What seems most important to understand about peerification and spousification is the sense of ambiguity children and adolescents appear to feel due to the mixed messages they receive about being in an equal relationship with their parents and their parents' fleeting ambivalence. One might argue that the modified parent–child hierarchy in mentored adultification and the reversal of the parent–child hierarchy experienced in parentification provide more predictability for children than the indecisive treatment they receive from being considered on an equal plane with their parents.

Parentification

A peerified child may periodically step into and out of a parental role with siblings, but a parentified child is a full-time quasi-parent to his/her siblings and parents. Parentification involves many roles. It may include being the family's primary breadwinner:

> My brother Joe had to quit school when he was 16 years old. He had to go out and get a job. But Joe was out gettin' a job at 16 to support all the kids ... He's our father. That's what he really is ... he's our father. Every fucking penny that my brother got he threw right into the family, right into the house. Cuz my mother can't work. (J. MacLeod, 1987 p. 51)

It could also involve being the family's social service advocate. Larry, from age 12, was the primary advocate for social services for his eight younger siblings and unemployed mother, who was chronically ill. On one occasion Larry entered the social worker's office with visible resolve. He said, "My family needs food, housing, and health care now. What do I have to do to get it?" After working with the social worker to procure services for his ailing mother, he returned home only to negotiate with the landlord about back rent and to piece together a meal for his sisters and brothers and his mother.

The most extreme forms of parentification are observed in economically disadvantaged families in which the parents are substance abusers. For example, children of alcoholics often take on parentified roles in relation to their parents, concerning themselves with the parents' well-being, attempting to guide them away from trouble, and quite often protecting the non-alcoholic parent from the alcoholic parent (Deutsch, 1982).

Evan, age 18, like many of the other parentified children we have worked with, reported that his adultification experiences began in middle childhood when his parents' drug addictions progressed. As noted earlier, poverty together with parents' substance abuse problems most likely occur in cases of childhood parentification. Evan's parents' drug habits led to the economic downfall of their family. As a result, Evan became responsible for raising his siblings, and he also took a heavy hand with his parents, who kept the family in dire financial straits. At one point, Evan's parents ran up his credit cards past their limit while Evan was trying to finish high school, parenting his younger siblings, and working three jobs to pay off the debt that his parents had incurred. He accomplished all his tasks successfully, including graduating from high school, maintaining his jobs and the family household, and monitoring his siblings' performance in school, but in the process of accomplishing these goals he "put his parents out of the house and forbade them to see their younger children."

With his parents out of the house, Evan believed that he would finally get a break. Unfortunately, shortly after his parents' departure and his father's death (which occurred soon thereafter), two young men stole Evan's car. Evan needed his car to get to work and to school, where he was taking courses to become an Emergency Medical Technician (EMT). Evan reported the loss to the police but also did some investigation on his own and found the perpetrators. Evan said, "I was so mad when I found them I beat them and beat them, screaming, how could you do this to me after all I've had to do. Everything inside me came out on them." For the beatings he delivered, Evan was arrested and imprisoned for a month. He was not able to complete his testing to become an EMT.

The outcomes of parentification are an interesting mix of life skills, successes and challenges that affect the child's or adolescent's sense of self and emotional expression. Perhaps because parentification is the extreme form of adultification, and the family circumstances that elicit it often require being in charge without parental back-up, the natural course for developing identity, intimacy, and other aspects of emotions are compromised for parentified children and adolescents. Weiss (1979, p. 109) states:

These children may soon learn that their need for parental care can only be realized partially, and then only by acting as their parents' helpers and companions; by acting, in effect, in ways that deny their very needs for dependency and nurturance. And this may be another reason why some of these young people describe themselves later as having become loners. They have learned not to express certain needs.

Parenting Adultified African American Boys and Teens

Now that we have thoroughly reviewed the four forms of adultification, let us turn our attention to the challenges that mothers and fathers may face in parenting low-income adultified male children. To explore this issue, we consider the PACC model of parenting mentioned earlier in this chapter (Stevenson, 2003; Stevenson et al., 2001; Winn et al., 2012). PACC is a strengths-based model for parenting minority children as compared to most parenting and child development models, which are deficit-based (V. McLoyd, 1990). It focuses on building boys' resilience and strengths, including their overlooked assets such as having a sense of humor, the ability to use language dynamically, the capacity to develop deep friendships, and a resolute spirituality that gives rise to profound levels of perseverance through adversity. PACC also acknowledges that these strengths are at times undermined by the adverse contexts and racial inequities that exist in US society.

PACC focuses specifically on four parenting behaviors – parents' capacity to protect, provide affection to, correct, and connect their children to viable and supportive networks. It also takes into account the normative experiences required for children's healthy development across the life course. According to the American Psychological Association Task Force on Resilience and Strength in Black Children and Adolescents (2008), those experiences are reflected in five developmental domains: (1) gendered racial identity development and racial socialization; (2) emotional expressions, regulation, and psychological development; (3) social development; (4) intellectual, language, academic, and vocational skill development; and (5) physical health and development. Children who progress in a healthy manner relative to these domains acquire proficiency and agency which serve as strengths and inner resources and complement parenting practices in ways that make a transition from normative development to adultification less likely or only minimally pronounced. Many African American male children, however, face caustic external realities (e.g., low expectations, racism, poverty, discrimination, marginalization, violent and dangerous community contexts) that can compromise their development and well-being in these domains and impede their healthy and timely life course progression. Some of these external realities pull for adultified responses by African American young boys in ways that add to or reinforce the adultification practices in which parents engage.

A key challenge of adultification in all of its forms is that as these boys develop strengths that allow them to cope with economically disadvantaged experiences and emotionally restrictive relationships, they move in and out of school, societal, and work contexts and relationships in which their strengths are not only unappreciated but seen as aggressive and arrogant. Racial rejection and fear that is coupled with gender undermining can be particularly stressful as these boys are trying to construct a functional and stable definition of manhood that works in their insular households and neighborhoods as well as the larger society. The stress of trying to be a different version of "the man" in these different relationships, particularly at school, can be overwhelming and can influence their relationships across the lifespan from childhood through later adulthood (Bentley, Thomas, and Stevenson, 2013; Cassidy and Stevenson, 2005; Stevenson, 2014; Thomas and Stevenson, 2009). Thus, as we think back to DeVaughn's situation, for example, the major question we pose in considering PACC and the corollary domains of normative development is whether mothers and fathers can provide adultified African American boys with the necessary behavioral and developmental aspects of parenting, especially when the realities of their everyday lives and aspects of extreme adultification run counter to what the model suggests low-income African American boys require.

PACC and adultification

According to the PACC model, *protection* comprises parents' intentional sheltering from, instruction about, and monitoring of threats or harm to their child's physical, emotional, and cultural identities. The purpose of protection is not defensiveness against improbable threats, but rather discernment of real threats that cause harm to children. To develop successfully, African American boys, like all children, require physically and emotionally safe spaces free from violence and ridicule where their inclinations to be active and strong are assets, not deficits. Moreover, the model argues that parents should be able to provide their sons with activities that promote healthy exploration, inquisitiveness, curiosity, love of learning and eagerness to excel. Not only should these boys be protected from prevailing negative stereotypes and narratives about African American males (e.g., lazy, athlete, drug dealer, school dropout, etc.) but parents have the added "minority tax" of protecting their sons from disproportionate system actions (arrests at school) taken against them that are fueled by these stereotypes.

Based on our observations of adultified children, protection is often a difficult parenting practice to employ, even at the most basic level of precocious knowledge. Low-income adultified African American boys are often made privy just by living in dangerous neighborhoods to harsh realities of life such as witnessing violence that it is difficult for their mothers, who are usually the custodial parent, to protect them from seeing. In the ethnographic and clinical cases we have studied, the closest mothers came to achieving this goal was through mentored adultification in which they appeared more vigilant about their sons' environmental exposures in general, and in which they explained the nature of their protectiveness toward their sons to them. For example, Jeffrey's mother kept a somewhat distant, but watchful eye on him and protected him by demanding temporal and geographic accountability from him. She told us, "It is hard to raise a good boy in this neighborhood with all the violence that goes on. But I protect Jeffrey by making sure I know where he is at all times and keeping him away from what's out there in the street.

To tell you the truth, he's so busy helping me, he doesn't have enough time to be out there." In contrast, boys who were peerified, spousified, or parentified experienced little in the way of parental protection. Rather, they were deemed the protectors of others.

In the PACC model, when parents provide *affection* they knowingly affirm, show that they care, and nurture the physical, social, emotional, and cultural identity of their sons. The purpose of affection is not indulgence but affirmation that African American boys are valued and important. Parents who engage their sons with affection provide healthy, predictable, consistent nurturance, and support as their sons try new behaviors, learn new ideas, and try, fail, and succeed at mastering aspects of life. According to PACC, parents who show their sons affection are not afraid to be humble and acknowledge the pain that unfair contexts and others' misinterpretations can cause. Mothers' and fathers' ability to be culturally attuned, interpreting their boys' behaviors, emotions, and gestures in the multiple ways that the boys' themselves intended, and not pathologizing them, are critical to their success in working with them. For example, caring parents are careful to not automatically ascribe pathological motives to the many reasons African American boys may choose to put distance between themselves and a hostile environment. Parents who display appropriate affection toward their sons get to know them, their stories and their motivations, finding strength and vulnerability where it exists, establishing common connections and bonds, and using their supportive relationships to help their children excel.

Our experiences have shown that regardless of the level of adultification African American boys in our ethnographies and clinical practices experience, most of their parents show them some form of affection. What we have not witnessed systematically from parents with adultified children, however, are displays of affection of as comprehensive a nature as the PACC model calls for. We believe that the day-to-day experiences of living in poverty likely dull one's senses, as dealing with uncertainty and painful situations do little in the way of spawning consistent merriment. Several of the boys we have studied, however, especially those in mentored adultification,

peerified, spousified, and parentified roles, have indicated that their parents' occasional expressions of thanks for what they do is good enough for them. Fourteen-year-old Curtis said of his mother, "I don't like all that huggin' and kissin' on me. Knowin' that she appreciates what I do is good enough."

Correction involves parents providing intentional support for their sons' healthy, adaptive behaviors while confronting maladaptive behaviors that undermine the physical, emotional, cultural identity, humanity, and voice of their children. The purpose of correction is not punishment but accountability, reconciliation and the building, enhancing or reconnecting of young African American males to their best selves, families, and community relationships. Correction includes those strategies that parents use to help children learn and do what is right. Intrinsic to correction is the attempt to teach young boys how to restore and repair relationships, as well as atone for any emotional or material damage they create. Developing stick-to-it-iveness and resilience to bounce back from setbacks are also critical. Finally, correction includes firm compassion and the creation of natural opportunities for boys to provide restitution for misdeeds and mistakes *and* to win, be powerful, and strong. So, according to PACC, rather than unfairly punishing their son, parents should work to ensure fairness and increase the opportunities their sons have to learn and contribute to their positive development.

Correction is clearly the most difficult parenting practice that mothers and fathers experience with adultified children, especially those who are peerified, spousified, and parentified. Once a boy has been adultified in the extreme, it usually means that his parents have relinquished their power to their child and that the usual parent–child hierarchy no longer exists. Under these circumstances it is difficult for a parent to guide the child or enforce rules, because the child is usually navigating the world for the parent. Herein lies a central paradox in adultification that often causes problems, particularly for boys, in other domains of their lives, leading them to have less success and greater difficulty in institutions that operate under traditional adult–child hierarchies and modes of correction. The comments of Jason, age 15, illustrate:

Sometimes I just don't believe how this school operates and thinks about us. Here I am a grown man. I take care of my mother and have raised my sisters. Then I come here and this know-nothing teacher treats me like I'm some dumb kid with no responsibilities. I am so frustrated. They are trying to make me something that I am not. Don't they understand I'm a man and have been a man longer than they have been women?

Connection highlights the importance of social, emotional, and cultural belongingness for African American boys. Research has shown that low-income boys, in particular, experience profound losses and interrupted connections mostly due to the absence of adult males in their lives. Parents who can help their sons build strong, positive connections to their culture and race and positive adults as role models tend to do better all around.

Again, the context of poverty and the labor that adultified boys engage in likely keeps them from being connected to others beyond the needs of their parents. Typically their parents have little in the way of social capital and some even shy away from trying to link their sons to others who can help them because the parents are embarrassed about their circumstances. Devon noted:

I ain't got no time to do nothing. Between taking care of my momma and my sisters and brothers and working I ain't got no time to hang out … I can't even throw down my rap and get a girlfriend. Damn, that's whack! Hmm … I wonder what it's like to be one of these rich White kids with mad money and nothin' to do but spend it? I wonder what it is like to be a kid?

Summary and Conclusions

In this chapter our goal was to sensitize readers to a situation that faces many low-income African American boys in America – childhood adultification – and how that situation intersects with their mothers' and fathers' abilities to parent them in ways that will lead them to having healthy and successful lives. As we have clearly shown, African American boys often begin life "behind the eight ball" and are consistently confronted by environmental, economic, social, psychological, and institutional (e.g., criminal justice system, schools)

assaults as they navigate a passage from childhood through adulthood. For some, that navigation involves considerable family responsibilities, which can compromise a young boy's normative development academically, socially, and psychologically. As a team of social scientists and clinicians, it has been our pleasure to introduce you to these very important issues. We hope that you will think long and hard about what we have shared with you. But, most importantly, we hope that the stories of young adolescent males, like DeVaughn, inspire you to do something civically minded about the challenging situations we have described.

Critical Thinking Questions

1. Have you observed instances of childhood adultification in your life and what do you see as the precipitating factors of the adultification? Do you think that adultification experiences are different for boys and girls? For youth of different races and ethnicities? For those who have notable economic wealth vs. those who do not?

2. The PACC model sets forth some useful standards for parenting children, especially those who live in uncertain and adverse conditions. What responsibilities do you think society and public policies have for helping parents to implement those parenting practices in raising their children?

3. It might appear, from what you have read, that nothing short of a targeted policy and programmatic approach at local, state, and federal levels to support the healthy development of African American boys is in order. What programs or considerations do you think school systems, for example, should put in place to deal with the issues discussed in this chapter?

Acknowledgments

We thank the National Science Foundation for their support of the research reported in this chapter through grants SES-1061591 and SES-0703968. We also acknowledge core support to the Three-City Study from the National Institute of Child Health and Human Development through grants HD36093 and HD25936 as well as the support of many government agencies and private foundations. We are particularly indebted to funding received from the W. K. Kellogg Foundation for their support of our work through the Promoting Academic Success in

Boys of Color Initiative. Most importantly, we express our heartfelt appreciation to all the African American boys and men who graciously participated in the research and clinical projects from which we drew the exemplar case studies presented in this chapter.

References

Abbott, A. (2004). *Methods of discovery: Heuristics for the social sciences*. New York: W. W. Norton.

American Psychological Association, Task Force on Resilience and Strength in Black Children and Adolescents. (2008). *Resilience in African American children and adolescents: A vision for optimal development*. Washington, DC: American Psychological Association. Retrieved May 30, 2014 from http://www.apa.org/pi/families/resources/resiliencerpt.pdf.

Anderson, E. (1990). *Streetwise: Race, class, and change in an urban community*. Chicago: University of Chicago Press.

Aratani, Y., Wight, V. R., and Cooper, J. L. (2011). *Racial gaps in early childhood: Socio-emotional health, developmental and educational outcomes among African American boys*. New York: National Center for Children in Poverty.

Arditti, J. A. (1999). Rethinking relationships between divorced mothers and their children: Capitalizing on family strengths. *Family Relations, 48*, 109–119.

Azar, S. T., Reitz, E. B., and Goslin, M. (2008). Mothering: Thinking is part of the job description. Application of cognitive views to understanding maladaptive parenting and doing intervention and prevention work. *Journal of Applied Developmental Psychology, 29*, 295–304.

Bentley, K. L., Thomas, D. E., and Stevenson, H. C. (2013). Raising consciousness: Promoting healthy coping among African American boys at school. In C. Clauss-Ehlers, Z. Serpell, and M. Weist (eds), *Handbook of culturally responsive school mental health: Advancing research, training, practice, and policy* (pp. 121–133). New York: Springer.

Bergmann, L. (2008). *Getting ghost: Two young lives and the struggle for the soul of an American city*. New York: New Press.

Bourgois, P. (2002). *In search of respect: Selling crack in El Barrio* (2nd edn) New York: Cambridge University Press.

Burton, L. M. (1990). Teenage childbearing as an alternative life-course strategy in multigeneration Black families. *Human Nature, 1*, 123–143.

Burton, L. M. (2007). Childhood adultification in economically disadvantaged families: A conceptual model. *Family Relations, 56*, 329–345.

Burton, L. M., and Clark, S. L. (2005). Homeplace and housing in the lives of low-income urban African American families. In V. C. McLoyd, N. Hill, and K. Dodge (eds), *African American family life: Ecological and cultural diversity* (pp. 166–188). New York: Guilford Press.

Burton, L. M., Garrett-Peters, R., and Eaton, S. (2009). "More than good quotations": How ethnography informs knowledge on adolescent development and context. In R. M. Lerner and L. Steinberg (eds), *Handbook of adolescent psychology*, vol. 1 (3rd edn) (pp. 55–92). Hoboken, NJ: John Wiley & Sons, Inc.

Burton, L. M., Lichter, D. T., Baker, R. S., and Eason, J. M. (2013). Inequality, family processes, and health in the "new" rural America. *American Behavioral Scientist, 5*, 1128–1151.

Burton, L. M., Obeidallah, D. O., and Allison, K. (1996). Ethnographic perspectives on social context and adolescent development among inner-city African American teens. In R. Jessor, A. Colby, and R. Shweder (eds), *Essays on ethnography and human development* (pp. 395–418). Chicago: University of Chicago Press.

Burton, L. M., and Stack, C. B. (2014). "Breakfast at Elmo's": Adolescent boys and disruptive politics in the kinscripts' narrative. In A. Garey, R. Hertz, and M. Nelson (eds), *Open to disruption: Time and craft in the practice of slow sociology*. Nashville, TN: Vanderbilt University Press.

Cassidy, E. F., and Stevenson, H. C. (2005). They wear the mask: Hypermasculinity and hypervulnerability among African American males in an urban remedial disciplinary school context. *Journal of Aggression, Maltreatment and Trauma, 11*, 53–74.

Crosnoe, R., and Cavanagh, S. E. (2010). Families with children and adolescents: A review, critique, and future agenda. *Journal of Marriage and Family, 72*, 594–611.

Davidson, G. O. (1996). *Broken heartland: The rise of America's rural ghetto*. Iowa City, IO: University of Iowa Press.

Davis, L. M., Kilburn, M. R., and Schultz, D. J. (2009). *Reparable harm: Assessing and addressing disparities faced by boys and men of color in California*. Santa Monica, CA: RAND Corporation.

Dei, G. J. S. (1997). *Reconstructing "dropout": A critical ethnography of the dynamics of Black students' disengagement from school*. Toronto, Canada: University of Toronto Press.

Deutsch, C. (1982). *Broken bottles, broken dreams: Understanding and helping children of alcoholics*. New York: Teachers College Press.

Edin, K., and Lein, L. (1997). *Making ends meet: How single mothers survive welfare and low-wage work*. New York: Russell Sage Foundation.

Elder, G. H., Jr. (1974). *Children of the Great Depression. Social change in life experience*. Chicago: University of Chicago Press.

Elder, G. H., Jr., and Shanahan, M. J. (2006). The life course and human development. In R. Lerner (ed.), *Handbook of child psychology*, vol. 1, *Theory* (pp. 665–715). Hoboken, NJ: John Wiley & Sons, Inc.

Ferguson, A. A. (2001). *Bad boys: Public schools in the making of Black masculinity*. Ann Arbor, MI: University of Michigan Press.

Foster, H., Hagan, J., and Brooks-Gunn, J. (2008). Growing up fast: Stress exposure and subjective "weathering" in emerging adulthood. *Journal of Health and Social Behavior, 49*, 162–177.

Harding, D. J. (2010). *Living the drama: Community, conflict, and culture among inner-city boys*. Chicago: University of Chicago Press.

Hughes, D. L., Johnson, D., Smith, E., Rodriguez, J., Stevenson, H. C., and Spicer, P. (2006). Parents' ethnic/racial socialization practices: A review of research and directions for future study. *Developmental Psychology, 42*, 747–770.

Johnson, M. K., and Mollborn, S. (2009). Growing up faster, feeling older: Hardship in childhood and adolescence. *Social Psychology Quarterly, 72*, 39–60.

Jurkovic, G. J. (1997). *Lost childhoods: The plight of the parentified child*. New York: Brunner/Mazel.

Jurkovic, G. J., Thirkield, A., and Morrell, R. (2001). Parentification of adult children of divorce: A multidimensional analysis. *Journal of Youth and Adolescence, 30*, 245–257.

Kotlowitz, A. (1991). *There are no children here: The story of two boys growing up in the other America*. New York: Doubleday.

Luthar, S. S. (2003). The culture of affluence: Psychological costs of material wealth. *Child Development, 74*, 1581–1593.

MacLeod, J. (1987). *Ain't no makin' it: Aspirations and attainment in a low-income neighborhood* (2nd edn). Boulder, CO: Westview Press.

McLoyd, V. C. (1990). The impact of economic hardship on Black families and children: Psychological distress, parenting, and socioemotional development. *Child Development, 61*, 331–346.

McLoyd, V. C. (1998). Socioeconomic disadvantage and child development. *American Psychologist, 53*, 185–204.

Minuchin, P., Colapinto, J., and Minuchin, S. (1998). *Working with poor families*. New York: Guilford Press.

Preston, P. (1994). *Mother father deaf: Living between sound and silence*. Cambridge, MA: Harvard University Press.

Roopnarine, J. L., and Hossain, Z. (2013). African American and African Caribbean fathers. In N. J. Cabreba and C. S. Tamis-Lemoda (eds), *Handbook on father involvement: Multidisciplinary perspectives* (pp. 223–243). New York: Routledge.

Sroufe, L. A., and Ward, J. J. (1980). Seductive behavior of mothers of toddlers: Occurrence, correlates, and family origins. *Child Development, 51*, 1222–1229.

Stack, C. B. (1974). *All our kin: Strategies for survival in a Black community*. New York: Harper and Row.

Stein, J. A., Riedel, M., and Rotheram-Borus, M. J. (1999). Parentification and its impact on adolescent children of parents with AIDS. *Family Process, 38*, 193–208.

Stevenson, H. C., Jr. (ed.) (2003). *Playing with anger: Teaching coping skills to African American boys through athletics and culture*. Westport, CT: Praeger.

Stevenson, H. C., Jr. (2014). *Promoting racial literacy in schools: Differences that make a difference*. New York: Teachers College Press.

Stevenson, H. C., Jr., Davis, G., and Abdul-Kabir, S. (2001). *Stickin' to watchin' over, and getting' with: An African American parent's guide to discipline*. San Francisco, CA: Jossey-Bass.

Strauss, A. L., and Corbin, J. M. (1998). *Basics of qualitative research: Techniques and procedures for developing grounded theory* (2nd edn). Thousand Oaks, CA: Sage Publications.

Sullivan, M. L. (1989). *Getting paid: Youth crime and work in the inner city*. Ithaca, NY: Cornell University Press.

Thomas, D., and Stevenson, H. C., Jr. (2009). Gender risks and education: The particular classroom challenges of urban, low-income African American boys. *Review of Research in Education, 33*, 160–180.

Venkatesh, S. A. (2008). *Gang leader for a day*. New York: Penguin Press.

Weiss, R. S. (1979). Growing up a little faster: The experience of growing up in a single-parent household. *Journal of Social Issues, 35*, 97–111.

Williams, T., and Kornblum, W. (1994). *The uptown kids: Struggle and hope in the projects*. New York: Grosset/Putnam.

Wilson, W. J. (1987). *The truly disadvantaged: The inner city, the underclass, and public policy*. Chicago: University of Chicago Press.

Wilson, W. J. (1996). *When work disappears: The world of the new urban poor*. New York: Alfred A. Knopf.

Winn, D. M., Iruka, I. U., Harradine, C., Buansi, A., McKinney, M., and Stevenson, H. (2012). *Providing opportunities to spite the obstacles: Countering the adverse conditions that undermine the success of African American boys*. Washington, DC: Grantmakers for Children, Youth, and Families.

Wood, G. (2001). Desperately seeking security. *Journal of International Development, 13*, 523–534.

Wood, G. (2003). Staying secure, staying poor: The "Faustian Bargain." *World Development, 31*, 455–471.

Part III

Family Challenges Over the Life Course

12

Family Resilience to Promote Positive Child Development, Strong and Flexible Families, and Intergenerational Vitality

Sharon Landesman Ramey, Robin Gaines Lanzi, and Craig T. Ramey

> Regardless of family composition, all families have goals and are dynamic systems that attempt to balance the needs of individual family members as well as the whole family. In this chapter, the authors advance a family resilience perspective that focuses on the most important ways that parents facilitate their young children's development. According to Ramey, Lanzi, and Ramey, both promotive processes and harmful factors and stressors are necessary for children to develop resilience. From this perspective, family challenges are an important opportunity for growth.

Family resilience is a psychological construct that encompasses many dimensions of how families function (Black and Lobo, 2008; Luthar, 2006; Masten and Obradovic, 2006; McCubbin and Patterson, 1983; McCubbin, McCubbin, Thompson, Han, and Allen, 1997). The essence of resilience is that families have a repertoire of approaches to help them survive – and even benefit from – the ebb and flow of challenges they encounter. The construct of resilience is strongly linked to the field of positive psychology (e.g., Seligman, Steen, Park, and Peterson, 2005) and to understanding the biosocial nature of human development itself (e.g., Wilson, 1979, 2012). In times of duress, families demonstrate their resilience; in times of calm, families may reflect on how they handle difficult periods and even take actions so that they are well prepared to be resilient in the face of future adversity.

Families provide the physical, social, emotional, and cognitive environment that serves as the primary means of protecting and nurturing children during their early period of dependence on others for survival. Families also serve as major facilitators of children's learning about the world and themselves as active agents in the world. Many of children's experiences within their own family environment provide the foundation for how they will negotiate with others outside the family unit. Above all, healthy families offer a trustworthy and stable haven where children are comfortable and can seek help to understand their own experiences both within and outside the family (Ramey and Ramey, 2012).

Family Problems: Stress, Risk, and Resilience, First Edition. Edited by Joyce A. Arditti.
© 2015 John Wiley & Sons, Inc. Published 2015 by John Wiley & Sons, Inc.

There can be little doubt that most families are goal-directed social units that fulfill vital societal functions. A chief function of families with children is ensuring that each child is healthy and shows progress toward becoming a competent, caring, and eventually independent and contributing member of society. At the same time, most families also place a value on interdependence among family members. Interdependence is not at odds with children becoming independent. Rather interdependencies are a complementary dimension of mature behavior that fosters efficiency and can promote flexibility, planning, and problem-solving for the family as a unit. Families recognize that as children mature, they too will form new and lasting social relationships in multiple realms of personal, work, recreational, and community life; these later relationships also will benefit from healthy forms of interdependence.

Another goal important for many families is that their own values, traditions, and history are shared and passed on through the generations. For some families, this goal may be one that is explicit and openly discussed; for others, this goal may be implicit or embedded within the family's encouragement that their children become "good people" and "show respect for their family's heritage." To achieve this goal of sustaining the identity of a family through the generations, many families often tell stories about how their ancestors and older family members have survived difficult situations. These shared memories reveal strategies for maintaining equilibrium when there are serious threats to the family or to family members. In some ways, these intergenerational reflections provide families with an opportunity to think about how to adapt to their current life situation and how they can strengthen their resilience in the future. Conversely, families that minimize, overlook, or actively deny the reality of "difficult times" may discover that their children have fewer opportunities to acquire strategies that contribute to individual or collective group resilience.

In this chapter we focus primarily on the features of the family environment that contribute to positive development of children, as indexed by an array of biological, educational, and psychosocial outcome measures. We rely on the construct of resilience as an organizing theme, and we explore the diverse ways in which family resilience contributes to the integrity of the family as a unit. Because we have investigated children's developmental trajectories by conducting longitudinal studies (often beginning during the prenatal period or shortly after birth and extending through childhood and sometimes into adulthood) that include both experimental interventions (designed to test the efficacy of early interventions to improve child and family outcomes) and naturalistic studies (often of large cohorts of children and families), we place a high priority on understanding the fluctuations that occur over the lifetime of a family (see C. Ramey, S. Ramey, and Lanzi, 2006 for representative longitudinal studies). Many of the fluctuations and transitions that occur in family life can be considered normative and fairly predictable, while others are far less so. Thus, with this longitudinal lens in place, we view families as dynamic biological and social systems that function according to a set of basic principles.

We present our perspective on family resilience in three sections. The first section identifies *key biosocial systems principles that characterize family units*. These principles inherently work to promote achieving homeostasis – that is, a healthy, balanced system of functioning. For families, however, what homeostasis "looks like" is far from a simple, static, or universal picture. This leads us to propose that "family homeostasis" represents a delicate and frequently changing state in which the roles and behavior of individual family members, subunits within the family, and the family as a whole accommodate the demands on the family and the availability of resources to achieve positive outcomes for both individual family members and the family as a whole. These systems principles help to identify strategies that can promote, but not always guarantee, a balanced family system. Under times of duress and particularly when adjusting to unexpected major fluctuations, the family's response can be viewed in terms of being more or less resilient. The second section provides a *succinct summary of longitudinal research findings* about parents that derive from a wealth of studies about the ways in which parents exert a significant influence over the course of their children's development. This summary emerged from a major scientific meeting sponsored by the National Institutes of Health (NIH) during a period when major questions arose about how great an influence parents truly exert on their children's development (Borkowski, Ramey, and Bristol-Powers, 2002). The NIH conference forum led to building a consensus among developmental scientists about the most important ways that parents do, in fact, affect their children's development. Briefly, the acronym of RPM3, representing Responsive care, Prevention and protection, and Monitoring, Mentoring, and Modeling, captures this summary (Borkowski, Ramey, and Bristol-Powers, 2002). In this second section, we elaborate on these distinct dimensions of parenting, and illustrate how these collectively represent family-level supports that strengthen a family's resilience. In essence, the practice of RPM3 simultaneously confers benefits to children and provides a robust biosocial systems framework that helps families to maintain equilibrium (or homeostasis) during periods of transition and duress. In the third and final section, we present an overview of *our model of human development* that underlines the complexity and interdependence of children and their family units. We have used this conceptual framework, known as Applied Biosocial Contextual Development – or the ABCD Model (Ramey *et al.*, 2006) – to guide many of our longitudinal research studies. The research projects that have been shaped by the ABCD framework have focused on testing hypotheses about how to increase the promotive and resilient factors in children and families, while also minimizing or avoiding the harmful or threatening factors. At the heart of the ABCD framework is the premise that resilience can be strengthened and learned, although undeniably there are biological and community environmental influences that also contribute to the expression of resilience. This core premise is now amply supported with scientific evidence that important components of resilience can be acquired, through systematic and intentional efforts, in addition to those that may occur naturally through the process of "living and learning."

Key Biosocial Systems Principles That Characterize Family Units

Biological systems theory presents a cohesive set of operational principles about how organisms develop and function at the individual and collective level (see Bertalanffy, 1968; Miller, 1978). These principles

inherently work to promote achieving *homeostasis* – that is, a healthy, balanced system of functioning. For families, however, there is no simple, trans-cultural, or static picture of what homeostasis "looks like" (Landesman, Jaccard, and Gunderson, 1991). Rather, "family homeostasis" is a composite of behaviors that are in dynamic flux to help the family as a whole unit balance the needs and demands of individual members while simultaneously ensuring that the subunits (such as specific parent–child dyadic relationships and sibling relationships) and the whole family itself have the essential resources to continue to thrive. Implicit in the family mission of realizing continued survival is the notion that the family's ability to handle multiple and sometimes serious threats and challenges will lead to greater resilience – that is, positive functioning even in times of duress. Among the most foundational principles from systems theory that are important to understanding family homeostasis are the following:

- that all of the elements of a system are interdependent;
- that the whole is greater than the sum of its individual parts;
- that changes in one unit can influence all of the other units within the system; and
- that threats to either the whole system or its subcomponents potentially impact the whole system.

These biosocial systems principles can be applied to help families identify strategies that can promote, but not always guarantee, a resilient family system. Under conditions of challenge – whether from outside or inside the family unit and whether expected or unexpected – the collective action of the family unit can be viewed in terms of being more or less resilient. Family resilience, however, does not necessarily imply that family agreement or harmony among all members is a response to a given problem or threat. In fact, depending on the nature of the situation, there may be strong advantages to a family system that tolerates and even welcomes diverse viewpoints about how to handle a problem. In such a situation, the family that has multiple cognitive and behavioral approaches to problem-solving may increase the likelihood of maintaining long-term homeostasis. On the other hand, a family system that is too extreme in its diverse approaches to a problem may be unable to make a firm decision or be able to coordinate the family members in a timely manner to enact a solution, thus minimizing the probability of a positive outcome. Further, if the diversity of approaches is so extreme that family members are constantly confronting one another, then this perpetual confrontation could distract the family unit from other important functions.

In today's world, the definition of family is sometimes itself a topic of deliberation. For purposes of scientific inquiry, we adopted a broad definition of family that is not restricted by strict dimensions of biological relatedness, the legal status of the unit, or the momentary arrangement of living and social relationships. Our operational definition of family is: a family is a collection of individuals who have a clearly stated long-term commitment to the general well-being of one another, who label themselves as a "family," and who are recognized in their community as an integral unit with designated responsibilities within their society (Landesman *et al.*, 1991; Ramey and Ramey, 2012).

We proposed this broad definition of family several decades ago, when we recognized how rapidly the profiles of families in the United States were changing. We also took into account a transcultural perspective. Above all, we wanted to ensure that collections of individuals who establish long-term commitments and agree to function in ways that promote the well-being of their individual members and their local communities and society as a whole are taken into account and, from a scientific perspective, included in our research in a way that is respectful and capable of revealing important dimensions about family resilience. We know of no scientific principle that a priori favors one type of family unit over another, although undoubtedly one can imagine certain types of family structures and composition that can be more (or less) challenging to operate. Because our primary interest is learning more about family resiliency patterns and how parents help to promote children who will be capable and resilient themselves, we have discovered that using this nonrestrictive definition of the family increases our opportunity to understand a fuller range of environments where children are, in fact, living and learning

on a daily basis. Several of the fascinating aspects of this functional definition of the family unit are that: (1) an individual may belong to more than one family unit at a time; (2) not all family members may include (or exclude) the same people in their own definition of "my family"; and (3) the "family environment" includes psychological and social resources that may strongly influence the behavior of family members, even in the absence of sharing the same physical environment (Landesman, 1986).

We recognize that the family's home environment expresses many things about the family, including the types and amounts of physical and financial resources the family has, what they value in terms of how to spend time and money, what their daily routines are and how stable (versus unpredictable) these routines are, how they assign and fulfill different responsibilities needed to keep the family functioning, and even the extent to which they show aspects of their spiritual beliefs and their sense of aesthetics (that is, diverse ways to represent beauty and "the cultural arts"). The family environment thus can help to promote resilience; alternatively, there may be environmental features that constrain or impede resilience in a family.

For almost all children, their family home environment (which for some children may include the linkage of two or more different physical settings where there are distinct social members) provides many examples of how adults, particularly their primary parents, behave when problems arise and when there are perceived or actual threats to the family unit. In addition, children's individual experiences of their family environment are linked with strong emotional meaning, almost always a mix of both positive and negative emotions. These emotions can drive memories as well as behavior. Over time, children often come to remember their experiences in ways that help to guide their own choices about future behaviors and negotiations outside the family environment. Undoubtedly, each family creates and stores memories of what has occurred at home. Sometimes, a family's memories become collective and widely shared, both within and outside the family unit. Other times, there can be divergence in what the individual family members experience and/or what they remember. Just as important to understanding the family system and environment are those things that do not happen. That is, because families exist within a community and societal context, family members notice the ways that their family is similar to and different from other families. Sometimes the *absence* of certain activities or resources can exert a strong, direct impact on the development of children. When assessing the family environment, a consideration of what is missing from the family environment, along with what is present, may help provide insights into how resilient the family is under particular conditions.

As a system, families distinguish themselves by their patterns of salient activities, relationships, and the emotional tone of how the family functions as a whole, and how well the subunits within the family operate. Each family environment is surrounded by a larger ecological context that has an influence of what occurs in the home. In highly supportive communities, the resources and strategies needed to achieve homeostasis are markedly different than in communities that are very low in their resources to support families. In more extreme situations, family homes located in hostile or dangerous ecological contexts face a dramatically different everyday situation in terms of how to protect their family and family members as they move in and out of the home for school, work, and recreation.

The practical and psychological consequences of certain aspects of the family environment and the family's homeostasis may be dependent to a large extent on whether the family functions in ways that are deemed normative, healthy, and desirable versus those that are considered deviant, harmful, or challenging to the stability of other families. The norms for families as well as the ideals promoted for a family vary tremendously across cultures, communities, and cohorts. The cohort effect is profound; across the generations, there have been vast changes in how families operate from day to day. For a cohort that views men and women as equal partners, for instance, who choose to jointly share many responsibilities related to parenting, earning wages, seeking personal fulfillment both inside and outside the family unit, planning their family's social and recreational activities, and maintaining the physical home, the family system works quite differently than for a cohort that defines the roles of men and women in a far more precise and differentiated way. Similarly, the presence

of re-configured families where one or both parents have brought children into a new family unit, single-parent families, families that adopt and/or foster children, and families with multi-generational living arrangements may exert strong effects of how a family functions and achieves its own form of family homeostasis.

Theoretically, there are some structural and physical characteristics of families that may appear to be highly advantageous for almost all families. Among these characteristics would be having sufficient social resources (for instance, enough adults or older siblings) to handle the everyday operations of the family unit and having sufficient and stable financial and physical resources to meet the family's current needs as well as the projected future needs of the family as a unit and as a support for children as they transition into independent adulthood and leave the family home. However, families that do not have optimal resources on a stable basis can be highly successful to the extent that they are able to enlist support in other ways, including establishing positive relationships with others outside the immediate family environment (friendships, extended kinship networks, societal institutions designed to support families), being frugal and creative in their use of limited physical and financial resources, and placing a strong priority on their family as a unit by encouraging the development and contributions of each family member. In many ways, when families do not have "everything" they need and want, this may create a natural opportunity for families to explore and learn new ways to adapt and achieve another level of homeostasis. Certainly, families that are stable as a unit and have adequate resources rarely have a guarantee that they will never face troubling times or situations. In families from all walks of life, challenges can arise from a multitude of sources, including unexpected economic downturns, natural disasters, serious health problems, injuries to family members or the family home, and major societal upheavals. Thus, family resilience is not something just for some families, but not needed in others. Family resilience applies to all family units, and active awareness of the importance of resilience strategies to maintain family homeostasis is vital for intergenerational survival and thriving of children. Indeed, resilience does not show until a family faces problems or challenges, although resilience preparedness that occurs during periods of stability and relatively ideal conditions is likely to exert a large and enduring effect on families and their children.

Application of Scientific Evidence about How Parents Promote Positive Development in Their Children: The RPM3 Approach

RPM3 is a term that summarizes an approach to parenting that has been endorsed by the National Institute of Child Health and Human Development (NICHD), based on a large body of scientific findings about what types of parenting are associated with children who are, on average, among the most healthy and socially and cognitively competent. RPM3 is a term that stands for five different dimensions of parenting. These are:

1. Responding to the child in an appropriate manner.
2. Preventing risky behavior or problems before they arise.
3. Monitoring the child's contact with his or her surrounding world.
4. Mentoring the child to support and encourage desired behaviors.
5. Modeling behavior to provide a consistent, positive example for the child.

RPM3 represents a synthesis from a scientific conference that was convened when the question arose "How much do parents really matter?" At an extreme, the position was advanced that children's development was virtually not affected in any major way by what parents did; rather, the claim was made, most vocally by Judith Harris (1998), that only biology (genetic influences) and peer influences (often from middle childhood through later adolescence) shaped a child's personality. This provocative position was not without some merit, since there is strong scientific support that both biology and peers do matter. Further, schools and teachers matter, and community opportunities and experiences (including non-parental

mentors and role models) also matter. The purpose of the scientific meeting was to identify which, if any, parenting behaviors showed a major influence on the course of a child's development; and to help parents and the public understand these within a broader appreciation for the fact that human development is a multi-determined process. (For a more detailed analysis of this controversy and the diverse responses, see the edited conference proceedings in Borkowski *et al.*, 2002.) In this chapter, we re-interpret the RPM3 model or advice to parents as representing a combined and evidence-based strategy that affords great promise as a broad way to maximize resilience in the next generation while at the same time increasing family homeostasis over the many years and decades that parents assume a distinct responsibility as "leaders" within the family unit.

Responding to the child in an appropriate manner

Although a guideline such as this may seem obvious, responding is much more than a parent paying attention to a child (see Box 12.1). The words actually are carefully chosen to convey two quite distinct things: (1) parents should be sure that they (individually or as a couple or team) are responding to their child, not merely reacting to their child's behavior or needs; and (2) parents need to focus on having their response be appropriate, not one that is overblown or out-of-proportion, too casual or minimal, or too late. The difference between reacting without reflection and awareness and responding to a child is profound. Many parents react (understandably) to their children. That is, they answer with the first words, feelings, or actions that come to mind. This is a fairly normal thing to do, especially with all the other things people do every day. When parents primarily react, however, they are not behaving in a way that reflects preparation and a decision about the outcome they want from the event or action. Even more than that, when parents rely on a habit of reacting as their usual way of parenting, they are far less likely to choose the best way to reach the outcome they want for themselves as parents, for their family as a unit, and for their child as someone who is actively learning and developing.

Box 12.1 Responding in an Appropriate Manner

JoAnn is 6 months old and has been a typical baby. One day she starts crying and just will not stop. Fredericka and Harvey, her thirtyish parents, try to comfort her to no avail. At 2 a. m. they decide to call her pediatrician to seek advice. Listing to JoAnn over the phone, the pediatrician advises them to take JoAnn to the emergency room. She is discovered to have otis media, which has caused her eardrum to bulge and is a very painful condition and the reason why the child was crying.

The discharge nurse at the emergency room notes that young babies cry for a reason, usually pain, and that Fredericka and Harvey were right to seek advice and take action because they could not figure out what was wrong or to alleviate JoAnn's suffering.

The approach of responding to each individual child, in contrast, means that the parents have taken a moment (or more) to think about what is really going on before they speak, feel, or act. Responding is a much more difficult parenting habit to adopt than reacting, because this takes more time and effort. The time that parents take between looking at the event and acting, speaking, or feeling can be vital to the parent–child relationship. That time, whether it be a few seconds, five minutes, or a day or two, can allow parents to see things more clearly, in terms of what is happening right now and what you want to happen in the long run.

What is an appropriate parental response? An appropriate response is one that fits the situation. As you can see in Box 12.1, baby JoAnn's parents attempt first to comfort her in the usual way, but when she persists in crying during the night, Fredericka and Harvey take a reasonable action to determine the source of her distress. These parents respond quickly and appropriately to their infant's signals that something is amiss and outside intervention is necessary. One of the most compelling things is a child's age and developmental understanding. A parenting

response that works very well for a 6-year-old child is unlikely to be effective with a 16-month-old or a 16-year-old. Another factor that determines whether a parental response will be effective concerns the specific facts of the occasion. For example, a fitting response for a baby who is crying differs from a fitting response for a 4-year-old or a 10-year-old who is crying. A fitting response for an instance in which a child is running depends on whether that child is running into a busy street or running to the swing set on the playground. Your child's physical or emotional needs may also shape your decision about a fitting response. Finally, recognizing the importance of each child's personality and individual history, parents respond in ways that help the child to learn and to grow in terms of their social, emotional, and cognitive maturity.

"Responding to each child in an appropriate manner" helps parents promote resilience in their family. This is because appropriate responses require the parents to think about options before they make a decision. Parents who take the time to anticipate and then to see typical problems from many sides, rather than only one side, are more likely to choose the most fitting response. For situations that happen often, parents who have well-thought-out responses discover these can become almost automatic. Parents often learn form their own parents (the child's grandparents), from professionals who help to care for their children (pediatricians, nurses, teachers, social workers, psychologists), from reading books about parenting (particularly those from trustworthy sources such as the American Academy of Pediatrics that issue excellent evidence-backed parenting guides that cover different age periods and take into account biological maturation, social-emotional needs, and a child's cognitive understanding, and also focus on children with special needs – see the website for the American Academy of Pediatrics for an up-to-date listing), and from talking with other parents who have children of a similar age or who have successfully learned about how to handle certain challenges in their own family life.

Parents who respond appropriately reflect on whether their words and their actions go together and help to get across what they are trying to accomplish. This involves parents being able to control their emotions well enough that they behave in mature and effective ways. Parents who respond appropriately are continuously seeking to understand the reasons for their child's actions or behavior (note: understanding the cause of a child's behavior does not mean the parents accept or condone all of the child's behavior, but rather this understanding leads them to choose responses that are likely to stop and/or minimize the same unacceptable behavior from recurring, and to increase the probability the child will show specific types of positive behavior more often).

Effective responsiveness to children becomes particularly challenging when parents have more than one child, and the children are different in their needs and comprehension. When parents have a general approach that they consistently (but not overly rigidly) apply, they can be fair and maximize maintaining family homeostasis. When children are old enough, parents can help children to anticipate the responses that will occur. Parents can consider previous, similar events and recall how they handled these. They can remind their child(ren) of these other times and the outcomes. Parents can use their past experiences within the family – as well as their family-of-origin experiences – to judge their current situation, decide the outcome they want, and figure out how to reach that outcome.

This approach promotes family resilience since children rapidly learn that their parents do not make decisions based on whim or just the immediate situation. This in turn invites children to seek responsive or anticipatory guidance from their parents when they encounter new problems or have questions. Warm, concerned, and sensitive or individualized parental responses will also increase the likelihood of maintaining long-term positive relationships, so that when truly major problems arise, a child can depend on his or her parents to be thoughtful and caring, rather than just reactive in the "heat of things."

Preventing risky behaviors or problems before they arise

Building on systems theory about the interdependence of elements within a system, parents know that there are many problems they can actively prevent. This is part of a proactive family resilience plan.

Parents recognize that they cannot entirely prevent difficulties, but that focusing on those that they can minimize helps to preserve their resources, time, and energy for solving the most serious problems that cannot be fully anticipated or prevented. Thus, depending on the age of the children and where the family lives, parents need to spot and, if feasible, prevent, possible problems in their home and community. Ways to spot problems before they turn into full-blown crises include parents being actively and appropriately involved in their child's life. This anticipation is important for all parents, no matter what the living arrangements. Knowing how a child usually thinks, feels, and acts will help parents notice when things begin to change and differentiate between those that may be signs of trouble. When parents set realistic limits and enforce them consistently within the family environment, they are preventing many potential problems. Parents need to be selective with setting limits, primarily by establishing boundaries on the most important behaviors their child is engaged in. Parents who work as a team (a subunit of the family system) to help the child "see" the limit clearly are far more likely to achieve success. If their child goes beyond the limit, either parent (or the parents together) will implement the same consequences for the child. This can promote family resilience in working as a team with the same functional rules. When parents decide to restrict or punish their child, they will be using the most effective methods, in a timely manner. Sometimes parents choose to have a child correct or make up for the outcome of his or her improper or harmful actions; when these are not overly harsh and when they "match" the child's transgressions well, these become valuable in both prevention of future "bad behavior" and promoting resilience in the child (through learning that mistakes can be corrected, at least in part). As children learn how limits work in their family unit, and what happens when he or she goes past those limits, he or she will trust parents to be fair. Family resilience often includes the need to be fair and balanced in addressing the wrongs or problems a family experiences. Adopting only short-term, immediate responses to major family problems rarely promote longer-term survival and building flexibility and resilience.

Interestingly the National Institutes of Health conference on parenting identified the importance of parents creating healthy ways for their children to express their emotions. How is this important for family resilience? Many problems within the family arise from children "acting out" when they have intense emotions that they cannot yet control or regulate; and other problems arise when children excessively withhold or hide their feelings (thus preventing early interventions to help children with their feelings). These childhood feelings can range widely, from frustration to anger to rage; from disappointment to sadness to depression; and from distress to anxiety to fear. If a child does not receive parental assistance in acknowledging that intense emotions are a part of life and that these emotions can be addressed, then both the children and the family are "at risk." Parents who are able to help their children label emotions and then find constructive ways to control these and use emotions to guide, but not dominate, their thoughts and actions are likely to be preparing their children for life's inevitable fluctuations. Emotional learning within the family extends beyond parents addressing each child's emotions individually; families need to promote compassion and patience in understanding that there is likely to be variation in how family members feel about themselves or their current life situation. The family as a whole can help to prevent emotional extremes that can be debilitating, while also recognizing that sharing emotions within a safe family setting can often prompt new levels of understanding and developing plans for action.

M3: monitoring, mentoring, and modeling

The "M3" in RPM3 describes three intertwined, yet differentiated principles of parenting: monitoring, mentoring, and modeling. At first, these words seem similar, but in terms of parenting and family dynamics, each of the three Ms is expressed in quite different ways. The first practice of monitoring (see Box 12.2) is one that requires a conscious level of engagement in assessing how individual family members are doing, both at the current time and in comparison to the past. Sometimes monitoring is placed in the context

---

Box 12.2 Monitoring

Julie is the 14-year-old daughter of Bart and Elaine. Recently Julie has become somewhat vague about her plans for weekend events. Last night (Thursday) she informed Bart and Elaine that she had been invited for a sleepover at her friend Betty's house. Friday around noon Elaine called Betty's mom to thank her for Julie's invitation and to ask if Bart and Elaine could treat the girls to an order-in pizza. Both mothers then chatted about the upcoming weekend. Elaine concluded that the invitation was genuine and that adults would be at Betty's house all weekend and that the girls would be well supervised by responsible adults.

---

of preparing a child for a planned transition, such as school entry or the transition to young adulthood. Being a monitor means that parents (and often older siblings as well) pay careful attention to younger children and their surroundings, especially to each child's adjustment to his or her groups of friends and peers and in getting used to external activities, such as going to school and participating in team sports. The primary goal of monitoring is to detect any potential problems early so that they can be effectively and appropriately addressed. The experience and knowledge of parents are vital to the well-being of children; yet monitoring does not imply that a child has no time alone or outside the view of parents and family members. Rather, monitoring is an ongoing process that could be equated with monitoring the weather or air quality, paying particular attention to extremes or warning signs that should be used to guide the behavior of the parents and/or children.

Being a mentor is quite an active role, but does not necessarily mean suggesting a resolution to a problem. As you can see from Box 12.3, Bill and Mary do not necessarily tell their son what to do with regard to guitar lessons, but provide input and advice in terms of how interests change and the importance of enjoying life and following one's interests or new opportunities. The hallmark of an effective parent

Box 12.3 Mentoring

Bill and Mary are the parents of their 15-year-old son, Jamie. Jamie has been taking guitar lessons since he was 12. Recently Jamie seems to have lost interest in the guitar and seems more interested in lacrosse. During a conversation at dinner, Bill makes the observation that lacrosse seems to have become Jamie's "passion." Jamie agrees and says that between schoolwork and lacrosse practice and games he is not doing as well in his guitar progress as he would like. Mary observes that something similar happened to her as a young teenager when she was taking ballet lessons. Bill notes that he dropped playing high school football after his sophomore year because he just wasn't very good at it. The conversation drifts to the various things that Bill, Mary, and Jamie have enjoyed over their lives – some of which they continue to enjoy and some of which are no longer active interests. Jamie asks their opinion about the guitar lessons. Bill and Mary agree that it is sometimes difficult to "fit it all in" and that Jamie should do what he thinks is best. Jamie says that he will think it over.

mentor is one who helps to teach children through a variety of direct interactions, instruction, and planned opportunities to explore and learn from others, including people and places outside the family home. A mentor is someone who helps the child to learn about himself or herself, as well as about how the world works, and what his or her roles in that world can be. As a mentor, a parent focuses on the learning needs of the child. Some of these learning needs include learning to be a good member of the family, cooperating, helping, and showing care for the well-being of others and the family as a whole. In a sense, the family environment is a microcosm of the world for the child, offering many opportunities to practice new behaviors and approaches and to become a con-tributing "citizen" within the family's world. When parents serve as mentors, their forms of teaching are thoughtful and well attached to a child's readiness to increase his or her skills and understanding.

Ideally, parents balance their mentoring across the full range of development, rather than focus narrowly on only one or two domains. That is, parents mentor their children in social development, language and cognitive development, physical development, safety and health-promoting behaviors, and emotional development. At the same time that parental mentor-ing facilitates the development of each child, this mentoring serves a stabilizing function for family homeostasis. Mentoring activities often are fun and engaging, varied, and multi-directional. That is, in the

process of mentoring their children, parents themselves often learn a lot from their children. This dynamic back-and-forth learning is one of the most apparent features of dynamic biosocial systems. Overly static or rigid systems that contain few opportunities for ongoing learning rarely yield systems that are highly successful and capable of surviving when the system – in this case, the family – encounters sudden change or difficult situations, most notably situations in which the solutions that worked in the past no longer produce the desired result in the changing times. Mentoring, thus, is a parenting skill that keeps parents mentally and socially agile and creates a subunit within the family for transmitting new knowledge when it becomes available. Rarely does a parent have a comprehensive, multi-year plan for everything that a child needs to "learn." Rather, mentoring evolves as a way of life, exchanging information and encouraging multiple ways of acquiring new skills and knowledge. The content of the mentoring is not entirely predictable, and thus becomes something that all family members contribute to over time. In most families, there will be special needs that arise as well as new opportunities that occur in the world; these will encourage both parents and children to pursue learning new things and helping one another.

Being a model as a parent means that what parents do serves as powerful, highly visible examples that show their beliefs, values, and attitudes on a daily basis. When children become adults, their memories of their parents as role models often are highly motivating, shaping both things they aspire to do in their own lives and identifying things they vigorously want to avoid. Being a model does not mean that parents can ever be, or should even aspire to be, "perfect." But when it comes to family resilience, allowing children to observe how their parents handle difficult situations and how parents themselves learn from mistakes and from feedback they receive (observing and reflecting on the consequences of their behavior as adults and as parents) offers a good model.

In practice, the M3 component of good parenting behavior often occurs quite naturally. Parents need not monitor everything, but rather they need to think about how to ask the right types of questions (sometimes of the child, sometimes of others), be observant when they see their child in new situations, set realistic limits along with consequences for not following these limits, and encourage their children's positive choices when they are not present. Helping children to know when to ask for help, and from whom they should ask help, is an aspect of mentoring. As role models, parents can both show the positive behavior they would like to promote in their children and discuss when things do not work out as planned. How parents solve problems and correct mistakes and the ways that parents learn from others are sources of good information for children when they cannot solve issues on their own.

One especially challenging issue for families is when they encounter what seems to be a serious clash of personalities or approaches within their own family. This can include a parent–child "personality clash" or sibling clashes. These often are not permanent, but if these are not recognized and addressed, they can weaken the family's ability to maintain homeostasis. Indeed, a parent's ability to monitor the child is often one of the first things to suffer from this type of clash. Thus finding ways to keep the lines of communication open becomes a vital coping or survival strategy. A delicate and complex reality is that families rarely have good times and good relationships "all the time." When parents model that they do not completely withdraw, retaliate, or quit being a parent even when interactions are problematic, then they are helping to convey a fundamental resilience strategy – namely, to continue to work toward solutions. Some aspects of family functioning include knowing when to take a break from working on problems, and when to seek help or advice from others who may offer new insights and perspectives when it seems that "nothing is working like it should."

In healthy families, children will be allowed to develop strong, healthy relationships with peers and with other adult mentors who may be able to provide advice, instruction, socialization, and sometimes just listen (from a different perspective) to the child. Formal mentoring programs that pair children with caring mentors have been highly successful in some communities; often these are designed for children whose families are not stable in terms of providing positive and stable parenting support for their children.

Mentors do what a good coach does. They develop a child's strengths; share a child's interests; offer advice and support; give praise; and listen. Mentors help kids reach their full potential, which includes mistakes and tears, as well as successes and smiles. Mentors know that failures often precede major successes; knowing this fact, they encourage kids to keep trying because those successes are right around the corner. Parenting programs have also been implemented for troubled teens. These focus on parents learning to show that they respect their child's thoughts and opinions without instantly judging them. Even when parents do not agree with their child, they can let them know that they are interested in their child's thoughts, without the constant threat of punishment, criticism, or harsh teasing. If a child is afraid of being punished or put down, then the child may stop sharing things entirely. In contrast, when the family system allows different points of view to coexist for a while, these may allow children to think more about an issue (this obviously does not extend to permitting dangerous and illegal behaviors). For a dynamic biosocial system such as the family, parents are well advised to acknowledge the important difference between "I disagree with you" and "You're wrong." If children are never allowed to make decisions, but only expected to obey (without thinking on their own), then the resilience skills they need for later life are being overlooked. Trial-and-error learning within the context of parents who monitor, mentor, and serve as role models is both natural and often quite effective.

All too often, parenting behavior and family functioning are guided by adults reacting to their own childhoods; that is, many parents think "I don't ever want to be like my parents"; or "It was good enough for me, so it's good enough for my kids." Remember that reacting instead of responding often prevents parents from making decisions that can change the outcome of a situation. The NIH produced an informational pamphlet generated by the scientific conference, filled with lots of practical advice and hints about many of the common challenges of being a parent. Of course, a pamphlet cannot serve as a full preparation course to be a parent. Above all, even our own experience with parenting advice books and television series (e.g., C. Ramey and S. Ramey, 1999; S. Ramey and C. Ramey, 1999, with the companion Public Broadcasting television series for parents about the first three years of life "Right from Birth," and about ages 3 to 8 "Going to School") has taught us as scientists that families are genuinely interested in learning all they can about ways that are effective (versus harmful or ineffective) to promote their children's well-being. We are optimistic that books such as these will encourage more vigorous study of the resilience framework, so that families can become better prepared and, in turn, demonstrate more effective and timely ways to promote resilience over their life course.

Application of the Applied Biosocial Contextual Development Conceptual Framework for Understanding Promotive and Resilient Factors in Families and Children

The model of human development that we developed and have used to guide our studies of families, which we refer to as the Applied Biosocial Contextual Development theoretical framework (or ABCD model) emphasizes the complexity and interdependence of children and their family units (Ramey, MacPhee, and Yeates, 1982; Ramey and Ramey, 1998; Ramey and Ramey, 1992; Ramey et al., 2006). ABCD incorporates both stress and resilience as key

components in the healthy development of families and children, and recognizes the importance of the resources that are available at multiple levels. ABCD is well suited for guiding family research projects that focus on testing hypotheses about how to increase the promotive and resilient factors in children and families, at the same time minimizing or avoiding the harmful or threatening factors that may be present, because ABCD addresses the whole social ecology of the family and child.

A fundamental premise of the ABCD model as a systems theory is that changes in the family and child may affect changes in their biology and experiences and that the community context and resources available to families will influence their strengths and the outcomes for their children. How the family and ultimately the child respond to these stressors in their lives is in large part a function of the resources available to them, the appropriateness and acceptability of these resources, and their experiential response to these resources. Figure 12.1 displays the ABCD conceptual framework. The processes that are involved in helping to promote resilience are displayed in the middle and categorized as "Promotive Processes" and "Harmful Factors and Stressors." From a developmental perspective, all children will have exposure to both types of processes. Without challenges to development, resilience may be virtually impossible to promote. In other words, if a child never experienced an event or decision that challenged his or her thinking or decision-making or ways of behaving, then the child would be unlikely to reach his or her full potential in terms of acquiring resiliency. It is this personal experiential component of the child within the family context (shown on the left of the figure) that presents an opportunity for growth for both the child as an individual and the family as a social system. The pathways by which the child influences the family and the family influences the child over time are interdependent and multi-faceted. They can be through supports and challenges that relate to day-to-day life events and decisions to the more complex, life-altering, major decisions.

How the family supports and promotes resilience in children can be conceptualized as a continuum of resilience supports controlled and applied by the parents (or family as a whole) or by the child (as he or she becomes more independent and engaged in diverse activities both inside and outside the family

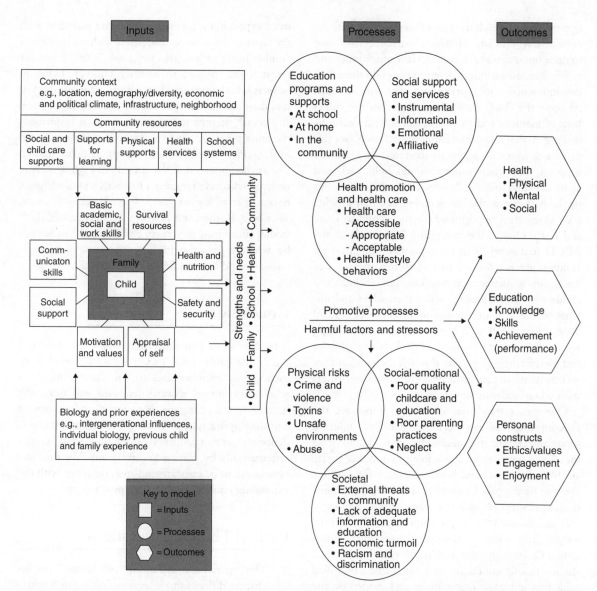

Figure 12.1 The Applied Biosocial Contextual Development (ABCD) model of human development (adapted from C. Ramey *et al.*, 2006).

environment). Whereas all life events involve an opportunity for families to support children in their development of resiliency, these events differ in the degree to which family members actually are able to control and direct the processes. At one end of this continuum, parents exert high control over decisions and direct the child in their response to adverse events; at the other end, the children themselves are given

control of the change process with family members sometimes providing backup assistance and supports when requested by the child (or when necessary to protect the child from imminent harm). When children have the opportunity to make a decision about how to respond, enact their decision, and reflect upon the results of their decision, they are more likely to "grow" in their resiliency because they are given opportunities to push the boundaries of what they are comfortable with and what life experiences they have to draw upon to make decisions. How much input and active decision-making is given to the child should be developmentally appropriate and take into account not only the child's chronological age, but the child's level of maturity and past experiences with decision-making. A vital role of the family unit throughout this process is to know when to intervene and provide supports, and when parents should hold back and allow the child to make decisions that may or may not be the best ones at the moment, but that may provide a developmental opportunity for their child to grow and learn. One of the interesting features about the ABCD framework is that the positive outcomes for children are not limited to just formal measures of health or academic achievement, but include the child's own set of feelings about themselves and life. That is, the goal of families to promote continued inter-generational well-being includes embedding within their children's values and goals that are positive and life-affirming to pass on through the families they will create when they grow up and choose life partners with whom to create new families.

Our own research has focused on improving the outcomes for children born into families enduring severe and chronic stressors and living in environments that have minimal or inadequate economic, social, and/or educational and health resources for families. We also have worked closely in developing interventions to support children born with biological risk conditions, such as prematurity and low birth-weight and with developmental disabling conditions. Collectively, the results of our longitudinal studies, usually conducted as randomized controlled trials that test new interventions and guided by the ABCD framework, demonstrate that high-quality and intensive interventions can transform children's developmental trajectories. For children living in extreme poverty, they can be transformed from having a high probability of showing delayed and sub-average cognitive and academic performance outcomes to being able to perform at least on national average – that is, comparable to children from relatively low-risk, well-resourced families and communities (Ramey, Sparling, and Ramey, 2012). Similarly, children with biological risks and medical conditions can exceed the usual expectations for them if they are provided with the types of experiences associated with what resilient families bring to bear (Ramey *et al.*, 2006). Even our research that helped to identify children living in poverty who became academic high-achievers showed that these families, despite highly challenging physical and social circumstances, found ways to implement the same types of effective parenting strategies (listed in the RPM3 model earlier) to support their children that are documented in the families of high-achieving children who have far greater financial and educational resources available to them (e.g., Robinson, Lanzi, Weinberg, Ramey, and Ramey, 2002). Together, these studies affirm how responsive children and families can be when provided with opportunities to increase resilience and to learn flexible coping skills.

Conclusion

It is clear to us that achieving family resilience is a highly desirable goal that results in benefits to each family member and to the family unit as a whole. Resilience requires learning and flexibility because it is a changing characteristic of a complex and developing system. We also believe that the evidence is clear that resilience can be learned and taught systematically by parents and programs. We find this conclusion to be encouraging and consistent with the expanding emphasis on positive psychology.

Critical Thinking Questions

1. The operational definition of "family" in this chapter differs from a legal definition or a structural definition. Think of two types of families that differ markedly from a conventional and legal definition. For each type of family, describe how the operational definition here is supportive of the child and helps to build resiliency. Contrast this with using only a legal definition of the family.

2. The summary of a scientific conference resulted in conclusions that endorse the RPM3 Model. Briefly define what RPM3 means. Next, describe how parents who do not live together but who are active in their child's life could fulfill the RPM3

"ideal." In your example assume the child attends school, has a learning disability, and is shy. Also assume the parent lives in the same city as the child.

3. Systems theory guides the ABCD Model. Look at Figure 12.1 and propose how a set of specific promotive factors could lead to a major change in the developmental trajectory for a child. How would these new promotive factors influence other areas of the child's life or the family's functioning? What outcomes might realistically be changed? How soon could this happen? Would these changes be enduring?

References

Bertalanffy, L. von (1968). *General systems theory*. New York: Braziller.

Black, K., and Lobo, M. (2008). A conceptual review of family resilience factors. *Journal of Family Nursing, 14*, 33–55. doi: 10.1177/1074840707312237.

Borkowski, J. G., Ramey, S. L., and Bristol-Powers, M. (eds) (2002). *Parenting and the child's world: Influences on academic, intellectual, and social-emotional development*. Mahwah, NJ: Lawrence Erlbaum Associates.

Harris, Judith R. (1998). *The nurture assumption: Why children turn out the way they do*. New York: Free Press.

Landesman, S. (1986). Toward a taxonomy of home environments. In N. R. Ellis and N. W. Bray (eds), *International review of research in mental retardation*, vol. 14 (pp. 259–289). New York: Academic Press.

Landesman, S., Jaccard, J., and Gunderson, V. (1991). The family environment: The combined influence of family behavior, goals, strategies, resources, and individual experiences. In M. Lewis and S. Feinman (eds), *Social influences and socialization in infancy* (pp. 63–96). New York: Plenum Press.

Luthar, S. S. (2006). Resilience in development: A synthesis of research across five decades. In D. Cicchetti and D. J. Cohen (eds), *Developmental psychopathology*, vol. 3, *Risk, disorder, and adaptation* (2nd edn) (pp. 739–795). Hoboken, NJ: John Wiley & Sons, Inc.

Masten, A. S., and Obradovic, J. (2006). Competence and resilience in development. *Annals of the New York Academy of Science, 1094*, 13–27. doi: 10.1196/annals.1376.003.

McCubbin, H. I., McCubbin, M. A., Thompson, A. I., Han, S. V., and Allen, C. T. (1997). Families under stress: What makes them resilient? *Journal of Family and Consumer Sciences, 89*, 2–11.

McCubbin, H. I., and Patterson, J. M. (1983). The family stress process: The Double ABCX Model of adjustment and adaptation. In H. I. McCubbin, M. Sussman, and J. M. Patterson (eds), *Social stress and the family: Advances in family stress theory and research* (pp. 7–38). New York: Haworth Press.

Miller, J. G. (1978). *Living systems*. New York: McGraw Hill.

Ramey, C. T., MacPhee, D., and Yeates, K. O. (1982). Preventing developmental retardation: A general systems model. In J. M. Joffee and L. A. Bond (eds), *Facilitating infant and early childhood development* (pp. 343–401). Hanover, NH: University Press of New England.

Ramey, C. T., and Ramey, S. L. (1998). Early intervention and early experience. *American Psychologist, 53*, 109–120.

Ramey, C. T., and Ramey, S. L. (1999). *Right from birth: Building your child's foundation for life*. New York: Goddard Press.

Ramey, C. T., Ramey, S. L., and Lanzi, R. G. (2006). Children's health and education. In I. Sigel and A. Renninger (eds), *The handbook of child psychology*, vol. 4 (pp. 864–892). Hoboken, NJ: John Wiley & Sons, Inc.

Ramey, C. T., Sparling, J. J., and Ramey, S. L. (2012). *Abecedarian: The ideas, the approach, and the findings*. Los Altos, CA: Sociometrics Corporation.

Ramey, S. L., and Ramey, C. T. (1992). Early educational intervention with disadvantaged children: To what effect? *Applied and Preventive Psychology, 1*, 131–140.

Ramey, S. L., and Ramey, C. T. (1999). *Going to school: How to help your child succeed*. New York: Goddard Press.

Ramey, S. L., and Ramey, C. T. (2012). Understanding the developmental influences of the family environment. In L. C. Mayes and M. Lewis (eds), *The environment of human development: A handbook of theory and measurement* (pp. 222–242). New York: Cambridge University Press.

Robinson, N. M., Lanzi, R. G., Weinberg, R. A., Ramey, S. L., and Ramey, C. T. (2002). Family factors associated with high academic competence in former Head Start children at third grade. *Gifted Child Quarterly, 46*, 281–294.

Seligman, M. E. P., Steen, T. A., Park, N., and Peterson, C. (2005). Positive psychology progress: Empirical validation of interventions. *American Psychologist, 60*, 410–421. doi:10.1037/0003-066X.60.5.410.

Wilson, E. O. (1979). *On human nature*. Cambridge, MA: Harvard University Press.

Wilson, E. O. (2012). *The social conquest of earth*. New York: Liveright Publishing Corporation.

13

Challenges and Changes
Stress and Resilience Among Military Families
Over the Life Course

Adrian Blow, Chris Marchiondo, and Lisa Gorman

Military families are as diverse as the organizations they serve. In order to thrive, service members and their families must successfully navigate the many challenges and changes associated with military life. For example, military families must navigate the unique stresses associated with active service during wars, deployment and then reintegration of a service member when he or she returns home, frequent relocations, and in some cases death and loss. Even during peacetime, training and tours of duty may require adjustments that tax the resources of family members. In response to the needs of military families, military-developed resilience programs that provide critical mental health and social supports for military families are becoming more common.

While the case example on the next page does not describe an actual family, it closely reflects many of the typical issues that military families endure as they undergo and adapt to numerous changes in their lives. Military-related events are occurring in the midst of other normal life experiences including births, sicknesses, and deaths. Developmental issues related to child and family changes also need to be absorbed into the many other transitions military families face. In this chapter we will summarize some of the major challenges these families deal with as they move through the life course and as well as some of the things that families do to overcome military-related changes and challenges. We will also describe two Department of Defense (DoD) programs developed to help service

members and their families develop resiliency in the face of these enormous challenges. While most of these families endure stress due to military life, we emphasize that most are extremely resilient, with a great deal of variability and difference among these families.

The State of the Military Family

The US Military is a large and diverse organization tasked with fulfilling many difficult missions in defense of the nation. There are more than 2.5 million uniformed members of the Armed Forces and more than 3.1 million military family members (Department of Defense, 2011). At any given moment, military

Family Problems: Stress, Risk, and Resilience, First Edition. Edited by Joyce A. Arditti.
© 2015 John Wiley & Sons, Inc. Published 2015 by John Wiley & Sons, Inc.

Case Example: Mike

Mike Brown is a 37-year-old soldier in the US Army. He enlisted after high school and requested training to become an infantrymen and paratrooper – the soldiers who engage in close-quarters battle with the enemy. After being assigned to the 82nd Airborne Division in North Carolina, Mike met a young college student named Diane. They fell in love, were married, and within a year had a son they named William. While Mike was on a training mission in Alaska, his wife tragically died in a car accident. With help from his parents, Mike raised William for six years as a single parent. He quickly rose through the ranks and was soon placed in charge of a 10-soldier squad. He met Jen (a first-grade school teacher) in 2001; they dated for little more than a year before Mike received orders to deploy to Iraq. He was gone for a year, but he and Jen stayed in contact (Mike's parents took care of William for the duration of the deployment). When he returned she helped him recuperate from a burn he received in battle. Within a year, they married; a year later Jen gave birth to a daughter, Jill, three weeks after William left on his second deployment to Afghanistan. After six months in Afghanistan, the Army granted him a two-week leave to return home, where he finally met his new daughter. Two years ago, Jen gave birth to another daughter, Stacy. Today, William is 17, Jill is 7, and Stacy is 2. The couple has moved three times since marrying, and Mike is preparing for his third combat deployment. Mike struggled with post-traumatic stress disorder after his second deployment, where his unit saw frequent combat with the enemy and five of his fellow soldiers died. He felt constant guilt for surviving when others close to him had died. Jen had difficulties coping with the changes in Mike, but a support group of spouses helped her tremendously. With the help of Jen and a therapist, Mike has recovered except for occasional nightmares. As he now prepares for his third deployment, he has learned that his mother has been diagnosed with cancer. Mike considered asking the Army for a reassignment to live near his parents, but his mother and father insisted he continue leading his soldiers. Mike reluctantly agreed. Jen reluctantly agreed as well and worries that she will be the one called on to be the caregiver for Mike's mom during the deployment. She also carries deep fears for his safety and for a return of his post-traumatic stress. She also has days when she is resentful due to his frequent absences. William is angry his father will miss his high school graduation, and his daughter Jill fears he will be killed like her friend's father.

personnel are serving in all fifty states, on all seven oceans, and in nearly every country on earth. Tens of thousands of service members and their family members live overseas in countries such as Germany, the UK, and Japan; thousands more live in Alaska and Hawaii. The average age of the force is fairly young, with 43% of service members 25 years old or younger, more than half are married, and 44% are parents (Department of Defense, 2011). Roughly half of military service members serve in a full-time, active-duty capacity, while the remainder serve generally part-time in the National Guard or Reserves.

Throughout the history of the nation, service members have repeatedly been asked to deploy for combat and peacekeeping missions. These dangerous and difficult assignments often entail a year or more away from family and friends; more than 1.2 million US soldiers, sailors, airmen, and marines have died in combat since the Revolutionary War (American war and military operations casualties, n.d.). Most recently, more than 2 million military service members have experienced repeated, dangerous, and typically year-long combat deployments as part of the Global War on Terror. More than 6,000 have died, and tens of thousands more have returned home with injuries, some severe. Improvements in battlefield armor and emergency medicine mean that many injuries that would have been fatal in previous wars are now survivable; thus thousands of wounded veterans and their families are struggling to overcome debilitating injuries such as the loss of sight, hearing, or limbs, and traumatic brain injuries (TBI) induced by roadside bomb explosions. In addition to these visible wounds, many service members return home with invisible mental health scars manifested in post-traumatic stress disorder (PTSD), anxiety, and depression (Gorman, Blow, Ames, and Reed, 2011; Hoge, Auchterlonie, and Milliken, 2006; Hoge *et al.*, 2004; Tanielian and Jaycox, 2008). These studies suggest that nearly 40% of returning Army veterans report heightened levels of anxiety, depression, or substance abuse, making the transition home after combat even more difficult. Suicide in the military is at an all-time high despite massive efforts to provide soldiers with mental health resources, to

reduce their deployments, and otherwise support them. War exacts a heavy toll on the military. (See Box 13.1.)

Perhaps not surprisingly, life for military family members can be challenging as well, even during peacetime. Active-duty service members, their spouses, and their children can expect to move frequently compared to civilian counterparts, sometimes more than once a year. With every move, families must say goodbye to friends, neighbors, and co-workers, pack their belongings, and move to another state or even country. Once there, they must begin the process of assimilation again, integrating into new schools, communities, military units, and other social institutions. Those serving on a part-time basis in the National Guard or Reserves are much less likely to move, and

---

Box 13.1   The Invisible Injuries of War and the Family

Family members face numerous tasks to make reintegration a successful experience after a deployment is over. This task is challenging for everyone involved, simply due to the fact that family members have changed during a deployment and need to find ways to get to know each other all over again. However, making this more complicated is that many of the changes observed in service members are due to what have become known as invisible wounds of war. These are non-physical wounds that affect the mental functioning of the individual and which may present the service member to the family (e.g., children, spouse) as someone very different from the individual who left home to go to war. Some of the signature wounds of recent wars are post-traumatic stress disorder (PTSD), depression, and traumatic brain injury (TBI). These wounds are acquired through exposure to traumatic events or to bomb blasts. Symptoms from these invisible wounds can affect all members of a family. For example, children may experience ambiguous loss due to the changes in the service member, or spouses could experience secondary traumatization due to witnessing the struggles of their loved one.

PTSD, Depression, TBI Symptoms

All three of these conditions have symptoms which could be confusing to family members. Symptoms of these disorders include flashbacks, avoidance, negative changes in beliefs and feelings, hyperarousal, changed mood, headaches, loss of coordination, feeling sad, and difficulty concentrating.

How to Help Children and Family Members

As with any disorder, finding ways to communicate with children about these conditions in developmentally appropriate ways is extremely important. Interventions should be tailored to each unique situation. There are many important resources available for family members. Examples of internet resources include:

1. http://www.extension.org/pages/63008/ effects-of-visible-and-invisible-parent-combat-injuries-on-children#.UvAAofldV8E;
2. http://www.brainlinemilitary.org/ content/2011/05/the-invisible-injuries-of-war-impact-on-military-families-and-children.html.

may instead serve in the same unit their entire careers. Like their active-duty counterparts, however, they and their families also face many unique challenges, particularly during combat deployments.

During such deployments, it would seem that most of the stress is felt by the deployed service member, since his or her life is often in danger while serving thousands of miles from home. Yet deployments bring an entirely new set of challenges to those at home as well. Military spouses who once shared responsibilities must quickly assume almost sole responsibility for parenting and the daily running of the household during deployments. All of the challenges of daily life – paying bills, getting children to school, going to work, preparing meals, maintaining homes and vehicles, paying taxes, dealing with difficult family members, and so on – must continue, except now only one adult is home to shoulder the burden. Moreover, the entire family must live with the possibility of the service member's death or severe injury, a reality made even more difficult by typically infrequent communication and limited information available during war. As with the case example above, it is not uncommon for spouses to give birth while their service member is deployed. Children continue to grow and change throughout lengthy deployments. These developmental changes are particularly noticeable during rapid development periods such as early childhood or adolescence. In addition, difficult family events such as illness continue to occur during these times, as is illustrated by the mother's illness in the case example. Service members in this case must cope with being far away during a time of need and may feel guilt and powerlessness as a result. The hardships of daily life for military families only increase during deployments.

The stress associated with military-related transitions is illustrated by studies that suggest that during a deployment, there is a higher risk for parenting distress and child maltreatment. Rentz et al. (2007), for example, conducted a time-series analysis of child maltreatment data in Texas from 2000 to 2003. They found that both departures for and returns from deployment imposed significant stress on the family (the parental unit in particular) and that rates of child maltreatment were twice as high in military families during years when soldiers were deployed in combat when compared to years of peace or minimal deployments.

Gibbs, Martin, Kupper, and Johnson (2007) replicated this finding in a separate study. Both of these studies concluded that among families of enlisted soldiers in the US Army with substantiated reports of child maltreatment, rates of maltreatment are greater when the soldiers are on combat-related deployments. These studies speak to the spike in stress surrounding a deployment and the need for increased support services for these families. From a family perspective, deployment increases vulnerability for children and stress for all members of the family.

Obviously, the sustained stress and uncertainty experienced by spouses at home can severely tax their ability to cope, and the service member is not the only family member at risk for mental health problems and substance abuse. Military spouses report strikingly high rates of anxiety disorders, depression, and even post-traumatic stress disorder (Gorman et al., 2011; Mansfield et al., 2010). Some struggle with what is known as secondary trauma, developing trauma symptoms after hearing of their service member's own life-threatening experiences in war. Not being present on the battlefield, it would seem, does not render family members immune to the ill effects of war. In our case example, Jen was under immense stress during the deployments, particularly from changes stemming from the recent birth of her child, becoming a stepmother, and caregiving for her mother-in-law, to name just a few, while at the same time holding down her own job as a school teacher.

Children, too, struggle to cope with a deployed parent. Younger children may struggle to understand the significance of the event and the risks involved. Older children may wrestle with considerable fears and worries, while others may resent the deployed parent out of the belief that he or she volunteered to leave the family for a year. From an attachment perspective, children may become anxious, avoidant, or insecure, due to frequent comings and goings of one parent, especially if these lead to increased stress in the other parent. In other cases, children may assume too much responsibility and become parentified, while others may challenge the authority of the parent at home – or the authority of the service member when he/she returns. These scenarios are even more complicated if there is a divorced family or stepfamily situation, or, as in the case study, a death of a parent, meaning that a stepparent or grandparent would need to step in during the deployment. Acting-out behaviors, school delinquency, falling grades, isolation, and depression are all known risk factors for children of deployed parents (Chandra, Martin, Hawkins, and Richardson, 2010; Gorman, Fitzgerald, and Blow, 2010).

Unfortunately, such difficulties do not end as soon as the service member returns from war. Coming home after combat – a process known as redeployment and reintegration – might initially seem to be a positive event for families. After a year away from home the service member's return is often a joyous, occasion – at least initially. For many families, though, significant challenges and difficulties may arise that they must carefully navigate. Whether active-duty or reserves, virtually every family will struggle to successfully negotiate the hurdles of reintegration. When the service member returns, he or she must reintegrate into a family that has grown and changed over the course of a year. New infant children may greet them at their arrival; divorce papers may await others; children may have blossomed into teenagers with new responsibilities and roles in the home; spouses may have become more independent; still others may be grieving the deaths of fellow soldiers or family members. For many families, the challenge of accommodating the return of an adult into the household may mean many changes. Whereas the spouse at home assumed most of the responsibilities, he or she will now need to relinquish some of that control to balance the partnership again. This is not a simple task and usually means that couples need to create time to negotiate and renegotiate roles, a painful process. In addition, the returning service member must work to find his or her place in a family that functioned and changed for a year during the deployment. He/she may feel left out or unwanted during this process, and children may reject the service member's attempts to become a part of family life again. Existing problems in the family may flare up, or new problems may arise. Military leaders often tell their personnel to expect a "honeymoon period" of a few weeks after redeployment, but to also know that the honeymoon cannot last indefinitely. In reality, this period of adjustment can take many months and in the case of multiple deployments can lead to years of disruption in family life.

Outside of the home, new problems and challenges can face both the service member and his or her family. This can be particularly true for those serving part-time in the National Guard or Reserves, whose experiences when returning home are often markedly different from those of their active-duty counterparts. When working with military families, it is essential to know whether the service member served on active or reserve duty, and to understand their unique experiences. Members of the active-duty military and their families generally live on large installations, sometimes surrounded by as many as 40,000 other service members. Within these secure military communities, service members and families have access to an extensive array of services including military hospitals, churches, schools, counseling services, support groups, shopping malls, and many other family support services. For most active-duty military and their families, it is comforting to live so close to others who have endured the same hardships. While deployed, these service men and women know that their families have access to strong social-support networks and services; when they redeploy after war, service members receive the same benefits of a tightly knit military community, both on duty and off, in addition to full-time work and competitive pay. While deployments are challenging for everyone involved, the members of the US military's active-duty forces have many built-in support systems to help them cope and even thrive in tough times.

Families and members of the National Guard and Reserve forces, however, often face very different experiences during and after war. They and their families generally do not live on military installations, and their largely civilian communities may not have any other military families living in them (especially in rural areas). These isolated families do not always have easy access to military support services, and often must travel long distances to take advantage of them. For example, travel to a Veterans (VA) facility may be several hours for those living in remote areas. Civilian support services (for example, mental health counselors, doctors, and schools) are often unfamiliar with the unique challenges and needs of military families, and they might not be able to tailor their services for the military. Neighbors may not even realize the service member has deployed. Even if they do know, they often have a very poor understanding of the many challenges the parent at home is facing, or the stress such deployments create for children. Many of these families report a strong sense of isolation and lack of understanding in their communities. Their burdens can be significantly greater than those placed on active-duty families.

Adding still more stress, service men and women in the Guard and Reserves do not return to full-time employment with the military like their active-duty counterparts. Instead, many struggle to find employment in tough economic times. Tough economic times have been present for many of the wars since 2001. Guard and Reserve members also lack the ready support of a military organization of their peers, since they typically meet for only two days a month to train. These Veterans often report that some of the hardest times occur when they have returned home and are struggling to come to terms with the often traumatic, always different experiences they endured overseas. Like their active-duty counterparts, many in the National Guard and Reserves have witnessed friends and members of their units being killed; some are haunted by the guilt of surviving when others died. Many struggle to find meaning in daily life after the intensely emotional experiences of war. In the moments when they most need understanding peers, they find themselves surrounded by neighbors, co-workers, and even family members who may understand very little about their needs and experiences. This can indeed be an extraordinarily difficult transition.

Despite the many challenges facing the military family during both peace and war, what remains clear is that most successfully navigate the turmoil, uncertainty, and difficulties they face. While the most recent deployments have lasted since 2001, military life has historically been challenging, even in peacetime. Even when there are no wars, military life always involves a great deal of training events, tours of duty in far-off places, and relocations.

Resiliency

In recent years, the military has increasingly adopted a resiliency focus as they grapple with how to help service members and their families successfully endure something as stressful as a year-long deployment to war. In fact, *resiliency* has become one of the mostly widely touted terms used to describe military life in recent years and entire programs now exist that focus on enhancing resiliency in military families. The goal of such resiliency programs is to assist soldiers and their families in overcoming hardships related to deployment so that they emerge from the situation stronger than before. One definition describes family resiliency as "the capacity of a dynamic system to withstand or recover from significant challenges that threaten its stability, viability, or development" (Masten, 2011, p. 494). In this regard, resilient families in the military utilize processes that allow them to withstand and recover from the stress of combat deployment. Key questions remain as to what exactly it is within resilient families that allows them to adapt well to multiple transitions. These processes include things like family communication, marital/relational strength, parenting style, and a coherent guiding family belief system along with fewer risk factors, including mental health difficulties, employment, and stress pile-up (Blow *et al.*, 2013; Saltzman *et al.*, 2011).

A family's ability to manage and cope with stress varies between and within families. It should also be noted that there is only a certain amount of stress that any one family can effectively endure. Unfortunately, some families face an accumulation of devastating stressors and family crises during deployments that make successful reintegration extremely difficult. External factors can also play havoc with families. For example, challenges associated with deployment and reintegration can be exacerbated by changes in the individual, family, and work contexts that naturally occur during the absence of the deployed service member. Most deployments last a lengthy period of time, typically 12 months in the war zone. This usually includes additional time spent in extensive trainings that prepare individuals to be successful on the deployment; such trainings, however, equate to more time away from home. During this separation, families experience normal developmental challenges, and some families will also experience life-changing events unrelated to deployment (e.g., a diagnosis of a life-threatening illness or loss of a significant loved one). In addition to the strains of the deployment experience, changes in the service member and in his or her family context during the deployment can place a strain on marriages and other relationships. Families adapt to this stress in different ways; some do not do well and may face negative outcomes such as divorce; while others go through a period of intense difficulty, but are able to recover and turn out better than before; still others negotiate this experience with little difficulty, and may report positive aspects of deployment and even personal growth. Much of military family research to date has emphasized the risk factors and negative outcomes associated with military deployments, such as mental health difficulties and combat-related challenges; however, this focus has often overlooked the majority of families who do quite well and who experience growth and resilience. A focus on both *risk* and *resilience* within and between families highlights factors that contribute to resilient outcomes in family members facing stressful events associated with deployment, separation, family, or community life.

Adaptability: Developmental Considerations across the Life Course

Adaptability is another important concept for military families. The major challenges of military life occur in the midst of normal developmental processes as well as at the same time as other unexpected life difficulties, as described above. For the family described in the case example, two deployments occurred during a time of rapid development for the two young children, who both underwent rapid changes while Mike was away fighting war. While different from those of his siblings, the changes experienced by William (the teenage son) were also vast during Mike's time fighting wars. These events occurred during other very stressful events including child births, employment, blended family issues, and unresolved issues that came up for William during the deployments related to the loss of his biological mother.

Military children

Children from military households are unique in that they experience many changes in household composition as well as community support and connection during deployment and military life transitions. Fortunately, there are entire organizations focused on helping these children, including the national Military Child Education Coalition (MCEC; http://www.militarychild.org/); military-focused projects initiated by ZERO TO THREE (http://www.zerotothree.org/), and Operation Military Kids (http://www.operationmilitarykids.org/public/home.aspx), to name just a few. Virtually all of these military children face the normal issues of childhood while often finding themselves moving to new communities with the challenge of making new friends and connections. They are in school systems where their connection to the military may go unnoticed, and they must deal with changes in family structure that are often quite stressful. Children of active-duty service members who live near or on military installations have different school experience from children of the National Guard (i.e., they go to school with other military children), but they endure more frequent moves than their National Guard counterparts (who may not even consider themselves military).

Military spouses

Military spouses also face unique issues. Most of these spouses are adept at juggling many different tasks at the same time, and many actually benefit from the personal growth that may result from a spouse's deployment. However, they also are faced with the consideration of how to maintain their own careers and personal interests as these dreams are continually upended due to the demands of military life. Changes in a military spouse can have deep effects on family life, especially during reintegration, and in some cases spouses may experience resentment that makes reconnection with the service member more difficult. In addition, factors may accumulate to make reconnection in the couple relationship more difficult post-deployment. Depression in both soldier and spouse post-deployment makes reconnection in the relationship difficult. Studies by the authors of this chapter suggest that depression after deployments is the most difficult hurdle to overcome as spouses reconnect post-deployment (Blow *et al.*, 2013; Gorman, 2009).

Aging families

Military life might also affect aging families in unique ways. Parents preparing for retirement may have been called upon to become caretakers for children during a deployment or called upon to devote a great deal of time and energy to ensuring a deployment goes well. These parents and grandparents are invaluable sources of support and assistance during a deployment, and families who have good relationships with these parents, and close proximity, are exceptionally lucky. Another challenge that aging families may face is related to aging veterans. These individuals must often face physical and mental health issues related to their own deployments in other wars going back to World War II, Korea, and Vietnam. These issues may all be a factor in successful aging experiences. Healthcare may be a factor, as these veterans depend on the US Department of Veterans Affairs for support. Moreover, end-of-life issues may bring up unresolved issues for both these veterans and their families.

Family configuration

Different types of family configuration can also lead to unique stress during a deployment. For example, single-parent households are faced with the choice of what to do with their children during the deployment and whether their career is worth the sacrifice of so much time away from home. While the military requires single parents to develop family care plans well in advance of deployments, these plans in and of themselves can be very difficult to create and enact. This is particularly difficult for women. Note, 5.3% of active-duty parents are single parents and this number is higher in the guard and reserves (9.4%; Department of Defense, 2011). Parents, siblings, and other relatives often step in to help soldiers in these situations. These situations grow increasingly complex and difficult when situations occur that involve divorce, ex-spouses, blended families, and changing households. For example, an ex-spouse might be angry and interfering if his or her children are raised by a step-parent while their father or mother is away on deployment. A couple going through a divorce during or after a deployment creates unusual disruptions for children (in addition to the deployment-related disruptions), and difficult

challenges for all involved. Finally, with the abolition of the ban on homosexuals in the military, increasing numbers of same-sex couples are a part of the military. These couples and their children may face additional layers of acceptance and stigma related to integrating well into military life. It is still as yet unclear how these families will integrate into the military as a whole, but it is likely that these families will face similar challenges to those faced by these families living in mainstream society, only with the added challenges of military life described above.

Social support

One of the most widely touted protective factors for all types of life difficulties is the presence of an effective system of social support. This is particularly important for military families, who need help and connection as they endure many changes and transitions. Unfortunately, the process of developing such networks of support is made more complex by the frequent moves active-duty military families experience. Post-deployment support is particularly important for successful reintegration. As soldiers return to normal civilian life, they are no longer surrounded by others who share similar lived experiences (i.e., their combat unit). In addition, family stress can create a negative environment, which can diminish support from within the family. Further, family roles often necessitate renegotiation when the service member's deployment ends – when he or she returns home, family life is disrupted; for example, spouses who are faced with making decisions without a partner must adapt to shared decision-making when the service member returns. This process may leave one or both partners feeling isolated and misunderstood.

If the service member witnessed a traumatic event during a deployment, social support may be even more important upon redeployment. Post-traumatic stress disorder (PTSD), for example, is a relatively common mental health concern among returning service members, and has been studied extensively. Social support following a traumatic event influences the emergence and development of PTSD symptoms (Guay, Billette, and Marchand, 2006). In one meta-analysis involving 77 studies, the absence of effective social support was found to be the strongest predictor of PTSD, with an effect size of 0.40 (Brewin, Andrews, and Valentine, 2000). A separate meta-analysis, involving 68 studies, found low social support to be among the strongest predictive factors of PTSD (Ozer, Best, Lipsey, and Weiss, 2003). In their review of PTSD studies, Guay *et al.* (2006) conclude that social support is related to the development and maintenance of PTSD as well as to the severity of PTSD symptoms. Several studies of social support have focused on military veterans exclusively. In one study (Barrett and Mizes, 1988), veterans who received high levels of social support after their return home from deployment experienced fewer PTSD symptoms. Solomon, Waysman, and Mikulincer (1990) studied 284 Israeli soldiers and concluded that poor family relations and lacking support from society was positively correlated with loneliness, which influenced mental health outcomes including PTSD.

It is not only the presence of social support that is important, but also the quality of relationships (Guay *et al.*, 2006). Negative social support can intensify the development of PTSD. Lepore and Greenberg (2002) show that inadequate support from significant people hinders the individual's ability to gain control over negative emotions. In other words, negative interactions with significant individuals can serve to exacerbate the development and maintenance of PTSD (Guay *et al.*, 2006). This is an important consideration for returning veterans, whose spouses/significant others are often experiencing their own levels of distress.

Ineffective help for spouses of service members with PTSD could lead to higher levels of their own personal distress. Some studies show, for example, that caregiver burden is a valid concern for those supporting soldiers diagnosed with PTSD. Calhoun, Beckham, and Bosworth (2002) studied caregiver burden in a sample of PTSD diagnosed Vietnam veterans. Partners of veterans (n = 51) diagnosed with PTSD experienced more caregiver burden and had poorer psychological adjustment than did partners of veterans without PTSD (n = 20). In addition, Dekel, Goldblatt, Keidar, Solomon, and Polliack (2005) conducted qualitative interviews of nine wives of PTSD-diagnosed veterans. Their findings reveal how the lives of these women largely revolved around their husbands' illness. The women in this study faced a constant struggle around maintaining their independence. When caregivers

are distressed and burdened, not only may the relationship with the PTSD soldier become strained, but other members of the family may also suffer. These studies all suggest that social support including support from both family and community are protective and can ease the adjustment of soldiers and affect everyone in the family.

Military-Developed Programs to Increase Resiliency in Service Members and Families

Out of the growing recognition of the critical importance of resiliency both in service members and their families, several programs designed to enhance resiliency have emerged within the Department of Defense. We will briefly highlight two such programs: the Army's Comprehensive Soldier and Family Fitness (CSF2) program, and the Navy's Families OverComing Under Stress (FOCUS) program. Both programs were designed specifically to help service members and families cope with and even thrive during the sometimes difficult experiences of military life. Importantly, both programs were developed in partnership with university researchers, and incorporate cutting-edge research on topics such as mental health, family dynamics, and positive psychology.

The Army's Comprehensive Soldier and Family Fitness program (CSF2)

This program began as an initiative to increase resiliency among soldiers. Developed through a partnership with university researchers committed to the ideas of strength-oriented, "positive psychology" the program focuses on helping soldiers develop five facets of well-being believed to be essential to mental health under times of stress: social, emotional, familial, spiritual, and physical fitness. Later, the program was expanded to include family members as well. (For an in-depth review, see http://csf2.army.mil/.)

The first of the five components is social fitness. Humans are highly social beings, and it has long been recognized that social support is often critical for sustaining mental health in difficult times. The research cited above on the benefits of social support for veterans with PTSD lends further support to this idea. By having strong social bonds and healthy relationships with others, soldiers – as is the case with all people – can receive support and have a "shoulder to lean on" in hard times, thus avoiding the need to cope with difficulties alone. Obviously the same is true for family members at home, who also benefit from a strong social network, both during deployments and after.

The second component of CSF2 is emotional strength. Here the emphasis is on a positive and optimistic outlook on life, even in the face of difficulties. As the research on depression and other mental illnesses has shown, those with a tendency to focus on the bad events and negative aspects of life are significantly more prone to negative mental health outcomes. In addition, the CSF2 program encourages soldiers and family members to develop and use self-control, stamina, and good character (Comprehensive Soldier and Family Fitness (CSF2), n.d.). Having an optimistic outlook or recommending the use of self-control and endurance does not mean or imply that one should ignore hard events or the realities of stressful times; rather the goal is to empower soldiers and their families to face life's challenges in ways that are healthy and productive, particularly by making choices and acting in ways that reflect one's strengths and capabilities.

It is hoped that this chapter has made it clear that families are critically important social units, and perhaps never more so than during the hard times of war. Thus, CSF2 considers families to be a key facet to soldier resiliency. Healthy families built around strong, loving, safe relationships provide their members with a "secure base" upon which they can rely in hard times.

Spiritual fitness is another component of the CSF2 program. The Army has long recognized the importance of having soldiers who possess strong values, a sense of purpose in life, and a life vision. Historically, the Army Chaplains have been responsible for helping interested soldiers find such a sense of purpose or meaning in life. That is still the case today, and CSF2 simply places a greater, Army-wide emphasis on the importance of developing one's spiritual side. The presence of a purpose or meaning for one's life has been shown through research to increase resiliency and the ability to cope with adversity. By contrast, the absence of meaning in one's life strongly correlates to the presence of depression, anxiety, and other negative social and emotional outcomes (Steger, Frazier, Oishi, and Kaler, 2006). In CSF2, the broader concept of spirituality is the basis of a person's character, and is a combination of that person's philosophical, psychological, personal, and religious beliefs. The spiritual component of CSF2 does not advocate for the adoption of any particular religious view or even for a religious orientation in general; rather each individual soldier or family member should decide what that means to him or her.

Finally, physical fitness has obvious and historical importance for soldiers in the Army. In fact, the first duty of the day for most soldiers is to participate in organized physical fitness training with the members of his or her unit. Soldiers are tested every six months to assess their physical readiness. Soldiers must respond to many vigorous demands both in combat and peacetime, and being physically fit is simply essential. CSF2, however, expands upon this idea by also encouraging soldiers to think in terms of their body's well-being; exercise, nutrition, an active lifestyle, and even sleep are important considerations for soldiers. Family members, too, are encouraged to adopt healthy, active lifestyles. Such lifestyles are associated with better mental and physical health, and improve well-being.

Soldiers and family members can receive training in CSF2 both online (csf2.army.mil/training.html) and in person. The Army has developed training programs for selected soldiers, civilians, and military spouses to serve as Master Resilience Trainers (MRT). MRTs receive a 10-day, intensive training course that prepares them to train many others in the principles of CSF2. There are other facets to the CSF2 program, including a Performance Enhancement program and higher-level trainings. In combination, the five facets of CSF2 – social, emotional, familial, spiritual, and physical fitness – are intended to help soldiers and their families enhance their own resources and strengths in order to maintain resiliency and health during hard times.

The Navy's FOCUS program: Family resiliency training

The US Navy has developed and instituted a similar resiliency-oriented program, also developed in conjunction with university researchers (Saltzman et al., 2011).

Known as FOCUS, short for Families OverComing Under Stress, this program places emphasis on resiliency in children and families. (For more about this program go to http://www.ncbi.nlm.nih.gov/pmc/articles/PMC3162635/.) Specifically, the goals of the program are to enhance resiliency, which the Navy defines as "the ability to cope with, adapt to, and overcome challenges" (FOCUS: What is resiliency?, n.d.). Researchers designed FOCUS so that trainers could instruct families in the use of practical skills to help them navigate the many challenges of deployments. These skills include understanding emotional reactions, clear communication, effective problem solving, and goal setting and achievement (FOCUS: What is resiliency?, n.d.).

The skill-based design of FOCUS seeks to provide service members, spouses, and even children with specific, time-tested skills to help them remain resilient during deployments. Service members learn a variety of skills: effective ways to talk with children about deployments; maintainence of social and emotional connections with children and spouses during deployments; methods of re-establishing effective family routines or developing new routines when needed; ways to reconnect with spouses and children upon redeployment; and methods of managing combat stress and painful reminders of deployment. It is critically important for overall well-being for families to establish and maintain routines that define family life in the midst of change. These may be related to values or faith traditons of a family. These can include things like mealtimes, family vacations, or special activities invloving parents and children. Families that do better seem to be more adept in switching out roles and routines.

Spouses can also receive training in a wide variety of practical skills, including: caretaking for children and themselves during long deployments; effective communication strategies for negotiating the many changes that will occur within the family during deployments; effective means of communicating with young children, particularly as it relates to the emotionally challenging topics of safety, both for their parents and themselves; child behavior management both at home and in school; how to help their children remain connected to the deployed service member; how to provide effective support while coping with the difficulties that may arise from combat stress

reactions in their military spouse; and how to know when someone in the family might need additional, outside support.

Children are vital members of the family and are certainly prone to feeling stress during long deployments. The Navy deliberately sought to develop a program that includes an emphasis on helping children cope with something that their civilian peers may never have to face. Skills taught include: developing effective communication skills to enable children to let parents know that they are struggling; how to communicate with parents about some of the many changes that are likely to occur during deployments; means of staying connected to the parent at home as well as the deployed service member and how to share important life events such as birthdays; preparing children for the inevitable changes that will occur when a deployed parent returns; and teaching children how to effectively communicate with their friends so that peers better understand the challenges they face. As with any major life event, it is important that families are able to communicate about their experiences. Families need to be able to communicate about what is bothering them (e.g., fears) and what is happening to them (e.g., role transitions). Families do well when they do not have a combative communication style and when they are able to be rely more on planning about how events will unfold. They work hard at figuring out how to make deployments and reintegrations work.

As with the Army's CSF2 program, the Navy has a program to educate what are known as "resiliency trainers" at many Navy installations around the globe. In addition, the program's website (www.focusproject.org) has helpful information and links for family members and professionals.

Summary

Military families must be resilient and they very often are. They face more stress than the population as a whole, especially in times of war. These families learn to adapt with the help of their communities, as well as formal and informal support services. There are cases where the stress may simply be too much (as in any family), where these families might need crisis intervention or added therapeutic help. This is no different from families in the general population. The recent wars have also led to a burgeoning literature on family resiliency and this literature will be instructive in family resiliency processes as a whole.

Critical Thinking Questions

Consider the case example at the beginning of the chapter in light of the following questions:

1. What kinds of supports would help the deployment processes work out well for this particular family?

2. How might the loss of his mother at a young age and the deployment to war affect the development of William?

3. How might deployment affect the involvement of the extended family in the life of a child like William? In your discussion, consider the extended family of William's deceased mother as well.

4. Given the challenge of deployment for Mike and Jen, how might they go about reconnecting after the deployment is over?

5. Many normal family processes occur during Mike's deployments. Discuss how these normal events exacerbate distress in the family.

References

Allen, E. S., Rhoades, G. K., Stanley, S. M., and Markman, H. J. (2010). Hitting home: Relationships between recent deployment, posttraumatic stress symptoms, and marital functioning for army couples. *Journal of Family Psychology, 24,* 280–288.

American war and military operations casualties: Lists and statistics. (n.d.). Retrieved May 30, 2014 from http://www.history.navy.mil/library/online/american%20war%20casualty.htm#t1.

Barrett, T. W., and Mizes, J. S. (1988). Combat level and social support in the development of posttraumatic stress disorder in Vietnam veterans. *Behavior Modification, 12,* 100–115.

Blow, A. J., Gorman, L., Ganoczy, D., Kees, M., Kashy, D. A., Valenstein, M., ... and Chermack, S. (2013). Hazardous drinking and family functioning in National Guard Veterans and spouses postdeployment. *Journal of Family Psychology, 27,* 303–313.

Brewin, C. R., Andrews, B., and Valentine, J. D. (2000). Meta-analysis of risk factors for post-traumatic stress disorder in trauma exposed adults. *Journal of Consulting and Clinical Psychology, 68,* 748–766.

Calhoun, P. S., Beckham, J. C., and Bosworth, H. B. (2002). Caregiver burden and psychological distress in partners of veterans with chronic posttraumatic stress disorder. *Journal of Traumatic Stress, 15,* 205–212.

Castaneda, L., Harrell, M., Varda, D., Hall, K., Beckett, M., and Stern, S. (2008). *Deployment experiences of guard and reserve families.* Santa Monica, CA: RAND Corporation.

Chandra, A., Martin, L. T., Hawkins, S. A., and Richardson, A. (2010). The impact of parental deployment on child social and emotional functioning: Perspectives of school staff. *Journal of Adolescent Health, 46,* 218–223.

Comprehensive Soldier and Family Fitness (CSF2). (n.d.). Retrieved May 30, 2014 from http://csf2.army.mil/fivedimensions.html.

Dekel, R., Goldblatt, H., Keidar, M., Solomon, Z., and Polliack, M. (2005). Being a wife of a veteran with posttraumatic stress disorder. *Family Relations, 54,* 24–36.

Department of Defense. (2011). 2011 Demographics: Profile of the military community. Retrieved May 30, 2014 from http://www.militaryonesource.mil/footer?content_id=267470.

FOCUS: What is resiliency? (n.d.) Retrieved May 30, 2014 from http://www.focusproject.org/how-it-works/resiliency-training.

Gewirtz, A., Erbes, C., Polusny, M., Forgatch, M., and DeGarmo, D. (2011). Helping military families through the deployment process: Strategies to support parenting. *Professional Psychology, Research and Practice, 42,* 56–62. doi: 10.1037/a0022345.

Gibbs, D. A., Martin, S. L., Kupper, L. L., and Johnson, R. E. (2007). Child maltreatment in enlisted soldiers' families during combat-related deployments. *Journal of the American Medical Association, 298,* 528–535.

Gorman, L. (2009). Dyadic factors associated with postdeployment adjustment for National Guard couples. Unpublished Ph.D. dissertation, Michigan State University.

Gorman, L., Blow, A. J., Ames, B., and Reed, P. (2011). National Guard families after combat: Mental health, use of mental health services, and perceived treatment barriers. *Psychiatric Services, 62*(1), 28–34.

Gorman, L., Fitzgerald, H., and Blow, A. J. (2010). Parental combat injury and early child development: A conceptual model for differentiating effects of visible and invisible injuries. *Psychiatric Quarterly, 81,* 1–21.

Guay, S., Billette,V., and Marchand, A. (2006). Exploring the links between posttraumatic stress disorder and social support: Processes and potential research avenues. *Journal of Traumatic Stress, 19*, 327–338.

Hoge, C. W., Auchterlonie, J. L., and Milliken, C. S. (2006). Mental health problems, use of mental health services, and attrition from military service after returning from deployment to Iraq or Afghanistan. *Journal of the American Medical Association, 296*(9), 1023–1032.

Hoge, C. W., Castro, C. A., Messer, S. C., McGurk, D., Cotting, D. I., and Koffman, R. L. (2004). Combat duty in Iraq and Afghanistan, mental health problems and barriers to care. *New England Journal of Medicine, 351*(1), 13–22.

Karney, B. R., and Crown, J. S. (2007). *Families under stress: An assessment of data, theory, and research on marriage and divorce in the military.* Santa Monica, CA: RAND Corporation.

Lepore, S. J., and Greenberg, M. A. (2002). Mending broken hearts: Effects of expressive writing on mood, cognitive processing, social adjustment, and mental health following a relationship breakup. *Psychology and Health, 17*, 547–560.

MacDermid Wadsworth, S. M. (2010). Family risk and resilience in the context of war and terrorism. *Journal of Marriage and Family, 72*, 537–556.

Mansfield, A., Kaufman, J., Marshall, S., Gaynes, B., Morrissey, J., and Engel, C. (2010). Deployment and the use of mental health services among U.S. Army wives. *New England Journal of Medicine, 362*, 101–109.

Masten, A. S. (2011). Resilience in children threatened by extreme adversity: Frameworks for research, practice, and translational synergy. *Development and Psychopathology, 23*, 493–506.

Nelson Goff, B. S., Crow, J. R., Reisbig, A. M. J., and Hamilton, S. (2007). The impact of individual trauma symptoms of deployed soldiers on relationship satisfaction. *Journal of Family Psychology, 21*, 344–353.

Newby, J., McCarroll, J., Ursano, R., Fan, Z., Shigemura, J., and Tucker-Harris,Y. (2005). Positive and negative consequences of a military deployment. *Military Medicine, 170*(10), 815–819.

Ozer, E. J., Best, S. R., Lipsey, T. L., and Weiss, D. S. (2003). Predictors of posttraumatic stress disorder and symptoms in adults: A meta-analysis. *Psychological Bulletin, 129*, 52–73.

Rentz, E. D., Marshall, S. W., Loomis, D., Casteel, C., Martin, S. L., and Gibbs, D. A. (2007). Effects of deployment on the occurrence of child maltreatment in military and nonmilitary families. *American Journal of Epidemiology, 165*, 1199–1206.

Riggs, D. S., Byrne, C. A., Weathers, F. W., and Litz, B. T. (1998). The quality of the intimate relationships of male Vietnam veterans: Problems associated with posttraumatic stress disorder. *Journal of Traumatic Stress, 11*, 87–101.

Saltzman, W. R., Lester, P., Beardslee, W. R., Layne, C. M., Woodward, K., and Nash, W. P. (2011). Mechanisms of risk and resilience in military families: Theoretical and empirical basis of a family-focused resilience enhancement program. *Clinical Child and Family Psychology Review, 14*, 213–230.

Solomon, Z., Waysman, M., and Mikulincer, M. (1990). Family functioning, perceived social support, and combat-related psychopathology: The moderating role of loneliness. *Journal of Social and Clinical Psychology, 9*, 456–472.

Steger, M. F., Frazier, P., Oishi, S., and Kaler, M. (2006). The meaning in life questionnaire: Assessing the presence of and search for meaning in life. *Journal of Counseling Psychology, 53*, 80–93.

Tanielian, T., and Jaycox, L. H. (2008). *Invisible wounds of war: Psychological and cognitive injuries, their consequences, and services to assist recovery.* Santa Monica, CA: Rand Monographs.

14

Intimate Partner Violence

Jennifer L. Hardesty and Kimberly A. Crossman

Intimate partner violence (IPV) is one of the most widespread and preventable family problems of our time. While women are more often victims of IPV, it is a problem with many nuances that profoundly affects both genders and cuts across socioeconomic status and family structures. In Chapter 14, Hardesty and Crossman explain the different types of IPV and explore risk factors that contribute to its occurrence. We see that different social locations can contribute to IPV and that the most disadvantaged women are the most likely to be victimized. IPV is a family challenge over the life course because it affects the whole family and has intergenerational implications. Children's exposure to IPV has negative effects that extend into their own adulthood.

Approximately one in four women experience physical or sexual violence by an intimate partner (IPV) in their lifetime (Black *et al.*, 2011). As the scenarios in the case example on page 214 illustrate, the type and context of these acts can vary greatly. When most people think about IPV they envision the scenario that describes Toni's relationship. Indeed, this is what we tend to see in movies (e.g., *Revolutionary Road*, *Enough*) and music videos (e.g., Eminem's *Love the Way You Lie*) and what typically receives the most attention in the news media. These are the situations that often end with the woman escaping the relationship after multiple attempts to leave or, in some cases, end in her death at the hands of her abusive partner. This is the typical face of IPV and is what Johnson (2008) refers to as

intimate terrorism or coercive controlling violence. This type of IPV often involves frequent and severe physical and/or sexual violence, but its distinguishing characteristic is that the violence occurs in a context of intensive efforts to control or dominate many aspects of the partner's life (e.g., employment, contact with friends and family).

Perhaps surprisingly, intimate terrorism, although much more visible and recognizable to us, appears to be less common than the type illustrated by Shari and Bren's story in the second case scenario (p. 214), which Johnson refers to as *situational couple violence* (2008). In the latter, a violent act happens in the context of a specific argument, but there is no motive to control or dominate one's partner beyond perhaps winning the

Family Problems: Stress, Risk, and Resilience, First Edition. Edited by Joyce A. Arditti.
© 2015 John Wiley & Sons, Inc. Published 2015 by John Wiley & Sons, Inc.

Case Example: Toni and Shari

Toni is a 40-year-old mother of one teenage son. She has been married to William, 44 years old, for almost 15 years. In hindsight, Toni can see that William showed signs of controlling her early on. For example, he insisted that they have a child soon after marriage and that she quit the job she loved to stay home with their son. It wasn't until her son was a toddler that the physical violence began. It started with pushing and shoving, but quickly escalated. Over the last 10 years, Toni has suffered repeated beatings and sexual violence at the hands of her husband. She is afraid he may someday kill her, but leaving feels impossible. She has no money, no job skills, and few friends. Plus, William has threatened that she'll never see her son again if she leaves.

Shari is a 28-year-old mother of two young children. She was never married to her children's 30-year-old father, Bren, but they have parented together since their children were born. For the most part, Shari and Bren get along well. They each describe the other as a loving and good parent. A few years ago, they encountered a rough patch in their relationship when Bren lost his job and was unable to contribute financially. On two occasions, their arguments became so heated that Bren pushed Shari. The second time it happened, Shari pushed and hit Bren back. They both expressed remorse and agreed to ground rules to take a time-out when arguments became too heated. Shari and Bren describe those incidents as a low point in their history that does not define their relationship as a whole, which they describe as mutually satisfying.

current argument. Instead, episodes of violence are more a reflection of poor conflict-management skills and hostility than indicative of an overall control dynamic in the relationship. We hear less about situational couple violence or, when we do, we assume it must be similar to the classic intimate terrorism with which we are most familiar. Importantly, both of the scenarios above involve violence that negatively affects relationships and families. Recognizing that IPV experiences differ, however, helps us avoid "one size fits all" approaches in our research, practice, and policy efforts.

In this chapter, we identify risk and protective factors associated with experiencing IPV and discuss the process of achieving resilient outcomes despite IPV. A feminist framework provides us with a critical lens for considering how larger social structures create or uphold power differences, gender inequalities, and patriarchal attitudes towards women that shape the risk and protective factors as well as the potential for resilient outcomes. Finally, to the extent possible, we discuss current knowledge with respect to different types of IPV to encourage critical thinking about the varied needs of families affected by violence.

Extent and Nature of Intimate Partner Violence

The US Department of Health and Human Services (2010) has identified IPV as one of the most significant and preventable public health problems in the United States. In 2010, approximately 4.7 million women experienced physical violence and approximately 686,000 women experienced sexual violence by an intimate partner (Black *et al.*, 2011). In 2009, 1,081 women were murdered by husbands or boyfriends (Federal Bureau of Investigation, 2010). IPV results in over 200 million injuries among women each year (National Center for Injury Prevention and Control, 2003), with significant implications for their physical and mental health. For example, IPV is associated with chronic pain, physical activity limitations, heart disease, depression, anxiety, low self-esteem, feelings of isolation, post-traumatic stress symptoms, suicide ideation, and homelessness (Bonomi *et al.*, 2006; Calvete, Corral, and Estavez, 2007; Carlson, McNutt, Choi, and Rose, 2002; Centers for Disease Control and Prevention, 2008; Coker, Weston, Creson, Justice, and Blakeney,

2005; Golding, 1999; Johnson and Leone, 2005; J. Lee, Pomeroy, and Bohman, 2007; Mitchell *et al.*, 2006).

IPV is also considered a major social problem (Basile and Black, 2011; Tierney, 1982). A *social problem* refers to a social condition that is recognized by society more generally as detrimental in its effects and warranting remedy. Social conditions become social problems through *social construction* – or a process of redefinition – usually as a result of the advocacy efforts of individuals, activities, and political groups (Tierney, 1982). Feminist scholars, who have been central to defining IPV as a social problem, have identified multiple social factors that may contribute to women's experiences of IPV, including patriarchal attitudes or institutions that could influence some men to commit IPV or allow women to be vulnerable to it (Basile and Black, 2011). However, scholars have debated for over a decade the extent to which gender and patriarchy contribute to IPV against women because women also perpetrate violence. This is referred to as the "gender-symmetry/asymmetry debate." As explained by Jasinski (2001), the study of IPV is generally approached from two diverging theoretical perspectives: the feminist perspective and the family violence perspective (see Table 14.1). Researchers examining IPV from either side of this conceptual debate often have conflicting reports on the "true" extent and nature of IPV and the role of gender. Specifically, feminist theorists view violence between heterosexual partners as perpetrated primarily by men against women (*gender asymmetric*) and occurring within larger and highly influential societal structures that uphold and reproduce power differences between men and women. Indeed, feminist researchers have found that women are primarily the victims of IPV committed by men who seek to control them (e.g., Dobash, Dobash, Wilson, and Daly, 1992). In stark contrast, family violence theorists conceptualize violence as *gender symmetric* and rooted in problematic family structures (e.g., unhealthy boundaries) and communication processes (e.g., poor conflict management). Their research indicates that women perpetrate violence as much as or more than men do (e.g., Fergusson, Horwood, and Ridder, 2005; Straus, 1999). Johnson's typology of violence helps us make sense of these seemingly contradictory findings.

Johnson's typology of domestic violence

Johnson's (2008) typology of domestic violence helps us make sense of these conflicting reports about the extent and nature of IPV because it underscores the importance of considering the context in which violent acts occur. Johnson (2008) makes an important distinction between intimate terrorism and situational couple violence as two qualitatively different types of IPV. Intimate terrorism involves violence that is used along with non-violent tactics to create a general pattern of control of one's partner, while situational couple violence is violence that occurs in the context of an argument and does not involve a motive to control one's partner. Johnson also identifies two related types of violence. Violent resistance describes

Table 14.1 Theoretical perspectives of intimate partner violence (IPV)

	Family violence perspective	*Feminist perspective*
Definition of IPV	Minor to severe physical, sexual, verbal, and emotional abuse in the context of a specific conflicting situation	Physical and sexual abuse in the context of control
Perpetrators of IPV	IPV is gender symmetric. Men and women perpetrate IPV equally	IPV is gender asymmetric. Men perpetrate violence against women in the majority of IPV cases
Causes of IPV	Family conflict and stress	Power differences between men and women
Sampling method in IPV studies	Community sampling for general survey research	Agency sampling from shelters, hospitals, or court records

Source: Based on information from Jasinski (2001).

violence that is used *in response* to intimate terrorism, such as acts used to defend against violence or other control tactics. Finally, in rare cases, both partners use intimate terrorism; Johnson refers to this type as mutual violent control.

Observing the context in which violence occurs provides an explanation for the inconsistent findings shown in research. When researchers make distinctions based on the type of violence, they find that violence that occurs in combination with other control tactics (intimate terrorism), such as monitoring a partner's activities, interfering in relationships with family and friends, or restricting contact with others out of jealousy, is primarily perpetrated by men in heterosexual relationships (89–97% of intimate terrorism incidences), while violence that occurs during conflict without a general pattern of control (situational couple violence) is perpetrated by both men (55–56% of situational couple violence incidences) and women (44–45% of situational couple violence incidences; Johnson, 2008). In line with research showing that women are primarily the victims of intimate terrorism, violence that occurs in response to intimate terrorism (violent resistance) is perpetrated primarily by women (85% of violent resistance cases) and less often by men (15% of violent resistance cases; Johnson, 2008). Both men and women perpetrate violence at equal rates in relationships within which *both* partners are violent and controlling (mutual violent control), although these situations appear to be quite rare (Johnson, 2008). These distinctions also highlight discrepancies in research on the broad range of consequences of IPV. Intimate terrorism appears to be more frequent, severe, and injurious than situational couple violence (Johnson, Leone, and Xu, 2008) and is associated with numerous mental health issues, including depression (Anderson, 2008) and post-traumatic stress disorder (Johnson and Leone, 2005). Less is known about the effects of violent resistance and mutual violent control because most researchers have focused on examining the more common forms of IPV, situational couple violence and intimate terrorism.

Johnson's work also reveals that the sampling procedures researchers use can influence their findings. Research based on samples from agencies (e.g., domestic violence shelters, hospitals, court records) is more likely to include women who have experienced intimate terrorism, whereas research that recruits participants from the community (e.g., general survey research) is more likely to include women who have experienced situational couple violence. Johnson (2008) explains that women who experience intimate terrorism are less likely to participate in general survey research due to fear of their partner finding out. Agencies also are more likely to serve women who have experienced more controlling and escalating violence by men (i.e., intimate terrorism; Johnson, 2008). Indeed, research using agency samples generally shows that women are primarily the victims of IPV by men because these samples are dominated by intimate terrorism cases. Similarly, the research showing that women and men perpetrate IPV equally includes participants recruited through community sampling, or samples dominated by situational couple violence.

Although many scholars have replicated Johnson's findings, providing credibility that different forms of IPV do exist (Ansara and Hindin, 2010; Frye, Manganello, Campbell, Walton-Moss, and Wilt, 2006; Graham-Kevan and Archer, 2003; Hardesty, Khaw, Chung, and Martin, 2008), there is no standardized or universally accepted way to measure or classify the types in research or practice. Furthermore, although practitioners agree that the typology is useful in their direct work with clients, it remains difficult for practitioners to determine which type of IPV a client is experiencing without a standard assessment tool (Derrington, Johnson, Menard, Ooms, and Stanley, 2010). Nonetheless, Johnson provides a theoretically useful framework to build upon and his typology is necessary for making sense of what we currently know about IPV.

Diversity and intimate partner violence

IPV affects all women, regardless of their age, race or ethnicity, socioeconomic status, sexual orientation, physical ability, or family structure. However, according to intersectionality theory (De Reus, Few, and Blume, 2005), these social identities or locations interact with and co-construct one another to create diverse experiences and unique challenges for abused women. For instance, a study comparing IPV victimization rates among African American, Latino, and Anglo-American women found no significant differences in the number of IPV cases reported annually across the three main racial groups (Bachman, 1994). However, other forms of oppression, such as prejudice and discrimination, could affect whether a woman of racial or ethnic minority status seeks or is able to obtain help from others in her community. Perhaps she would be reluctant to report the incident to avoid increasing negative perceptions of her community, already stigmatized by mainstream society (Richie and Kanuha, 1993). Or she may simply be discriminated against and denied resources in a community that is hostile towards minorities. Similarly, in same-sex relationships, homophobia may interfere with a victim's ability to obtain help and resources (Mahoney, Williams, and West, 2001).

Different social locations (e.g., social class) also may contribute to the occurrence of IPV. For example, studies demonstrate that women with lower socioeconomic status are at greater risk for violence (Cunradi, Caetono, and Schafer, 2002). One explanation is that couples with lower socioeconomic status are exposed to more social stressors (e.g., unemployment or underemployment) with fewer economic resources to cope (e.g., limited access to physical or mental health care or quality childcare), which may contribute to situational couple violence (Cunradi et al., 2002; Johnson, 2008; Renzetti, 2011). Status incompatibilities that favor women in heterosexual relationships (e.g., she earns more money than he does) are also associated with IPV risk for women, particularly nonviolent controlling tactics (Kaukinen, 2004). Kaukinen posits that for some men, such status incompatibilities threaten their sense of manhood. Thus, they may use controlling behaviors to reassert their dominance and power in the relationship, which is consistent with the dynamics of intimate terrorism. Finally, we know less about IPV among women of higher socioeconomic status, in part because their greater access to resources may enable them to cope more privately and, particularly for affluent women, because community norms emphasize keeping family problems hidden (Haselschwerdt, 2013; Weitzman, 2000). In sum, IPV cuts across all groups but does not necessarily impact all women equally. It is important to recognize how the cultural and social contexts within which women live shape their experiences.

Child Abuse and Exposure to Intimate Partner Violence

Based on a number of large-scale studies, Carlson (2000) conservatively estimates that from 10% to 20% of US children are exposed to adult IPV each year, which translates to approximately 7 to 14 million children (Edleson et al., 2007). Exposure to IPV can take many forms, including direct (e.g., seeing or being involved in the violence) or indirect (e.g., hearing the sounds, but not seeing the act or seeing the aftermath, such as physical injury or changes in the mother's demeanor) exposure (Jaffe, Wolfe, and Campbell, 2012). Child exposure to adult IPV has generally been understudied compared to the vast attention paid to child physical abuse (Fantuzzo, Boruch, Beriama, Atkins, and Marcus, 1997). Only since the 1990s have researchers considered exposure to IPV as a form of maltreatment in and of itself (McGee and Wolfe, 1991; Somer and Braunstein, 1999). Indeed, exposure to IPV is associated with multiple negative outcomes in children (Evans, Davies, and DiLillo, 2008; Wolfe, Crooks, Lee, McIntyre-Smith, and Jaffe, 2003). Developmentally, exposure has been related to disruption in the development of secure attachment, self-regulation, and social competence (Gewirtz and Edleson, 2007). Emotionally and psychologically, it has been associated with anxiety (Marks, Glaser, Glass, and Horne, 2001), depression (Marks et al., 2001), and post-traumatic stress disorder (PTSD; Levendosky, Huth-Bocks, Semel, and Shapiro, 2002; Moretti, Obsuth, Odgers, and Reebye, 2006). Finally, research has found associations with aggression (Gewirtz and Edleson, 2007; Margolin, 1998; Moretti et al., 2006), conduct disorders (Jouriles, Norwood, McDonald, Vincent, and Mahoney, 1996), withdrawing from others (Marks et al., 2001), and delinquent behavior (Marks et al., 2001).

There is no question that exposure negatively affects children; however, an important limitation of this research is the reliance on mothers' reports of children's IPV exposure as well as their adjustment and behavior (Ware et al., 2001). Research suggests that mothers may overreport their children's externalizing problems, especially if under distress at domestic violence shelters (Brody and Forehand, 1986; Hughes and Luke, 1998; Jouriles and Thompson, 1993; Moore and Pepler, 1998). Parents also generally underreport children's exposure to IPV (Richters and Martinez, 1993; Wolfe *et al.*, 2003). This may be due to the mother not being aware of the child's exposure (e.g., if the child hides in another room or pretends to be asleep) or the mother's reluctance to admit her child's exposure. Cultural factors, such as race and social class intersections, may also contribute to the invisibility of children (Hardesty, Oswald, Khaw, Fonseca, and Chung, 2008). Poor African American mothers, for example, may attempt to actively shield their children from IPV to avoid adding to the burdens of minority stress (e.g., economic insecurity, discrimination; Collins, 1990). Struggling to survive, they may be in denial of their children's knowledge of IPV. Furthermore, marginalized women (e.g., poor women, racial/ethnic minorities, immigrant women) may distrust the police or child welfare system and thus be reluctant to disclose concerns related to their children and may also socialize their children to avoid disclosures (Dodson and Schmalzbauer, 2005).

Finally, another possible limitation of this research is the use of shelter samples, which may present confounding variables because children in shelters are likely to have been exposed to multiple traumas and co-occurring risks in addition to IPV, including poverty, stress from residing in a shelter, and maternal distress or depression. However, in an analysis of 60 studies of children's exposure to IPV, Evans *et al.* (2008) found no differences between clinical (e.g., shelter) and community samples in terms of children's externalizing and internalizing behaviors.

In addition to children's exposure to IPV, some children may also experience direct physical or sexual abuse. Rates of co-occurrence of direct abuse and exposure to parental IPV, however, are not clear as studies are limited methodologically and have presented a broad range of percentages. For example, a review of 31 studies shows a co-occurrence rate from 6% to 100% depending on how scholars define child abuse and recruit their sample (Appel and Holden, 1998). A more recent report shows a co-occurrence rate between 19% and 60% (Casanueva, Kotch, and Zolotor, 2007). Furthermore, although IPV and child abuse appear to co-occur within families, only two studies have shown a direct, causal link between the

two (L. Lee, Kotch, and Cox, 2004; Rumm, Cummings, Krauss, Bell, and Rivara, 2000). Research on co-occurrence of IPV and direct child abuse, as well as the effects of IPV exposure on children in general, also has not made distinctions between different types of violence. Therefore, it remains unknown whether direct child abuse is more likely to co-occur with a specific type of IPV or whether exposure to different types relates to different outcomes for children. Nonetheless, child abuse in addition to IPV exposure has been found to increase negative effects on children above and beyond IPV exposure alone (Wolfe *et al.*, 2003). Studies also indicate that child abuse and IPV exposure are risk factors for children perpetrating abusive behaviors in adolescence and adulthood (Wolfe, Crooks, Chiodo, and Jaffe, 2009). However, many children abused or exposed to their parents' IPV never become violent themselves (Barnett, Miller-Perrin, and Perrin, 2005); thus, there are opportunities for resilient outcomes among children affected by violence (Wolfe *et al.*, 2009).

Intimate Partner Violence and the Process of Resilience

Resilience refers to the process of positive adaptation or competent functioning despite exposure to significant adversity (Garmezy, 1993; Luthar and Cicchetti, 2000). Significant adversity is distinguished from normal, everyday challenges in that most people exposed to such adversity demonstrate poor outcomes (Patterson, 2002). Researchers became interested in the process of resilience after observing positive adaptation among children when maladaptive outcomes were expected due to growing up in extreme poverty with mentally ill or alcoholic parents (e.g., Werner and Smith, 1982) or being raised by a schizophrenic parent (Masten, Best, and Garmezy, 1990). This led to a consideration of how protective factors might moderate the effects of exposure to significant adversity such that some people are able to thrive despite their high-risk status (Luthar, Cicchetti, and Becker, 2000). In this section, we take a resilience-theoretical approach to move beyond the negative effects of IPV to consider how individuals recover and achieve positive outcomes despite adversity. Importantly, individuals who experience adversity are not mere bystanders to this process; they are active agents for change and recovery (Walsh, 2006). At the same time, it is important to understand the social factors and background characteristics that individuals may not have control over that can interfere with or enhance their ability to be resilient.

Risk factors for intimate partner violence

Resilience is a dynamic process involving a complex interplay between risk and protective factors (Luthar, Cicchetti, and Becker, 2000). *Risk factors* (also referred to as vulnerability factors) include individual-, family-, and community-level characteristics or variables that are associated with the likelihood of experiencing adversity (Luthar and Cicchetti, 2000). The US Department of Justice (2007) has identified early parenthood, severe poverty, and unemployment as risk factors for experiencing IPV. Specifically, women who have children before age 21 are two times as likely to experience IPV, and men who have children before the age of 21 are three times as likely to perpetrate IPV. Low household income and women's unemployment also increase the risk of experiencing IPV. Although findings are mixed, some research suggests that exposure to IPV as a child may increase the risk for adult IPV victimization (Bensley, Van Eenwyk, and Simmons, 2003). Furthermore, women who were abused as a child are also at greater risk for victimization as an adult (Coid *et al.*, 2001).

Risk factors that have been identified are primarily from survey data, which likely taps into situational couple violence (Johnson, 2008). Because situational couple violence arises from situational stressors, it makes sense that variables such as early parenthood, poverty, and unemployment pose risks. Some researchers have begun to examine risk factors for intimate terrorism in comparison to situational couple violence specifically. For instance, marital status has been identified as a risk factor for intimate terrorism but not situational couple violence. Macmillan and Gartner (1999) found that the odds for experiencing intimate terrorism increased when transitioning from singlehood or cohabitation to marriage, while the odds decreased for situational couple violence. It is possible

that marriage reinforces feelings of entitlement among controlling abusers (i.e., intimate terrorists; Johnson, 2008). The likelihood of experiencing intimate terrorism also decreases as a man's education increases, even while controlling for race and income (Johnson, 2008).

Additional cultural and social factors can serve as potential barriers (or risk factors) by influencing a woman's appraisal of herself and the situation and her use of resources. After all,

> abuse is both a social problem and a personal issue, as it is perpetrated by men against women in their social locations as wives and/or intimate partners. As a social problem, it can be viewed as a point of convergence of broader patterns of economic, social, and political discrimination against women. (Lempert, 1996, p. 269)

For instance, cultural expectations of Asian women and families may influence how Asian American women respond to IPV. Specifically, an Asian American woman may face challenges to leaving an abusive partner due to cultural pressures to keep the family unit intact and maintain interdependence (J. Lee *et al.*, 2007). Likewise, African American women may feel reluctant to seek help or leave an abusive partner because of idealized notions of the "strong African American woman" who always "stands by her man" (Mitchell *et al.*, 2006).

Protective factors

Much of the research on IPV has focused on risk factors and potential negative outcomes. Less attention has been paid to factors that may lessen the impact of IPV, known as *protective factors*. Protective factors include individual-, family-, and community-level characteristics or variables that moderate the relations between exposure to significant adversity and potential negative consequences (Luthar and Cicchetti, 2000). Some studies have shown that social and practical support are important protective factors that buffer the potential negative mental health effects of IPV for women (Arias, Lyons, and Street, 1997; Beeble, Bybee, and Sullivan, 2009; Coker *et al.*, 2002; Levendosky, Leahy, Bogat, Davidson, and von Eye, 2006; Thompson *et al.*, 2000). Indeed, women have reported that having someone to confide in helps them cope with the violence and enhance their self-esteem. Social support also has been shown to play a significant role in women's decision to leave a violent partner (Ulrich, 1991). Importantly, however, women must also perceive that social support is available and that an empathic response will be provided (Waldrop and Resick, 2004). Perceived and available social support may play a key role in psychological functioning for women who experience intimate terrorism specifically because the abuser in these relationships is likely to isolate his partner from family and friends (Levendosky and Graham-Bermann, 2001).

In addition to social support, a survey of 557 women found five other factors that served as a buffer for abused women's development of depression and anxiety: good health, advanced education, low economic hardship, high self-esteem, and employment (Carlson et al., 2002). Additional studies have shown that self-esteem (Campbell, Miller, Cardwell, and Belknap, 1994), self-efficacy (Sullivan, Campbell, Angelique, Eby, and Davidson, 1994), and self-care (Campbell et al., 1994) also help mitigate the negative effects of IPV. To our knowledge, no work has been done to identify protective factors specific to different types of IPV.

Adaptive and maladaptive outcomes

Most women do eventually leave abusive partners and recover from the abuse (Campbell et al., 1994; Chang et al., 2006; Khaw and Hardesty, 2007). Although the process of leaving tends to be gradual and often consists of multiple cycles of leaving and returning, agency, perseverance, and the very act of leaving itself demonstrate women's strengths in overcoming adversity (Chang et al., 2006; Khaw and Hardesty, 2007). Carver (2010) identified several possible outcomes following exposure to adversity. These include the concepts of succumbing (i.e., despair or surrendering to the adversity), survival with impairment (i.e., functioning at a lower level than pre-abuse), resilience (i.e., recovering from the negative effects and returning to pre-abuse functioning), and thriving (i.e., obtaining higher functioning than pre-abuse, which may also be considered resilience). Given the variability in possible risk and protective factors for women who experience IPV, each of these outcomes seems theoretically conceivable.

Succumbing to the adversity seems possible given reports of suicide ideation and attempts by women experiencing IPV, particularly for African American women with low incomes (Meadows, Kaslow, Thompson, and Jurkovic, 2005). Substance abuse of painkillers, antidepressants, and tranquilizers may also be evidence of succumbing to the adversity for women experiencing intimate terrorism (Johnson and Leone, 2005). Survival with impairment appears to be another possible outcome as abused women may frequently miss work due to the effects of violence, experience depressive and PTSD symptoms, and suffer from lower self-esteem (Coker et al., 2005; Johnson and Leone, 2005; Khaw and Hardesty, 2007). Low-income minority women who experienced intimate terrorism, in particular, report greater physical health problems in comparison to women who experienced situational couple violence, even when controlling for the severity and frequency of violence (Leone, Johnson, Cohan, and Lloyd, 2004).

Positive outcomes may also result despite one's experience of violence. These include recovery and thriving. Research evidence supports these ideas of "bouncing back" and "bouncing forward" in the midst of IPV. Research by Oke (2008), for instance, demonstrates how some women who increase their focus on education and work following separation from an abusive partner are able to develop an even stronger and more empowered identity than before the abuse (i.e., they thrived). Others simply, but just as notably, regain their prior sense of self, demonstrating recovery and resilience (Khaw and Hardesty, 2007; Oke, 2008).

Other longitudinal studies of women who have left abusive partners also show that trauma-related symptoms reduce over time, providing further evidence that recovery is attainable once the violence ends (Dutton and Painter, 1993; Mertin and Mohr, 2001). This recovery may be due, in part, to women's creative use of a variety of strategies to escape or avoid violence and protect themselves (Campbell, Rose, Kub, and Nedd, 1998). Although efforts to differentiate positive outcomes after intimate terrorism from situational couple violence are rather limited, studies have revealed that recovery is possible even for severe cases of intimate terrorism. For example, a study by Ford-Gilboe and colleagues found that women's health improved over time despite the mental and physical effects they experienced during violent, controlling relationships and immediately after separation (Ford-Gilboe, Wuest, and Merritt-Gray, 2005).

An additional factor that influences a woman's experience after facing IPV is coping. *Coping* has been defined as "a response aimed at diminishing physical, emotional, and psychological burden that is linked to stressful life events and daily hassles" (Snyder and Dinoff, 1999, p. 5). Active problem-solving and negotiating with oneself and one's partner are effective coping strategies that women use in response to IPV (Campbell *et al.*, 1998). Although the goal of coping is to reduce burden, coping can sometimes be adaptive or, surprisingly, maladaptive. Whether adaptive or maladaptive, how coping develops depends directly on the woman's appraisal of herself, the situation, and the resources available to her (Calvete *et al.*, 2007). For instance, the presence of resources (e.g., social support) and the woman's perception that resources are both available and useful increase adaptive coping styles that lead to equal or higher levels of functioning after experiencing IPV (Calvete *et al.*, 2007; J. Lee *et al.*, 2007; Meadows *et al.*, 2005). Furthermore, although most studies have identified negative effects of maladaptive coping (e.g., denial of abuse), there has been some speculation regarding the development and impact of these coping styles, and, more specifically, if they may actually be beneficial to some women in the midst of IPV:

> Women employ a variety of coping efforts, some of which may appear perplexing to those outside the situation, but which may have served a woman well in helping her to continue with other aspects of her life while living with an abusive partner or with the aftermath of violence. (Lindhorst, Nurius, and Macy, 2005, p. 336)

For example, placating the abuser, which was previously considered a helpless response by abused women, is now recognized as an active strategy of survival (Gondolf and Fisher, 1988). Thus, a woman may deliberately choose to appease her partner's controlling demands to stave off a violent attack that could leave her unable to show up for her new job the following day. Likewise, a woman may fight back in response to her partner's demands in an effort to control the timing of his use of violence against her (e.g., while the children are away from home). Thus,

these seemingly maladaptive coping mechanisms, at times, may be appropriate and beneficial for a woman's survival and everyday functioning when facing IPV.

The type of coping style and its effect on a woman's functioning may also depend on other factors. Some evidence suggests that certain cultural ideals and types of violence may lessen the typically positive effects of adaptive coping. For instance, an adaptive coping style demonstrated through active problem-solving, such as direct confrontation or efforts toward leaving the abuser, may lead to increased acts of violence and lower functioning (e.g., feeling powerless) in cases of intimate terrorism or in communities where oppression and discrimination against women prevail (Johnson and Leone, 2005; Mitchell *et al.*, 2006). For example, within African communities there are cultural sanctions for husbands to physically abuse their wives, and wives face cultural pressures to accept the violence and remain passive to conform to cultural definitions of femininity and marriage (Rotimi, 2007). Thus, women in severe situations of coercive control or who live where cultural ideologies uphold IPV may be more likely to use hidden and "passive" coping styles, which are often labeled maladaptive, to get by (J. Lee *et al.*, 2007, pp. 710). Therefore, a woman's perception and resources, both influenced by the type of IPV and the broader cultural and societal contexts in which she lives, can impact the development of coping styles and ultimately her potential for resilient outcomes.

Responding to Intimate Partner Violence

As reflected in Toni's and Shari's stories at the beginning of this chapter, women's experiences with IPV can vary greatly. Johnson's (2008) typology helps us make sense of these differences and highlights the need to make distinctions in types of violence in our responses to it. For Toni and Shari, and any woman who experiences violence, safety must be the top priority. Safety planning and risk assessment guidelines are available to assist in this process and can be adapted to fit specific cases or contexts (see Hardesty and Campbell, 2004). Beyond safety, their needs are likely very different.

Toni, for example, faces unique barriers to achieving nonviolence in the context of intimate terrorism. Because of William's control over her, Toni has little access to social and financial support and is at risk of harm to herself or her children if she decides to leave the relationship. She may be experiencing the potentially debilitating effects of depression and PTSD due to years of physical and sexual abuse. Her children also may be struggling with effects of exposure to their father's violence and control. Thus, Toni is in need of comprehensive services that are not only intended to prevent physical harm (e.g., legal system intervention, batterer intervention programs) but that also foster recovery and healing for her and her children (e.g., mental and physical health care, financial and employment services, access to social support). In contrast, Shari and Bren may benefit from interventions to improve communication and conflict management as they continue to parent together (e.g., anger management programs, parent education classes) and help them plan for how to respond should violence become an issue in the future (e.g., seeking legal and/or mental health interventions).

Regardless of the type of IPV, our responses should focus on reducing risk factors for IPV while increasing the protective factors that promote resilient outcomes. Goodmark (2011) distinguishes between first-generation and second-generation issues in responding to IPV. First-generation responses over the last 30 years have focused on using the legal system to ensure immediate safety of abused women and to hold abusers accountable for their actions. As a result, we have institutionalized police policies and civil remedies, such as mandatory arrest policies, no-drop prosecution policies, civil protection orders that include provisions for housing and child custody and support, and stalking laws. Second-generation responses have expanded beyond these immediate issues to address the broader consequences of IPV. This has included the creation of policies to protect abused women from discrimination in the workplace and in housing practices. For example, states have developed policies against eviction or denying housing or terminating employment due to IPV. To address the mental and physical health consequences of IPV, health care professionals advocate for routine assessment of IPV among all women to identify violence and assess safety needs, connect women with resources and support, and provide comprehensive trauma-informed care (Ford-Gilboe, Varcoe, Wuest, and Merritt-Gray, 2011).

Despite tremendous progress, challenges remain in preventing IPV and ensuring the safety and health of all women and children affected by IPV. These ongoing challenges were apparent most recently in the US House of Representatives' initial failure to reauthorize the Violence Against Women Act (VAWA). The VAWA, first passed into law in 1994, provides assistance to women and families in the form of law enforcement protections and funding for services and programs (National Network to End Domestic Violence, 2013). Objections to the new bill centered on extending certain protections to Native Americans, undocumented immigrants, and lesbian, gay, bisexual, and transgender victims of violence (Bendery, 2013). After great debate, the VAWA was finally reauthorized to provide protection and services to all individuals, regardless of their sexual orientation, gender identity, or citizenship status. New policies also provide legal authority for tribal communities to prosecute non-tribal abusers for crimes that take place on their reservations. The VAWA 2013 offers additional protections and grant programs to improve services for college students, youth, public housing residents, and victims of cyber-stalking. However, concerns remain as to how to successfully implement the new policies and programs when social service organizations, including VAWA programs, continue to face dramatic budget cuts by the federal government. Although political tensions and disagreements will likely persist regarding the best ways to respond to IPV, there are ways individuals can respond to women we know who are affected by IPV.

Our responses to women who experience IPV should acknowledge their strengths and empower them to remain active agents in achieving health and safety and recovering from violence. Helping women identify resources in their local communities should they choose to seek help is one way to support empowerment. Anyone can call the National Domestic Violence Hotline (1-800-799-SAFE), 24 hours a day, seven days a week, to talk to an advocate who can provide immediate safety planning and crisis intervention if needed, but can also provide information about local resources, such as domestic violence shelters, mental health services, and batterer treatment programs. Callers do not have to be in crisis to use this resource and the caller can remain anonymous.

Additional responses that can promote resilience are to help women increase or maintain social support and foster their economic independence. Support from family members and friends as well as professionals should involve a nonjudgmental, empathic understanding of the complexity of IPV. If a woman is contemplating leaving her partner, those who provide support should recognize that different pathways are possible for leaving and that many women often leave multiple times before they are completely free from the relationship (Chang et al., 2006). Thus, being aware that leaving is a complex process rather than a single event helps us offer support that recognizes women's agency and choice. It is also important to recognize that not all women who are abused wish to end their relationships (Campbell et al., 1998). Social support is crucial to help women choose the path that is right for them while remaining attuned to their own feelings of emotional and physical safety (Sullivan et al., 1994). Focusing on a woman's strengths is also important for creating a sense of empowerment for women to take charge of their lives while maintaining or increasing their self-esteem. As individuals, we can also advocate for efforts aimed at supporting resilience among abused women and their children, such as anti-poverty policies and programs related to cash and food assistance, subsidized housing access, job placement services, and access to education (Williams Shanks and Danzinger, 2011).

Conclusion

As the chapter illustrates, the extent and nature of violent acts by an intimate partner can vary greatly across social locations and attention must be paid in both research and practice to making distinctions in the type of IPV that all women experience, regardless of their socioeconomic status, race, ethnicity, or the culture in which they live. This chapter provides a review of the prevalence of IPV with attention to the unique qualities of intimate terrorism and situational couple violence, two types of IPV identified by Johnson (2008). More research is needed to fully understand how our responses to IPV can be informed by Johnson's typology, but the different contexts do suggests different approaches. The process of resilience provides an explanation for how women and their children can recover and thrive despite a history of IPV and informs how our responses to IPV can promote resilient outcomes. Consideration of the social, economic, and cultural pressures or challenges that women may face in the midst of IPV must continue in future research, policy, and practice efforts to address the needs of women of all backgrounds and promote their safety and well-being.

Critical Thinking Questions

1. How have sampling procedures contributed to the debate/tensions between feminist and family violence perspectives?
2. How does Johnson's typology address the tensions between feminist and family violence perspectives?
3. What is gained by using Johnson's typology to assess Toni's and Shari's situations described at the beginning of the chapter?
4. What are some adaptive and maladaptive outcomes that result from IPV and how might women's coping promote or hinder achieving resilient outcomes?
5. Using the knowledge you have gained about IPV and resilience, in what ways would you approach Toni and Shari similarly and differently in a practical setting?

References

Anderson, K. L. (2008). Is partner violence worse in the context of control? Journal of Marriage and Family, 70(5), 1157–1168.

Ansara, D. L., and Hindin, M. J. (2010). Exploring gender differences in the patterns of intimate partner violence in Canada: A latent class approach. Journal of Epidemiology and Community Health, 64, 849–854.

Appel, A. E., and Holden, G. W. (1998). The co-occurrence of spouse and physical child abuse: a review and appraisal. Journal of Family Psychology, 12, 578–599.

Arias, I., Lyons, C. M., and Street, A. E. (1997). Individual and marital consequences of victimization: moderating effects of relationships efficacy and spouse support. Journal of Family Violence, 12(2), 193–210.

Bachman, R. A. (1994). *Violence against women: A national crime victimization survey report*. NCJ 145325. Washington, DC: US Department of Justice, Bureau of Justice Statistics.

Barnett, O. W., Miller-Perrin, C. L., and Perrin, R. D. (2005). *Family violence across the lifespan: An introduction* (2nd edn) Thousand Oaks, CA: Sage Publications.

Basile, K. C., and Black, M. C. (2011). Intimate partner violence against women. In C. M. Renzetti, J. L. Edleson, and R. Kennedy Bergen (eds), *Sourcebook on violence against women* (2nd edn) (pp. 111–130). Thousand Oaks, CA: Sage Publications.

Beeble, M. L., Bybee, D., and Sullivan, C. M. (2009). Main, mediating and moderating effects of social support on the well-being of survivors of intimate partner violence across two years. *Journal of Consulting and Clinical Psychology, 77*(4), 718–729.

Bendery, J. (2013). VAWA reauthorization will get Senate vote next week. Retrieved May 30, 2014 from http://www.huffingtonpost.com/2013/01/28/vawa-reauthorization_n_2568872.html.

Bensley, L., Van Eenwyk, J., and Simmons, K. W. (2003). Childhood family violence history and women's risk for intimate partner violence and poor health. *American Journal of Preventive Medicine, 25*(1), 38–44.

Black, M. C., Basile, K. C., Breiding, M. J., Smith, S. G., Walters, M. L., Merrick, M. T., … and Stevens, M. R. (2011). *The National Intimate Partner and Sexual Violence Survey (NISVS): 2010 summary report*. Atlanta, GA: National Center for Injury Prevention and Control, Centers for Disease Control and Prevention.

Bonomi, A. E., Thompson, R. S., Anderson, M., Reid, R. J., Carrell, D., Dimer, J. A., and Rivara, F. P. (2006). Intimate partner violence and women's mental, physical, and social functioning. *American Journal of Preventive Medicine, 30*(6), 458–466.

Brody, G. H., and Forehand, R. (1986). Maternal perceptions of child maladjustment as a function of the combined influence of child behavior and maternal depression. *Journal of Consulting and Clinical Psychology, 54*(2), 237–240.

Calvete, E., Corral, S., and Estavez, A. (2007). Cognitive and coping mechanisms in the interplay between intimate partner violence and depression. *Anxiety, Stress and Coping: An International Journal, 20*(4), 369–382.

Campbell, J. C., Miller, P., Cardwell, M. M., and Belknap, R. A. (1994). Relationship status of battered women over time. *Journal of Family Violence, 9*(2), 99–111.

Campbell, J. C., Rose, L., Kub, J., and Nedd, D. (1998). Voices of strength and resistance: A contextual and longitudinal analysis of women's responses to battering. *Journal of Interpersonal Violence, 13*(6), 743–762.

Carlson, B. E. (2000). Children exposed to intimate partner violence: Research findings and implications for intervention. *Trauma, Violence, and Abuse, 1*(4), 321–342.

Carlson, B. E., McNutt, L., Choi, D. Y., and Rose, I. M. (2002). Intimate partner abuse and mental health: The role of social support and other protective factors. *Violence Against Women [Special Issue]: Health Care and Domestic Violence, 8*(6), 720–745.

Carver, C. S. (2010). Resilience and thriving: Issues, models, and linkages. *Journal of Social Issues [Special Issue]: Thriving: Broadening the Paradigm Beyond Illness to Health, 54*(2), 245–266.

Casanueva, C., Kotch, J., and Zolotor, A. (2007). Intimate partner violence and child abuse and neglect. In K. A. Kendall-Tackett, and S. M. Giacomoni (eds), *Intimate partner violence* (pp. 23-1–23-17). Kingston, NJ: Civic Research Institute.

Centers for Disease Control and Prevention (CDC). (2008). Adverse health conditions and health risk behaviors associated with intimate partner violence – United States 2005. *Morbidity and Mortality Weekly Report, 57*, 113–117.

Chang, J. C., Dado, D., Ashton, S., Hawker, L., Cluss, P. A., Buranosky, R., and Scholle, S. H. (2006). Understanding behavior change for women experiencing intimate partner violence: Mapping the ups and downs using the stages of change. *Patient Education and Counseling, 62*(3), 330–339.

Coid, J., Petruckevitch, A., Feder, G., Chung, W., Richardson, J., Moorey, S. (2001). Relation between childhood sexual and physical abuse and risk of revictimisation in women: A cross-sectional study. *The Lancet, 356*, 450–455.

Coker, A. L., Smith, P. H., Thompson, M. P., McKeown, R. E., Bethea, L., and Davis, K. E. (2002). Social support protects against the negative effects of partner violence on mental health. *Journal of Women's Health and Gender-Based Medicine, 11*(5), 465–476.

Coker, A. L., Weston, R., Creson, D. L., Justice, B., and Blakeney, P. (2005). PTSD symptoms among men and women survivors of intimate partner violence: The role of risk and protective factors. *Violence and Victims, 20*(6), 625–643.

Collins, P. H. (1990). *Black feminist thought: Knowledge, consciousness, and the politics of empowerment*. New York: Routledge.

Cunradi, C. B., Caetano, R., and Schafer, J. (2002). Alcohol-related problems, drug use, and male intimate partner violence severity among US couples. *Alcoholism: Clinical and Experimental Research, 26*(4), 493–500.

De Reus, L., Few, A., and Blume, L. (2005). Multicultural and critical race feminisms: Theorizing families in the third wave. In V. Bengston, A. Acock, K. Allen, P. Dilworth-Anderson, and D. Klein (eds), *Sourcebook of family theory and research* (pp. 447–468). Newbury Park, CA: Sage Publications.

Derrington, R., Johnson, M., Menard, A., Ooms, T., and Stanley, S. (2010). *Making distinctions among different types of intimate partner violence: A preliminary guide*. Oklahoma City, OK: National Healthy Marriage Resource Center and the National Resource Center on Domestic Violence.

Dobash, R. P., Dobash, R. E., Wilson, M., and Daly, M. (1992). The myth of sexual symmetry in marital violence. *Social Problems, 39*, 71–91.

Dodson, L., and Schmalzbauer, L. (2005). Poor mothers and habits of hiding: Participatory methods in poverty research. *Journal of Marriage and Family, 67*(4), 949–959.

Dutton, D., and Painter, S. (1993). Emotional attachments in abusive relationships: A test of traumatic bonding theory. *Violence and Victims, 8*(2), 105–120.

Edleson, J. L., Ellerton, A. L., Seagren, S. L., Kirchbert, S. O., Schmidt, S. O., and Ambrose, A. T. (2007). Assessing child exposure to adult domestic violence. *Children and Youth Services Review, 29*(7), 961–971.

Evans, S. E., Davies, C., and DiLillo, D. (2008). Exposure to domestic violence: A meta-analysis of child and adolescent outcomes. *Aggression and Violent Behaviors, 13*, 131–140.

Fantuzzo, J., Boruch, R., Beriama, A., Atkins, M., and Marcus, S. (1997). Domestic violence and children: Prevalence and risk in five major U.S. cities. *Journal of the American Academy of Child and Adolescent Psychiatry, 36*(1), 116–122.

Federal Bureau of Investigation. (2010, September). Crime in the United States, 2009: Expanded homicide data. Retrieved May 30, 2014 from http://www2.fbi.gov/ucr/cius2009/offenses/expanded_information/homicide.html.

Fergusson, D. M., Horwood, L. J., and Ridder, E. M. (2005). Partner violence and mental health outcomes in a New Zealand birth cohort. *Journal of Marriage and Family, 67*(5), 1103–1119.

Ford-Gilboe, M., Varcoe, C., Wuest, J., and Merritt-Gray, M. (2011). Intimate partner violence and nursing practice. In J. Humphreys and J. C. Campbell (eds), *Family violence and nursing practice* (2nd edn) (pp. 115–153). New York: Springer.

Ford-Gilboe, M., Wuest, J., and Merritt-Gray, M. (2005). Strengthening the capacity to limit intrusion: Theorizing family health promotion in the aftermath of woman abuse. *Qualitative Health Research, 15*(4), 477–501.

Frye, V., Manganello, J., Campbell, J. C., Walton-Moss, B., and Wilt, S. (2006). The distribution of and factors associated with intimate terrorism and situational couple violence among a population-based sample of urban women in the United States. *Journal of Interpersonal Violence, 21*(10), 1286–1313.

Garmezy, N. (1993). Risk and resilience. In D. C. Funder, R. D. Parke, C. Tomlinson-Keasey, and K. Widaman (eds), *Studying lives through time: Personality and development* (pp. 377–398). Washington, DC: American Psychological Association.

Gewirtz, A. H., and Edleson, J. L. (2007). Young children's exposure to intimate partner violence: Towards a developmental risk and resilience framework for research and intervention. *Journal of Family Violence, 22*(3), 151–163.

Golding, J. M. (1999). Intimate partner violence as a risk factor for mental disorders: A meta-analysis. *Journal of Family Violence, 14*(2), 99–132.

Gondolf, E. W., and Fisher, E. R. (1988). *Battered women as survivors: An alternative to treating learned helplessness.* Lexington, MA: Lexington Books.

Goodmark, L. (2011). State, national, and international legal initiatives to address violence against women: A survey. In C. M. Renzetti, J. L. Edleson, and R. Kennedy Bergen (eds), *Sourcebook on violence against women* (2nd edn) (pp. 191–207). Thousand Oaks, CA: Sage Publications.

Graham-Kevan, N., and Archer, J. (2003). Intimate terrorism and common couple violence: A test of Johnson's predictions in four British samples. *Journal of Interpersonal Violence, 18*(11), 1247–1270.

Hardesty, J. L., and Campbell, J. C. (2004). Safety planning for abused women and their children. In P. G. Jaffe, L. L. Baker, and A. J. Cunningham (eds), *Protecting children from domestic violence: Strategies for community intervention* (pp. 89–110). New York: Guilford Press.

Hardesty, J. L., Khaw, L., Chung, G. H., and Martin, J. M. (2008). Coparenting relationships after divorce: Variations by type of marital violence and fathers' role differentiation. *Family Relations, 57*(4), 479–491.

Hardesty, J. L., Oswald, R. F., Khaw, L., Fonseca, C., and Chung, G. H. (2008). Lesbian mothering in the context of intimate partner violence. *Journal of Lesbian Studies, 12*(2/3), 191–210.

Haselschwerdt, M. L. (2013). Managing secrecy and disclosure of domestic violence in affluent communities: A grounded theory ethnography. Unpublished doctoral dissertation, University of Illinois at Urbana-Champaign.

Hughes, H. M., and Luke, D. A. (1998). Heterogeneity in adjustment among children of battered women. In G. W. Holden, R. Geffner and E. N. Jouriles (eds), *Children exposed to marital violence: Theory, research, and applied issues* (pp. 185–221). Washington, DC: American Psychological Association.

Jaffe, P. G., Wolfe, D. A., and Campbell, M. (2012). *Growing up with domestic violence: Assessment, intervention, and prevention strategies for children and adolescents.* Cambridge, MA: Hogrefe.

Jasinski, J. L. (2001). Theoretical explanations for violence against women. In C. M. Renzetti, J. L. Edleson, and R. K. Bergen (eds), *Sourcebook on violence against women* (pp. 5–21). Thousand Oaks, CA: Sage Publications.

Johnson, M. P. (2008). *A typology of domestic violence: Intimate terrorism, violent resistance, and situational couple violence.* Boston, MA: Northeastern University Press.

Johnson, M. P., and Leone, J. M. (2005). The differential effects of intimate terrorism and situational couple violence: Findings from the National Violence Against Women Survey. *Journal of Family Issues, 26*(3), 322–349.

Johnson, M. P., Leone, J. M., and Xu, Y. (2008, November). Gender, intimate terrorism, and situational couple violence in general survey data: The gender debate revisited – again. Paper presented at the annual meeting of the National Council on Family Relations, Little Rock, AR.

Jouriles, E. N., Norwood, W. D., McDonald, R., Vincent, J. P., and Mahoney, A. (1996). Physical violence and other forms of marital aggression: Links with children's behavior problems. *Journal of Family Psychology, 10*(2), 223–234.

Jouriles, E. N., and Thompson, S. M. (1993). Effects of mood on mothers' evaluations of children's behavior. *Journal of Family Psychology, 6*(3), 300–307.

Kaukinen, C. (2004). Status compatibility, physical violence, and emotional abuse in intimate relationships. *Journal of Marriage and Family, 66*(2), 452–471.

Khaw, L., and Hardesty, J. L. (2007). Theorizing the process of leaving: Turning points and trajectories in the stages of change. *Family Relations, 56*(4), 413–425.

Lee, L. C., Kotch, J. B., and Cox, C. E. (2004). Child maltreatment in families experiencing domestic violence. *Violence and Victims, 19*(5), 573–591.

Lee, J., Pomeroy, E. C., and Bohman, T. M. (2007). Intimate partner violence and psychological health in a sample of Asian and Caucasian women: The roles of social support and coping. *Journal of Family Violence, 22*(8), 709–720.

Lempert, L. B. (1996). Women's strategies for survival: Developing agency in abusive relationships. *Journal of Family Violence, 11*(3), 269–289.

Leone, J. M., Johnson, M. P., Cohan, C. M., and Lloyd, S. (2004). Consequences of male partner violence for low-income minority women. *Journal of Marriage and Family, 66*(2), 471–489.

Levendosky, A. A., and Graham-Bermann, S. A. (2001). Parenting in battered women: The effects of domestic violence on women and their children. *Journal of Family Violence, 16*(2), 171–192.

Levendosky, A. A., Huth-Bocks, A. C., Semel, M. A., and Shapiro, D. L. (2002). Trauma symptoms in preschool-age children exposed to domestic violence. *Journal of Interpersonal Violence, 17*(2), 150–164.

Levendosky, A. A., Leahy, K. L., Bogat, G. A., Davidson, W. S., and von Eye, A. (2006). Domestic violence, maternal parenting, maternal mental health, and infant externalizing behavior. *Journal of Family Psychology, 20*(4), 544–552.

Lindhorst, T., Nurius, P., and Macy, R. J. (2005). Contextualized assessment with battered women: Strategic safety planning to cope with multiple harms. *Journal of Social Work Education, 41*(2), 331–352.

Luthar, S. S., and Cicchetti, D. (2000). The construct of resilience: Implications for interventions and social policies. *Development and Psychopathology, 12*(4), 857–885.

Luthar, S. S., Cicchetti, D., and Becker, B. (2000). The construct of resilience: A critical evaluation and guidelines for future work. *Child Development, 71*(3), 543–562.

Macmillan, R., and Gartner, R. (1999). When she brings home the bacon: Labor-force participation and the risk of spousal violence against women. *Journal of Marriage and the Family, 61*(4), 947–58.

Mahoney, P., Williams, L. M., West, C. M. (2001). Violence against women by intimate relationship partners. In C. M. Renzetti, J. L. Edleson, and R. K. Bergen (eds), *Sourcebook on violence against women* (pp. 143–178). Thousand Oaks, CA: Sage Publications.

Margolin, G. (1998). Effects of domestic violence on children. In P. K. Trickett and C. J. Schellenbach (eds), *Violence against children in the family and the community* (pp. 57–101). Washington, DC: American Psychological Association.

Marks, C. R., Glaser, B. A., Glass, J. B., and Horne, A. M. (2001). Effects of witnessing severe marital discord on children's social competence and behavioral problems. *Family Journal, 9*(2), 94–101.

Masten, A. S., Best, K., and Garmezy, N. (1990). Resilience and development: Contributions from the study of children who overcome adversity. *Development and Psychopathology, 2*(4), 425–444.

McGee, R. A., and Wolfe, D. A. (1991). Psychological maltreatment: Toward an operational definition. *Development and Psychopathology [Special Issue]: Defining Psychological Maltreatment, 3*(1), 3–18.

Meadows, L. A., Kaslow, N. J., Thompson, M. P., and Jurkovic, G. J. (2005). Protective factors against suicide attempt risk among African American women experiencing intimate partner violence. *American Journal of Community Psychology [Special Issue]: Theoretical and Methodological Innovations in Research on Intimate Partner Violence, 36*(1/2), 109–121.

Mertin, P., and Mohr, P. (2001). A follow-up study of posttraumatic stress disorder, anxiety, and depression in Australian victims of domestic violence. *Violence and Victims, 16*(6), 645–654.

Mitchell, M. D., Hargrove, G. L., Collins, M. H., Thompson, M. P., Reddick, T. L., and Kaslow, N. J. (2006). Coping variables that mediate the relation between intimate partner violence and mental health outcomes among low-income, African American women. *Journal of Clinical Psychology, 62*(12), 1503–1520.

Moore, T. E., and Pepler, D. J. (1998). Correlates of adjustment in children at risk. In G. W. Holden, R. Geffner, and E. N. Jouriles (eds), *Children exposed to marital violence: Theory, research, and applied issues* (pp. 157–184). Washington, DC: American Psychological Association.

Moretti, M. M., Obsuth, I., Odgers, C. L., and Reebye, P. (2006). Exposure to maternal vs. paternal partner violence, PTSD, and aggression in adolescent girls and boys. *Aggressive Behavior, 32*(4), 385–395.

National Center for Injury Prevention and Control. (2003). *Costs of intimate partner violence against women in the United States.* Atlanta, GA: Centers for Disease Control and Prevention.

National Network to End Domestic Violence. (2013). Reauthorization of the Violence Against Women Act (VAWA). Retrieved May 30, 2014 from http://www.nnedv.org/docs/Policy/VAWA_Reauthorization_Fact_Sheet.pdf.

Oke, M. (2008). Remaking self after domestic violence: Mongolian and Australian women's narratives of recovery. *Australian and New Zealand Journal of Family Therapy, 29*(3), 148–155.

Patterson, J. M. (2002). Integrating family resilience and family stress theory. *Journal of Marriage and Family, 64*(2), 349–360.

Renzetti, C. M. (2011). Economic issues and intimate partner violence. In C. M. Renzetti, J. L. Edleson, and R. Kennedy Bergen (eds), *Sourcebook on violence against women* (2nd edn) (pp. 171–188). Thousand Oaks, CA: Sage Publications.

Richie, B. E., and Kanuha, V. (1993). Battered women of color in public health care systems: Racism, sexism, and violence. In B. Bair and S. E. Cayleff (eds), *Wings of gauze: Women of color and the experience of health and illness* (pp. 288–299). Detroit, MI: Wayne State University Press.

Richters, J. E., and Martinez, P. (1993). The NIMH community violence project: I. Children as victims of and witnesses to violence. *Psychiatry: Interpersonal and Biological Processes [Special Issue]: Children and Violence, 56,* 7–21.

Rotimi, A. (2007). Violence in the family: A preliminary investigation and overview of wife battering in Africa. *Journal of International Women's Studies, 9,* 234–252.

Rumm, P. D., Cummings, P., Krauss, M. R., Bell, M. A., and Rivara, F. P. (2000). Identified spouse abuse as a risk factor for child abuse. *Child Abuse and Neglect, 24*(11), 1375–1381.

Snyder, C. R., and Dinoff, B. L. (1999). Coping: Where have you been? In C. R. Snyder (ed.), *Coping: The psychology of what works* (pp. 3–19). New York: Oxford University Press.

Somer, E., and Braunstein, A. (1999). Are children exposed to interparental violence being psychologically maltreated? *Aggression and Violent Behavior, 4*(4), 449–456.

Straus, M. A. (1999). The controversy over domestic violence by women: A methodological, theoretical, and sociology of science analysis. In X. B. Arriaga and S. Oskamp (eds), *Violence in intimate relationships* (pp. 17–44). Thousand Oaks, CA: Sage Publications.

Sullivan, C., Campbell, R., Angelique, H., Eby, K., and Davidson, W. (1994). An advocacy intervention program for women with abusive partners: Six-month follow-up. *American Journal of Community Psychology, 22*(1), 101–122.

Thompson, M. P., Kaslow, N. J., Kingree, J. B., Rashid, A., Utett, R., Jacobs, D., and Matthews, A. (2000). Partner violence, social support, and distress among inner-city African American women. *American Journal of Community Psychology, 28*(1), 142–161.

Tierney, K. J. (1982). The battered women movement and the creation of the wife-beating problem. *Social Problems, 29*(3), 207–220.

Ulrich, Y. C. (1991). Women's reasons for leaving abusive spouses. *Health Care for Women International, 12,* 465–473.

US Department of Health and Human Services. (2010). *Healthy people 2010* (2nd edn). Washington, DC: US Government Printing Office.

US Department of Justice, National Institute of Justice. (2007). Causes and consequences of intimate partner violence. Washington, DC: US Department of Justice. Retrieved May 30, 2014 from http://www.nij.gov/nij/topics/crime/intimate-partner-violence/causes.htm.

Waldrop, A., and Resick, P. (2004). Coping among adult female victims of domestic violence. *Journal of Family Violence, 19*(5), 395–415.

Walsh, F. (2006). *Strengthening family resilience* (2nd edn). New York: Guilford Press.

Ware, H. S., Jouriles, E. N., Spiller, L. C., McDonald, R., Swank, P. R., and Norwood, W. D. (2001). Conduct problems among children at battered women's shelters: Prevalence and stability of maternal reports. *Journal of Family Violence, 16*(3), 291–307.

Weitzman, S. (2000). *Not to people like us: Hidden abuse in upscale marriages.* New York: Basic Books.

Werner, E. E., and Smith, R. (1982). *Vulnerable but invincible: A longitudinal study of resilient children and youth.* New York: McGraw-Hill.

Williams Shanks, T. R., and Danzinger, S. K. (2011). Anti-poverty policies and programs for children and families. In J. M. Jensen and M. W. Fraser (eds), *Social policy for children and families: A risk and resilience perspective* (2nd edn) (pp. 25–56). Thousand Oaks, CA: Sage Publications.

Wolfe, D. A., Crooks, C. C., Chiodo, D., and Jaffe, P. G. (2009). Child maltreatment, bullying, gender-based harassment, and adolescent dating violence: Making the connections. *Psychology of Women Quarterly, 33,* 21–24.

Wolfe, D. A., Crooks, C. V., Lee, V., McIntyre-Smith, A., and Jaffe, P. G. (2003). The effects of children's exposure to domestic violence: A meta-analysis and critique. *Clinical Child and Family Psychology Review, 6*(3), 171–187.

15

Abuse in Late Life
Unsuspecting Elders and Trusted Others

Karen A. Roberto, Pamela B. Teaster, and Marya C. McPherson

With the aging of society, elder abuse is fast becoming a pressing social problem with profound health, emotional, and economic effects for victims. Unfortunately, all too often the mistreatment of elders is unrecognized and underreported. Many perpetrators are family members or other individuals who have an ongoing relationship with the aged person and may be dependent on the elder for their sustenance. In Chapter 15, the authors outline ways for older adults to prevent abuse in their lives. Central to these efforts is the need for elders to stay informed, active, and socially engaged.

You may never have encountered an older adult like Eleanor who was experiencing abuse, and you probably are not aware of it even if you have (see case example on p. 229). Elder abuse is a largely hidden problem in community and facility settings. With the aging of the population in the United States and across the globe, however, elder abuse is becoming a pressing public health, criminal justice, and public policy concern (Acierno *et al.*, 2010; Amstadter *et al.*, 2011b; Krienert, Walsh, and Turner, 2009). Elder abuse most often occurs close to home and infiltrates elders' daily lives. The vast majority of perpetrators of abuse are family members, friends, neighbors, or others who have gained the trust of older adults (Krienert *et al.*, 2009).

Society's recognition and understanding of elder abuse is still emerging. Comparing findings of the growing body of literature on perceived and substantiated cases of elder abuse is challenging because no uniform term or agreed–upon definition is used among state governments, researchers, health and professional service providers, and advocates. For example, "elder mistreatment" is a common term used to describe abuse of older adults perpetrated by persons with whom there is an expectation of trust. In a report to the National Academy of Science, Bonnie and Wallace (2003, p. 40) described elder mistreatment as:

> (a) intentional actions that cause harm or create a serious risk of harm (whether or not harm is intended) to a vulnerable elder by a caregiver or other person who stands in a trust relationship to the elder or (b) failure by a caregiver to satisfy the elder's basic needs or to protect the elder from harm.

Similarly, the National Center on Elder Abuse (NCEA, n.d.a) suggests the use of "domestic elder abuse" to refer to any "maltreatment of an older person by

Family Problems: Stress, Risk, and Resilience, First Edition. Edited by Joyce A. Arditti.
© 2015 John Wiley & Sons, Inc. Published 2015 by John Wiley & Sons, Inc.

Case Example: Eleanor Vogel

A year ago, Eleanor Vogel, age 76, lost her 82-year-old husband, Ralph, to lung cancer. For over 30 years, Eleanor had been an elementary school teacher in their small Ohio community, and Ralph was the principal of the local high school. They have two sons. Jonah, a successful investment banker, lives in New York with his wife and children. Their other son, Jeb, is a chemist and lives in Cleveland. Since a divorce that occurred in his early thirties, Jeb has been unable to keep a steady job. For the 10 years after his divorce, Eleanor and

Ralph sent Jeb money at least yearly so that he could "get back on his feet." After the 2008 recession, Jeb's pleas for money increased. He came to help Eleanor with Ralph during the last months of Ralph's life and insisted on remaining there upon his father's death. Jeb reminds Eleanor daily that she is very forgetful and increasingly exerts control over decisions about her finances and interactions with others. Eleanor feels quite capable of managing her daily affairs and wants Jeb to leave her home as soon as possible.

Table 15.1   Types of elder abuse

Type of abuse	Definition	Examples
Physical	Use of physical force that may result in bodily injury, physical pain, or impairment	Hitting; slapping; pushing; shoving; kicking; pinching; burning; biting; beatings; restraining with ropes or chains
Sexual	Non-consensual sexual contact of any kind with an elderly person	Unwanted touching; making the person look at pornography; forcing sexual contact with a third party; coerced nudity; unwanted sexualized behavior; rape; sodomy
Emotional/ psychological	Infliction of anguish, pain or distress through verbal or non-verbal acts	Name-calling; yelling, swearing, insulting, disrespectful or threatening comments; threats; intimidation; isolating the person from others
Financial	Illegal or improper use of an elder's funds, property, or assets	Misuse of funds; taking money under false pretenses; forgery; forced property transfers; purchasing expensive items with the older person's money without that person's knowledge or permission; denying the older person access to his or her own funds; embezzlement
Neglect/ abandonment	Refusal, or failure, to fulfill any part of a person's obligations or caregiving duties to an elderly adult; may be intention or unintentional	Withholding appropriate attention; failure to provide food, water, clothing, medications, and assistance with activities of daily living; failing to meet the physical, social, or emotional needs of the older person

Source: NCEA, n.d.b.

---

someone who has a special relationship with the elder (a spouse, a sibling, a child, a friend, or a caregiver)," that occurs in the elder's home or in the home of a caregiver. NCEA also recommends the term "institutional abuse" to refer to the abuse of older adults that occurs in residential facilities (e.g., nursing homes, assisted living facilities), but identifies a formal relationship between these elderly victims and their *perpetrators*, with perpetrators defined as "persons

who have a legal or contractual obligation to provide elder victims with care and protection." Perpetrators of elder abuse can also be strangers – persons who target older adults with the intent to harm or commit fraudulent acts (e.g., scams, theft, muggings). Regardless of focus, most definitions recognize five forms of elder abuse: physical abuse, sexual abuse, psychological and emotional abuse, financial abuse and exploitation, and neglect and abandonment (see Table 15.1).

In this chapter, we use the terms *elder abuse* and *elder mistreatment* interchangeably to refer collectively to the various forms of abuse, exploitation, and neglect perpetrated by family members, friends and neighbors, and strangers who have befriended or gained the trust of an older person. Drawing primarily from the empirical elder abuse literature as well as from public policy documents, we (a) provide elder abuse prevalence and incidence rates; (b) explore characteristics of elderly victims and their perpetrators; (c) address the costs and potential consequences of elder abuse; (d) describe an ecological-community framework that sheds light on the unique dynamics of late-life abuse; and (e) discuss potential individual, family, community, and policy-level solutions. When available, we highlight information about specific types of elder abuse. However, it is highly unlikely that any one type of abuse occurs in the same way or in isolation. Rather, older adults who experience abuse often are subjected to "polyvictimization," wherein multiple types of abuse or mistreatment are perpetrated simultaneously (Finkelhor, Ormrod, and Turner, 2007). Issues of elder self-neglect are equally important and present many challenges for families, but this type of abuse is beyond the scope of this chapter. (For information on self-neglect see: Dong, Simon, Mosqueda, and Evans, 2012; Paveza, VandeWeerd, and Laumann, 2008.)

Prevalence and Incidence Rates

Research on the prevalence and incidence of elder abuse (EA) is limited, and exact state or national rates of EA are not yet definitive. Different sources (e.g., older adult surveys, adult protective services records, police reports, domestic violence shelter data) suggest varying rates of abuse and victimization. There is agreement across studies, however, that elder abuse threatens the health, safety, dignity, and overall well-being of far too many older Americans. Recent large-scale, community-based studies have provided preliminary insights into the magnitude of this issue, suggesting that elder abuse is much more common than previously thought.

In the most recent national survey of Adult Protective Services (APS) agencies (the principal public agencies responsible for investigating abuse), 253,426 incidents

involving elder abuse were reported by the 32 states responding to the survey (Teaster, Otto *et al.*, 2006). This represented 8.3 reports of abuse for every 1,000 older Americans. Self-neglect was the most common category of investigated reports (29.4%), followed by caregiver neglect (26.1%), and financial exploitation (18.5%).

In one of the first nationally representative studies of elder abuse, 9% of 3,005 community-dwelling older individuals (aged 57–85) reported recent verbal mistreatment by a family member, 3.5% reported financial abuse by a family member, and 0.2% reported physical mistreatment by a family member (Laumann, Leitsch, and Waite, 2008). A second nationally representative survey found that more than 1 in 10 respondents aged 60 and older had experienced some type of abuse or potential neglect by a family member in the year prior to the study. Specifically, 5.2% experienced financial abuse, 4.6% reported emotional abuse, 1.6% specified physical abuse, <1% described experiences of sexual abuse, and 5.1% indicated potential neglect (Acierno *et al.*, 2010). According to the study participants reporting abuse, family members perpetrated the majority of the most recent abuse events in their lives: 57% of emotional abuse events, 76% of physical abuse events, 52% of sexual abuse events, and 74% of neglect.

State-level studies have also found prevalence and incidence patterns that mirror national statistics and reveal the surprising frequency of elder abuse. Amstadter and colleagues (2011b), for example, surveyed South Carolinians aged 60 and older and found a prevalence rate of 12.9% for emotional abuse, 2.1% for physical mistreatment, 0.3% for sexual abuse, and 6.6% for financial exploitation by a family member. Similar to the national rates (Acierno *et al.*, 2010), the authors of the South Carolina study found that 1 in 10 of the adults surveyed reported experiencing some type of past-year mistreatment. In addition, 2 in 10 older adults reported experiencing some type of abuse since turning 60 years of age. Findings from a comprehensive statewide survey of New York residents aged 60 and older also suggested alarming rates of elder abuse. Researchers documented an estimated total one-year incidence rate of 76 per 1,000 older residents encountering some type of abuse, with the incidence of financial exploitation being most common, affecting 41 of 1,000 adults 60 and older in the course of a year

(Lifespan of Greater Rochester, Inc., Weill Cornell Medical Center of Cornell University, and New York City Department for the Aging, 2011). These high rates of victimization are clearly a serious concern as we approach the coming decades, with the number of persons aged 65 and older anticipated to more than double between 2010 and 2050 (Vincent and Velkoff, 2010).

Researchers and practitioners alike consistently assert that a dramatic discrepancy exists between the actual prevalence of elder abuse and the number of cases that reach the attention of various authorities. The magnitude of underreporting has varied across study findings, and reporting rates vary by abuse type (Acierno et al., 2010; Lifespan of Greater Rochester, Inc., et al., 2011). For example, the National Elder Mistreatment Survey (Acierno, Hernandez-Tejada, Muzzy, and Steve, 2009) found that some types of abuse were more likely to reach the attention of the police than others. Only 8% of older respondents who experienced emotional mistreatment in the past year had reported an incident to the police, compared to 16% experiencing sexual abuse and 31% who were victims of physical abuse. One reason for the underestimation of the occurrence of abuse is that older victims do not discuss their situation with others and rarely report incidences to the authorities. Reasons older adults give for not disclosing abuse include embarrassment, belief that they are responsible for what happened, worry that the perpetrator might harm them even more, a desire for their family member to stay out of jail, fear that they will be placed in a nursing home, not believing that help is available if they expose the abuse, acceptance of a long-standing abusive situation as one that must be tolerated, and not recognizing their situation as an abusive one.

Although recognition and reporting of abuse typically starts with the older individual, underreporting also occurs at the community level. Reasons for underreporting include an overall lack of community awareness, reluctance to recognize elder abuse as a problem occurring in a community, hesitance to take responsibility for getting involved in such a difficult issue, and inability of community members to act to remedy such harmful situations (Roberto, Teaster, McPherson, Mancini, and Savla, 2013).

Victims and Perpetrators of Elder Abuse

A multitude of interacting factors contribute to late-life vulnerability to abuse. Changes associated with aging as well as intrapersonal characteristics can place an older person at risk for abuse. The relationships between older adults and potential perpetrators are complex and often cited as a factor contributing to abuse.

Individual risk factors

One of the most commonly thought of risk factors for elder abuse is age. However, support for the significance of age as a risk factor is mixed. State agencies (e.g., APS; Teaster, Otto et al., 2006) and empirical studies focused on specific types of abuse (e.g., sexual, financial) have identified adults aged 75 and older as being particularly susceptible (Burgess, Dowdell, and Prentky, 2000; MetLife Mature Market Institute, 2011a). However, recent national community-based studies that assessed all types of abuse found that young-old individuals (60–69) were more susceptible to abuse, particularly emotional and physical abuse (Acierno et al., 2009) and that the risk of abuse did not increase with age (Laumann et al., 2008).

The association between age and risk of abuse may also be a result of the increasing number of adults in the late stages of life. These individuals often experience a decline in health, which results in a greater dependence on others for care than is typical of the general population of older adults. With advancing age, individuals also may experience decreasing interactions with members of their social network whose presence may protect them from abuse and mistreatment. In addition, as individuals proceed through the later stages of life, they tend to judge others' trustworthiness less stringently than younger individuals (Carstensen, 1992; Charles and Carstensen, 2010) and thus may be more vulnerable to fraud and financial exploitation. An investigation of age differences in perceived trust using neuroimaging methodology revealed differences between younger and older adults in activation of the anterior insula, a region of the brain believed to contribute to decision-making

(Castle *et al.*, 2012). The study authors posited that "older adults might have a lower visceral warning signal in response to cues of untrustworthiness, which could make deciding whom to trust difficult" (p. 20851).

Although older women are more likely to be victimized than older men (Hightower, 2004; Krienert *et al.*, 2009; Wisconsin Coalition Against Domestic Violence, 2009), gender differences in the risk for elder abuse, such as age, require further consideration (Thompson, Buxton, Gough, and Wahle, 2007). Older women's high rates of abuse might result, at least in part, from their longer lifespan (and associated vulnerabilities mentioned above), which may bring them into greater contact with potential abusers (Krienert *et al.*, 2009). In addition, women are subjected to higher rates of family violence across the lifespan, and researchers have shown that previous exposure to a traumatic life event (e.g., interpersonal and domestic violence) elevates an elder's risk of late life mistreatment (Acierno *et al.*, 2010). Thus, unique vulnerabilities related to gender and power dynamics need to be considered as a component of risk for elder abuse (Wisconsin Coalition Against Domestic Violence, 2009). (See Box 15.1.)

Lachs and colleagues (1997) reported race as a risk factor for abuse. They found more Black elders at risk for abuse than their White counterparts, but cautioned that their findings were predicated on the use of APS

cases and may overestimate the contribution of race. Similarly, Tatara (1999), using APS data from 31 states, found that both Black and Hispanic elders were over-represented in the state data on elder abuse victims. Nearly one in three victims known to authorities was a minority elder. One possible explanation for differences in reports of abuse of majority and minority elders is that knowledge about elder abuse is derived from European-American definitions, perceptions, and experiences with abuse. Distinct cultural norms and beliefs about what constitutes elder abuse may contribute to risk for abuse among minority elders (DeLiema, Gassoumis, Homeier, and Wilber, 2012; Horsford, Parra-Cardona, Post, and Schiamberg, 2010; Tauriac and Scruggs, 2006).

Dakin and Pearlmutter (2009) analyzed responses from focus groups conducted with African American, Latina, and White women aged 60 and older of varying socioeconomic backgrounds. They found that African American and White women with high socioeconomic status (SES), as well as Latina women, did not identify financial abuse as a type of elder abuse. Working-class White women did not identify verbal abuse as elder mistreatment, whereas working-class African American women included societal maltreatment (i.e., systemic mistreatment by HMOs) and financial abuse in their definitions of elder abuse, but did not include physical abuse. The Latina women (all characterized as low SES) exhibited higher tolerance for spousal abuse than women in the other groups.

Face-to-face interviews with 100 African American, 95 Korean American, and 90 White adults aged 60 and older also revealed several differences in perceptions of elder abuse (Moon and Benton, 2000). African American respondents were slightly less tolerant than White respondents of involving non-family members in cases of potential abuse, whereas White respondents exhibited a significantly higher tolerance for verbal abuse than either African American or Korean American elders. Korean elders were the most tolerant of elder abuse overall, particularly financial exploitation. Also, they were significantly more likely than respondents in the other groups to blame the victims for the occurrence of elder abuse and held significantly more negative attitudes toward involvement of people outside the family in elder mistreatment incidents and reporting of elder abuse to authorities.

Box 15.1   IPV

Edcouch, Texas: A home health care provider reached out to local authorities after she learned the 80-year-old husband of a couple she served had threatened to bury his wife in the backyard. The care provider reported that the man was repeatedly verbally abusive to his wife and she herself was fearful of him. When police investigated, they found a machete, rifle, and knives allegedly used to abuse the wife. Despite mounting evidence against the man for emotionally and physically abusing his wife, he continued to state that he had done nothing wrong.

ValleyCentral.com, February 25, 2010

It is also important to remember that cultural interpretations and perceptions can differ within minority communities. For example, whereas Tauriac and Scruggs's (2006) examination of the perceptions of 35 African Americans (age range 16 to 63) of elder abuse by an adult child found high consistency in their perceptions and depictions of physical abuse, verbal abuse and neglect and abandonment, differences emerged based on the age and sex of the study participants. When asked about what constitutes extreme abuse, older respondents gave more examples of verbal abuse than younger respondents, while younger respondents gave more examples of verbal abuse when asked to provide examples of a mild form of abuse. Female respondents offered more examples of neglect or abandonment and provided more varied examples of abuse behaviors, regardless of the level of severity of the abuse, than male respondents.

Poor overall health and disabilities that require older adults to seek assistance in order to live independently increase their risk for abuse. Laumann and colleagues (2008) found that older adults who reported any type of physical vulnerabilities were approximately 13% more likely to report verbal mistreatment than study participants who indicated that they had no physical vulnerabilities. In addition, the better the respondents rated their health, the lower their odds of financial mistreatment. Acierno et al. (2009) reported that the likelihood of financial exploitation by both family members and strangers was higher among older adults with more severe physical disabilities, and poor health predicted neglect. Amstadter and colleagues (2011b) also found that the need for assistance with activities of daily living and poor health status were significant correlates of emotional abuse, physical abuse, neglect, and financial abuse and exploitation of older adults.

Changes in cognitive functioning, including declining memory, also have been associated with increased risk of physical abuse, emotional abuse, caregiver neglect, and financial exploitation. In a study of 8,932 older adults in Chicago, of whom 238 were identified as victims of elder abuse by social service professionals, Dong and colleagues (Dong, Simon, Rajan, and Evans, 2011) noted several different types of age-related cognitive change contributed to elder abuse risk. After controlling for other known risk factors (e.g., medical conditions, depressive symptoms, little social support), lower levels of global cognition, higher dementia severity, lower levels of episodic memory, and slower perceptual speed were all independently associated with an increased risk of abuse.

Cognitive impairment increases exponentially with age and is perhaps the most pervasive and salient risk factor for financial abuse and exploitation (Sherod et al., 2009). Decline in financial capacity, defined as the ability to manage one's financial affairs in a manner consistent with self-interest, usually occurs very early in the course of cognitive impairment, with older adults and those who care for them often remaining unaware of encroaching deficits in financial skill (Widera, Steenpass, Marson, and Sudore, 2011). Compromises in decision-making capacity make older adults particularly susceptible to *undue influence* (UI), a tactic used by the large majority of individuals perpetrating financial abuse (Blum, 2012). This type of manipulation can take two forms: (a) overt UI, which involves intimidating or instilling fear in an older adult (i.e., person recognized that he or she is being forced to do something against his or her will); and (b) covert UI, or "false goodwill," which involves the betrayal of a trusting relationship (Blum, 2012; Steigel and Wood, 2011). Covert UI is most common and much more difficult to detect or address than overt UI. For a high-profile example of UI, read about the case of New York City socialite and philanthropist Brooke Astor (http://www.aarp.org/money/estate-planning/info-06-2009/newsmaker_susan_robbins_thy_will_be_undone.html) and how the five-year dispute ended (http://www.huffingtonpost.com/2012/03/28/brook-astor-estate-settle_n_1386121.html).

Another consistent finding is that lower levels of social support are strongly associated with the occurrence of all types of elder abuse (Acierno et al., 2010; Amstadter et al., 2011b). Older adults who are lonely or isolated are much more vulnerable to elder abuse than elders who have strong and actively engaged support systems. Acierno and colleagues (2009, 2010) noted that low social support was associated with more than triple the likelihood that mistreatment of any form would be reported by older adults. Similarly, Amstadter and colleagues (2011b) reported that low levels of social support significantly predicted the likelihood of older adults experiencing emotional and physical mistreatment.

An examination of loneliness as a risk factor for elder abuse among 141 elderly women who presented to an urban medical center in China also revealed that social support was protective against elder abuse risk (Dong, Beck, and Simon, 2009). Initial analyses showed that each 1-point increase in loneliness scores was associated with a 44% increase in elder abuse risk. However, having high levels of social support negated the higher risk for mistreatment that was associated with higher loneliness scores. The authors of this study concluded that whereas low levels of social support contribute to elder abuse risk, high levels of social support may buffer or minimize other risk factors that place older adults at greater risk for abuse. Thus, the interactions of social support and other risk factors merit further exploration.

Having limited social support also increases the likelihood of more severe outcomes for elders who encounter mistreatment. A review of APS substantiated cases involving 113 older adults revealed that lower levels of both social network and social engagement were associated with higher mortality risk for abuse victims (Dong, Simon, Beck et al., 2011). Specifically, older victims of abuse with low or average levels of social network support or social engagement had increased mortality risk associated with elder abuse.

Place of residence may also contribute to elders' vulnerability for abuse. Although the abuse of older adults is prevalent and problematic in both rural and urban settings, patterns of abuse vary considerably in different types of communities. An examination of elder abuse experienced by 7,178 rural and 7,615 urban older women found that significantly more rural women were victims of physical abuse, emotional abuse, and active caregiver neglect than urban women, while more urban women had experienced more passive caregiver neglect than rural women (Dimah and Dimah, 2003).

The structure and culture of rural environments also may inadvertently conceal and alternatively facilitate abuse and inhibit prevention and treatment efforts (Riddell, Ford-Gilboe, and Leipert, 2009; Teaster, Roberto, and Dugar, 2006). Geographic isolation combined with economic stressors, strong social and cultural pressures, and lack of available services in rural jurisdictions significantly compound the problems confronted by older adults seeking support and services to end abuse. For example, interviews with 10 older women who had experienced intimate partner violence and 24 community service professionals in a rural community in eastern Kentucky revealed that the unique characteristics of this rural setting played an important role in concealing abuse and created barriers to providing appropriate services for victims. Lack of appropriate shelter services and affordable transitional housing within the community or surrounding area, close social ties with emergency responders and service providers in the "tight knit" community, and low levels of education and economic security among the older victims all exacerbated the abuse experiences of rural residents (Teaster et al., 2006). These factors also can create difficulties for service providers in identifying and assisting victims of elder abuse and complicate the ability of the criminal justice system to investigate and prosecute.

The findings from the research literature suggest that many factors – demographic, social, cultural, historical, behavioral, and psychological – alone or in conjunction, may heighten, moderate, or reduce the risk for elder abuse. Neither the contributions of individual risk factors nor the complex interactions between and among these factors are fully understood and will continue to garner the attention of scholars. In practice, service providers rely on experience, instinct, and a broad spectrum of factors, or "red flags" when trying to discern whether abuse is occurring in the lives of the older adults they encounter. A summary of these practical indicators, developed by the Center of Excellence on Elder Abuse and Neglect, is available at http://www.centeronelderabuse.org/docs/Red_Flags_2012.pdf.

Perpetrators of elder abuse

The large majority of perpetrators have an ongoing relationship with their elderly victims before mistreatment occurs (Jackson and Hafemeister, 2012; Krienert et al., 2009). Outsiders often perceive alleged perpetrators as primary sources of support for elders rather than individuals who are causing them harm; they are family members, caregivers, friends, service providers, church members, and neighbors. Perpetrators may also have unique characteristics that help them hide their abusive actions from others in the family and community. In the MetLife Mature Market Institute (2011a) study of elder financial abuse and exploitation, for example, perpetrators shared several traits: they were good at cultivating relationships and convincing older adults that they were worthy of their trust; they were charming, attentive, and exhibited excellent persuasion skills.

The majority of individuals who perpetrate emotional abuse are intimate partners or spouses (25%) or acquaintances (25%), followed by children and grandchildren (19%), and other relatives (13%; Acierno et al., 2009). In cases of elder sexual abuse, perpetrators tend to be husbands or adult sons (Ramsey-Klawsnik, 1991; Teaster and Roberto, 2004). In a study where sexual abuse of elders occurred in care facilities, employees were the most commonly alleged perpetrators (43%), followed by facility residents (40%; Ramsey-Klawsnik and Teaster, 2012). Most accused (78%) were male. Two accused staff and four accused residents had criminal histories.

Although both men and women perpetrate abuse against older adults, research studies and state investigations consistently show that men are more likely than women to be abusers (Krienert et al., 2009; MetLife Mature Market Institute, 2011a; Teaster, Otto et al., 2006; Wisconsin Coalition Against Domestic Violence, 2009). Krienert and colleagues, for example, reviewed a large cross-national sample of elder abuse incidents reported to the criminal justice system and found that 72% of offenders were male. Similarly, an examination of 127 elder sexual abuse cases investigated by Medicare Fraud Control Units over a 10-year time span also determined that 80% of perpetrators were male (Payne, 2010). Examination of nation-wide financial abuse and exploitation cases (n = 314) reported in the news (MetLife Mature Market Institute, 2011a) also revealed that nearly 60% of perpetrators in these cases, most of which involved multiple types of abuse, were males. Male perpetrators were typically older than female perpetrators. The majority of males were between the ages of 30 and 59, while most of the female perpetrators were between the ages of 30 and 49. (See Box 15.2.)

Perpetrators are often dependent on the older person for shelter, finances, and emotional support (Jackson and Hafemeister, 2012; Lachs et al., 1997).

Box 15.2   Sweetheart Scam

Boston, Massachusetts: Edward, an 85-year-old retired judge, was allegedly swindled by his long time "friend," "love interest," and power of attorney. City council woman Kimberly (age 39), whose mother was friends with the Judge long before his mental decline, claimed they were just "close friends" and that she began "looking out for him to protect him from his family" after he was diagnosed with Alzheimer's disease. Over four years, Kimberly had twice influenced the Judge to make changes to his will, leaving the bulk of his assets to her and her two children. She had also accepted a "generous gift" from the judge of $380,000 to pay for her new condominium. Once inquiries into the nature of the relationship began, Kimberly's only response was, "If I was some horrible woman like they are making me out to be, who wanted his money, wouldn't I have married him and had his pension for the rest of my life? And I didn't do that."

Boston Globe, April 8, 2010

It is also commonly reported that they are addicted to alcohol or other illicit drugs (Jogerst, Daly, Galloway, Zheng, and Xu, 2012; Krienert et al., 2009) and have a history of mental or emotional illness (Acierno et al., 2009; Jackson and Hafemeister, 2011). According to one national survey, perpetrators of emotional, physical, and sexual abuse have a much higher incidence of probable substance abuse problems (21–56%) than the general population (11%; Amstadter et al., 2011a). Substance abuse by perpetrators was particularly salient in cases of physical abuse, with 53.8% of female victims and 65.9% of male victims reporting excessive substance use by alleged perpetrators. A survey of 401 older victims of reported domestic abuse who sought criminal justice assistance in New York identified 161 of the perpetrators (74%) as having a mental impairment (Brownell, Berman, and Salamone, 2000). Of these perpetrators, 51% were substance abusers, 26% had a mental illness,

17% had a mental illness and chemical dependency, and 6% had dementia.

Among cases of elder abuse brought to the attention of authorities in South Carolina (Amstadter *et al.*, 2011b), 15% of known perpetrators had a problem with substance abuse at the time mistreatment occurred, almost 50% were unemployed and socially isolated, 16% had prior problems with the police, and about 19% had a prior mental health treatment history. An analysis of Virginia cases also revealed that almost a third of elder abuse perpetrators were chronically unemployed, employed in the unskilled or semi-skilled labor force (43%), or unemployed (53%) at the time elder abuse incidents actually occurred. Forty-two percent of these perpetrators were financially dependent on the elder whom they abused. Additionally, 50% of perpetrators had either drug dependence/addiction, alcohol dependence/addiction, or both (Jackson and Hafemeister, 2011).

When an older person is highly dependent on a family member, the caregiver may experience frustration, anger, and resentment that can lead to a range of abusive behaviors from verbally assaulting the elder to depriving them of daily essentials, care, and services (Amstadter *et al.*, 2011a). Findings from interviews with 265 informal caregiver/older adult care dyads indicated that poorer caregiver health, caregiver cognitive impairments, caregiver risk for clinical depression, spousal caregiving relationships, and greater care recipient needs for assistance with activities of daily living (ADL/IADL) were all associated with increased risk for mistreatment within caregiver–care receiver relationships (Beach *et al.*, 2005). In a national survey of 5,777 older adults, Amstadter and colleagues (2011a) revealed that one out of seven victims of emotional mistreatment reported that he or she would be unable to live independently without the assistance provided by the perpetrator. Female victims of multiple types of elder abuse were more likely to be dependent on perpetrators for physical care and were more likely to live with their abusers. "Deviance" among perpetrators (e.g., substance abuse, criminal activity), on the other hand, was more likely in cases involving male victims.

It is important to note that caregivers who abuse do not typically do so because they are stressed by the responsibility of providing care (Lachs and Pillemer,

2004), but rather because they are dependent on the care recipient (Nerenberg, 2008; Pillemer, 2004). A frequently occurring scenario (see the case example at the beginning of this chapter) involves an adult child who has never become completely independent from the parent because of personal (e.g., mental illness, drug dependence), relational (e.g., unable to sustain intimate relations), or financial issues (e.g., unable to keep a job). These relationships may become abusive or violent when the older adult declines or refuses to provide more money or other types of support, particularly when the dependent adult child becomes desperate. (See Box 15.3.)

As evident from the information provided in this section, we actually know very little about the perpetrators of elder abuse beyond their demographic characteristics and personal behaviors. It is important to be aware, however, that abuse can take place with or without any of these perpetrator characteristics being apparent, and many families with extensive risk factors (e.g., life circumstances, substance abuse, interdependency of caregiver and old person) do not manifest abuse. The complex interactions between unique factors of different abuse types, dependence, deviance, social isolation, and other relational factors such as gender or family history of abuse play a powerful role in patterns of perpetration and merit further exploration.

Box 15.3   Dependent Perpetrator

Hollywood, California: An elderly woman who was discovered housed in a backyard shed was moved from a hospital to a Hollywood nursing home, according to the Department of Children and Families. The 84-year-old woman was malnourished and dehydrated when the Sheriff's Office found her without food or water in a sweltering storage shed behind the beach house of her son, Pastro, age 54. An accounting tutor at a local college, Pastro told authorities he moved his mother into the shed because he needed to rent her room to make money.

Sun Sentinel, June 2, 2011

Costs and Consequences of Elder Abuse

The costs and consequences of elder mistreatment are intersecting, cumulative, and pervasive in the lives of abuse victims (Scott-Storey, 2011; Thomas, Joshi, Wittenberg, and McCloskey, 2008). Some are overt or material in nature, such as physical injuries or the loss of money and valued possessions (MetLife Mature Market Institute, 2011a; Wiglesworth, Austin, Corona, and Mosqueda, 2009). Other outcomes of elder abuse can be insidious and, according to reports of victims, even more detrimental than readily observable damages. These less tangible costs and consequences include long-term emotional or psychological damages (Begle *et al.*, 2011; Cisler, Begle, Amstadter, and Acierno, 2012; MetLife Mature Market Institute, 2011a), new or exacerbated health problems (Fisher and Regan, 2006; Thomas *et al.*, 2008), and social isolation and loneliness (Winterstein and Eisikovits, 2005). Exposure to one type of abuse or violence puts victims at greater risk of experiencing other types of violence, triggering a pattern of ongoing or multiple victimizations (Acierno *et al.*, 2010) and resultant complex trauma. *Polyvictims*, those who have repeated exposures to violence, crime, and abuse, are even more distressed than those who have experienced chronic victimization or abuse of a single type (Finkelhor *et al.*, 2007).

Elder abuse can cause physical injuries ranging widely from bruises and sprains, to broken bones and lost teeth, to severe brain trauma, sometimes resulting in long-term health problems, functional limitations, or even death. One case-control study of severe physical abuse of older adults found that victims were assaulted with a wide variety of weapons and predominantly suffered injuries to the head and torso (Friedman, Avila, Tanouye, and Joseph, 2011). Eighty-five percent of perpetrators in these cases were family members or intimate partners, with spouses/partners and children perpetrating an equal number of cases (31.7% each). Nearly 60% of victims were female. Among victims of violence aged 60 and older identified through two different trauma centers, specific injuries suffered included: (a) fractures of the head, neck, upper extremities and lower extremities; (b) open wounds on the head and neck, torso, lower and upper extremities, and other unspecified areas of the body; and (c) internal injuries including chest and brain trauma. Compared to the study control group (n = 123), composed of elders who did not experience abuse, but were admitted for accident-related injuries, abused elders suffered more severe injuries as determined by longer hospital stays, treatment in an intensive care unit, assisted breathing, and in-hospital case fatality rates.

The impact of sexual abuse, perhaps the most egregious and underreported type of elder abuse (Teaster and Roberto, 2004), has not been explored as thoroughly in the research literature as other types of abuse. Ramsey-Klawsnik (2004) described some of the medical forensic markers consistent with elder sexual abuse, including genital injuries, human bite marks, imprint injuries such as finger marks, and bruising on the thighs, buttocks, breasts, and other body areas. Not surprisingly, older sexual abuse victims also exhibited substantial psychosocial indicators of trauma including symptoms of post-traumatic stress disorder. (See Box 15.4.)

In a sample of intimate partner violence victims that included older women, Bonomi, Anderson, Rivara, and Thompson (2007) also found that sexual intimate

---

Box 15.4 Sexual Abuse

Bronx, New York: A nursing home worker was indicted after the worker was allegedly caught sexually assaulting a woman in her 80s with Alzheimer's disease. This employee, who was a non-clinical staff member at the facility, was naked in a laundry closet with the woman when a co-worker opened the closet. The co-worker reported it to authorities. The worker accused of sexual abuse had been working at the nursing home for 12 years. The nursing home administrator responded, "We are shocked that an incident of this nature could have occurred at our center – it is in no way reflective of the care and compassion that our staff shows residents on a daily basis."

NBC 4 New York, December 7, 2012

partner violence exposure, alone or in combination with physical abuse, resulted in numerous adverse health effects that "persisted for many years after the abuse stopped" (p. 993). Outcomes of sexual violence included higher likelihood of depression, twice the probability of reporting fair or poor health, and low scores on standardized measures of general health and physical, social, and mental functioning.

The full extent of emotional mistreatment among older adults remains unclear, though it appears to have a pivotal role in most personal accounts of elder abuse. The intangible nature of psychological abuse makes it difficult to quantify in data collection measures, and often means it goes unrecognized even by victims themselves. Though about 15% of substantiated APS cases involve confirmed emotional abuse (Teaster, Otto et al., 2006), it is the type of abuse least often reported to the police (Acierno et al., 2009). Studies of intimate partner violence (IPV) in late life have suggested that emotional or psychological abuse may increase in frequency or severity as partners age, and physical abuse becomes less common (Roberto, McPherson, and Brossoie, 2013), with reports of psychological mistreatment from partnered older adults as high as 32% (Daly, Hartz, Stromquist, Peek-Asa, and Jogerst, 2008) to 45% (Fisher and Regan, 2006).

What we do know about emotional mistreatment is that it is one of the most damaging forms of elder abuse. For example, Begle and colleagues (2011) found that emotional abuse had a more powerful effect on long-term mental health of victims than did physical abuse. After controlling for other distress factors among a study of surveyed adults 60 and older, emotional, but not physical, abuse correlated with higher levels of negative emotional symptoms (e.g., anxiety, depression) of elder abuse victims. Older adults who experience chronic emotional mistreatment may internalize their abuser's verbal aggression, thus leading to increased physical health symptoms, lower sense of self-efficacy, learned helplessness, and an external locus of control, factors associated with depression and anxiety (Begle et al., 2011). Cisler and colleagues (2012), in further analysis of results from the National Elder Mistreatment Study, arrived at similar conclusions about the powerful, lasting impacts of emotional violence. When other known correlates of poor mental health were accounted for, only psychological mistreatment was found to be a significant predictor of late-life negative emotional symptoms and functional impairment. While acknowledging that physical and sexual abuse impact the victims' psychological health, the study authors suggested that "emotional abuse may have a more potent and direct effect on mental health, whereas the effects of sexual and physical mistreatment are shared with other factors in the environment, such as social support and physical health" (Cisler et al., 2012, p. 226).

Elder financial abuse, regarded by some as the "Crime of the Twenty-First Century," costs older Americans nearly 3 billion dollars annually (MetLife Mature Market Institute, 2011a). Falling victim to financial abuse can eradicate nearly all of an elder's financial resources at a point in their lives when they have little or no ability to recoup financial losses (MetLife Mature Market Institute, 2009). However, the losses to elderly victims extend far beyond dollars and cents. "Elder financial abuse engenders health care inequities, fractures families, reduces available health care options … increases rates of mental health issues among elders [and] … invariably results in losses of human rights and dignity" (MetLife Mature Market Institute, 2011a, p. 4).

Elder abuse, in all its forms, has a profound impact on overall health and quality of late life of victims. Broad health outcomes can be indirect and cumulative in nature. In one of the first studies to examine the long-term health implications of abuse, Fisher and Regan (2006) found that women who had experienced psychological/emotional abuse, threats, physical violence, or sexual abuse since age 55 had significantly increased odds of reporting bone or joint problems, digestive problems, depression or anxiety, chronic pain, and high blood pressure or heart problems.

The most dramatic outcome of elder abuse and neglect is premature death (see Box 15.5). In a seminal study addressing mortality risk among abused elders, Lachs, Williams, O'Brien, Pillemer, and Charlson (1998) cross-linked the New Haven Established Population for Epidemiologic Studies for the Elderly (EPESE) and Connecticut Ombudsman/Elderly Protective Service records. Of the 175 reported and substantiated cases of adults who experienced abuse, the risk of death for those who had experienced elder mistreatment was higher than for those who had not. When Dong and colleagues (Dong, Simon

Box 15.5   Premature Death

Whitesburg, Kentucky: A mother, her two daughters, and her son were placed in jail on suspicion of abuse and neglect that led to the premature death of the family's paternal grandmother. The indictment said they inflicted unreasonable confinement on their mother-in-law/grandmother, Mildred, resulting in physical pain and injury. Charges also indicated the four deprived Mildred of the services necessary to maintain her basic health and welfare. Theresa, the mother of the three others accused in this case, admitted no wrongdoing by herself or her children.

WYMT TV Mountain News, December 6, 2012

Death as an outcome of elder abuse is a serious concern for service providers who work with older adults. In response, many communities have created multi-disciplinary teams known as Elder Abuse Fatality Review Teams (National Center on Child Fatality Review, 2004). The teams use a formal or informal deliberative process that: identifies deaths caused by or are traceable to elder abuse; examines the multi-agency systemic interventions and community involvement in and knowledge of elder abuse related deaths; and explores social changes and new systemic interventions to avert future deaths and reduce and eliminate elder abuse.

Theorizing Pathways and Response to Abuse in Late Life

et al., 2009) cross-referenced data on 9,318 Chicago residents 65 and older with APS data, both reported and confirmed cases of elder abuse were significantly correlated with increased risk for mortality. The one-year mortality rate for elders without any reported elder abuse was 5.91 deaths per 100 persons each year; for those with reported elder abuse it was 13.49 deaths per 100 persons; and for those individuals with confirmed cases of elder abuse, the one-year mortality rate rose to 18.33 deaths per 100 persons.

A 10-year retrospective post-mortem examination of 74 records on persons aged 60 and older by the Chief Medical Examiner in Louisville, Kentucky sheds light on how elder abuse can lead directly to death (Shields, Hunsaker, and Hunsaker, 2004). Of the elder abuse cases reviewed for this study, 52 were determined to be elder homicide, and 22 cases were victims of neglect. Of the homicide deaths among older adults, 42.3% resulted from a gunshot wound, 36.5% were the outcome of severe beatings, 19.2% of the elders died from stab wounds, and 9.6% of the deaths resulted from asphyxia. Closer examination of the neglect cases revealed that 50% of these elders died because of bronchopneumonia, 22.7% succumbed to sepsis, 9.1% died because of severe dehydration, and others passed away because of heart disease (9.1%), falls (4.5%), or undetermined causes (1 elder; Shields *et al.*, 2004).

It was stated earlier that elder abuse is a complex problem that stems from the convergence of multiple individual, family, and systemic causes. While there is no one explanation or unifying theory of elder abuse (Biggs and Goergen, 2010; Laumann *et al.*, 2008), several theories and conceptual perspectives provide promising avenues for understanding older victims' experiences with abuse and identifying pathways for effective elder abuse prevention and intervention. In this section, we describe one such framework, socio-ecological theory (Bronfenbrenner, 1986), which, with the integration of salient concepts from other theoretical approaches (e.g., life course perspective, feminist theories), has the potential to advance understanding of elder abuse and guide societal responses to address this growing problem.

The basic premise of socioecological theory is that individuals are embedded in a series of environmental systems that interact with one another and with the individual to influence all types of human development. As an organizing template for the study of elder abuse, the model provides a focus on the characteristics of the older adult and four influencing systems (see Figure 15.1): (a) the microsystem, or the immediate context in which the abuse takes place (e.g., community, residential setting); (b) the mesosystem, or the relationship between the older adult and the abuser (e.g., relative, friend, caregiver); (c) the exosystem, or

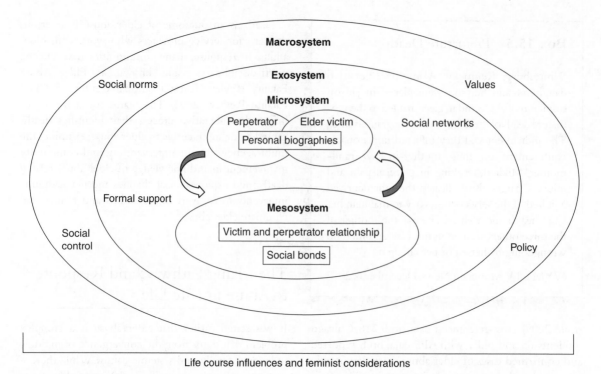

Figure 15.1 Ecological framework for elder abuse (adapted from Horsford *et al.*, 2010 and Teaster *et al.*, 2006).

environments that are external to the older adult (e.g., community services, law enforcement) that may affect their well-being; and (d) the macrosystem, which includes broad ideological values, norms, and institutional patterns of a particular culture (Parra-Cardona, Meyer, Schiamberg, and Post, 2007; Horsford *et al.*, 2010; Teaster *et al.*, 2006). The socioecological model facilitates an understanding that elder abuse is a complex problem requiring coordinated responses from different levels of intervention.

Understanding the influence of micro- and meso-systems in older adults' lives also necessitates the inclusion of life course concepts (Elder, 1998), including an examination of older individuals' histories or personal biographies, family relationships, and social and historical contexts. Life course investigators acknowledge the importance of social bonds in life trajectories and transitions. Specifically, the life course perspective posits the principle of "linked lives," which emphasizes relational interconnectedness (Elder, 1998). Individual lives are embedded within relationships with family and other social

network members and are influenced by them. Although the immediate relevance of these social relationships may wax and wane over time, relationship stories are integral to how older adults make meaning of their lives.

Feminist frameworks also offer an important avenue for examining the complex intersection of social and historical context, age, gender, race, ethnicity, socioeconomics and sexual orientation in the lives of an increasingly diverse population of potential elder abuse victims. For example, scholars focusing on late-life intimate partner violence have demonstrated that power inequities and abusive behaviors within violent intimate relationships tend to persist over time, in many cases even after perpetrators become sick and frail and recipients of care from the partners they have abused (Band-Winterstein and Eisikovits, 2009; Montminy, 2005). Incorporating a feminine lens within the socioecological model focuses attention on the power and control dynamics that typically characterize late-life abuse, the caregiving arrangements and exchanges that may complicate interactions among intimate partners or other family care relationships, and age-related changes in power dynamics (e.g., reversal of child/parent roles, role changes within marriages) that may contribute to late-life experiences of abuse (Roberto *et al.*, 2013).

Tenets of social organization provide a community framework that informs the explication of the exosystem and macrosystem in the ecological model. Social organization pertains to how people in a community interrelate, cooperate, and provide mutual support. It includes social support norms, social controls that regulate behavior and interaction patterns, and the networks that operate in a community (Furstenberg and Hughes, 1997; Mancini, Martin, and Bowen, 2003; Mancini, Nelson, Bowen, and Martin, 2006). Community members share norms that govern behaviors and expectations that can be provided for both licit and illicit activities (Furstenberg and Hughes, 1997); activity considered unacceptable by the general population might be more tolerated among certain subgroups of individuals. These subgroups may be characterized by particular demographic characteristics (i.e., age, race) and by psychographic characteristics, including attitudes about gender, sense of self, beliefs about others, and so on.

Community capacity, a dynamic group process, reflects the degree to which people in a community demonstrate a sense of shared responsibility for the welfare of the community and its individual members (Bowen, Martin, Mancini, and Nelson, 2000). It also demonstrates collective competence by taking advantage of opportunities for addressing community needs and confronting situations that threaten the safety and well-being of community members. Community capacity as an aspect of social organization enables researchers to capture the process of community influence on older adults and their relationships. Specifically, this perspective focuses on older adults and their informal networks of relationships (e.g., partners, children, other family members, friends, neighbors), formal support systems available to them (e.g., justice system, community/victim services, health care professionals, religious leaders), and the broader ideological values, norms, and institutional patterns of the communities in which they live (Mancini *et al.*, 2006; Mancini and Bowen, 2013).

Responding to the Challenges of Elder Abuse

As depicted in Figure 15.1, to understand elder abuse requires an examination of multiple interwoven systems that are influenced by the complex intersection of social and historical context, age, gender, race, ethnicity, and socioeconomic variables. Likewise, to prevent elder abuse and address it when it happens requires active involvement from members of each of the systems.

Individuals and families

Elder abuse occurs for a variety of reasons, and although there is not one definitive factor that places an older person at risk for mistreatment, older adults can do a variety of things to help prevent abuse in their lives, including (MetLife Mature Market Institute, 2011c; 2012):

- being informed;
- staying alert;
- organizing and keeping legal and financial documents in a safe place;
- being active and socially engaging with others;
- keeping in touch with family members;
- participating in community activities;
- being cautious when making financial decisions;
- monitoring financial affairs;
- never being pressured into making an immediate decision; discussing with a trusted family member or other before taking action;
- being wary of family members or caregivers who might have a need for financial assistance or who have substance abuse issues;
- being wary of people who ask about changing a will or adding their names to bank accounts or titles on property;
- discussing concerns about actual or suspected abuse with a trusted family member or professional.

Although the focus of this chapter is on elder abuse perpetrated by relatives, friends, and trusted others, family members are more likely to be in a position to help prevent their elderly relatives from abuse than contribute to it. Strategies for family members include (MetLife Mature Market Institute, 2011b; 2012):

- watch for warning signs that might indicate elder abuse;
- encourage the older adult to organize legal and financial documents;
- stress to the older adult the importance of monitoring financial affairs;
- suggest that the older adult be cautious in making any decisions that will influence their finances or resources;
- maintain open dialogue with the older adult;
- take the older adult's concerns seriously;
- call and visit the older adult as often as possible;
- be especially vigilant for signs of abuse or neglect if your family member has a cognitive problem;
- if abuse is suspected, discuss concerns with the older adult and encourage him or her to disclose any concerns that he or she has now or at any time in the future, and do not hesitate to seek professional help to address the issue.

Community programs and services

Whenever a potential abusive situation is identified, either by the victim or some third party, in most states APS is the principal public agency responsible for investigating the situation. It operates under a mandate to protect safety, health, and civil liberties (Office of Justice Programs, 2000). When APS receives reports of elder abuse, workers go into the home to investigate and ameliorate the situation with legal, medical, psychological, and social services. In non-emergency cases, however, APS workers cannot enter private residences to investigate alleged abuse without consent from the older individual or his or her caregiver or legal guardian, a court order, or a search warrant (Roby and Sullivan, 2000). If consent to enter is denied, APS can petition the court for assistance upon showing of probable cause. The authority of APS in long-term care settings varies from state to state. Although all state APS programs have the authority to investigate in domestic settings, only 68.5% have the authority to investigate in institutional settings (Teaster, 2003).

Beyond each state's APS services, there are national, state, and local initiatives that have found creative and successful ways to prevent and address elder abuse, although services and programming may vary considerably between different geographic areas. Model programs often incorporate the use of multidisciplinary response teams, inter-agency collaboration, and/or comprehensive, coordinated community education efforts. For example, the National Association of Triads (NATI) supports partnerships between law enforcement, older adults, and community groups that are tailored to the needs of local communities. With the goal of promoting older adult safety, many local triads have helped put protections in place for seniors that can reduce their risk of elder abuse. Examples of specific supports provided by Triad groups include Escort Partnerships, Safe Walks, Safe Shopping, Older Adult Referral Cards for law enforcement officers, Telephone Reassurance, Adopt-a-Senior, and an Older Adult Buddy System. To learn more about the national Triad system, visit the NATI website at www.nationaltriad.org.

The National Center on Elder Abuse (NCEA) has identified an array of regional and local coalitions nationwide focused on aspects of elder abuse prevention and intervention, as well as "promising practices" in this field (NCEA, 2007). They also provide the NCEA's Innovative Practices Database, which is an online tool that can locate program models and information resources around the country related to elder abuse prevention, intervention, and public education (NCEA, n.d.c). To learn more about best practices and other leading national, state, and local initiatives, we encourage you to explore information provided by the NCEA (www.ncea.aoa.gov), the National Clearinghouse on Abuse in Later Life (NCALL; www.ncall.us), and the National Committee for Prevention of Elder Abuse (NCPEA; www.preventelderabuse.org).

Policy initiatives

Although there are numerous examples of state and federal legislation and policy initiatives that address elder abuse, there has been only one successful initiative at the federal level. The Elder Justice Act (EJA), otherwise known as Title VI, Section H of the Patient Protection and Affordability Act (United States Government Printing Office, 2010), became law on

March 23, 2010. Advocates, practitioners, researchers, and supportive legislators worked diligently for many years to give elder abuse the legislative attention they believed it deserved. Their efforts finally bore fruit as attention and support grew concerning this pervasive but under-recognized crime.

The purpose of the EJA is to increase awareness and knowledge of elder abuse, neglect, and exploitation at the national level, train individuals from various disciplines on these issues, combating elder abuse, and prosecuting cases of elder abuse where appropriate. It is the first bill to state specifically that it is the right of older adults to be free of abuse, neglect, and exploitation and will provide federal resources to address present situations of elder abuse and prevent future abuse. The passing of the EJA has already significantly raised a national focus on elder abuse, and particularly, elder financial abuse. However, many of the programs and activities authorized (e.g., research, training) cannot be implemented until Congress appropriates the funding.

Conclusion

With the aging of the population, there is growing awareness of elder abuse among individuals, families, communities, and societies at large. Understanding of and efforts to address the problems surrounding elder abuse have been enhanced through the advancement of theory, research, and practice. Local, state, and national entities have taken up this widespread problem through a variety of programmatic and legislative initiatives and events. For example, in 2012, a ground-breaking White House Special Event on Elder Abuse and Financial Exploitation (see http://www.youtube.com/watch?v=49g5h-x1sGg) unveiled a deep commitment by the Department of Health and Human Services to address the problem, with a particular emphasis on elder financial abuse. Numerous entities, both public and private, are now working together to prevent and confront elder mistreatment and more comprehensively address the devastating impact elder abuse has on individuals, families, and communities.

In recognition of elder abuse as a global social issue affecting the health and human rights of millions of older persons around the world, the United Nations General Assembly, in its resolution 66/127, designated June 15 as World Elder Abuse Awareness Day (WEAAD; United Nations, 2012). The purpose of WEAAD is to provide an opportunity for communities to join forces around the world in an effort to promote a better understanding of the abuse of older persons. The hope is that through a visible, worldwide call to enthusiastically and innovatively raise awareness of the myriad cultural, social, economic and demographic processes affecting elder abuse, one day the scourge of this form of mistreatment will not be tolerated and thus eradicated.

Critical Thinking Questions

1. Revisit the case example presented at the beginning of the chapter and answer the following questions. Provide the rationale for your response using information from the research literature provided in this chapter and available elsewhere.

   (a) On a scale from 1 (very unlikely) to 10 (very likely), how likely is it that Eleanor is being financially exploited?

   (b) By interfering with Eleanor's interactions with other family members or friends, is Jeb mistreating his mother?

   (c) On a scale from 1 (very unlikely) to 10 (very likely), how likely is it that Eleanor's situation is happening in the county in which you live?

   (d) Does Eleanor need outside help? If so, on a scale from 1 (very unlikely) to 10 (very likely), how likely is it that Eleanor will get the help she needs?

   (e) Would you intervene in this situation? If so, what would you do?

2. Choose two of the news stories about actual elder abuse cases presented in this chapter. As you review these stories, think carefully about risk factors or "red flags" for elder abuse and answer the following questions.

   (a) What characteristics of the alleged perpetrators suggest they do or do not fit the profile of an elder abuse perpetrator?

(b) What factors increased the older adult's vulnerability for abuse?

(c) Describe measures the older adult victim, their family members, and the community could have taken to reduce the chance of the abuse ever taking place.

(d) What are the immediate and potential long-term outcomes of the abuse for the older adult and the alleged perpetrator(s)?

(e) What information would you share with an older adult in your own family or community who may be vulnerable to abuse like the victims in these stories?

3. Compare and contrast efforts to address elder abuse in two communities (e.g., rural and urban; minority- and non-minority-populated areas) in the state in which you live. Based on the following, what can you conclude about each community's response to elder abuse?

(a) local news story about elder mistreatment;

(b) local community and state agency efforts and resources;

(c) state laws or policies that define or address elder abuse.

References

Acierno, R., Hernandez, M. A., Amstadter, A. B., Resnick, H. S., Steve, K., Muzzy, W., and Kilpatrick, D. G. (2010). Prevalence and correlates of emotional, physical, sexual, and financial abuse and potential neglect in the United States: The National Elder Mistreatment Study. *American Journal of Public Health, 100*, 292–297. doi: 10.2105/ajph.2009.163089.

Acierno, R., Hernandez-Tejada, M., Muzzy, W., and Steve, K. (2009). *National elder mistreatment study*. Rockville, MD: US Department of Justice. Retrieved May 30, 2014 from https://www.ncjrs.gov/pdffiles1/nij/grants/226456.pdf.

Amstadter, A. B., Cisler, J. M., McCauley, J. L., Hernandez, M. A., Muzzy, W., and Acierno, R. (2011a). Do incident and perpetrator characteristics of elder mistreatment differ by gender of the victim? Results from the National Elder Mistreatment Study. *Journal of Elder Abuse and Neglect, 23*, 43–57. doi: 10.1080/08946566.2011.534707.

Amstadter, A. B., Zajac, K., Strachan, M., Hernandez, M. A., Kilpatrick, D. G., and Acierno, R. (2011b). Prevalence and correlates of elder mistreatment in South Carolina: The South Carolina Elder Mistreatment Study. *Journal of Interpersonal Violence, 26*(15), 2947–2972. doi: 10.1177/0886260510390959.

Band-Winterstein, T., and Eisikovits, Z. (2009). "Aging out" of violence: The multiple faces of intimate violence over the life span. *Qualitative Health Research, 19*, 164–180. doi: 10.1177/1049732308329305.

Beach, S. R., Schulz, R., Williamson, G. M., Miller, L. S., Weiner, M. F., and Lance, C. E. (2005). Risk factors for potentially harmful informal caregiver behavior. *Journal of the American Geriatrics Society, 53*, 255–261. doi: 10.1111/j.1532-5415.2005.53111.x.

Begle, A. M., Strachan, M., Cisler, J. M., Amstadter, A. B., Hernandez, M., and Acierno, R. (2011). Elder mistreatment and emotional symptoms among older adults in a largely rural population: The South Carolina Elder Mistreatment Study. *Journal of Interpersonal Violence, 26*(11), 2321–2332. doi: 10.1177/0886260510383037.

Biggs, S., and Goergen, T. (2010). Theoretical development in elder abuse and neglect. *Ageing International, 35*(3), 167–170. doi: 10.1007/s12126-010-9066-z.

Blum, B. (2012). Elder abuse, financial loss, and undue influence: FAQs. Retrieved May 30, 2014 from http://www.bennettblummd.com/interview_with_dr__blum.html.

Bonnie, R. J., and Wallace, R. B. (eds) (2003). *Elder mistreatment: Abuse, neglect, and exploitation in an aging America*. Washington, DC: National Academies Press.

Bonomi, A. E., Anderson, M. L., Rivara, F. P., and Thompson, R. S. (2007). Health outcomes in women with physical and sexual intimate partner violence exposure. *Journal of Women's Health, 16*, 987–997. doi:10.1089/jwh.2006.0239.

Bowen, G. L., Martin, J. A., Mancini, J. A., and Nelson, J. P. (2000). Community capacity: Antecedents and consequences. *Journal of Community Practice, 8*, 1–21. doi: 10.1300/J125v08n02_01.

Bronfenbrenner, U. (1986). Ecology of the family as a context for human development: Research perspectives. *Developmental Psychology, 22*, 723–742. doi:10.1037/0012-1649.22.6.723.

Brownell, P., Berman, J., and Salamone, A. (2000). Mental health and criminal justice issues among perpetrators of elder abuse. *Journal of Elder Abuse and Neglect, 11*, 81–94. doi: 10.1300/J084v11n04_06.

Burgess, A. W., Dowdell, E. B., and Prentky, R. A. (2000). Sexual abuse of nursing home residents. *Journal of Psychosocial Nursing and Mental Health Services, 38*, 10–18.

Carstensen, L. L. (1992). Social and emotional patterns in adulthood: Support for socioemotional selectivity theory. *Psychology and Aging, 7*, 331–338. doi: 10.1037/0882-7974.7.3.331.

Castle, E., Eisenberger, N. I., Seeman, T. E., Moons, W. G., Boggero, I. A., Grinblatt, M. S., and Taylor, S. E. (2012). Neural and behavioral bases of age differences in perceptions of trust. *Proceedings of the National Academy of Sciences, 109*, 20848–20852. doi: 10.1073/pnas.1218518109.

Charles, S. T., and Carstensen, L. L. (2010). Social and emotional aging. *Annual Review of Psychology, 61*, 383–409. doi: 10.1146/annurev.psych.093008.100448.

Cisler, J. M., Begle, A. M., Amstadter, A. B., and Acierno, R. (2012). Mistreatment and self-reported emotional symptoms: Results from the National Elder Mistreatment Study. *Journal of Elder Abuse and Neglect, 24*, 216–230. doi: 10.1080/08946566.2011.652923.

Dakin, E., and Pearlmutter, S. (2009). Older women's perceptions of elder maltreatment and ethical dilemmas in adult protective services: A cross-cultural, exploratory study. *Journal of Elder Abuse and Neglect, 21*, 15–57. doi: 10.1080/08946560802571896.

Daly, J. M., Hartz, A. J., Stromquist, A. M., Peek-Asa, C., and Jogerst, G. J. (2008). Self-reported elder domestic partner violence in one rural Iowa county. *Journal of Emotional Abuse, 7*, 115–134.

DeLiema, M., Gassoumis, Z. D., Homeier, D. C., and Wilber, K. H. (2012). Determining prevalence and correlates of elder abuse using promotores: Low-income immigrant Latinos report high rates of abuse and neglect. *Journal of the American Geriatrics Society, 60*, 1333–1339. doi: 10.1111/j.1532-5415.2012.04025.x.

Dimah, K. P., and Dimah, A. (2003). Elder abuse and neglect among rural and urban women. *Journal of Elder Abuse and Neglect, 15*, 75–93. doi: 10.1300/J084v15n01_06.

Dong, X., Beck, T., and Simon, M. A. (2009). Loneliness and mistreatment of older Chinese women: Does social support matter? *Journal of Women and Aging, 21*(4), 293–302. doi: 10.1080/08952840903285252.

Dong, X., Simon, M. A., Mosqueda, L., and Evans, D. A. (2012). The prevalence of elder self-neglect in a community-dwelling population. *Journal of Aging and Health, 24*, 507–524. doi: 10.1177/0898264311425597.

Dong, X., Simon, M., Rajan, K., and Evans, D. A. (2011). Association of cognitive function and risk for elder abuse in a community-dwelling population. *Dementia and Geriatric Cognitive Disorders, 32*, 209–215. doi: 10.1159/000334047.

Dong, X. D., Simon, M., Mendes, C., Fulmer, T., Beck, T., Hebert, L., ... and Evans, D. (2009). Elder self-neglect and abuse and mortality risk in a community-dwelling population. *JAMA: Journal of the American Medical Association, 302*, 517–526. doi: 10.1001/jama.2009.1109.

Dong, X. Q., Simon, M. A., Beck, T. T., Farran, C., McCann, J. J., Mendes de Leon, C. F., ... and Evans, D. A. (2011). Elder abuse and mortality: The role of psychological and social wellbeing. *Gerontology, 57*, 549–558. doi: 10.1159/000321881.

Elder, G. H., Jr. (1998). The life course and human development. In R. M. Lerner (ed.), *Handbook of child psychology*, vol. 1, *Theoretical models of human development* (5th edn) (pp. 939–991). New York: John Wiley & Sons, Inc.

Finkelhor, D., Ormrod, R. K., and Turner, H. A. (2007). Polyvictimization and trauma in a national longitudinal cohort. *Development and Psychopathology, 19*, 149–166. doi: 10.1017/S0954579407070083.

Fisher, B. S., and Regan, S. L. (2006). The extent and frequency of abuse in the lives of older women and their relationship with health outcomes. *The Gerontologist, 46*, 200–209. doi: 10.1093/geront/46.2.200.

Friedman, L. S., Avila, S., Tanouye, K., and Joseph, K. (2011). A case-control study of severe physical abuse of older adults. *Journal of the American Geriatrics Society, 59*, 417–422. doi: 10.1111/j.1532-5415.2010.03313.x.

Furstenberg, F. F., and Hughes, M. E. (1997). The influence of neighborhoods on children's development: A theoretical perspective and research agenda. In J. Brooks-Gunn, G. J. Duncan, and J. L. Aber (eds), *Neighborhood poverty: Policy implications in studying neighborhoods* (pp. 22–47). New York: Russell Sage Foundation.

Hightower, J. (2004). Age, gender and violence: Abuse against older women. *Geriatrics and Aging, 7*, 60–63.

Horsford, S. R., Parra-Cardona, J. R., Post, L. A., and Schiamberg, L. (2010). Elder abuse and neglect in African American families: Informing practice based on ecological and cultural frameworks. *Journal of Elder Abuse and Neglect, 23*, 75–88. doi: 10.1080/08946566.2011.534709.

Jackson, S. L., and Hafemeister, T. L. (2011). *Financial abuse of elderly people vs. other forms of elder abuse: Assessing their dynamics, risk factors, and society's response*. Rockville, MD: US Department of Justice.

Jackson, S. L., and Hafemeister, T. L. (2012). Pure financial exploitation vs. hybrid financial exploitation co-occurring with physical abuse and/or neglect of elderly persons. *Psychology of Violence, 2*, 285–296. doi: 10.1037/a0027273.

Jogerst, G. J., Daly, J. M., Galloway, L. J., Zheng, S., and Xu, Y. (2012). Substance abuse associated with elder abuse in the United States. *American Journal of Drug and Alcohol Abuse, 38*, 63–69. doi: 10.3109/00952990.2011.600390.

Krienert, J. L., Walsh, J. A., and Turner, M. (2009). Elderly in America: A descriptive study of elder abuse examining National Incident-based Reporting System (NIBRS) data, 2000–2005. *Journal of Elder Abuse and Neglect, 21*, 325–345. doi: 10.1080/08946560903005042.

Lachs, M. S., and Pillemer, K. (2004). Elder abuse. *The Lancet, 364*, 1263–1272. doi: 10.1016/S0140-6736(04) 17144-4.

Lachs, M. S., Williams, C., O'Brien, S., Hurst, L., and Horwitz, R. (1997). Risk factors for reported elder abuse and neglect: A nine-year observational cohort study. *The Gerontologist, 37*, 469–474. doi: 10.1093/geront/37.4.469.

Lachs, M. S., Williams, C. S., O'Brien, S., Pillemer, K. A., and Charlson, M. E. (1998). The mortality of elder mistreatment. *JAMA: Journal of the American Medical Association, 280*, 428–432.

Laumann, E. O., Leitsch, S. A., and Waite, L. J. (2008). Elder mistreatment in the United States: Prevalence estimates from a nationally representative study. *Journals of Gerontology Series B: Psychological Sciences and Social Sciences, 63*, S248–S254.

Lifespan of Greater Rochester, Inc., Weill Cornell Medical Center of Cornell University, and New York City Department for the Aging. (2011). *Under the radar: New York State Elder Abuse Prevalence Study. Self-reported prevalence and documented case surveys.* Retrieved May 30, 2014 from http://www.lifespan-roch.org/documents/UndertheRadar051211.pdf.

Mancini, J. A., and Bowen, G. L. (2013). Families and communities: A social organization theory of action and change. In G. W. Peterson and K. R. Bush (eds), *Handbook of marriage and the family* (3rd edn) (pp. 781–813). New York: Springer.

Mancini, J. A., Martin, J. A., and Bowen, G. L. (2003). Community capacity. In T. P. Gullotta and M. Bloom (eds), *Encyclopedia of primary prevention and health promotion* (pp. 319–330). New York: Kluwer Academic/Plenum.

Mancini, J. A., Nelson, J. P., Bowen, G. L., and Martin, J. A. (2006). Preventing intimate partner violence: A community capacity approach. *Journal of Aggression, Maltreatment and Trauma, 13*, 203–227.

MetLife Mature Market Institute. (2009). *Broken trust: Elders, family, and finances.* Westport, CT: MetLife Mature Market Institute. Retrieved May 30, 2014 from http://www.gerontology.vt.edu/docs/mmi-studies-broken-trust.pdf.

MetLife Mature Market Institute. (2011a). *The MetLife study of elder financial abuse: Crimes of occasion, desperation and predation against America's elders.* New York: MetLife Mature Market Institute. Retrieved May 30, 2014 from http://www.metlife.com/assets/cao/mmi/publications/studies/2011/mmi-elder-financial-abuse.pdf.

MetLife Mature Market Institute. (2011b). Planning tips: Preventing elder financial abuse for family caregivers. Retrieved May 30, 2014 from http://www.gerontology.vt.edu/docs/MetLife%20Elder%20Abuse_Family%20Tips_051711.pdf.

MetLife Mature Market Institute. (2011c). Planning tips: Preventing elder financial abuse for older adults. Retrieved May 30, 2014 from http://www.gerontology.vt.edu/docs/MetLife%20Elder%20Abuse_Older%20Adults%20Tips_051711.pdf.

MetLife Mature Market Institute. (2012). The essentials: Preventing elder abuse. Retrieved May 30, 2014 from https://www.metlife.com/assets/cao/mmi/publications/essentials/mmi-preventing-elder-abuse-essentials.pdf.

Montminy, L. (2005). Older women's experiences of psychological violence in their marital relationships. *Journal of Gerontological Social Work, 46*, 3–22. doi: 10.1300/J083v46n02_02.

Moon, A., and Benton, D. (2000). Tolerance of elder abuse and attitudes toward third-party intervention among African American, Korean American, and White elderly. *Journal of Multicultural Social Work, 8*, 283–303. doi: 10.1300/J285v08n03_05.

National Center on Child Fatality Review. (2004). *Elder abuse fatality review.* Retrieved May 30, 2014 from http://ican-ncfr.org/hmElderAbuseFatality.asp.

National Center on Elder Abuse. (2007). Local elder abuse coalitions at work. Promising Practices issue briefs. Retrieved May 30, 2014 from http://www.ncea.aoa.gov/Resources/Publication/docs/PromisingPracticesElderAbuseCoalitions.pdf.

National Center on Elder Abuse. (n.d.a). What is elder abuse? Retrieved May 30, 2014 from http://www.ncea.aoa.gov/faq/index.aspx.

National Center on Elder Abuse. (n.d.b). Types of elder abuse. Retrieved May 30, 2014 from http://www.ncea.aoa.gov/FAQ/Type_Abuse/index.aspx.

National Center on Elder Abuse. (n.d.c). NCEA innovative practices database. Retrieved May 30, 2014 from http://www.ncea.aoa.gov/Stop_Abuse/EBP/Database/index.aspx.

Nerenberg, L. (2008). *Elder abuse prevention: Emerging trends and promising strategies.* New York: Springer.

Office of Justice Programs. (2000). *Our aging population: Promoting empowerment, preventing victimization, and implementing coordinated interventions.* US Department of Justice. Retrieved May 30, 2014 from http://www.ojp.usdoj.gov/docs/ncj_186256.pdf.

Parra-Cardona, J. R., Meyer, E., Schiamberg, L., and Post, L. (2007). Elder abuse and neglect in Latino families: An ecological and culturally relevant theoretical framework for clinical practice. *Family Process, 46*, 451–470. doi: 10.1111/j.1545-5300.2007.00225.x.

Paveza, G., VandeWeerd, C., and Laumann, E. (2008). Elder self-neglect: A discussion of a social typology. *Journal of the American Geriatric Society, 56*, S271–S275. doi: 10.1111/j.1532-5415.2008.01980.x.

Payne, B. K. (2010). Understanding elder sexual abuse and the criminal justice system's response: Comparisons to elder physical abuse. *Justice Quarterly, 27*, 206–224. doi: 10.1080/07418820902763087.

Pillemer, K. (2004). Elder abuse is caused by the deviance and dependence of abusive caregivers. In D. Loseke, R. Gelles, and M. Cavanaugh (eds), *Current controversies on family violence* (2nd edn) (pp. 207–220). Newbury Park, CA: Sage Publications.

Ramsey-Klawsnik, H. (1991). Elder sexual abuse: Preliminary findings. *Journal of Elder Abuse and Neglect, 3*, 73–90. doi: 10.1300/J084v03n03_04.

Ramsey-Klawsnik, H. (2004). Elder sexual abuse within the family. *Journal of Elder Abuse and Neglect, 15*, 43–58. doi: 10.1300/J084v15n01_04.

Ramsey-Klawsnik, H., and Teaster, P. B. (2012). Sexual abuse of health care facility residents: Adult Protective Services and facility policy and practice implications. *Generations, 36*, 53–59.

Riddell, T., Ford-Gilboe, M., and Leipert, B. (2009). Strategies used by rural women to stop, avoid, or escape from intimate partner violence. *Health Care for Women International, 30*, 134–159. doi: 10.1080/07399330802523774.

Roberto, K. A., McPherson, M. C., and Brossoie, N. (2013). Intimate partner violence in late life: A review of the empirical literature. *Violence Against Women, 19*, 1538–1558.

Roberto, K. A., Teaster, P. B., McPherson, M. C., Mancini, J. A., and Savla, J. (2013). A community capacity framework for enhancing criminal justice response to elder abuse. *Journal of Crime and Justice* (published online July 2). doi:1 0.1080/0735648X.2013.804286.

Roby, J., and Sullivan, R. (2000). Adult Protective Service laws: A comparison of state statutes from definition to case closure. *Journal of Elder Abuse and Neglect, 12*, 17–51. doi: 10.1300/J084v12n03_02.

Scott-Storey, K. (2011). Cumulative abuse: Do things add up? An evaluation of the conceptualization, operationalization, and methodological approaches in the study of the phenomenon of cumulative abuse. *Trauma, Violence, and Abuse, 12*(3), 135–150. doi: 10.1177/1524838011404253.

Sherod, M. G., Griffith, H. R., Copeland, J., Belue, K., Krzywansky, S., Zamrini, E. Y., … and Marson, D. C. (2009). Neurocognitive predictors of financial capacity across the dementia spectrum: Normal aging, mild cognitive impairment, and Alzheimer's disease. *Journal of the International Neuropsychological Society, 15*, 258–267. doi: 10.1017/S1355617709090365.

Shields, B. E., Hunsaker, D. M., and Hunsaker, J. C., III. (2004). Abuse and neglect: A ten-year review of mortality and morbidity in our elders in a large metropolitan area. *Journal of Forensic Science, 49*, 1–6. doi: 10.1520/JFS2003161.

Steigel, L., and Wood, E. F. (2011). The role of undue influence in elder abuse. National Consumer Law Center. Retrieved May 30, 2014 from http://www.nclc.org/images/pdf/conferences_and_webinars/webinar_trainings/presentations/2011/the_role_of_undue_influence_in_elder_abuse.pdf.

Tatara, T. (1999). Introduction. In T. Tatara (ed.), *Understanding elder abuse in minority populations* (pp. 1–9). Philadelphia: Taylor and Francis.

Tauriac, J. J., and Scruggs, N. (2006). Elder abuse among African Americans. *Educational Gerontology, 32*, 37–48. doi: 10.1080/03601270500338625.

Teaster, P. B. (2003). *A response to the abuse of vulnerable adults: The 2000 Survey of State Adult Protective Services.* Washington, DC: National Center on Elder Abuse. Retrieved May 30, 2014 from http://www.ncea.aoa.gov/Resources/Publication/docs/apsreport030703.pdf.

Teaster, P. B., Otto, J. M., Dugar, T. A., Mendiondo, M. S., Abner, E. L., and Cecil, K. A. (2006). *The 2004 survey of Adult Protective Services: Abuse of adults 60 years and older.* Washington, DC: National Center on Elder Abuse. Retrieved May 30, 2014 from http://www.ncea.aoa.gov/Resources/Publication/docs/2-14-06_FINAL_60_REPORT.pdf.

Teaster, P. B., and Roberto, K. A. (2004). The sexual abuse of older adults: APS cases and outcomes. *The Gerontologist, 44*, 788–796. doi: 10.1093/geront/44.6.788.

Teaster, P. B., Roberto, K. A., and Dugar, T. A. (2006). Intimate partner violence of rural aging women. *Family Relations, 55*, 636–648. doi: 10.1111/j.1741-3729.2006.00432.x.

Thomas, K. A., Joshi, M., Wittenberg, E., and McCloskey, L. A. (2008). Intersections of harm and health: A qualitative study of intimate partner violence in women's lives. *Violence Against Women, 14*(11), 1252–1273. doi: 10.1177/1077801208324529.

Thompson, E. H., Buxton, W., Gough, C. P., and Wahle, C. (2007). Gendered policies and practices that increase older men's risk of elder mistreatment. *Journal of Elder Abuse and Neglect, 19*, 129–151. doi: 10.1300/J084v19n01_09.

United Nations. (2012). World Elder Abuse Awareness Day: 15 June. Retrieved May 30, 2014 from http://www.un.org/en/events/elderabuse.

United States Government Printing Office. (2010). Public law 111-148-MAR. 23, 2010. Retrieved May 30, 2014 from http://www.gpo.gov/fdsys/pkg/PLAW-111publ148/pdf/PLAW-111publ148.pdf.

Vincent, G. K., and Velkoff, V. A. (2010). The next four decades: The older population in the United States: 2010–2050. Washington, DC: US Census Bureau.

Widera, E., Steenpass, V., Marson, D., and Sudore, R. (2011). Finances in the older patient with cognitive impairment: "He didn't want me to take over." *JAMA: Journal of the* *American Medical Association, 305*, 698–706. doi: 10.1001/jama.2011.164.

Wiglesworth, A., Austin, R., Corona, M., and Mosqueda, L. (2009). Bruising as a forensic marker of physical elder abuse. Washington, DC: US Department of Justice.

Winterstein, T., and Eisikovits, Z. (2005). The experience of loneliness of battered old women. *Journal of Women and Aging, 17*(4), 3–19. doi: 10.1300/J074v17n04_02.

Wisconsin Coalition Against Domestic Violence. (2009). *Elder abuse, neglect, and family violence: A guide for health care professionals.* Madison, WI: Wisconsin Coalition Against Domestic Violence and Wisconsin Bureau of Aging and Disability Resources.

16

Adolescent Development and Romantic Relationships

Jennifer Kerpelman, Alyssa McElwain, and
Hans Saint-Eloi Cadely

Adolescent romantic relationships are contexts for self-development and skill building. In Chapter 16, we learn that these relationships also introduce two primary challenges in the lives of youth: risky sexual behavior and dating aggression. It is no surprise that high-quality and communicative parent–adolescent relationships are a protective factor for youth in navigating the often complicated and technologically infused waters of intimacy. Yet many teens are at risk for STDs and unintended pregnancies, with GLBT and ethnic minority youth at even greater risk for unhealthy sexual outcomes due to a lack of social support and acceptance. Kerpelman and colleagues explore the role of youth-focused relationship education as a means to facilitate healthy adolescent relationships.

I love you not only for what you are, but for what I am when I am with you. I love you not only for what you have made of yourself, but for what you are making of me. I love you for the part of me that you bring out.
Elizabeth Barrett Browning

Direct experience with romantic relationships often begins during the adolescent years (Collins, 2003). These relationships serve as important contexts for adolescents' discovery of themselves and their sense of identity (Kerpelman *et al.*, 2012). The quotation from Elizabeth Barrett Browning is consistent with Caryl Rusbult's "Michelangelo phenomenon," a model of relationships and development holding that "close partners sculpt one another's selves shaping one another's skills and traits and promoting versus inhibiting one another's goal pursuits" (Rusbult, Finkel, and Kumashiro, 2009, p. 308). In healthy, loving relationships, the sculptor carefully brings out the best in the partner, but in an unhealthy, troubled relationship, the artist's rendering may be a quite different, often unflattering version of the partner. Adolescents' romantic relationships are informed by models they have observed around them. These models may be positive, such as a caring, supportive relationship between parents, or they can be negative where adolescents observe high conflict, infidelity, and lack of effective communication among couples. Adolescents may not recognize what healthy romantic relationships are like, and even if they do see positive adult models, they may not know what it means to have a healthy romantic relationship during their teenage years. As adolescents gather information about relationships, they often seek out answers from their peers. Although parents remain important in their adolescents' lives and can serve as a valued source for information about romantic relationships, the roles of parents evolve as peer relationships rise in prominence during adolescence (Hill, Bromell, Tyson, and Flint, 2007; Meeus, 2003). The challenges for researchers, practitioners, and policymakers are to understand influences on adolescents' romantic relationships, as well as the benefits and costs of these relationships, and determine ways to maximize healthy adjustment outcomes. Recent work has acknowledged the developmental significance of romantic relationships in adolescents' lives (Collins, 2003; Furman and Shaffer-Hand, 2006; Giordano, Manning, and Longmore, 2006; Laursen and Mooney, 2007). Such relationships can help foster positive growth in areas of self-development, including adolescents' considerations of their future goals and aspirations (Bouchey and Furman, 2003; Furman and Shaffer, 2003), as well as offer opportunities for adolescents to develop interpersonal skills (Barber and Eccles, 2003). Importantly, romantic relationships serve as an important context for identity formation and developing the capacity for intimacy (Beyers and Seiffge-Krenke, 2010; Dyk and Adams, 1987; Markstrom and Kalmanir, 2001; Montgomery, 2005; Pittman, Keiley, Kerpelman, and Vaughn, 2011). Identity formation is a central task of adolescence (Erikson, 1968), and experiences with peers and romantic partners help adolescents explore who they are, both as an individual and as a partner within a relationship, and afford adolescents the chance to develop their understanding of intimacy outside family relationships (Kerpelman et al., 2012). Although the intimacy experienced in adolescent romantic relationships is not as mature and complex as that experienced in adult romantic relationships, they do bear resemblances. The patterns established in romantic relationships during adolescence set the stage for the nature and quality of adult relationships. In fact, in early adulthood intimacy and identity processes converge as young people navigate

toward new adult roles (Pittman et al., 2011). Thus, through experiences with romantic partners, adolescents explore their identities, consider their future goals, develop communication and conflict management skills, learn about intimacy and sexuality, and experience feelings of closeness and support. However, adolescents' romantic relationships also bring challenges.

What follows is in-depth coverage of two primary challenges of adolescents' romantic relationships: risky sexual behavior and dating aggression. A final section addresses future opportunities for research and practice, highlighting adolescents' use of technology in their romantic relationships, as well as the value of youth-focused relationship education. Critical thinking questions are offered at the end of the chapter.

Challenges of Adolescent Romantic Relationships

Romantic relationships during adolescence can be a double-edged sword. Whereas they are normative and part of healthy development, they also can introduce unhealthy risk-taking behaviors and experiences that are associated with a host of negative consequences for adolescents and their families. In particular, engaging in romantic relationships increases the potential for adolescents to become sexually active. Sexual activity increases adolescents' risks of unintended pregnancy, contracting sexually transmitted diseases (Centers for Disease Control and Prevention (CDC; 2012), and experiencing negative emotional consequences such as anxiety, depression, and suicidal ideation (Hallfors, Waller, and Ford, 2004; Welsh, Grello, and Harper, 2003). Romantic relationships also increase the likelihood of experiencing jealousy, possessiveness, and relationship violence (Giordano, Soto, Manning, and Longmore, 2010). Many adolescents may confuse jealousy with love or believe erroneously that controlling behaviors indicate caring. The next two sections address adolescent sexual relationships and dating aggression, noting influences, consequences, and the role of family in these two challenging areas of adolescent romantic relationships.

Sexual relationships in adolescence

Adolescent romantic relationships play a key role in the development of sexuality, with most first sexual experiences occurring in the context of committed relationships (Furman and Shaffer, 2003). Adolescents are building intricate and unique sexual identities as they begin to engage in sexual behaviors (Tolman and McClelland, 2011). Despite sexual exploration being developmentally normative, there are several behaviors that can place adolescents' health and well-being at risk. Risky behavior, such as sexual intercourse at a young age, having multiple sexual partners, and lack of contraceptive use may lead to unintended pregnancy and sexually transmitted diseases (STDs).

Sexual activity increases with age across adolescence (CDC, 2012; Fergus, Zimmerman, and Caldwell, 2007); the average age of first intercourse in the United States is between the ages of 16 and 17 years (Chandra, Martinez, Mosher, Abma, and Jones, 2005; Martinez, Copen, and Abma, 2011). By the end of high school, approximately 47% of adolescents have had sexual intercourse, with more males than females reporting having had sex (CDC, 2012). The prevalence of having had sexual intercourse during high school differs by ethnicity, with African American youth reporting the highest rates (60%), followed by Hispanic youth (48%) and European American youth (44%; CDC, 2012). Older adolescents are more likely to be sexually active and also are more likely to use birth control methods such as birth control pills, intrauterine devices, and other hormonal contraceptives than are younger adolescents. However, older adolescents are less likely to report using condoms during sexual intercourse than are younger adolescents (CDC, 2012), indicating a focus of older adolescents on pregnancy prevention more than STD prevention. Approximately 6% of adolescents have sexual intercourse before age 13, and 15% of adolescents report having had four or more sexual partners in their lifetime (CDC, 2012). During first sexual intercourse, 79% of females and 87% of males report using some method of contraception (Abma, Martinez, and Copen, 2010) and contraceptive use has increased over the past decade among adolescents (Martinez et al., 2011).

Contrary to popular belief – and what most teens might say – not everyone is "doing it" (see Box 16.1).

Box 16.1

- The age of sexual initiation is increasing and more young people are refraining from all types of sexual experiences including oral, anal, and vaginal intercourse (Chandra, Mosher, and Copen, 2011).

- Many teens are choosing to delay sexual intercourse until after high school and the percentage of sexually experienced teens in the United States has declined slightly over the past two decades (CDC, 2012). This decrease is possibly due to more sexual health education in schools, awareness of sexual risks, and changing social attitudes (Kan, Cheng, Landale, and McHale, 2010).

- Among sexually inexperienced teens, the most common reasons given for refraining from sexual intercourse are related to the potential social, emotional, and physical consequences of sexual activity (Michels, Kropp, Eyre, and Halpern-Felsher, 2005). Sexually inexperienced adolescents, especially females, expect sex to occur when they are in love, sexually attracted, or in a committed relationship (Parkes, Henderson, Wight, and Nixon, 2011), emphasizing the co-development of sexuality and romantic relationships.

When they do have sex, the majority of adolescents have sex within an exclusive, committed romantic relationship (Abma et al., 2010; Martinez et al., 2011), where they progress from less to more intimate sexual behaviors (e.g., from kissing to intercourse; de Graaf, Vanwesenbeeck, Meijer, Woertman, and Meeus, 2009). Some evidence suggests that progressing from less to more intimate behaviors is not detrimental to adolescent health, but that beginning sexual activity at a young age and beginning sexual exploration with more intimate behaviors is linked with less frequent use of contraceptives, particularly for females (de Graaf et al., 2009). The expectation that sexual activity will occur within the context of a committed romantic relationship is associated with delayed first intercourse and more consistent condom use (Parkes, Henderson, Wight, and Nixon, 2011). Although it seems that the trend regarding teenage sexuality involves couple intimacy with sexual exploration, some adolescents (25%) are engaging in casual, or uncommitted sexual relationships, often referred to as "hooking up" (de Graaf *et al.*, 2009; Manning, Giordano, and Longmore, 2006).

Casual sexual relationships or "hook ups" carry potential risk because partners are relatively unknown and these relationships increase adolescents' risks for experiencing emotional and physical consequences such as pregnancy, STDs, or feeling used and rejected. Another concern is that adolescents are using sexual activity as a means to build relationships, as one study found that almost a third of teens who had sex with someone they just met wanted the relationship to progress into a typical dating relationship (Manning *et al.*, 2006). Uncommitted relationships, such as sexual relationships with acquaintances, friends or ex-boyfriends/girlfriends are likely to lead to feelings of jealousy. Although experiencing jealousy and negative relationship dynamics are associated with not using condoms consistently, adolescents who report causal, non-exclusive sexual relationships (e.g., sex with someone they just met) are more likely to use condoms than adolescents in committed relationships (Manning, Flanigan, Giordano, and Longmore, 2009). (See Box 16.2.)

Consequences of risky sexual behavior

There are two consequences of adolescent risky sexual behavior that warrant considerable attention: unintended pregnancy and transmission of STDs. The highest number of diagnoses of STDs (e.g., chlamydia, gonorrhea, syphilis, and human papillomavirus) is among young people aged 15–24 (CDC, 2012). Females are more likely than males to have contracted an STD by late adolescence (CDC, 2012) and experiencing physical neglect and abuse during childhood increase the odds of contracting an STD by adulthood (Haydon, Hussey, and Tucker-Halpern, 2011). High rates of STD infections among adolescent populations reflect a lack of knowledge and skills about practicing safe sex, as well as barriers to getting access to quality prevention and testing services (CDC, 2012). Research consistently shows that some ethnic minority groups (i.e., American Indian, Hispanic, and African American) have more diagnosed STDs than non-Hispanic white individuals (CDC, 2012).

The teen pregnancy rate peaked in 1990 at 117 pregnancies per 1,000 females age 15–19, then steadily decreased by 44% to 66 per 1,000 in 2009 (Curtin, Abma, Ventura, and Henshaw, 2013). Safe sex practices affect the teen pregnancy rate, as do delaying intercourse and increased effective contraceptive use. However, the teen pregnancy rate in the United States remains the highest in any industrialized Western nation (Santelli, Lindberg, Finer, and Singh, 2007).

Box 16.2   Hooking Up

Morgan went to a party and met an attractive boy her age. They ended up having sex that night and continued to "hook up" occasionally during the following several weeks until their relationship soured and they stopped speaking altogether.

What is Morgan thinking? It's not uncommon for two people who "jump into bed" together to quickly learn that they have very little in common and do not get along well. Sexual desire, attraction, and sometimes drugs and/or alcohol can cloud judgment when it comes to sexual decision-making. "Hooking up" can seem fun and appealing

to young people, but has many unintended physical and emotional consequences.

How can parents/adults help? Adults can talk to teens about the benefits of starting relationships slowly and gradually becoming physically intimate with a relationship partner. Taking time to get to know a partner provides an opportunity to establish trust, open communication, and determine if individual values are aligned. Teens can ask themselves about their own sexual boundaries, what characteristics they seek in a dating partner, and how they plan to move slowly in a dating relationship.

Almost 750,000 US women aged 15–19 become pregnant each year and approximately 60% result in birth (Kost, Henshaw, and Carlin, 2010). Although pregnancy and birth rates are declining across all ethnic groups, Hispanic and African American girls continue to have higher rates of pregnancies, abortions, and births during adolescence than do their European American peers (Kost et al., 2010). Children born to mothers ages 15–17 often have less stimulating home environments, more behavior problems, worse educational achievement, and higher likelihood of experiencing teen pregnancy themselves (Hoffman, 2006).

Gay, lesbian, and bisexual youth

In addition to considering the emotional, physical and social consequences of risky sexual behavior for heterosexual youth, it is important to address the experiences of sexual minority youth. Young people who identify (or later identify) as gay, lesbian, bisexual, or transexual (GLBT) also begin engaging in sexual behavior with partners during adolescence. In one nationally representative survey, approximately 2% of boys and 10% of girls aged 15–17 reported experiencing same-sex sexual behavior (Chandra, Mosher, and Copen, 2011). GLBT youth face potentially negative consequences after "coming out" or self-identifying as GLBT to friends and family (D'Augelli, Grossman, Starks, and Sinclair, 2010). By adolescence, several studies showed that approximately half of GLBT youth have already come out to friends and parents while 26% report they are in the process of self-disclosure, and 15% state they have not shared their sexual orientation with family members or friends (D'Augelli et al., 2010; Padilla, Crisp, and Rew, 2010). Feelings of rejection from both society at large and family members can lead to internalized homophobia, or a fear or hatred of one's own homosexual identity (more common among males; D'Augelli et al., 2010). Youth who do not feel comfortable coming out to parents report more fear of harassment and negative reactions from their parents and report that their parents' religious beliefs were a significant barrier to them coming out (D'Augelli et al., 2010; Padilla et al., 2010). In fact, severe family conflict may drive GLBT youth to homelessness (Saewyc, 2012). The consequences for GLBT youth can include poor self-esteem, suicidal ideation, and substance abuse (Padilla et al., 2010; Saewyc, 2012). Not only do GLBT youth face possible rejection at home, the vast majority of sexual health programs taught in schools are focused on preventing sexual risk behaviors among heterosexual youth. It is possible that GLBT youth feel ignored and unimportant as a result and do not receive the necessary knowledge and skills to protect their sexual health. Compared to heterosexual youth, GLBT youth are more likely to have early sexual debut, more sexual partners, less condom use, and higher risk of contracting STDs and HIV (Saewyc, 2012).

The role of family in adolescent sexuality

There are many ways in which the family environment is associated with the tendency of some adolescents to engage in risky sexual behavior. Family structure can influence parenting, and research indicates that when adolescents live in homes with two biological or adoptive parents they are less likely to engage in early sexual intercourse or risky sexual behavior than are adolescents in stepfamilies or single-parent families (Pearson, Muller, and Frisco, 2006; Zimmer-Gembeck and Helfand, 2008). For instance, a single parent with multiple children may not be able to monitor and support each child if the parent's time with the children is limited. While family structure is frequently studied, these studies find only modest associations among structure and adolescent sexual outcomes, indicating that other family-related variables may be more important (Zimmer-Gembeck and Helfand, 2008). Specifically, parental control and involvement are suggested as factors that more directly influence adolescent sexual behavior rather than simply family structure (Davis and Friel, 2001). Parents can help to prevent these risky behaviors through their parenting style and relationship quality and communication with their adolescents.

Parents use a combination of control, emotional support, and discipline strategies with adolescents, which can either promote or inhibit healthy sexual development. Behavioral control refers to parents' attempts to be aware of the child's behavior and monitor their whereabouts and actively set boundaries. Parental monitoring is a combination of parental knowledge, the child's willingness to share information, and the parents' actions in response to the child's disclosure (Stattin and Kerr, 2000). More parental monitoring during early adolescence is associated with having fewer sexual partners (Landsford et al., 2010). Parental monitoring is a very important factor in preventing sexual victimization or unwanted sexual experiences among females (Small and Kerns, 1993). If adolescents perceive their parents to have adequate justification for rules, they are more likely to comply (Baxter, Bylund, Imes, and Routsong, 2009). Therefore, having open conversations and explaining justification for rules or boundaries regarding sexual activity and dating relationships appears more effective than prohibiting sexual behavior in adolescence.

In contrast to parental monitoring and behavioral control, which are important and developmentally healthy aspects of parenting, psychological control refers to the attempt to use manipulation and intimidation to control another person's thoughts or beliefs. This parenting behavior can inhibit or interfere with healthy adolescent development and is associated with more sexual risk taking (Barber, Stolz, and Olsen, 2005; Kincaid, Jones, Cuellar, and Gonzalez, 2011). Adolescents whose parents are psychologically controlling have higher numbers of sexual partners by age 16 (Landsford et al., 2010). Psychological control can interfere with healthy decision-making because the adolescent is discouraged by parents from exploring their own thoughts and beliefs about their sexuality (Kincaid et al., 2011).

Making decisions about sex can be overwhelming to adolescents, who are new to this social domain. Having a positive, supportive relationship with an adult is essential, as many adolescents consult with family members (e.g., parents, siblings, aunts, uncles) as they explore their sexuality (Michels, Kropp, Eyre, and Halpern-Felsher, 2005). Low parent–child relationship quality is associated with younger sexual initiation and lack of condom use among adolescents under age 16 (Zimmer-Gembeck and Helfand, 2008). Sexually inexperienced teens reported more supportive parents than their sexually experienced counterparts (Parkes et al., 2011) and young girls with high-quality relationships with their mothers are more likely to delay intercourse (Davis and Friel, 2001). More specifically, when parents have high

expectations, provide support when listening to the adolescent's problems, and try to understand their adolescent's perspective, adolescents report being sexually abstinent (Aspy et al., 2007). Further, when adolescents perceived their parents to have high educational aspirations for them and also perceived high relationship quality, they were less likely to have been diagnosed with an STD during late adolescence (Deptula, Henry, and Schoeny, 2010). Parental support and relationship quality provide a foundation for parents to educate their child and transmit values about sexuality, which can be protective factors for adolescents.

Children and adolescents learn about sexuality from a variety of sources in their environment (Lefkowitz and Stoppa, 2006); however, parents are in a unique position because they can directly educate their children about sexual health within the framework of their unique family values, an advantage that schools and community groups do not have. Having discussions about sexuality before the adolescent becomes sexually active can help protect them from risky behaviors (Clawson and Reese-Weber, 2003). It appears that the way parents discuss sexual topics with their child can make a difference in how the information is received. When parents reported more discussion of sexual consequences (e.g., dangers of getting an STD, negative impact on social life due to a loss of peer respect, the moral issues of not having sex, and negative consequences of pregnancy) with their child, the child was actually less likely to use condoms during intercourse (Deptula et al., 2010). Parental disapproval of sex did not delay initiation and discussion of sexual consequences was actually associated with more STD diagnoses at a later time (Deptula et al., 2010). This may indicate that providing young adolescents messages about the negative moral and social implications of having sex to the exclusion of education does not serve to protect them. In fact they seem to be very aware of these consequences (Michels et al., 2005). It may be difficult for some parents to put aside their anxiety and overcome the *cultural myth that information equals permission.*

Communication about sex does not encourage risky sexual behavior. Several studies suggest that adolescents' comfortable communication about sex with mothers predicted not being sexually active and intending to delay sexual intercourse (Guzman et al., 2003) and more use of contraceptives (Clawson and Reese-Weber, 2003; DiClemente et al., 2001). What seems to be the most important is the adolescents' perceptions of the emotional tone of sexual conversations rather than the parents' perceptions and the actual content of conversations (Deptula et al., 2010). Especially among higher-risk minority group samples, comfortable and frequent communication about sexual topics with mothers promotes healthier decision-making especially among females (DiClemente et al., 2001; Guzman et al., 2003). For example, adolescents reported more contraceptive use, greater self-efficacy in declining unwanted sexual activity, and greater confidence discussing STDs and HIV and safer sex practices with a potential sexual partner. Research indicates that parents and families have an influential role in the prevention of unplanned pregnancy and prevention programs are often designed with this in mind (e.g., Blake, Simkin, Ledsky, Perkins, and Calabrese, 2001; Dittus, Miller, Kotchick, and Forehand, 2004). Some pregnancy and STD prevention programs have begun involving parents in the education process both in and out of the classroom (e.g., Blake et al., 2001; Dittus et al., 2004; Lederman, Chan, and Roberts-Gray, 2008). Even if parents cannot attend sexual health classes with their child, completing homework assignments together that address sexual issues helps adolescents feel more confident in avoiding high-risk sexual behaviors more so than sexual health classes alone (Blake et al., 2001).

Summary

Having high-quality parent–adolescent relationships with open communication can be a protective factor, especially when adolescents perceive high levels of support and high expectations for their futures. Although rates of teen pregnancy have slowly declined, there is still evidence that many teens are at risk for STDs and unintended pregnancies. GLBT and ethnic minority youth, many of whom live in low-resource families, are at particular risk for unhealthy sexual outcomes given the barriers to support and acceptance they face. Sexual exploration and experiences occur within romantic relationships and the commitment and dynamics of the relationship context matters for sexual health outcomes. Even when parents have good quality relationships and open communication with their adolescents, addressing emerging sexuality and the choices adolescents make can be challenging for parents. While parents remain important in their adolescents' lives, other influences, such as peers and social media greatly affect adolescents' sexual decision-making.

Dating Aggression in Adolescence

Dating aggression, defined as aggression that occurs within the context of romantic relationships, is very broad and difficult to describe, particularly because such behaviors vary in how and why they are being enacted. It is often thought that one individual is the perpetrator (initiating aggressive behaviors towards one's romantic partner) while the other is the victim (receiving the aggressive behavior from one's romantic partner). However, research suggests that among adolescent and young adult couples, perpetration and victimization of dating aggression tend to co-occur. Those who report having been victimized also report perpetrating such behaviors towards their romantic partners (Bookwala, Frieze, Smith, and Ryan, 1992; Connolly, Friedlander, Pepler, Craig, and Laporte, 2010; Williams, Connolly, Pepler, Craig, and Laporte, 2008). Rates of aggression in adolescents' dating relationships vary, with some studies finding rates of over 50% (Ellis, Crooks, and Wolfe, 2009; Fritz and Slep, 2009). Silverman, Raj, Mucci, and Hathaway (2001) found that one in five high school-aged adolescent girls experienced physical and/or sexual abuse from a dating partner. More recent studies have shown that dating aggression is becoming common among middle school students. According to the Research Triangle Institute International (RTI International, 2012), among a sample of 1,430 seventh graders, approximately 37% of students reported being psychologically abused by their dating partner, 15% of students reported being physically abused by their dating partners, and 31% reported being victims of electronic dating aggression (e.g., aggression on social networking sites, through texting, etc.). These findings suggest a relatively high number of adolescents who are involved in an abusive or aggressive relationship in the United States.

Adolescents who are involved in a violent romantic relationship are more likely to report negative mental health outcomes such as depression, suicidal thoughts, interpersonal problems (e.g., lack of assertiveness, avoidance, and maliciousness), anxiety, and post-traumatic stress disorder (Barnyard and Cross, 2008; Callahan, Tolman, and Saunders, 2003; Champion, Collins, Reyes, and Rivera, 2009; Chase, Treboux, and O'Leary, 2002; Rich, Gidycz, Warkentin, Loh, and Weiland, 2005). Other health consequences related to dating aggression include high levels of substance use, unhealthy weight control (overuse of laxatives, diet pills, and vomiting to lose weight), sexual risk behaviors, and teenage pregnancy (Alleyne, Coleman-Cowger, Crown, Gibbons, and Vines, 2011; Chase et al., 2002; Foo and Margolin, 1995; Howard, Wang, and Yan, 2007; Schiff and Zeira, 2005; Silverman et al., 2001). Factoring in health costs (medical and mental health), and loss of efficiency in the workplace that can occur from involvement in an aggressive relationship, dating aggression is an economic expense that costs the United States approximately 6.2 billion dollars annually (in 2003 dollars; Centers for Disease Control and Prevention, 2003). Such outcomes and costs highlight the concerns dating aggression brings to adolescent development.

Dating aggression behaviors

Dating aggression behaviors can vary according to whether they are psychological, physical, or sexual. *Psychological aggression* is defined as demeaning forms of aggression directed toward one's romantic partner. Such behaviors may range from yelling at, insulting, swearing at, or threatening to hurt one's romantic partner, as well as destroying something belonging to one's romantic partner (Straus, Hamby, Boney-McCoy, and Sugarman, 1996). *Physical aggression* involves physically attacking one's romantic partner. Examples of such behaviors are: grabbing, pushing, slapping, punching, and/or kicking one's romantic partner (Straus et al., 1996). More severe forms of physical dating violence include burning one's romantic partner, using a knife or gun, or dumping one's romantic partner out of a car (Foshee et al., 2009;

Straus et al., 1996). Although psychological dating aggression and physical dating aggression are distinct forms of aggression, research indicates a strong linkage between these two types of aggression. Specifically, individuals who perpetrate and/or are victims of psychological aggression often are perpetrators and/or victims of physical aggression (Cano, Avery-Leaf, Cascardi, and O'Leary, 1998). Furthermore, psychological aggression is thought to precede physical aggression (Hamby and Sugarman, 1999; O'Leary, Malone, and Tyree, 1994; O'Leary and Slep, 2003), and has been shown to occur more frequently than physical aggression within adolescent romantic relationships (Foshee et al., 2009). Whereas 10–30% of adolescents and young adults report to have perpetrated or to have been victimized by physical aggression in a dating relationship (Giordano et al., 2010; Gomez, 2011; Silverman et al., 2001), approximately 70–90% of couples within this age group have either engaged in or been victimized by psychological aggression (Barnyard, Arnold, and Smith, 2000; Champion et al., 2009; Jelz, Molidor, and Wright, 1996; Lawrence, Yoon, Langer, and Ro, 2009). In these studies psychological aggression was defined broadly such as insulting one's partner, cruel putdowns, or yelling at one's partner. Negative outcomes of psychological aggression include lower self-esteem, and lower levels of positive relationship behaviors (Jelz et al., 1996; Kasian and Painter, 1992). It is noteworthy that individuals who report being victimized by both forms of aggression indicate that psychological aggression was more damaging than physical aggression to their self-worth (Follingstad, Rutledge, Berg, Hause, and Polek, 1990; Lawrence et al., 2009). (See Box 16.3.) Finally, *sexual aggression* is described as using psychological or physical force to engage in sexual activities/intercourse with one's romantic partner. Approximately 25–59% of high school and college students report being victims of sexual aggression (Barnyard et al., 2000; Champion et al., 2009; Silverman et al., 2001; Young and Furman, 2008). Sexual aggression was defined in these studies as either being hurt sexually or using force to engage in sexual activities/intercourse (e.g., "Have you had sexual intercourse when you didn't want to because a person threatened or used some degree of physical force [twisting your arm, holding you down, ...]?";

Box 16.3   Dating Aggression and Psychological Abuse

Sam and Robin have been dating for a few months and the relationship seemed wonderful at first. Recently, Robin insults Sam by calling him names and telling him that he doesn't deserve her. Whenever he says he's not sure about staying in the relationship, she tells him that no other girls would want to date him and threatens to tell everyone really personal information about him. Sam feels worthless and isn't sure what to do about the relationship.

What are Robin and Sam thinking? Psychological abuse can go unrecognized as abuse by teens, but can include name-calling, making threats, and generally demeaning one's partner. A person may use psychological aggression toward a partner because of their own feelings of insecurity or they may be modeling what they have observed others do in their relationships. It is common for a person experiencing emotional abuse to feel low self-worth and to wonder whether they should end the relationship.

How can parents/adults help? Communicate with teens about what is a normal and healthy part of relationships. For example, conflict and arguments are common even in healthy relationships. Name-calling and degrading one's partner is not healthy relationship behavior and is considered psychological abuse. Parents and adults can also look for changes in the adolescent's mood, because lowered self-esteem, anxiety, and depression can all result from unhealthy dating relationships.

Young and Furman, 2008, p. 300). On an important note, dating aggression is linked with unhealthy sexual behaviors for the victims such as a higher number of sexual partners throughout adolescence, a lower likelihood of condom usage during intercourse, and a higher likelihood of adolescents having their first sexual experience at an early age (Alleyne *et al.*, 2011; Halpern, Spriggs, Martin, and Kupper, 2009; Howard *et al.*, 2007). All three types of dating aggression behaviors vary according to severity. Examples of minor and severe forms of dating aggression are as follows: psychological (minor: insulting one's partner; severe: threatening to hit one's partner), sexual (minor: making one's partner have sex without a condom; severe: using force to have sex with one's partner without his or her consent), and physical (minor: grabbing one's partner; severe: choking one's partner; Straus *et al.*, 1996). Moreover, minor forms of dating aggression occur more frequently than severe forms of dating aggression (Foshee *et al.*, 2009; Schnurr and Lohman, 2008). A popular belief is that males are more violent than females are. On the contrary, some studies have shown that among adolescents, males and females report similar rates of physical dating aggression (Cano *et al.*, 1998; Giordano *et al.*, 2010), while other findings indicate that females are more likely than males to perpetrate

physical aggression (Alleyne *et al.*, 2011; Archer, 2000; Bookwala *et al.*, 1992; Fernandez-Fuertes and Fuertes, 2010; Foo and Margolin, 1995; Jelz *et al.*, 1996; Lichter and McCloskey, 2004; Ozer, Tschann, Pasch, and Flores, 2004; Schnurr and Lohman, 2008). Qualifying these findings is that male adolescents are more likely than female adolescents to engage in more severe forms of physical aggression (Archer, 2002; Bookwala *et al.*, 1992; Callahan *et al.*, 2003; Foshee *et al.*, 2009; Foo and Margolin, 1995; Hamby and Sugarman, 1999). However, in the perpetration of psychological aggression, female adolescents engage in higher levels of such behaviors than males do (Archer, 2004; Fernandez-Fuertes and Fuertes, 2010; Jelz *et al.*, 1996). Finally, adolescent males are more likely than females to engage in sexual aggression towards their romantic partners (Alleyne *et al.*, 2011; Barnyard and Cross, 2008; Ozer *et al.* 2004; Young and Furman, 2008).

Aggression, problem behaviors, and vulnerability

Research shows that relationship aggression co-occurs with other problem behaviors. For example, adolescents who engage in delinquent or violent behaviors with their peers (e.g., fighting, carrying a gun) are more likely to engage in aggressive behaviors toward their dating partners (Ozer et al., 2008; Schnurr and Lohman, 2008; T. Williams et al., 2008). Moreover, adolescents who interact with peers who hold positive attitudes toward dating aggression are more likely to regard such behaviors as acceptable, which, in turn, may lead to them actually engaging in some form of dating aggression toward their dating partner (Foo and Margolin, 1995; T. Williams et al., 2008). Endorsing positive attitudes about dating aggression can range from holding strong gender stereotypes (i.e., attitudes about how someone should behave in a relationship based on their gender; Lichter and McCloskey, 2004) to accepting the use of dating aggression depending on the circumstance (e.g., feeling that it is acceptable to hit one's romantic partner if he/she is cheating or humiliates the other partner throughout the relationship; Foo and Margolin, 1995). Importantly, adolescents found to be aggressive in their previous dating relationships (Cano et al., 1998) and/or exposed to community violence (Malik, Sorenson, and Aneshensel, 1997) are more likely to perpetrate or to become victims of dating aggression.

Finally, it has been shown that adolescents with vulnerable characteristics are more likely to engage in dating aggression. Vulnerable adolescents are those who are generally aggressive (i.e., engage in violent behaviors with their peers), engage in delinquent or antisocial behaviors (Bookwala et al., 1992; Cui et al., 2013; Ozer et al., 2004; Schnurr and Lohman, 2008), report poor academic performance (Barnyard and Cross, 2008; Schnurr and Lohman, 2008), or who have emotional problems (e.g., adolescents who experience high levels of jealousy; Bookwala et al., 1992; Fernandez-Fuertes and Fuertes, 2010; Giordano et al., 2010). In addition, adolescents who report high levels of engagement in substance use, particularly cigarettes, marijuana, and alcohol, are at greater risk of engaging in dating aggression (Barnyard and Cross, 2008; Foo and Margolin, 1995; Howard et al., 2007; Malik et al., 1997; Schnurr and Lohman, 2008; Silverman et al., 2001). A recent study by Galliher and Bentley (2010) demonstrated that adolescents who were rejection-sensitive (i.e., easily disturbed or distressed when they perceive they are being rejected) were more likely to perpetrate aggression and less likely to be satisfied in their romantic relationships.

Other research shows that adolescents who are preoccupied with their romantic relationships (i.e., highly dependent on their romantic partner) are more likely to engage in dating aggression (Miga, Hare, Allen, and Manning, 2010).

The role of family in adolescent dating aggression

When addressing dating aggression among adolescents, the quality of family relationships needs to be considered. Three frameworks are used to explain the role of the family in adolescent and adult dating aggression: social learning theory, the cycle of violence hypothesis, and attachment theory. Research findings on interparental aggression have often been explained through Bandura's (1978) social learning theory that states that children who witness their parents behaving aggressively towards one another in which such behaviors lead to "positive outcomes" (i.e., the perpetrator getting what he/she wants), are likely to imitate such behaviors in their adolescent or young adult romantic relationships. Research in support of this theory suggests that children who are exposed to parental violence (i.e., interparental aggression) are more likely to engage in violent behaviors in their adolescent and/or adult romantic relationships (Fite et al., 2008; Foo and Margolin, 1995; Foshee, Bauman, and Linder, 1999; Hare, Miga, and Allen, 2009; Jouriles, Mueller, Rosenfield, McDonald, and Dodson, 2012; Malik et al., 1997; O'Leary et al., 1994). Such children are also more likely to endorse positive attitudes regarding dating aggression (i.e., more likely to think that dating aggression is acceptable under certain circumstances) as they become adolescents and/or young adults (Lichter and McCloskey, 2004).

The cycle of violence hypothesis not only states that children who are exposed to interparental aggression are more likely to perpetrate such behaviors in their future romantic relationships, but also that children who are victims of child abuse are more likely to become involved in an aggressive/abusive relationship as adolescents and young adults (Widom, 1989). This has been supported in previous studies indicating that children who were abused physically and/or sexually are more likely to perpetrate and/or be victimized by dating aggression in their adolescent/

young adult romantic relationships (Barnyard *et al.*, 2000; Gomez, 2011; Malik *et al.*, 1997; Simons, Lin, and Gordon, 1998).

Finally, attachment theory (Bowlby, 1980, 1990) has been a commonly used theory in addressing dating aggression among adolescents and young adults. According to this theory, children who develop a secure attachment with their parents or caregivers are more likely to view the world as a safe or secure place, and in turn will be more likely to view their involvement in romantic relationships as safe and secure as adolescents and/or young adults, whereas the opposite is expected for those who develop an insecure bond with their parents as children (Hazan and Shaver, 1987). Furthermore, adolescents with an insecure attachment style are more likely to perpetrate aggressive behaviors towards their romantic partner (Hare *et al.*, 2009; Miga *et al.*, 2010). In particular, such individuals may also endorse high levels of anxiety (i.e., fear of losing their partner) and may engage in aggressive behaviors towards their romantic partner out of a sense of insecurity (Miga *et al.*, 2010).

Other ways that families influence adolescent dating aggression involve the quality of relationship between adolescents and their parents. Research indicates that lack of parental involvement and monitoring, lack of parental closeness and support, low levels of parental discipline, and high levels of harsh discipline (i.e., corporal punishment) are related to dating aggression perpetration and victimization among adolescents (Chase *et al.*, 2002; Jouriles *et al.*, 2012; Miller, Gorman-Smith, Sullivan, Orpinas, and Simon, 2009; Pflieger and Vazsonyi, 2006; Simons, Burt, and Simons, 2008). Miller and colleagues (2009) also showed that parental support of aggressive behaviors (e.g., parents telling their kids that it is fine to hit someone first if being challenged to a fight) was linked with dating aggression perpetration among adolescents.

Based on findings across the research, it can be concluded that parents play a pivotal role in how adolescents view aggression and whether they will engage in dating aggression. Therefore, it is important that parents are aware of how their children interact with their romantic partners. Parents must also talk to their children about the dangers and consequences of dating aggression. Furthermore, parents must be mindful of *how* they are arguing with their spouse/ significant other. Children learn through observation what behaviors are deemed acceptable within an argument and are likely to imitate what they observe as they become romantically involved.

Summary

Dating aggression is an unfortunate, yet common occurrence among adolescents and young adults. Such behaviors may occur in the form of psychological, physical, or sexual aggression. When adolescents do not recognize the various forms of dating aggression, they may unknowingly engage in these negative behaviors during a conflict in their romantic relationships (e.g., belittling, insulting, or threatening a partner during an argument). Therefore it is imperative to increase adolescents' knowledge of dating aggression in order to decrease the likelihood that such behaviors will occur or be repeated throughout their relationships. Lastly, parents must address these issues with their children and be positive role models for how to engage in effective conflict management so that their children do not adopt negative habits in resolving disagreements with their significant others.

Challenges: Concluding Points

Risky sexual behavior and dating aggression are important social problems that need to be addressed through youth- and family-focused programs and policies designed to support and promote adolescent health. Substantial research has highlighted the contributing factors to each of these challenges, as well as the associated consequences. Families, in particular, play important roles in both producing and preventing these challenges in adolescent romantic relationships. It also is important to acknowledge that risky sexual behaviors and dating aggression can impede healthy adolescent development in areas of identity, intimacy, and academics, among others. Current research efforts need to continue to explore patterns in families, and the broader contexts in which families are situated, that exacerbate adolescents' engagement in risky sexual behavior and dating aggression. Such exploration will assist in uncovering opportunities for education and intervention with adolescents and families that help reduce the rate of these relationship problems occurring across generations.

Future Opportunities
for Research and Practice

Adolescents' relationships and technology

As technology continues to be integrated into all aspects of our daily lives, the use of technology to form, maintain, and end relationships is increasing, especially among younger generations (Subrahmanyam and Greenfield, 2008). Although not extensive, emerging research on adolescents' use of online communication in their romantic relationships shows several important trends, including, using technology to maintain connections with friends and romantic partners, finding romantic partners online, and engaging in sexual communication online. Adolescents' online communication can result in added stress for adolescents and their parents; however, it also offers ways to stay connected with partners and address relationship needs and goals.

Adolescents' online communication and romantic relationships

Being online is a daily part of contemporary adolescents' lives. Included in their online activities are communication with family members, friends, and romantic partners through social networking sites, tweeting, instant messaging, texting, and other electronic modes of communication. Increasing evidence suggests that adolescents are using online means to address needs for intimacy and connection to others (Reich, Subrahmanyam, and Espinoza, 2012). Of particular interest is research addressing adolescents' use of online communication to establish and maintain peer relationships, including those with romantic partners. When adolescents use online methods of communicating with romantic partners and friends, such methods can enhance the in-person contact they have with their close peers. They are able to stay up to date on one another's activities and to communicate thoughts and feelings instantaneously. The small, but

growing body of research addressing adolescents' use of online communication to find or connect with a romantic partner shows positive and negative consequences. Adolescents primarily use online communication to support and extend their interactions with romantic partners, and the majority do not appear to use electronic communication to form initial relationships or to find casual sex partners. In fact, recent research shows that adolescents primarily use social networking sites to connect with people they already know (Reich et al., 2012). Only a minority of teens have used instant messaging to ask someone out or to end a relationship, and few adolescents use online communication to connect with strangers. Adolescents with more troubled relationships with family member or peers, as well as adolescents with limited interpersonal skills, are more likely to seek out exchanges with strangers online (Reich et al., 2012). A one-year longitudinal study of almost 900 middle adolescents indicated that Internet activity choice influenced later relationship quality in both best friendships and romantic relationships (Blais, Craig, Peplar, and Connolly, 2008). Using instant messaging was positively associated with most aspects of romantic relationship and best-friendship quality. In contrast, visiting chat rooms was negatively related to best-friendship quality, and using the Internet to play games and for general entertainment predicted decreases in relationship quality with best friends and with romantic partners. These findings reflect the important and complex functions of online socialization for the development and maintenance of relationships in adolescence. Another longitudinal study (Cheng, Missari, Ma, and Yi, 2011) showed that Internet use and Internet café visits increased the occurrence of Taiwanese adolescents' first romantic relationship experiences and their first exposure to sexual intercourse. The effects were found above and beyond the influence of family bonds, parental supervision, socio-demographic and educational variables on romantic relationship and sexual intercourse experiences. In particular, girls who visited Internet cafés were more vulnerable to early sexual experiences than were boys or their female counterparts who did not visit Internet cafés. Furthermore, Internet use and Internet café visits were found to increase the likelihood of having sexual intercourse before experiencing a first romantic relationship.

The good news is that most adolescents do not meet their online-only contacts in person. One study (van den Heuvel, van den Eijnden, van Rooij, and van de Mheen, 2012) found that 17% of the adolescents participating in the study met online contacts in person; among the youth that had these in-person encounters, about a third had parents who were unaware of such activities. This study showed that the likelihood of having in-person meetings with online contacts increased when an adolescent had low self-esteem. Although most adolescents are using technology to connect with current friends and romantic partners, it is important to consider implications for the minority of adolescents who may be putting themselves at risk by connecting online with virtual strangers, especially those adolescents who have in-person contacts without their parents' knowledge.

Online sexual behavior

When communicating with a romantic partner includes *sexting* (sending sexually explicit messages or images) this can result in unintended consequences such as the information being shared with others without the sender's consent, or being used for emotional blackmail purposes. Sexting can potentially lead to a young person being arrested if the sexually explicit material sent is classified as illegal. Recent work by Drouin and Landgraff (2012) demonstrated that attachment style (relationship anxiety and avoidance) helps explain young adults' use of sexting to communicate with romantic partners. Young adults with higher levels of attachment anxiety (worried that a partner does not return one's love and affection) were more likely than those with low anxiety to send a sex text; whereas young men with higher levels of attachment avoidance (discomfort with relationship closeness) were more likely than those low in anxiety/avoidance to send sex text and pictures (see Box 16.4).

Male and female adolescents vary in their willingness to engage in online sexual disclosure, with males significantly more willing than females to communicate online about sexual material regardless of how intimate the relationship. Interestingly, Yang, Yang, and Chiou (2010) found that female adolescent participants were more likely to communicate online

about sexual material when relationship intimacy was either high or low but not moderate. Willingness to communicate about sexual material was higher for online communication than in-person communication for both males and females. An assessment of early and middle adolescents' perceptions of their risky sexual online behavior showed that those who believed their friends were engaged in risky behaviors were more likely to engage in risky behaviors themselves (Baumgartner, Valkenburg, and Peter, 2010). It also was found that the more perceived risks and vulnerability an adolescent believed might occur due to online sexual behavior, the less likely the adolescent was to engage in such behavior six months later. Thus, adolescents' perceptions of their friends' behaviors matter, but so do adolescents' beliefs about risk and vulnerability when attempting to understand adolescents' decisions about online sexual behavior.

Families and adolescents' use of technology

Clearly it is important for parents to be aware of their adolescents' (especially young adolescents') online, texting, and other social networking activities. Learning how to use the technology themselves can help parents be more attuned to their children's activities and have a language for discussing technology-based communication. Texting, tweeting, and posting are ways that family members can stay in touch with one another and be aware of what is occurring in each other's lives. A. Williams and Merten (2011) contend that social media technology has the potential to strengthen family bonds, noting that how parents and adolescents negotiate the role of the Internet in their families has implications for adolescents' exposure to potential harm from outside the family system. Research examining the effects of adolescent online communication with romantic partners on families and how such communication is affected by parents and family members is in its infancy (Subrahmanyam and Greenfield, 2008). It will be important for future research to pose questions that help elucidate benefits and costs of the technology-supported communication that increasingly permeates close interpersonal relationships and family life.

Box 16.4   Sexting

Jayla recently started texting with Antonio, a guy she likes at her school. Antonio is very popular and her friends are really excited for Jayla because he is showing interest in her. After a couple weeks of texting and talking, Antonio asks her to send a nude picture of herself. Worried that he might stop talking to her if she refused, and feeling lucky that he even wants this picture, Jayla sent him an explicit photo of herself. Soon afterwards, she found out that Antonio showed this picture to all his friends and they were sending it to many other people at the school. Jayla was very embarrassed and hurt.

What are Jayla and Antonio thinking? Adolescents have a strong urge to belong and are often concerned about rejection from their peers. Especially during adolescence, dating relationships that offer social benefits like increased status or popularity can be pretty appealing. As adolescents develop a sense of identity and a greater understanding of their values they can be more assertive and stand up for their values. Jayla thought she could get Antonio's love by sharing the nude photo of herself with him; Antonio was looking to increase his status with his peers when he shared Jayla's picture with them.

How can parents/adults help? Parents/adults can talk to adolescents about what they value and how they would stand up for their values in certain social situations. They can discuss the consequences of sending messages or posting images or words that they may regret. Not only are there potential emotional or social consequences, some states have enacted laws that make sending sexually explicit images a crime. It is important for parents/trusted adults to explain to teens, that although technology can be a great way to communicate and further develop a romantic relationship, it also offers ways for teens to have their privacy violated. In Jayla's case, she thought she could trust Antonio and that the picture she shared with him was private. But Antonio did not respect Jayla and took advantage of her trust. Now Jayla has to face the consequences of engaging in sexting and the embarrassment of her picture being shared with many other boys. And Antonio is at risk for getting in trouble for sharing the picture of Jayla without her knowledge or permission. It is important to remind teens that once information or pictures are shared electronically they cannot be controlled by the person who sent them.

Summary

The growing literature addressing online communication and romantic relationships reveals both healthy and unhealthy online communication engaged in by adolescents. When online communication is used to contact strangers, share sexting messages, or communicate in hurtful ways, this can bring stress into adolescents' lives as well as those of their family members. Conversely , online communication can increase timely communication among friends and romantic partners, strengthening their connections with one another (Lee, 2009). Not only will future research need to address increasingly complex questions about the infusion of social technology in adolescents' close relationships, the use of technology for relationship education will likely become a growing method for reaching adolescents with the timely information they need (Braithwaite and Fincham, 2007, 2009, 2011).

Youth-Focused Relationship Education

Most adolescents are interested in romantic relationships and actively seeking information about dating and related topics (Collins, 2003; Furman and Shaffer, 2003). If adolescents are unable to obtain information from reputable sources, they may believe faulty information about romantic relationships. Inaccurate messages about relationships can come from family members and peers, on websites, and from other sources. Relationship education offers a means to counter the faulty messages adolescents may receive, and can help youth learn and practice skills to communicate effectively, manage disagreements productively, and engage in activities that help to build respect, intimacy, and trust within a romantic relationship. Developmentally, it is normal for adolescents to make decisions based on immediate needs and wants, often giving little thought to future implications or consequences. This is especially true when adolescents find themselves strongly attracted to another person, and they have limited experience negotiating within relationships. Relationship education offers steps that adolescents can take prior to being in the "heat of the moment," helping them make the link between current choices and potential future consequences. Youth-focused relationship education uses a developmentally appropriate approach and typically covers areas of self-development, values, decision-making in relationships, recognizing healthy, unhealthy, and abusive relationships, and skills necessary for good communication and managing conflict within relationships (Adler-Baeder, Kerpelman, Schramm, Higgenbotham, and Paulk, 2007; Kerpelman, 2007). When youth do not have positive relationship models, not only are they unlikely to have a clear understanding of what healthy relationships look like, they are also unlikely to appreciate how healthy relationships can be beneficial. Relationship education helps adolescents understand the different ways that healthy relationships foster physical and mental health, support educational and career aspirations, and enhance quality of life (Gardner and Boellaard, 2007; Kerpelman, Pittman, Adler-Baeder, Eryigit, and Paulk, 2009). Through relationship education youth can learn ways to manage negative emotions and to employ interpersonal skills that support healthy relationship functioning (Adler-Baeder et al., 2007; Gardner, Giese, and Parrot, 2004; Kerpelman, 2007; Kerpelman et al., 2009). Youth-focused relationship education also helps adolescents learn to recognize warning signs that indicate they are in an unhealthy, possibly abusive, relationship and provides them with knowledge and skills to address such circumstances (Pittman and Kerpelman, 2013). Education can address alternatives to dating aggression, helping adolescents learn healthy ways to manage feelings of anger, hurt, or jealousy within a dating relationship. Relationship education also can complement sexuality information, helping adolescents understand that sexuality is connected with relationships. By linking sexuality with processes that occur within close relationships, a more comprehensive view of sexuality and health can be offered to adolescents.

Evaluation of youth-focused relationship education programs

During the past decade, a number of evaluation studies addressing youth-focused relationship education have been published, yet the overall number of peer-reviewed evaluation publications remains sparse. Research to date shows that educating adolescents about healthy relationships increases their understanding of how relationships function (Adler-Baeder et al., 2007; Gardner et al., 2004), and builds skills and behaviors associated with maintaining healthy romantic relationships (Gardner and Boellaard, 2007; Kerpelman et al., 2009). Evaluation results of the federally funded Healthy Couples, Healthy Children: Targeting Youth project (Kerpelman, Pittman, and Adler-Baeder, 2005–2010) showed that relationship education was effective in helping adolescents decrease the use of verbal aggression toward dating partners (Adler-Baeder et al., 2007), as well as decrease faulty relationship beliefs and increase conflict management skills (Kerpelman, Pittman, and Adler-Baeder, 2008; Kerpelman et al., 2009, 2010). Importantly, relationship education was found to be effective with adolescents from diverse backgrounds, with such education being particularly beneficial for adolescents who faced multiple obstacles to having healthy relationships (Kerpelman et al., 2010). Finally, relationship education enhanced adolescents' beliefs that aggression within relationships is not acceptable, which in turn was concurrently and longitudinally associated with less use of physical aggression toward a dating partner (Pittman and Kerpelman, 2013). Collectively the findings from these evaluation studies highlight the importance of considering what youth bring to the relationship education context, such as their family and cultural backgrounds, past and current dating experiences, and their beliefs about romantic relationships, so that the learning experiences are sensitive to the needs of the adolescents being served. To be most effective, it is critical that programs be evaluated rigorously in experimental studies (randomized controlled trials where people are randomly assigned to either the intervention group or the control group) or quasi-experimental studies (where program participants are compared to a group of people similar to the program participants, but participants are not randomly assigned to the intervention and control groups). Such designs increase the certainty that changes in knowledge, skills and/or behaviors are due to the program rather than to other factors. Being able to show that a program works and to replicate the results is the ultimate goal when one is trying to effect change. Developing new ways to offer educational information, in various settings where adolescents spend time, including online, will be important if education is to reach diverse adolescents, especially those who need it most, to ensure healthy decision-making as they navigate important relationship decisions and challenges.

Conclusions

Adolescent romantic relationships offer opportunities for self-development and skill building, while also introducing challenges and risks for youth and their families. Family members, especially parents/caregivers, provide a context in which adolescents gain information and make decisions about romantic relationships. Depending on the health of the family system and the broader community in which the family resides, the adolescent may observe positive modeling and receive support needed to navigate challenges successfully and avoid costly risks. Conversely, the adolescent without support and other factors that promote resilience may encounter situations and choices that are difficult to manage and engage in behaviors that lead to negative outcomes that derail development, health, and future potential. Research needs to continue investigating how adolescent sexual health and experiences with dating aggression are associated with family functioning and adolescent adaptation. In addition, avenues for intervening at the individual and family level are needed when sexual, emotional, or physical health is compromised. Research is just beginning to examine

how the increasing use of social media affects adolescent romantic relationships and ways that families can interface with technology that offer positive influences on how adolescents use social networking and online communication to support healthy relationships. Finally, youth-focused relationship education in schools, community settings, and online can increase the likelihood that more youth are accurately informed and armed with skills needed to form and maintain healthy relationships with friends and romantic partners.

Critical Thinking Questions

1. Although dating aggression consists of a variety of behaviors, what do adolescents consider to be dating aggression behaviors? How do we help adolescents understand that psychological forms of aggression can be as detrimental as physical forms of aggression?

2. Researchers generally agree that sexual desire and exploration during adolescence is a normal part of development. Do you think that families typically treat an adolescent's sexual and romantic relationship development as normal and healthy? Why or why not?

3. If you were to design a prevention program for reducing unintended teen pregnancy and STDs, or to prevent adolescent dating violence, what kinds of information and activities would you include? How might you reach youth that are particularly vulnerable (i.e., sexual minority youth, low-income, and/or ethnic minority youth)? How would you involve parents?

4. How can parents respect their teens' privacy while still being a positive influence on their teens' online communication with romantic partners?

References

Abma, J., Martinez, G., and Copen, C. (2010). Teenagers in the United States: Sexual activity, contraceptive use, and child-bearing, National Survey of Family Growth 2006–2008. *Vital Health Statistics, 23*(30). Retrieved May 30, 2014 from http://www.cdc.gov/nchs/data/series/sr_23/sr23_030.pdf.

Adler-Baeder, F., Kerpelman, J. L., Schramm, D. G., Higgenbotham, B., and Paulk, A. (2007). The impact of relationship education on adolescents of diverse backgrounds. *Family Relations, 56*, 291–303. doi: 10.1111/j.1741-3729.2007.00460.x.

Alleyne, B., Coleman-Cowger, V. H., Crown, L., Gibbons, M. A., and Vines, L. N. (2011). The effects of dating violence, substance use and risky sexual behavior among a diverse sample of Illinois youth. *Journal of Adolescence, 34*, 11–18. doi: 10.1016/j.adolescence.2010.03.006.

Archer, J. (2000). Sex differences in aggression between heterosexual partners: A meta-analytic review. *Psychological Bulletin, 126*, 651–680. doi: 10.1037//0033-2909.126.5.681.

Archer, J. (2002). Sex differences in physically aggressive acts between heterosexual partners: A meta-analytic review. *Aggression and Violent Behavior, 7*, 313–351. doi: 10.1037/0033-2909.126.5.651.

Archer, J. (2004). Sex differences in aggression in real-world settings: A meta-analytic review. *Review of General Psychology, 8*(4), 291–322. doi: 10.1037/1089-2680.8.4.291.

Aspy, C., Vesely, S., Oman, R., Rodine, S., Marshall, L., and McLeroy, K. (2007). Parental communication and youth sexual behavior. *Journal of Adolescence, 30*, 449–466. doi:10.1016/j.adolescence.2006.04.007.

Bandura, A. (1978). Social learning theory of aggression. *Journal of Communication, 28*, 12–29. doi: 10.1111/j.1460-2466.1978.tb01621.x.

Barber, B. K., Stolz, H. E., and Olsen, J. A. (2005). Parental support, psychological control, and behavior control: Assessing relevance across time, culture and method. *Monographs of the Society of Research on Child Development, 70*, 1–103.

Barber, B. L., and Eccles, J. S. (2003). The joy of romance: Healthy adolescent relationships as an educational agenda. In P. Florsheim (ed.), *Adolescent romantic relations and sexual behavior: Theory, research, and practical implications* (pp. 355–370). Mahwah, NJ: Lawrence Erlbaum Associates.

Barnyard, V. L., Arnold, S., and Smith, J. (2000). Childhood sexual abuse and dating experiences of undergraduate women. *Child Maltreatment, 5*, 39–48. doi:10.1177/1077559500005001005.

Barnyard, V. L., and Cross, C. (2008). Consequences of teen dating violence: Understanding intervening variables in ecological context. *Violence Against Women, 14*, 998–1013. doi: 10.1177/1077801208322058.

Baumgartner, S. E., Valkenburg, P. M., and Peter, J. (2010). Assessing causality in the relationship between adolescents' risky sexual online behavior and their perceptions of this behavior. *Journal of Youth and Adolescence, 39*, 1226–1239. doi:10.1007/s10964-010-9512-y.

Baxter, L. A., Bylund, C. L., Imes, R., and Routsong, T. (2009). Parent–child perceptions of parental behavior control through rule-setting for risky health choices during adolescence. *Journal of Family Communication, 9*, 251–271. doi: 10.1080/15267430903255920.

Beyers, W., and Seiffge-Krenke, I. (2010). Does identity precede intimacy? Testing Erikson's theory on romantic development in emerging adults of the 21st century. *Journal of Adolescent Research, 25*(3), 387–415. doi: 10.1177/0743558410361370.

Blais, J. J., Craig, W. M., Peplar, D., and Connolly, J. (2008). Adolescents online: The importance of internet activity choices to salient relationships. *Journal of Youth and Adolescence, 37*, 522–536. doi: 10.1007/s10964-007-9262-7.

Blake, S., Simkin, L., Ledsky, R., Perkins, C., and Calabrese, J. (2001). Effects of a parent–child communications intervention on young adolescents' risk for early onset of sexual intercourse. *Family Planning Perspectives, 33*, 52–61. Retrieved May 30, 2014 from http://www.guttmacher.org/pubs/journals/3305201.pdf.

Bookwala, J., Frieze, I. H., Smith, C., and Ryan, K. (1992). Predictors of dating violence: A multivariate analysis. *Violence and Victims, 7*, 297–308.

Bouchey, H. A., and Furman, W. (2003). Dating and romantic experiences in adolescence. In G. R. Adams and M. D. Berzonsky (eds), *The Blackwell handbook of adolescence* (pp. 313–329). Oxford: Blackwell.

Bowlby, J. (1980). *Attachment and loss.* New York: Basic Books.

Bowlby, J. (1990). *A secure base: Parent–child attachments and healthy human development.* New York: Basic Books.

Braithwaite, S. R., and Fincham, F. D. (2007). ePREP: computer based prevention of relationship dysfunction, depression and anxiety. *Journal of Social and Clinical Psychology, 26*, 609–622. doi: 10.1521/jscp.2007.26.5.609.

Braithwaite, S. R., and Fincham, F. D. (2009). A randomized clinical trial of a computer based preventative intervention: Replication and extension of ePREP. *Journal of Family Psychology, 23*, 32–38. doi: 10.1037/a0014061.

Braithwaite, S. R., and Fincham, F. D. (2011). Computer-based dissemination: A randomized clinical trial of ePREP using the actor partner interdependence model. *Behaviour Research and Therapy, 49*, 126–131. doi: 10.1016/j.brat.2010.11.002.

Callahan, M. R., Tolman, R. M., and Saunders, D. G. (2003). Adolescent dating violence victimization and psychological well-being. *Journal of Adolescent Research, 18*(6), 664–681. doi: 10.1177/0743558403254784.

Cano, A., Avery-Leaf, S., Cascardi, M., and O'Leary, D. (1998). Dating violence in two high school samples: Discriminating variables. *Journal of Primary Prevention, 18*(4), 431–446. doi: 10.1023/A: 1022653609263.

Centers for Disease Control and Prevention. (2003). *Costs of intimate partner violence against women in the United States.* Atlanta, GA: CDC. Retrieved May 30, 2014 from http://www.cdc.gov/ncipc/pub-res/ipv_cost/ipvbook-final-feb18.pdf.

Centers for Disease Control and Prevention. (2012). Youth risk behavior surveillance – United States, 2011. Surveillance Summaries 61 (no. 4). Retrieved May 30, 2014 from http://www.cdc.gov/mmwr/pdf/ss/ss6104.pdf.

Champion, J. D., Collins, J. L., Reyes, S., and Rivera, R. L. (2009). Attitudes and beliefs concerning sexual relationships among minority adolescent women. *Issues in Mental Health Nursing,* 30, 436–442. doi: 10.1080/01612840902770475.

Chandra, A., Martinez, G., Mosher, W., Abma, J., and Jones, J. (2005). Fertility, family planning, and reproductive health of U.S. women: Data from the 2002 National Survey of Family Growth. National Center for Health Statistics. *Vital Health Statistics,* 23(25). Retrieved May 30, 2014 from http://www.cdc.gov/nchs/data/series/sr_23/sr23_025.pdf.

Chandra, A., Mosher, W., and Copen, C. (2011). Sexual behavior, sexual attraction, and sexual identity in the United States: Data from the 2006–2008 National Survey of Family Growth. *National Health Statistics Reports, 36,* 1–36.

Chase, K. A., Treboux, D., and O'Leary, D. K. (2002). Characteristics of high-risk adolescents' dating violence. *Journal of Interpersonal Violence, 17,* 33–49. doi: 10.1177/0886260502017001003.

Cheng, S., Missari, S. A., Ma, K. J., and Yi, C. (2011). The effects of internet use on adolescents' first romantic and sexual relationships in Taiwan. Retrieved May 30, 2014 from http://www.typ.sinica.edu.tw/upfiles/4_01.pdf.

Clawson, C., and Reese-Weber, M. (2003). The amount and timing of parent–adolescent sexual communication as predictors of late adolescent sexual risk-taking behaviors. *Journal of Sex Research, 40,* 256–265. doi: 10.1080/00224490309552190.

Collins, W. A. (2003). More than myth: The developmental significance of romantic relationships during adolescence. *Journal of Research on Adolescence, 13,* 1–24. doi: 10.1111/1532-7795.1301001.

Connolly, J., Friedlander, L., Pepler, D., Craig, W., and Laporte, L. (2010). The ecology of adolescent dating aggression: Socio-demographic risk factors. *Journal of Aggression, Maltreatment and Trauma, 19,* 469–491. doi: 10.1080/10926771.2010.495028.

Cui, M., Ueno, K., Gordon, M., and Fincham, F. (2013). The continuation of intimate partner violence from adolescence to young adulthood. *Journal of Marriage and Family, 75,* 300–313. doi: 10.1111/jomf.12016.

Curtin, S. C., Abma, J. C., Ventura, S. J., and Henshaw, S. K. (2013). Pregnancy rates for U.S. women continue to drop. National Center for Health Statistics, Data Brief, no. 123. Retrieved June 1, 2013 from http://www.cdc.gov/nchs/data/databriefs/db136.htm.

D'Augelli, A. R., Grossman, A. H., Starks, M. T., and Sinclair, K. O. (2010). Factors associated with parents' knowledge of gay, lesbian, and bisexual youths' sexual orientation. *Journal of GLBT Family Studies, 6,* 178–198. doi: 10.1080/15504281003705410.

Davis, E. C., and Friel, L. (2001). Adolescent sexuality: Disentangling the effects of family structure and family context. *Journal of Marriage and Family, 63,* 669–681. doi: 10.1111/j.1741-3737.2001.00669.x.

de Graaf, H., Vanwesenbeeck, I., Meijer, S., Woertman, L., and Meeus, W. (2009). Sexual trajectories during adolescence: Relation to demographic characteristics and sexual risk. *Archives of Sexual Behavior, 38,* 276–282. doi:10.1007/s10508-007-9281-1.

Deptula, D., Henry, D., and Schoeny, M. (2010). How can parents make a difference? Longitudinal associations with adolescent sexual behavior. *Journal of Family Psychology, 24,* 731–739. doi: 10.1037/a0021760.

DiClemente, R., Wingood, G., Crosby, R., Cobb, B., Harrington, K., and Davies, S. (2001). Parent–adolescent communication and sexual risk behaviors among African American adolescent females. *Journal of Pediatrics, 139,* 407–412.

Dittus, P., Miller, K. S., Kotchick, B. A., and Forehand, R. (2004). Why Parents Matter! The conceptual basis for a community-based HIV prevention program for the parents of African American youth. *Journal of Child and Family Studies, 13,* 5–20. doi: 10.1023/B:JCFS.0000010487.46007.08.

Drouin, M., and Landgraff, C. (2012). Texting, sexting, and attachment in college students' romantic relationships. *Computers in Human Behavior, 28,* 444–449. doi:10.1016/j.chb.2011.10.015.

Dyk, P. A., and Adams, G. R. (1987). The association between identity development and intimacy during adolescence: A theoretical treatise. *Journal of Adolescent Research, 2*(3), 223–235. doi: 10.1177/074355488723004.

Ellis, W. E., Crooks, C. V., and Wolfe, D. A. (2009). Relational aggression in peer and dating relationships: Links to psychological and behavioral adjustment. *Social Development, 18,* 253–269. doi: 10.1111/j.1467-9507.2008.00468.x.

Erikson, E. H. (1968). *Identity: Youth and crisis.* Oxford: Norton.

Fergus, S., Zimmerman, M., and Caldwell, C. (2007). Growth trajectories of sexual risk behavior in adolescence and young adulthood. *American Journal of Public Health, 97,* 1096–1101. doi:10.2105/AJPH.2005.074609.

Fernandez-Fuertes, A. A., and Fuertes, A. (2010). Physical and psychological aggression in dating relationships of Spanish adolescents: Motives and consequences. *Child Abuse and Neglect, 34,* 183–191. doi: 10.1016/j.chiabu.2010.01.002.

Fite, J. E., Bates, J. E., Holtzworth-Munroe, A., Dodge, K. A., Nay, S. Y., and Pettit, G. S. (2008). Social information processing mediates the intergenerational transmission of aggressiveness in romantic relationships. *Journal of Family Psychology,* 22(3), 367–376. doi: 10.1037/0893-3200.22.3.367.

Follingstad, D. R., Rutledge, L. L., Berg, B. J., Hause, A. S., and Polek, D. S. (1990). The role of emotional abuse in physically abusive relationships. *Journal of Family Violence,* 5, 107–120. doi: 10.1007/BF00978514.

Foo, L., and Margolin, G. (1995). A multivariate investigation of dating aggression. *Journal of Family Violence,* 10, 351–377. doi: 10.1007/BF02110711.

Foshee, V. A., Bauman, K. E., and Linder, F. (1999). Family violence and the perpetration of adolescent dating violence: Examining social learning and social control processes. *Journal of Marriage and the Family,* 61, 331–342.

Foshee, V. A., Benefield, T., Suchindran, C., Ennett, S. T., Bauman, K. E., Karriker-Jaffe, K. J., ... and Mathias, J. (2009). The development of four types of adolescent dating abuse and selected demographic correlates. *Journal of Research on Adolescence,* 19(3), 380–400. doi: 10.1111/j.1532-7795.2009.00593.x.

Fritz, P. A. T., and Slep, A. M. S. (2009). Stability of physical and psychological adolescent dating aggression cross time and partners. *Journal of Clinical Child and Adolescent Psychology,* 38, 303–314. doi:10.1080/15374410902851671.

Furman, W., and Shaffer, L. (2003). The role of romantic relationships in adolescent development. In P. Florsheim (ed.), *Adolescent romantic relations and sexual behavior: Theory, research, and practical implications* (pp. 3–22). Mahwah, NJ: Laurence Erlbaum Associates.

Furman, W., and Shaffer-Hand, L. (2006). The slippery nature of romantic relationships: Issues in definition and differentiation. In A. C. Crouter and A. Booth (eds), *Romance and sex in adolescence and emerging adulthood: Risks and opportunities* (pp. 171–178). Mahwah, NJ: Laurence Erlbaum Associates.

Galliher, R. V., and Bentley, C. G. (2010). Links between rejection sensitivity and adolescent romantic relationship functioning: The mediating role of problem-solving behaviors. *Journal of Aggression, Maltreatment and Trauma,* 19, 603–623. doi:10.1080/10926771.2010.502066.

Gardner, S. P., and Boellaard, R. (2007). Does youth relationship education continue to work after a high school class? A longitudinal study. *Family Relations,* 56, 490–500. doi: 10.1111/j.1741-3729.2007.00476.x.

Gardner, S. P., Giese, K., and Parrot, S. M. (2004). Evaluation of the connections: Relationships and marriage curriculum. *Family Relations,* 53, 521–527. doi: 10.1111/j.0197-6664.2004.00061.x.

Giordano, P. C., Manning, W. D., and Longmore, M. A. (2006). Adolescent romantic relationships: An emerging portrait of their nature and developmental significance. In A. C. Crouter and A. Booth (eds.), *Romance and sex in adolescence and emerging adulthood: Risks and opportunities* (pp. 127–150). Mahwah, NJ: Lawrence Erlbaum Associates.

Giordano, P. C., Soto, D. A., Manning, W. D., and Longmore, M. A. (2010). The characteristics of romantic relationships associated with teen dating violence. *Social Science Research,* 39, 863–874. doi: 10.1016/j.ssresearch.2010.03.009.

Gomez, A. M. (2011). Testing the cycle of violence hypothesis: Child abuse and adolescent dating violence as predictors of intimate partner violence in young adulthood. *Youth and Society,* 43, 171–192. doi:10.1177/0044118X09358313.

Guzman, B., Schlehofer-Sutton, C., Villanueva, C., Stritto, M., Casad, B., and Feria, A. (2003). Let's talk about sex: How comfortable discussions about sex can impact teen sexual behavior. *Journal of Health Communication,* 8, 583–598. doi: 10.1080/716100416.

Hallfors, D., Waller, M., and Ford, C. (2004). Adolescent depression and suicide risk: Association with sex and drug behavior. *American Journal of Preventive Medicine,* 27, 224–230. doi: 10.1016/j.amepre.2004.06.001.

Halpern, C. T., Spriggs, A. L., Martin, S. L., and Kupper, L. L. (2009). Patterns of intimate partner violence victimization from adolescence to young adulthood in a nationally representative sample. *Journal of Adolescent Health,* 45, 508–516. doi: 10.1016/j.jadohealth.2009.03.011.

Hamby, S. L., and Sugarman, D. B. (1999). Acts of psychological aggression against a partner and their relation to physical assault and gender. *Journal of Marriage and the Family,* 61, 959–970. doi: 10.2307/354016.

Hare, A. L., Miga, E. M., and Allen, J. P. (2009). Intergenerational transmission of aggression in romantic relationships: The moderating role of attachment security. *Journal of Family Psychology,* 23, 808–818. doi: 10.1037/a0016740.

Haydon, A., Hussey, M., and Tucker-Halpern, C. (2011). Childhood abuse and neglect and the risk of STDs in early adulthood. *Perspectives on Sexual and Reproductive Health,* 43, 16–22. doi: 10.1363/4301611.

Hazan, C., and Shaver, P. (1987). Romantic love conceptualized as an attachment process. *Journal of Personality and Social Psychology,* 52(3), 511–524. doi: 10.1037/0022-3514.52.3.511.

Hill, N. E., Bromell, L., Tyson, D. F., and Flint, R. (2007). Developmental commentary: Ecological perspectives on parental influences during adolescence. *Journal of Clinical Child and Adolescent Psychology,* 36, 367–377. doi: 10.1080/15374410701444322.

Hoffman, S. (2006). By the numbers: The public cost of adolescent childbearing. Washington DC: The National

Campaign to Prevent Teen Pregnancy. Retrieved May 30, 2014 from www.thenationalcampaign.org/resources/pdf/pubs/BTN_Full.pdf.

Howard, D. E., Wang, M. Q., and Yan, F. (2007). Psychosocial factors associated with reports of physical dating violence among U.S. adolescent females. *Adolescence, 42,* 311–324.

Jelz, D. R., Molidor, C. E., and Wright, T. L. (1996). Physical, sexual, and psychological abuse in high school dating relationships: Prevalence rates and self-esteem issues. *Child and Adolescent Social Work Journal, 13,* 69–87. doi: 10.1007/BF01876596.

Jouriles, E. N., Mueller, V., Rosenfield, D., McDonald, R., and Dodson, M. C. (2012). Teens' experiences of harsh parenting and exposure to severe intimate partner violence: Adding insult to injury in predicting teen dating violence. *Psychology of Violence, 2,* 125–138. doi: 10.1037/a0027264.

Kan, M., Cheng, Y., Landale, N., and McHale, S. (2010). Longitudinal predictors of change in number of sexual partners across adolescence and early adulthood. *Journal of Adolescent Health, 46,* 25–31. doi: 10.1016/j.jadohealth.2009.05.002.

Kasian, M., and Painter, S. L. (1992). Frequency and severity of psychological abuse in a dating population. *Journal of Interpersonal Violence, 7,* 350–364. doi: 10.1177/088626092007003005.

Kerpelman, J. L. (2007). Youth-focused relationships and marriage education. *Forum for Family and Consumer Issues, 12.* Retrieved May 30, 2014 from http://ncsu.edu/ffci/publications/2007/v12-n1-2007-spring/kerpelman/fa-7-kerpelman.php.

Kerpelman, J. L., Pittman, J. F., and Adler-Baeder, F. M. (2005–2010). Healthy Couples, Healthy Children: Targeting Youth. Five-year federally funded evaluation study of youth focused relationship education. Grant (#90OJ2017) received by Auburn University from the United States Office of Planning, Research, and Evaluation/Administration for Children and Families, Washington, DC.

Kerpelman, J. L., Pittman, J. F., and Adler-Baeder, F. (2008). Identity as a moderator of intervention-related change: Identity style and adolescents' responses to relationships education. *Identity: An International Journal of Theory and Research, 8,* 151–171. doi: 10.1080/15283480801940073.

Kerpelman, J. L., Pittman, J. F., Adler-Baeder, F., Eryigit, S., and Paulk, A. L. (2009). Evaluation of a statewide youth-focused relationships education curriculum. *Journal of Adolescence, 32,* 1359–1370. doi: 10.1016/j.adolescence.2009.04.006.

Kerpelman, J. L., Pittman, J. F., Adler-Baeder, F., Stringer, K. J., Eryigit, S., Cadely, H. S., and Harrell-Levy, M. (2010). What adolescents bring to and learn from relationships education classes: Does social address matter? *Journal of Couple and Relationship Therapy, 9,* 95–112. doi: 10.1080/15332691003694877.

Kerpelman, J. L., Pittman, J. F., Cadely, H. S., Tuggle, F. J., Harrell-Levy, M. K., and Adler-Baeder, F. M. (2012). Identity and intimacy during adolescence: Connections among identity styles, romantic attachment and identity commitment. *Journal of Adolescence, 35,* 1427–1439. doi: 10.1016/j.adolescence.2012.03.008.

Kincaid, C., Jones, D., Cuellar, J., and Gonzalez, M. (2011). Psychological control associated with youth adjustment and risky behavior in African American single mother families. *Journal of Child and Family Studies, 20,* 102–110. doi: 10.1007/s10826-010-9383-6.

Kost, K., Henshaw, S., and Carlin, L., (2010). U.S. teenage pregnancies, births and abortions: National and state trends and trends by race and ethnicity. New York and Washington, DC: Guttmacher Institute. Retrieved May 30, 2014 from http://www.guttmacher.org/pubs/USTPtrends.pdf.

Landsford, J., Yu, T., Erath, S., Pettit, G., Bates, J., and Dodge, K. (2010). Developmental precursors of number of sexual partners from ages 16–22. *Journal of Research on Adolescence, 20,* 651–677. doi: 10.1111/j.1532-7795.2010.00654.x.

Laursen, B., and Mooney, K. S. (2007). Individual differences in adolescent dating adjustment. In R. C. M. E. Engels, M. Kerr, and H. Stattin (eds), *Friends, lovers and groups: Key relationships in adolescence* (pp. 81–92). Hoboken, NJ: John Wiley & Sons, Inc.

Lawrence, E., Yoon, J., Langer, A., and Ro, E. (2009). Is psychological aggression as detrimental as physical aggression? The independent effects of psychological aggression on depression and anxiety symptoms. *Violence and Victims, 24,* 20–35. doi: 10.1891/0886-6708.24.1.20.

Lederman, R., Chan, W., and Roberts-Gray, C. (2008). Parent–adolescent relationship education (PARE): Program delivery to reduce risks for adolescent pregnancy and STDs. *Behavioral Medicine, 33,* 137–143. doi:10.3200/BMED.33.4.137-144.

Lee, S. J. (2009). Online communication and adolescent social ties: Who benefits more from internet use? *Journal of Computer-Mediated Communication, 14,* 509–531. doi:10.1111/j.1083-6101.2009.01451.x.

Lefkowitz, E., and Stoppa, T. (2006). Positive sexual communication and socialization in the parent–adolescent context. *New Directions for Child and Adolescent Development, 112,* 39–55. doi: 10.1002/cd.161.

Lichter, E. L., and McCloskey, L. A. (2004). The effects of childhood exposure to marital violence on adolescent gender-role beliefs and dating violence. *Psychology of Women Quarterly, 28,* 344–357. doi: 10.1111/j.1471-6402.2004.00151.x.

Malik, S., Sorenson, S. B., and Aneshensel, C. S. (1997). Community and dating violence among adolescents: Perpetration and victimization. *Journal of Adolescent Health, 21*, 291–302. doi: 10.1016/S1054-139X(97)00143-2.

Manning, W., Flanigan, C., Giordano, P., and Longmore, M. (2009). Relationship dynamics and consistency of condom use among adolescents. *Perspectives on Sexual and Reproductive Health, 41*, 181–190. doi: 10.1363/4118109.

Manning, W., Giordano, P., and Longmore, M. (2006). Hooking up: The relationship contexts of "nonrelationship" sex. *Journal of Adolescent Research, 21*(5), 459–583. doi: 10.1177/0743558406291692.

Markstrom, C. A., and Kalmanir, H. M. (2001). Linkages between the psychosocial states of identity and intimacy and the ego strengths of fidelity and love. *Identity: An International Journal of Theory and Research, 1*, 179–196. doi: 10.1207/S1532706XID0102_05.

Martinez, G., Copen, C., and Abma, J. (2011). Teenagers in the United States: Sexual activity, contraceptive use, and childbearing, National Survey of Family Growth 2006–2010. *Vital and Health Statistics, 23*(31). Retrieved May 30, 2014 from: http://www.cdc.gov/nchs/data/series/sr_23/sr23_031.pdf.

Meeus, W. (2003). Parental and peer support, identity development and psychological well-being in adolescence. *Psychology: The Journal of the Hellenic Psychological Society, 10*, 192–201.

Michels, T., Kropp, R., Eyre, S., and Halpern-Felsher, B. (2005). Initiating sexual experiences: How do young adolescents make decisions regarding early sexual activity? *Journal of Research on Adolescence, 15*, 583–607. doi: 10.1111/j.1532-7795.2005.00112.x.

Miga, E. M., Hare, A., Allen, J. P., and Manning, N. (2010). The relation of insecure attachment states of mind and romantic attachment styles to adolescent aggression in romantic relationships. *Attachment and Human Development, 12*, 463–481. doi: 10.1080/14616734.2010.501971.

Miller, S., Gorman-Smith, D., Sullivan, T., Orpinas, P., and Simon, T. R. (2009). Parent and peer predictors of physical dating violence perpetration in early adolescence: Tests of moderation and gender differences. *Journal of Clinical Child and Adolescent Psychology, 38*(4), 538–550. doi: 10.1080/15374410902976270.

Montgomery, M. J. (2005). Psychosocial intimacy and identity: From early adolescence to emerging adulthood. *Journal of Adolescent Research, 20*(3), 346–374. doi: 10.1177/0743558404273118.

O'Leary, K. D., Malone, J., and Tyree, A. (1994). Physical aggression in early marriage: Prerelationship and relationship effects. *Journal of Consulting and Clinical Psychology, 62*(3), 594–602. doi: 10.1037/0022-006X.62.3.594.

O'Leary, K. D., and Slep, A. M. (2003). A dyadic longitudinal model of adolescent dating aggression. *Journal of Clinical Child and Adolescent Psychology, 32*(3), 314–327. doi: 10.1207/S15374424JCC3203_01.

Ozer, E. J., Tschann, J. M., Pasch, L. A., and Flores, A. (2004). Violence perpetration across peer and partner relationships: Co-occurrence and longitudinal patterns among adolescents. *Journal of Adolescent Health, 34*, 64–71. doi: 10.1016/j.jadohealth.2002.12.001.

Padilla, Y., Crisp, C., and Rew, D. (2010). Parental acceptance and illegal drug use among gay, lesbian, and bisexual adolescents: Results from a national survey. *Social Work, 55*, 265–275. doi: 10.1093/sw/55.3.265.

Parkes, A., Henderson, M., Wight, D., and Nixon, C. (2011). Is parenting associated with teenagers' early sexual risk-taking, autonomy and relationship with sexual partners? *Perspectives on Sexual and Reproductive Health, 43*, 30–40. doi: 10.1363/4303011.

Pearson, J., Muller, C., and Frisco, M. (2006). Parental involvement, family structure, and adolescent sexual decision-making. *Sociological Perspectives, 49*, 67–90. doi: 10.1525/sop.2006.49.1.67.

Pflieger, J. C., and Vazsonyi, A. T. (2006). Parenting processing and dating violence: The mediating role of self-esteem in low- and high-SES adolescents. *Journal of Adolescence, 29*, 495–512. doi: 10.1016/j.adolescence.2005.10.002.

Pittman, J. F., Keiley, M. K., Kerpelman, J. L., and Vaughn, B. E. (2011). Attachment, identity, and intimacy: Parallels between Bowlby's and Erikson's paradigms. *Journal of Family Theory and Review, 3*, 32–46. doi: 10.1111/j.1756-2589.2010.00079.x.

Pittman, J. F., and Kerpelman, J. L. (2013, May). A cross-lagged model of adolescent dating aggression attitudes and behavior: Relationship education makes a difference. Presented at Hawaii International Social Science Conference, Waikiki, HI.

Reich, S. M., Subrahmanyam, K., and Espinoza, G. (2012). Friending, IMing, and hanging out face-to-face: Overlap in adolescents' online and offline social networks. *Developmental Psychology, 48*, 356–368. doi: 10.1037/a0026980.

Rich, C. L., Gidycz, C. A., Warkentin, J. B., Loh, C., and Weiland, P. (2005). Child and adolescent abuse and subsequent victimization: A prospective study. *Child Abuse and Neglect, 29*, 1373–1394. doi:10/1016/j.chiabu.2005.07.003.

RTI International. (2012). New study of 1,430 7th-grader students reports teen dating violence behaviors and risk factors occurring among middle school students. Retrieved May 30, 2014 from http://www.rwjf.org/vulnerablepopulations/product.jsp?id=74129.

Rusbult, C. E., Finkel, E. J., and Kumashiro, M. (2009). The Michelangelo phenomenon. *Current Directions in Psychological Science, 18,* 305–309. doi: 10.1111/j.1467-8721.2009.01657.x.

Saewyc, E. (2012). Research on adolescent sexual orientation: Development, health disparities, and resilience. *Journal of Research on Adolescence, 21,* 256–272. doi: 10.1111/j.1532-7795.2010.00727.x.

Santelli, J. S., Lindberg, L. D., Finer, L. B., and Singh, S. (2007). Explaining recent declines in adolescent pregnancy in the United States: The contribution of abstinence and improved contraceptive use. *American Journal of Public Health, 97,* 150–156. doi: 10.2105/AJPH.2006.089169.

Schiff, M., and Zeira, A. (2005). Dating violence and sexual risk behaviors in a sample of at-risk Israeli youth. *Child Abuse and Neglect, 29,* 1249–1263. doi: 10.1016/j.chiabu.2005.04.007.

Schnurr, M. P., and Lohman, B. J. (2008). How much does school matter? An examination of adolescent dating violence perpetration. *Journal of Youth and Adolescence, 37,* 266–283. doi: 10.1007/s10964-007-9246-7.

Silverman, J. G., Raj, A., Mucci, L. A., and Hathaway, J. E. (2001). Dating violence against adolescent girls and associated substance use, unhealthy weight control, sexual risk behavior, pregnancy, and suicidality. *JAMA: Journal of the American Medical Association, 286*(5), 572–579. doi: 10.1001/jama.286.5.572.

Simons, L. G., Burt, C. H., and Simons, R. L. (2008). A test of explanations for the effect of harsh parenting on the perpetration of dating violence and sexual coercion among college males. *Violence and Victims, 23,* 66–82. doi: 10.1891/0886-6708.23.1.66.

Simons, R. L., Lin, K., and Gordon, L. (1998). Socialization in the family of origin and male dating violence: A prospective study. *Journal of Marriage and the Family, 60,* 467–478.

Small, S., and Kerns, D. (1993). Unwanted sexual activity among peers during early and middle adolescence: Incidence and risk factors. *Journal of Marriage and the Family, 55,* 941–952.

Stattin, H., and Kerr, M. (2000). Parental monitoring: A reinterpretation. *Child Development, 71,* 1072–1085.

Straus, M. A., Hamby, S. L., Boney-McCoy, S., and Sugarman, D. S. (1996). The revised conflict tactics scales (CTS2): Developmental and preliminary psychometric data. *Journal of Family Issues, 17*(3), 283–316. doi: 10.1177/019251396017003001.

Subrahmanyam, K., and Greenfield, P. (2008). Online communication in adolescent relationships. *Future of Children,* 18, 119–146. Retrieved May 30, 2014 from http://www.http://futureofchildren.org/publications/journals/article/index.xml?journalid=32&articleid=59.

Tolman, D., and McClelland, S. (2011). Normative sexuality development among adolescents: A decade in review, 2000–2009. *Journal of Research on Adolescence, 21,* 242–255. doi: 10.1111/j.1532-7795.2010.00726.x.

Van den Heuvel, A., van den Eijnden, R. J. J. M., van Rooij, A. J., and van de Mheen, D. (2012). Meeting online contacts in real life among adolescents: The predictive role of psychosocial wellbeing and internet-specific parenting. *Computers in Human Behavior, 28,* 465–472. doi:10.1016/j.chb.2011.10.018.

Welsh, D., Grello, C., and Harper, M. (2003). When love hurts: Depression and adolescent romantic relationships. In P. Florsheim (ed.), *Adolescent romantic relations and sexual behavior: Theory, research, and practical implications* (pp. 185–211). Mahwah, NJ: Lawrence Erlbaum Associates.

Widom, C. S. (1989). Does violence beget violence? A critical examination of the literature. *Psychological Bulletin, 106,* 3–28. doi: 10.1037/0033-2909.106.1.3.

Williams, A. L., and Merten, M. J. (2011). iFamily: Internet and social media technology in the family context. *Family and Consumer Sciences Research Journal, 40,* 150–170. doi: 10.1111/j.1552-3934.2011.02101.x.

Williams, T. S., Connolly, J., Pepler, D., Craig, W., and Laporte, L. (2008). Risk models of dating aggression across different adolescent relationships: A developmental psychopathology approach. *Journal of Consulting and Clinical Psychology, 76,* 622–632. doi: 10.1037/0022-006X.76.4.622.

Yang, M., Yang, C., and Chiou, W. (2010). Differences in engaging in sexual disclosure between real life and cyberspace among adolescents: Social penetration model revisited. *Current Psychology, 29,* 144–154. doi: 10.1007/s12144-010-9078-6.

Young, B. J., and Furman, W. (2008). Interpersonal factors in the risk for sexual victimization and its recurrence during adolescence. *Journal of Youth and Adolescence, 37,* 297–309. doi: 10.1007/s10964-007-9240-0.

Zimmer-Gembeck, M., and Helfand, M. (2008). Ten years of longitudinal research on U.S. adolescent sexual behavior: Developmental correlates of sexual intercourse, and the importance of age, gender and ethnic background. *Developmental Review, 28,* 153–224. doi:10.1016/j.dr.2007.06.001.

Part IV

Policy and Practice Responses to Family Problems

17

Strengthening Family Resilience
A Community Capacity Approach

Anne F. Farrell, Gary L. Bowen,
and Samantha A. Goodrich

Communities are defined not only by place and geographical surroundings, but by social connections. Strong and vital communities can enable a sense of belonging and provide a protective "web" of support that influences how families respond to challenge. In Chapter 17, Farrell, Bowen, and Goodrich use a "road of life" metaphor to illustrate the importance of healthy relationships as a source of family resilience through life's journey. The authors advance a community-capacity approach to respond to family problems, which capitalizes on family strengths and mobilizes informal and formal community assets.

Introduction: The Road of Life

Life is a road, and the journey down that road can be long. It has twists and turns, arduous climbs, and hills to coast down. It is smooth and bumpy, meandering and straight. There are sharp curves and potholes; inviting vistas appear and recede. Sight distance can be limited. On the road, it is possible to anticipate some of what is ahead and to look back at what has passed, all the while paying attention to the surroundings.

Writers from philosopher-poet Robert Frost to the band Green Day have described life as a road, an apt metaphor because it represents essential aspects of the human condition. In the social sciences field, Bowen and Martin (2011) use the "road of life" metaphor to describe the experiences of military families and to explain how they adapt, cope, and thrive in the face of the ongoing and acute stress associated with multiple moves, deployment, family separation, combat, and reentry. As these authors explain it, individuals and families of all types set out on the journey of life in a given *context* (a place and time) equipped with personal *assets*, both innate and acquired through experience. They experience *normative life events* (schooling, graduations, friendships, and so on) and *non-normative life events* (illness, extraordinary accomplishment, trauma) along the way.

Moreover, the journey is influenced by events in the *individual's* life (e.g., friendships, breakups), *family* events (e.g., marriage, births), and *historical* context (e.g., economy, war, and political changes). These three contexts create variations in the condition of the road such that no two people follow exactly the

Family Problems: Stress, Risk, and Resilience, First Edition. Edited by Joyce A. Arditti.
© 2015 John Wiley & Sons, Inc. Published 2015 by John Wiley & Sons, Inc.

same road in the same way. Success on the road of life then stems from the individual and collective skills and resources that family members bring to the journey that enable the family to cope with the risks, liabilities, and dangers that the road of life poses. In addition, individuals and families often have the support of others as they attempt to navigate the road of life. In other words, informal and formal supports are the guardrails that guide families, keep them on course, and help them return to safe travels. A fundamental concern of this chapter is how formal and informal supports can help shift the balance of family risks and assets, enabling families to take care of themselves and contribute to the well-being of the community.

Overall, some families seem quite able to stay on course and "bounce back" quickly following setbacks, while others struggle. Those that flourish throughout the journey are said to demonstrate *resilience* in spite of the challenges they face. An additional question is how communities cultivate family resilience in a way that members of the community might benefit. In this chapter, we pose and address questions about the road of life as experienced by families:

- In the face of adversity, what keeps families on the road? What types of assets, prevention strategies, and interventions might be effective in supporting families?
- Can families benefit from facing challenge and adversity? In other words, can the experience of surmounting challenge leave families and communities better prepared to handle the next stressor that comes along?
- Once off the road, what distinguishes those families who return? What distinguishes those families who can use available resources to assist them in recovery versus those who do not? Do these families use formal and informal supports in different ways?
- How do we build family resilience? Can we purposefully construct what occurs naturally in many families and communities to bring people back to the road?
- What is community capacity? How can we support communities to develop the capacity to sustain families and to support a diverse range of families in building that capacity?

Through explanation and example, we define family resilience (and distinguish it from individual resilience), discuss and distinguish formal and informal support at the individual and community levels, and introduce the concept of community capacity. We touch upon theory that explains how families develop skills that help them to "rally" in times of strife. Finally, we outline ways that community capacity is constructed, maintained, and sustained, including forms of prevention and intervention. These concepts are illustrated through families in three contexts: families in the child welfare system, families of children with disabilities, and military families (see Box 17.1).

Resilience

Individual resilience

Individuals face a range of stressors, adverse conditions, and risk factors, which may be acute, chronic, or compounded by the presence of multiple negative influences. Consider a child who is born into a single-parent family living in poverty. The family lives in substandard housing (overcrowding, vermin, etc.) in a crime-ridden neighborhood (little access to safe outdoor recreation). Supporting the family requires the equivalent of three full-time, low-wage jobs, resulting in persistent, high parental stress and significant time spent out of the home working. The community's schools are struggling. The quality of education and child care is poor. Whereas the odds are stacked against a child born and raised in this environment, one can imagine that she can succeed and thrive, graduate from college, attend graduate school, and start her own family with hope and confidence.

How is this success possible? We can view this child's success through the lens of individual resilience. When faced with adversity, some individuals cope, thriving in spite of the adversity. In other words, they are resilient. In the 1980s, the terms *invulnerability* and *invincibility* were attempts to explain children who experienced normal outcomes in spite of risk, including family problems, problematic parenting, school transitions, negative peer influence, poverty, high geographic mobility, and community disorganization. Although the terms invulnerability and invincibility

---

Box 17.1   Family–Community Examples

To promote a working understanding and application of family resilience, we depict these concepts through the lens of three specific and relatable contexts.

Families in the Child Welfare System

Most reports to child welfare authorities stem from child neglect. Within the child welfare population, there is a subset of families who are in the system (e.g., have children in foster care, are being monitored by child protective services) primarily because they are unable to provide consistent, stable housing for their family and meet the basic needs of their children. This issue is in large part a consequence of poverty, yet it also reflects a complex array of challenges and problems. Family resilience can be built through combined approaches to interventions that address both the child welfare needs and environmental needs of the family.

Families of Children with Disabilities

The birth or diagnosis of a child with a disability can derail a family and shake their sense of collective competence. In spite of this, the vast majority of families who have children with disabilities demonstrate resilience that can be observed over time and in response to developmental change. Intervention programs incorporate concepts such as family-centeredness and strength orientation, which tend to be rare in other systems, but offer unique opportunities to acknowledge and build family resilience.

Military Families

The exigencies of military life include frequent geographic moves, the deployment of service members, and the realities of combat. These place extraordinary demands on the families of service members. At the same time, military installation communities are tight-knit and organized around a particular way of life. This offers a unique opportunity to build capacity within the community, helping families thrive in spite of their challenging circumstances.

---

were not ultimately seen as helpful ones to describe children's actual characteristics and experiences (i.e., no child is invulnerable or invincible), researchers identified a number of traits that seemed to "buffer" children against risk: personal disposition, intelligence, communication skills, parental warmth, and community members and supports that endorsed positive values and norms (Masten, 2001; Masten, Best, and Garmezy, 1990; Walsh, 1996).

Resilience is the capacity for successful adaptation, positive functioning, or competence, despite risk, stress, or trauma (Egeland, Carlson, and Sroufe, 1993; Masten et al., 1990). In our example, the resilient child would emerge from her stressful family and community environment with skills that support her success in high school and transition to college, where she develops a supportive social network, achieves, and successfully applies to graduate school. In Ellis and Boyce's (2008) terms, she adapts in a way that is similar to a *daffodil*,

flourishing and thriving regardless of the natural environment. Viewed from the lens of individual resilience, she succeeds (with some help) because of a unique set of personal assets. Alternatively, an *orchid* child is one who is much more sensitive to context, and more easily affected by both nurturing and deleterious experiences. This child's success is more strongly tied to the nurturing capacity of the environment. A child of this nature may flourish in the environment described above if she has a coach, teacher, or mentor along the way who sees her potential, encourages her, and nurtures her resilient leanings.

Originally conceived as quite rare, resilience is now thought to be a common process, "ordinary magic" that emerges from youth's remarkable capacity for adaptation (Masten, 2001, p. 227). Beyond the idea of having good outcomes in spite of threat, more recent conceptualizations incorporate an element of growth. After veering off course temporarily, a resilient individual copes with the adversity, adapting where necessary and resuming a healthy path, often *with greater resources than before* (Boss, 2006; Hawley and DeHaan, 1996; Norris, Stevens, Pfefferbaum, Wyche, and Pfefferbaum, 2008). Hence, resilience does not refer simply to the absence of stress or adversity; it focuses on individual assets that prevent and protect from the effects of adversity, leaving greater capability (Bowen, Martin, and Mancini, 2013).

Family resilience

Resilience can be examined at multiple levels or units of analysis (Bowen *et al.*, 2013; Bowen and Martin, 2011; Walsh, 2013). According to Bronfenbrenner's (1979, 1986) ecological model, individuals exist (are "nested") within their families, which are nested within the community. These levels have reciprocal influence, such that communities affect the way individuals and families function, and vice versa. Because individuals are profoundly affected by the contexts in which they grow, it is logical to consider resilience as emerging from an interaction of the person and their life contexts, rather than simply viewing it as a sum of individual traits. From this point forward, we focus on family resilience as an important lever for positive coping within the context of the community.

Family resilience is more than the sum of the separate capacities of its members. Stressful life challenges impact the entire family, which responds and adapts as a unit, not as a simple collection of persons (i.e., the family response is more than the sum of the individual responses; Walsh, 2013). Family resilience is the dynamic process that fosters positive adaptation, which is in turn productive for family well-being in the context of stress or crisis (Hawley and DeHaan, 1996; Walsh, 1996). A variety of paths to family resilience exist, as each family has its own unique interaction of risk and protective factors, and no single coping response or set of responses is effective in all situations (Walsh, 2013). Family resilience is more than just managing stress; it includes the opportunity for personal and relational growth as a result of struggle (Walsh, 2013).

Family resilience rests on a balance of *risk factors* that may pose barriers to effective functioning (poverty, war, illness, divorce, job loss, etc.) and *protective*

factors or *assets* that enable families to resist disruption (Hawley, 2000; H. McCubbin and McCubbin, 1988). Risks and assets are dynamic and changing, such that an asset in one situation may be a liability in another. For example, a very tight-knit and highly cohesive family may function very well under typical circumstances. Since this family pattern affords a great deal of support, cohesion may be highly adaptive for a family around the time they face a challenge, such as the birth of a child with a significant disability. Over time, however, the family will need to loosen its structure and open itself to external influences if it is to receive information, help, and support that is instrumental to the child's development. Without opening themselves up to external supports, the family may develop a rigid structure that leaves its members isolated in a time of need, potentially causing or compounding problems.

The influence of time

Returning to Bowen and Martin's (2011) "road of life" metaphor, consider the influence of time. Understanding how a family prepares for and manages adversity requires a longitudinal perspective (Bowen *et al.*, 2013; Walsh, 2013). Four relevant dimensions of time include (1) family experiences and characteristics during the "baseline" period before adversity; (2) the characteristics and length of adversity; (3) the timing or life stage during which adversity occurs; and (4) the evolving internal and external sources of support that the family uses in the context of adversities across the lifespan (Bowen *et al.*, 2013; Simon, Murphy, and Smith, 2005).

First, the family's reaction is influenced by its values, past experiences, and general functioning, including cohesion, flexibility, and communication (Luthar, Cicchetti, and Becker, 2003). Olson (2000) states that healthy families have a balanced sense of togetherness and individuality, are sufficiently flexible to accommodate change, and have clear, open, and consistent communication. During crisis, they alter their patterns of functioning and then return to less extreme patterns once crisis passes. These individual family characteristics interact with the influences of time to shape family resilience.

Second, responses to adversity of short duration may be very different from those to a more long term, or chronic, set of adverse conditions. The pattern and severity of the stressor also matters. Families adapt more readily to normative transitions (such as the birth of a child, minor illness, or launching a teenager into work or college) than they do to crises such as major illness, divorce, death, or the military deployment of a family member. More substantial stressors or crises place greater demands on individual family members and on the family as a whole. The diagnosis of developmental disability in a young child, for example, may involve both a short-term stressor (adjusting to an altered perspective) and a long-term set of conditions to manage (Hemmeter et al., 2005). So, the family of a young child with autism first adjusts to the idea or meaning of that disability (Will my child be able to live independently as an adult? Who will ensure that my child is well cared for when I am gone? What is the experience of siblings?). Over time, the child diagnosed with autism may demonstrate repetitive self-stimulatory behaviors or self-injurious behavior (e.g., hand-biting) to which the family needs to create adaptive responses. A balanced family can adapt by relying on community supports, both formal and informal.

Third, the life stage or developmental timing of an event for individuals within the family influences the type of crisis a family faces as well as how it responds (Olson, 2000; Walsh, 1996). For example, families with small children are apt to experience vocational, economic, and gender-role strain at first, which may be viewed as normative. For families whose young children present higher care-management pressure due to a developmental disability, the normative stresses of early parenting are layered with this additional dimension, which may require additional adjustments in the long term. In other words, the impact of events and the capacity to be resilient are dependent on the type and the timing of disturbance within family and individual life journeys (McCubbin, Futrell, Thompson, and Thompson, 1998). If we are to understand resilience as a process of coping with and adapting to stress, it is necessary to observe family patterns before, during, and after the event, and over time. The assets that a family brings to crisis influence how they manage; in fact, the notion of assets (discussed below) is critical to our understanding of family coping.

Fourth, families tap various internal and external supports when facing adversity. Variations in the form and accessibility of resources are a by-product of changes in the physical and social environment and the characteristics of the family unit and its members (Bowen et al., 2013; Simon et al., 2005). In other words, families may resort to external supports (outside the family) at different points in time, owing to the family's appraisal of their own capacity to manage a particular challenge; depending on whether they experience social stigma related to either their problems or about help-seeking; because an apt, acceptable, and convenient resource presents itself; or due to the family's prior experiences with particular forms of support. For example, consider a family that has never sought support from a mental health professional (formal) that might also generally seek informal support from extended family. That family might not feel the need to consult mental health professionals or support groups when their newborn child is diagnosed with a disability. Yet, the family has positive experiences with the hospital social worker and with a parent of a child with a disability who offers parent-to-parent information and support. Consequently, the family is open to additional *formal* supports in the future when they face adversity. Research suggests that families who are open to the social support offered by schools, care providers, religious organizations, and communities tend to be more resilient (Dunst and Trivette, 2009; Perry, 2004). Consistent with the Circumplex Model, adaptive responses include "flexing" to consider external supports during difficulty. This flexibility varies over the life course, depending on the challenge, the context, and the family's own sense of its ability to surmount the challenge.

Assets

Let's return to the girl growing up in an impoverished neighborhood. In spite of her family's minimal resources, and the frequent absence of her mother due to long work hours, the family is cohesive and flexible. Her mother is warm, dedicated, communicative, affectionate, and has high standards for school performance. She stays apprised of her daughter's school activities, monitors her social network, supports her decision-making, ensures good dietary and sleep habits, and is resourceful, availing her family of free and low-cost cultural opportunities such as the library and museum. The family faces a chronic set of stressors with ample personal assets and community resources. The road of life is challenging, but the family is navigating it safely owing in part to their assets. The term *asset* refers to internal strengths, resources, and skills (within the family) and the opportunities and supports available in the environment (Bowen and Martin, 2011).

Assets can play three distinct roles in determining the relationship between risk and outcome (Bowen *et al.*, 2013). First, an asset may serve a preventive function, reducing the occurrence or intensity of adversity, for example, when a parent's social ties avail them of specific help for combating the presenting situation. Second, an asset may increase the likelihood of positive outcomes, thus promoting them, as when a family "rallies" to meet the challenges posed by a particular stressor. Third, an asset can protect a family by buffering the negative influence of adversity. A single asset or set of assets may engage all three of these functions, thereby helping to *prevent* adversity, *promote* good outcomes, and *protect* the family.

Return to our example of the family living in poverty. Should the family face a new crisis, those assets may be sufficient or they may be inadequate to the presenting situation. What if the family loses access to an afterschool program they had relied on? Perhaps there is a neighbor or relative to whom the family has shown kindness and that person offers to provide child care temporarily. This reciprocity is evidence of *social capital* (i.e., resources through relationship connections) that is present in some social networks and protective of families. In this eventuality, additional crisis is averted. Another, less desirable outcome is possible: with no alternative, the girl stays home alone after school and is left vulnerable to threats made by older youth in the neighborhood. Eventually the police become involved, it becomes clear that she is unsupervised, and child welfare authorities are notified. Her mother responds to this threat with great distress, relapses into substance use that she had refrained from for years, becomes irate with her caseworker, loses her job because she fails to report, and ultimately loses her child to foster care. In this eventuality, the family's lack of access to community resources hampers their ability to cope and results in very undesirable outcomes. This example makes clear how individual and family coping occur in a communal context. As Lyons, Mickelson, Sullivan, and Coyne (1998) put it, "solo performances are rare, and each event draws a cast of characters who confront the issue individually and together" (p. 580).

How do today's families experience assets? In the most recent edition of the Search Institute's American Family Assets study (Syvertsen, Roehlkepartain, and Scales, 2012), a national youth and family survey, the least common asset was close relations with others in community. The number of family assets did not differ by parent education, income, single- vs. two-parent homes, immigration status, sexual orientation of parents, or gender. This suggests that there are ample assets within the incredibly diverse range of families and family structures present in our culture. Overall, families that lacked transportation, health insurance, adequate meals, and stable housing had fewer assets all together. Black and Latino families had more assets than all other ethnic groups. Urban families had more assets than rural. These results might not be altogether surprising; however, they present communities with interesting challenges. How can we construct a network of support for vulnerable families? Should we do so? Will an imposed or artificial network be less effective than small, informal networks? Research in the field of disabilities suggests that small, informal social supports are most effective for families. Beyond a certain "threshold," more support is not better (Perry, 2004). In other words, social isolation is detrimental, but sometimes less is more.

Strengths orientation
In the last decade or two, the field of family studies underwent a paradigm shift from traditional clinical approaches that were remedial in focus to models that acknowledge and capitalize on strengths over deficits, commonly called a wellness or strength-based orientation (Hemmeter *et al.*, 2005). What does this actually mean in terms of work with families? We use resilience as the example of a strength-based approach that is used widely today and contrast that with older deficit-based orientations in order to bring these terms into context.

The concept of resilience is optimistic and strength-oriented, emphasizing positive capacity in a *salutogenic* orientation (Hawley, 2000; Hawley and DeHaan,

1996). Family-centered models of care and support are responsive to the family's self-identified needs over those of professionals (Bailey, Nelson, Hebbeler, and Spiker, 2007). This is in opposition to deficit-oriented approaches to working with families. Historically, research and common perceptions have focused on the negative and stressful experiences of family members (Perry, 2004). From a remedial or deficit orientation, families who are experiencing hardship or difficulty are viewed as impaired and therefore incapable of helping themselves or bouncing back without formal professional support. Deficit orientations *pathologize* a family, label them as broken, focus predominantly on weaknesses and negative experiences, and entertain a problem-focused view that minimizes future hopes.

To contextualize the difference between deficit- and strength-oriented approaches, return to our earlier example of a child living in a single-parent home. The child welfare system provides family-based living environments (foster care) for children when parents are unable to provide a nurturing, healthy home. Within the child welfare system, some caseworkers may believe that a subset of parents are incapable of improving their skills, becoming more stable, and learning to better meet the needs of their children. Those families are deemed helpless and damaged. In our example, the family lives far from extended family members, the mother works long hours, the afterschool program is defunded, and other child care is exorbitantly priced. Child welfare authorities are called and a finding of neglect is made. By focusing on parent lapses, the caseworker misses the fact that the parent is exhausted from working hard to provide for her family and is still not able to make ends meet. The mother becomes enraged at the prospect of losing her child to the foster care system, and screams at the caseworker, who then deems her to be out of control. The parent is not empowered to focus on her own or the community's assets to improve her family's situations.

Alternatively, a resilience- or strength-based case management approach views the adversity as temporary and contextual and not an inherent flaw of the family (Leitz, 2011). This perspective highlights assets and successes and recognizes the potential to use assets toward a brighter future. In the child welfare system, family preservation and reunification programs connect birth parents with supports to harness strengths and "get back on the road." Following our example, the caseworker may step back to understand the circumstances and find that the mother is in fact dedicated, loving, and attentive to the best of her ability. She is a competent parent facing acute financial and environmental stressors. Rather than remove the child from the home, the caseworker refers the parent to a family preservation and supportive housing program that provides an opportunity to improve her life circumstances, ensure a healthy home for her daughter, and keep her family together. The referral to a supportive housing program results in an assets-focused approach to case management, referral to community resources (substance abuse treatment, counseling), and assistance in applying for a permanent federal rental subsidy in a preferred neighborhood to reduce financial burden (Farrell, Britner, Guzzardo, and Goodrich, 2010).

Formal and informal supports

Research across an array of contexts informs us that formal and informal supports enhance adaptation and that successfully meeting a challenge leaves families more confident and capable. Formal and informal supports are distinct yet interdependent resources that can contribute to resilience. *Formal supports* are intentionally constructed networks, systems, and help-giving sources, often comprising professional or expert providers such as human service agencies and health providers; these providers might include education, health, and mental health professionals (teachers, physicians, counselors, social workers), child welfare caseworkers, afterschool/out-of-school staff (camp counselors, recreation therapists, tutors), visiting nurses, and mentors (Bowen, Richman, and Bowen, 2000).

Informal supports are less organized or structured, including group associations and networks of personal and social relationships maintained voluntarily, such as spouse or partner, extended family, co-workers, neighbors, and friends (Bowen, Martin, Mancini, and Nelson, 2000). These informal supports include both primary or "core" relationships, such as close friends, as well as secondary or "peripheral" ties, such as acquaintances (Fingerman, 2009, p. 70). Researchers define the functions of informal networks as emotional, instrumental (e.g., access to financial resources, equipment), companionate, informational (e.g., about a child's disability, services, and community resources), and validation (Gottlieb, 2000; McWilliam, 2005). Informal supports are commonplace within our social networks; most individuals and families rely primarily on pre-existing, natural social relationships (family, friends, neighbors, co-workers) and turn to formal supports only when those resources are inadequate. Informal supports are readily accessed and have no financial cost. An individual who delivers a prepared dinner to a neighbor following a death in the family is providing informal support. That act of support also builds the relationship, making it more likely that the neighbors will support each other in the future. In this way, acts of informal support build social reciprocity and enhance relationships.

An important function of formal supports is to strengthen informal community connections (Huebner, Mancini, Bowen, and Orthner, 2009). Further, it is important that formal supports do not supplant informal ones, as it is undesirable and costly, for formal systems take over tasks that natural, informal networks could easily address. Yet, formal supports have their role and can provide assistance to families with small or limited informal networks of support to help them to build a larger informal network. Identifying assets and coping resources is a critical aspect of formal early intervention programs for young children with disabilities. These programs use formal supports and interventions as means of building the family's capacity to advocate, such that they gradually assume roles and functions that were initially the work of a paid service coordinator. Beyond improving a child's functional skills, effective early intervention programs employ formal supports as a means of building informal family supports, laying the groundwork for family resiliency (Dunst and Trivette, 2009).

Community Capacity

The ways in which formal and informal supports operate in a community can be conceptualized at two levels. First, as discussed above, social scientists examine individual families in the context of the formal and informal supports that serve as guardrails on the road of life. The study of adaptation and resilience from the individual family perspective (e.g., evaluating the relative strength and weakness of their support systems) is a micro-level approach (Mancini and Bowen, 2013). Although the grouping or clustering of families within communities or other geographic areas is neglected in this approach, most community studies that examine outcomes such as family resilience adopt the micro-level perspective (Wiens and Boss, 2006).

Second, the operation of formal and informal supports can be conceptualized across families who live in a certain geographic area, such as a neighborhood, zip code, census tract, military installation, political district, or larger geographic unit (city, town). To what extent are families within an area nested in formal and informal support systems? Think about the neighborhood or community you lived in as a child. Did neighbors know one another, and did members of the community come together for events and celebrations? Perhaps your neighborhood had a Community Watch program, which was initiated through a neighborhood group (informal) and local law-enforcement officials (formal). We know that families are advantaged when they live in communities where formal and informal supports are dense and strong. In these communities, families are more likely to demonstrate resilient patterns in the context of challenge and adversity, including improved health and overall well-being (Mancini, Arnold, Martin, and Bowen, 2014). Mancini and Bowen (2013) label this macro-level perspective a *contextual effects* approach – formal and informal supports at the community level influence families beyond their own particular links to support systems. That is, formal and informal family and community assets form an interactive and protective "web" of support that influences how families respond to challenge.

Social organization theory of action and change

Mancini and Bowen (2013) developed a social organization theory of action and change to account for the operation of formal systems and informal networks at this macro-level. Unlike numerous theories constructed to understand how communities disintegrate, this work is grounded in a strengths-oriented view, focuses in particular on informal networks, and guides an understanding of how communities build and sustain assets. The concept of social organization is foundational to the theory and describes "how people in a community interrelate, cooperate, and provide mutual support; it includes social support norms, social controls that regulate behavior and interaction patterns, and networks that operate in a community" (Mancini and Bowen, 2013, p. 781).

Community is defined as any geographic unit of aggregation from small (e.g., a family's apartment building) to large (the county where the apartment building is located). Although families have connections with others that are not tied to a geographic location (e.g., social networking media), Mancini and Bowen (2013) focus on the nature and pattern of loose ties, close alliances, and formal supports within these locally anchored geographic communities – the places where families live and work. Importantly, geographic communities are nested within one another (e.g., neighborhoods comprise sections of towns with mutual influence on each other). Communities are thus defined not only by place – human-made surroundings (buildings, parks, etc.) and geographic boundaries (neighborhoods, towns, and

counties, etc.) – but also by social connections. They host individuals, enable a sense of belonging, and include social patterns from culture and language to helping behaviors.

Bowen, Martin, and colleagues (2000, p. 7) define *community capacity* as:

> the extent to which community members (a) demonstrate a sense of shared responsibility for the general welfare of the community and its members, and (b) demonstrate collective competence in taking advantage of opportunities for addressing community needs and confronting situations that threaten the safety and well-being of community members.

Community capacity is a central social organizational process that results from the particular configuration and operation of formal and informal networks in a given community. Bowen, Martin, and colleagues (2000) use the verb *demonstrate* intentionally: community capacity is anchored in *action* that produces positive results for community members and their families, including family resilience. Figure 17.1 depicts how social networks, including the intersections between formal and informal networks (network effect levels),

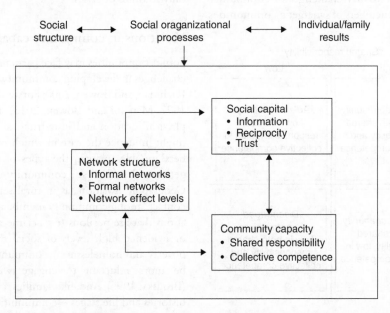

Figure 17.1 Social organizational processes, social structure, and individual/family results. Reprinted with permission from Mancini, Bowen, and Martin (2005). © 2005, John Wiley and Sons.

and social capital (i.e., information exchange, reciprocity, and trust) interact to influence community capacity. Note that community capacity itself influences the presence of social capital and the nature of the social support networks. In this way, community capacity can be self-sustaining.

Four types of communities

Mancini and Bowen (2009) divide each of the two dimensions of community capacity into low and high levels and then cross the dimensions to propose four types of communities: synergetic (high shared responsibility, high collective competence); relational (high shared responsibility, low collective competence); able (low shared responsibility, high collective competence); and disengaged communities (low shared responsibility, low collective competence). See Figure 17.2, which illustrates this *typology*. Viewed in this way, positive family functioning and outcomes, including resilience, are more likely in synergetic communities, in which members exhibit common identity and pride, see the community as worthy of their investments in time and energy, and assume responsibility for handling the more common and day-to-day challenges of community living. Moreover, members of synergetic communities

pull together in times of crisis and challenge to make things happen whether the presenting concern involves one family (e.g., a missing or ill child) or multiple families (neighborhood cleanup in the aftermath of a hurricane).

Thus, in synergetic communities, community capacity is anchored in action that produces positive results for member families. Shared responsibility is a necessary and prerequisite condition for demonstrating collective competence. As the *motivational dimension* in the community capacity model, shared responsibility derives from the accumulated and shared experiences of community members, rather than from conformity to external authority. In other words, highly adaptive communities unite spontaneously in crisis rather than waiting for formal agencies such as law enforcement, public health, or disaster management to direct their activities. Applying this typology, the number of able communities is likely to be very low (Mancini and Bowen, 2009). Without external pressure, community members are unlikely to demonstrate collective competence unless they share a sense of responsibility for the community and its members. Communities with high degrees of capacity make use of every opportunity for improvement rather than be active only in times of crises.

Variations in community capacity

Some communities may face particular difficulties and challenges in developing community capacity (Bowen, Richman, and Bowen, 2000; Furstenberg and Hughes, 1997; Mancini and Bowen, 2013). For example, the physical location and infrastructure of a community might influence the ease in which community members are able to form the types of relationships that generate the "fuel" for community capacity building. Geographic isolation (as in rural settings) may make contact among community members difficult. In situations that are perilous (e.g., crime and delinquency) or evidence high levels of social disadvantage (e.g., poverty and homelessness), community members may be more reluctant to engage with one another (Brodsky, 1996). And, like families, communities have histories and life stages – communities that have been through significant adversity and difficulty may find it difficult to initiate community-building efforts

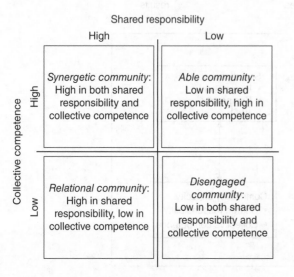

Figure 17.2 A typology of community capacity (adapted from Mancini and Bowen, 2009, p. 255). © Lexington Books.

in the face of new challenges and adversities (The Harwood Group, 1999).

As instruments of socialization, social control, and social support, the operation of formal supports (e.g., police, human service agencies), including those both inside and outside of community boundaries, may also frame and inform patterns of social interaction. Community members may struggle to generate community capacity and to deal with adversities and challenges when institutional resources are weak; when these resources are strong they have the potential to provide direct support as well as leveraging informal community capacity building.

Community capacity across the family life cycle

Families may need to "tap" community capacity in varying amounts across the life cycle (Bowen *et al.*, 2000). For example, a neighborhood with high community capacity (synergetic) may be a particularly important asset for parents with children in the early and middle adolescent years – a developmental period when children spend less time at home and more time in the community. Importantly, families both potentially benefit from living in a community with high capacity, and they have influence over the level of capacity in the community, which is consistent with a strengths orientation. The level of fit between the needs and abilities of the family and the resources of the community influence the success of families in making transitions, in fulfilling the individual and collective needs of family members, and in responding to internal and external demands (Bowen *et al.*, 2000).

How might we envision community capacity operating across a family's life cycle? Let's turn to an example of service members with families. Many of these families have endured major challenges associated with wartime deployments and related stressors since September 11, 2001 (Bowen *et al.*, 2013; MacDermid Wadsworth, 2010). Some children have faced significant hardships, including feelings of ambiguous loss, psychological health problems, and lower academic achievement, as their service member parent has faced repeated and often lengthy deployments in support of the war effort (Engel, Gallagher, and Lyle, 2008; Huebner *et al.*, 2009). The strength of

community supports (both formal and informal) may be especially important to military families at this point in the family life cycle, especially for dual military parents (both spouses in the military) and for nonmilitary spouses who must shoulder increased parental responsibilities when their spouses are deployed.

Take the example of a young man, age 12, whose Marine Corps father is deployed for the third time and whose mother is home keeping the family together in her husband's absence at a base in San Diego, CA. This family is fortunate enough to live in an area where the local schools serve as a major support system for military families and their school-age children by developing school cultures that are military-friendly and by reaching out to provide direct support to nonmilitary parents and caretakers. In particular, the Building Capacity project in the San Diego area works to increase collaborative partnerships between formal and informal networks in support of promoting "military-connected schools" for students and their families.[1] The boy and his family from our example become involved with the services that are in the community that promotes the family's resilience against the stress of the father's employment.

Policy and Practice Responses to Family Problems

We end our discussion of family resilience with illustrations of how policies can spur practices that help build community capacity in service of family resilience. Whereas policymaking at the federal and state level may seem distant and perhaps even irrelevant, these policies in fact determine the kinds of formal preventive programs and interventions that are developed, tested, funded, and available in the community. In this way, "macro" policies are developed and implemented nationally, in states, and in communities, with the hopes that they operate at the "micro" level (at the level of individual families). Although the nature and scope of these policies differ, they are in general oriented toward helping families avoid adversity (prevent), achieve positive outcomes (promote), and build capacity at the individual, family and community levels for meeting challenges (protect). From this perspective, policies and the practices that result from these policies are intended to operate as securing and sustaining assets in the lives of families.

Families in the child welfare system

For decades, US child welfare policy was mostly reactive: family problems (neglect, abuse) came to the attention of authorities when they were extreme, and the interventions that followed were intrusive. Thousands of children experienced extended stays in foster care as communities faced shortages in access to supportive services, and, steeped in deficit models of family, officials rarely deemed families "ready" for reunification. By the 1990s, Congress enacted laws with swifter timetables to child welfare decision-making and policies that resulted in better coordination of services and programs for these families, including child welfare, mental health, substance abuse, economic, nutritional, housing, and health supports. Historically, well-intentioned programs in these areas have operated out of separate "silos" that often challenged rather than supported the organizational capacities of families.

Increasingly, policymakers and researchers note the intertwined nature of housing and child welfare for a substantial portion of child welfare-involved families referred for neglect (Courtney, Terao, and Bost, 2004; Culhane, Webb, Grim, Metraux, and Culhane, 2003) and the need for service integration. Because housing problems (crowding, poor conditions) place families at risk for separation and decrease chances of reunification, a call to action implored federal agencies to address housing barriers as a fundamental component of child welfare interventions.

Newer service delivery models envision housing as a platform for addressing family needs: families are referred to intensive, strengths-based community programs where a single case manager coordinates services across categorical systems, enables family access to federal and state housing vouchers which defray the cost of housing, and supports families as they locate housing in desired neighborhoods once they establish initial stability (see Farrell et al., 2010, for a description). Family assets are enabled through case management efforts aimed at bolstering supports, and community capacity is cultivated through positive relations with landlords (ensure security deposits). Such an intervention would be ideal for the child welfare-involved family depicted in this chapter. The federal child welfare agency has undertaken a major initiative to further test the model (ACF, 2012), which also provides for trauma-informed interventions and evidence-based mental health services through community-based service providers, and evaluations that examine the process, outcomes, and costs of implementation. This example demonstrates how a community intervention that is tailored to local family and community characteristics can promote a more coordinated and supportive service delivery experience for families living at the margins.

Families of children with disabilities

Until the 1970s, children with disabilities lived in institutions and inclusion models were unheard of. The deinstitutionalization of children and the development of school- and community-based programs is the consequence of advocacy efforts by family members, court decisions that forced the desegregation of children, and shifts in federal policy (Turnbull, Stowe, Turnbull, and Schrandt, 2007). Federal policy that guides the form and quality of early intervention and special education programs for children with disabilities and their families rests most substantially in the Individuals with Disabilities Education Act (IDEA).[2] The IDEA acknowledges the fundamental notion that families are the most important persons in the lives of children and mandates strength-based services.

Dunst and Trivette (2009) note that effective services acknowledge family needs and aspirations, functioning styles, and supports and resources, all in keeping with their priorities. In the field of disabilities, the definition of intervention includes both formal and informal supports, which is a rare blending across the human service spectrum. Importantly, families' experiences of informal support relate to their optimism about the future and their confidence in parenting (Bailey et al., 2007). As a matter of policy, the formal disability service system (macro-level) capitalizes on informal family supports (micro-level) as a means of providing timely, accessible resources that build family capacity. Consistent with Huebner and colleagues' (2009) concern that the provision of formal supports should not supplant family and community resources, Dunst and Trivette (2009) point out that families perceive professional social support positively only when it is offered in response to an indicated need for help.

Two specific aspects of disability services warrant mention here because of the use of formal supports to cultivate sustainable informal supports and family assets. The first is parent-to-parent support programs, which match "veteran" parents with others whose children are newly diagnosed with disabilities (Singer et al., 1999). These programs produce significant change over interventions that include only professional support providers. The second, alluded to earlier, is an aspect of formal service coordination in early intervention. Historically, service providers are at an advantage over families by virtue of their formal knowledge and formal and informal connections in the service arena. IDEA mandates a paid service coordinator to collaborate with families to ensure that services are coherent and responsive. The collaboration helps parents build skills that will serve them through a lifetime of support, empowering them to advocate for appropriate services within and across a fragmented bureaucracy (Thompson et al., 1997).

Thompson and colleagues (1997) conclude that effective programming enables parent empowerment through two main avenues. First, family-centered practices lead to greater family involvement and empowerment. The second route is indirect: Family-centered practices relate to the amount of support families receive, most likely because the service coordinator assists families in connecting to natural supports (family, community). Those supports facilitate coping, which reduces family stress, which is negatively related to empowerment (when stress is high, empowerment is low, and vice versa).

Military families

In the military community, there has been growing recognition of the increased rate of stress-related problems among military families and a need to provide preventive community services that promote the long-term health and well-being of these families and bolster them against the hardships associated with military life, including multiple deployments, extended separations, and post-traumatic stress symptoms (Bowen et al., 2013). As a result, the US military began to seek out and support efforts to implement preventive services for military families and create policies that addressed the well-being of the family. At the macro-level of intervention, the Department of Defense has issued a new instruction (Number 1342.22) addressing military family readiness, which applies to all service branches, including the National Guard and Reserve (Department of Defense, 2012).

A key focus on this instruction is linking formal and informal networks in support of military service members and their families. The aim is to promote family strengths and increase family resilience. In particular, through its partnership with the United States Department of Agriculture, the Office of the Secretary of Defense for Military Community and Family Policy is sponsoring the development of an online community capacity building training and curriculum that aligns with this instruction. The University of Georgia and the University of North Carolina at Chapel Hill are developing an online training system based in the Social Organization Theory of Action and Change (Mancini and Bowen, 2013) and focused on instructing family service providers in both military and civilian communities in ways to build more collaborative and integrative systems of social care, including mobilization of informal networks (e.g., extended family, friends, neighbors, work associates, and so forth) in support of service members and families. Training modules include information on forming a community performance team; assessing a community and its needs; using results-focused planning; working with formal and informal networks, military leaders, and employers; monitoring progress; and making efforts more sustainable. This training effort is intended to promote the ability of service providers to create community capacity to support the families within their community. Having service providers work from a community capacity perspective will create an environment that facilitates shared responsibility and collective competence through all levels of the community, therefore promoting community capacity in the long term.

Conclusion: Navigating Life's Journey

We began this chapter by describing life as a journey, using a road of life metaphor to capture the experiences of families – a road replete with adversities and challenges, opportunities and resources. In some cases, adversities and challenges are anticipated, like deployment demands; in other cases, they are not, such as a birth of a child with a disability. Without doubt, the road of life for many families is difficult and precarious – the level of drag from the surface of the road and the number of obstacles on the road are significant. We used three types of families to illustrate unique demands on the road of life: families in the child welfare system, families of children with disabilities, and military families. We ended the chapter by discussing policy and practice responses to promote the resilience of these families. Between the "book ends," we introduced a number of concepts to examine variation in the ability of families to navigate the road of life, such as individual and family resilience, time, assets, formal and informal supports, community capacity, and the family life cycle. We adopted a strengths orientation, which is consistent with a focus on family resilience – what moves families toward health and well-being.

Although the popular press is filled with stories of families drawing upon their internal strengths to overcome incredible odds, these stories may be more the exception than the rule. No family is invincible or invulnerable in the face of life challenges and adversities, and relatively few families successfully manage high-risk conditions when they travel on the road of life alone. However, families do vary in their resilience – the ability to stay on the road (meet demands and address the needs of the family and its individual members) and return to the road over time when faced with significant challenges. Yet, by virtue of getting back on the road, all families have the potential to emerge from adversity with improved capacity to navigate the curves ahead.

Clearly, personal and family strengths play a role in the ability of families to demonstrate resilience; however, these strengths are not the whole story.

Formal and informal supports also play an important role, both at the level of individual families (micro approach) and across families within geographic locations (macro approach). These supports operate like guardrails and tow trucks on the road of life – they keep families on the road and help if they run off. The most effective formal supports promote informal supports, enable family and community members to support each other, and leave them better able to do so in the future, encouraging the development of synergetic communities. Our examples of policies and practices in support of families illustrate how formal and informal supports combine to keep families on the road. Families do not have to make life's journey alone.

In the context of our review, we conclude that family scholars and practitioners have given inadequate attention to viewing families in the context of the communities in which they live and work (see also, Mancini and Bowen, 2013). We assert that the operation of formal and informal supports in these communities offer viable leverage points to both understand variation in the resilience of these families and to assist them in more successfully negotiating adversities and challenges that they meet on the road of life. Scholars and practitioners are encouraged to give more nuanced attention to how these supports may operate differently within the context of race, ethnicity, class and culture, as well as over the life course.

Critical Thinking Questions

1. What are some strategies that formal systems, such as human service agencies and organizations, might use to engage informal networks in support of families? Imagine yourself in a position as a case manager supporting youth aging out of foster care, a service coordinator working with families who have young children with disabilities, a hospital social worker on a geriatric floor, a school social worker in an elementary school serving predominantly military families, or an outreach worker for homeless families. What strategies might your employing agency to use to enable the individuals you support to gain social

capital, become more self-sufficient, and experience positive outcomes? What efforts could you make to ensure that these individuals become more connected with community?

2. In what ways might informal supports for families (e.g., extended family, friends, neighbors, work associates) operate differently within the context of race, ethnicity, class and culture, as well as over the life course? Consider how various aspects of diversity interact with community assets and risks; individual, family and historical time; and policies and practices.

3. How might the traditional "social safety net"[3] reflect (or not) propositions for building and sustaining social capital? Family resilience? Community capacity? How might you revise it?

4. You have the opportunity to provide major funding for projects intended to support either:

- poor families who have a child with a disability in a urban community;
- military families facing multiple deployments; and
- parents who have substance abuse problems and child welfare involvement.

Discuss the elements you'd like to see in place among agencies who are applying for funding. As a fundamental, ensure that programs and supports are sustainable, that is, that they will persist in the absence of diminished external support. You also want to know that the individuals served in the project might also leave with new and sustainable assets. What can you do to help ensure these forms of sustainability?

Notes

1. See http://buildingcapacity.usc.edu/. The project is sponsored by the School of Social Work at the University of Southern California, and it is funded by a grant from the Department of Defense Education Activity (DoDEA).

2. Currently enacted as The Individuals with Disabilities Education Improvement Act of 2004, Public law 108-446.

3. Governmental supports such as Temporary Assistance to Needy Families, Medicaid, Social Security Disability, Women and Children's housing subsidies, free and reduced lunch, Special Supplemental Nutrition Program for Women, Infants, and Children (WIC); and supports provided by NGOs and community non-profits.

References

Administration for Children and Families (ACF). (2012). Partnerships to demonstrate the effectiveness of supportive housing for families in the child welfare system. Washington, DC: US Department of Health and Human Services, Administration for Children and Families.

Bailey, D. B., Nelson, L., Hebbeler, K., and Spiker, D. (2007). Modeling the impact of formal and informal supports for young children with disabilities and their families. *Pediatrics, 120*(4), e992–e1001.

Boss, P. (2006). *Loss, trauma, and resilience.* New York: W. W. Norton.

Bowen, G. L., and Martin, J. A. (2011). The resiliency model of role performance for service members, veterans, and their families: A focus on social connections and individual assets. *Journal of Human Behavior in the Social Environment, 21*, 162–178.

Bowen, G. L., Martin, J. A., and Mancini, J. A. (2013). The resilience of military families: Theoretical perspectives. In M. A. Fine and F. D. Fincham (eds), *Family theories: A content-based approach* (pp. 417–438). New York: Routledge.

Bowen, G. L., Martin, J. A., Mancini, J. A., and Nelson, J. P. (2000). Community capacity: Antecedents and consequences. *Journal of Community Practice, 8*, 1–21.

Bowen, G. L., Richman, J. M., and Bowen, N. K. (2000). Families in the context of communities across time. In S. J. Price, P. C. McKenry, and M. J. Murphy (eds), *Families across time: A life course perspective* (pp. 117–128). Los Angeles, CA: Roxbury Publishers.

Brodsky, A. E. (1996). Resilient single mothers in risky neighborhoods. *Journal of Community Psychology, 24*, 347–363.

Bronfenbrenner, U. (1979). *The ecology of human development: Experiments by nature and design.* Cambridge, MA: Harvard University Press.

Bronfenbrenner, U. (1986). Ecology of the family as a context for human development: Research perspectives. *Developmental Psychology, 22,* 723–742.

Courtney, M., Terao, S., and Bost, N. (2004). *Midwest evaluation of the adult functioning of former foster youth: Conditions of the youth preparing to leave state care.* Chicago: Chapin Hall at the University of Chicago.

Culhane, J., Webb, D., Grim, S., Metraux, S., and Culhane, D. (2003). Prevalence of child welfare services involvement among homeless and low-income mothers: A five-year birth cohort study. *Journal of Sociology and Social Welfare, 3,* 79–97.

Department of Defense. (2012). Instruction no. 1342.22: Military family readiness. Retrieved May 30, 2014 from http://www.dtic.mil/whs/directives/corres/pdf/134222p.pdf.

Dunst, C. J., and Trivette, C. M. (2009). Capacity-building family-systems intervention practices. *Journal of Family Social Work, 12*(2), 119–143.

Egeland, B., Carlson, E., and Sroufe, L. (1993). Resilience as process. *Development and Psychopathology, 5,* 517–528.

Ellis, B. J., and Boyce, W. T. (2008). Biological sensitivity to context. *Current Directions in Psychological Science, 17*(3), 183–187.

Engel, R. C., Gallagher, L. B., and Lyle, D. S. (2008). Military deployments and children's academic achievement: Evidence from Department of Defense education activity schools. *Economics of Education Review, 29*(1), 73–82.

Farrell, A. F., Britner, P. A., Guzzardo, M., and Goodrich, S. (2010). Supportive housing for families in child welfare: Client characteristics and their outcomes at discharge. *Child and Youth Services Review, 32,* 145–154.

Fingerman, K. L. (2009). Consequential strangers and peripheral ties: The importance of unimportant relationships. *Journal of Family Theory and Review, 1,* 69–86.

Furstenberg, F. F., Jr., and Hughes, M. E. (1997). The influence of neighborhoods on children's development: A theoretical perspective and a research agenda. In J. Brooks-Gunn, G. J. Duncan, and J. L. Aber (eds), *Neighborhood poverty,* vol. 2 (pp. 23–47). New York: Russell Sage Foundation.

Gottlieb, B. H. (2000). Self-help, mutual aid, and support groups among older adults. *Canadian Journal on Aging, 19,* 58–74.

Harwood Group. (1999). *Community rhythms: Five stages of community life.* Bethesda, MD: The Harwood Group and the Charles Stewart Mott Foundation.

Hawley, D. R. (2000). Clinical implications of family resilience. *American Journal of Family Therapy, 28*(2), 101–116.

Hawley, D. R., and DeHaan, L. (1996). Toward a definition of family resilience: Integrating life span and family perspectives. *Family Process, 35,* 283–298.

Hemmeter, M.L., Santos, R., Snyder, P., Hyson, M., Harris-Solomon, A., Bailey, D., … and Fewell, R. (2005). Young children with, or at risk for, developmental disabilities. In K.C. Lakin and A. Turnbull (eds), *National goals and research for people with intellectual and developmental disabilities* (pp. 15–37). Washington, DC: American Association on Mental Retardation.

Huebner, A. J., Mancini, J. A., Bowen, G. L., and Orthner, D. K. (2009). Shadowed by war: Building community capacity to support military families. *Family Relations, 58,* 216–228.

Leitz, C. A. (2011). Theoretical adherence to family centered practice: Are strengths-based principles illustrated in families' descriptions of child welfare services? *Children and Youth Services Review, 33,* 888–893.

Luthar, S. S., Cicchetti, D., and Becker, B. (2003). Research on resilience: Response to commentaries. *Child Development, 71,* 573–575.

Lyons, R. F., Mickelson, K. D., Sullivan, M. J. L., and Coyne, J. C. (1998). Coping as a communal process. *Journal of Social and Personal Relationships, 15,* 579–605.

MacDermid Wadsworth, S. M. (2010). Family risk and resilience in the context of war and terrorism. *Journal of Marriage and Family, 72,* 537–556.

Mancini, J. A., Arnold, A. L., Martin, J. A., and Bowen, G. L. (2014). Community and primary prevention. In T. P. Gullotta and M. Bloom (eds), *Encyclopedia of primary prevention and health promotion* (2nd edn). New York: Springer.

Mancini, J. A., and Bowen, G. L. (2009). Community resilience: A social organization theory of action and change. In J. A. Mancini and K. A. Roberto (eds), *Pathways of human development: Explorations of change* (pp. 245–265). Lanham, MD: Lexington Books.

Mancini, J. A., and Bowen, G. L. (2013). Families and communities: A social organization theory of action and change. In G. W. Peterson and K. R. Bush (eds), *Handbook of marriage and the family* (pp. 781–713). New York: Springer.

Mancini, J. A., Bowen, G. L., and Martin, J. A. (2005). Community social organization: A conceptual linchpin in examining families in the context of communities. *Family Relations, 54,* 570–582.

Masten, A. S. (2001). Ordinary magic: Resilience processes in development. *American Psychologist, 56*(3), 227–238.

Masten, A. S., Best, K. M., and Garmezy, N. (1990). Resilience and development: Contributions from the study of children who overcome adversity. *Development and Psychopathology, 2,* 425–444.

McCubbin, H. I., and McCubbin, M. A. (1988). Typologies of resilient families: Emerging roles of social class and ethnicity. *Family Relations, 37,* 247–254.

McCubbin, J. A., Futrell, E. A., Thompson, E. A., and Thompson, A. I. (1998). Resilient families in an ethnic and cultural context. In H. I. McCubbin, E. A. Thompson, A. I. Thompson, and J. E. Fromer (eds), *Resiliency in families* (pp. 329–351). Thousand Oaks, CA: Sage Publications.

McWilliam, R. A. (2005). Assessing the resource needs of families in the context of early intervention. In M. J. Graßnick (ed.), *A developmental systems approach to early intervention* (pp. 215–234). Baltimore, MD: Paul H. Brookes Publishing Co.

Norris, F. H., Stevens, S. P., Pfefferbaum, B., Wyche, K. F., and Pfefferbaum, R. L. (2008). Community resilience as a metaphor, theory, set of capacities, and strategy for disaster readiness. *American Journal of Community Psychology, 41,* 127–150.

Olson, D. H. (2000). Circumplex model of marital and family systems. *Journal of Family Therapy, 22*(2), 144–167.

Perry, A. (2004). A model of stress in families of children with developmental disabilities: Clinical and research applications. *Journal on Developmental Disabilities, 11*(1), 1–16.

Simon, J. B., Murphy, J. J., and Smith, S. M. (2005). Understanding and fostering family resilience. *Family Journal, 13*(4), 427–436.

Singer, G. H., Marquis, J., Powers, L. K., Blanchard, L., Devenire, N., Santelli, B., ... and Sharp, M. (1999). A multi-site evaluation of parent to parent programs for parents of children with disabilities. *Journal of Early Intervention, 22,* 217–229.

Syvertsen, A. K., Roehlkepartain, E., and Scales, P. C. (2012). Key findings from the American Family Assets Study. Minneapolis, MN: The Search Institute.

Thompson, L., Lob, C., Elling, R., Herman, S., Jurkiewicz, T., and Hulleza, C. (1997). Pathways to family empowerment: Effects of family-centered delivery of early intervention services. *Exceptional Children, 64,* 99–114.

Turnbull, H. R., Stowe, M. J., Turnbull, A. P., and Schrandt, M. (2007). Public policy and developmental disabilities: A 35-year retrospective and a five-year prospective based on the core concepts of disability policy. In S. L. Odom, R. H. Horner, M. E. Snell, and J. Blacher (eds), *Handbook of developmental disabilities* (pp. 15–34). New York: Guilford Press.

Walsh, F. (1996). The concept of family resilience: Crisis and challenge. *Family Process, 35,* 261–281.

Walsh, F. (2013). Community-based practice applications of a family resilience framework. In D. S. Becvar (ed.), *Handbook of family resilience* (pp. 65–82). New York: Springer.

Wiens, T. W., and Boss, P. (2006). Maintaining family resiliency before, during, and after military separation. In C. A. Castro, A. B. Adler and T. W. Britt (eds), *Military life: The psychology of serving in peace and combat,* vol. 3, *The military family* (pp. 13–38). Westport, CT: Praeger Security International.

18

Family Policy through a Human Rights Lens

Elaine A. Anderson and Bethany L. Letiecq

Vulnerable groups such as children, persons with disabilities, the poor, elderly or the infirm are often those targeted by social policies. The application of a human rights lens helps reveal the extent to which government policies promote functioning, health, and well-being of some families, while failing to address the human needs of other families. In their critique of key policies centered on family formation and family care, Anderson and Letiecq argue that the individualistic and often fragmented nature of US social policies may contribute to further marginalization of at-risk families. The fact that certain social policies do not appear to uphold rights to human dignity, nondiscrimination, and social justice suggests the need for a more explicit family policy agenda which recognizes all families in all of their diversities.

Family Policy through a Human Rights Lens

One might ask why a chapter on family policy is included in a book on family risk, resilience, and social justice. Hopefully the answer will become very clear as you read this chapter and gain an understanding of how policy is an essential component to promoting healthy families and communities. Indeed, understanding policy is critical for those interested in working with families or planning to work in human services because, to a large extent, policy shapes family life and the ways in which professionals interact with families. Policies can determine which services are available to address the risks families face, as well as who can use these services. Policies can dictate which risks are most critical to address in society and which programs will be funded. Policies can promote (or hinder) the ability of families

to positively cope and adapt to their circumstances and thus can promote resilient outcomes. And policies can foster a society that is more equitable, fair, and just. However, in the policy arena, the intent or goal of policies for families is not always obvious or explicitly stated and – more often than not – policies aimed at families are driven by values and political ideology (Hays, 2003).

Throughout US history, there are numerous examples of ideological influence and differing goals for families across administrations and political leaders. Let's look at a few recent examples, starting with President Clinton. Often considered a conservative or moderate Democrat, President Clinton during his terms in office emphasized such contrasting legislation as the Family and Medical Leave Act (FMLA) and the Defense of Marriage Act (DOMA). FMLA was the first federal policy to acknowledge that family structure had changed, that more women were both working and

Family Problems: Stress, Risk, and Resilience, First Edition. Edited by Joyce A. Arditti.

providing family care, and that the work environment needed to assist families with greater flexibility to both earn wages and care for their members. In contrast, DOMA designated marriage to be exclusively between a man and a woman, thus limiting the rights of those in same-sex relationships and asserting what types of families would be recognized and valued in the policy arena. President George W. Bush, often considered a moderate Republican, ushered in policies favoring marriage promotion, abstinence-only sex education, and faith-based fatherhood initiatives. These policies reflected a rather traditional view of family life promoted in Christian doctrine and conservative thought and further delineated which types of families would be supported under the law (Cahill, 2005). Most recently, President Obama, considered to be a more liberal Democrat, has focused on overturning DOMA and overhauling health care, recognizing greater relationship diversity in family life and the importance of health care access for reducing health disparities. Presidents and other policymakers are heavily influenced by their values and the values of their constituents, and have significant power in shaping how our society approaches matters of risk, resilience, and justice.

Throughout this chapter, we will explore what social policy is and how families are included in those social policies, with particular focus on policies related to family formation and health. We chose to utilize a human rights perspective in our analyses because we are interested in understanding the extent to which US policies uphold or violate human rights and how families fare when, for example, the right to nondiscrimination is not upheld in our laws and policies. By using a human rights lens, we offer a critique of how social policies often fall short of actualizing justice for all families and consider the implications of such injustice for family risk and resilience. We aim to promote discussion on the intersections of family policy and human rights and how a human rights perspective can be useful when studying families and the social policies that matter for promoting family health, resilience, and justice.

Definitions of social and family policy

As Zimmerman (1976, 2001) states, *social policy* is a system of interrelated principles and actions that influence the well-being of members of a society. These principles can determine the nature of relationships among individuals, social groups such as families, and society as a whole. The actions resulting from social policies influence family relationships and our quality of life. Social policies are developed for a variety of reasons, but the primary goal of social policies is to provide for a range of needs (e.g., financial, social, educational, or health) that the economy cannot satisfy for all segments of the population (Titmuss, 1969). Often those targeted by and potentially benefitting from social policies are vulnerable groups such as children, persons with disabilities, the poor, elderly, or the infirm, who may not be able to meet their own needs and are often at risk for poor outcomes and health disparities.

Historically, US social policy has focused on protecting those most vulnerable from harm, abuse and neglect, unnecessary suffering, and social injustice, and removing the barriers to an individual's pursuit of life, liberty, and happiness. You may have heard the adage that if you work hard, you can achieve whatever level of success you choose, which may be more than what your family has achieved. This perspective – the American Dream – grew from the philosophy that an individual's opportunity should not be limited by the background of the family in which s/he was born. This emphasis on the individual is seen throughout the United States Constitution, which holds no guaranteed protection of family life (Kamerman and Kahn, 2001).

And while family is not mentioned in the US Constitution, many policies and laws exist at both the federal and state levels that either directly or indirectly influence family life. Thus, as noted by family policy scholars Kamerman and Kahn (1976, 1997), *family policy* can be defined as everything that government does to or for families. Giele (1979) added that family policy is a social policy with clear, important consequences for families, generally oriented either to helping target groups or individuals (within families) or to supporting family functions, including family formation, child socialization, economic provision, and care. These definitions recognize the role of government in promoting policies to benefit families, but also recognize that, perhaps because of our individualistic roots, the United States lacks an explicit family policy agenda or a comprehensive package of social policies specifically aimed at family well-being. The tension between individualism and family well-being has resulted in limiting the role of government in helping families meet their basic needs. Because most family policies are targeted, a perhaps unintended consequence is that not all families have equal access to policy-supported services, programs, and benefits, resulting in disparate risks, disparate health outcomes, and social injustices. Examining family policies using a human rights perspective allows us to more closely study the relationships between family needs, risks, resilience, and justice.

A human rights perspective

What do we mean by a human rights perspective? Wronka (2008) argues that human rights do not technically exist – only human needs do. But human rights provide us with the legal and ethical mandates to help humans meet their needs. These human needs must be met in order to survive and include, but are not limited to, components related to biological, psychological, emotional, social, and spiritual needs. Human rights are a reflection of the values and ethical codes of conduct that serve as principles for how we should behave. When we implement policies that attempt to help people meet their basic needs, the result can be a more just world, where we reduce risks born out of social inequality and promote more resilient families.

A human rights perspective is deeply rooted in our global history, especially following the many human rights atrocities that occurred during World War II. To provide an international human rights "roadmap," the General Assembly of the United Nations in 1948 adopted the Universal Declaration of Human Rights, which comprises 30 Articles or common standards for all peoples and all nations to strive for (United Nations, 2014). The document is a reflection of much of our international law (Buergenthal, Sheldon, and Stewart, 2002) and represents five core human rights encompassing human dignity; nondiscrimination; civil and political rights; economic, social, and cultural rights; and solidarity rights. So what do these rights mean for social policy, those principles and actions that influence risk, resilience, and family well-being? Let's consider.

Article 1 includes the core human right to dignity, where "all humans are born free and equal in dignity and rights" (United Nations, 2014). This notion appears to emanate from the core concepts of Judeo, Christian, and Islamic traditions that were probably the perspectives

of many of the nations involved in developing the document. The second core right centers on nondiscrimination, where it is asserted that to have rights, the only criterion is that a person is a human being. As stated in Article 2, nondiscrimination means that one acts justly towards others regardless of their "race, color, sex, language, religions, political or other opinion, national or social origin, property, birth or other status" (United Nations, 2014). Today, nondiscrimination policies also often include ability and sexual orientation, gender identity, and gender expression. There are many examples throughout history where people's dignity was violated, ignored, or destroyed because of acts of discrimination that were codified in US laws and social policies (e.g., Native American forced migration; African American slavery and Jim Crow segregation; Japanese internment camps; anti-miscegenation laws). It should come as no surprise that the communities who faced (and, in some cases, continue to face) violations of their human rights to dignity and nondiscrimination are some of the very same communities who are vulnerable to poor educational, social, and health outcomes.

Civil and political rights is the third core concept outlined in Articles 3 to 21 and is best represented with the statements that "everyone has the right to life, liberty and security of person," "everyone has the right to freedom of thought, conscience and religion" and "everyone has the right to freedom of opinion and expression" (United Nations, 2014). These rights emphasize that government should not interfere with the basic need to express oneself whether orally or in writing and may sound familiar to elements of the United States Declaration of Independence and the Bill of Rights, which hold that all men are created equal and have certain unalienable rights, including the right to life, liberty and the pursuit of happiness. Perhaps most relevant to this chapter is Article 16 under civil and political rights, which states, "The family is the natural and fundamental group unit of society and is entitled to protection by society and the State" (United Nations, 2014).

Earlier in the chapter we suggested that US social policies are developed to meet the needs of those in our society who may not be able to provide for themselves. The fourth core set of rights – that of economic, social and cultural rights – is captured in Articles 22 through 27 in the Universal Declaration and mirrors the purpose of social policy, that is, that government should provide for certain basic necessities that will ensure human dignity. For example, according to Article 25 of the Universal Declaration of Human Rights, "Everyone has the right to a standard of living adequate for the health and well-being of himself and his family, including food, clothing, housing, and medical care" (United Nations, 2014). These core rights also emphasize the provision of education and special protections for vulnerable groups such as the young, elderly and persons with disabilities.

Solidarity rights are outlined in Articles 28 through 30 in the Declaration and grew out of the international communities' failure to address global issues such as war, disasters, pollution, the oppression of indigenous and other peoples, and development that impinge upon the rights of all peoples (Wronka, 2008). Solidarity rights emphasize social and international order and call for the rights to peace, self-determination, cultural diversity, a clean environment, disaster relief, and distributive justice (Claude and Weston, 1992). Can you think of policies that uphold solidarity rights and those policies that fail to uphold such rights? When solidarity rights or other human rights are violated, how are individuals and families affected?

Examination of family policies through a human rights lens

By examining family policies using a human rights perspective, we seek to understand how family policies address risks and promote resilience among families and how policies promote social justice more broadly. We have chosen to focus on two important and hotly debated policy topics – those of marriage and health care. These topics correspond to two central functions of families, including family formation and the provision of care to family members; as noted earlier, both of these family functions are recognized as human rights.

A key facet of a human rights perspective is its unconditional regard for human beings. Yet in the United States, we have built a system of policies and laws that are conditional. In other words, not all human beings in the United States have the same rights or the same access to the same benefits. Indeed, we have attached rights and benefits to one's social location within two important institutions – our economic institution and the institution of marriage – both of which are undergoing change. Historically, one needed to be employed in the primary labor market (that is, in a job that offers benefits) or be married to someone who is employed in the primary labor market in order to access those benefits, which often included health care and retirement benefits among others. Some states and some employers do recognize domestic partners as eligible for certain benefits today. And with the passage of the Affordable Care Act (discussed in Box 18.1), those who are eligible can now purchase health care insurance irrespective of labor market policies, but this still leaves millions of people uninsured and tens of millions more with limited, inadequate, or no retirement benefits (Kaiser Family Foundation, 2012; Saad-Lessler and Ghilarducci, 2012). Thus, rather than providing rights and benefits universally as some other industrialized nations do, the United States has developed conditions or institutional "gates" where people are eligible or ineligible for certain rights and benefits depending on their social location.

Marriage as a Human Right for Some, but Not All?

In the case of marriage, Article 16 of the Universal Declaration of Human Rights states: "Men and women of full age, without any limitation due to race, nationality or religion, have the right to marry and found a family … [and] … Marriage shall be entered into only with the free and full consent of the intending spouses" (United Nations, 2014). The focus of Article 16 likely reflects the issues confronting the institution of marriage at the time in which the Declaration was adopted in 1948. Yet marriage is an ever-evolving institution and, most recently, debates about marriage policies and laws in the US have shifted to focus on marriage equality for same-sex couples and marriage as an antidote for poverty. Today, policymakers at all levels of governance, as well as members of the judiciary and laypersons alike, have been engaged in debate over who can legally enter the institution of marriage and thereby connect their loved ones to rights and benefits – in other words, who gets a key to the gate – and who cannot obtain access to that institution. Policymakers have also looked to the institution of marriage as a key ingredient for

---

Box 18.1 Obamacare

The Patient Protection and Affordable Care Act (often referred to as Obamacare) was passed by Congress in 2010. The intent of the legislation was to provide health care insurance and access to nearly 47 million uninsured Americans – many of whom are at risk of poor health outcomes as a result of being uninsured. The Act requires that everyone have health insurance in 2014 or be subject to a tax. To help people pay for their insurance, Medicaid was extended to those who earn up to 133% of the Federal poverty level – in 2013, that was $15,281 for an individual or $31,321.50 for a family of four. If you live in a state that does not give you this coverage, you won't be taxed if you can't get insurance. If you earn too much for Medicaid, tax credits will be given for incomes below 400% of the poverty level – in 2013 that was $45,960 for an individual or $92,000 for a family of four.

If you already have health insurance, all insurance plans must provide services in 10 essential health benefit categories. Some of these new benefits include preventive and wellness visits, maternity and newborn care, mental and behavioral health treatment, services to help people with chronic pre-existing conditions, and dental and vision care. These mandated benefits will allow more people to address chronic diseases before they require more expensive treatments. More younger and healthier people will have access to insurance, which could lower health care costs for all. Finally, low-income persons who might have addiction or mental health challenges will get coverage for their conditions. Ultimately, the Affordable Care Act will likely make insurance more affordable and provide insurance more fairly for more people, which is consistent with the human right to health care and will likely lead to increased health equity.

Resource: www.hhs.gov/healthcare/rights/.

---

ameliorating poverty in America in an effort to address the single most important risk factor for family well-being. First, let's review the changing landscape of marriage laws and policies leading up to the marriage equality movement and the Defense of Marriage Act (DOMA).

A brief history of marriage

Marriage and "the family" are often discussed as if static and monolithic (or uniform; Struening, 2002). Yet, historians argue that marriages and families have been changing for centuries to keep pace with changing economic pressures and changing social and cultural forces (Cherlin, 2004; Coontz, 2005). As Coontz (1992) reminds us, the revered traditional nuclear model of the 1950s was not the historical norm or the utopian experience. Indeed, women's rights within marriage have only recently changed *by law* to accord women more equal standing to men and, consequently, more gender justice.

For hundreds of years, marriage followed the Doctrine of Coverture, where a wife had no independent legal identity (Mason, Fine, and Carnochan, 2001). The long-standing patriarchal-marriage model assumed that men were heads of households and women and children were property owned by the husband (Cott, 2000; Ferree, 2004). Under Coverture, a woman could not sign a contract, own property or money, or file a lawsuit (Polikoff, 2008). Upon marriage, a woman gained her husband's surname and often lost her job and control over her body. During the first women's rights convention in 1848 (100 years before the Universal Declaration of Human Rights was adopted), the focus was largely on a woman's right to vote – which was granted in 1920. However, the convention also recognized that women's legal status in marriage affected the rights and legal protections of all women (Polikoff, 2008).

As the production of goods and services moved out of the home and women gained more legal rights, a "separate but equal" division of labor became the legal basis for a new kind of marriage – that of husband as provider and wife as homemaker and child care provider (Cott, 2000; Ferree, 2004). Within this formation, both men and women were expected to work in concert to advance the man's critical bread-winning role and laws sanctioned these gendered efforts. Thus, the wife legally owed her husband domestic support and the husband legally owed his family financial support, and would pay alimony to the wife upon divorce (Mason *et al.*, 2001; Polikoff, 2008). This marriage model was securely in place until the second wave of the women's movement began to challenge the "separate but equal" character-istics of the traditional nuclear model. During the 1960s and 70s, there were seismic shifts in American culture that were reflected in changes to marriage and family laws. In 1963, for example, under the Equal Pay Act, it became illegal to pay women less than men for equal work (Mason *et al.*, 2001). The once socially condemned behaviors of non-marital sex and out-of-wedlock childbirth gave way to a growing acceptance of cohabitation and single-parenthood.

During this period, the legal distinction between children born to a married mother versus those born to an unmarried mother was abolished. Thus, "illegiti-mate" children could no longer be denied inheritance, death benefits, and child support (Polikoff, 2008) – all of which hold implications for which children are placed at risk and which children thrive in our society. Divorce laws also shifted from fault-based to no-fault, allowing married couples to legally exit their union without establishing fault (Carbone, 1994). Significantly, nearly all states rewrote family and employment laws to reflect the equal standing now shared by couples (Mason *et al.*, 2001). The women's movement was essential to moving from a dependent marriage model where women had few rights to the current partner-ship model where rights are equally shared.

Today, a partnership marriage model is legally framed as a contractual relationship between two indi-viduals who enter the relationship by personal choice (Mason *et al.*, 2001). This new marriage model enforces the rights and responsibilities of both partners while respecting their independent legal identities. Thus, support obligations and responsibility for a spouse's debts are now placed equally on men and women. Upon divorce, assets are often split 50–50 and custody of children is typically shared jointly by parents (Carbone, 1994). No longer does the labor market support a man's "family wage" (Fernandez-Kelly,

2008). By 1988, a majority of single mothers, mothers in dual-parent families, and mothers of young children were in the labor market. Such employment patterns continued to grow in the 2000s, challenging women (and men) to balance the demands of earning and caring and placing increased pressure on employers to better support all families (Gornick and Meyers, 2003; Hochschild and Machung, 2003).

DOMA and the battle over same-sex marriage

It is critical for understanding the changing nature of the institution of marriage to understand why same-sex marriage has emerged as such a hot topic and fodder for human rights discourse. Alongside the civil rights and women's movements, the gay liberation movement was also in full swing. With the emergence of partner-ship marriage, where gender roles within marriage were no longer sanctioned by law, the gay community saw an opening to pursue marriage rights and marital justice (Polikoff, 2008). Indeed, in the early 1990s, three same-sex couples filed a lawsuit (*Baehr vs. Lewin*, 1993) against the state of Hawaii challenging the con-stitutionality of a "heterosexuals-only" marriage law. After the Hawaii Supreme Court found an early ruling in the case to be unconstitutional due to sexual dis-crimination, we waited to see if Hawaii would be the first state to recognize same-sex marriage (Oswald and Kuvalanka, 2008).

With the possibility of gay marriage being legalized at the state level, in 1996 Congress passed and President Clinton signed into law DOMA (Zimmerman, 2001). At the federal level, DOMA defined marriage as between one man and one woman as husband and wife – and reintroduced gender back into marriage law. DOMA also declared, contrary to the Full Faith and Credit Clause (Article IV, Section 1 of the US Constitution), that states are not required to recognize same-sex marriages performed in other states. With the passage of federal DOMA, the majority of states also passed laws banning same-sex marriage and 15 states "adopted even more restrictive laws that threaten or would ban more limited forms of partner recognition, such as domestic partner health benefits and hospital visitation rights" (Cahill, 2005, p. 179). However, other states moved to recognize same-sex marriage, with 17 states as well as the District of Columbia and eight Native American tribal jurisdictions legalizing same-sex marriage (as of January 2014). Oswald and Kuvalanka (2008) noted that even as same-sex couples in some states were granted marriage rights, under federal DOMA, they were not protected by federal laws and not eligible for 1,138 statutory provisions where marital status is a factor in determining benefits, rights, and privileges (e.g., death benefits, filing joint tax returns; US Government Accountability Office, 2004). In an unprecedented declaration, President Obama, during his second inaugural address in 2013, called for DOMA to be overturned and for gay marriage rights to be recognized federally. And in June of 2013, by a five to four majority, the US Supreme Court struck down part of DOMA, overturning the law that denied federal benefits to same-sex couples. While the Court decision does not guarantee the right to same-sex marriage, it now allows same-sex couples who are married to receive the same federal benefits as heterosexual couples (see Box 2.1 in Chapter 2 of this volume).

Opponents of same-sex marriage have employed mainly values-based and religious arguments in the fight over gay marriage (e.g., heterosexual marriage is best for children and society; marriage is a sacred institution sanctioned by a higher power), and offer little empirical evidence to support claims that legitimizing gay couples places the institution of marriage at risk or that same-sex parents harm their children (Crowl, Ahn, and Baker, 2008; Meezan and Rauch, 2005; Polikoff, 2008). Indeed, results from Crowl and colleagues' study suggest that children raised by same-sex parents fare as well as children raised by heterosexual parents. As Biblarz and Stacey (2010) note, "At this point no research supports the widely held conviction that the gender of parents matters for child well-being … We predict that even 'ideal' research designs will find instead that ideal parenting comes in many different genres and genders" (p. 17).

Proponents of same-sex marriage have relied mainly on constitutional arguments (e.g., DOMA violates the Due Process Clause and the Equal Protection Clause of the 14th Amendment, Full Faith and Credit, and the separation of church and state), and human rights arguments (Croghan and Letiecq, 2009; Zimmerman, 2001). From a human rights perspective, it has been argued that DOMA fails to uphold the right to human dignity and is discriminatory at its base, particularly if the institution of marriage continues to recognize a partnership marriage model, where gender neutrality and equality are protected under the law. Further it is argued that the right to marry the person whom you love and "found a family" is central to the ability of each of us to create a secure, stable, and dignified life. From a human rights perspective, legalizing gay marriage is a logical next step in the era of partnership marriage, where couples are free to choose the roles they will perform in marriage and family life regardless of their gender. A question that remains is how marriage recognition or the failure to recognize same-sex unions has legally affected the health and well-being of same-sex couples and their families. Will same-sex marriages be more vulnerable to dissolution because of historical violations to the human rights of dignity and nondiscrimination or more resilient? How might we promote more positive outcomes across the diverse array of relationships that exist in our communities today?

Marriage promotion among the poor and communities of color

At the same time that policymakers and society at large have been debating marriage equality, the federal government also looked to the institution of marriage as a solution to such social "problems"[1] as teen pregnancy, non-marital births, single parenting, and poverty. Indeed, a major component of welfare reform under President Clinton's administration and a major thrust of anti-poverty programming under President Bush's administration (which continues to date) was marriage promotion. At the time, the promotion of heterosexual marriage was based on research suggesting that "children who grow up in healthy, married, two-parent families do better on a host of outcomes than those who do not" (Administration for Children and Families (ACF), n.d.). Further, it was suggested that married couples, on average, appear to build more wealth than single parents or cohabiting couples, "thus decreasing the likelihood that their children will grow up in poverty" (ACF, n.d.).

Under both the Bush and Obama Administrations, the federal government has committed millions of dollars per year in funding to promote heterosexual marriage as a means to ending poverty. Activities have included marriage and healthy relationships education, marriage-skills training, advertising campaigns, high school educational programs, and marriage mentoring programs (Pate, 2010). Marriage promotion policies have not just targeted low-income families; they have also focused on communities of color, including African American, Hispanic, Asian/Pacific Islander, and Native American communities. The intended goals of these social policies are to reduce divorce rates, single parenting, and poverty, all of which hold significant risks for family well-being. However, the unintended consequences of diverting funds away from established anti-poverty programs to promote marriage have been persistent poverty rates, especially among women and children, with little evidence that marriage promotion efforts work at all to stabilize relationships and promote more resilience among at-risk families (ACF, 2005; Pate, 2010).

Paternity establishment, fatherhood initiatives, and child support enforcement

In partnership with marriage promotion efforts, we saw the implementation of paternity establishment programs and Responsible Fatherhood Initiatives (ACF, 2005). These initiatives have two purposes: (1) to connect fathers with their children to promote father involvement, and (2) to encourage and/or sanction fathers to financially support their children (Anderson, Kohler, and Letiecq, 2002). Many fatherhood initiatives also support participants' economic viability by providing educational programming and job training. Under welfare reform, child support efforts were also revamped. Policymakers revised rules governing the distribution of child support collection among federal and state governments and welfare families, required states to establish an automated registry of child support cases, and required states to provide information to a federal parent locator service (Lockie, 2009). Welfare reform also required all welfare recipients to cooperate with state child support enforcement orders and to hand over their child support rights to the state. Under the new laws, enforcers of child support now have the option to implement harsher penalties, such as jail time, for

fathers who refuse or are unable to pay child support (Lockie, 2009), which raises questions about justice, particularly among poor men who often face discrimination and unequal treatment in both the labor market and US prison system.

Coupling marriage promotion with paternity establishment, responsible fatherhood initiatives, and child support enforcement paints a complicated picture. Proponents argue that these policies are supported by empirical evidence linking traditional heterosexual marriage to positive child outcomes and are thus in the best interests of children (Blankenhorn, 2007; Waite and Gallagher, 2000; Whitehead, 1993). Critics of marriage promotion question the underlying pro-heterosexual-marriage assumptions, arguing that correlational data linking child outcomes to family structure variables have been interpreted as if cause and effect relationships were established – in other words, that single parenthood "causes" poverty or that marriage "causes" the acquisition of wealth (Biblarz and Stacey, 2010; Coltrane, 2001; Hardisty, 2008). It is also possible that the most attractive and privileged members of our society "self-select" into the institution of marriage. Moreover, policymakers' assumptions regarding the reasons poor single mothers are less likely to marry have been based on deficit-based perspectives centering on father absence, cultural deviance, immorality or loose sexual values. However, Edin and Reed (2005) found in their study of low-income single mothers that these women truly value marriage; however, their economic insecurity, coupled with their male partners' economic challenges, are obstacles to entering the institution.

Finally, critics of marriage promotion argue that these efforts do little to address the structural and systematic barriers to economic self-sufficiency experienced by low-income families, who are disproportionately families of color (Pate, 2010; Trzcinski, 1995). These policies, it is argued, fail to resolve the institutionalized sexism, racism, and classism that persist to delegitimize the status of low-income families and fail to address all families' rights to nondiscrimination and their economic, social, and cultural rights (Heath, 2009). From a human rights perspective, questions remain about privileging one family form over all others. Would we experience a more just society (and perhaps more resilient families) if we equally valued and supported single-parent families, same-sex couples and same-sex parents, and cohabitating couples as we do traditional nuclear families? As Polikoff (2008) posits, what would our society look like if we valued all families under the law?

US Health Care: Not Necessarily Equal for All

The United States spends more per capita on health care and as a percentage of gross domestic product (GDP; projected to rise to around 20% by 2015) than any other developed nation, but life expectancy and infant mortality rates (among other outcomes) remain among the poorest of comparison industrialized countries (McLaughlin and McLaughlin, 2008). When *Healthy People 2010* was published in 2000 by the US Department of Health and Human Services (DHHS), goals outlined were to increase the health lifespan, reduce health disparities, and achieve access to preventive services for all Americans. However, to date we have not met these goals. African Americans, Hispanics, Native Americans, and Asian/Pacific Islanders, who represent 25% of the US population, experience striking health disparities, including shorter life expectancy and higher rates of diabetes, cancer, heart disease, stroke, substance abuse, infant mortality and low birth weight than whites (Williams and Dilworth-Anderson, 2006; Zsembik, 2006). These poor health outcomes also have social class and gender determinants (McLaughlin and McLaughlin, 2008). How have we so profoundly missed the mark in health care today and failed to uphold the human right to a standard of living adequate for the health and well-being of all families (United Nations, 2014)?

The present US health care system grew out of a variety of policy initiatives introduced and passed over the past 100 years. A major shift in US health care occurred during the Great Depression in 1929, when health insurance systems emerged to stabilize the cash flows of providers (McLaughlin and McLaughlin, 2008). Health insurance systems grew during World War II, and a series of reforms followed, including the Hill–Burton Act of 1946, which expanded hospital facilities. As noted by McLaughlin and McLaughlin, the political "give and

take" in the development of health care policy over the decades has left us with an incredibly complex system of "federally-financed programs, each of which has its own often-changing sets of regulations" (p. 39). We have identified several, particularly family-relevant, health policy initiatives to illustrate where we have come from, where we are now, and where health care reforms, recently passed under the Obama Administration, are taking us. The selected policies focus on three emerging at-risk groups: long-term care and the elderly, immigrants and their children, and the mentally ill. For each of these policies, we utilize a human rights lens to discuss the policy limitations related to risk, resilience and social justice.

Medicare and long-term care

The history of the US health care system reflects a focus on individual health rather than the health of family systems or communities. An early example of an individual focus on health care was Medicare, a health policy initiative established under the Johnson Administration with the passage of the Social Security Amendments of 1965 (Ford, 1989; Kerschner and Hirschfield, 1975). Medicare, which mirrored the structure of health insurance in the private sector, was designed to benefit the well-being of the elderly (those 65 or older), yet lacked adequate coverage for prevention and long-term care. With 59% of the elderly in the United States at risk of needing long-term care (e.g., assistance with daily living skills; Feder, Komisar, and Niefeld, 2000), and 75% of these people receiving this care from family, the increased burden on families has been extensive. One evident risk to families is stress arising from long-term caregiving. Also, the risks of depression and other mental health symptoms are higher among elderly caregivers than for the general population (Shields, 1992). In addition, families must be resilient in order to respond when protective long-term care services, such as respite care or home health care assistance, are inaccessible, either because no services exist in the community or because of exorbitant cost.

The legislative framework for policies on elders' long-term care has predominately been based on a respond-to-the-crisis approach. Today, long-term care is funded by multiple federal programs, including

Medicare and Medicaid, which provide cash, in-kind transfers such as housing and transportation, and/or goods and services (O'Shaughnessy, Price, and Griffiths, 1987). Family continues to be the major protective factor behind policies on elder long-term care. Thus, if one has no family who can obtain or provide necessary services, then the right to be able to fulfill such basic necessities as caring for one's daily living needs is threatened and may result in differential elder protection and disparate health outcomes.

One provision of Obama's health care reform under the Patient Protection and Affordable Care Act (PPACA) is the Community Living Assistance Services and Supports (CLASS) Act. This Act, originally introduced by the late Senator Ted Kennedy, establishes a national voluntary long-term care payroll deduction insurance program for employed individuals. Workers pay premiums and, when eligible, receive benefits averaging $50 a day to purchase home and community long-term care assistance (Wiener, Hanley, Clark, and Van Nostrand, 1990). This program allows all workers to become vested after five years, regardless of pre-existing conditions. The Act increases protection by making long-term care financially accessible to more individuals through automatic enrollment for workers 18 and older, although employees and employers can choose not to participate. Both low-income individuals and full-time students who are working can pay a monthly premium of only $5 to be in the program. However, the terms do not provide for non-working spouses or other non-working individuals, raising questions about equity, fairness, and justice for all. As with the majority of US health care policies, the CLASS Act is tied to an employment-based healthcare system that is exclusionary and discounts coverage for those who are unemployed (McLaughlin and McLaughlin, 2008).

Immigrants and health care access

In addition to policies focused on the elderly, legislation has also attempted to address the health needs of some, but not all low-income children. Children of immigrants comprise a large share of the young child population – in fact, they are the fastest-growing component of this population and are at significant risk for health disparities (Hernandez, 1999). Yet, immigrant children still are not adequately covered under either Medicaid (Federal Register, 2009) or the Children's Health Insurance Program (CHIP; Kenney and Cook, 2007), the major policies enacted to provide health care for poor children. Because documented and undocumented immigrant parents may be fearful of having their right of freedom rescinded and being deported, they often do not use health-based services. Consequently, the children of these immigrants use public benefits less often (Fix and Zimmerman, 1999). Lower benefit-usage for noncitizen children is due to ineligibility for such programs as food stamps, Medicaid, or CHIP. Noncitizen children who are undocumented are ineligible for all benefits except some emergency Medicaid health care (Rodriguez, Hagen, and Capps, 2004). This policy clearly violates children's rights of nondiscrimination and provision of certain basic necessities such as health care and fails to uphold the notion that everyone should receive the human dignity of equality.

Immigrant children are more likely to lack health insurance or any source of health care than native-born children, resulting in risks for poor health outcomes. Children of immigrants are twice as likely to be uninsured despite an increase in coverage through Medicaid between 1999 and 2002 (Kaiser Family Foundation, 2003) and their health is reported to be fair or poor at twice the rate of children of natives (Ku and Blaney, 2000). In 2005, more than 3.2 million Latino children had no access to health coverage (Huang, Yu, and Ledsky, 2006), facing obstacles to accessing both Medicaid and CHIP (Ku, 2007). Federal laws restrict most noncitizens, including children, arriving in the US after 1996 from accessing health programs for the first five years of residence.

Current immigration policy on children's health care access is a perfect example of social injustice and the lack of the right of distributive justice, as the US health care system determines eligibility or merit for receipt of health care based upon the time frame for entering the country. Few systems of universal health care worldwide determine one's worthiness to receive health care assistance utilizing a situated place-in-time determinant. A positive outcome of health care reform is the eradication of a time restriction for children's receipt of health care. States can now opt to use federal funds to make Medicaid and CHIP available to otherwise eligible legal immigrant children and all children born in the United States, even if their parents are undocumented. It is important that child advocates continue to observe the universal and more just implementation of this state-level protection for some of society's most vulnerable.

Mental health parity

Discussion about health care policy disproportionately focuses on physical health care services and does not attend to mental health care coverage. A debate in the health care arena in recent years has been about mental health care parity, providing the same amount of insurance coverage for mental health benefits as are allowed for medical/surgical benefits. Mental health coverage is important, given that half of the leading causes of disability worldwide are mental disorders and nearly 30% of the US adult population is affected by at least one mental illness during any given year (National Institute of Mental Health, 2009). About 33% of mental illnesses are classified as severe (e.g., schizophrenia, eating disorders, PTSD), and often these illnesses include substance abuse. Severe illnesses tend to be excluded from health benefits because they typically require expensive, long-term treatment (Friedman, n.d.). The protection of mental health coverage becomes a family-centered health policy issue because over 20% of adult Americans provide informal care for a family member with a mental illness (Guarnaccia and Parra, 1996). Further, the mortality rate for some of these disorders (e.g., schizophrenia, eating disorders) is much higher than the national average, devastating affected families.

Prior to 1996, families did not have equal access to health and mental health care. For medical/surgical benefits there was no annual cap on the amount of coverage that could be provided and there was a $1 million lifetime benefit cap. In contrast, for mental health benefits, there was a $5,000 annual cap on the amount of coverage and a $50,000 lifetime cap on benefits. If one was diagnosed with a severe mental illness, it is possible one could use all of one's lifetime benefit

coverage in one year (USDHHS, 1999). In 1996, the first mental health parity legislation was introduced into Congress and, in 1997, the Mental Health Parity Act of 1996 was signed into law (Centers for Medicare and Medicaid Services, 1997). Passage of this legislation forced states to revise existing or create new parity laws. For the first time, families began to receive some protection and assistance with increased inpatient treatment days and more coverage for outpatient treatment and hospitalization. However, employers could choose whether to offer mental health benefits; not all mental illnesses were covered; many programs such as Medicare and Medicaid were not required to provide benefits; and great variation remained in the amount, duration, or scope of allowed treatment. Consequently, the right of nondiscrimination was not ensured, but rather depended on one's employer, diagnosis, and health insurer.

Finally, in 2008, Congress passed the Paul Wellstone and Pete Domenici Mental Health Parity and Addiction Equity Act effective January 2010 (Pear, 2008). The Act prohibits employer health plans from imposing caps or limitations on mental health and substance abuse benefits that also are not applied to medical/surgical benefits. For those businesses with 50 or more employees that provide mental health coverage, parity is required. Co-payments, deductibles, and number of visits or frequency of treatment limitations can also be no more restrictive on mental health and substance abuse benefits than those imposed on medical and surgical benefits. Under the PPACA reform, mental health benefits are now a mandatory part of basic care, and insurance companies are required to provide coverage that is equal to coverage provided for any other medical condition. With such policy changes, greater equality of the right of dignity, nondiscrimination, basic necessities, and preservation of self-determination may occur for many individuals and their families.

From a human rights perspective, we recognize that there are intended and unintended consequences of US health care policy that have perpetuated health care inequalities and health disparities. However, we also recognize that much of our health is the result of social determinants, such as housing, education, social capital, and the natural and built environment around us (McLaughlin and McLaughlin, 2008). Taken together, social policy decisions have not brought human rights and health justice to all, but rather have privileged some groups and disadvantaged others. Indeed, our brief analysis of health care policy over time reveals that individuals and families across the lifespan face myriad challenges in meeting their health care needs, even while the US invests the largest share of GDP in health care of all industrialized nations (McLaughlin and McLaughlin, 2008). From inadequate policy attention and funding for preventative care, prescription drugs and long-term care needs of elders to denying care coverage to immigrant children (regardless of their status), the US health care system has any number of cracks for individuals and families to fall through. These cracks mean that too many will suffer poor health consequences, and tragically, too many will face premature death. And even with greater attention paid to health disparities disproportionately felt by low-income communities and communities of color, the US continues to fail to meet the needs of our most vulnerable members. Indeed, in the US, health care remains a privilege and not a human right.

Conclusions

Throughout this chapter, we have examined social policies that target individuals and families across two domains of family functioning – that of family formation and family care – that are recognized as human rights (United Nations, 2014). Our goal was to promote understanding of the ways in which targeted policies can promote the functioning, health, and well-being of some families, while failing to address the human needs and rights of other families. Because US social policies tend to focus on individuals and are not universal, a perhaps unintended consequence is that we fail to ameliorate many of the known risks to family well-being. For example, by promoting heterosexual marriage as an anti-poverty strategy, we systematically exclude those who choose not to marry, those who for any number of reasons are unmarriageable, and those who legally cannot enter the institution of marriage. By excluding the most vulnerable in

our anti-poverty strategies, we further marginalize at-risk families and fail to uphold rights to human dignity, nondiscrimination, and social justice. By excluding same-sex couples from marriage, we likewise disenfranchise people from their right to found a family that is legitimized and recognized under both state and federal laws and human rights doctrine. In these instances, we miss opportunities to promote family resilience and create a more fair and just society.

According to the Universal Declaration of Human Rights, one of the most basic of human rights is the right to medical care (United Nations, 2014). In the US, we have developed a wildly complex health care system that is one of the most expensive to operate in the world, yet yields disparate results as a function of one's social location in our society. As we discussed, low-income families, communities of color, immigrant parents and their children, and those with mental health disorders face unequal access to care, increased risks to poor health, resultant health disparities, and tragic personal and familial losses. Policymakers and the general public seem uneasy with the solutions to disparate and unjust health outcomes, as we have witnessed with President Obama's Affordable Care Act, famously referred to as "Obamacare" by health reform critics and ultimately embraced by Obama as recognition that he really does care about health!

As family scholars, we urge you and political leaders to continue to engage in these complicated discussions and grapple with the tensions inherent in our individual-focused society when attempting to meet the human needs and rights of all families. We would argue that a shift to a more explicit family policy agenda would serve the US well and better position it to confront familial risks to health and well-being and promote resilience and health equity. We agree with the Universal Declaration that "the family is the natural and fundamental group unit of society and is entitled to protection by society and the State" (United Nations, 2014). The question remains, which families merit and are deserving of this protection? And are we willing to recognize all families in all of their diversities under the law to actualize a more civil, fair, and just society?

Critical Thinking Questions

1. What is it about the United States (its history, social structure, model of governance, and values-orientations, etc.) that challenges the ability to promote an explicit family policy agenda and ensure the human rights of all?

2. From a policy perspective, how might we promote positive adaptation and resilience among diverse family forms? How might we value all families under the law?

3. From a policy perspective, how might we promote better individual, family, and community health outcomes, particularly among those populations most at risk for disparate and poor health?

Note

1. We use quotes around the word "problems" recognizing that not all people and not all scholars of family science problematize such family phenomena.

References

Administration for Children and Families (ACF). (2005). *Framing the future: A fatherhood and healthy marriage forum. Summary report.* Retrieved May 30, 2014 from http://www.fullspectrumpr.net/wyofams/winshape_report_final.pdf.

Administration for Children and Families (ACF). (n.d.). Healthy Marriage and Promoting Responsible Fatherhood demonstration grants by region. Retrieved May 30, 2014 from http://archive.acf.hhs.gov/healthymarriage/about/factsheets_hm_matters.html.

Anderson, E. A., Kohler, J. K., and Letiecq, B. L. (2002). Low-income fathers and "responsible fatherhood" programs: A qualitative investigation of participants' fathering experiences and perceptions of program efficacy. *Family Relations, 51,* 148–155.

Biblarz, T. J., and Stacey, J. (2010). How does the gender of parents matter? *Journal of Marriage and Family, 72*(1), 3–22.

Blankenhorn, D. (2007). *The future of marriage.* New York: Encounter Books.

Buergenthal, T., Sheldon, D., and Stewart, D. (2002). *International human rights law in a nutshell.* St. Paul, MN: West.

Cahill, S. (2005). Welfare moms and the two grooms: The concurrent promotion and restriction of marriage in US public policy. *Sexualities, 8,* 169–187.

Carbone, J. R. (1994). A feminist perspective on divorce. *Future of Children, 4*(1), 183–209.

Centers for Medicare and Medicaid Services. (1997). Health Insurance Portability and Accountability Act of 1996 (HIPAA). Retrieved May 30, 2014 from http://www.hhs.gov/ocr/privacy/hipaa/administrative/statute/hipaastatutepdf.pdf.

Cherlin, A. (2004). The deinstitutionalization of American marriage. *Journal of Marriage and Family, 66*(4), 848–861.

Claude, R., and Weston, B. (1992). *Human rights in the world community.* Philadelphia: University of Pennsylvania Press.

Coltrane, S. (2001). Marketing the marriage solution: Misplaced simplicity in the politics of fatherhood. *Sociological Perspectives, 44,* 387–418.

Coontz, S. (1992). *The way we never were: American families and the nostalgia trap.* New York: Basic Books.

Coontz, S. (2005). *Marriage, a history: From obedience to intimacy or how love conquered marriage.* New York: Viking Books.

Cott, N. (2000). *Public vows: A history of marriage and the nation.* Cambridge, MA: Harvard University Press.

Croghan, R., and Letiecq, B. L. (2009). Arguments for and against same-sex marriage. Unpublished manuscript.

Crowl, A. L., Ahn, S., and Baker, J. (2008). A meta-analysis of developmental outcomes for children of same-sex and heterosexual parents. *Journal of GLBT Family Studies, 4,* 385–407.

Edin, K., and Reed, J. M. (2005). Why don't they just get married? Barriers to marriage among the disadvantaged. *Future of Children, 15*(2), 117–137.

Feder, J., Komisar, H. L., and Niefeld, M. (2000). Long-term care in the United States: An overview. *Health Affairs, 19*(3), 40–46.

Federal Register. (2009). 2009 poverty guidelines. *Federal Register, 74*(14), 4199–4201.

Fernandez-Kelly, P. (2008). Gender and economic change in the United States and Mexico, 1900–2000. *American Behavioral Scientist, 52*(3), 377–404.

Ferree, M. M. (2004, May). The gay marriage backlash: A threat to modern marriage. *Newsday.* Retrieved May 30, 2014 from http://www.newsday.com/opinion/a-threat-to-modern-marriage-1.527035.

Fix, M. E., and Zimmerman, W. (1999). All under one roof: Mixed-status families in an era of reform. Research report. Washington, DC: Urban Institute.

Ford, D. (1989). Translating the problems of the elderly into effective policies: An analysis of filial attitudes. *Policies Studies Review, 8,* 704–716.

Friedman, G. (n.d.). The case for mental health parity. Retrieved May 30, 2014 from http://www.abilitymagazine.com/Mental_Health_Parity.html.

Giele, J. Z. (1979). Social policy and the family. *Annual Review of Sociology, 5*, 275–302.

Gornick, J. C., and Meyers, M. K. (2003). *Families that work: Policies for reconciling parenthood and employment.* New York: Russell Sage Foundation.

Guarnaccia. P. J., and Parra, P. (1996). Ethnicity, social status, and families' experiences of caring for a mentally ill family member. *Community Mental Health Journal, 32*(3), 243–260.

Hardisty, J. (2008). *Pushed to the altar: The right wing roots of marriage promotion.* Somerville, MA: Political Research Associates and the Women of Color Resource Center. Retrieved May 30, 2014 from http://www.publiceye.org/pushedtothealtar.

Hays, S. (2003). *Flat broke with children: Women in the age of welfare reform.* New York: Oxford University Press.

Heath, M. (2009). State of our unions: Marriage promotion and the contested power of heterosexuality. *Gender and Society, 23*(1), 27–48.

Hernandez, D. J. (1999). *Children of immigrants: Health, adjustment, and public assistance.* Washington, DC: National Research Council Committee on the Health and Adjustment of Immigrant Children and Families.

Hochschild, A., and Machung, A. (2003). *The second shift.* New York: Penguin Books.

Huang, Z. J., Yu, S., and Ledsky, R. (2006). Health status and health service access and use among children in U.S. immigrant families. *American Journal of Public Health, 96*(4), 634–640.

Kaiser Family Foundation. (2003). Immigrants' health care coverage and access. Report no. 2231-03, August 2003. Washington, DC: The Henry J. Kaiser Family Foundation. Retrieved from www.kff.org.

Kaiser Family Foundation. (2012). The uninsured: A primer. Washington, DC: The Henry J. Kaiser Family Foundation. Retrieved May 30, 2014 from http://www.kff.org/uninsured/upload/7451-08.pdf

Kamerman, S. B., and Kahn, A. J. (1976). Explorations in family policy. *Social Work, 21*, 181–186.

Kamerman, S. B., and Kahn, A. J. (1997). *Family change and family policies in Great Britain, Canada, New Zealand, and the United States.* Oxford: Clarendon Press.

Kamerman, S. B., and Kahn, A. J. (2001). Child and family policies in the United States at the opening of the twenty-first century. *Social Policy and Administration, 35*(1), 69–84.

Kenney, G. M., and Cook, A. (2007). Coverage patterns among SCHIP-eligible children and their parents. Urban Institute Research of Record, no. 15, February 6, 2007. Washington, DC: Urban Institute. Retrieved May 30, 2014 from http://www.urban.org/url.cfm?ID=311420.

Kerschner, P. A., and Hirschfield, I. S. (1975). Public policy and aging: Analytic approaches. In D. S. Woodruff and J. E. Birren (eds), *Aging: Scientific perspectives and social issues* (pp. 391–408). New York: Van Nostrand.

Ku, L. (2007). Reducing disparities in health coverage for legal immigrant children and pregnant women. Washington, DC: Center on Budget and Policy Priorities. Retrieved May 30, 2014 from http://www.cbpp.org/cms/?fa=view&id=143.

Ku, L., and Blaney, S. (2000). Health coverage for legal immigrant children: New census data highlight importance of restoring Medicaid and SCHIP coverage. Washington, DC: Center on Budget and Policy Priorities, October 10, 2000. Retrieved from http://www.cbpp.org/cms/index.cfm?fa=view&id=1348.

Lockie, A. J. (2009). Multiple families, multiple goals, multiple failures: The need for limited equalization as a theory for child support. *Harvard Journal of Law and Gender, 32*, 1–26.

Mason, M. A., Fine, M. A., and Carnochan, S. (2001). Family law in the new millennium: For whose families? *Journal of Family Issues, 22*(7), 859–881.

McLaughlin, C. P., and McLaughlin, C. D. (2008). *Health policy analysis: An interdisciplinary approach.* Sudbury, MA: Jones and Bartlett Publishers.

Meezan, W., and Rauch, J. (2005). Gay marriage, same-sex parenting, and America's children, *Future of Children, 15*(2), 97–115.

National Institute of Mental Health. (2009). Transforming the understanding and treatment of mental illness. The National Institute of Mental Health, August 6, 2009. Retrieved from http://www.nimh.nih.gov/health/publications/the-numbers-count-mental-disorders-in-america/index.shtml.

O'Shaughnessy, C., Price, R., and Griffiths, J. (1987). *Financing and delivery of long-term care services for the elderly.* Washington, DC: Congressional Research Service.

Oswald, R. F., and Kuvalanka, K. A. (2008). Same-sex couples: Legal complexities. *Journal of Family Issues, 29*(8), 1051–1066.

Pate, D. J. (2010). Fatherhood responsibility and the marriage-promotion policy: Going to the chapel and we're going to get married? In R. Coles and C. Green (eds), *The myth of the missing Black father.* New York: Columbia University Press.

Pear, R. (2008). House approves bill on mental health parity. *The New York Times, March 6,* 2008.

Polikoff, N. (2008). *Beyond (straight and gay) marriage: Valuing all families under the law.* Boston, MA: Beacon Press.

Rodriguez, N., Hagan, J., and Capps, R. (2004). State poverty rates: Do the new welfare policies make a difference. *Review of Policy Research, 23*, 657–680.

Saad-Lessler, J., and Ghilarducci, T. (2012). Near retirees' defined contribution retirement account balances (fact sheet). New York: Schwartz Center for Economic Policy

Analysis (SCEPA) at The New School. Retrieved May 30, 2014 from http://www.economicpolicyresearch.org/images/docs/SCEPA_blog/guaranteeing_retirement_income/Fact_Sheet_Retirement_Balances_july_2012_revised_FINAL.pdf.

Shields, C.G. (1992). Family interaction and caregivers of Alzheimer's disease patients: Correlates of depression. *Family Process, 31*, 19–33.

Struening, K. (2002). *New family values: Liberty, equality, diversity*. Lanham, MD: Rowman and Littlefield.

Titmuss, R. (1969). The social division of welfare. In *Essays on the welfare state* (pp. 35–55). Boston, MA: Beacon Press.

Trzcinski, E. (1995). An ecological perspective on family policy: A conceptual and philosophical framework. *Journal of Family and Economic Issues, 16*(1), 7–33.

United Nations. (2014). The Universal Declaration of Human Rights. Retrieved May 30, 2014 from http://www.un.org/en/documents/udhr/index.shtml.

US Department of Health and Human Services. (USDHHS) (1999). *Mental Health: A report of the Surgeon General. Executive summary.* Rockville, MD: US Department of Health and Human Services, Substance Abuse and Mental Health Services Administration, Center for Mental Health Services, National Institutes of Health, National Institute of Mental Health. Retrieved May 30, 2014 from www.surgeongeneral.gov/library/mentalhealth/pdfs/ExSummary-Final.pdf.

US Government Accountability Office. (2004). Defense of Marriage Act: Update to prior report, GAO-04-353R. Washington, DC: US Government Accountability Office. Retrieved May 30, 2014 from http://www.gao.gov/new.items/d04353r.pdf.

Waite, L., and Gallagher, M. (2000). *The case for marriage: Why married people are happier, healthier, and better off financially*. New York: Doubleday.

Whitehead, B. F. (1993). Dan Quayle was right. *Atlantic Monthly*, April, pp. 47–84.

Wiener, J. M., Hanley, R. J., Clark, R., and Van Nostrand, J. F. (1990). Measuring the activities of daily living: Comparisons across national survey. *Journal of Gerontology, 45*(6), 229–237.

Williams, S. W., and Dilworth-Anderson, P. (2006). Chronic disease and African American families. In D. R. Crane and E. S. Marshall (eds), *Handbook of families and health* (pp. 80–95). Thousand Oaks, CA: Sage Publications.

Wronka, J. (2008). *Human rights and social justice*. Thousand Oaks, CA: Sage Publications.

Zimmerman, S. L. (1976). The family and its relevance for social policy. *Social Casework, 57*, 547–554.

Zimmerman, S. L. (2001). *Family policy: Constructed solutions to family problems*. Thousand Oaks, CA: Sage Publications.

Zsembik, B. A. (2006). Health issues in Latino families and households. In D. R. Crane and E. S. Marshall (eds), *Handbook of families and health* (pp. 40–61). Thousand Oaks, CA: Sage Publications.

19

Multisystemic Therapy as a Strength-Based Model for Working with Multiproblem Families

Stacy R. Ryan, Phillippe B. Cunningham, Patricia A. Brennan,
and Sharon L. Foster

Multisystemic Therapy (MST) is a family treatment grounded in ecological theory, which articulates the interdependence of developmental contexts. MST has been widely used in the US and abroad because of its success in dealing with families who experience multiple problems such as poverty, youth delinquency, and child maltreatment. In Chapter 19, Ryan and colleagues apply MST principles through a strength-based lens which helps empower families to mobilize change and overcome their challenges by drawing out existing resources and client defined goals. Assessment of family strengths is important when working with multiple problem families as it instills hope and helps families see that their goals might be within reach.

Multisystemic Therapy (MST) is a family treatment for changing youths' antisocial behavior (e.g., delinquency, drug abuse). Because of its success in reducing problem behavior and improving family functioning, MST is widely used in the United States, and is particularly applicable to families who experience multiple problems beyond youth delinquency, such as poverty, family disruption, school problems, and the like (see Henggeler, 2011a, for a review). A reason for the success of MST is that it is guided by research on factors that contribute to youth problem behavior. Therapists follow treatment principles that focus on improving the youth's functioning in day-to-day interactions and that emphasize youth, family, and community strengths (Henggeler, Schoenwald, Borduin, Rowland, and Cunningham, 2009). This strength-based practice (e.g., Rapp, Saleebey, and Sullivan, 2005; Walsh, 2002) is an example of a general approach that many have argued is the best practice response to challenges faced by multiple-problem families (Boyd-Franklin, 2003).

This chapter is divided into two parts. In the first part, we describe the MST model that explains how risk and stress impact families, and provide an overview of MST. This overview includes a discussion of MST treatment principles and procedures and research support for the effectiveness of MST. In the second part, we discuss the characteristics of a strength-based approach and explain why these principles are particularly important for treating multiple-problem families. We also show how the strength-based approach applies to MST treatment

Family Problems: Stress, Risk, and Resilience, First Edition. Edited by Joyce A. Arditti.
© 2015 John Wiley & Sons, Inc. Published 2015 by John Wiley & Sons, Inc.

principles. To help with this demonstration, we provide a case example, which is woven into our discussion of how therapists use MST to help families change and to promote family members' ability to cope with the challenges they encounter. We conclude this chapter with a discussion of social policies that promote the use of MST in community settings. We also comment on policies that are needed to further encourage and enable community settings to make MST available to families.

Part 1   Multiple Problem Families: Ecological Overview

Prior to 1986 (Henggeler *et al.*, 1986), most researchers and clinicians felt that "nothing worked" in treating adolescents from multiple-problem families who exhibited such serious antisocial behavior problems as delinquency and substance abuse. Borduin and Henggeler (1982) argued, however, that a major reason why existing treatments were ineffective was that they failed to consider or target the actual causes of these seemingly recalcitrant problems. Numerous studies have found that a consistent set of factors are associated with and/or predict the development of serious antisocial behavior in youth (Henggeler, 1989). Antisocial behavior is defined by

behaviors that violate social and cultural norms that infringe upon the rights of others and often include aggressive acts (both covert and overt). Whether the behavior examined was conduct disorder, delinquency, or substance abuse, this research has shown that many families have multiple problems – they simultaneously experience day-to-day challenges in the family, the neighborhood, and the broader community.

As a result, these families often enter psychotherapy with chronic problems (Henggeler, Schoenwald, Borduin, Rowland, and Cunningham, 1998). Researchers in the field of family-based treatments have organized these factors into a social-ecological model (see Figure 19.1) of youth problems (e.g., Swenson, Henggeler, Taylor, and Addison, 2005) – a model that serves as a theoretical framework for how to approach treatment (Henggeler, 1999). This model sees the youth as part of many systems, including the family, a peer group, a school environment, a neighborhood, and a community. Once youth become criminally involved, they also become part of the juvenile justice or the mental health system and come in contact with agencies that provide services to young people.

All of these systems influence the youth, whose behavior in turn influences the systems. Each system can encourage youth strengths and resistance to engaging in problem behavior. Alternatively, misguided aspects of each system can place youth at risk

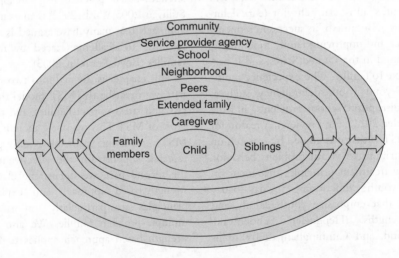

Figure 19.1   Social-ecological model of influences on youth behavior (adapted from Swenson *et al.*, 2005). Reproduced with permission of Guilford Publications, Inc.

for greater delinquency. For example, youth who spend time with non-delinquent friends (part of the peer system) are less likely to engage in problem behavior than those who surround themselves with friends who regularly break rules, use drugs, and engage in illegal activities. MST is guided by this social-ecological model. Therapists aim to intervene in the relevant systems in which the youth is embedded to engineer circumstances that will promote adaptive, positive, successful functioning at home, at school, and in the community while reducing factors that increase risk for delinquency.

Overview of the MST model

Theoretical basis of MST

MST's social-ecological model (Figure 19.1) is based primarily on Urie Bronfenbrenner's (1979) theory of "social ecology." The theory of social ecology states that all behavior is multi-determined by the nested "social structures" in which an individual is embedded. In other words, the individual is part of groups that are part of larger groups – the individual child is a member of a family and a peer group, which exist within schools and neighborhoods, which are part of larger communities. These nested structures, which Bronfenbrenner likened to a set of Russian dolls, each one inside the next one (Henggeler *et al.*, 2009), can directly or indirectly influence behavior. Regarding adolescent antisocial behavior, these nested "social structures" (individual, family, peers, school, community) each provides unique risk and protective factors that influence the others and add up over time to give rise to problem behavior. Risk factors make problem behavior more likely, whereas protective factors reduce the chances that the youth will develop difficulties. For example, one important predictor of adolescent problem behavior (delinquency, drug use) is association with deviant peers, a risk factor. But association with deviant peers is influenced by parental monitoring (parents knowing where the youth is and with whom – a protective factor). This shows how risk and protective factors work together to affect one another as well as the youth's behavior. Similarly, parental monitoring is itself influenced by aspects of the family's social ecology such as the parents' work schedule or physical and or mental health. MST is

Table 19.1 Overview of factors that contribute to delinquency

Component of social ecological model	Well-established contributors to delinquency
Family level	Poor parental supervision
	Inconsistent or lax discipline
	Poor affective relations between youth, caregivers, and siblings
	Parental substance abuse and mental health problems
Peer level	Association with drug-using and/or delinquent peers
	Poor relationship with peers, peer rejection
School level	Academic difficulties, low grades, having been retained
	Behavioral problems at school, truancy, suspensions
	Negative attitude toward school
	Attending a school that does not flex to youth needs
Community level	Availability of weapons and drugs
	High environmental and psychosocial stress (violence)
	Neighborhood transience – neighbors move in and out

Source: Adapted from Henggeler *et al.* (2009).

designed to assess and clinically address these factors in the adolescent's and family's social ecology. Table 19.1 summarizes different risk factors related to youth problem behavior at different parts of the social structure that have particularly strong research support. MST is particularly likely to target one or more of these factors, depending on the family.

The MST theory of change is consistent with both the research on the known determinants of antisocial behavior and the theory of social ecology. MST assumes that adolescent problem behavior (delinquency, drug use) is the net result of the interplay of these interconnected systems (individual, family, peers, school, community). Furthermore, to be clinically effective with antisocial adolescents, treatment must be sufficiently comprehensive and flexible to address each of these multiple systems that are directly or indirectly associated with a particular youth's problem behavior. Because families have different risk and

Table 19.2 MST treatment principles

Principle 1	The primary purpose of assessment is to understand the fit between the identified problems and their broader systemic context.
Principle 2	Therapeutic contacts emphasize the positive and use systemic strengths as levers for change.
Principle 3	Interventions are designed to promote responsible behavior and decrease irresponsible behavior among family members.
Principle 4	Interventions are present focused and action oriented, targeting specific and well-defined problems.
Principle 5	Interventions target sequences of behavior with and between multiple systems that maintain the identified problems.
Principle 6	Interventions are developmentally appropriate and fit the developmental needs of the youth.
Principle 7	Interventions are designed to require daily or weekly efforts by family members.
Principle 8	Intervention effectiveness is evaluated continuously from multiple perspectives, which provides assuming accountability for overcoming barriers to successful outcomes.
Principle 9	Interventions are designed to promote treatment generalization and long-term maintenance of therapeutic change by empowering caregivers to address family members' needs across multiple systemic contexts.

Source: Adapted from Henggeler *et al.* (1998).

protective factors, treatment must also be able to be adapted to the specific problems and strengths of each family. A further assumption of MST is that treatment must be collaborative, empowering, and hope-instilling, so that the youth's caregivers are able to acquire and use the skills, competencies, and resources required to effectively manage the difficulties that inevitably arise in raising adolescents.

MST treatment principles and procedures

MST is not a set of specific treatment techniques. Instead, it is a comprehensive conceptual model in which the therapist determines those factors across a youth's and a family's social ecology that contribute directly or indirectly to problem behavior (e.g., delinquency, drug use). The therapist then prioritizes these factors and develops a treatment plan by fitting family strengths with community resources and employing interventions that have research support for changing the factors the therapist has identified. In order to be effective, MST therapists need to be well trained in a variety of therapies that have been shown to be effective in promoting strengths and changing risk factors. These include cognitive behavior therapy, parent training, communication skills training, and strategic and structural family therapies.

The therapist bases the exact design, selection, and implementation of interventions on nine treatment principles that serve to operationalize MST (see Table 19.2). These principles guide the therapist to focus on the here-and-now, day-to-day interactions between the youth, family members, and members of other systems. They also heavily involve the family as active partners in the change process, and focus on strengths to promote change.

Home-based model of service delivery

MST differs from other more traditional therapies in which individuals or families come to a clinic once a week to meet with the therapist. Clinic-based therapies often inadvertently create barriers for multiple-problem families, who may have difficulty scheduling and making it to therapy sessions due to factors such as work schedules and lack of transportation or babysitting. Instead, MST is a home-based model of service delivery: therapists provide services in the home, school, and/or community settings at times that are convenient to the family (usually during evenings and weekends when youth are prone to engage in antisocial behavior). Therapists are available to families 24 hours a day, 7 days a week. Such availability greatly reduces missed appointments and minimizes barriers to getting treatment and, importantly, puts therapists in the position of being able to quickly respond to clinical emergencies that are inevitable when working with youth with antisocial behavior problems.

In addition to permitting therapists to respond in a timely fashion to crises and removing barriers to receiving treatment, a home-based model of service delivery has several added benefits. First, it allows the therapist to assess the youth, the family, and the environment directly, by experiencing what their real day-to-day lives are like. This provides more ecologically valid assessment information to inform the design and implementation of interventions. Second, it improves the chances that treatment will have a lasting effect, because interventions are implememented in the settings where behavior problems typically occur. Finally, a home-based model of service delivery enhances the relationship between the therapist and the family, because the family knows that the therapist understands their daily lives and environment (Henggeler et al., 2009).

Because of the intensity of MST treatment, therapists have low caseloads of four to six families per therapist. Treatment is time-limited – each family receives three to five months of services. In addition, because of the many needs of multiple-problem families, therapists provide comprehensive care. For example, a therapist might help a family member to make contact with a judge or probation officer, find treatment for their own individual physical or mental health problems, connect with appropriate social services, and the like.

MST quality assurance system
Simply telling therapists "use MST with your families" does not always result in their using the conceptual framework that guides MST correctly. At the same time, research clearly shows that therapists who do a better job following the MST model are able to bring about change in multiple-problem families (e.g., Ellis, Naar-King, Templin, Frey, and Cunningham, 2007; Huey, Henggeler, Brondino, and Pickrel, 2000; Sundell et al., 2008). Therapists who follow a treatment model appropriately are said to be adherent to the model – they conduct the treatment as it was meant to be done, a process called "treatment fidelity." Published findings on MST have demonstrated that greater clinician, supervisor, and consultant adherence to the model, as measured by standardized adherence measures, is associated with better outcomes for youth, such as fewer arrests and less drug involvement.

MST developers learned over time that an intensive and standardized quality assurance system was needed to ensure that therapists followed MST's nine treatment principles with fidelity. This system includes manuals for therapists, supervisors, consultants, and organizations that describe what is required to provide MST with fidelity. MST is usually provided by master's level therapists who participate in a five-day orientation and quarterly booster trainings. They also receive on-site clinical supervision from trained MST supervisors and weekly case consultation with an off-site MST expert. In addition, MST organizations measure adherence for therapists, supervisors, and consultants (Henggeler et al., 2009), so that those involved in delivering MST receive regular feedback about how well they are staying on track with delivering MST as it was designed to be delivered. In addition, the organization housing the MST program can consult with experts and have access to a web-based tracking and feedback system that allows program leaders to see how well therapists and the families they treat are doing.

Research support for MST
More than 30 years of research and 26 published studies looking at whether MST works to improve youth and family functioning over time have clearly demonstrated that MST is an effective way to treat serious antisocial behavior problems. These studies have included more than 5,200 participating families, including one study that involved inner-city delinquents (Henggeler et al., 1986), 11 studies with serious juvenile offenders (Borduin et al., 1995; Butler, Baruch, Hickey, and Fonagy, 2011; Curtis, Ronan, Heiblum, and Crellin, 2009; Glisson et al., 2010; Henggeler, Melton, Brondino, Scherer, and Hanley, 1997; Henggeler, Melton, and Smith, 1992; Henggeler et al., 1986; Ogden, Hagen, and Anderson, 2007; Ogden and Halliday-Boykens, 2004; Sundell et al., 2008; Timmons-Mitchell, Bender, Kishna, and Mitchell, 2006), two studies with substance-abusing or dependent juvenile offenders (Henggeler, Halliday-Boykins, Cunningham, Randall, and Shapiro, 2006; Henggeler, Pickrel, and Brondino, 1999), and three studies with juvenile sexual offenders (Borduin, Henggeler, Blaske, and Stein, 1990; Borduin, Schaeffer, and Heiblum, 2009; Letourneau et al., 2009). Most of these studies have compared MST with

the usual services that youth receive (such as being placed in juvenile hall or other forms of incarceration, being on probation, etc.), and have shown MST to be superior.

Research has also demonstrated that MST is effective with families in which child abuse is a problem (Brunk, Henggeler, and Whelan, 1987; Swenson, Schaeffer, Henggeler, Faldowski, and Mayhew, 2010), and can be adapted to treat youth with serious psychiatric conditions (Henggeler, Rowland et al., 1999; Rowland et al., 2005; Stambaugh et al., 2007) and with chronic health conditions (Ellis et al., 2004; Ellis et al., 2005; Naar-King et al., 2009). However, the efficacy of MST has been most firmly established with serious juvenile offenders (many of who are at imminent risk of out-of-home placements such as incarceration or residential treatment).

Across MST studies, a number of consistent positive outcomes have emerged. Clinically, in comparison to control groups, MST has: (a) improved family relations and functioning; (b) increased school attendance; (c) decreased adolescent psychiatric symptoms; (d) decreased adolescent substance use; and (e) decreased long-term rates of re-arrest ranging from 25% to 70%. A recent 21-year follow-up study (Sawyer and Bourduin, 2011) found that youth who received MST compared to those who received individual therapy exhibited 36% fewer felony arrests, 75% fewer violent arrests, 33% fewer days incarcerated, and 37% fewer divorce, paternity, and child support suits. MST also has better results in terms of attending therapy and the need for additional services. MST has: (a) 97% and 98% rates of treatment completion; (b) decreased long-term rates of days in out-of-home placement ranging from 47% to 64%; (c) higher consumer satisfaction than treatment as usual. This has produced considerable cost savings, for example, the Washington State Institute on Public Policy (Aos, Phipps, Barnoski, and Roxanne, May 1999) concluded that MST produced more than $60,000 in savings per youth, compared with usual methods of intervening. A more recent cost-benefit analysis of MST with serious and violent juvenile offenders (Klietz, Borduin, and Schaeffer, 2010) found that MST produced cost benefits ranging from $75,110 to $199,374 per youth. This strong track record of outperforming the ways most

communities deal with delinquency has led to MST being used in more than 30 states and 14 countries. MST currently has more than 500 teams of therapists and supervisors who annually treat approximately 23,000 youths.

Part 2 Case Example: MST with Derek and His Family

Armed with background information presented in Part 1, we now turn to a discussion of how MST is applied, and consider MST as a strength-based model. Before moving on to the specifics of MST treatment, let's meet Derek and his family.

Case Example: Derek

Andrea is a 30-year-old single African American mother of three: Derek, age 15 years, Darrious, age 12 years, and Devin, age 3 years. Devin was recently diagnosed with cystic fibrosis. Andrea's live-in boyfriend, Marcus, has two adult children and was recently released from prison following being jailed for marijuana possession. This is Andrea's fifth live-in boyfriend over the past three years. Andrea works as a home-health nurse; however, she risks losing this job because she is often late to work because she experiences hangovers most mornings as a result of having been drunk the night before.

Derek was referred to MST by a Family Drug Court case manager as part of a diversion program, due to his truancy and physical violence at home (he has been arrested several times for assaulting his mother's boyfriend), at school (he has been involved in several fights involving gang activity), and in the neighborhood (he has been arrested for fighting). Derek's placement in this diversion program was following a recent arrest for possession and sale of marijuana. Derek admits that he uses marijuana and alcohol daily.

Derek enjoys football and made it onto a school team in the past. Derek spends time with his younger brother, Darrious, but much of this time is when Darrious is also engaged in illegal activities. Derek often babysits his younger brother, Devin, without complaint – keeping him safe in their one-bed room apartment. Derek also likes to take Devin to the neighborhood recreation center and church playground.

Andrea has a permissive style of parenting and does not pay much attention to where Derek and Darrious are, or what they are doing when away from the home. A lot of her spare time consists of working or caring for Devin, who is currently on a feeding tube and requires a home health nurse for physical development sessions.

Deficit- vs. strength-based models of intervention

As discussed above, MST sees family members as part of complex social systems made up of smaller subsystems (e.g., parent subsystem, children subsystem, sibling subsystem). Interactions among family members and with members of other systems show patterns that influence the behavior of members of the systems. Particular patterns of interactions contribute to problems that exist within families (Henggeler et al., 1998; Patterson, 1982). Family-based treatments aim to alter styles of interaction as a way to improve functioning among and between subsystems. Historically, psychotherapy treatments sought to treat multiproblem families using a deficit-based model approach – looking at what was wrong or missing, and trying to correct this. Some current psychotherapy treatments like MST, however, focus on the use of a strength-based model, which emphasizes what is positive and adaptive in the family and makes use of these factors to promote change. Deficit- and strength-based models would have very different ways of thinking about Derek and his family.

Deficit-based model

Deficit-based treatments spend considerable time exploring *how* families got to the place they are in when they enter treatment. A rationale for this method is that once the therapist and the family better understand how problems developed, then they will be better able to change the negative patterns that lead to problem behaviors. Interventions that are driven by a deficit model view multiple-problem families through the lens of what went wrong, what is absent and or what is insufficient. Approaching treatment from a deficit perspective has sometimes been shown to be ineffective (Madsen, 1999), and may in fact have negative effects for disadvantaged racial groups because it can perpetuate negative stereotypes and undermines the process of building a strong alliance capable of empowering families (Boyd-Franklin, 1989). A therapist trying to understand Derek's circumstances and plan his treatment from this perspective might talk about him in this way:

Derek is a 15-year-old African American male. He was mandated to treatment for aggressive behavior and substance use. At least two factors contribute to his excessive involvement in substances: (1) caregivers who model substance use, and (2) a mother with a permissive parenting style that includes a lack of parental monitoring. To help reduce Derek's substance use, parent management training will be provided to Andrea. Although Derek enjoys taking care of his younger brother, the process of taking on parental responsibilities is likely related to his sense of obligation to make additional money for the family by dealing drugs. To address this, Andrea's pattern of alcohol use will be treated. Andrea's problems with alcohol create an unstable environment for Derek, likely causing feelings of insecurity which may be directly related to Derek's aggressive behavior. To partially address this problem, Derek will be provided with skills to cope with his feelings and manage his anger. This problem should also be addressed by the substance use treatment that Andrea will receive. Collectively, the risk factors in Derek's family and environment limit his opportunities for different choices.

Strength-based model

An alternative approach to treating families uses a strength-based model of practice. The focus of strength-based practice is to focus on existing strengths within a family system and larger environmental contexts (Walsh, 2003). A focus on deficits can leave families feeling hopeless. This is especially the case for multiple-problem families, who are faced with a barrage of challenges. Providers working from a strength-based perspective aim to help families discover strengths that they can use to meet life's challenges.

Focusing on strengths with multiple-problem families helps increase feelings of hope for a successful outcome. A therapist trying to understand Derek's circumstances and plan his treatment from this perspective might talk about him in this way:

> Derek is a 15-year-old African American male. He and his family are seeking treatment for aggressive behavior and substance use. Derek and his family have several strengths that will facilitate meeting these goals. Andrea cares deeply for her children. This is demonstrated in her commitment to seeking and obtaining resources to help her children (e.g., she followed through on treatment for Derek and has sustained care provided for Devin). Andrea's community is rich with resources (i.e., church and community center), which might be able to provide resources to help Andrea manage her alcohol use and/or manage the parental responsibility of caring for Devin so she is able to distribute her attention to her other sons as well. Derek is athletic, providing the opportunity for him to engage in prosocial activities that involve football. His established relationship with the neighborhood community center and the church provides an opportunity to join leagues, which will also present opportunities to engage with prosocial peers. Derek's ability to maintain a relationship with community resources and his past involvement in school sports shows that Derek has interpersonal skills that can be utilized when participating in prosocial activities.

Key differences between the deficit- and strength-based models within a therapeutic context
The examples above illustrate several important differences between the two ways of understanding Derek and his family. First, deficit-based models focus on the past. Strength-based models focus on the present and the future. Second, deficit-based models focus on how problems started and on understanding factors that led to a problematic behavior. Strength-based models focus on strengths to use as leverage for change. Third, deficit-based models tend to ignore family strengths, as those aspects of life are going well, and the goal is to understand what is wrong. The strength-based model focuses on providing families with emotional resources via articulation of strengths in order to tackle the challenges that they face. The goal is to mobilize change using strength as the vehicle. Fourth, deficit-based models focus on changing family dynamics in order to prevent problematic behavior. Strength-based models

focus on re-affirming family strengths so that families can deal with present and future challenges.

A misconception of the strength-based approach is that it ignores the challenges that exist for multiple-problem families. It is important to understand that the strength-based model does not ignore challenges. This approach uses particular principles (see below) to draw out and upon strengths to empower families to mobilize change, overcoming challenges. As shown in the two case conceptualizations, the deficit perspective focused on the problem and how individuals in the family and the larger environment were responsible for these problems. The strength-based perspective, on the other hand, focused on aspects in the system that could be used to help overcome the challenges that serve as the goals for treatment.

MST practices through a strength-based lens

The implementation of MST treatment principles is guided by an underlying strength-based model. In this section, we examine MST treatment principles that fit with strength-based practice (Rapp *et al.*, 2005). The following subsections are organized according to six strength-based practice principles. For each principle, the strength-based approach is discussed first and then a comparison is made with MST. The discussion of each principle ends with information about why the particular principle is important for working with multiple-problem families.

Goal-oriented
Practice from a strength-based perspective is driven by goals that are set by the family. Although therapists help families articulate their goals, the actual goal is based on family-defined values and aspirations for their future. Setting goals from the client's perspective is central to strength-based practice. Identified strengths are then used to help move families in the direction of their goals. Using client defined goals helps to ensure a match between identified strengths and goal attainment (Rapp *et al.*, 2005).

MST principle 4 is directly in line with this strength-based principle. MST principle 4 states "Interventions are present focused and action oriented, targeting specific and well-defined problems"

(Henggeler et al., 1998). A fundamental assumption of MST is that the youth's family or caregiver is the key to favorable long-term outcomes, even if the caregiver presents serious clinical challenges. Treatment goals are therefore largely defined by the family and the vast majority of MST clinical resources are devoted to developing the capacity of the caregiver to achieve those goals.

Two types of well-specified treatment goals that result from this process: overarching goals and intermediate goals. Overarching goals refer to the family's ultimate aims by the end of treatment (e.g., Derek will attend a full day of school, five days a week) and are determined by the family. Intermediate goals refer to the daily nuts and bolts of reaching the overarching goals (e.g., Andrea will ask her neighbor and good friend to provide Derek with a ride to school so that he can avoid the bus stop where delinquent friends congregate). Formulation of intermediate goals is led by the therapist, confirmed by the family. Even though the therapist leads this specification of intermediate goals, this practice is consistent with the strength-based model. This is because the family-led (overarching) goals drive the therapists-led (intermediate) goal-setting process (Henggeler et al., 2009). Because goal setting is the first task of therapy, goal setting serves as a guide for when and where to incorporate specific strengths. Goal setting also steers treatment in a clear direction, providing criteria that are used to measure whether goals have been met by the end of treatment.

Maintaining a goal-oriented focus during treatment with multiple-problem families is important. As discussed, multiple-problem families face many complex challenges, often existing within and between systems. Without measureable goals, these continued challenges can easily overshadow progress. Having a measureable goal (e.g., Derek will attend a full day of school, five days a week) allows the therapist and family to evaluate progress in an unambiguous way, which can motivate subsequent efforts to change and provide a clear indication of when the family no longer needs treatment.

Assessment of strengths

The systematic assessment of strengths lies at the heart of the strength-based model (Rapp et al., 2005). Assessing strengths at the start of treatment allows this information to serve as the foundation for all future work. From this perspective, the assessment process directs therapists to focus on strengths, steering treatment providers away from a focus on problems. A key aspect of this assessment is the focus on "what already works, exceptions to the problems, and identifying coping strategies already in the client's repertoire" (Rapp et al., 2005, p. 81). Strengths uncovered as part of this assessment help families set goals that feel more achievable, thus enhancing hope and the probability of success.

MST principle 1 is directly in line with this strength-based principle. MST principle 1 states: "The primary purpose of assessment is to understand the fit between the identified problems and their broader systemic context" (Henggeler et al., 1998). Adherence to this treatment principle involves three steps. The first step involves systematically (with the use of a specific MST record form) examining the strengths in each system. The next two steps revolve around systematically understanding problem areas. The goal of understanding these problem areas is to identify how to leverage individual strengths to initiate and maintain change. Knowing individual need areas allows the therapist to begin matching environmental resources and areas of strength to address family needs.

Assessment of strengths is particularly important when working with multiple-problem families. Multiple-problem families typically have a number of need areas that can easily cloud their recognition of their competencies and resources, and interfere with attempts to use existing capabilities. Reminding families of their strengths and the things they are doing well is hope-instilling and helps families to see that their goals might be within reach.

Explicit methods for using family and environmental strengths to help clients achieve goals

Strength-based practice utilizes information about strength areas to match families with existing resources in the community that can provide opportunity and supports. Rapp et al. (2005) argue that this is one of the most important aspects of strength-based practice. Using a family strength to take advantage of a community resource matched with the needs/challenges of a family becomes part of the family's problem-solving repertoire. For example, Derek could use his familiarity with the recreation center and church, as well as individuals within this establishment, to become involved in organized sports activities. This would provide a place for Derek to choose to meet prosocial peers instead of hanging out with deviant peers. Having such a resource builds resilience for future challenges. For example, in the future should a challenge arise, Derek and his family will now consider and examine the recreation center and church as a place that could help with a challenge.

MST was founded on the notion that the families should be treated within the context of their environment, using community resources to meet their needs (Henggeler *et al.*, 2009), and therefore has this strength-based principle as a part of the therapeutic framework. Procedurally, MST principle 1 is also in line with this strength-based principle. MST begins with a "fit assessment." This assessment assesses each system (e.g., family members, neighborhood, and service provider agencies) for strengthens and needs. The overall goal is to establish fits between family needs and community resources. As mentioned above, MST therapist forms help to guide this assessment. In addition therapists, supervisors, and consultants use a structured format for talking about cases. This allows them to track progress and fine-tune family–community resource fits.

Unfortunately, multiple-problem families often have serious difficulties such as parental drug abuse and child maltreatment. To treat multiple-problem families successfully, therapists need a thorough understanding of the case and a comprehensive plan for treatment. An explicit method for gathering information about strength areas and fit between family needs and community resources is important and helps the therapist (1) stay strength-focused in the face of the kinds of serious problems that can engender negative emotions which can adversely affect the family–therapist relationship, and (2) work through momentary crises as another example in which strengths may be used to overcome the challenge.

Therapeutic relationship and content instill hope
A core element of strength-based practice is that the therapeutic relationship is accepting and empowering, allowing the client to feel comfortable enough to embrace strengths and use them to bring about change. Rapp and colleagues (2005, p. 82) explain that "the relationship is accepting, purposeful, and empathetic; [and as] empowering the relationship should: increase the client's perceptions of their abilities, increase the client's options and perception of options, and increase the opportunities and confidence of the client to choose and act on those choices."

MST principle 9 states: "Interventions are designed to promote treatment generalization and long-term maintenance of therapeutic change by empowering caregivers to address family members' needs across multiple systemic contexts." To accomplish this goal for families and meet this MST principle, the MST therapist must create a strong therapeutic relationship with families and empower clients throughout the therapeutic process. Empowerment from an MST perspective includes several therapist attitudes and behaviors: (1) therapists should avoid presenting themselves as the expert and imparting change directly through their own efforts. Instead therapists should focus on leveraging the family's abilities and capacities to bring about change; (2) therapists should treat families with respect, recognizing that families have the right to decide what happens to them – allowing families to set goals for treatment; and (3) therapists should not get discouraged but instead be creative when finding ingenious resources for a family to use to leverage change.

Multiple-problem families who enter therapy with significant problems especially need a therapeutic relationship that kindles their sense of optimism. Multiple-problem families often enter treatment feeling hopeless. A hope-instilling relationship facilitates treatment engagement, a willingness to try new things, and the belief that existing strengths can lead to behavior change. Because multiproblem families face many challenges, it is likely that additional challenges will arise after treatment. During therapy, empowering families instills hope that things will get better and they can meet their goals. Following therapy, this empowerment promotes the belief that the family can successfully conquer challenges as they arise.

Collaborative approach to treatment
The strength-based model of practice includes a collaborative approach to treatment. That is, although the therapist has skills and knowledge relevant to the therapeutic process, the therapist does not enter the relationship as the expert. Instead, the therapist understands that the family is the expert on their family. This forces the therapist to use his or her skills

and knowledge to present options to families, allowing families to select from and ultimately choose their therapeutic course. Such a process guarantees that the family's wishes and desires are heard at each step of treatment: formulating an understanding of the case, treatment planning, and treatment implementation.

As discussed earlier, one of the main assumptions of MST implementation is that therapists work collaboratively with families (Henggeler *et al.*, 2009). Effective collaboration between therapist and families is necessary for MST therapist to adhere to the MST principles. An accurate strength and fit assessment (principle 1) requires the family and the therapist to work together. This allows for an effective process of fitting family strengths with environmental resources (principle 2), leading to a level of trust whereby families feel comfortable communicating whether matches were successful or require modification (principles 6, 7) – a process capable of leveraging the most behavior change (principles 3, 5). A collaborative approach facilitates family engagement so that treatment sessions can be present-focused and action-oriented, targeting specific and well-defined challenges (principle 4). Successful collaboration between families and therapists creates a relationship in which the therapist can help the family feel empowered to use strengths to overcome daily challenges (principle 9) and achieve goals (principle 8).

Maintaining a collaborative relationship with multiproblem families is important. Unfortunately, most multiple-problem families who are in treatment are often receiving services from many different agencies. This can be overwhelming and lead to service burnout, such that no one service is able to work effectively (Hennessy, 2010). Research has shown that providing choice to multiple-problem families and believing that they are competent to choose their own path towards better outcomes are related to staying in treatment, better relationships with the therapist, and better outcomes (Norcross and Wampold, 2011).

Leveraging change with multiple-problem families

Strategies for identifying indicators of strength within multiproblem families
It is important to examine each system (see Figure 19.1) to identify available strengths. This includes looking for positive features of the child, parent, family, peer,

school, neighborhood, and community systems – including other agencies that may be providing the family with services. Identifying strengths within and between systems can lead to collective strengths that move families in the direction of change. Henggeler and colleagues (1998) provide examples of strengths within each system:

- *child*: individual competencies and abilities (e.g., social skills, academic skills), attractiveness, intelligence, hobbies and interests, hygiene, motivation, temperament;
- *parent*: social skills, concern, problem-solving ability, attractiveness, frustration tolerance, patience, altruism, motivation;
- *family*: financial resources (money, property, welfare benefits, employment income), basic needs are met (housing and food), child care is provided, transportation is available, strong affective and instrumental relationship between spouses, number and variety of social supports, characteristics of the extended family, recreational and leisure activities;
- *peers*: individual competencies and abilities of peers, prosocial activities, hobbies and interests, family monitoring and involvement in peer activities;
- *school*: appropriate and effective classroom management practices, school-wide discipline procedures, concerned school personnel, teacher involvement in the community, availability of prosocial after-school activities;
- *neighborhood*: recreational and leisure activities, voluntary associations, law enforcement, business and industry, human services, concerned and involved neighbors.

Looking at the case of Derek, several strengths are readily identifiable that can be used to help this family change, despite their many challenges. At the individual level, Derek shows social skills (indicated by established relationships with others in the community center and church and participation in a team sport), academic skills (maintained good academic standing to participate in football), interest in spending time with his family (evident in his care for his younger brother and time spent with middle brother), and motivation (evident in his desire to support his family). At the parental level, Andrea shows various strengths: social skills (evident in the job that she has) and concern (evident in her ability to provide services for her youngest son and follow through on services for Derek). At the familial level, the family has financial resources (Andrea has employment income), their basic needs are met (the youngest brother receives necessary treatment, they have a home, the family is clothed and fed), child care is provided (the youngest child has nurse care and Derek is capable of watching his younger two brothers without complaint). At the peer level, Derek appears to have access to peers with individual competencies and to opportunities for prosocial activities (Derek has access through the community center and the church). At the school level, we see evidence of prosocial after-school activities (because the school has football one can assume that they have other activities as well). At the neighborhood level, recreational and leisure opportunities are present.

This analysis shows how important it is to look beyond obvious problem behaviors when looking for strengths. For example, it is clear that Derek cares about his brothers and finds it important to have a close relationship with them – even though he seems to be pulling one of his brothers into criminal behavior. This desire to be close to his family is a strength because the family is a significant source of support in the intervention process. Derek's and Darrious's substance involvement should not overshadow the clear strength that Derek and his brother enjoy being together. As another example, it is clear that Derek's mother believes it is important to work and provide for her family. Her substance use problems should not obscure this strength.

Social policy

Over the past three decades, MST has advanced from a single study with 80 participants to an internationally implemented program the provides service to more than 15,000 youths and their families each year (Henggeler, 2011b). This wide dissemination of MST has coincided with the increased support by national funding agencies and mental health organizations for empirically validated mental health treatments – treatments that have been shown to work using rigorous scientific approaches. The many studies that show that MST leads to improved mental health and

behavioral functioning across a variety of youth populations (Borduin et al., 1990; Henggeler et al., 2006; Swenson et al., 2010) provide a strong basis for the widespread adoption of MST. However, successful dissemination depends on more than empirical evidence that a treatment works. Many families who receive MST do not pay for these services. Instead, MST may be provided by community agencies that receive government funding to offer services to reduce youth delinquent or antisocial behavior as an alternative to incarceration. Policies at the local, state, and federal level influence who received funding for what types of programs, and influence whether mental health and juvenile justice agencies will offer MST or continue with their usual methods of dealing with these youth. For example, the US Office of Juvenile Justice and Delinquency Prevention and its Blueprints for Violence Prevention program have helped to focus federal funding priorities on a relatively limited number of violence prevention programs (including MST) that have shown strong research support. In addition, state funding initiatives have provided support for the dissemination of MST in states such as South Carolina, Ohio, and Washington. Continued funding support is crucial in terms of maintaining the kind of quality control and treatment fidelity required for MST to be used properly.

As communities consider whether to adopt MST, it is important to consider the costs of offering this treatment in a broader context. While MST is a relatively costly intervention, costing approximately $4,743 (in 2001 dollars) per youth/family treated, juvenile justice systems cost society over $14 billion a year (law enforcement, courts, incarceration, etc.), which more than doubles when one includes costs associated with such things as probation, health care, child welfare, treatment, school, and victims. In fact, it costs approximately $240.99 per day to hold a juvenile in a juvenile justice facility at a yearly cost of approximately $88,000 (American Correctional Association, 2008). Thus, it is not surprising that MST has been estimated to return $12.40 to $28.33 to taxpayers and future victims for every dollar spent on MST – a net return of approximately $131,918 per participant (Aos, 2002).

Particular types of communities may present unique difficulties that make successful implementation of

MST harder. For example, communities in rural areas may require therapists to spend more hours driving to community settings and may provide limited local resources for positive peer support. These community-level factors can lead to decreased therapist adherence and, in turn, reduce MST treatment benefits. Recent studies have begun to test whether additional community organizational interventions in these settings might improve MST outcomes (Glisson *et al.*, 2010). Initial findings suggest that community-level interventions designed to reduce barriers between organizations may be useful when starting to implement MST in rural communities.

Summary

MST is a family intervention for youth with serious antisocial behavior problems. Therapists provide MST in community settings. Treatment addresses factors known to promote delinquency at the individual, family, peer, school, and community levels. Therapists are guided by strength-based principles. These include assessing strengths in the various systems that affect the youth and family, explicitly connecting strengths to intervention planning, involving the family as an active collaborator in the treatment process, and instilling hope and a belief that change is possible, even for families with multiple, serious problems.

Over the last three decades, studies have again and again shown that MST can help youth stay in the community and reduce their delinquent and substance use behavior, as long as therapists implement MST with fidelity. Although it is a very intensive treatment, analyses of the cost of MST relative to the outcomes it produces show that MST is considerably less costly than other ways of dealing with delinquent, substance-using youth. Because of its success and associated cost savings, numerous agencies across the United States and abroad have adopted MST. Public policies that support funding for treatments that (a) show solid scientific evidence that they work, and (b) reduce taxpayer burden can encourage communities and organizations to adopt MST as an effective, family-empowering strategy for reducing youth antisocial behavior.

Critical Thinking Questions

1. What is the underlying philosophical viewpoint of the strength-based perspective and how does this parallel the underlying therapeutic framework of MST?
2. Compare the strength- and deficit-based ways of describing Derek and his family you read about in the chapter. Where do you see specific examples of each of the four differences between deficit- and strength-based approaches in how the therapist talks about the family using the two different approaches?
3. What therapeutic aspects of MST make it especially easy to implement as a strength-based model?
4. What other therapeutic approaches have you read about that might align with the strength-based perspective?
5. What policy recommendation would you make at the state and federal level to make MST more widely available to the community?

References

American Correctional Association. (2008). *Adult and juvenile correctional departments, institutions, agencies, and probation and parole authorities.* Alexandria, VA: American Correctional Association.

Aos, S. (2002). The juvenile system in Washington State: Recommendations to improve cost-effectiveness. Olympia, WA: Washington State Institute for Public Policy. Retrieved May 30, 2014 from www.wsipp.wa. gov/rptfiles/WhatWorksJuv.pdf.

Aos, S., Phipps, P., Barnoski, R., and Roxanne, L. (1999, May). The comparative cost and benefits of programs to reduce crime (4.0). Olympia, WA: Washington State Institute for Public Policy. Retrieved May 30, 2014 from http://www. wsipp.wa.gov/pub.asp?docid=01-05-1201.

Borduin, C. M., Cone, L. T., Mann, B. J., Henggeler, S. W., Fucci, B. R., Blaske, D. M., and Williams, R. A. (1995). Multisystemic treatment of serious juvenile offenders: Long-term prevention of criminality and violence. *Journal of Consulting and Clinical Psychology, 63*(4), 569–578. doi: 10.1037/0022-006x.63.4.569.

Borduin, C. M., and Henggeler, S. W. (1982). Psychosocial development of father-absent children. In S.W. Henggeler (ed.), *Delinquency and adolescent psychopathology: A family-ecological systems approach* (pp. 63–98). Littleton, MA: John Wright-PSG Publishers Inc.

Borduin, C. M., Henggeler, S. W., Blaske, D. M., and Stein, R. J. (1990). Multisystemic treatment of adolescent sexual offenders. *International Journal of Offender Therapy and Comparative Criminology, 34*(2), 105–113. doi: 10.1177/0306624x9003400204.

Borduin, C. M., Schaeffer, C. M., and Heiblum, N. (2009). A randomized clinical trial of Multisystemic Therapy with juvenile sexual offenders: Effects on youth social ecology and criminal activity. *Journal of Consulting and Clinical Psychology, 77*(1), 26–37. doi: 10.1037/a0013035.

Boyd-Franklin, N. (1989). *Black families in therapy: A multi-systems approach.* New York: Guilford Press.

Boyd-Franklin, N. (2003). *Black families in therapy: Understanding the African American experience* (2nd edn). New York: Guilford Press.

Bronfenbrenner, U. (1979). Contexts of child-rearing: Problems and prospects. *American Psychologist, 34*(10), 844–850. doi: 10.1037//0003-066x.34.10.844.

Brunk, M., Henggeler, S. W., and Whelan, J. P. (1987). Comparison of Multisystemic Therapy and parent training in the brief treatment of child-abuse and neglect. *Journal of Consulting and Clinical Psychology, 55*(2), 171–178. doi: 10.1037//0022-006x.55.2.171.

Butler, S., Baruch, G., Hickey, N., and Fonagy, P. (2011). A randomized controlled trial of Multisystemic Therapy and a statutory therapeutic intervention for young offenders. *Journal of the American Academy of Child and Adolescent Psychiatry, 50*(12), 1220–1235. doi: 10.1016/j.jaac.2011.09.017.

Curtis, N. M., Ronan, K. R., Heiblum, N., and Crellin, K. (2009). Dissemination and effectiveness of multisystemic treatment in New Zealand: A benchmarking study. *Journal of Family Psychology, 23*(2), 119–129. doi: 10.1037/a0014974.

Ellis, D. A., Frey, M. A., Naar-King, S., Templin, T., Cunningham, P. B., and Cakan, N. (2005). The effects of Multisystemic Therapy on diabetes stress among adolescents with chronically poorly controlled type 1 diabetes: Findings from a randomized, controlled trial. *Pediatrics, 116*(6), e826–e832. doi: 10.1542/peds.2005-0638.

Ellis, D. A., Naar-King, S., Frey, M., Templin, T., Rowland, M., and Greger, N. (2004). Use of Multisystemic Therapy to improve regimen adherence among adolescents with Type 1 diabetes in poor metabolic control: A pilot investigation. *Journal of Clinical Psychology in Medical Settings, 11*(4),315–324.doi:10.1023/B:JOCS.0000045351. 98563.4d.

Ellis, D. A., Naar-King, S., Templin, T., Frey, M. A., and Cunningham, P. B. (2007). Improving health outcomes among youth with poorly controlled type I diabetes: The role of treatment fidelity in a randomized clinical trial of Multisystemic Therapy. *Journal of Family Psychology, 21*(3), 363–371. doi: 10.1037/0893-3200.21.3.363.

Glisson, C., Schoenwald, S. K., Hemmelgarn, A., Green, P., Dukes, D., Armstrong, K. S., and Chapman, J. E. (2010). Randomized trial of MST and ARC in a two-level evidence-based treatment implementation strategy. *Journal of Consulting and Clinical Psychology, 78*(4), 537–550. doi: 10.1037/a0019160.

Henggeler, S. W. (1989). *Delinquency in adolescents.* Newbury Park, CA: Sage Publications.

Henggeler, S. W. (1999). Multisystemic Therapy: An overview of clinical procedures, outcomes, and policy implications. *Child Psychology and Psychiatry Review, 4*(1), 2–10.

Henggeler, S.W. (2011a). Efficacy studies to large-scale transport: The development and validation of Multisystemic Therapy programs. *Annual Review of Clinical Psychology, 7*, 351–381.

Henggeler, S.W. (2011b). Multisystemic Therapy (MST) for treating adolescent antisocial behavior: The journey from efficacy research to international transport. *Child and Adolescent Mental Health, 16*, 18–18.

Henggeler, S. W., Halliday-Boykins, C. A., Cunningham, P. B., Randall, J., and Shapiro, S. B. (2006). Juvenile drug court: Enhancing outcomes by integrating evidence-based treatments. *Journal of Consulting and Clinical Psychology, 74*(1),42–54.doi:10.1037/0022-006x.74.1.42.

Henggeler, S.W., Melton, G. B., Brondino, M. J., Scherer, D. G., and Hanley, J. H. (1997). Multisystemic Therapy with violent and chronic juvenile offenders and their families: The role of treatment fidelity in successful dissemination. *Journal of Consulting and Clinical Psychology, 65*(5), 821–833.

Henggeler, S. W., Melton, G. B., and Smith, L. A. (1992). Family preservation using Multisystemic Therapy: An effective alternative to incarcerating serious juvenile offenders. *Journal of Consulting and Clinical Psychology, 60*(6), 953–961. doi: 10.1037/0022-006x.60.6.953.

Henggeler, S. W., Pickrel, S. G., and Brondino, M. J. (1999). Multisystemic treatment of substance-abusing and dependent delinquents: Outcomes, treatment fidelity, and transportability. *Mental Health Services Research, 1*(3), 171–184. doi: 10.1023/a:1022373813261.

Henggeler, S.W., Rodick, J. D., Hanson, C. L., Watson, S. M., Borduin, C. M., and Urey, J. R. (1986). Multisystemic treatment of juvenile offenders: Effects on adolescent behavior and family interaction. *Developmental Psychology, 22*(1), 132–141. doi: 10.1037/0012-1649.22.1.132.

Henggeler, S. W., Rowland, M. D., Randall, J., Ward, D. M., Pickrel, S. G., Cunningham, P. B., ... and Santos, A. B. (1999). Home-based Multisystemic Therapy as an alternative to the hospitalization of youths in psychiatric crisis: Clinical outcomes. *Journal of the American Academy of Child and Adolescent Psychiatry, 38*(11), 1331–1339. doi: 10.1097/00004583-199911000-00006.

Henggeler, S. W., Schoenwald, S. K., Borduin, C. M., Rowland, M. D., and Cunningham, P. B. (1998). *Multisystemic treatment for antisocial behavior in children and adolescents.* New York: Guilford Press.

Henggeler, S. W., Schoenwald, S. K., Borduin, C. M., Rowland, M. D., and Cunningham, P. B. (2009). *Multisystemic Therapy for antisocial behavior in children and adolescents* (2nd edn). New York: Guilford Press.

Hennessy, K. D. (2010). Quality improvement. In B. L. Levin, K. D. Hennessy, and J. Petrila (eds), *Mental health services: A public health perspective* (3rd edn). Oxford: Oxford University Press.

Huey, S. J., Henggeler, S. W., Brondino, M. J., and Pickrel, S. G. (2000). Mechanisms of change in Multisystemic Therapy: Reducing delinquent behavior through therapist adherence and improved family and peer functioning. *Journal of Consulting and Clinical Psychology, 68*(3), 451–467. doi: 10.1037//0022-006x.68.3.451.

Klietz, S. J., Borduin, C. M., and Schaeffer, C. M. (2010). Cost-benefit analysis of Multisystemic Therapy with serious and violent juvenile offenders. *Journal of Family Psychology, 24*(5), 657–666. doi: 10.1037/a0020838.

Letourneau, E. J., Henggeler, S. W., Borduin, C. A., Schewe, P. A., McCart, M. R., Chapman, J. E., and Saldana, L. (2009). Multisystemic Therapy for juvenile sexual offenders: 1-year results from a randomized effectiveness trial. *Journal of Family Psychology, 23*(1), 89–102. doi: 10.1037/a0014352.

Madsen, W. (1999). *Collaborative therapy with multi-stressed families.* London: Guilford Press.

Naar-King, S., Ellis, D., Kolmodin, K., Cunningham, P., Jen, K. L. C., Saelens, B., and Brogan, K. (2009). A randomized pilot study of Multisystemic Therapy targeting obesity in African-American adolescents. *Journal of Adolescent Health, 45*(4), 417–419. doi: 10.1016/j.jadohealth.2009.03.022.

Norcross, J. C., and Wampold, B. E. (2011). Evidence-based therapy relationships: Research conclusions and clinical practices. *Psychotherapy, 48*(1), 98–102. doi: 10.1037/a0022161.

Ogden, T., Hagen, K. A., and Anderson, O. (2007). Sustainability of the effectiveness of a programme of multisystemic treatment (MST) across participant groups in the second year of operation. *Journal of Child Services, 2*, 4–14.

Ogden, T., and Halliday-Boykens, C. A. (2004). Multisystemic treatment of antisocial adolescents in Norway: Replication of clinical outcomes outside of the US. *Child and Adolescent Mental Health, 9*, 77–83.

Patterson, G. R. (1982). *Coercive family process.* Eugene, OR: Castalia.

Rapp, C. A., Saleebey, D., and Sullivan, W. P. (2005). The future of strengths-based social work. *Advances in Social Work, 6*(1), 79–90.

Rowland, M. D., Halliday-Boykins, C. A., Henggeler, S. W., Cunningham, P. B., Lee, T. G., Kruesi, M. J. P., and Shapiro, S. B. (2005). A randomized trial of Multisystemic Therapy with Hawaii's Felix Class youths. *Journal of Emotional and Behavioral Disorders, 13*(1), 13–23. doi: 10.1177/10634266050130010201.

Sawyer, A. M., and Bourduin, C. M. (2011). Effects of Multisystemic Therapy through midlife: A 21.9-year follow-up to a randomized clinical trial with serious and violent juvenile offenders. *Journal of Consulting and Clinical Psychology, 79*(5), 643–652.

Stambaugh, L. F., Mustillo, S. A., Burns, B. J., Stephens, R. L., Baxter, B., Edwards, D., and DeKraai, M. (2007). Outcomes from wraparound and Multisystemic Therapy in a Center for Mental Health Services system-of-care demonstration site. *Journal of Emotional and Behavioral Disorders, 15*(3), 143–155.

Sundell, K., Lofholm, C. A., Gustle, L. H., Hansson, K., Olsson, T., and Kadesjo, C. (2008). The transportability of Multisystemic Therapy to Sweden: Short-term results from a randomized trial of conduct-disordered youths. *Journal of Family Psychology, 22*(4), 550–560. doi: 10.1037/0012790.

Swenson, C. C., Henggeler, S. W., Taylor, I. S., and Addison, O. W. (2005). *Multisystemic Therapy and neighborhood partnerships.* New York: Guilford Press.

Swenson, C. C., Schaeffer, C. M., Henggeler, S. W., Faldowski, R., and Mayhew, A. M. (2010). Multisystemic Therapy for child abuse and neglect: A randomized effectiveness trial. *Journal of Family Psychology, 24*(4), 497–507. doi: 10.1037/a0020324.

Timmons-Mitchell, J., Bender, M. B., Kishna, M. A., and Mitchell, C. C. (2006). An independent effectiveness trial of Multisystemic Therapy with juvenile justice youth. *Journal of Clinical Child and Adolescent Psychology, 35*(2), 227–236. doi: 10.1207/s15374424jccp3502_6.

Walsh, F. (2002). A family resilience framework: Innovative practice applications. *Family Relations, 51*(2), 130–137. doi: 10.1111/j.1741-3729.2002.00130.x.

Walsh, F. (2003). Family resilience: A framework for clinical practice. *Family Process, 42*, 1–18.

20

Risk and Resilience among Latino Immigrant Families

Implications for Community-Based Programs of Services and Cultural Adaptation Research

José Rubén Parra-Cardona, Sara Lappan, Ana Rocío Escobar-Chew, and Michael Whitehead

Latinos have become the largest ethnic minority group in the United States, yet immigrant families face many challenges such as economic hardship, discrimination, and unhealthy working conditions. The "Latino paradox," whereby foreign-born Latinos report better physical and mental health than their US-born counterparts, is indicative of how cultural practices and a positive migration outlook (i.e., gratitude for life in the United States in comparison to even worse living conditions in the family's home country) may be protective factors for Latino immigrant families. In Chapter 20 we see how collaborative parenting interventions that engage the community and capitalize on existing family strengths such as cultural identity and close-knit family values are effective.

Although the United States is a nation of immigrants, we have witnessed in recent years an intense debate focused on Latino immigration.[1] Regardless of personal positions on this issue, Latinos have become the largest ethnic minority group in the United States and the vast majority of children in Latino immigrant families are US citizens by birth (US Census Bureau, 2010). Thus, a pressing challenge for the nation refers to the urgent need to address the health and mental health needs of this young generation. Unfortunately, a large proportion of US Latino children and youth continue to experience intense health disparities as they do not have access to services aimed at ensuring their well-being (Alegría *et al.*, 2008).

This chapter is divided into two major sections. First, we will talk about Latino immigrants in the United States, reflect on their most pressing needs, their history of migration to the United States, and their most relevant life experiences as immigrants. In the second half of the chapter, we will present an alternative to address their mental health needs by describing a case example of a services-research

Family Problems: Stress, Risk, and Resilience, First Edition. Edited by Joyce A. Arditti.

model aimed at supporting their parenting efforts. For clarity, we consider a *services-research model* to be any approach aimed at integrating research methodologies and the provision of direct services with "real-world" utility and impact (Garland, Hurlburt, and Hawley, 2006).

Latino Immigrants in the United States

Latinos have become the largest ethnic minority group in the United States (US Census Bureau, 2010). However, Latino immigrants are exposed to multiple and intense contextual challenges such as limited access to social services, work exploitation, inadequate health and mental health care, racial discrimination, and cultural challenges (Flores *et al.*, 2002; Suárez-Orozco, Yoshikawa, Teranishi, and Suárez-Orozco, 2011).

Much remains to be done to effectively address the multiple needs of this population. For example, once Latino children transition into adolescence, they are more likely to experience suicidal thoughts, depression, anxiety, and school drop-out than their Euro-American counterparts (Kataoka, Zhang, and Wells, 2002). Latino youth are also overrepresented among drug abusing and delinquent adolescents in the United States (Pantin, Schwartz, Sullivan,

Coatsworth, and Szapocznik, 2003). Furthermore, Latino families face considerable challenges in accessing culturally relevant mental health interventions (Flores *et al.*, 2002). Thus, there is a great need to effectively overcome the multiple barriers that prevent Latino immigrants from accessing culturally relevant health and mental health services aimed at enhancing their quality of life (Castro *et al.*, 2006; Suárez-Orozco *et al.*, 2011).

Historical Understanding of Latino Immigration

Historically, the US government has modified its immigration policies according to national priorities (see Box 20.1). Specifically, in times of economic expansion, the United States government has set in motion aggressive initiatives to encourage Latino immigration. When facing austerity and limited economic growth, immigration policies have become restrictive (Akers Chacón and Davis, 2006). For example, as a result of the US involvement in World War II, the "Bracero [manual laborer] program" was strongly promoted to address the intense need for economic expansion. Although the program started in the early 1940s by offering work visas to Mexican agricultural workers, the program soon spread to alternative areas of the economy such as railroads and

Box 20.1   Historical Milestones of Latino Immigration

Time period	Milestone
World War II (1940s)	Bracero program was initiated, strongly fostering immigration based on US economic needs.
1940–1963	Bracero program was consistently renewed and expanded to cover workforce needs in railroad and construction industries.
1964	Bracero program ended due to a diminished need to support critical areas of the economy (e.g., agriculture, railroad, construction).
1986	The Immigration Reform and Control Act made immigrants who entered the United States before 1982 eligible for legalization.
1986–present	Immigration policies became considerably stringent towards Latin American immigrants, particularly by increasing security at the Mexican border.

construction. Based on active demands from US employers, the Bracero program was consistently renewed until 1963.

Through this program, thousands of Latino immigrants were actively recruited by the US government from the 1940s to address key economic challenges facing the nation. The Bracero program became essential for US economic prosperity as it provided a much-needed labor supply for multiple agricultural needs. As the nation experienced the need to expand infrastructure, braceros were also recruited as railroad workers.

Unfortunately, the historical and active role of the US government in generating an intense and long-term program of immigration, which did not contemplate clear paths to achieve permanent citizenship, is rarely addressed in current immigration debates. Thus, during times of economic crisis and austerity, undocumented Latinos are often portrayed as individuals willing to violate the law and abuse US economic resources (González and Price, 2010). Such a depiction overlooks the past and current critical economic contributions that Latino immigrants offer to the US. For example, approximately one in three Latino immigrant workers in the food service industry are cooks, compared to one in seven US-born workers (National Council of La Raza (NCLR), 2013). Thus, during times of economic expansion, Latino immigrants are used, but overlooked by not recognizing their critical contributions to the country. In times of economic crisis, Latino immigrants become unique targets with public discourses commonly portraying them as a burden to the US economy or a threat to national security (Buchanan, 2006; Hayworth and Eule, 2006; Krikorian, 2008; Wucker, 2006).

Latino immigration in the United States also needs to be analyzed by examining the significant "push" factors that Latinos are likely to experience in their countries of origin. It is well documented that several Latin American countries are still affected by unstable democracies and economies, weak law enforcement systems, and corruption in the government and private sectors (Dodson and Jackson, 2004). Civil wars in some Latin American countries have also led to intense poverty and totalitarian regimes (Butler, 2003). These historical challenges continue to place a considerable percentage of the Latin American population in extreme hardship due to extreme poverty and inability to meet their basic needs (Hoffman and Centeno, 2003). Thus, a primary motivation for low-income Latino families to leave their home countries refers to their desire to increase their overall quality of life (Parra-Cardona, Cordova, Holtrop, Villarruel, and Wieling, 2008).

Understanding the Life Experiences of Latino Immigrants in the United States: Risk and Protective Factors

In this section, we discuss risk and protective factors that impact the lives of Latino parents. We focus on parents, as the focus of our work is helping Latino immigrants with their parenting practices. Thus, we provide relevant examples of risk and protective factors by giving voice to participants from our research projects. We consider that their voices are the best way to "bring to life" and communicate the variety of challenges that negatively impact their lives, as well as their testimonies of success in the face of adversity.

Risk factors

Lack of recognition of within-group diversity
There is a permanent risk for service and mental health professionals to overlook the wide heterogeneity associated with Latino cultural groups (Cardemil, 2008). That is, professionals may consider that all Latinos are alike and share the same cultural values and traditions, whereas in reality, different Latino subgroups vary extensively with regard to contextual and cultural experiences. According to the US Census (US Census Bureau, 2010), 63% of Latino immigrants in the United States reported Mexican origins, 9.2% Puerto Rican, 3.5% Cuban, 3.3% Salvadoran, 2.8% Dominican, 2.1% Guatemalan, 1.8% Colombian, and the remainder identified various regions of Central and South America. Identifying differences among various Latino sub-groups is of critical importance. For example, Puerto Ricans enjoy the benefits of US citizenship, whereas Latinos from Mexico, Central, and South America may be exposed to intense

challenges when interacting with the immigration system if their goal is to permanently reside in the United States. In contrast, Puerto Ricans may experience cultural identity challenges that Latin Americans may not face due to the historical challenges between Puerto Rico and the United States Continental government.

Because there is a critical need to avoid considering "that all Latinos are the same," service providers must constantly investigate the specific cultural and life experiences that have impacted the lives of their Latino clients.

Racism and discrimination

Exposure to racism and discrimination constitutes a particularly dramatic experience with deleterious physical and mental health effects, as well as negative effects on personal and intimate relationships (Falicov, 2007). Although these challenges affect all Latinos, they are particularly detrimental to foreign-born Latinos as this sub-group may experience unique barriers to cope with discrimination such as significant language barriers, limited social support networks, and pending documentation status (Parra-Cardona et al., 2008). The negative effects of discrimination are well expressed by a Latino father who described how powerless he felt when he was being discriminated against: "Discrimination is a bitter drink that you need to swallow ... you have to swallow it ... because you say 'If I get rebellious or do not behave, they can throw me into jail' ... So, you just have to swallow that drink" (Parra-Cardona et al., 2008, p. 163).

Poverty and economic barriers

The 2011 median income of US Latino households was $38,624 compared to the national median income of $50,054. The poverty rate among Latinos in 2010 was 26.6%, an increase from 25.3% in 2009 (US Census Bureau, 2012). Approximately 21% of children in immigrant families live in poverty, compared to 14% in US-born families (Greenberg et al., 2004). Hardship is also more pronounced for children of immigrant families than for children of US natives, as it involves limited access to adequate nutrition, housing, and healthcare (Edberg, Cleary, and Vyas, 2010).

We constantly face this challenging reality with the Latino immigrant families we serve in Detroit. Sadly,

although the average number of children in these families is two, their average annual family income ranges from $20,000 to $22,000. These figures impose dramatic challenges on families and parents as they have to make extraordinary efforts to make ends meet (Parra-Cardona et al., 2008). Unfortunately, fighting adversity ends up negatively impacting whole families, as one father affirmed: "You get home and you just want to sleep ... we feel frustrated for feeling so tired ... and we give our kids the worst moment of the day because we are so frustrated because of work" (p. 164). One mother also reported with sadness: "I lost many years of my children because I had to work at night ... I saw my daughter very little when she was small ... Because of work, I lost a lot of years of seeing my children grow up" (p. 164).

Educational barriers

Latino youth by far have the highest school drop-out rate in the nation (29%), compared to Blacks (13%) and non-Latino Whites (7%). Furthermore, educational achievement is low among Latinos, as only 13% of Latinos 25 years of age and older achieved a high school degree by 2010, and only 6.2% were enrolled as full-time college students (US Census Bureau, 2012). Educational disparities particularly affect Latino immigrants, as they are exposed to increased barriers such as language difficulties and intense poverty (Flores et al., 2002).

Health and mental health disparities

Latinos born in Latin America tend to have better health than US-born Latinos, a phenomenon known as the Latino health paradox. It is hypothesized that their better health has to do with the fact that Latino immigrants arrive in the United States with health practices that contrast with habits and practices of Latinos in the United States. However, whenever Latino immigrants experience health problems, they are very likely to face significant barriers to access to health and mental health care services such as long waiting times, decreased preventive screening, and lack of health care insurance (Cummings, Wen, and Druss, 2011; Flores et al., 2002). Latinos are also the least likely ethnic minority group in the United States to have health insurance (Cubanski, Huang, Damico, Jacobson, and Neuman, 2010). With regard to mental health disparities, Latinos report a lower risk of having a psychiatric disorder compared to Euro-Americans, but those who develop a mental health problem tend to have more persistent and severe symptoms, as well as greater disability (US Census Bureau, 2012).

Furthermore, several reports indicate that Latino immigrants engaged in occupations avoided by US citizens are exposed to dangerous occupational hazards that put their health at risk. As one Latina migrant worker in one of our studies explained: "our boss would spray something on the field that made you have headaches ... Once, my brother told him 'Stop, it's making us feel sick' and he said, 'It doesn't hurt you ... If it would hurt you, I wouldn't be spraying'" (Parra-Cardona, Bulock, Imig, Villarruel, and Gold, 2006, p. 369).

Language

Language barriers can constitute a considerable challenge for Latinos because English proficiency is associated with higher wages and occupational status (Sorenson, 1988). In addition, immigrants who are not English-proficient are restricted to health and mental health providers who offer services in Spanish. This constitutes a significant risk factor that can lead to failure to engage with health and mental health services, particularly if providers are not perceived as culturally competent and trustworthy by Latino clients (Eggerth and Flynn, 2010).

Work exploitation

Latino immigrants are at high risk of being exposed to exploitative working conditions, particularly if they lack documented immigration status (Dalla and Christensen, 2005). For example, Latino agricultural workers have provided detailed narratives of long working hours, poor housing conditions, and exposure to dangerous pesticides (Parra-Cardona et al., 2006). In other areas such as construction, landscaping, and meat packaging, studies have documented extensive work shifts, lack of insurance for work-related accidents, limited job training, and poor quality of working conditions (e.g., Dalla and Christensen, 2005). A Latina immigrant mother reflected on the work exploitation she has witnessed in food processing plants: "there have been times that they treat [Latino workers] bad ... they leave them without a

break up to eight hours ... I think they treat Americans different" (Parra-Cardona et al., 2006, p. 369).

Transnational experience

Immigration often demands that Latinos leave behind loved ones in their home countries, as relocating with family members is not feasible. Thus, Latino immigrants are likely to experience significant losses associated with their immigration experience. These families are identified by scholars as *transnational families* (Falicov, 2007). Symptoms associated with the process of immigration and separation can include depression, anxiety, psychosomatic illnesses, and addictions (Falicov, 1998).

The transnational experience has also promoted a shift with regard to cultural expectations among immigrants. For example, whereas cultural expectations have historically identified Latino men as the leaders of the immigration experience, Latina women have increasingly taken on this role and often have done so by leaving family members behind. This shift has brought about important challenges with regard to how best support transnational families. For example, in addition to having to endure intense significant risks to their personal safety during the process of relocation (e.g., increased risk for abduction, rape), immigrant women with pending documentation are also highly likely to experience abuse and exploitation in a variety of US contexts without feeling empowered to reach out for help (e.g., sexual harassment in the workplace, domestic violence by a partner who holds documented immigrant status).

Cultural challenges

Assimilation perspectives refer to belief systems holding that immigrant groups must fully assimilate into the mainstream host society even if it is at the expense of their cultural identities. For example, some critics have proposed that immigrants should abandon their cultural identities by fully assimilating into US society and culture, as Huntington (2004) affirms: "[T]he central issue is not immigration but immigration with or without assimilation. To what extent will these immigrants, their successors, and descendants follow the path of earlier immigrants and be successfully assimilated into American society and culture?" (p. 178). This perspective considers that immigrants must relinquish any type of language, cultural values, and traditions that are not considered "American." Thus, assimilation pressures demand that cultural differences must be diminished, and ideally eliminated, in order to maintain a homogeneous society (Huntington, 2004; Lorenzo-Hernandez, 1998).

Several studies have confirmed the negative effects resulting from a pressure to assimilate (Schwartz, Unger, Zamboanga, and Szapocznik, 2010). Specifically, Latino immigrants can experience intense challenges as they strive to define their cultural identity, a process known as *acculturative stress* (Finch, Hummer, Kolody, and Vega, 2001). In fact, acculturative stress has been associated with serious physical and mental health problems (Finch *et al.*, 2001).

Protective factors

Cultural values and traditions

Culture constitutes a powerful resource to cope with adversity, particularly as it refers to relevant Latino cultural values and traditions. For example, *familismo* (familism) is a Latino value that emphasizes the importance of being rooted in family life and unity (Falicov, 1998). *Colectivismo* (collectivism) refers to having a strong sense of orientation toward others, including the importance of experiencing life as a member of a reference group rather than living in isolation. Closely related, *personalismo* (personalism) highlights the importance of establishing meaningful interpersonal relationships in a variety of social contexts. *Respeto* (respect) denotes the importance of informing interpersonal relationships according to deference and consideration toward others (Falicov, 1998).

Some studies have explored the influence of cultural values on health and mental health outcomes. For example, *familismo* (i.e., the emphasis on family unity) has been found to have a strong protective effective against external stressors (Hovey and King, 1996; Rivera *et al.*, 2008; Sabogal, Marin, and Otero-Sabogal, 1987). The importance of a strong family orientation was highlighted by a Latina mother as she reflected on her expectations for parenting programs: "In Latin American countries, there is a lot of love for the family.... For these groups [parenting groups], first focus on the family and the importance of having a healthy family (Parra-Cardona *et al.*, 2009, p. 222).

Resilience and the Latino paradox

Resilience refers to the capacity to overcome challenges and rebound from adversity strengthened and more resourceful (Walsh, 2003). According to Walsh, resilience can be embraced whenever families adapt their belief systems in order to make meaning of adversity. For example, recent Latino immigrants are likely to report that life in the United States offers a level of stability and safety that they cannot experience in their countries of origin (e.g., better incomes, education, lower levels of community violence). Our work with Latino migrant workers has confirmed this premise. As one Latina woman stated: "I got in the United States more than other people, who don't have a life. I got a place to live, and somebody else doesn't have a place" (Parra-Cardona *et al.*, 2006, p. 368).

These findings are consistent with the "Latino immigrant paradox," which refers to the fact that foreign-born Latinos report higher levels of health and mental health than US-born individuals (Alegría *et al.*, 2008). According to social comparison theories (Campbell, Garcia, Granillo, and Chavez, 2012), the Latino paradox can be explained because individuals make comparisons with respect to existing social structures and tend to place themselves along specific points of a continuum (e.g., low vs. high SES). Thus, Latino immigrants who have been exposed to intense poverty and hardship in their countries of origin may experience challenges in the United States to be more tolerable than the extraordinary stressors experienced in their home countries (Campbell *et al.*, 2012). A migrant worker illustrates this theory as she explained her motivation to bring her family to the United States: "[L]ife is very hard in Mexico ... here there is work ... the children study ... there's something to eat ... to live" (Parra-Cardona *et al.*, 2006, p. 368).

Spirituality and religion

Several researchers agree about the critical influence that spirituality and religion have in the lives of Latino immigrants (Elizondo, 1994; Hilton, Gonzalez, Saleh, Maitoza, and Anngela-Cole, 2012). Scholars have stated that despite centuries of oppression and exploitation dating back to the European invasion of Indian territories, Latino history consistently shows the ways in which spirituality has been critical for Latinos as they have overcome adversity (Bartolome, 1997). For instance, in a qualitative study with Latino community organizers, Garrido (2009) found that the experience of communal suffering served as a "catalyst for spiritual growth which challenged the participants to rethink their own personal spirituality" (p. 82). Thus, it is critical to remain aware that the spiritual experience for Latinos is not only restricted to individual religious practices but, most importantly, it constitutes a powerful source for creating a sense of community and meaning-making in the face of adversity (Garrido, 2009).

Implications for Community-Based Programs: A Model of Services Research with a Cultural Adaptation Focus

The identification of salient risk and protective factors constitutes a critical step before engaging in programs of services research with underserved Latino immigrant populations, as barriers must be clearly identified and resources fully utilized. In what follows we describe how a model of services research with a cultural adaptation focus has guided our work by remaining attentive to specific risk and protective factors that we identified in the city of Detroit, Michigan.

Figure 20.1 describes a proposed model for implementing community-based programs of services research with Latino populations. We emphasize the term *services research* as scholars highlight the need to empirically examine the impact of delivering interventions (Southam-Gerow, Ringeisen, and Sherrill, 2006). That is, programs can offer multiple and highly relevant benefits to communities, but the impact of programs can be lost if indicators of success are not adequately identified and measured. For illustrative purposes, we provide examples of how the proposed model has informed our community-based work with Latino immigrants. However, this model should be used only as a case example and specific adaptations must be made when applying these concepts with Latino populations in various contexts.

Engaging the community

According to Community-Based Participatory Research (CBPR) principles, active community involvement is essential in the processes that shape the design and implementation of applied research

Figure 20.1 Proposed model of services research.

(Fielden *et al.*, 2007). Thus, the identification of community health and mental health problems should result from a participatory process between researchers and key members of the community (O'Fallon and Dearry, 2002). Participatory approaches have been found to be effective in research with diverse populations because there is an emphasis on collaborating with community members to identify the stressors that affect their lives (Kumpfer, Alvarado, Smith, and Bellamy, 2002; Pantin *et al.*, 2003).

Thus, the initial step of our proposed model consists of engaging community leaders and members of the targeted community. In our program of applied research, we initiated contact with leaders of key mental health, health, and religious organizations in Detroit. Once we learned from them about the history of the Latino community in this context, we invited them to establish with us a collaborative relationship aimed at supporting their efforts and meeting pressing needs of the community. We also communicated to them the importance of monitoring the impact of our work through a rigorous research protocol. However, the design of this protocol had to be produced through the joint collaboration of community members, organizational leaders, and researchers.

Learning from community members

In order to fully embrace collaboration, an initial step consisted of conducting a large qualitative study with 83 Latino parents from Detroit to learn about their life experiences and parenting needs. Table 20.1 summarizes the findings from this investigation (see Parra-Cardona *et al.*, 2008, 2009). In summary, we learned about the intense struggles and contextual challenges that Latino immigrants have experienced in Detroit, such as work exploitation, social isolation, community violence, and, most recently, a strong anti-immigration climate. In consonance with the Latino paradox, we also learned that the vast majority of parents reported that these challenges were much more manageable compared to the intense challenges that they experienced in their countries of origin.

We also learned that although parents were highly committed to their parenting efforts, many of them did not have a model of effective parenting (Parra-Cardona *et al.*, 2009), particularly if they were exposed only to harsh models of parenting in their families of origin. When we presented to Latino parents the possibility of offering a community-based parenting program aimed at supporting their parenting needs, the vast majority of participants reacted with high enthusiasm.

Learning directly from Latino parents about their parenting challenges and aspirations was critical for two main reasons. First, we confirmed, as community leaders have previously reported to us, the high need for a community-based parenting program aimed at supporting their parenting efforts. Second, the information provided by parents helped us to adapt the intervention in ways that was culturally relevant to them.

Designing programs according to risk and protective factors

Risk factors

Having confirmed with community members their strong desire to participate in a parenting program, we proceeded to evaluate how risk and protective factors in this community should inform our work.

We first became aware that we did not face a situation of extreme within-group diversity as 98% of parents in our sample are of Mexican origin. However, this required ensuring that the intervention was culturally relevant to the few parents born in Central American countries. Furthermore, the decision to focus on Spanish-speaking Latino immigrants as the target population resulted from considering that it was critical to first achieve success on a parenting project with this Latino sub-group, prior to extending our efforts to additional Latino sub-populations such as US-born Latinos. We also confirmed that Latino immigrants in Detroit are exposed to several risk factors, such as extensive working hours, poverty, and educational barriers. These barriers demanded from us to carefully design our intervention procedures accordingly in order to make sure we supported parents willing to attend parenting programs. Thus, we realized that we had to offer dinner, child care, and transportation support.

Table 20.1 Life experiences and parenting needs

	Shared ancestry study (Parra-Cardona et al., 2008)			Queremos aprender (We want to learn) study (Parra-Cardona et al., 2009)	
Sample size	64 participants: 44 female (24 foreign-born; 20 US-born); 20 male (12 foreign-born; 8 US-born)			83 participants: 64 female and 19 male (all foreign-born, first-generation immigrants)	
Brief description of sample	Participants identified as Latino or Hispanic and had a child between the ages of 3 and 17 years. Immigrant parents reported an average of 2.4 years living in the United States			Breakdown of country of origin: Mexico, 60; Cuba, 7; Colombia, 4; Costa Rica, 3; Guatemala, 3; Honduras, 2; Nicaragua, 2; El Salvador, 2	
Major findings	Coding category	Foreign-born parents	US-born parents	Coding category	Findings
	Being a good parent	Both groups concurred that being a parent constitutes one of their most central life commitments as well as a very important source of satisfaction. Contextual challenges affect parenting efforts		"We want to learn, but don't offer White parenting classes"	Want culturally relevant parenting interventions where educators are respectful and collaborative
	Adversity and discrimination	Examples: language barriers, exposure to long and stressful working conditions, lack of familiarity with the school and social service systems, and fear of immigration authorities	Perceive that Latinos continue to be excluded from service provision, experience discriminatory practices in the workplace, or are treated based on stereotypes and preconceptions	"Instilling values in children"	Would like parenting interventions that are based on an awareness of relevant Latino cultural values
	Latino cultural values	Importance of adhering to traditional Latino cultural values	Emphasized the importance of transmitting to their children cultural values associated with the importance of respect toward others, as well as the importance of family life and a supportive community	"My kid tells me she's calling 911"	Being able to implement effective discipline with their children is a major parenting goal. They want parenting classes based on the awareness of cultural challenges that influence implementation of parenting practices
	Gender roles	The participants' descriptions of gender roles indicated traditional expectations about the roles that mothers and fathers should have	More likely to report that they inform their lives based on egalitarian gender roles	"How can we protect our kids from drugs?"	Parents expressed fear and concern over the possibility that their children might engage in alcohol and drug use at an early age
	Testimonies of resilience	Ways in which they have been able to adapt after their relocation to the United States, as well as the strategies used to cope with contextual challenges	Ways in which parents perceived life challenges as an opportunity to create a better legacy for their children and to offer them opportunities they did not have	"Learning and helping each other"	Parents expressed the importance of facilitating learning experiences by promoting a sense of community with group participants

We also implemented parenting groups in community settings preferred by participants, as ensuring easy access and safety is essential. With regard to cultural challenges, parents reported cultural differences with their US-born adolescent children as particularly challenging. Although we recognized that families with adolescent children present the most critical need for help, we were also aware that because this was our first project in the community, we had to achieve success and learn from our mistakes. Thus, we decided to first focus on families with young children (ages 4–11) as we needed to gain experience in delivering a comprehensive parenting program with a population that is not likely to present intense parenting challenges. After achieving success with this population, we are now seeking funding to implement a program of applied services research focused on Latino families with middle-school children, as this population is likely to present more complex challenges such as premature sex, gang involvement, and substance use/abuse (Prado *et al.*, 2009).

Protective factors
Participants in our qualitative studies strongly confirmed the critical importance that culture has in their lives. For example, the desire to strongly promote *family unity* (i.e., *familismo*) was consistently reported by parents as a main motivator to engage in parenting interventions. We also confirmed that *respeto* constitutes an important cultural value that parents would like to see reflected in parenting interventions. Specifically, parents reported their desire to be in a parenting program that would help them with strategies to teach their children how to be respectful of others, without having to rely on harsh parenting practices to achieve this goal.

In concordance with the Latino paradox, we have confirmed with parents in our program that despite exposure to intense contextual challenges, Latino immigrant parents constantly refer to quality of life in the United States as significantly better than in their home countries. We have used this perception of better life in the United States as a motivator in our parenting groups by inviting parents to reflect about the type of activities they can do as a family that they could not experience in their home countries (e.g., small vacations, camping trips, etc.).

Finally, because we have witnessed the key role that spirituality and religion have in the lives of parents in our studies, our main intervention delivery site is the building of a major religious organization in Detroit that is highly trusted by Latino residents. In addition, in the initial sessions we invite parents to reflect on the meaning of parenthood, and they have frequently reflected on this issue by making reference to spiritual interpretations of what constitutes being a good parent.

Culturally adapting the intervention

Having engaged with communities and identified salient risk and protective factors, our work shifted towards culturally adapting an existing parenting intervention to make it attractive and culturally relevant to the target population. Specifically, cultural adaptation refers to "the systematic modification of an evidence-based treatment (EBT) or intervention protocol to consider language, culture, and context in such a way that is compatible with the client's cultural patterns, meaning, and values" (Bernal, Jimenez-Chafey, and Domenech Rodríguez, 2009, p. 362). In our program of services research, we have focused on culturally adapting the evidence-based parenting intervention known as *Parent Management Training, the Oregon Model* (PMTO™). We selected this intervention for two main reasons. First, the PMTO long-term intervention effects have been documented in a prevention trial extending over a nine-year follow-up period, indicating sustained reductions in child and youth internalizing (e.g., depression, anxiety) and externalizing (e.g., delinquent) behaviors. Second, empirical research with Hispanic families has demonstrated that Latino populations find the PMTO intervention to be responsive to their cultural values and traditions (Domenech Rodríguez, Baumann, and Schwartz, 2011). Adapting an intervention does not only refer to translating it into a specific language or finding people who match the ethnicity of the beneficiaries of the intervention. In contrast, cultural adaptation requires interventionists to consider multiple levels of adaptation in order to make an intervention culturally relevant.

In our program of research, we have followed a theoretical framework known as the *Ecological Validity*

Framework developed by Bernal, Bonilla, and Bellido (1995). This model focuses on eight specific dimensions that are necessary to address in order to produce relevant cultural adaptations for Latinos: (a) language, (b) persons, (c) metaphors, (d) content, (e) concepts, (f) goals, (g) methods, and (h) context.

According to this framework, *language* refers to the importance of delivering interventions in the native language of the target population. Dr. Domenech Rodriguez is a leading Co-Investigator in our Detroit project and the original translation and linguistic refinement of the PMTO manual was conducted by her research team following the tenets of the Ecological Validity Framework. We refer the reader to the original source for a detailed description of this work (Domenech Rodríguez et al., 2011).

The dimension of *persons* refers to the type and quality of the relationship between the recipients of interventions and the professionals who deliver the intervention. In our work, parenting groups are implemented by fully bilingual Latinos who are members of the community they serve. These community members foster a stronger level of trust with participants than university-based students. This is due to the fact that they are members of the target community and, unlike students, they do not rotate off programs after obtaining academic degrees. *Metaphors* refers to the symbols and concepts that are shared by a particular cultural group. For example, we have adapted our manuals according to cultural metaphors in the Latino culture that denote the importance of parents in the lives of children, which is an important cultural value in the Latino culture. The dimension of *content* refers to the cultural knowledge that is communicated as embedded within the original intervention, particularly as it refers to the cultural values, customs, and traditions of a target population. For example, we address with parents the challenges and opportunities resulting from becoming a bicultural family integrated by foreign-born parents and US-born children.

Concepts refers to the theoretical models utilized in a culturally adapted intervention, which should be culturally relevant for the target population. The principles of the PMTO intervention allow us to address this cultural dimension as the intervention

places parents in a position of high influence and authority with regard to their children, which constitutes an important cultural expectation among Latinos. The dimension of *goals* refers to the objectives that are pursued when implementing interventions. In our project, we focus on three major objectives that have high cultural relevance in the Latino culture: (1) helping parents acquire effective parenting skills, (2) increasing family unity and emotional intimacy as a result of parents utilizing effective and non-punitive parenting skills, and (3) supporting families as they navigate challenging cultural experiences, such as learning to cope with immigration and becoming a bicultural family.

Methods refers to ensuring that all characteristics of implementation procedures are culturally relevant and respectful. For instance, we never force parents to participate with verbal contributions in parenting groups as they may have experienced discrimination from previous service providers. In fact, parents have reported that allowing them "to take their time" to become verbally active in groups has been essential for them to trust the parenting groups, as they describe top-down approaches in previous experiences with counselors to be disrespectful. Finally, *context* refers to consideration of economic and social variables that impact a specific population. Because a large proportion of participants in our groups come directly from work to our parenting sessions, offering hot and complete dinners is a top priority in our project.

Implementation

Recruitment of participants

When approaching Latinos for participation in community-based programs, it is essential to do so in a way that trust is promoted, particularly because Latino immigrants tend to fear formal institutions due to potential discrimination (Domenech Rodríguez, Rodríguez, and Davis, 2006). Thus, although traditional forms of participant engagement can be useful (e.g., posting flyers), our experience with low-income Latinos has strongly confirmed that face-to-face recruitment is the most effective strategy. In addition, our high success in recruiting Latinos is related to the fact that most of our face-to-face recruitment is carried out by community members rather than university staff. Our recruitment coordinator is also a Mexican-origin professional who is actively involved in the local Latino community as a community organizer and his reputation and knowledge of the community have been essential to our success.

Evaluation

A program of services research demands rigorous evaluation (Southam-Gerow *et al.*, 2006). Collecting useful data is critical to demonstrate to community stakeholders and funders that the services being offered to the community are relevant and worth supporting in the future. For example, our assessments consists of parental self-reports of child behaviors and behavioral observations of parent–child interactions. These combined data constitute strong evidence for the impact of parenting programs.

We have followed in our work important guidelines for evaluation procedures, as recommended by researchers with expertise with Latino populations (Knight, Roosa, Calderón-Tena, and Gonzales, 2009). First, it is essential to remain aware that as a result of past experiences of discrimination or exploitation, Latino participants may be distrustful of any type of evaluation. Thus, communicating in full detail to participants all evaluation procedures is a top priority. In addition, participants need to be assured that no questions regarding immigration status will be asked and that all raw data will be kept confidential. This is essential, in view of the recent anti-immigration climate experienced in several regions of the United States. Whereas participants need to be assured of protection of their confidentiality, they also need to receive a detailed explanation of situations when confidentiality cannot be maintained such as instances of child or elder abuse.

Finally, researchers must address literacy limitations, particularly if consent forms will be signed. In our project, reading with parents and completing consent forms usually takes 30 minutes if parents are illiterate as we ensure that they understand all sections of consent forms. Thus, a regular assessment session lasting an hour with parents who can read and write can take up to three hours with parents experiencing literacy limitations.

Advocacy

Serving Latino communities carries the responsibility of remaining accountable for supporting Latino families facing unique challenges. Often, interventionists from our team have assisted families with referrals to community resources aimed at helping them address basic needs such as food, job placement, and immigration counseling. Thus, when working with underserved populations it is critical to identify members of the research team who will be capable of engaging in advocacy activities, as it is not sufficient to "refer" participants to adequate services, but, most importantly, it is essential to confirm that Latinos are respected and supported when requesting services and interacting with formal institutions.

Impact of the intervention

By now, you must wonder whether all this preliminary work, adaptations, and planning have a real impact in the everyday lives of our target population. The answer is "Yes!" To date, we have successfully delivered the intervention to approximately 106 families (180 individual parents). Despite the fact that some studies report how "challenging" it is to retain Latinos in parenting programs, 86% of participants in our project completed at least 7 out of 12 parenting sessions, which constitutes a remarkable accomplishment considering the multiple contextual challenges that they experience in their lives. The remaining of parents completed a range of one to five sessions.

In terms of impact, parents have provided very detailed narratives of the benefits they have experienced in our parenting groups. We refer you to the original publication if you are interested in learning more about specific outcomes (see Parra-Cardona *et al.*, 2012), but we summarize below the top three areas in which parents report benefiting the most from the intervention. Although the quotations come from individual parents, the areas of change that we report refer to the consensus of the majority of participants as reported in the final group evaluations.

Recognizing parenting mistakes

In our intervention, we never tell parents "you are doing your parenting wrong." Instead, we communicate to parents, "you are the experts in your family and we will show you a new way of parenting that has been very useful to other parents. In the end, you will decide which parenting skills are best for you." As a result of exposing parents to new parenting techniques, a common reaction we have observed in participants consists of them becoming aware of struggles that they experience when facing specific parenting situations (e.g., losing temper after children ignore their commands). As one parent commented: "I was able to see all the mistakes we make as parents. We were not giving good directions and our children were not responding like we wanted. We also learned how to control our emotions, which is fundamental" (Parra-Cardona et al., 2012, p. 67).

Thus, the first major positive impact that parents commonly report refers to reaching an awareness of deficiencies they had in their parenting style, as another parent affirmed:

> We all want to provide a good upbringing for our children but we were on a wrong path until we came to group and realized what we were doing wrong. Our task as parents is just beginning and we're starting to change the habits we had. We have a big task ahead of us and I believe it will be much better from now on. (Parra-Cardona et al., 2012, p. 68)

This outcome is particularly important when considering that approximately 60% of female children and 47% of male children in Mexico suffer some form of maltreatment (e.g., physical, emotional, etc.) or neglect during their childhood (Secretaría de Seguridad Pública (SSP), 2010). Unfortunately, we have confirmed these strong patterns of punitive parenting in our work with Mexican-born Latino immigrant parents. However, we have also witnessed that the vast majority of participants in our parenting groups achieve highly positive parenting changes if they are offered the help they need.

Improving family relations
Once parents recognize deficiencies in their parenting practices and focus on improving their parenting skills by testing some of the techniques shared in the intervention, they witness gradual positive changes in their family relations. One parent reflected a sentiment commonly reported by group participants: "We have

improved with regards to the quality of time we spend as a family. We are devoting more time to our family and it has had a positive effect on everyone in our family" (Parra-Cardona et al., 2012, p. 68).

In addition to improving the emotional family climate, parents talk about how specific parenting skills helped them achieve a better relationship with their children. For example, a common complaint that parents expressed at the beginning of groups is that "children do not do enough things on their own" or that "children do not follow directions." Thus, the PMTO intervention has specific techniques such as incentive charts through which parents teach children to accomplish big behaviors (e.g., cleaning their room) by breaking them down into small steps (e.g., making their bed, picking up dirty clothes, etc.). As children achieve success with small behaviors, they receive small incentives (e.g., a token) that they can then use in exchange for big rewards (e.g., going out to the park for an extra hour) at the end of the week if they accomplish the more complex behaviors.

Some people mistakenly perceive this parenting practice as a simple token system. It's much more than that, as we help parents coach their children to be successful by helping them develop key skills that they will need in life. In the process, parents and children must work together by strengthening their relationship. Thus, if you picture a parent that constantly yells at his children and spanks them when they don't follow directions, being able to promote this type of change in his parenting practices constitutes a monumental task.

The voice of one parent summarizes the positive changes that participants commonly report in our groups after experiencing this dramatic change in their parenting practices:

> I used to say to my child, "Do this right now!" and I would snap my fingers. Now, I say, "It's five steps you need to do [incentive chart] and you will win two points …" Now, they smile as I motivate them. It's a big difference. Before, they had a sad face because I was yelling all the time. Now, I use motivation and they smile and follow my directions.

Considering that *familismo* and *respeto* are strong cultural values in the Latino culture, these findings are highly relevant because improvement of parenting practices leads to more harmonious family relations, which consequently reinforces critical cultural values focused on family unity.

Implementing discipline with love
Implementing discipline in a caring and firm way is one of the major accomplishments for parents attending our groups. As we mentioned before, many of them were raised with very harsh parenting practices from their parents and, to their dismay, they see themselves repeating these patterns with their own children. Thus, being able to implement discipline in a firm but peaceful way has been one of the most important benefits reported by a vast majority of participants. The following quotation provides a very good description of the sentiment expressed by several parents who have experienced this positive impact of the intervention:

> The way I was educating my children was wrong. How I punished them was not right … It's the behaviors you learned as a kid and the domestic violence and hitting that you experienced with your parents … I have tried very hard not to spank my kids, but you grow up with how your parents treated you … I learned about discipline here and I will offer my kids something that is much better … I'm learning how to control myself now. It's hard but I'm changing. (Parra-Cardona *et al.*, 2012, p. 67)

As we have previously explained, the reduction of punitive parenting practices is highly relevant as Latino immigrants are very likely to have been exposed to various forms of parental abuse or neglect (SSP, 2010), particularly if they were raised in impoverished communities with low literacy. A large proportion of participants in our project were raised in rural Mexico and they have vivid memories of how emotionally distressing it was to be exposed to these types of parenting practices as children. Thus, parents in our groups frequently report how they will keep the beautiful aspects of parenting given to them by their parents, but also replace the deleterious practices with parenting skills that promote harmony, unity, and well-being.

The importance of culture
Finally, parents have strongly communicated to us the importance of culture in their parenting practices.

Once parents have mastered new and effective parenting skills, they have repeatedly reported their desire to address important cultural themes in more depth, such as how to become bicultural families. That is, they recognize that their Latino cultural values and traditions contrast with those that their children learn in school or with friends, which tend to be more oriented toward US culture. Thus, addressing cultural issues in depth constitutes a highly relevant goal for parents, as one mother affirmed:

> I need to get into my child's culture that is outside of our home, the American culture. I need help so I can understand it better. For example, my kid goes to school with many American children and sometimes he comes home with questions about the Americans that my husband and I don't know how to respond. We need to help our kids being in these two cultures [Latino and American cultures]. (Parra-Cardona *et al.*, 2012, p. 68)

A strong focus on culture is critical because even if parents learn new parenting skills, such learning must be positioned within a cultural realm that is meaningful to them. Otherwise, recently acquired parenting skills are at risk of not becoming culturally grounded and may wane over time because parents did not perceive them to be at the core of their cultural life (Bernal *et al.*, 2009).

Long-term sustainability

A final but particularly critical step refers to achieving long-term sustainability of community-based programs. That is, ensuring that efficacious mental health programs remain in the community on a permanent basis. The move towards ownership by the community can be a long and painstaking process, particularly if substantial funding is no longer present.

In our program of services research, we are currently facing the need to achieve long-term sustainability now that the funding provided to study the efficacy of the intervention is ending. Thus, we are working with community partners to develop a long-term sustainability plan focused on achieving permanent funding, continuing training of interventionists, and large-scale dissemination.

Conclusion

In this chapter, we have attempted to justify the high need for developing programs of services research aimed at empowering underserved Latino immigrant populations in the United States. Regardless of one's personal position concerning the current immigration debate, the reality is that millions of Latino children and youth born in the United States do not receive the health and mental health care that they deserve and need. We want to be part of the solution by committing our efforts to supporting the parenting needs of Latino immigrant parents. We expect that in these pages, you will find useful resources that will motivate you to serve a population that has played a critical role in the construction of the United States.

Critical Thinking Questions

1. Please provide four examples of ways in which service provision to Latino immigrants can have a negative impact with this population, particularly if there is a lack of understanding of their life and cultural experiences.
2. Please elaborate on three protective factors that you consider particularly relevant in service provision to Latino populations.
3. Please elaborate on why you consider it is relevant to develop programs of services research with Latino immigrants according to a community-level framework, rather than solely relying on family-based interventions.

Note

1. We recognize that the term "Latinos/as" appropriately makes reference to men and women. However, for clarity, we will employ the term "Latinos" as this is widely utilized in the literature on Latino populations. We define as a Latino immigrant any individual whose origins can be traced back to Latin America, specifically Mexico, Central, and South America, including the Caribbean.

References

Akers Chacón, J., and Davis, M. (2006). *No one is illegal: Fighting violence and state repression on the U.S.–Mexico Border.* Chicago: Haymarket Books.

Alegría, M., Canino, G., Shrout, P., Woo, M., Duan, N., Vila, D., ... and Meng, X. L. (2008). Prevalence of mental illness in immigrant and non-immigrant Latino groups. *American Journal of Psychiatry, 165,* 359–369.

Bartolome, M. A. (1997). *Gente de costumbres y gente de razón: Las identidades étnicas en México* [People of customs and reason: The ethnic identities in Mexico]. Mexico City, Mexico: Siglo XXI.

Bernal, G., Bonilla, J., and Bellido, C. (1995). Ecological validity and cultural sensitivity for outcome research: Issues for the cultural adaptation and development of psychosocial treatments with Hispanics. *Journal of Abnormal Child Psychology, 23,* 67–82.

Bernal, G., Jiménez-Chafey, M. I., and Domenech Rodríguez, M. M. (2009). Cultural adaptation of treatments: A resource for considering culture in evidence-based practice. *Professional Psychology: Research and Practice, 40,* 361–368.

Buchanan, P. J. (2006). *State of emergency: The third world invasion and conquest of America.* New York: St. Martin's Press.

Butler, M. J. (2003). U.S. military intervention in crisis, 1945–1994: An empirical inquiry of just war theory. *Journal of Conflict Resolution, 47,* 226–248.

Campbell, K., Garcia, D. M., Granillo, C. V., and Chavez, D. V. (2012). Exploring the Latino paradox: How economic and citizenship status impact health. *Hispanic Journal of Behavioral Sciences, 34,* 187–207.

Cardemil, E. (2008). Cultural sensitivity treatments: Need for an organizing framework. *Culture and Psychology, 14,* 357–367.

Castro, F. G., Barrera, M., Pantin, H., Martinez, C., Felix-Ortiz, M., Rios, R., ... and Lopez, C. (2006). Substance abuse prevention intervention research with Hispanic populations. *Drug and Alcohol Dependence, 48* (Supplement), S29–S42.

Cubanski, J., Huang, J., Damico, A., Jacobson, G., and Neuman, T. (2010). *Medicare chartbook* (4th edn). Menlo Park, CA: The Henry J. Kaiser Family Foundation.

Cummings, J. R., Wen, H., and Druss, B. G. (2011). Racial/ethnic differences in treatment for substance use disorders among U.S. adolescents. *Journal of the American Academy of Child and Adolescent Psychiatry, 50*(12), 1265–1274.

Dalla, R. L., and Christensen, A. (2005). Latino immigrants describe residence in rural Midwestern meatpacking communities: A longitudinal assessment of social and economic change. *Hispanic Journal of Behavioral Sciences, 27,* 23–42.

Dodson, M., and Jackson, D. W. (2004). Horizontal accountability in transitional democracies: The Human Rights Ombudsman in El Salvador and Guatemala. *Latin American Politics and Society, 46,* 1–27.

Domenech Rodríguez, M. M., Baumann, A. A., and Schwartz, A. L. (2011). Cultural adaptation of an evidence-based intervention: From theory to practice in a Latino/a community context. *American Journal of Community Psychology, 47,* 170–186.

Domenech Rodríguez, M. M., Rodríguez, J., and Davis, M. (2006). Recruitment of first-generation Latinos in a rural community: The essential nature of personal contact. *Family Process, 45,* 87–100.

Edberg, M., Cleary, S., and Vyas, A. (2010). A trajectory model for understanding and assessing health disparities in immigrant/refugee communities. *Journal of Immigrant Minority Health, 13,* 576–584.

Eggerth, D. E., and Flynn, M. A. (2010). When the third world comes to the first: Ethical considerations when working with Hispanic immigrants. *Ethics and Behavior, 20*(3), 229–242.

Elizondo, V. (1994). Popular religion as the core of cultural identity based on the Mexican American experience in the United States. In A. M. Stevens-Arroyo and A. M. Diaz-Stevens (eds), *An enduring flame: Studies on Latino popular religiosity* (pp. 113–132). New York: Bildner Center.

Falicov, C. J. (1998). *Latino families in therapy: A guide to multicultural practice.* New York: Guilford Press.

Falicov, C. J. (2007). Working with transnational immigrants: Expanding meanings of family, community, and culture. *Family Process, 46,* 157–171.

Fielden, S. J., Rusch, M. L., Masinda, M. T., Sands, J., Frankish, J., and Evoy, B. (2007). Key considerations for logic model development in research partnerships: A Canadian case study. *Evaluation and Program Planning, 30,* 115–124.

Finch, B., Hummer, R., Kolody, B., and Vega, W. (2001). The role of discrimination and acculturative stress in the physical health of Mexican-origin adults. *Hispanic Journal of Behavioral Sciences, 23,* 399–429.

Flores, G., Fuentes-Afflick, E., Barbot, O., Carter-Pokras, O., Claudio, L., Lara, M., … and Weitzman, M. (2002). The health of Latino children: Urgent priorities, unanswered questions, and a research agenda. *JAMA: Journal of the American Medical Association, 288,* 82–90.

Garland, A. F., Hurlburt, M. S., and Hawley, K. M. (2006). Examining psychotherapy processes in a services research context. *Clinical Psychology: Science and Practice, 13,* 30–46.

Garrido, A. (2009). Relationship between spirituality and critical consciousness development of Latino immigrants involved in social justice. Unpublished doctoral dissertation, Loyola University Chicago. ProQuest Information & Learning, 2010. AAI3377749.

González, G. G. (producer/director), and Price, V. (director). (2010). *Cosecha triste: El programa Bracero/Harvest of loneliness: The Bracero program* [documentary]. (Available from Films Media Group, Films for the Humanities and Sciences 132 West 31st Street, 17th Floor, New York, NY 10001.)

Greenberg, M., Rahmanou, H., Miller, H. N., Kaufmann, K. M., Lay, J. C., Novelli, W. D., and Goyer, A. (2004). Looking to the future. *Future of Children, 14,* 138–159.

Hayworth, J. D., and Eule, J. (2006). *Whatever it takes: Illegal immigration, border security, and the war on terror.* Washington, DC: Regnery Publishing.

Hilton, J. M., Gonzalez, C. A., Saleh, M., Maitoza, R., and Anngela-Cole, L. (2012). Perceptions of successful aging among older Latinos, in cross-cultural context. *Journal of Cross-Cultural Gerontology, 27,* 183–199.

Hoffman, K., and Centeno, M. A. (2003). The lopsided continent: Inequality in Latin America. *Annual Review of Sociology, 29,* 363–390.

Hovey, J. D., and King, C. A. (1996). Acculturative stress, depression, and suicidal ideation among immigrant and second-generation Latino adolescents. *Journal of the American Academy of Child Adolescent Psychiatry, 35,* 1183–1192.

Huntington, S. P. (2004). *Who are we? The challenges to America's national identity.* New York: Simon & Schuster.

Kataoka, S. H., Zhang, L., and Wells, K. B. (2002). Unmet need for mental health care among U.S. children: Variation by ethnicity and insurance status. *American Journal of Psychiatry, 159,* 1548–1555.

Knight, G. P., Roosa, M. W., Calderón-Tena, C. O., and Gonzales, N. A. (2009). Methodological issues in research on Latino populations. In F. A. Villarruel, G. Carlo, J. M. Grau, M. Azmitia, N. J. Cabrera, and T. J. Chahin (eds), *Handbook of U.S. Latino psychology: Developmental and community-based perspectives* (pp. 45–62). Washington, DC: Sage Publications.

Krikorian, M. (2008). *The new case against immigration: Both legal and illegal.* New York: Sentinel.

Kumpfer, K. L., Alvarado, R., Smith, P., and Bellamy, N. (2002). Cultural sensitivity and adaptation in family-based prevention interventions. *Prevention Science, 3*, 241–246.

Lorenzo-Hernandez, J. (1998). How social categorization may inform the study of Hispanic immigration. *Hispanic Journal of Behavioral Sciences, 20*, 39–57.

National Council of La Raza (NCLR). (2013). Latinos working hard to strengthen America's economy. Retrieved May 30, 2014 from http://www.nclr.org/images/uploads/publications/Analysis_Labor_Day_2010_FNL.pdf.

O'Fallon, L. R., and Dearry, A. (2002). Community-based participatory research as a tool to advance environmental health sciences. *Environmental Health Perspectives, 110*, 155–159.

Pantin, H., Schwartz, S. J., Sullivan, S., Coatsworth, J. D., and Szapocznik, J. (2003). Preventing substance abuse in Hispanic immigrant adolescents: An ecodevelopmental, parent-centered approach. *Hispanic Journal of Behavioral Sciences, 25*, 469–500.

Parra-Cardona, J. R., Bulock, L., Imig, D. R., Villarruel, F. A., and Gold, S. (2006). "Trabajando duro todos los días": Learning from the life experiences of Latino/a migrant families. *Family Relations, 55*, 361–375.

Parra-Cardona, J. R., Cordova, D., Holtrop, K., Villarruel, F., and Wieling, E. (2008). Shared ancestry, evolving stories: Similar and contrasting life experiences described by foreign born and U.S. born Latino parents. *Family Process, 47*, 157–172.

Parra-Cardona, J. R., Holtrop, K., Córdova, D., Escober-Chew, A. R., Horsford, S., Tams, L., … and Fitzgerald, H. (2009). "Queremos aprender": Latino immigrants' call to integrate cultural adaptation with best practice knowledge in a parenting intervention. *Family Process, 48*, 211–231.

Prado, G., Huang, S., Schwartz, S. J., Maldonado-Molina, M. M., Bandiera, F. C., de la Rosa, M., and Pantin, H. (2009). What accounts for differences in substance use among U.S.-born and immigrant Hispanic adolescents? Results from a longitudinal prospective cohort study. *Journal of Adolescent Health, 45*, 118–125.

Rivera, F. I., Guarnaccia, P. J., Mulvaney-Day, N., Lin, J.Y., Torres, M., and Alegría, M. (2008). Family cohesion and its relationship to psychological distress among Latino groups. *Hispanic Journal of Behavioral Sciences, 30*, 357–378.

Sabogal, F., Marin, G., and Otero-Sabogal, R. (1987). Hispanic familism and acculturation: What changes and what doesn't? *Hispanic Journal of Behavioral Sciences, 9*, 397–412.

Schwartz, S. J., Unger, J. B., Zamboanga, B. L., and Szapocznik, J. (2010). Rethinking the concept of acculturation: Implications for theory and research. *American Psychologist, 65*, 237–251.

Secretaría de Seguridad Pública (SSP). (2010). *Maltrato y abuso infantil en México: Factor de riesgo en la Comisión de Delitos*. Mexico, DF: Subsecretaria de Prevención y Participación Ciudadana, Gobierno Federal.

Sorenson, A. (1988). The fertility and language characteristics of Mexican-American and non-Hispanic husbands and wives. *Sociological Quarterly, 29*, 111–130.

Southam-Gerow, M. A., Ringeisen, H. L., and Sherrill, J. T. (2006). Integrating interventions and services research: Progress and prospects. *Clinical Psychology: Science and Practice, 13*, 1–8.

Suárez-Orozco, C., Yoshikawa, H., Teranishi, R. T., and Suárez-Orozco, M. M. (2011). Growing up in the shadows: The developmental implications of unauthorized status. *Harvard Educational Review, 81*(3), 438–472.

US Census Bureau. (2010). USA quick facts. Retrieved May 30, 2014 from http://quickfacts.census.gov/qfd/states/00000.html.

US Census Bureau. (2012). *Latin Americans by the numbers*. Washington, DC: US Census Bureau. Retrieved May 30, 2014 from http://www.infoplease.com/spot/hhmcensus1.html.

Walsh, F. (2003). Family resilience: A framework for clinical practice. *Family Process, 42*, 1–18.

Wucker, M. (2006). *Lockout: Why America keeps getting immigration wrong when our prosperity depends on getting right*. New York: Public Affairs.

21

Harm Reduction as a Model for Families Responding to Substance Abuse

Patt Denning

Principles of harm reduction are based on a public health model, which seeks to lessen risky behavior, reduce disease transmission, and maximize healthy lifestyles. Harm-reduction approaches to substance abuse are particularly attractive because they respect human rights, are inclusive, and non-discriminatory. In Chapter 21, Patt Denning outlines how harm-reduction treatment strategies are best applied to families dealing with substance abuse. Rather than pathologizing drug-affected persons as well as family coping behaviors that may have evolved in response to substance abuse (e.g., codependency), harm-reduction strategies offer alternative interventions that forge a solution based on realistic expectations, compassion, and patience for the process of change.

Introduction

How would you react if your son or daughter told you they were using drugs? What about if you saw your father doing drugs? Would you even know what to think, let alone what to do? You find that the Internet offers too much information that doesn't quite fit with your situation. This is what happens to thousands of people each day – a sudden awareness of something scary and unknown disrupting what you thought of as your "normal" family. This chapter is meant to bridge the gap between what has already been suggested as ways to help families dealing with addiction and the current understanding of complex family dynamics. It begins with a discussion of what

underlies the development of substance problems and then introduces the reader to the ongoing development of therapy and counseling models based on harm reduction, an international movement to improve the lives of people who misuse substances. A description of a model developed by this author and others then includes an explanation of the differences between this model and treatment-as-usual in the United States, and the primary clinical principles and techniques of harm-reduction psychotherapy (HRP).

The rest of the chapter describes and illustrates the ongoing development of a treatment for working with families and friends of drug users using harm-reduction principles. The author was instrumental in applying harm-reduction principles to substance

Family Problems: Stress, Risk, and Resilience, First Edition. Edited by Joyce A. Arditti.
© 2015 John Wiley & Sons, Inc. Published 2015 by John Wiley & Sons, Inc.

abuse and has used these same principles to help families and friends deal with the pessimism, pain, and grief that accompany their relationship to a person with an active substance abuse problem. The treatment involves learning decision-making processes based on both self-care and love for the substance misuser and is based on the values of harm reduction, caring, and increment change, rather than those of codependency, tough love, and abrupt behavior change.

Vulnerability to Substance Misuse

Why do some people misuse drugs while other don't? This is a question whose answer is much more complicated than the brain disease model currently in vogue can account for. We have several large studies, as well as clinical evidence from thousands of practitioners, to point us to a multifactorial understanding. Primary to this is the role of trauma in predicting substance misuse. This section offers a brief description of this literature.

In the current climate of time-limited therapies, psychopharmacological treatments, and a general move towards what can be observed, most treatment models focus on symptom management, behavioral problems, or relational difficulties. Less attention is paid to the underlying (or overriding) factors that contribute to these manifestations of emotional pain and the ensuing substance misuse. It is only by gaining information about these underlying factors that we can begin to formulate a risk-and-resiliency model that may aid not only in treatment, but in the prevention of substance use disorders. In addition, by focusing primarily on behavior, the context of a person's identity and history is often placed in the background. Yet culture, experiences of trauma, and the resulting disruption of affect and attachment are vital factors in the development of the personality, in mental health, and in the functioning of the whole person. (Anda *et al.*, 2002; Felitti, 2004). In harm-reduction therapy, these are given fundamental weight and attention.

Unfortunately, while the epidemiological data on the co-incidence of drug abuse and trauma is overwhelming, there is little reference in the substance abuse literature to childhood trauma as a causative factor in the development of substance abuse. This is in stark contrast to the considerable attention paid to this topic in both the child development literature and in work on attachment. But the substance abuse field has largely remained silent on the topic.

For example, in Miller and Carroll's (2006) collection representing the "state of the art" in addiction research and practice, only one chapter in this otherwise excellent book refers to family violence, and the authors caution against making too much of it, stating: "While alcohol use and violence are clearly associated, the causal relationship between parental alcoholism, family violence, and later alcohol problems among the offspring has not been firmly established" (Hesselbrock and Hesselbrock, 2006, p. 103).

There are a few exceptions to the lack of interest within the substance abuse literature. Early on, Wurmser (1980) asserted the relationship between trauma and drug abuse: "Many compulsive drug users were severely traumatized as children. Child abuse, is, in the simplest and strongest terms, one of the most important etiologic factors for later drug abuse" (p. 2). He goes on to explain that drug abuse, among other risk-taking behaviors, is an attempt, through taking action, to take control of and to reverse overwhelming feelings of helplessness. The most compelling research on the role of trauma in the initiation of substance misuse can be found in the ACE Study of adverse childhood experiences (Felitti, 2004). This population-based analysis of over 17,000 middle-class American adults undergoing comprehensive, biopsychosocial medical evaluation indicated that three common categories of addiction are strongly related in a proportionate manner to several specific categories of adverse experiences during childhood. These experiences include:

- recurrent and severe physical abuse (11%);
- recurrent and severe emotional abuse (11%);
- caregiver sexual abuse (22%);
- growing up in a household with:
  o   an alcoholic or drug-user (25%)
  o   a member being imprisoned (3%)
  o   a mentally ill, chronically depressed, or institutionalized member (19%)
  o   the mother being treated violently (12%)
  o   both biological parents *not* being present (22%).

These facts, coupled with related information, suggest that the basic cause of addiction is predominantly experience-dependent during childhood and not substance-dependent. This challenge to the usual concept of the cause of addictions has significant implications for medical practice and for treatment programs. If childhood experiences are the primary underlying cause of substance abuse, then our fear of even occasional drug use should be tempered and attention paid instead to family and community child-rearing. The *Just Say No* culture that teaches people to fear any exposure to drugs would be seriously undermined, and perhaps the stigma of having a drug problem be reduced.

One of the limitations of this study is the use of a middle-class population; consequently issues of poverty, violence, and racism are less obvious contributing factors to substance abuse in this particular study. For example in highly disadvantaged environments, there is a greater risk that children may be exposed to violence occurring outside the home (e.g., in the neighborhood), which in turn can traumatize a child and contribute to poor developmental outcomes (Leventhal and Brooks-Gunn, 2000). Resiliency within the family system can be overwhelmed by the impact of the outside world and children can grow up traumatized and at risk for substance abuse and other developmental problems (Straussner, 2001).

Harm Reduction as a Public Health and Clinical Model

What is harm reduction?

Harm reduction is an approach to working with drug users that aims to reduce drug-related harm to individuals, their families, and communities without necessarily reducing the consumption of drugs and alcohol. The damage done by drug and alcohol use, not necessarily the drug use itself, is the focus of attention (Marlatt, Larimer, and Witkiewitz, 2012). The term "harm reduction" was coined in the 1980s to describe public health approaches to working with drug use. At that time, the goal of harm-reduction interventions was to reduce the transmission of blood-borne

diseases, specifically hepatitis B and HIV. It was based on the reality that all behavior change (leaving a relationship, changing sexual habits, changing diet, getting psychiatric treatment, deciding to take meds for HIV, deciding to reduce or quit drugs or alcohol) requires a process of decision-making for successful implementation of a plan of change. Ambivalence and resistance are normal and expected parts of the change process. From a harm-reduction perspective, it was deemed far too important to save lives by offering immediate practical interventions than to get involved in whether people should or should not be using drugs (Marlatt *et al.*, 2012). In this way, one decreases a natural defensiveness that people often feel when confronted about their use: instead they are offered a pragmatic and compassionate ear and guidance.

Currently in the United States, harm reduction is practiced in three broad arenas:

- *Public health* approaches such as needle exchange, non-discriminatory health care, overdose prevention, and pill testing in clubs to reduce physical harm (e.g., HIV/HCV transmission) related to drug use. Under the public health umbrella, harm-reduction services include low-threshold housing that does not discriminate against drug users and that provides adequate and relevant supportive services. They also include older interventions such as drug substitution therapies (e.g., methadone).
- *Advocacy* for the decriminalization of drug use, fair sentencing laws, medical marijuana to reduce harm done by the War on Drugs, and other sane drug policies. Most recently, the treatment "industry" is coming under scrutiny by drug policy analysts.
- *Harm-Reduction Therapy*, a clinical approach to facilitate change in harmful drug using behaviors. The approach is unique in that treatment is offered to active drug users and it is entirely client-centered. The goals and the pace of treatment are determined by the client, not the therapist or counselor. HRP is based on sound evidence that the components of the treatment model are effective in both engaging clients and in facilitating change (Miller and Carol, 2006; Miller and Rollnick, 2012; Prochaska and Velicer, 1997).

Principles of harm reduction

The first principles were articulated by the Harm Reduction Coalition to protect the rights of active intravenous drug users (IDUs) and to offer public health interventions such as syringe exchange to save lives and prevent disease transmission (Sorge and Kershnar, 1998). The principles begin with the bold statement that no one should be punished simply for what they choose to put into their body, absent harm to others.

The principles of harm reduction are sufficiently broad that they have been applied to any low-threshold, inclusive, and non-discriminatory approach to working with problem behaviors, including working with people with severe mental and behavioral disturbances and with chronically homeless individuals. It is these principles of harm reduction that are the foundation for the principles of a harm-reduction-informed treatment model.

1. *Not all drug use is abuse.* Some is fun, some is medicine, some is just a part of life. Most people in the United States use some type of drug, and most do not have problems. Moreover, most can and do make rational choices about, and while, using drugs. Our confusion about use vs. abuse has its origins in both moral conviction and the ideology of substance abuse treatment. This confusion constitutes a significant barrier for people who want to honestly discuss their use and decide for themselves if it is a problem.
2. *Drug use occurs on a continuum from benign to chaotic,* and people move back and forth between those poles throughout their drug-using lifespan, most never reaching the point of chaos. People vary widely in their ability to manage drugs. Many can and do make rational decisions while using drugs, and do not necessarily have to quit to do less harm to self or others. In fact, research shows that many people manage formerly abusive or dependent drug use patterns by spontaneous recovery, moderation, or *reduction* in drug use or drug-related harms. There is no way to predict at the outset who will attain which of these goals.
3. *Drug abuse is a health, not a legal or moral concern.* There should be no punitive sanctions for what a person chooses to, or refuses to, put into her/his body. This principle is in stark contrast to the current climate that allows for drug testing in order to secure public housing, or to join the debate club at school.
4. *People use drugs for specific reasons.* They work! New learning in *neurobiology* supports the fact that people, especially those with physical, mental, or emotional illness, get significant relief from street drugs. People do not necessarily have the disease of addiction, they have a *relationship with drugs.*
5. *Harm is relative,* depending on one's reason for using, drugs may be preferable to one's experience without them.
6. *Incremental change is normal* and motivation is fluid.

History of harm-reduction psychotherapy (HRP)

The origins of HRP are multiple and can largely be credited to Alan Marlatt (1998) and Edith Springer (1991). Marlatt and Springer returned from visits to Dutch public health clinics to begin the efforts to transform American substance abuse treatment using the principles of harm reduction they learned in the Netherlands. Marlatt borrowed the term "come as you are" (from Nirvana's 1991 album *Nevermind*) to represent harm reduction's determination to work with all people no matter what their motivation for change might be. Springer repeatedly told stories of "then and now" – how she moved her treatment program away from rigid rules and confrontation tactics to a harm-reduction flexibility and supportive stance. This author (Denning, 2000; Denning and Little, 2012; Denning, Little, and Glickman, 2004), along with other clinicians (e.g., Tatarsky, 2002), began the task of transforming harm-reduction public health principles into treatment theory and practice. Denning (2000; Denning and Little, 2012) published the first comprehensive book describing the rationale for and the clinical principles and techniques of this new paradigm in drug treatment. The rationale for a harm-reduction-based treatment approach lies in the well-documented inadequacies of traditional treatment based on the Minnesota Model to help clients achieve lasting abstinence (Peele and Brodsky, 1991). The Minnesota Model combines a firm belief that "addiction" is a medical disease with the conviction that the 12-Step model is the best way to help people. In addition, the traditional practice of refusing treatment or terminating treatment in the face of occasional or continuing substance use does not measure up to the standard of care for other medical or psychiatric disorders. For example, patients with high cholesterol are not denied statin medication if they continue to eat a high-fat diet; people with depression or schizophrenia are not required to be symptom-free before or during treatment episodes.

The clinical models and methods of HRP as developed and practiced by this author and the staff at the Harm Reduction Therapy Center (HRTC) are a combination of evidence-based approaches (primarily the cognitive behavioral therapy work of Hester and Miller, 1989; Marlatt *et al.*, 2012; Miller and Rollnick, 2012; and Rotgers, 2003). Further methods were derived from the neurobiological understanding of the effects of trauma (van der Kolk, McFarlane, and Weisaeth, 1996) and the use of attachment theory and other psychodynamics relational models (Bowlby, 1988; Khantzian, 1999; Walant ,1995). These authors described how early childhood experiences of trauma disrupt both brain chemistry and healthy attachment. Dysfunction of brain reward systems, impulsivity, and intolerance to psychic pain create an individual whose biology will reinforce the use of substances to excess. In addition, disruptions in attachment lead a person to form attachments to substances as a means of feeling whole.

Harm-reduction treatment, collectively referred to as harm-reduction psychotherapy (HRP) by its developers, is client-driven, collaborative, holistic, respectful, and empowering. Contrary to the dominant paradigm of substance abuse treatment where abstinence is the goal, *harm-reduction treatment does not state that abstinence either is or is not the goal of treatment*, but rather that it is up to the client to choose and pursue appropriate and realistic goals. These might be total abstinence, abstinence from their most problematic drug only, or some combination of reduction in frequency, in amount, or in dangerous behaviors associated with drug or alcohol use. It is the belief of harm-reduction (HR) developers and practitioners that all treatment should be harm-reduction-informed because it allows the widest possible diversity of clients to enter a treatment relationship, not only those who have a will to quit using altogether. Smaller problems can be addressed before they become bigger ones, saving the person and their family much suffering.

Principles of harm-reduction psychotherapy (HRP)

As mentioned above, the principles of HRP were first derived from the principles of the harm-reduction movement, both the public health and the advocacy arms. This author then used the literature on cognitive behavioral and psychodynamic evidence-based practices to add the clinical perspective to those principles.

1. *Incremental change is normal and motivation is fluid.* Just because we want to change something doesn't mean we can "just do it." The Stage Model of Change (Prochaska and DiClementi, 1992), based on research, explains the process that we go through stages to make major behavior change and asserts that change is *most* effective if we work through the stages one at a time, thoroughly, in order, and preferably with support. Change in addictive behavior is usually gradual, relies on the resolution of ambivalence about one's relationship with drugs, and passes through a series of stages. These stages are best negotiated with the help of *motivational enhancement therapy*, which aims to engage clients in goal setting and help them develop their own internal motivations for change (Miller and Rollnick, 2012).

2. *People have the right to make choices, even bad ones.* Self-determination is one of the major components of reliable and stable behavior change.

3. *Abstinence is one of many harm-reduction goals*, it just isn't the only one. At any point in time, most people in the United States with drug problems are not abstinent. Outcomes are as varied as the people seeking change; this is not only real, it is desirable! No counselor or program can say what each person's success will look like.

4. *Treatment-as-usual has less than optimal abstinence outcomes*, but much better harm-reduction outcomes. That is, clients may not have stopped using completely, but risk has been reduced (Project MATCH, 1997).

5. *Each person's relationship with drugs is unique.* Therefore, harm reduction is a collaborative model in which the goals and the pace of treatment are established together between client and the therapist, not preordained by "the program." Rather than a disease, harm-reduction practitioners consider addiction a *biopsychosocial* phenomenon in which the relative importance of biology (for example, genetics, health status, age, gender), psychology (mental health/illness, identity, motivation, and expectation), and environment (environmental stressors as well as setting of use) vary from individual to individual. Harm-reduction psychotherapy aligns with a model of "drug, set, and setting" which illustrates this biopsychosocial phenomenon and its interrelated aspects (adapted from Zinberg, 1984; see Denning and Little, 2012). This model articulates how the experience of drug use and its outcomes are the result of complex interactions between characteristics of the *drug* itself (e.g., its potency, legality, how it is used), the mind*set* or psychological, physical, cultural, and health qualities of the person using the drug, and the *setting*, which encompasses how stressful or supportive the environment is, as well as the meaning a person ascribes to drug use within a particular community or culture. The idea that drug-related harm is a result of the interplay between drug, set, and setting is in contrast to traditional models (discussed in the next section) of addiction that claim it is only the drug itself that is causing harm.

Differences between harm-reduction and traditional models

There are distinct differences between various models that are used to treat substance use disorders. The most recognized treatment model utilized in the United States is called the Minnesota Model. It is an approach comprised of the disease theory of addiction coupled with 12-Step participation. Advocates of this model point to the traditionally poor outcomes of older models of psychotherapy for substance use disorders, which focused primarily on treating personality and mood disturbances (see, e.g., Khantzian, 1985), as reason for the Minnesota Model's emphasis

on a peer-based and spirituality-based supportive community. This approach has indeed helped many people and saved their lives and those of their family; however, its overutilization during the past few decades may have inadvertently squelched innovation in substance abuse treatment. Many lay people, as well as professionals, are unaware of the emergence of diverse ways of thinking about and treating substance use disorders that are proving to be more effective.

Table 21.1 compares the major models on dimensions such as basic beliefs about addiction and about drug users, treatment style, etc. In many ways, the biopsychosocial mix of elements as conceptualized from a harm-reduction perspective (rather than a disease model) is a much more comprehensive and useful way of seeing substance misuse than competing approaches. Harm reduction acknowledges how different elements, originating from multiple contexts, contribute to the origin and maintenance of addictive behavior (Miller and Carroll, 2006; Morgenstern and Leeds, 1993). In this manner, harm reduction is a multi-pronged approach, similar to Multisystemic Therapy (MST; see Chapter 19, this volume), that aligns with principles of ecological theory whereby behavior is multiply determined. Such a perspective points, then, to specific interventions targeted to each component (bio, psycho, or environmental) that may affect change. This way of seeing things is also inclusive of the many other connections, systems, and resources that a person and their family may have to marshal a plan for helping change occur. Figure 21.1 provides a visual roadmap to this understanding.

Harm-Reduction Psychotherapy: Working with Family Systems

Traditional approaches to substance misuse in family systems

Families and friends of people suffering from substance misuse are often given the same rules to live by as their drug-using loved ones. From an abstinence perspective this might involve strict adherence to a 12-Step program. Although more psychotherapists are using developmental models in their treatment of relational and family problems, many continue to

Table 21.1 Major models of substance use disorders

	Minnesota Model	Self-medication hypothesis	Cognitive/behavioral models	Harm reduction treatment
Basic beliefs about addiction: etiology and course	Biopsychosocial disease; progressive; loss of control; can't moderate.	Significant problems managing feelings. May mask underlying problems.	Combination of learned behaviors, habit, and cognitive distortions. Ambivalence about change is normal. Brain changes make control more difficult, not impossible.	Biopsychosocial phenomena, not disease. Different for different people. Trauma plays a large role in development of addiction.
Basic beliefs about people with addictions and their needs	In denial; loss of control; lie or minimize use.	Misuse due to the need to cope with life. Poor self-care. Co-occurring is the rule.	Clients have trouble with cognitive styles (black and white thinking). Can learn skills to make changes. Loss of control isn't inevitable.	Not in denial – afraid of punishment and shaming. Can learn to modify use. Ambivalence is normal. Self-medication.
Goal of treatment and who sets the goal	Life-long abstinence from all drugs. Program sets goal.	Generally abstinence from problematic drug. Therapist sets goal.	Return person to healthy functioning with or without abstinence. Client may set goal usually.	Reduce drug-related harm. May or may not be abstinence from some or all drugs. Client decides.
Modalities available and preferences	Inpatient, detoxification, outpatient, residential, IOP.	Outpatient, some inpatient.	Outpatient, generally short-term.	Currently outpatient. Brief and/or ongoing.
Methods of treatment	Former "addicts" seen as best to treat clients. Group work dominates. Families often involved in treatment.	Mental health professionals. Mostly individual, some group. No family involvement.	Individual and groups.	Both individual and group sessions primary. Family treatment and support. Drop-in.
Techniques of treatment	Confrontation of denial. Education about disease. 12-Step facilitation.	Dynamic psychotherapy. Confrontation of lack of self-care.	Focus on "here and now, not there and then." Behavior rehearsal and skills training.	Motivational interviewing. Substance use management. Decisional balance. Cognitive and psycho-dynamic therapy. Psychiatric meds.
Beliefs and interventions regarding relapse	Relapse returns person to beginning of recovery again. Exposure to triggers must be avoided.	Relapse indicates being overwhelmed by feelings. No adjustment of treatment. Causes explored.	Relapse is an educational opportunity to fine-tune skills.	Natural part of change. Learning opportunity.
Cultural sensitivity and competency	"Equal Opportunity Disease" dominant. Recent focus on activities for different populations.	Not mentioned in literature.	Not generally a focus.	Primary focus on developmental differences: race, gender, class, etc. How they affect drug use, addiction, and relative harms suffered.

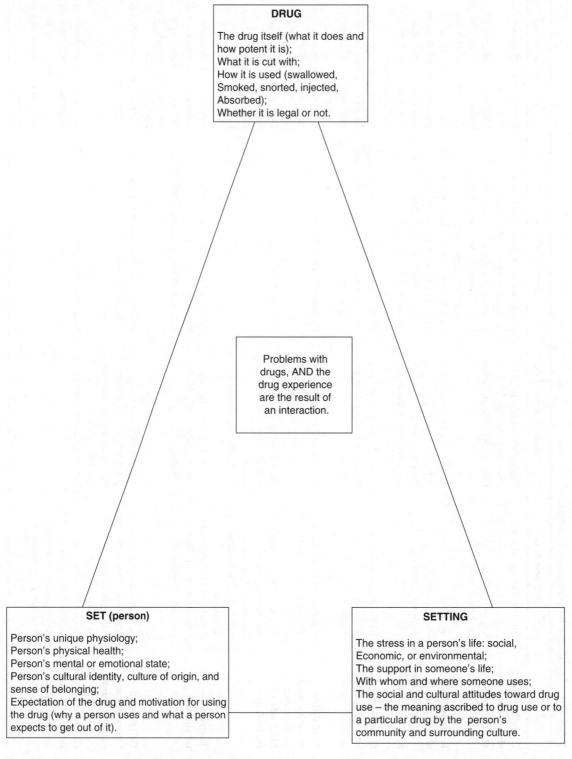

Figure 21.1   Drug, set, setting (from Zinberg, 1984). Compiled by Jeannie Little and Patt Denning.

view codependency in the context of the disease model and 12-Step recovery. Even when clinicians use harm-reduction-informed methods for drug users, the families and friends of these clients are frequently left with traditional self-help groups such as Al Anon and Co-Dependents Anonymous. While helpful to many family members, many more are often confused and upset by a "tough love" or "loving detachment" approach that may differ from their values of friendship, family, community, and love.

The codependency movement

Popular literature overflows with books and articles on the difficulties of people who love people abusing drugs and alcohol. The names associated with these self-help publications (e.g., Melodie Beattie, John Bradshaw) are well known. The overwhelming premise of these books is that the people closest to addicted individuals may be troubled themselves and in attempting to "help" the addicted individual, actually enable unhealthy behavior and become sick themselves (Beattie, 1987, 1990). In effect, these writers assert that codependency is a disease in the same way that drug addiction is a disease. The codependent bases her identity and self-esteem on the well-being of their addicted loved one and becomes hypervigilant and controlling. Self-help books offer lists of codependent characteristics that can be quite extensive. Low self-esteem, difficulty expressing anger, and passivity are all components of this disorder. The lists are so all-encompassing that most people, especially women, could easily check off a number of the characteristics and diagnose themselves as codependent. Many of these books point to cycles of behavior and feelings that are termed codependent in that they are unhealthy for both the person misusing drugs and their loved ones (Beattie, 1987). For example, Beattie states that any rescuing behavior aimed at the drug user or alcoholic results in the helper first feeling angry, but ultimately leads to him or her feeling victimized. To break this cycle of self-victimization, advice for codependents centers on detachment and abstinence (from helping the person). Although it is true that many people involved with a person with a serious substance disorder do engage in this type of controlling cycle, the literature leads one to believe that it is invariably

unhealthy and leads to a delay in the addicted person hitting bottom and changing for the better (Gordon and Barrett, 1993). In essence, the standard definition of codependency has two components: failure of self-care, and protecting/enabling the drug user (Beattie, 1990). Although the first component is an important point and a source of suffering for the loved one, the latter means any attempt of family members to protect the drug user from suffering the harms of his or her addiction is seen as pathological. This author questions how realistic such a premise actually is, as it precludes any self-sacrifice, or practical efforts to manage a loved one's addiction to prevent job loss or other events that could further damage the family.

Al-Anon, Al-Ateen, Nar-Anon, or ACOA (adult children of alcoholics) support groups often offer similar support and guidance. Members of these groups are told they need to stop "enabling" and practice "tough love." This advice may not work for many people, who view it as overly harsh or restrictive. No professional argues against exposing that interactions between loved ones and their addicted family members are fraught with conflict, secrecy, attempts to control, and attempts to hide. But it is imperative to understand the motivation for such interactions and to be open to the possibility that not all such coping strategies are pathological. One alternate perspective is that people are trying to maintain attachment, family, and/or community in the face of a disabling problem. Demonizing a helper who is reacting to a bad situation with less than perfect responses may inadvertently pathologize the family system. This, in turn, undermines the possibility of moving toward healthier interactions and behaviors and contributes to a need for intervention, a need for long-term and often expensive treatment (Peele, 1989; Szalavitz, 2006). There are essential racial, class, gender, and other cultural differences that play an enormous role in how loved ones and their communities react to substance abuse issues (Straussner, 2001; White and Sanders, 2004). Cultural differences in dealing with shame, sickness, and deviant behavior lead to an enormous variety of responses. Ostracizing the offending member is not a universal response. Often, families rally together with extended relatives, church members, etc. to help the troubled person return to a normal state.

Critics argue that "tough love" is particular to the current dominant (White) American culture and an extension of the nation's "tough on crime" ideology. This ideology originates in part from puritanical doctrine whereby persons were either to be saved or condemned, with the condemned seen as deserving of harsh and swift punishment from God (Arditti, 2012).

Regardless of their origins, pathologizing beliefs and attitudes about codependency are mirrored in the larger society and give rise to rigid, punitive approaches to drug use and addiction such as the War on Drugs, which has resulted in the mass incarceration of people for drug-related offenses, many of whom are nonviolent and whose only crime may be taking an illegal drug (see Alexander, 2010; Loury, 2008).

The dilemmas that families and friends face

The belief that "going to rehab" will cure an addiction in 28 days is the stuff of "reality" television shows, not reality. Moving through a substance abuse problem often takes years and is characterized by many setbacks along the way (Marlatt *et al.*, 2012; Miller and Carroll, 2006). This author has observed that unrealistic expectations regarding the nature of substance abuse treatment and its ability to quickly cure addiction can contribute to family members' disappointment, as they often engage in a cycle of hope, despair, and rage over time. Members of this author's family support group have said that there is something about being encouraged to detach from those one loves that feels harsh or dogmatic, and their own inability to do this contributed to their own sense of personal failure.

For the reader to experience the emotional nature of this topic, it may be helpful to write as if you are a family member. For example, imagine that you have loved your daughter since before she was born, and it is unthinkable to abandon her to her addiction in the hopes that she will hit bottom and get better before it kills her. Everyone agrees that one never fully recovers from the death of a child, and so every ounce of your parental soul seeks a way to help her. Or as a spouse, you do not believe that your life will be better if you leave your husband, even though his drinking is out of control. From a traditional treatment perspective, your only alternative has been to stand out of the way and let someone you care about fall until they hit bottom. You may find yourself hoping they will recognize some area of harm that they do not see. You may want them to really notice the devastation of their children, or that they are inches from losing a good job. But the truth is that people can only see what they are ready to see, and sometimes all you can do is simply appreciate with them the giant step undertaken in looking at any harm at all.

On the other hand, suppose you are in a situation and have had it with the lies and the promises and the suffering that a family member's drug use has caused you and others. Maybe you're also ashamed of your loved one, or hold awful regrets about others whom they have hurt. You don't feel like being patient, and loving, and *passive* in the face of all this. You're about to take the advice to get tough. The problem is, though, tough love may not work and may feel really awful to everyone involved. From a harm-reduction perspective, it is unrealistic to expect people to change complicated behaviors *just like that*. Any approach that limits you to an all-or-nothing choice, an either-or, ignores the reality of how people go about making changes. People change in incremental steps, practicing new behaviors and altering emotional reactions in stages, over time (Prochaska and DiClementi, 1992). The other crucial ingredient in making lasting changes is support. People often do not make significant changes without an enormous amount of support during the process. When we expect immediate change and refuse to be with a person during this process, we undermine the very goal we're trying to accomplish. Banishment seldom leads to reconciliation. Inclusion and connection rather than exclusion and alienation are the keys to successful resolution of family problems (Ryan and Deci, 2000). It is important to remember that even an absent family member continues to be a part of the family system. Cutting one member off (as in the case of "tough love") does not mean that they are not continuing to exert an influence on people's feelings and actions.

In relation to Brenda's case on p. 347, a harm-reduction approach has some similarities to Network Therapy (Galanter, 2002): A friendship group was formed to support a woman in trouble with drugs. But there are several important differences. The friends made no demands on Brenda to change and offered

Case Example: Brenda

Brenda was wearing out her friends. She had always been a party girl, and at age 27, Brenda and her friends didn't worry about the long-term effects of their lifestyle. Over the past year, however, Brenda had started spinning out of control. She routinely got blind drunk and was using both cocaine and Ecstasy as well (although she wouldn't readily admit to the cocaine). She resisted her friends' attempts to talk with her and avoided them after bad weekend binges. One of Brenda's friends called for a consultation and arrived with two others. Ted and Bob had known Brenda since college, and Laura had known her since childhood. They were roommates after college until relationships resulted in different living situations. Recently Laura had wondered if it might help to have Brenda move in with her. They all expressed worry that Brenda was reacting badly to some setbacks over the past year. She was laid off from a job and was having trouble finding anything but part-time work. Her cat had gotten cancer, and she had to put him to sleep. And a man that she had hoped to marry decided that he wasn't ready. The friends assumed that these events were to blame for Brenda's erratic behavior with alcohol and drugs. But Brenda wasn't talking.

At first the friends were asking for help doing an "intervention" and demanding that Brenda go to "rehab." They knew that she would resist, and were afraid that it would ruin their friendship. I let them know that forced interventions often do cause alienation, and that without at least some interest on Brenda's part, she would not benefit much from such a short, coerced treatment. We reviewed several other options for their involvement, including having Brenda move in with Laura. They decided on a direct approach, one that was in keeping with their slightly "in-your-face" style with one another. They went out for drinks and talked to Brenda about what they noticed – more about her stress than about her use, how worried they were, and asked if she thought she ought to get psychotherapy. She wasn't totally opposed, but didn't acknowledge her increased drug use. Surprisingly, she accepted Laura's invitation to move in rent-free for a few months, saying that she was feeling lonely a lot since the breakup. After weeks of making and breaking appointments, Brenda began individual therapy with one of HRTC's therapists. During a period of six months of weekly sessions, she revealed other significant sources of stress that she hadn't shared with her friends. At first, she talked little about her substance use, but as she relaxed and realized that her therapist was not going to force the issue, she opened up and admitted that she wasn't happy with how she was partying lately. Brenda was engaged in working on the other sources of stress and became interested in making a "party plan" so she wouldn't embarrass herself. She stopped using cocaine altogether, limited her Ecstasy use to once a month, and learned how to moderate her drinking by attendance at Moderation Management self-help meetings. Her friends kept in phone contact with me and reported that they felt much relief that she was in good hands and confirmed the changes that Brenda had made.

unconditional support. Brenda's psychotherapy was segregated from the friends' consultations, and Brenda was never confronted by her individual therapist with any information that came to her via the friends. This allowed a confidential relationship that was independent of others' worries and wishes and, I believe, contributed to her willingness to continue in treatment. After six months, she reined in her alcohol and drug use significantly and is now able to focus her therapy on other important issues in her life.

Harm-reduction family treatment

Despite the continued predominance of the Minnesota Model and related approaches, there is a growing international movement of families who are trying to support one another as they struggle to stay connected with their loved ones who are in trouble with alcohol or other drugs, while also struggling to take care of themselves (see, e.g., support groups such as: From Grief to Action, www.fgta.ca; or Family Drug Support, www.familydrugsupport.com). This section provides some guidance, using harm-reduction principles to illustrate the power of family connection, resilient support groups, and society in the healing process, as well as the dangers of detachment and alienation. As we have discussed, being the loved one of a person with an alcohol or other drug problem can be excruciating. People experience profound helplessness, frustration, anger, and fear. Today's optimism, induced by fervent promises of "never again," is replaced by tomorrow's disappointment when those promises are broken. Loved ones struggle with extraordinary questions about loyalty, love, support, and limits. How much help is too much? How long should you put up with it? With a broader view, the question becomes "How can we address the real harm and suffering of the families and friends of people with serious alcohol and drug problems?"

In harm-reduction psychotherapy, working with families often involves working within the grey areas – the not knowing, the struggle to define what is best to do, the limits to set, the concessions to make. Rather than viewing codependency as a disease that runs parallel to the disease of addiction, harm-reduction therapy views these behaviors through the same biopsychosocial lens as addiction. Family members may develop problematic behaviors or develop ineffective coping strategies in the face of a loved one who is abusing alcohol or other drugs. Helpful interventions can, thus, follow the same process as with the drug-affected person: analyze the conflict, respect the ambivalence, and forge a solution from realistic expectations, compassion, and patience for the process of change.

With regard to the role of family members, the line that separates healthy caretaking from destructive helping is not always easily identified or defined. Clinicians can choose to explore this line in each individual rather than make a priori judgments about the ways loved ones cope. Reliance on the self-determination theory is a cornerstone to this approach (Ryan and Deci, 2000). Self-determinism claims that the strength to change is based on one's sense of power to effect change, and the

motivation for change is most powerful when it is intrinsic (within the person) rather than extrinsic (external to the person).

Harm-reduction principles uphold people's right to make decisions, even if those decisions lead to harm (Denning and Little, 2012; Denning et al., 2004). Family members have to come to grips with this reality for themselves as well as for their loved one. Freedom to choose, even if it may not always be in one's best interests, and having understanding for the addicted family member does not mean, however, that limits are not set. Just as one must set limits with a 2-year-old, one must set limits with an adult. Within a harm-reduction framework, the focus of limits are on behavior. Limits keep a child from running into traffic, touching a hot stove, and eating poison. Adults need somewhat different limits. "You can't yell at me" and "I won't let you take all of our money and spend it on drugs" are some of the limits a person might need to set. It is more useful clinically to separate a person from her behavior. For example, running into traffic, touching a hot stove, or eating poison doesn't mean a child is stupid. Spending all of her money on drugs doesn't mean she is a stupid adult. They may just be ignorant of the consequences, curious, or overcome by need.

Principles and practices for assisting families

There is an array of principles and practices that can assist family members manage both their own involvement and their reactions to loved ones struggling with addiction. These strategies and principles are based on the same concepts that form the underpinnings of harm-reduction psychotherapy with drug users. Note the emphasis on collaboration rather than prescription, choice, acceptance of ambivalence, and the reality that change takes place over time.

1. "Promises, Promises": The Reality of Failures and Relapses
Families who have been dealing with a drug-abusing loved one for a while may be feeling a bit cynical about their promises to quit, or stay in treatment, or pay back money that was taken. On the one hand, family members are reluctant to hope that it'll be any

different this time. But they also hate to see the hurt in a loved one's eyes when they express skepticism in the face of new promises. The reality is that most people with significant alcohol or drug problems try a lot of different times and a lot of different ways to help themselves. The norm is that they cycle through problems and solutions many times before they make lasting changes. It's important for loved ones not to ask for promises. This usually just results in lying and secrecy. And it's the lying and secrecy as much as it is the broken promises that strain relationships. What harm reduction suggests is to hold a paradox: people don't have to put up with behaviors that hurt them and can make demands and state hopes and expectations of the person. Loved ones can express the full range of their feelings. At the same time, family members have already realized that demands and pleas do not usually result in lasting change on the part of the person with a problem. Loved ones have their own *decisional balance* at work. Taking one action or another is a matter of weighing the pros and cons of each. Successfully holding the paradox, then, means that a person can be at the end of his or her rope, and still know that change is incremental, with many setbacks along the way. Loved ones can be angry and frustrated and still understand that the process of change takes time. One can expect a person to change their behavior while at the same time openly discussing the lack of change.

The present author has found that most people who are drawn to harm reduction bring with them a pervasive sense of failure and self-reproach. The harsh "observer" finds fuel in self-directed anger at their inability to "get with the program," or "face their problem." In fact, the isolation and hopelessness that grows from this sense of failure often drives continued use. What I have learned to advise them is this: as a family member or a friend, **it is vital that you grab any opportunity to *not* reinforce the addict's "observer."** When addicts beat themselves up for relapsing, it is not an invitation for you to join in.

2. There Are No Rules Except the Rules You Make
This is not exactly what a family member may want to hear, given the often desperate need for a solution, but the fact is, no one knows what another person should do. All the advice about not "enabling" a

person, all the talk about not being "codependent" tries to force a family member into making up rules that they might not really want to enforce, or maybe don't have the power to enforce. Other people might tell them to do things that violate their own values about loyalty and family. Then if they don't abide by their advice, they get labeled as a problem, as someone who is supporting another's addiction. Harm-reduction principles can help guide loved ones to figure out what might be best for all concerned

3. Identify the Harms You Are Suffering
This author asked family clientele to make a detailed list of the harms that another person's drug problem is causing. For example: *Are you losing sleep? Are you paying their bills and not having enough money to buy your medicine or food? Are they bringing home people who might endanger you or your children? Are they acting up in public when you're out together? Are they stashing illegal drugs at your house, putting you at risk of arrest or losing your home?*

Next, the person needs to try to be objective about this list. Which things are actually related directly to drug or alcohol abuse? Trying to make distinctions between the actual activity of drug using and the behaviors that might go along with it is helpful because it clarifies what is most important to the person rather than oversimplifying the issue as simply drug use. An example of this distinction might be: *Is the harm really that your cousin smokes weed, or that he smokes in your car when you are going somewhere together? Or how about your girlfriend who is using a lot of speed and staying up all night so you can't get to sleep. Again, while she may have a drug problem, your problem is about her behavior of keeping you up.*

4. Distinguish between Being Harmed and Being "Hurt"
Harm implies physical damage, whereas *hurt* can mean emotional reactions. It might not be possible to tease apart the distinction between harm and hurt, but for many people, what is happening is not that they are actually suffering a lot of harm because of a loved one's drug or alcohol problem, but that they are really hurt and disappointed in them, and maybe angry as well. All such feelings are important and serve as a guide to one's decisions and behaviors. From a clinical standpoint, what is more helpful is to help the person to assess the difference between their emotional reactions to a loved

one's drug use and problem behaviors (which may range from anger to disappointment to worry to hopelessness, etc.) and actual destructive results that come down on them: *Are you losing money, sleep, your job? Are your other family members being victimized? Or are you suffering from the disappointment of failed expectations and hopes, or from watching a good person spiral down?*

5. Identify What's Most Important to You

Family members differ in the amount of stress, involvement, or detachment that they feel comfortable with in relation to their relationship with the substance-affected person. It may have to do with temperament or personal values. Clinicians can help each person identify their wishes for peace and quiet in order to function at their best vs. excitement and challenge, for example. Some people are basically loners, but may still want some family involvement. Others are very social, enjoying interacting with lots of different kinds of people. It is also helpful to have the person think about how they came to be involved with this person who has a drug or alcohol problem. What did they enjoy and admire about them? Has it all gone away or just sometimes? Knowing what's important and what one needs to feel relatively content can help a person decide on how they will interact with problem people.

6. Affirm Your Values: Beware of Tough Love

People generally have some values about loyalty between loved ones – the belief that one is supposed to stick with a person through hard times. In fact, marriage vows say just that: "for better or worse." Such ideas of loyalty and self-sacrifice are too often criticized in modern American society when it comes to people with alcohol and other drug problems. The stigma of mental illness (see Chapter 3, this volume) or physical handicap is changing, and the role of the caretakers of these people is a valued one. However, a more tolerant perspective may not apply for people with addictions. On one hand, addiction is a disease and we should help people. But on the other hand, we shouldn't "enable" a person by really helping them out when they need it, when they are suffering the worst consequences of their problems. Why do we think that they should suffer because of their problems when we don't think that way about others? Consider how we treat people with other problems

that are called diseases. Both diabetes and schizophrenia are chronic disorders that have a course that is often deteriorating. While there are certain things the patient can do to prevent or slow down the progressive damage, the disorder has its own course. We spend a lot of time encouraging these people to monitor their food intake, exercise, take their medicine, avoid stress, etc. But when they (invariably) don't always follow medical advice, or the wishes of their family, we may feel frustrated or worried, but we don't usually throw them out! We try to protect them from serious negative consequences while attempting to motivate them to take better care of themselves. What harm reduction suggests is that we adopt the same attitude towards people with alcohol and other drug problems. As previously mentioned, "tough love" is a questionable approach in helping people overcome a drug or alcohol problem (Szalavitz, 2006). In fact, such an approach can cause considerable pain on both sides and has separated people from those who are most important to them. One may need to practice "tough love" at some point, but hopefully not until other, more healing types of intervention have been tried.

7. Establish Your Absolute Limits

It may be helpful for family members to realize that their attempts to try and figure out what they want to do about a loved one's alcohol or other drug problem is a similar process to what the drug user is going through. Each person is coming at the problem from a different perspective, perhaps, but the guidelines are pretty much the same. What is your bottom line? What will you not tolerate and what has got to change? What can you live with, if only with minor adjustments? There is probably at least one thing that feels "non-negotiable." For example stealing money is a common bottom line for many families affected by substance abuse. Loved ones need to remember, though, that even if a person accepts treatment, there will probably be relapses and they need to decide what to do in that situation. Will the person be allowed any choices or negotiation or second chances? The more strict the limits and demands are, the more likely they will lose the person, at least in the short run.

The main thing for families to remember is that limits are about *each family member*. Limits are not necessarily the only things that can be done and they may not even be the right thing for the person. It is important to remember that no one really knows what's right for the other person (*and neither does any counselor or expert*).

8. Planning Your Response: What Do You Want to Do First?

Put yourself in the following situation. Let's consider a family example whereby *the cousin smokes marijuana when the two of you are out driving in your car. You really think he has a problem with pot. And you get really nervous with the drug in your car. What if you get stopped and the police smell it? You could go to jail. You've been trying to talk to him about how come he smokes so much and maybe he should quit, but he just tells you that you're trying to stop his fun. He doesn't think he has a problem. He just likes it to relax after a hard day at work. The two of you are at a stalemate in terms of defining a problem, let alone solving it. You aren't getting anywhere trying to convince him that he has a problem. And, in fact, your biggest problem may be that he smokes in your car and puts you at risk. You don't have to talk to him any more about smoking pot. Save your energy. Just set a limit about smoking in your car: "Put it out or get out. Now." You might also decide not to let him smoke in your presence, or around your parents and kids. In this way, you reduce the harms to you and those around you without trying to force him to change.*

The point is to generate a number of possible solutions by separating out drug or alcohol use from problem behaviors associated with it. Each possible action probably has risks and benefits associated with it, just like a person's drug or alcohol use has certain risks and benefits.

Put yourself in another family scenario: *Let's say your son, a crack addict, comes by your home while you're at work and steals your TV. By the time you discover it, he has pawned the TV for cash and is getting high. You consider your options. Have him arrested. Demand that he go get the TV back. Offer him cash to get it. Bargain with him that you won't turn him in if he goes for treatment. Kick him out of the house. Do nothing.*

Figure 21.2 offers a diagrammatic representation of what harm or help might be offered in each of these alternatives.

Dealing with substance misuse that is complicated by mental illness

Another situation that is excruciating for families is when one member is both drug addicted and mentally ill. This is the meaning of the term "comorbid," or dual diagnosis. Many schizophrenic people use alcohol as a way of soothing auditory hallucinations. Some also use marijuana because it makes them feel less agitated. Some

Action	Harm	Help
Have him arrested	Physical risks of jail. Creates animosity	Wake-up call. Teach him a lesson. Get him away from you and your stuff
Demand that he get it back	He'll fail, because he doesn't have money or doesn't know where it is	Force him to deal with you and work to get your forgiveness
Offer cash	Uses it to buy more drugs	You get your TV back
Bargain	He might call your bluff	Maintains relationship
Kick him out of the house	He'll be homeless and a target for other harms (violence, poor nutrition, prostitution, etc.)	Forces him to make a choice. Lets him know you want him, just not his drugs
Do nothing	You'll lose more of your stuff	He'll eventually feel bad and stop stealing from you. Maybe stop using, too

Figure 21.2 Risks and benefits associated with possible solutions.

also smoke crack as a way of making them feel more alive, a feeling they've lost since becoming ill or from taking their medications. The majority of people with schizophrenia also smoke cigarettes. This mixture of drugs can often cause disturbing symptoms and pose dangers in the house, such as fires. Using their money for alcohol and drugs often means that they don't pay their rent and end up on the streets. If family members have the financial resources, they could consider a number of interventions short of demanding that the person quit using all drugs. For example, paying their rent for them (directly to the landlord) so as to prevent the harms associated with homelessness. One might put up good smoke detectors so that if they pass out with a cigarette burning, they won't burn down the house and themselves. Someone might arrange to drive them to their doctor's appointment and give them money to fill their medication prescription. In this way, loved ones reduce both the harms to themselves (worry, anger), but also to their troubled family member or friend.

One final word: *Abstinence is a harm-reduction strategy.* Loved ones should not be afraid to ask for it, but remember that the person might not be able or willing to quit right now. Even for people who *have* decided to quit, most find that relapses are the rule, and they stop and start numerous times before achieving lasting abstinence. How loved ones respond to these natural "slips" is an important decision. Anything that suggests to the person that they'd better not admit when they've used again will set up the possibility of lying, secrecy, and broken communication.

Conclusion

The major principle of harm reduction is *any change in a positive direction.* This means to look for specific harms one experiences, and perhaps also harms that loved ones are suffering, and steps to take to reduce harms. At first, this may or may not have to do with how much the person is actually using alcohol or other drugs. In fact they will likely continue to use as they begin to obtain more control over their lives in their effort to *reduce the harm* done by drugs or alcohol.

The main goal of this chapter is to challenge people to think from a radically different perspective about loved ones who are suffering with substance abuse problems. This author believes that only by using a model that respects all of the components – biological factors, psychological vulnerabilities and strengths, and social/cultural realities – can we begin to change the current climate of hatred, fear, and punishment of people who are suffering with drug- and alcohol-related difficulties – along with their families and their communities. Harm reduction offers a new perspective based on compassion, reason, and collaboration to minimize how drug users are pathologized and to bring them back into the families, friendship networks, and social institutions that are the source of strength and healing.

Critical Thinking Questions

1. What are the critical differences between a traditional view of substance abuse within a family system and a harm-reduction approach?
2. What are the strengths and weakness of such an approach (harm reduction)?
3. Could this approach strengthen family and friendship networks in such a way as to restore resiliency to all members? If so, explain why you think this. If not, also explain.

References

Alexander, M. (2010). *The new Jim Crow: Mass incarceration in the age of colorblindness.* New York. New Press.

Anda, R., Whitfield, C., Felitti, V., Edwards, V. J., Dube, S. R., and Williamson, D. F. (2002). Adverse childhood experiences, alcoholic parents, and later risk of alcoholism and depression. *Psychiatric Services, 53*(8), 1001–1009.

Arditti, J. A. (2012). *Parental incarceration and the family: Psychological and social effects of imprisonment on children, parents, and caregivers.* New York: NYU Press.

Beattie, M. (1987). *Codependent no more: How to stop controlling others and start caring for yourself.* New York: Harper/Hazeldon.

Beattie, M. (1990). *Codependent's guide to the twelve steps.* New York: Fireside.

Bowlby, J. (1988). *A secure base: Parent–child attachment and healthy human development.* New York: Basic Books.

Denning, P. (2000). *Practicing harm reduction psychotherapy: An alternative approach to the addictions.* New York: Guilford Press.

Denning, P., and Little, J. (2012). *Practicing harm reduction psychotherapy: An alternative approach to addictions* (2nd edn). New York: Guilford Press.

Denning, P., Little, J., and Glickman, A. (2004). *Over the influence: The harm reduction guide to managing drugs and alcohol.* New York: Guilford Press.

Felitti, V. J. (2004). The origins of addiction: Evidence from the Adverse Childhood Experiences study. Original article published in German. English version available: http://www.acestudy.org/files/OriginsofAddiction.pdf.

Galanter, M. (2002). Network therapy. In D. Brook and H. Spitz (eds), *The group therapy of substance abuse.* New York: Haworth Medical Press.

Gordon, J., and Barrett, K. (1993). The codependency movement: Issues of context and differentiation. In J. Baer, A. Marlatt, and R. J. McMahon (eds), *Addictive behaviors across the life span: Prevention, treatment and policy issues* (pp. 307–339). Newbury Park, CA: Sage Publications.

Hesselbrock, V. M., and Hesselbrock, M. N. (2006). Developmental perspectives on the risk for developing substance abuse problems. In W. R. Miller and K. M. Carroll (eds), *Rethinking substance abuse: What the science shows, and what we should do about it* (pp. 97–114). New York: Guilford Press.

Hester, R. K., and Miller, W. R. (eds). (1989). *Handbook of alcoholism treatment approaches: Effective alternatives.* New York: Pergamon Press.

Khantzian, E. J. (1985). The self-medication hypotheses of addictive disorders: Focus on heroin and cocaine dependence. *American Journal of Psychiatry, 142,* 1259–1264.

Khantzian, E. J. (1999). *Treating addiction as a human process.* Northvale, NJ: Jason Aronson.

Leventhal, T., and Brooks-Gunn, J. (2000). The neighborhoods they live in: The effects of neighborhood residence on child and adolescent outcomes. *Psychological Bulletin, 126,* 309–337.

Loury, G. C. (2008). *Race, incarceration, and American values.* Cambridge, MA: MIT Press.

Marlatt, G. A. (ed.). (1998). *Harm reduction: Pragmatic strategies for managing high-risk behaviors.* New York: Guilford Press.

Marlatt, G. A., Larimer, M. E., and Witkiewitz, K. (eds). (2012). *Harm reduction: Pragmatic strategies for managing high-risk behaviors.* New York: Guilford Press.

Miller, W. R., and Carroll, K. M. (eds). (2006). *Rethinking substance abuse: What the science shows and what we should do about it.* New York: Guilford Press.

Miller, W. R., and Rollnick, S. (2012). *Motivational interviewing: Preparing people for change* (3rd edn). New York: Guilford Press.

Morgenstern, J., and Leeds, J. (1993). Contemporary psychoanalytic theories of substance abuse: A disorder in search of a paradigm. *Psychotherapy, 30,* 194–206.

Peele, S. (1989). *The diseasing of America: Addiction treatment out of control.* Lexington, MA: Lexington Books.

Peele, S., and Brodsky, A. (1991). *The truth about addiction and recovery.* New York: Simon & Schuster.

Prochaska, J. O., and DiClemente, C. C. (1992). In search of how people change: Applications to addictive behaviors. *American Psychologist, 47,* 1102–1114.

Prochaska, J. O., and Velicer, W. F. (1997). The transtheoretical model of health behavior change. *American Journal of Health Promotion, 1,* 38–48.

Project MATCH Research Group. (1997). Matching alcoholism treatments to client heterogeneity: Project MATCH posttreatment drinking outcomes. *Journal of Studies on Alcohol, 58,* 7–29.

Rotgers, F. (2003). Cognitive-behavioral theories of substance abuse. In F. Rotgers, J. Morgenstern, and S. Walters (eds), *Treating substance abuse: Theory and technique* (pp. 166–189). New York: Guilford Press.

Ryan, R., and Deci, E. (2000). Self-determination theory and the facilitation of intrinsic motivation, social development, and well-being. *American Psychologist, 55,* 68–78.

Sorge, R., and Kershnar, S. (1998). *Getting off right: A safety manual for injection drug users.* New York: Harm Reduction Coalition.

Springer, E. (1991). Effective AIDS prevention with active drug users: The harm reduction model. In M. Shernoff (ed.), *Counseling chemically dependent people with HIV illness* (pp. 141–158). New York: Harrington Park Press.

Straussner, S. L. A. (ed.) (2001). *Ethnocultural factors in substance abuse treatment.* New York: Guilford Press.

Szalavitz, M. (2006). *Help at any cost. How the troubled-teen industry cons parents and hurts kids.* New York: Riverhead Books.

Tatarsky, A. (2002). *Harm reduction psychotherapy: A new treatment for drug and alcohol problems.* Northvale, NJ: Jason Aronson.

van der Kolk, B. A., McFarlane, A. C., and Weisaeth, L. (1996). Dissociation and information processing in posttraumatic stress disorder. In B. A. van der Kolk, A. C. McFarlane, and L. Weisaeth (eds), *Traumatic stress: The effects of overwhelming experience on mind, body, and society* (pp. 303–327). New York: Guilford Press.

Walant, K. (1995). *Creating the capacity for attachment: Treating addictions and the alienated self.* Northvale, NJ: Jason Aronson.

White, W., and Sanders, M. (2004). Recovery management and people of color: Redesigning addiction treatment for historically disempowered communities. Retrieved May 30, 2014 from www.bhrm.org/papers/peopleofcolor.pdf.

Wurmser, L. (1980). Drug use as a protective system. In D. J. Lettieri, M. Sayers, and H. W. Pearson (eds), *Theories on drug abuse: Selected contemporary perspectives (NIDA Monograph 30)* (pp. 71–74). Washington, DC: US Department of Health and Human Services.

Zinberg, N. (1984). *Drug, set, setting.* New Haven: Yale University Press.

Part V

Conclusion

22

Responding to Family Problems

Joyce A. Arditti

We began this book with a conceptual overview that helped situate family problems "in context" – that is, within their social worlds and environments. Throughout the chapters we examined how family problems are multiply determined and saw how risk and protective factors operate on various systemic levels to influence the well-being of families and children. Sometimes family problems emerge because of the structural complexity of the family (e.g., grandparent-headed households) or the types of problems faced (e.g., military families or families with a parent in prison). Family problems may be related to particular developmental periods, as in the case of elders and children, when individuals must rely on others for their care. Or perhaps there is a developmental mismatch in terms of caregiving demands and developmental status as in the case of childhood adultification. Other times family problems stem from an imbalance when the demands of a situation outweigh a families capability to deal with those demands. For example, severe poverty can connect with child neglect – material deprivation can be so extreme that it overwhelms the family. And yet, as pointed out in Chapter 7 (Jarrett, Bahar, and McPherson), and in Chapters 19 (Ryan and colleagues) and 17 (Farrell, Bowen, and Goodrich), even in the face of impoverished conditions, resilience, either by virtue of resilient parents as in the case of the extraordinary strategies utilized by poor mothers, or by virtue of interventions that capitalize on family and community strengths and perhaps buffer economic shortfalls through meaningful assistance and social support, better outcomes for children and families are possible.

When it comes to deciding how families will be affected by a particular set of problems or conditions, the answer will almost always be "it depends" (Garbarino, 1995). From a developmental science perspective, family problems always connect with the broader social environment. This is good news, because not only do we consider the factors that lead to vulnerability and risk, but we can also identify factors that connect with *agency* and *resilience*. The concepts of agency and resilience imply that individuals, and collectively families, are producers of their own development and can influence, shape, and even transcend toxic contexts of development (Brandstaedter and Lerner, 1999; Garbarino, 1995). In other words, throughout the chapters in this book we have seen how families and children are not necessarily passive, but make choices and decisions that represent active attempts to solve problems, locate resources, or find meaning in difficult circumstances. We have seen how individuals and family members are not simply victims of their life situations but may have diverse responses to family problems and adapt in multiple ways. Yet we must be cautious in our consideration of resilience, as it should never be an excuse to "do nothing." That is, families' inherent agency, as well as strength-based interventions aimed at bolstering resilience in families, may not be enough for families in trouble (Rutter, 1987; Seccombe, 2002). We must also try and change the odds for families, particularly those that are disadvantaged and marginalized, by attending to the interplay of political, economic, social, and racial climates that shape family life and development.

The Pyramid of Principles

How do we change the odds for families in trouble, while also recognizing their unique strengths, agency, and basic human rights? The pyramid of principles, initially developed to respond to the challenges associated with parental incarceration, is applicable in thinking about a wide range of family problems and the interlocking systems between parents, children, caregivers, and the social environment. We have seen throughout the book how complicated family problems are, and that most difficulties have multiple determinants. For example, as Hardesty and colleagues point out, there is no one single cause for relationship violence, and many factors contribute to its occurrence. In Chapter 4 (Loper, Whalen, and Will), we learned that multiple family background characteristics and environmental stressors contribute to the likelihood of a parent's criminal justice involvement. Thus a social policy and practice agenda aimed at ameliorating family problems must be multi-pronged, and attend to core ecological tenets of development that focus on "social justice, risk reduction, and enhancing opportunity with the ultimate goal of

promoting human capacity and agency" (Arditti, 2012, p. 144). In Part IV of this book, we saw chapters that focused on these various tenets, including using a human rights lens to craft family policy, multisystemic interventions which attend to all ecological layers, harm-reduction approaches to substance abuse, and strength-based approached aimed at mobilizing community capacity. The pyramid of principles integrates these approaches fully and furthers our discussion of understanding and responding to family problems. Figure 22.1 presents these principles as a hierarchical pyramid. For maximum efficacy, each level of the pyramid depends on the previous level being met. For example, a program developed to help children with parents in prison (see Chapter 4), or help someone like Gloria succeed after a period of incarceration (see this volume, p. 50), will be far more effective within a context of sweeping policy reform that addresses our overreliance on incarceration in the first place.

Principle 1: Advance social justice

A theme of this book, particularly in Part I, involved the issue of marginalization and how social exclusion can impact family life. In Chapter 2 for example, van Eeden-Moorefield and Benson articulate how gay, lesbian, transgendered, and bisexual people and their families are systematically excluded from certain privileges and protections (e.g., the risk of being fired due to sexual orientation). As discussed by Anderson and

Figure 22.1   The pyramid of principles (from Arditti, 2012). Reprinted with permission of New York University Press.

Letiecq (Chapter 18), social justice defines whether families will be included in a particular policy or program, and we learned that many social policies directed toward families "fall short of actualizing justice for all families in … their diversities" (Anderson and Letiecq, this volume, p. 291). In "falling short" and failing to recognize diversity, policy may intentionally, and also unintentionally, contribute to social inequality by deepening racial, ethnic, and economic disparities among individuals and their families. For example, while it is a fairly well-known fact that African Americans (and in particular males) are disproportionately represented among the prison inmate population in the United States, Hispanics have been the fastest-growing ethnic or racial group in the past decade. Hispanics are now the largest single ethnic group in the federal prison system and critics argue that this growth has been fueled in part by changes in immigration policies that have multiplied the ways in which undocumented immigrants can be prosecuted and imprisoned (Lopez and Light, 2009). Immigration law may not have intentionally been developed as a means to intensify social inequality or exclude people from opportunities, yet, arguably, is increasingly a pathway into the criminal justice system. Social inequality is intensified by penal involvement and has multifold implications for families (Western and Pettit, 2010). This is but one example of how important it is to attend to social justice when thinking about policy and programs that either target a particular group (e.g., undocumented immigrants) or ignore another (e.g., the exclusion of GLBT individuals from fair hiring and firing practices in some states).

The foundation of the pyramid specifies the need to advance social justice and truly recognize family diversity in terms of the many different ways people live as families, care for one another, and carry out key family functions such as child-rearing and economic provision. Social justice can be defined as the "elimination of institutionalized domination and oppression" (Young, 1990, p. 15). It has two important aspects. The first aspect involves the inclusion of everyone in the full benefits of society and the second involves the empowerment of people to participate fully in the economic, social, and cultural life of their communities and countries. So if we were to go back to our example about the plight of undocumented immigrants, we can

see how both inclusion and empowerment are necessary to improve the situations of Hispanic families in the United States. Parra-Cardona and colleagues (Chapter 20, this volume) give us a good picture of some of the barriers Latino immigrants face, and develop a community-based program aimed at empowering Latino parents and breaking their isolation in the community. Their inclusion in the program from the bottom-up is important and consistent with social justice principles.

Social justice demands a reversal of practices that disenfranchise individuals and families. Many of these practices are invisible, that is, unknown to others who are unaffected by them. Felon disenfranchisement laws are good examples of "invisible punishments" (Travis, 2002) that accompany incarceration and extend beyond prison walls after release. These laws involve denying ex-prisoners access to resources (e.g., student loans), benefits (e.g., federal public assistance), and political participation (e.g., voting rights) that are available to other United States citizens. In some states, it is perfectly legal to deny a person these things if they have a felony record. Undocumented immigrants are another group of people who are routinely denied resources, benefits, and political participation because they lack citizenship. Invisible punishments and barriers that stem from disenfranchisement is a social justice issue because they cause difficulties for those parents and families that are most in need. We can also see how many family problems stem from material hardships (e.g., food shortages, child neglect) and carry social stigma (e.g., mental illness, substance abuse, family violence) that contributes to isolation and invisibility that in turn undermine family and child well-being. Thus advancing a social justice agenda for families involves deconstructing social stigma, and confronting social and economic inequality through innovative programs and policies that include, rather than exclude, those most in need over the life course. For example, many states are opting out of the permanent ban on welfare benefits for ex-drug offenders who were incarcerated (see Arditti, 2012, for a review). Comprehensive immigration reform is another example of policy that is driven by a social justice agenda. Elements of reform aim to "include and empower" by providing opportunities for undocumented immigrants to earn citizenship (and thus gain access to important resources and federal and state aid), restore due process protections for immigrants, and examine the root causes of immigration (e.g., economic hardship, political oppression) (Vásquez, 2013).

Anti-poverty efforts as social justice
More broadly, anti-poverty measures are particularly important tools for enhancing social justice given record high numbers of families and children in poverty. Approximately 46.2 million Americans lived in poverty in 2011 (about 15%) and approximately 16.1 million, or 22% of all children live in poverty as of 2011 (US Department of Health and Human Sciences, 2012). Material hardship poses direct and indirect harms for children by contributing to parenting and environmental risks as well as negative health and educational outcomes. While children from all race groups were added to the poverty population, increasingly we see two worlds of childhood that reflect growing inequality and racial disparities. White and Asian children are on average much less likely to live in poverty than African American and Latino children (Macartney, 2011). For African American children, the poverty rate reported was 37.4% for 2011, Hispanic children have a rate of 34.1%, and for non-Hispanic White children the rate was 12.5% (US Department of Health and Human Sciences, 2012).

What factors are behind these racial differences? Obviously the answer is complicated, but, as shown by the arguments made by Comeau and Avison (Chapter 5, this volume), stem partly from the "second demographic transition" and the disparate social locations of families. Children and adults in two-parent married families are much less likely to live in poverty (10.9%), with children living in female-headed families with no spouse present having four times the rate of children in poverty (47.6%). We know race "intersects" with marital status (that is, Black children disproportionately spend time in single-mother households), contributing to their ranks among the poor. But the picture is even more complicated. Not only are Black children much more likely to be poor than White children, but they spend more years in poverty: Black children are seven times more likely than Whites to be "persistently poor" (longer cycles of poverty) and experience more frequent poverty cycles. Further, Black children are more likely to be born into poverty, which has powerful implications throughout the life course. Children born into poverty have substantially higher poverty rates than children who are not poor at birth and are likely to be poor as adults. Poor-at-birth children are at even greater risk (compared to those children who become poor at some other point during childhood) to drop out of high school and have a teen non-marital birth (Ratcliffe and McKernan, 2010).

Other factors contribute to growing poverty in general and race and ethnic disparities. Poverty has increasingly become concentrated among urban areas and in geographically isolated rural "ghettos" (e.g., the southern "Black Belt", rural Hispanic "boomtowns" in the Midwest and West; Lichter, 2012). Income and geographic segregation has grown most rapidly among Blacks and Hispanics with poor Whites less segregated from non-poor Whites than their minority counterparts. Neighborhood poverty (20–40% residents below the poverty line) is much greater for children of color (Lichter, 2012). Thus neighborhood poverty and isolation from non-poor communities and individuals mark social inequality and perpetuate it further. Recall the importance of community capacity in supporting strong families of all kinds (Chapter 17, this volume). Clearly, many poor families live in communities that are the least likely to provide the informal and formal supports that are needed to optimize strengths, enhance well-being, and leverage them into better living conditions.

The profile that has emerged with respect to poverty reflects growing income inequality, disparities in assets, and racial, ethnic and family structure inequalities. We may espouse ideologies that "celebrate" diversity, but specific types of diversity (i.e., single parenthood, race) connect with very real disadvantages, at least in the United States. How do we turn around growing social inequality? Social justice confronts the realities of family diversity and demands health security, enfranchisement of the poor, and evidence-based, rather than ideologically driven, anti-poverty measures. Marriage promotion is an example of an ideologically driven anti-poverty approach. From a statistical standpoint, there is no denying the demographic facts that marriage is connected with social and economic advantage. Part of the reason for this connection could be the fact that marriage is more *important* in the United States than other industrialized societies such as Western Europe or Canada (Cherlin, 2010). Marriage is so important in the United States that it is a special legal relationship status with many rights and privileges. Those that are not married are excluded from receiving these benefits, such as tax and inheritance breaks. And yet, as Anderson and Letiecq note in Chapter 18, there is no clear evidence that marriage in and of itself is an anti-poverty solution.

A recent evaluation of the New Hope program gives us some insight regarding the issue of marriage promotion as a means to lift single-mother families out of poverty (Gassman-Pines and Yoshikawa, 2006). The New Hope program offered work support supplements to poor women. Eligibility in the program included a willingness and ability to work 30 hours or more a week. The researchers conducting the study controlled for baseline differences between married and never-married women and included mediators such as parenting stress and depression in studying the effects of the program. The findings revealed that almost twice as many women who were in the New Hope program (21%) were married at the five-year follow up compared to 12% of the controls. For marriage promotion advocates, this could be defined as "success." But let's look more carefully at what happened to the women in the study. The researchers also found that the program increased income, wage growth, and goal efficacy among never-married mothers and decreased maternal depression. These benefits occurred before some of the mothers got married. Could it be that women who felt better and earned more income became more likely to get married? Other research suggests that greater income leads to marriage (rather than marriage causing greater income), also known as the "marriage premium" (Gassman-Pines and Yoshikawa, 2006). Social justice demands not that people get married, but that marriage does not characterize and perpetuate social inequality as it currently does. The New Hope program is a good anti-poverty program because it promotes employment (Lieb and Thistle, 2005) and empowers women and enhances their well-being, regardless of whether they get married.

Another example of how social justice can be a foundation for anti-poverty measures is through health policy. We have seen how health is a critical dimension of well-being and many family problems stem from a lack of physical and mental health. Health is fundamental for parental competency, family functioning, and positive developmental trajectories in children. The Patient Protection and Affordable Care Act (PPACA), signed into law in March, 2010, is an important anti-poverty measure that stands to advantage many families who previously lacked either health insurance or access to health care. Beginning in 2014, the Health Care and Education Affordability Reconciliation Act (HCEARA) and PPACA will fund expanded Medicaid coverage for all individuals whose incomes are under 133% of the federal poverty level. The PPACA also provides a promising mechanism to establish community health centers to provide basic health services in underserved areas (Beddoes, 2010), thus strengthening community capacity.

Regardless of the specific issue being addressed (e.g., poverty, immigration policy), a social justice agenda aligns with a resilience framework that threads throughout the chapters in this book. Of the many factors identified in the research on resilience and coping, social support from persons outside the family is considered crucial and often the heart of intervention and policy efforts (Garbarino, 1998). The twin foci of inclusion and empowerment that characterize social justice are a means to break the isolation of the disenfranchised, ensure due process, and encourage access to critical resources and social connections that help solve family problems.

Principle 2: Do no harm

One of the fundamental ideas of a resilience framework involves a recognition of family strengths and people's basic right to be treated with dignity, even in the face of very challenging and difficult circumstances. Several authors in the present volume discussed differences between a "deficit" and "strengths-based" approach to working with youth (Chapter 19 by Ryan and colleagues), families, and communities (Chapter 17 by Farrell and colleagues).

Part of the reason for the movement away from a deficit model of intervention, is that we know that in pathologizing families, we may do more harm than good, even when we have the best of intentions to help. The way a problem is framed to a large extent shapes how we will respond to it (Shlonsky, Friend, and Lambert, 2007). Harm reduction acknowledges that sometimes our responses to problems exacerbate them and can make a situation even worse.

Harm reduction is a fundamental strategy to reduce risk for individuals and their families that is based on a public health philosophy that seeks to lessen the consequences of risky behavior. A core tenet of public health is that people should have the knowledge, facilities, and freedom to maintain and improve their own health (World Health Organization (WHO), 2005). A "do no harm" principle rests on a social justice foundation that is nondiscriminatory, respects civil liberties and human rights, and provides alternatives to high-risk lifestyle choices that are non-stigmatizing and reduce public health harms (Hathaway, 2001; Nodine, 2006; WHO, 2005). In Chapter 21 of this volume, Denning applies harm-reduction principles for families responding to substance abuse. Additionally, we can see its value in a wide range of circumstances such as dealing with families' problems associated with mental illness (RachBiesel, Scott, and Dixon, 1999), adolescent problem behaviors (Dishion, McCord, and Poulin, 1999), and family violence (Shlonsky et al., 2007).

Harm reduction and parental incarceration
Utilizing a family perspective means we must calculate harm not only in terms of the individual who may have a presenting problem (such as substance abuse), but also the broad consequences one individual's risky behavior may have for the rest of the family. The study of parental incarceration is a good context to consider harm-reduction principles and examine some of the barriers that exist in implementing such an approach (Arditti, 2012). As noted in Chapter 4 by Loper and colleagues, a great deal of attention has recently been directed to the effects of a parent's incarceration on children. We can easily imagine a scenario whereby a parent's substance misuse can not only create health harms, but also lead to involvement in the criminal justice system with the potential for incarceration. Incarceration creates a "ripple effect" for the family, and has "collateral consequences" that go beyond the offender's confinement (Hagan and

Dinovitzer, 1999). These consequences involve the costs associated with the incapacitation of the offender stemming from incarceration upon release (such as a lack of employability), as well as the children who must bear the diminished economic and social capital of their families and communities that result from the widespread use of incarceration as a response to drug use and drug-related activity.

Applying a harm-reduction principle in this instance involves determining the extent to which incarceration creates more harm than good with respect to public safety, substance misuse and abuse, and the reduction of drug-related crime committed by parent offenders, as well as the effects over time incarceration has on children and families of the offender. Despite evidence that points to the inefficacy of incarceration to deter the use of illicit drugs (Csete, 2010; Druker, 1999; Global Commission on Drug Policy, 2011), harsh criminal sanctions are still widely used in the United States as a response to drug use and drug-related activity. The underlying roots of America's predominantly punitive approach can be traced to intense moral judgments associated with crime and risky behaviors such as drug use. Additionally, as we have seen throughout this text, agenda setting, legislation, and policy are also shaped by social constructions about the shared characteristics of a particular group of people and judgments about who is deserving of help. Negatively constructed (i.e., value-laden stereotypes) and powerless groups will usually be the target of punishment policy and the extent of their burdens will often be greater than needed to achieve the desired results (e.g., stopping substance abuse; Schneider and Ingram, 1992).

A shift away from punishment policy to harm reduction involves many things – including the construction of more positive images about those populations that disproportionately end up in prison (drug users, unauthorized immigrants, the mentally ill). Moving away from incarceration, especially for non-violent drug offenders, would be consistent with a harm-reduction strategy. Ultimately such a harm-reduction approach conceives of incarceration as a last resort rather than a first response and implies using specific strategies to reduce harm such as alternatives to incarceration (e.g., drug courts), sentencing reform, special arrest procedures when children are present, humane treatment in prison, rehabilitation programs for offenders, and so forth (Arditti, 2012).

A "do no harm" principle can be applied to many kinds of family problems. Harm reduction promotes a consideration of a wide range of options aimed at diminishing harm to a particular client, family, or group, *including the harm caused by the intervention itself* (e.g., incarceration as a response to illicit drug use; removing a child from his or her parents and community). The model encourages choice and responsibility without stigma (Shlonsky *et al.*, 2007). While total abstinence from a behavior may be ideal, harm reduction considers risk on a continuum. Thus any movement toward reducing negative behaviors can be considered a success and holds great promise in terms of involving families in solving problems.

Principle 3: Promote human development

While principles of social justice and harm reduction serve to broadly influence the social, legal, and economic contexts in which human development occurs, Principle 3 involves applying the tenets of developmental science to strengthen families and enhance the well-being of parents, children, and the communities in which they live (Arditti, 2012). Principles of developmental science focus on person–context interactions, proximal processes, and an ecological approach to human development (Bronfenbrenner, 1979; Lerner, 1998; Lerner, Sparks, and McCubbin, 1999). These principles translate to interventions and policy that focus on people's natural environments and day-to-day relationships and promote a systemic reorganization so that positive change can occur.

The importance of healthy relationships

From a developmental science perspective one of the best ways to solve family problems would be to promote resilience by encouraging and supporting healthy relationships. It is no surprise that a theme throughout this volume is that *family process matters*. In their discussion of what young children need from parents, developmental scientists Sharon Ramey and colleagues (Chapter 12) point out that process may be more important than family structure. That is good news, because we can think of many instances where,

as human services professionals, we may not be in a position to change structural factors in the families' world (such as family composition or neighborhood), and even if we try, these attempts may not yield results. However, we *may* be in a position to find ways to help family members relate to and care for one another, as well as strengthen connections between family members and important social institutions such as schools, workplace, or health settings. For example, with regard to health, Comeau and Avison (Chapter 5, this volume) point out that supportive relationships between children and their teachers serve a critical protective function for the most economically disadvantaged families.

As we have discussed, the federal government's marriage promotion efforts (see Chapter 18, this volume) were implemented to encourage marriage among single parents in order to reduce poverty. Underlying these efforts was the belief that children in married families are better off on a host of outcomes than children in single-parent families. Was the federal government wrong about this? Not necessarily, because as Comeau and Avison point out, there is solid research indicating differences along indicators of well-being between children in single-parent families and children in married families. It is a well-known fact that children in single-parent households are at much greater risk for poverty and a host of poverty-related outcomes such as poor school achievement and high school drop-out (see, e.g., McLanahan, 1994; McLoyd, 1998). Yet marriage promotion did not necessarily promote resilience among at-risk families or improve the lives of children. One reason could be that the focus was not on the quality of children's relationships, but on their family structure. Developmental scientists often emphasize that "resilience rests fundamentally on relationships" (Luthar, 2006, p. 780). In our example about marriage promotion policy, this would mean that resilience may be more effectively promoted by encouraging healthy family relationships rather than trying to directly encourage marriage.

Socioeconomic disadvantage and parenting

What do healthy relationships look like? Obviously the answer to that question is complicated and depends on many factors such as family type (e.g., parent–child or intimate partnership) and social location.

Research suggests that healthy families communicate; are affirming, respectful, and committed to one another; share responsibilities; have a healthy lifestyle free of violence and substance abuse; are connected to friends and community members; and are able to respond to and seek help with problems. Enhancing interventions are mindful of these qualities, but also sensitive to individual, socioeconomic, and cultural differences, so there are a range of possibilities with regard to strengthening families, parenting, and facilitating connections between families and other important institutions such as schools. For example, socioeconomic disadvantage is an important context that bears on how adults parent their children and child outcomes related to parenting. We can see this clearly in the literature on parental socialization. In a seminal study on social class and parental socialization, sociologist Annette Lareau found that in contrast to more affluent parents, economically disadvantaged parents tend to facilitate the accomplishment of "natural growth" in their children in which children experience "long stretches of leisure time, child-initiated play, clear boundaries between adults and children, and daily interactions with kin" (Lareau, 2011, p. 3). This type of socialization stands in stark contrast to middle-class parents who engage in a process of "concerted cultivation" characterized by organized activities for their children, and interaction with central institutions in society such as schools. Lareau argues that these differences in socialization style have implications for child outcomes, with more affluent children gaining important institutional advantages that translate into greater success as adults. The point here is that dominant discourses in society shape family behavior and, ultimately, how people fare in contemporary life.

Studies about parental discipline also point to cultural and socioeconomic variation in terms of how children are corrected and the outcomes associated with physical discipline. Low-income, and in particular African American, parents are more likely to use harsh discipline characterized by physical punishment with their children. This type of approach runs counter to "dominant cultural repertoires" of how children should be raised, centering on the importance of reasoning and teaching children to "solve problems with reasoning rather than with physical force" (Lareau, 2011, p. 4). A closer inspection, however, reveals the presence of family strengths even in conjunction with harsh discipline. Arditti, Burton, and Neeves-Bothelho (2010) found in their study that while some mothers utilized harsh discipline, they also invested in considerable energy advocating for their children (labeled "survivalist mothers" in the study). Other studies have found that although poor African American parents may use harsh discipline, these parents were affectionate and nurturing with their children (Deater-Deckard and Dodge, 1997). In these examples, family process may be shaped by the realities of everyday life in the context of economic disadvantage. That is, harsh discipline, while not necessarily endorsed by experts, can be viewed as adaptive, particularly in dangerous neighborhoods where children's obedience is necessary for their survival (Russell, Mize, and Bissaker, 2002). Yet positive family processes (such as affection and advocacy) in socioeconomically disadvantaged families may mitigate deleterious child effects (Deater-Deckard and Dodge, 1997) and point to the need to consider interventions and policy that build on these strengths and are in sync with the realities of people's environmental conditions and cultural understandings.

We can see how there is a great deal of variation in families in terms of how they may interact with each other and socialize their children. Burton and colleagues' (Chapter 11, this volume) discussion of childhood adultification illustrates perhaps the most extreme adaptation of parenting roles (i.e., children caring for adults rather than adults caring for their children) in response to severe economic hardship and other family difficulties such as addiction. Yet the preceding discussion of parental discipline demonstrates how certain family processes such as affection and advocacy may mitigate harm to children. We can also see from Lareau's study how a lack of fit with regard to family process and the dominant culture may lead to differential advantages for children. Ultimately, the take-away message from work on parental socialization, as well as the coverage provided by the chapters in this volume, point to the primacy of family process as a potential mechanism for change amongst vulnerable families. When we look carefully, we see evidence of healthy relationships, even among the most disadvantaged families (Valladares and Moore, 2009), pointing to the value of examining family strengths, not just family problems.

Goodness-of-fit

In addition to the importance of family process, the concept of "goodness-of-fit" is relevant in thinking about intervention and policy aimed at vulnerable families and children. Goodness-of-fit, originally an idea advanced by ecological systems theory (Bronfenbrenner, 1979), specified that healthy development and family functioning depend on the match between the needs of the developing individual or family and the resources, supports, and capacities of the multiple environments within which the person (or family) is located. In the case of marriage promotion, the lack of a positive effect likely suggests that the "intervention" did not necessarily promote human development in a manner that fit the needs and challenges of the poor families targeted by the program. Thus marriage promotion may not be the best "fit" for combating poverty and optimizing youth outcomes.

Another reason a program or policy may not fit is because of misinformation and stereotypes about the families or people that are targeted for service. We can see this lack of fit very clearly with regard to poor families, who are commonly at the core of policy debates given that poverty is acknowledged as a risk factor for many problems experienced by youth and their family members (Shanks and Danzinger, 2011). Many myths exist about poor children and their families. These myths stem from a "culture of poverty" concept, which basically encompasses the idea that poor people all share the same set of beliefs, values, and behaviors. Critics of the culture of poverty idea argue that the concept is constructed from a set of stereotypes that are not based on fact. Examples of these stereotypes include the belief that poor people are lazy and have weak work ethics, and are uninvolved in their children's learning (Gorski, 2008). Research does not support these stereotypes. For example, there is good evidence to suggest that many poor parents have close relationships with their children, care about their children's education, use specific strategies to help them with their school work, and are strong advocates for them in the school system (Arditti et al., 2010; Gutman and McLoyd, 2000; Valladares and Moore, 2009).

A culture of poverty perspective obscures the strengths of families and ignores the importance of family relationships in supporting youth outcomes such as school success. It ignores how individuals in families attempt to pursue lives marked by healthy contributions to self, family, and community (Lerner, Fisher, and Weinberg, 2000). And perhaps most importantly, it ignores the voices and concerns of vulnerable youth and families.

The case of family preservation

As in the case of the inefficacy of marriage promotion programs as an anti-poverty solution, we see a similar problem with family preservation programs and policies aimed at caregivers and children who are in the child welfare system. Unfortunately, many family preservation efforts "fail" in that they do not successfully improve parenting, prevent further maltreatment of children, or keep families together (Barth et al., 2005; Roberts, 1999). A goodness-of-fit lens can help us understand why these programs may fail. Family preservation is an alternative to foster care and requires states to make "reasonable efforts" to prevent the removal of children from their homes, and if they are in fact removed, ensure their return as soon as possible (Cytryn, 2010). Critics argue that the failure of these programs stems from a lack of fit between the reasons most families are involved in the child welfare system and the focus of legislation, reform, and programming aimed at children in the system (Barth et al., 2005; Cytryn, 2010; Roberts, 1999). As specified by McWey and Stevenson-Wojciak (Chapter 8, this volume), the majority of substantiated cases of child maltreatment are due to child neglect, which stems largely from material deprivation. Thus family preservation in these cases must entail meaningful services to children who are combating homelessness and poverty. As Farrell and colleagues point out in Chapter 17, housing problems place families at risk for separation and lessen their changes of reunification. Unfortunately, the majority of states have reported that they lack the appropriate funding and services to support families. Given that 90% of this limited funding is devoted to foster care and adoption (Cytryn, 2010), family preservation efforts are woefully underfunded. Additionally, apart from foster care and adoption, existing preservation services often focus on parental performance (Barth et al., 2005), which may be only part of the reason why families are in the system, particularly in the cases of child neglect stemming from material deprivation. Subsequently family preservation may not work because there is a lack of "fit" between the causes of child maltreatment and the services and resources available to families in the child welfare system. This lack of "fit" between families and the system may inadvertently contribute to an *overreliance* on foster care and adoption as a means to solve the problem of child neglect, running counter to the true mission of family preservation (Cytryn, 2010).

In sum, a hallmark of the promotion of human development involves the development of programs and policies that "fit" and the recognition that committed and loving relationships have a "high protective potential" (Luthar and Brown, 2007, p. 943). We see that this is true throughout the life course, whether we are discussing young children and their need for responsive care from parents (Ramey *et al.*, Chapter 12, this volume), or vulnerable elders dependent on family members for their care (Roberto *et al.*, Chapter 15, this volume; Piercy, Chapter 10, this volume). Throughout this volume and as emphasized in Part IV, programs and polices that are multi-pronged, strengths-based, and "acknowledge family needs and aspirations, functioning styles, and supports and resources" (Farrell *et al.*, p. 284, this volume) hold the most promise in terms of promoting positive human development.

Final Words: The Need for Evidence-Informed Practice and Policy

Much has been written about troubled families and how best as a society to respond to their problems. The theoretical perspectives and themes advanced in this textbook culminate in a pyramid of principles based on social justice, harm reduction, and the promotion of human development. But these principles alone are not sufficient to change the odds for distressed families. Practice and policy efforts aimed at addressing family problems must be "evidence-informed." In Chapter 1 (this volume) we discussed how important scientific evidence was in optimizing policy and practice responses to family problems. Evidence-informed practice and policy is based on research and evaluation

findings about what interventions are effective as well as the knowledge of practitioners (Arney, Lewis, Bromfield, and Holzer, 2010). Yet too often policy and interventions are based on cultural myths and panacea approaches to solving complicated problems such as poverty, poor health, substance use and abuse, and family violence. Panacea approaches reflect the search for "simple cures for difficult social problems" (Petrosino, Turpin-Petrosino, and Finckenauer, 2000, p. 357). In utilizing a panacea approach, governments typically adopt an intervention for a short time, and when it fails to work, either search for another "easy cure" or continue utilizing a failed approach even when it has been demonstrated not to work (Finckenauer, Gavin, Hovland, and Storvoll, 1999). For example, we can clearly see how the decades-long "war on drugs," characterized by lengthy periods of incarceration for even nonviolent drug offenders, is a panacea for responding to drug use and abuse. Although costing trillions of dollars for law enforcement, the courts, and prisons to enact criminal sanctions for drug-related offenses, many experts argue that the drugs war has done little to stop the demand for and use of drugs in the United States (Global Commission on Drug Policy, 2011), and has caused far more harm than good, particularly for children and families of offenders (Arditti, 2012; Hagan and Dinovitzer, 1999).

The implementation of a program or policy, even if it has not been demonstrated to be effective, sometimes happens because it is harmonious with widely held cultural beliefs and popular emotions (Finckenauer *et al.*, 1999). Returning to our marriage promotion example, we can see how cultural ideology about married nuclear families contributes to the popularity of these programs, even in the absence of strong evidence indicating their efficacy in alleviating poverty. This ideology specifies marriage as the most desirable family form and the most ideal form of human relationships, and contributes to the view that unmarried persons are deficient (Byrne and Carr, 2005). Subsequently pro-marriage ideology may add to the stigmatization and exclusion of the unmarried poor. Recall that social stigma can serve as a barrier regarding people's access to services and benefits (see for example van Eeden-Moorefield and Benson, Chapter 2, this volume; Loper *et al.*, Chapter 4, this volume). The lack of access to services and benefits is *already* an issue for economically disadvantaged families (Valladares and Moore, 2009). We can see then how myths concerning the culture of poverty as well as pro-marriage ideology perpetuate panacea policies and programs that oversimplify the highly challenged lives of those in poverty and may in fact further marginalize them.

In contrast to a panacea approach to solving complex problems and helping troubled and vulnerable families, evidence-informed practice ensures a greater likelihood that a program or policy will fit the needs of those families impacted by a specific government policy or targeted for service by a program or intervention. Evidence-informed practice is important because interventions and policies may inadvertently be unhelpful or, at worst, harmful to those they are intended to help. Ineffective programs also divert money and attention from effective programs and policies and innovative approaches to solving family problems (Petrosino *et al.*, 2000). The lack of evidence-informed practice and policy is apparent in critical areas of family intervention such as child and family welfare (Barth *et al.*, 2005). A major challenge is that vulnerable families in the social welfare system have very complex needs (see, e.g., McWey and Stevenson Wojciak, Chapter 8, this volume) and there is actually very little evidence detailing the parenting problems of caregivers involved in child welfare services (Barth *et al.*, 2005). It is often difficult or unethical to conduct the kinds of research (i.e., randomized experiments) that would provide definitive answers about the causes of problems such as child maltreatment that brings families into the system or whether a treatment "works" (Arney *et al.*, 2010).

The lack of evidence-informed practice is also widespread for many justice programs and policies, which are widely disseminated without pilot testing or implemented without evaluation (Petrosino *et al.*, 2000). The program "Scared Straight" is a case in point. This program, which was wildly popular through the late 1990s, was developed in the United States during the 1970s to deter juvenile offenders from a life of crime. Youth were brought to Rahway State Prison in New Jersey to participate in a "realistic and confrontational rap session run by prisoners serving life sentences" (Petrosino *et al.*, 2000, p. 356). In these rap sessions, prison life was graphically depicted by inmates – including stories of rape

and murder. The idea behind the program, rooted in deterrence theory, was that troubled youth would refrain from crime because they would not want to experience the trauma and deprivations of prison life as described by the inmates. Since its inception, Scared Straight programs similar to the one in New Jersey cropped up all over the country. Yet, "tough on crime" ideology and public perceptions about how the fear of consequences would deter crime fueled the program despite a lack of research demonstrating the program's efficacy. In fact, a systematic evaluation of the program suggested that it may have done more harm than good in that Scared Straight youth participants in some localities were actually *more* likely to commit additional delinquent acts (Petrosino *et al.*, 2000).

Conclusion

In this book, broad perspectives have been applied to an array of contemporary family problems. Specifically, constructivist perspectives have highlighted how social attitudes contribute to social exclusion, as well as how people make meaning of their experience and attempt to solve their problems. Family stress theory shows us how change, loss, and disturbance can create an imbalance in families in which the demands of a situation exceed the family's capabilities and resources to deal with it. And yet, we have seen throughout the book how families cope and adapt to their circumstances and are often successful in responding to adversity and crisis. Ecological theory highlights systemic interdependence and the importance of proximal processes in driving development. These multiple influences and the balance of risk and protective factors contribute to both vulnerability and resilience. We see evidence of families actively engaging with their environments and developing positive adaptations in the context of significant risk.

While we have learned that families can be resilient even under hardship and duress, evidence-based applications of the pyramid of principles can help change the odds for families in trouble. The concepts of risk and resilience cut across theoretical perspectives and substantive research. In changing the odds, the bottom line involves not only developing policy and interventions aimed at families that lessen risk and social inequality, but that also promote critical protective factors such as healthy relationships and agency. Such promotive practices for dealing with family problems must in part occur before difficulties occur or at least overwhelm. Too often public policy is risk-focused and reactive to "catalyzing events such as epidemics or disasters" (Jenson and Fraser, 2011, p. 276). Responding to crises and great need is of course important, but we must go beyond reacting, and embrace a proactive approach to preventing family problems rooted in the promotion of human development.

References

Arditti, J. A. (2012). *Parental incarceration and the family: Psychological and social effects of imprisonment on children, parents, and caregivers.* New York: NYU Press.

Arditti, J. A., Burton, L. M., and Neeves-Bothelho, S. E. (2010). Maternal distress and parenting in the context of cumulative disadvantage. *Family Process, 49,* 142–164.

Arney, F., Lewis, K., Bromfield, L., and Holzer, P. (2010). Using evidence-informed practice to support vulnerable families. In F. Arney and D. Scott (eds), *Working with vulnerable families: A partnership approach* (pp. 247–274). New York: Cambridge University Press.

Barth, R., Landsverk, J., Chamberlain, P., Reid, J., Rolls, J., Hurlburt, M., ... and Kohl, P. (2005). Parent-training programs in child welfare services: Planning for a more evidence-based approach to serving biological parents. *Research on Social Work Practice, 15,* 353–371.

Beddoes, P.V. (2010). How did NACo priorities fair in the final health reform law? *Courthouse Journal, 11,* April 9. Retrieved May 30, 2014 from http://www.wacounties.org/CHJ/2010/CHJ-1110.pdf.

Brandstaedter, J., and Lerner, R. (1999). Development, action, and intentionality: A view of the issues. In J. Brandstaedter and R. M. Lerner (eds), *Action and self-development: Theory and research through the life-span* (pp. ix–xx). Thousand Oaks, CA: Sage Publications.

Bronfenbrenner, U. (1979). *The ecology of human development: Experiments by nature and design.* Cambridge, MA: Harvard University Press.

Byrne, A., and Carr, D. (2005). Caught in the cultural lag: The stigma of singlehood. *Psychological Inquiry, 16,* 84–141.

Cherlin, A. (2010). *The marriage-go-round: The state of marriage and the family in America today.* New York: Vintage.

Csete, J. (2010). *From the mountaintops: What the world can learn from drug policy change in Switzerland.* Open Society Foundations Drug Policy Program. New York: Open Society Foundations. Retrieved May 30, 2014 from http://www.soros.org/initiatives/drugpolicy/articles_publications/publications/csete-mountaintops-20101021.

Cytryn, S. (2010). What went wrong? Why family preservation programs failed to achieve their potential. *Cardozo Journal of Law and Gender, 17,* 81–108.

Deater-Deckard, K., and Dodge, K. (1997). Externalizing behavior problems and discipline revisited: Nonlinear effects and variation by culture, context, and gender. *Psychological Inquiry, 8,* 161–175.

Dishion, T., McCord, J., and Poulin, F. (1999). When interventions harm: Peer groups and problem behavior. *American Psychologist, 54,* 755–764.

Drucker, E. (1999). Drug prohibition and public health: 25 years of evidence. *Public Health Reports, 114,* 14–29.

Finckenauer, J., Gavin, P., Hovland, A., and Storvoll, E. (1999). *Scared Straight: The panacea phenomenon revisited.* Prospect Heights, IL: Waveland Press.

Garbarino, J. (1995). *Raising children in a socially toxic environment.* San Francisco: Jossey-Bass.

Garbarino, J. (1998). Supporting parents in a socially toxic environment. Retrieved May 30, 2014 from http://parenthood.library.wisc.edu/Garbarino/Garbarino.html.

Gassman-Pines, A., and Yoshikawa, H. (2006). Five-year effects of an anti-poverty program on marriage among never-married mothers. *Journal of Policy Analysis and Management, 25,* 11–30.

Global Commission on Drug Policy. (2011). *War on drugs: Report of the Global Commission on Drug Policy.* Retrieved May 30, 2014 from http://www.globalcommissionondrugs.org.

Gorski, P. (2008). The myth of the culture of poverty. *Poverty and Learning, 65,* 32–36.

Gutman, L., and McLoyd, V. (2000). Parents' management of their children's education within the home, at school, and in the community: An examination of African-American families living in poverty. *Urban Review, 32,* 1–24.

Hagan, J., and Dinovitzer, R. (1999). Collateral consequences of imprisonment for children, communities, and prisoners. *Crime and Justice, 26,* 121–142.

Hathaway, A. (2001). Shortcomings of harm reduction: Toward a morally invested drug reform strategy. *International Journal of Drug Policy, 12,* 125–137.

Jenson, J., and Fraser, M. (2011). Toward the integration of child, youth, and family policy. In J. Jenson and M. Fraser (eds), *Social policy for children and families: A risk and resilience perspective* (pp. 265–279). Thousand Oaks, CA: Sage Publications.

Lareau, A. (2011). *Unequal childhoods*. Berkeley and Los Angeles: University of California Press.

Lerner, R. (1998). Theories of human development: Contemporary perspectives. In W. Damon and R. Lerner (eds), *Handbook of child psychology*, vol. 1, *Theoretical models of human development* (5th edn) (pp. 1–24). New York: John Wiley & Sons, Inc.

Lerner, R., Fisher, C., and Weinberg, R. (2000). Toward a science for and of the people: Promoting civil society through the application of developmental science. *Child Development, 71*, 11–20.

Lerner, R., Sparks, E. E., and McCubbin, L. D. (1999). Developmental contextualism and the developmental systems perspective. In R. Lerner, E. Sparks, and L. McCubbin (eds), *Family diversity and family policy: Strengthening families for America's children* (pp. 213–221). Norwell, MA: Kluwer.

Lichter, D. (2012). The geography of exclusion: Race, segregation, and concentrated poverty. *Social Problems, 59*, 364–388.

Lieb, H., and Thistle, S. (2005). The changing impact of marriage, motherhood and work on women's poverty. *Journal of Women, Politics, and Policy, 27*, 5–22.

Lopez, M., and Light, M. (2009). A rising share: Hispanics and federal crime. Washington, DC: Pew Research Center. Retrieved May 30, 2014 from http://pewhispanic.org 2009/02/18/a-rising-share-hispanics-and-federal-crime/.

Luthar, S. S. (2006). Resilience in development: A synthesis of research across five decades. In D. Cicchetti and D. Cohen (eds), *Developmental psychopathology*, vol. 3, *Risk, disorder, and adaptation* (2nd edn) (pp. 739–795). Hoboken, NJ: John Wiley & Sons, Inc.

Luthar, S. S., and Brown, P. J. (2007). Maximizing resilience through diverse levels of inquiry: Prevailing paradigms, possibilities, and priorities for the future. *Developmental Psychopathology, 19*, 931–955.

Macartney, S. (2011). Child poverty in the Unites States 2009 and 2010: Selected race groups and Hispanic origin (ACSBR/10-05). Retrieved May 30, 2014 from http://www.census.gov/prod/2011pubs/acsbr10-05.pdf.

McLanahan, S. (1994). *Growing up with a single parent: What helps, what hurts*. Cambridge, MA: Harvard University Press.

McLoyd, V. (1998). Socioeconomic disadvantage and child development. *American Psychologist, 53*, 185–204.

Nodine, E. (2006). Harm reduction: Policies in public health. In *Public health management and policy*, online textbook.

Retrieved May 30, 2014 from http://www.cwru.edu/med/epidbio/mphp439/Harm_Reduction_Policies.htm.

Petrosino, A., Turpin-Petrosino, C., and Finckenauer, J. (2000). Well-meaning programs can have harmful effects! Lessons from experiments of programs such as Scared Straight. *Crime and Delinquency, 46*, 354–379.

RachBiesel, J., Scott, J., and Dixon, L. (1999). Co-occurring severe mental illness and substance use disorders: A review of recent research. *Psychiatric Services, 50*. Retrieved May 30, 2014 from http://journals.psychiatryonline.org/article.aspx?articleid=83559.

Ratcliffe, C., and McKernan, S. (2010). Child poverty persistence: Facts and consequences. Urban Institute Brief 14, June. Washington, DC: Urban Institute. Retrieved May 30, 2014 from http://www.urban.org/UploadedPDF/412126-child-poverty-persistence.pdf.

Roberts, D. (1999). Is there justice in children's rights? The critique of federal family preservation policy. *Journal of Constitutional Law, 2*, 112–140.

Russell, A., Mize, J., and Bissaker, K. (2002). Parent–child relationships. In P. Smith and C. Hart (eds), *The Blackwell handbook of child social development* (pp. 205–222). Oxford: Blackwell.

Rutter, M. (1987). Psychosocial resilience and protective mechanisms. *American Journal of Orthopsychiatry, 57*, 316–331.

Schneider, A., and Ingram, H. (1993). Social construction of target populations: Implications for politics and policy. *American Political Science Review, 87*, 334–347.

Seccombe, K. (2002). "Beating the odds" versus "changing the odds": Poverty, resilience, and family policy. *Journal of Marriage and Family, 64*, 384–394.

Shanks, T., and Danzinger, S. (2011). Anti-poverty policies and programs for children and families. In J. Jenson and M. Fraser (eds), *Social policy for children and families: A risk and resilience perspective* (pp. 25–56). Thousand Oaks, CA: Sage Publications.

Shlonsky, A., Friend, C., and Lambert, L. (2007). From culture clash to new possibilities: A harm reduction approach to family violence and child protection services. *Brief Treatment and Crisis Intervention: A Journal of Evidence-Based Practice, 7*, 345–363.

Travis, J. (2002). Invisible punishment: An instrument of social exclusion. In M. Mauer and M. Chesney-Lind (eds), *Invisible punishment: The collateral consequences of mass imprisonment* (pp. 15–36). New York: New Press.

US Department of Health and Human Services, Assistant Secretary for Planning and Evaluation. (2012). Information on poverty and income statistics: A summary of 2012 current population survey data. ASPE Issue Brief. Retrieved May 30, 2014 from http://aspe.hhs.gov/hsp/12/povertyAndIncomeEst/ib.shtml.

Valladares, S., and Moore, K. (2009). The strengths of poor families. Research Brief Publication #2009-26. Washington, DC: Child Trends. Retrieved May 30, 2014 from http://childtrends.org/wp-content/uploads/2009/05/Child_Trends-2009_5_14_RB_poorfamstrengths.pdf.

Vásquez, J. (2013). Five key elements for immigration reform. Statesman.com., April 13. Retrieved May 30, 2014 from http://www.statesman.com/news/news/opinion/vasquez-five-key-elements-for-immigration-reform/nXKwb/.

Western, B., and Pettit, B. (2010). Incarceration and social inequality. *Daedalus, 139*, 8–19.

World Health Organization (WHO). (2005, May). Status paper on prisons, drugs and harm reduction. Copenhagen, Denmark: WHO Regional Office for Europe. Retrieved May 30, 2014 from http://www.euro.who.int/__data/assets/pdf_file/0006/78549/E85877.pdf.

Young, I. M. (1990). *Justice and the politics of difference.* Princeton, NJ: Princeton University Press.

Index

Note: Page numbers in *italics* refer to figures, those in **bold** refer to tables.

Family Problems: Stress, Risk, and Resilience, First Edition. Edited by Joyce A. Arditti.
© 2015 John Wiley & Sons, Inc. Published 2015 by John Wiley & Sons, Inc.